Preface

Welcome to the proceedings of the f[illegible]nference of the Humaine Association on Affect[illegible]teraction (ACII 2011), which was held in Memphis, Te[illegible]1 to 12th, 2011. Since its inception in 2005, the ACII conference series ha[illegible]ed some of the most innovative and fascinating basic and applied research in the burgeoning research area centered on emotions, affective computing, user modeling, and intelligent systems. This tradition of exemplary interdisciplinary research has been kept alive in 2011 as evident through the imaginative, exciting, and diverse set of papers spanning the fields of computer science, engineering, psychology, education, neuroscience, and linguistics.

The ACII 2011 conference program featured a rich tapestry of original research embodied through oral presentations, posters, invited talks, workshops, interactive demos, and a doctoral consortium. In all, we received 196 submissions (124 regular papers and 72 papers for workshops, Doctoral Consortium, and demos). Each paper was reviewed by at least two expert reviewers (most papers received three reviews) and vetted by members of the Senior Program Committee and organizers of various events. Forty-four out of the 124 regular papers were accepted as oral presentations (36 percent), and an additional 35 papers were accepted for poster presentations (an overall acceptance rate of 64 percent).

The conference also featured invited talks by three outstanding researchers: Rosalind Picard (MIT), Arvid Kappas (Jacobs University Bremen), and James Lester (North Carolina State University). The conference was kick-started by a full day of workshops on cutting-edge topics including affective brain-computer interfaces, machine learning for affective computing, emotions in games, as well as the first International Audio/Visual Emotion Challenge and Workshop. The conference also included an interactive events session where a number of researchers traveled the globe to demonstrate their affective interfaces and technologies. In keeping with ACIIs tradition of encouraging and scaffolding the next generation of researchers, the conference featured a Doctoral Consortium where 15 students presented their dissertation research. In all, the proceedings featured 138 papers, 79 regular papers (oral presentations and posters), and 59 additional papers for the workshops, Doctoral Consortium, demos, and invited speaker abstracts.

The ACII 2011 conference would not have been possible without the vision and dedicated effort of a number of people. We are indebted to the Program Committee and the Senior Program Committee for their exceptional work in reviewing the submissions and helping us select the best papers for the conference. We would like to acknowledge Kostas Karpouzis and Roddy Cowie, who along with Jean-Claude Martin, organized the Doctoral Consortium. Thanks to

Ginevra Castellano, who joined Björn Schuller to organize the workshops, and to Rafael Calvo and Tanner Jackson who joined Sidney D'Mello to organize the interactive events. We are grateful to Brendan Allison, Stephen Dunne, Dirk Heylen, and Anton Nijholt for organizing the Affective Brain-Computer Interfaces workshop; Georgios Yannakakis, Ana Paiva, Kostas Karpouzis, and Eva Hudlicka for organizing the Emotion in Games workshop; M. Ehsan Hoque, Dan McDuff, Louis Philippe, and Rosalind Picard for organizing the Machine Learning for Affective Computing workshop; and to Michel Valstar, Roddy Cowie, and Maja Pantic who, along with Björn Schuller, organized the First International Audio/Visual Emotion Challenge and Workshop. We would like to thank members of the Humaine Associations Executive Committee for their advice and support. Finally, thanks to the authors for sending us their best work and to all the attendees who bring ACII to life.

Sidney D'Mello and Art Graesser would also like to thank Cristina Conati for encouraging the Memphis team to host the 2011 conference and Jonathan Gratch for his invaluable support and assistance throughout the year leading up to the conference. We are indebted to the student volunteers from the Institute of Intelligent Systems, particularly Blair Lehman, Caitlin Mills, and Amber Strain, who were invaluable in numerous respects. Thanks to the staff of Conference Planning and Operations at the University of Memphis (with a special acknowledgement to Lauren Coggins) for all the local arrangements. Finally, we would like to thank our sponsors, the Institute for Intelligent Systems, the University of Memphis (Office of the Provost), the FedEx Institute of Technology, and Aldebran Robotics, who generously provided funds to help offset the registration costs for students.

In summary, 2011 appears to be an excellent year for Affective Computing and Intelligent Interaction. The keynotes, oral and poster presentations, live demos, Doctoral Consortium, opening workshops, attendees from all over the world, and the fall weather in Memphis (the Home of the Blues and the birth place of Rock and Roll) undoubtedly made the first ACII conference to be held in North America an intellectually stimulating, enjoyable, and memorable event.

October 2011

Sidney D'Mello
Art Graesser
Björn Schuller
Jean-Claude Martin

Organization

General Conference Chairs

Sidney D'Mello	University of Memphis, USA
Art Graesser	University of Memphis, USA

Program Chairs

Sidney D'Mello	University of Memphis, USA
Art Graesser	University of Memphis, USA
Björn Schuller	Technical University of Munich, Germany
Jean-Claude Martin	LIMSI-CNRS, France

Doctoral Consortium Chairs

Jean-Claude Martin	LIMSI-CNRS, France
Kostas Karpouzis	National Technical University of Athens, Greece
Roddy Cowie	Queen's University, Belfast, UK

Interactive Events (Demos) Chairs

Sidney D'Mello	University of Memphis, USA
Rafael Calvo	University of Sydney, Australia
Tanner Jackson	University of Memphis, USA

Workshop Chairs

Björn Schuller	Technical University of Munich, Germany
Ginevra Castellano	Queen Mary University of London, UK

Organizers of Affective Brain-Computer Interfaces (aBCI 2011) Workshop

Brendan Allison	TU Graz, Austria
Stephen Dunne	Starlab Barcelona, Spain
Dirk Heylen	University of Twente, The Netherlands
Anton Nijholt	University of Twente, The Netherlands

Organizers of Emotion in Games Workshop

Georgios Yannakakis	IT University, Denmark
Ana Paiva	Instituto Superior Técnico/INESC-ID, Portugal
Kostas Karpouzis	National Technical University of Athens, Greece
Eva Hudlicka	Psychometrix Associates, Inc., USA

Organizers of Machine Learning for Affective Computing (MLAC) Workshop

M. Ehsan Hoque	MIT, USA
Dan McDuff	MIT, USA
Louis Philippe	USC, USA
Rosalind Picard	MIT, USA

Organizers of the First International Audio/Visual Emotion Challenge and Workshop (AVEC)

Björn Schuller	Technical University of Munich, Germany
Michel Valstar	Imperial College London, UK
Roddy Cowie	Queen's University Belfast, UK
Maja Pantic	Imperial College London, UK

Senior Program Committee (Oral Presentations and Posters)

Anton Batliner	University of Erlangen-Nuremberg, Germany
Rafael Calvo	University of Sydney, Australia
Jean-Claude Martin	LIMSI-CNRS, France
Ben Du Boulay	University of Sussex, UK
Dirk Heylen	University of Twente, The Netherlands
Eva Hudlicka	Psychometrix Associates, USA
Qiang Ji	Rensselaer Polytechnic Institute, USA
Diane Litman	University of Pittsburgh, USA
Anton Nijholt	University of Twente, The Netherlands
Peter Robinson	University of Cambridge, UK
Nilanjan Sarkar	Vanderbilt University, USA
Björn Schuller	Technical University of Munich, Germany
Georgios Yannakakis	IT University of Copenhagen, Denmark

Program Committee (Oral Presentations and Posters)

Omar Alzoubi	University of Sydney, Australia
Elisabeth André	Augsburg University, Germany
Ivon Arroyo	University of Massachusetts Amherst, USA
Ruth Aylett	Heriot Watt University, UK
Gerard Bailly	CNRS, France
Ryan Baker	Worcester Polytechnic Institute, USA
Anton Batliner	University of Erlangen-Nuremberg, Germany
Christian Becker-Asano	University of Freiburg, Germany
Nadia Bianchi-Berthouze	University College London, UK
Luis Botelho	Superior Institute of Labour and Enterprise Sciences, Portugal
Ioan Buciu	University of Oradea, Romania
Win Burleson	Arizona State University, USA
Roberto Bresin	KTH, Sweden
Antonio Camurri	University of Genoa, Italy
Ginevra Castellano	Queen Mary University of London, UK
Jeffery Cohn	University of Pittsburgh, USA
Darren Cosker	University of Bath, UK
Ellen Cowie	Queen's University Belfast, UK
Kerstin Dautenhahn	University of Hertfordshire, UK
Eugénio De Oliveira	University of Porto, Portugal
Laurence Devillers	LIMS-CNRS, France
Anna Esposito	Second University of Naples, Italy
Kate Forbes-Riley	University of Pittsburgh, USA
Jonathan Gratch	University of Southern California, USA
Hatice Gunes	Imperial College London, UK
Jennifer Healey	Intel, USA
Emile Hendriks	Delft University of Technology, The Netherlands
Keikichi Hirose	University of Tokyo, Japan
Julia Hirschberg	Columbia University, USA
Ian Horswill	Northwestern University, USA
David House	Royal Institute of Technology, Sweden
Kostas Karpouzis	ICCS, Greece
Jarmo Laaksolahti	SICS, Sweden
Brent Lance	University of Southern California, USA
John Lee	The University of Edinburgh, UK
James Lester	North Carolina State University, USA
Henry Lieberman	MIT, USA
Christine Lisetti	Florida International University, USA
Patricia Maillard	Universidade do Vale do Rio dos Sinos, Brazil
Carlos Martinho	Instituto Superior Técnico, Portugal
Cindy Mason	Stanford University, USA
Matteo Matteuci	Politecnico di Milano, Italy

Peter Mcowan	Queen Mary University of London, UK
Scott Mcquiggan	SAS Institute, USA
Rada Mihalcea	University of North Texas, USA
Luís Morgado	ISEL, Portugal
Helen Pain	University of Edinburgh, UK
Ana Paiva	INESC-ID and Instituto Superior Técnico, Lisbon
Ioannis Patras	Queen Mary University of London, UK
Christian Peter	Fraunhofer Institute for Computer Graphics, Germany
Paolo Petta	Austrian Research Institute for Artificial Intelligence, Austria
Mannes Poel	University of Twente, The Netherlands
Frank Pollick	University of Glasgow, UK
Alexandros Potamianos	Technical University of Crete, Greece
Thierry Pun	University of Geneva, Switzerland
Ma. Mercedes T. Rodrigo	Ateneo de Manila University, The Philppines
Matthias Scheutz	Tufts University, USA
Magy Seif El-Nasr	Simon Fraser University, Canada
Hiroshi Shimodaira	University of Edinburgh, UK
Mark Shröder	DFKI, Germany
Stefan Steidl	University of Erlangen-Nuremberg, Germany
Jianhua Tao	Institute of Automation of the Chinese Academy of Sciences, China
Daniel Thalmann	Nanyang Technological University, Singapore
Barry-John Theobald	University of East Anglia, UK
Isabel Trancoso	Instituto Superior Técnico / INESC-ID, Portugal
Jan Treur	Vrije Universiteit Amsterdam, The Netherlands
Matthew Turk	University of California, Santa Barbara, USA
Egon L. Van Den Broek	University of Twente, The Netherlands
Juan Velasquez	MIT, USA
Ning Wang	Arizona State University, USA
Joyce Westerink	Philips Research, The Netherlands
Beverly Woolf	University of Massachusetts Amherst, USA
Chung-Hsien Wu	National Cheng Kung University, Taiwan
Lijun Yin	Binghamton University, USA

Additional Reviewers (Oral Presentations and Posters)

Fiemke Both
Hana Boukricha
Guillaume Chanel
Amber Strain
Maria-Elena Chavez-Echeagaray
Jeffrey Girard
Javier Gonzalez-Sanchez
Hatice Gunes

Kaoning Hu
Md. Sazzad Hussain
Blair Lehman
Chee Wee Leong
Peng Liu
Nataliya Mogles
David Pereira
Hector Perez Martinez
Stefan Rank
Matthew Rosato
Maria Ofelia Clarissa San Pedro
Stefan Scherer
C. Natalie Van Der Wal
Rianne Van Lambalgen
Arlette Van Wissen
Rainer Wasinger
Joyce Westerink

Program Committee (Workshops, Doctoral Consortium, Demos)

Aggelos Pikrakis	University of Piraeus, Greece
Albert Rilliard	LIMSI-CNRS, France
Alessandro Vinciarelli	University of Glasgow, UK
Anton Batliner	University of Erlangen-Nuremberg, Germany
Anton Nijholt	University of Twente, The Netherlands
Ashish Kapoor	Microsoft Research, USA
Athanassios Katsamanis	University of Southern California, USA
Audrey Girouard	Carleton University, Canada
Brent Lance	US Army Research Laboratory - Translational Neuroscience Branch, USA
Carlos Busso	The University of Texas at Dallas, USA
Catherine Pelachaud	CNRS Telecom ParisTech, France
Céline Clavel	LIMSI-CNRS, France
Christian Muhl	University of Twente, The Netherlands
Dan Bohus	Microsoft Research, USA
Egon L. Van Den Broek	University of Twente, The Netherlands
Elisabeth André	Augsburg University, Germany
Felix Burkhardt	Deutsche Telekom, Germany
Femke Nijboer	University of Twente, The Netherlands
Fernando De La Torre	Carnegie Mellon University, USA
Gary Garcia Molina	Philips Research Europe, The Netherlands
George Caridakis	ICCS-NTUA, Greece
Ginevra Castellano	Queen Mary University of London, UK
Gualtiero Volpe	InfoMus Lab - DIST - University of Genoa, Italy
Hatice Gunes	Imperial College London, UK
Hector P. Martinez	IT University of Copenhagen, Denmark
Iain Matthews	Disney Research Pittsburgh, USA
Ioannis Patras	Queen Mary University of London, UK
Jan B.F. Van Erp	TNO Human Factors - Perceptual and Cognitive Systems, The Netherlands

Jianhua Tao	Chinese Academy of Sciences, China
Jonathan Gratch	University of Southern California, USA
Jonghwa Kim	University of Augsburg, Germany
Joris Janssen	Philips, The Netherlands
Julia Hirschberg	Columbia University, USA
Julian Togelius	IT University of Copenhagen, Denmark
Julien Epps	The University of New South Wales, Australia
Kai Kuikkaniemi	HIIT, Finland
Laurence Devillers	LIMSI-CNRS, France
Magalie Ochs	NII, Japan
Magy Seif El-Nasr	Simon Fraser University, Canada
Marc Cavazza	University of Teesside, UK
Marc Schröder	DFKI GmbH, Language Technology Lab, Germany
Marcello Mortillaro	Swiss Center for Affective Sciences, Switzerland
Marian Bartlett	University of California, San Diego, USA
Mashfiqui Rabbi	Bangladesh University of Engineering and Technology, Bangladesh
Matthew Turk	University of California, USA
Matti Pietikainen	University of Ouly, Finland
Mohamed Chetouani	University Pierre and Marie Curie, France
Nadia Berthouze	University College London, UK
Nicolas Sabouret	LIP6, France
Nicu Sebe	University of Trento, Italy
Olga Sourina	Nanyang Technological University, Singapore
Ouriel Grynszpan	CNRS, France
Patricia Jaques	UNISINOS, Brazil
Peter Desain	Radboud University Nijmegen, The Netherlands
Peter Robinson	University of Cambridge, UK
Rafael Bidarra	Delft University of Technology, The Netherlands
Raul Fernandez	IBM Research, USA
Robert Leeb	Ecole Polytechnique Federale de Lausanne (EPFL), Switzerland
Ruth Aylett	Heriot-Watt University, UK
Shri Narayanan	University of Southern California, USA
Simon Lucey	CSRIO-ICT, Australia
Sophie Rosset	LIMSI-CNRS, France
Stefan Kopp	University of Bielefeld, Germany
Stefan Steidl	University of Erlangen-Nuremberg, Germany
Stephen Fairclough	Liverpool John Moores University, UK
Tanja Schultz	Universität Karlsruhe, Germany
Tetsunori Kobayashi	Waseda University, Japan

Thierry Pun	University of Geneva, Switzerland
Thomas J. Sullivan	NeuroSky, USA
Thorsten Zander	TU Berlin, Germany
Touradj Ebrahimi	Ecole Polytechnique Federale de Lausanne (EPFL), Switzerland
Victoria Eyharabide	UNICEN University, Argentina
Winslow Burleson	Arizona State University, USA
Yannick Mathieu	CNRS - Université Paris 7, France

Additional Reviewers (Workshops, Doctoral Consortium, Demos)

Ruth Aylett
Florian Eyben
Gangadhar Garipelli
Theodoros Giannakopoulos
Brais Martinez
Angeliki Metallinou
Antonios Oikonomopoulos
Ana Paiva
Fabien Ringeval
Marieke Thurlings
Felix Weninger
Martin Woellmer
Ramin Yaghoubzadeh

Steering Committee

Nick Campbell	Trinity College, Ireland
Ginevra Castellano	Queen Mary University of London, UK
Jeffery Cohn	University of Pittsburgh, USA
Cristina Conati	University of British Columbia, Canada
Roddy Cowie	Queen's University Belfast, UK
Jonathan Gratch	University of Southern California, USA
Dirk Heylen	University of Twente, The Netherlands
Arvid Kappas	Jacobs University Bramen, Germany
Kostas Karpouzis	National Technical University of Athens, Greece
Jean-Claude Martin	LIMSI-CNRS, France
Maja Pantic	Imperial College, UK
Catherine Pelachaud	CNRS, TELECOM ParisTech, France
Paolo Petta	Austrian Research Institute for Artificial Intelligence, Austria
Helmut Prendinger	National Institute of Informatics, Japan
Marc Schröder	German Research Center for Artificial Intelligence, Germany
Björn Schuller	Munich University of Technology, Germany
Jianhua Tao	Chinese Academy of Sciences, China

Local Assistance

Lauren Coggins
Blair Lehman
Caitlin Mills
Amber Strain
Staff and Students of the Institute for Intelligent Systems

Sponsors

University of Memphis
HUMAINE Association
FedEx Institute of Technology
Institute for Intelligent Systems
Aldebaran Robotics

Table of Contents – Part I

Invited Talks

Oral Presentations

Poster Papers

Table of Contents – Part II

Poster Papers

Doctoral Consortium

Interactive Event (Demo Papers)

The First Audio/Visual Emotion Challenge and Workshop

Affective Brain-Computer Interfaces Workshop (aBCI 2011)

Emotion in Games Workshop

Machine Learning for Affective Computing Workshop

To Our Emotions, with Love: How Affective Should Affective Computing Be?

Arvid Kappas

Jacobs University Bremen
School of Humanities and Social Sciences, Campus Ring 1, 28759 Bremen
a.kappas@jacobs-university.de

Abstract. "Affective computing" has become the rallying call for a heterogeneous group of researchers that, among other goals, tries to improve the interaction of humans and machines via the development of affective and multimodal intelligent systems. This development appears *logical* based on the popular notion that emotions play an important part in social interactions. In fact, research shows that humans missing the possibility to express or perceive/interpret emotions, seem to have difficulties navigating social conventions and experience a negative impact on their relationships.

However, while emotions are certainly somewhat important, the desire to implement affect in machines might also be influenced by *romantic* notions, echoed in the plight of iconic science fiction characters, such as Star Trek's Data, who struggles to achieve humanity via emotions. The emphasis on emotions in the psychological research on nonverbal communication is in part due to theoretical discussions in that community. However, taken out of this context, there is the risk to overestimate the importance of discrete emotional expressions. Inversely, behaviors relevant to successful interaction will be underestimated in psychology because they might be culturally variable and perhaps even idiosyncratic for smaller groups or individuals. In other words, what might be noise for the emotion theorist could be the data to create believable conversational agents.

I will discuss how much emotion might or might not be needed when trying to build emotional or emotion-savvy systems, depending on the type of application that is desired, based on a multi-level approach. At one level of analysis, a clear distinction of encoding and decoding processes is required to know what (real) people actually show in certain situations, or what people might in fact perceive. It is not obvious how much information is actually "read" from faces, as opposed to "read" into faces. In other words, context plays a large role for the interpretation of nonverbal behavior. Some of this context is verbal, but some is situational.

At a different level of analysis, interactive characteristics in conversation need to be considered. This refers to issues such as responsiveness, synchrony, or imitation that are often neglected in affective computing applications *and* in basic psychological research. For example, an artificial system that will only react to observed patterns of verbal/nonverbal behavior might be too slow and create strange delayed effects, as opposed to systems that seem to react, but that, in fact, anticipate the interactant's reactions. It is these areas where much interesting work is, should be, and will be happening in the next few years.

Keywords: Emotion theory, nonverbal behavior, social context.

S. D'Mello et al. (Eds.): ACII 2011, Part I, LNCS 6974, p. 1, 2011.

Affect, Learning, and Delight

James C. Lester

Department of Computer Science, North Carolina State University,
Raleigh, North Carolina, USA 27695
lester@ncsu.edu

Abstract. Because of the growing recognition of the role that affect plays in learning, affective computing has become the subject of increasing attention in research on interactive learning environments. The intelligent tutoring systems community has begun actively exploring computational models of affect, and game-based learning environments present a significant opportunity for investigating student affect in interactive learning. One family of game-based learning environments, narrative-centered learning environments, offer a particularly compelling laboratory for investigating student affect. In narrative-centered environments, learning activities play out in dynamically generated interactive narratives and training scenarios. These afford significant opportunities for investigating computational models of student emotion. In this talk, we explore the role that affective computing can play in next-generation interactive learning environments, with a particular focus on affect recognition, affect understanding, and affect synthesis in game-based learning.

Keywords: Affective computing, intelligent tutoring systems, game-based learning.

S. D´Mello et al. (Eds.): ACII 2011, Part I, LNCS 6974, p. 2, 2011.

Measuring Affect in the Wild

Rosalind W. Picard

MIT Media Laboratory; 75 Amherst Street; Cambridge, MA 02139
picard@media.mit.edu
Affectiva, Inc; 411 Waverley Oaks Road; Waltham, MA 02452
picard@affectiva.com

Abstract. Our teams at MIT and at Affectiva have invented mobile sensors and software that can help sense autonomic stress and activity levels comfortably while you are on the go, e.g. the Affectiva Q™ Sensor for capturing sympathetic nervous system activation, or without distracting you while you are online, e.g. webcam-based software capturing heart rate variability and facial expressions. We are also developing new technologies that capture and respond to negative and positive thoughts, combining artificial intelligence and crowd-sourced online human computation to provide just-in-time emotional support through a mobile phone with texting. Our technologies are all opt-in, and are currently being used robustly for "outside the lab, mobile" studies where core emotional processes are involved in autism, PTSD, sleep disorders, eating disorders, substance abuse, epilepsy, stressful workplaces and learning environments, online customer experiences, and more. The new technologies enable collecting orders of magnitude more data than previous lab-based studies, containing many fascinating variations of "what people really do" especially when making expressions such as smiles. This talk will highlight some of the most interesting findings from recent work together with stories of personal adventures in emotion measurement out in the wild.

Keywords: Emotion measurement, ambulatory sensing, electrodermal activity, skin conductance, autonomic nervous system, physiology, facial expression analysis, cardiocam, Q™ Sensor, Affdex, positive psychology, mobile sensing.

S. D´Mello et al. (Eds.): ACII 2011, Part I, LNCS 6974, p. 3, 2011.

Affective Modeling from Multichannel Physiology: Analysis of Day Differences

Omar Alzoubi[1], Md. Sazzad Hussain[1], Sidney D'Mello[2], and Rafael A. Calvo[1]

[1] School of Electrical and Information Engineering, University of Sydney, Australia
[2] Institute for Intelligent Systems, University of Memphis, Memphis, USA
{Omar.Al-Zoubi,Sazzad.Hussain,Rafael.Calvo}@sydney.edu.au,
SDmello@memphis.edu

Abstract. Physiological signals are widely considered to contain affective information. Consequently, pattern recognition techniques such as classification are commonly used to detect affective states from physiological data. Previous studies have achieved some success in detecting affect from physiological measures, especially in controlled environments where emotions are experimentally induced. One challenge that arises is that physiological measures are expected to exhibit considerable day variations due to a number of extraneous factors such as environmental changes and sensor placements. These variations pose challenges to effectively classify affective sates from future physiological data; this is a common problem for real world requirements. The present study provides a quantitative analysis of day variations of physiological signals from different subjects. We propose a classifier ensemble approach using a Winnow algorithm to address the problem of day-variation in physiological signals. Our results show that the Winnow ensemble approach outperformed a static classification approach for detecting affective states from physiological signals that exhibited day variations.

Keywords: Affect detection, classifier ensembles, non-stationarity, physiology.

1 Introduction

There is considerable motivation for measuring affect from physiological signals (for detailed review see [1]). Heart activity, respiration, facial muscle activity, galvanic skin response, body temperature, and blood pressure have all been considered as potential physiological channels for recognizing affective states [2, 3]. The literature is rife with a number of physiological-based affect detection systems that classify discrete emotions as well as primitive affective dimensions such as valence and arousal [4-6]. Despite impressive classification performance under controlled laboratory conditions [7, 8], the stochastic nature of physiological signals poses significant challenges when one moves from the lab and into the real world [9]. In particular, physiological data is expected to exhibit day variations [6], which introduce problems when previously trained models are used to generate predictions in the future; this is an important requirement for real world applications. This research addresses this problem by utilizing an updatable classifier ensemble

S. D'Mello et al. (Eds.): ACII 2011, Part I, LNCS 6974, pp. 4–13, 2011.

approach, which combines decisions from multiple classifiers. This approach was validated on physiological affective data collected from multiple subjects over multiple sessions that spanned several days.

1.1 Day Differences and Non-stationarity of Affective Physiological Data

Picard and colleagues [6] convincingly demonstrated that affective physiological data recorded from one subject across multiple days exhibited considerable day to day variations. They found that physiological data for a given emotion in a particular day (*day data*) yielded a higher clustering cohesion or tightness compared to data for the same emotion across multiple days. They attempted to address this problem by including day information as additional classification features; however, this did not yield a significant improvement in accuracy.

The day variation phenomena can be attributed to the non-stationarity nature of physiological signals [10], which may occur due to a number of factors such as: 1) mood changes across days, 2) electrode drift, 3) changes in the electrode impedance, and 4) modulations by other mental states such as attention and motivation [6]. Non-stationarity indicates that the signal changes its statistical characteristics (means, standard deviation, etc) as a function of time. These changes are propagated in the feature values extracted from the signal over time.

Day variation in physiological data represents a major problem for building reliable classification models that span multiple days. This is because classification methods assume that training data is obtained from a stationary distribution [11]. In real world contexts, however, this assumption of stationarity is routinely violated. According to Kuncheva [12], every real-world classification system should be equipped with a mechanism to adapt to the changes in the environment. Therefore, a more sophisticated approach is required to handle these day to day variations for physiological-based affect detection systems.

Understanding environment changes is essential for developing effective affect detection systems that can be deployed in real world affective computing applications. There is a critical need for basic research on how physiological signals vary over time before effective solutions can be proposed. This study contributes to this goal by systematically analyzing day variations in physiological data collected from four subjects over five recording sessions each. We also propose and evaluate an algorithm that has the potential to capitalize on, instead of being crippled by day variations in physiological signals.

1.2 Ensemble Approach for Classifying Physiological Data

The main motivation to use classifier ensembles is to increase the generalization capability of a classification system by combing decisions from multiple classifiers (e.g. averaging or voting) rather than relying on a single classifier [13]. Ensembles have been known to provide improved and/or more robust performance in many applications [14]. The present study uses *updatable classifier ensembles* to address changes in the classification environment over the life span of the classifier [15]. These changes can be minor fluctuations in the underlying probability distribution of data, steady trends, random or systematic change in classes (substitution of one class with another), and changes in class distribution, among others.

There are different strategies used for building and updating classifier ensembles that can work in non-stationary environments; see [12] for a detailed review. Winnow is an ensemble based algorithm that is similar to a weighted majority voting algorithm because it combines decisions from ensemble members based on their weights. However, it utilizes a different updating approach for member classifiers. This includes promoting ensemble members that make correct predictions and demoting those that make incorrect predictions. Updating of the weights is done automatically based on incoming data, which makes this approach suitable for online applications. The pseudo code presented in Table 1 describes the major steps of the algorithm.

Table 1. Winnow ensemble algorithm

- Initialization: Given a classifier ensemble D = {D1,….,Dn}, Initialize all classifier weights; $w_i = 1.\ i = 1{:}n$
- Classification: For a new example x, calculate the support for each class as the sum of the weights of all classifiers D_i that suggest class label c_k for x. Set x to the class with largest support. *k=1:number of classes*
- Updating: if x is classified correctly by classifier D_i then its weight is increased (promotion) by $w_i = alpha * w_i$, where alpha > 1. If classifier D_i incorrectly classifies x, then its weight is decreased by $w_i = w_i / alpha$ (demotion).

Ensemble based approaches appear to be a potential solution to the "*day data*" problem that arises during affective physiological modeling. We hypothesize that an ensemble classification approach might be able to handle environment related changes which include 1) data distribution changes (feature space), as is the case when data is obtained from different days or sessions, 2) changes in class distributions, which is quite prevalent during naturalistic interactions, 3) changes in diagnostic features, where features for discrimination particular affective states may change over time, 4) the introduction of new users over time; i.e. building person-independent models. Therefore, updatable ensemble-based modeling technique might be a more practical option for building real life affect detection systems than static approaches, where a classifier is trained on some initial data and is never updated in light of new data. As an initial step towards this goal, we evaluate the performance of the winnow ensemble algorithm in a laboratory study that was designed to systematically model day variations.

2 Measures, Methods, and Data

2.1 Participants and Measures

The participants were four male students between 24 and 39 years of age from the University of Sydney. Subjects were paid $100 for their participation in the study. Participants were equipped with electrocardiography (ECG), galvanic skin response (GSR), electromyography (EMG), and respiration (RESP) sensors for offline recording of physiological signals. The physiological signals were acquired using a BIOPAC MP150 system and AcqKnowledge software with a sampling rate of 1000 Hz for all channels. The ECG signal was collected with two electrodes placed on the wrist. EMG was recorded from the corrugator and zygomatic muscles on the face. GSR was recorded from the index and middle finger of the left hand. Participants wore a respiration belt around the chest to measure their respiration rate.

A set of 400 images, selected from the International Affective Picture System (IAPS) collection [16], served as the affect-inducing stimuli. The images were selected on the basis of their normative valence and arousal ratings. The mean valence norm scores ranges from 1.40 to 8.34, and mean arousal norm scores ranges from 1.72 to 7.35 (on a scale from 1 to 9). The valence dimension was divided into three categories (positive, neutral and negative), only images from the positive and negative categories were selected. Besides, the arousal dimension was divided into two categories (low or high). The selected images were then mapped into four categories: PositiveValence-LowArousal (mean IAPS valence norm > 6.03 and mean IAPS arousal norm < 5.47), PositiveValence-HighArousal (mean IAPS valence norm > 6.03 and mean IAPS arousal norm > 5.47), NegativeValence-HighArousal (mean IAPS valence norm < 3.71 and mean IAPS arousal norm > 5.47), and NegativeValence-LowArousal (mean IAPS valence norm < 3.71 and mean IAPS arousal norm < 5.47). The set of 400 images was then divided into 5 sets of 80 images each (20 images from each category).

2.2 Procedure

The study consisted of recording the physiological signals while subjects viewed the selected set of emotionally charged IAPS images for approximately 60 minutes over 5 sessions. Trials consisted of presenting each image for 12 seconds, followed by a self report questionnaire, where subjects had to select one of the four categories mentioned above. A blank screen was presented for 8 seconds to allow physiological activity to return to baseline levels before every new image appeared. Five images were presented consecutively from each category in order to maintain a stable emotional state for that category. The 80 images were organized into four blocks of 20 images each, with a pause that showed a blank screen for 2-3 minutes in order to give subjects an opportunity to return to the baseline neutral state before viewing images from the next block. Each subject participated in five recording sessions, each separated by one week. A different set of images were presented for each session in order to prevent habituation effects, however each set contained 20 images from each of the four categories mentioned earlier.

2.3 Feature Extraction and Classification Methods

The Matlab based Augsburg Biosignal Toolbox [2] was used to preprocess and extract features from the raw physiological data. A total of 214 statistical features (e.g. mean, median, standard deviation, maxima and minima) were extracted from the five physiological channels using window sizes of 6, 8, 10 and 12 seconds from each trial. Preliminary classification results showed no statistically significant differences in performance between the different window sizes, so a feature extraction window of

12 seconds was used in all subsequent analysis. It is known that the temporal resolution for these autonomic measures vary in response to emotional stimuli. In general, GSR changes were observed 1-3 sec after stimulus presentations. EMG responses are substantially faster, however, the frequency of the muscle activity can be summed up over a period of time e.g. 10 or 12 seconds to indicate a change in behavioral pattern [17]. While ECG and respiration responses are considered slower, we were constrained to use a window size of 12 seconds or less because this was the length of a single trial. However, estimating cardiac and respiratory patterns from short periods of time is not uncommon in psychophysiological research [18]. 84 were extracted from ECG, 21 from GSR, 21 from each of the EMG channels, and 67 from the RESP channel.

The Waikato Environment for Knowledge Analysis (Weka), a data mining package [19], and PRTools 4.0 [20], a pattern recognition Matlab library, were used for the classifications. Chi square feature selection was used to reduce the dimensionality of the feature space in order to avoid various problems associated with large feature spaces. The top five features were selected from all datasets used in subsequent analysis (data sets are described in the next section). We relied on five features because some preliminary analysis indicated that five features were sufficient to produce consistent classification results without sacrificing performance. Weka's support vector machine (SMO) classifier with a linear kernel was utilized for training classification models. Many successful applications of SVMs have demonstrated the superiority of this objective function over other classification approaches [21]. The choice of SMO classifier as a base classifier is independent from the classification approach adopted by the ensemble algorithm described in Table 1. However, the performance of the algorithm is expected to reflect the performance/s of its member classifier/s. Multiple classification algorithms could be used as base classifiers if needed, this is yet to be evaluated in future work.

3 Results and Discussions

Cohen's kappa was used to assess the agreement between subjects' self reports and IAPS mapped ratings for valence and arousal. The kappa for valence was .89 (95% CI = .87 - .91). The kappa score for arousal was = .41 (95% CI =.37 - .46). Clearly, the IAPS stimuli was quite successful in eliciting valence, but was much less effective in influencing arousal.

3.1 Classification Results for Day Datasets

Day datasets were constructed separately for the two affective measures valence (positive/negative) and arousal (low/high). Additionally, Separate datasets were constructed using IAPS ratings (Instances were labeled by the corresponding image category) and self reports of subjects. In total there were 80 (4 subjects x 5 recording session's x 2 affective measures (valence and arousal) x 2 ratings (IAPS ratings and self reports)) datasets with 80 instances in each data set. IAPS ratings datasets had a balanced distribution of labels 40:40 for positive/negative valence or low/high arousal. On the other hand, self report datasets had unbalanced distribution of classes, so a down sampling procedure (Weka's SpreadSubsample which produces a random subsample of a dataset) was applied to obtain a balanced distribution of classes. On average, 34% of data was lost for self report arousal datasets and 15% of data was lost on average for self report valence datasets. Therefore, baseline accuracy is (50%) for both types of data sets.

Table 2 presents average classification scores across the five day's datasets for each subject using 10 cross validation for both IAPS ratings and self reports ratings. A one-sample t-test indicated that the mean classification accuracy for both IAPS ratings and self reports ratings was significantly ($p < .05$) different from the baseline (.50). On the other hand, and despite the small sample size, a paired-samples t-test yielded significant differences ($p = .015$) between IAPS valence ratings ($M = .678$) and self reported valence ($M = .625$). While the difference was not significant ($p = .848$) for IAPS arousal ratings ($M = .578$) from self reported arousal ($M = .583$).

Table 2. Mean for day classification results for both IAPS ratings and self reports

	IAPS ratings		*Self Reports*	
Subject ID	*Valence*	*Arousal*	*Valence*	*Arousal*
Subject 1	.76	.57	.71	.58
Subject 2	.62	.59	.57	.55
Subject 2	.69	.59	.61	.57
Subject 3	.64	.56	.61	.63

3.2 Day Cross Validation Classification Results (Static Classifiers)

The basic assumption behind using classification techniques to model affective physiological data is that pre-trained models can be used to predict affect from future unseen input. A day cross validation procedure was then devised, where training data comprised data from four days and the fifth day data was used for testing. This procedure was repeated five times to test on all day datasets. The objective of this analysis is to assess the accuracy of classifiers that are trained on different day data to predict exemplars from other days.

Table 3. Day cross validation average of accuracy over 5 runs for both IAPS ratings and self reports

Subject ID	*Valence (IAPS)*	*Arousal (IAPS)*	*Valence (self report)*	*Arousal (self report)*
Subject 1	.59	.52	.52	.50
Subject 2	.54	.51	.53	.49
Subject 3	.50	.52	.51	.51
Subject 4	.50	.48	.50	.52

Table 3 shows day cross validation results (average) for both IAPS ratings datasets and self report datasets. A one-sample t-test indicated that the mean classification accuracy for both IAPS ratings and self reports ratings was not significantly ($p > .05$) different from the baseline (.50). The low detection rate for both IAPS ratings and self report ratings can be attributed to changes to data characteristics across the five days. In the next section we focus on understanding some of these changes.

3.3 Quantitative Analysis of Day Differences

In order to investigate day differences we pooled day data for each subject, while maintaining day information schemes. For example, the NegativeValence label of day one would be labeled D1_NV. The purpose is to assess how valence and arousal cluster in a physiological space on different days. Overall there were 16 datasets (4 subjects x 2 labeling valence/arousal). Top five features were separately selected from each dataset using chi square feature selection. Figure 1 presents a dendrogram obtained from hierarchical clustering on the data for one subject. The clusters were computed using the single linkage method [22] based on distances (Mahalanobis) between group means. It is clear from the dendrogram that there are different clusters for each day. In addition, day 3 data forms a cluster with day 5 data, however within this cluster D5_PV (the positive valence class of day 5) and D5_NV forms a cluster, days 2, 3, and 4 form distinct clusters. Similar patterns have been found from the other four subjects' data.

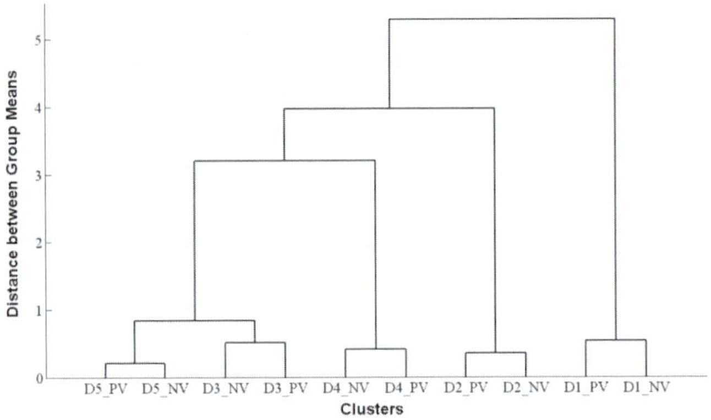

Fig. 1. Shows clusters of subject 1 data across 5 days for two classes (NV negative valence, PV positive valence)

From pattern recognition point of view, we would like to see distinct clusters for (negative and positive valence) classes across days. This poses challenges to classifiers that are not equipped with a suitable mechanize to handle changes to the classification environment. In the next section we present a procedure for training a winnow ensemble algorithm that is able to handle day variations in physiological data. We also provide a comparison between winnow ensemble classification results and results obtained using static classifiers.

3.4 Winnow Algorithm Results

The winnow ensemble algorithm described in section 1.2 was used to classify day data for each subject. There are different strategies for training ensemble classifiers. We adopted a training procedure that resembles day cross validation procedure, in order to make comparison with the static procedure possible. The ensemble used four base classifiers (SVM with linear kernels) each trained on one different day dataset, and the remaining day dataset was used for testing. The procedure was repeated five times, and averaged accuracy scores (proportion correct) were obtained across the five runs.

Table 4 shows averaged accuracy scores produced by winnow ensemble algorithm using 4 base classifiers, and alpha = 2; alpha is the parameter that is used to update the weights of classifier ensemble members. Acceptable results have been achieved using an alpha value of 2 in previous research [12].

Table 4. Averaged accuracy scores produced by Winnow ensemble algorithm with 4 base classifiers

Subject ID	*Valence (IAPS)*	*Arousal (IAPS)*	*Valence (self report)*	*Arousal (self report)*
Subject 1	.74	.72	.73	.63
Subject 2	.63	.69	.62	.65
Subject 3	.74	.75	.79	.76
Subject 4	.76	.73	.70	.69

A comparison of Table 3 with Table 4 indicates that the Winnow algorithm has clearly outperformed the *static* classifiers (classifiers that don't have an update mechanism to classifier weights). The winnow algorithm achieved higher accuracies on multi day data for both valence and arousal. A paired-sample t-test indicated that there was a significant (p = .018) difference in accuracy scores for IAPS valence ratings when Winnow results (M = .718) was compared to the static classifiers (M = .533). Similarly, Winnow accuracy scores for IAPS arousal ratings (M = .723) were significantly higher ($p < .05$) than static classifiers (M = .506). There was also a significant (p = .017) difference in self reported valence when Winnow results (M = .71) was compared to the static classifiers (M = .515). Finally, Winnow results for self reported arousal (M = .683) were significantly higher (p = .006) than the static classifier (M = .505).

The strategy of updating ensemble members' weights ensures classifiers are rewarded according to their performance. This is in contrast to a static approach to classification where classifiers are given the same weight irrespective of their performance. The ensemble approach can be viewed as a constantly emerging mechanism, so we expect its generalization capability will increase as the ensemble size grows. This requires developing strategies to manage the ensemble size and its structure.

4 Conclusions, Limitations and Future Work

We have shown that physiological data exhibits day variations. The challenge that this phenomenon introduces is of paramount importance to physiological based affect detection systems. In order to be able to detect affect from future physiological data, there is a need for a classification system that can handle these day variations. We have shown that classifier ensemble approaches offer such a capability by combining multiple classifiers decisions that have their weights updated according to their performance, which enhances the generalization capability of the system on future data. There are two primary limitations with the present study. One limitation of our work is the relatively small sample size, so replication with a larger sample is warranted. We should point out that several of the key comparisons (section 3.4) were statistically significant despite the small sample size. This leaves us with some confidence that we can draw some generalizations from the present results. The second limitation is that the emotions were artificially induced rather than spontaneously experienced. This approach was adopted because strict laboratory control was desired in the present experiment which systematically focused on assessing and remedying the day data phenomenon. Replicating this research in more naturalistic contexts is an important step for future work.

Finally, there are some additional issues to be considered for future work. These include: 1) analysis of day differences in diagnostic physiological features/channels of affect, 2) validating the efficacy of person-independent affect detectors, 4) deciding on the best approach for setting the ensemble size (fixed or dynamic ensemble size), 5) alternate strategies for training and updating ensemble members (training window size for adding new classifier members, weighting mechanism for ensemble members), and 6) change detection; i.e. when to update the ensemble members.

Acknowledgments. Sidney D'Mello was supported by the National Science Foundation (ITR 0325428, HCC 0834847). Any opinions, findings and conclusions, or recommendations expressed in this paper are those of the authors and do not necessarily reflect the views of the NSF.

References

1. Calvo, R.A., D'Mello, S.: Affect Detection: An Interdisciplinary Review of Models, Methods, and Their Applications. IEEE Transactions on Affective Computing 1, 18–37 (2010)
2. Wagner, J., Kim, J., Andre, E.: From Physiological Signals to Emotions: Implementing and Comparing Selected Methods for Feature Extraction and Classification. In: IEEE International Conference on Multimedia and Expo, ICME 2005, pp. 940–943 (2005)
3. Whang, M., Lim, J.: A Physiological Approach to Affective Computing. In: Affective Computing: Focus on Emotion Expression, Synthesis, and Recognition, pp. 310–318. I-Tech Education and Publishing, Vienna (2008)
4. Haag, A., Goronzy, S., Schaich, P., Williams, J.: Emotion Recognition Using Bio-sensors: First Steps towards an Automatic System. In: André, E., Dybkjær, L., Minker, W., Heisterkamp, P. (eds.) ADS 2004. LNCS (LNAI), vol. 3068, pp. 36–48. Springer, Heidelberg (2004)

5. Kim, J., Andre, E.: Emotion Recognition Based on Physiological Changes in Music Listening. IEEE Trans. Pattern Anal. Mach. Intell. 30, 2067–2083 (2008)
6. Picard, R.W., Vyzas, E., Healey, J.: Toward Machine Emotional Intelligence: Analysis of Affective Physiological State. IEEE Trans. Pattern Anal. Mach. Intell. 23, 1175–1191 (2001)
7. Kim, K., Bang, S., Kim, S.: Emotion recognition system using short-term monitoring of physiological signals. Medical and Biological Engineering and Computing 42, 419–427 (2004)
8. Lichtenstein, A., Oehme, A., Kupschick, S., Jürgensohn, T.: Comparing Two Emotion Models for Deriving Affective States from Physiological Data. In: Peter, C., Beale, R. (eds.) Affect and Emotion in Human-Computer Interaction. LNCS, vol. 4868, pp. 35–50. Springer, Heidelberg (2008)
9. Plarre, K., Raij, A., Hossain, M., Ali, A., Nakajima, M., Al'Absi, M., Ertin, E., Kamarck, T., Kumar, S., Scott, M., Siewiorek, D., Smailagic, A., Wittmers, L.: Continuous Inference of Psychological Stress from Sensory Measurements Collected in the Natural Environment. In: Proceedings of the 10th ACM/IEEE International Conference on Information Processing in Sensor Networks (IPSN), Chicago, IL (April 12-14, 2011)
10. Popivanov, D., Mineva, A.: Testing procedures for non-stationarity and non-linearity in physiological signals. Mathematical Biosciences 157, 303–320 (1999)
11. Last, M.: Online classification of nonstationary data streams. Intell. Data Anal. 6, 129–147 (2002)
12. Kuncheva, L.I.: Classifier Ensembles for Changing Environments. In: Roli, F., Kittler, J., Windeatt, T. (eds.) MCS 2004. LNCS, vol. 3077, pp. 1–15. Springer, Heidelberg (2004)
13. Sinha, A., Chen, H., Danu, D.G., Kirubarajan, T., Farooq, M.: Estimation and decision fusion: A survey. Neurocomputing 71, 2650–2656 (2008)
14. Oza, N.C., Tumer, K.: Classifier ensembles: Select real-world applications. Information Fusion 9, 4–20 (2008)
15. Muhlbaier, M., Polikar, R.: An Ensemble Approach for Incremental Learning in Nonstationary Environments. In: Haindl, M., Kittler, J., Roli, F. (eds.) MCS 2007. LNCS, vol. 4472, pp. 490–500. Springer, Heidelberg (2007)
16. Lang, P.J., Bradley, M.M., Cuthbert, B.N.: International affective picture system (IAPS): Technical manual and affective ratings. The Center for Research in Psychophysiology, University of Florida, Gainesville, FL (1995)
17. Andreassi, J.L.: Psychophysiology: Human behavior and physiological response. Lawrence Erlbaum Associates Publishers, New Jersey (2007)
18. Kreibig, S.D.: Autonomic nervous system activity in emotion: A review. Biological Psychology 84, 394–421 (2010)
19. Witten, I.H., Frank, E.: Data Mining: Practical Machine Learning Tools and Techniques, 2nd edn. Morgan Kaufmann Series in Data Management Systems. Morgan Kaufmann, San Francisco (2005)
20. Heijden, F.v.d., Duin, R.P., Ridder, D.d., Tax, D.M.: Classification, parameter estimation and state estimation - an engineering approach using Matlab. John Wiley & Sons, Chichester (2004)
21. Jain, A.K., Duin, R.P.W., Jianchang, M.: Statistical pattern recognition: a review. IEEE Transactions on Pattern Analysis and Machine Intelligence 22, 4–37 (2000)
22. Jain, A.K., Murty, M.N., Flynn, P.J.: Data clustering: a review. ACM Comput. Surv. 31, 264–323 (1999)

The Dynamics between Student Affect and Behavior Occurring Outside of Educational Software

Ryan S.J.d. Baker[1], Gregory R. Moore[1], Angela Z. Wagner[2], Jessica Kalka[2], Aatish Salvi[1], Michael Karabinos[3], Colin A. Ashe[3], and David Yaron[3]

[1] Department of Social Science and Policy Studies
Worcester Polytechnic Institute Worcester MA, USA
[2] Human-Computer Interaction Institute
Carnegie Mellon University
Pittsburgh PA, USA
[3] Department of Chemistry, Carnegie Mellon University, Pittsburgh PA, USA
{rsbaker,gregmoore}@wpi.edu, {awagner,jkalka,yaron}@cmu.edu,
aatishsalvi@gmail.com, {mk7,cashe}@andrew.cmu.edu

Abstract. We present an analysis of the affect that precedes, follows, and co-occurs with students' choices to go off-task or engage in on-task conversation within two versions of a virtual laboratory for chemistry. This analysis is conducted using field observation data collected within undergraduate classes using the virtual laboratory software as part of their regular chemistry classes. We find that off-task behavior co-occurs with boredom, but appears to relieve boredom, leading to significantly lower probability of later boredom. We also find that on-task conversation leads to greater future probability of engaged concentration. These results help to clarify the role that behavior outside of educational software plays in students' affect during use of that software.

Keywords: Affect dynamics, off-task behavior, virtual laboratory.

1 Introduction

In recent years, there has been increasing interest in studying the dynamics of affect, and the interplay between affect and behavior, within real-life contexts of human-computer interaction. In specific, considerable recent research has investigated affective dynamics, and the dynamics between affect and behavior, within the context of students using educational software. In early theoretical work in this area, Kort, Reilly, and Picard [9] produced a set of hypotheses for the transitions between affective states, based on Piagetian theories of cognitive equilibrium and disequilibrium. D'Mello, Taylor, and Graesser [6] conducted fine-grained analysis on student affect within educational software in a laboratory setting and found that few transitions between states occur significantly more or less than chance. However, they found evidence that some affective states were significantly more likely to have self-transitions (e.g. persistence over time) than others. In specific, their results provided evidence for a vicious cycle of boredom, and a virtuous cycle of flow (renamed "engaged concentration" in later work [e.g. 1]). This finding was replicated in

S. D´Mello et al. (Eds.): ACII 2011, Part I, LNCS 6974, pp. 14–24, 2011.

classroom settings in [1]. Later analysis where self-transitions were eliminated from analysis found evidence that transitions from confusion to frustration are common, but also found that frustration may lead to several different affective patterns, including alleviated frustration, frustration alternating with confusion, and frustration leading into boredom [5]. It has also been found that altering interactive learning environments to display empathy can disrupt vicious cycles of boredom and frustration [15], although not all types of motivational messages have this effect [19].

Researchers have also extended research on affective dynamics, to study the interplay between affect and specific behaviors associated with differences in learning outcomes, at a fine-grained level. In [1], two studies on affect-behavior dynamics were conducted for high school students using an intelligent tutor or an educational game in class. In both studies, analysis was presented showing that student boredom was likely to be followed by gaming the system [cf. 3], a behavior where students engage in systematic guessing or rapid help requests to obtain answers without thinking through the learning material. In [20], it was reported that off-task behavior leads to different affective consequences, depending on whether off-task behavior follows confusion or frustration; confusion followed by off-task behavior leads to frustration or boredom, whereas frustration followed by off-task behavior leads to positive engagement. Other research on the relationships between affect and behavior in similar educational contexts has typically been conducted at a coarser-grained level (e.g. self-report of overall prevalence of affect and behavior rather than transitions over seconds or minutes). For instance, Pekrun et al. [17] found that boredom was positively associated with attention problems in undergraduate students, and negatively associated with the use of elaboration and self-regulation strategies. Nottelmann and Hill [16] analyzed the relationship between anxiety and off-task behavior during high-stakes testing, finding a positive correlation. Larson and Richards [12] found that a student's overall frequency of boredom in school was not statistically significantly correlated to their overall incidence of disruptive behavior (considered an extreme form of off-task behavior) as reported by their teacher.

Within the current study, we investigate the interplay between student affect and two forms of student behavior among students learning from educational software: off-task behavior, and on-task conversation (defined below). These behaviors are distinguished from other forms of behavior during learning from educational software in that these behaviors occur outside the software, even though they may have significant impact on learning from the software. Analyzing these behaviors helps to expand our understanding of the overall process of learning from educational software, which includes student behavior and learning processes in the human-computer interaction between the student and the software, as well as behavior and learning processes in the social interactions surrounding the use of the software [cf. 22].

Off-task behavior consists of behaviors that do not involve the learning software or its domain in any way, and often stems from the types of attentional difficulties studied by Pekrun et al. [17]. On-task conversation consists of talking to another student or the instructor about the educational software or its domain, rather than interacting solely with the educational software. Both of these behaviors pertain to what the student does beyond just interacting with the educational software. Both behaviors also occupy significant amounts of student time during use of educational software [22]. For instance, [3] found that students learning from educational software in middle school mathematics classes spent 19% of the time engaging in these behaviors. However, there are some important differences between these behaviors.

Time spent engaging in off-task behavior is (by definition) time not spent learning, and off-task behavior has been repeatedly shown to be associated with poorer learning outcomes during individual learning [cf. 8, 11, 13], including within educational software [3]. In addition, off-task behavior is often an early harbinger of more serious forms of disengagement, such as skipping class or dropping out of high school [7, 23].

By contrast, on-task conversation plays a substantial and positive role in learning from educational software. On-task conversation has been observed even in software designed for individual use, when that software is used in classroom settings [e.g. 3, 22]. Several types of on-task conversation have been noted [22]: students collaborating on learning difficult material; students seeking help from the instructor; and instructors spontaneously providing help to a struggling student.

By studying what affect precedes these two categories of behavior during learning, and what affect accompanies the behaviors' emergence, we can improve the theoretical understanding of how affect influences outcomes during real-world tasks. We can also enrich our understanding of how behavior outside of the human-computer interaction is driven by affect occurring during the human-computer interaction, and in turn how this shapes later affect when the student is again focused on interacting with the computer.

2 Data Collection and Data Labeling

This paper examines students in first-year undergraduate chemistry classes using virtual laboratory software (Fig. 1) [24]. The software allows students to design and carry out their own experiments by retrieving chemical solutions from the stockroom (left panels of Fig. 1), and manipulating these solutions using standard glassware and equipment such as Bunsen burners, pH meters and balances (center panels). The right panels provide information on several properties of the contents of the selected solution, including the temperature, pH, and a list of chemical species and their concentrations (the list of species is not available for activities involving identification of unknowns, such as those considered here). Past research on this virtual learning environment suggests that having students design and carry out experiments involves a deeper level of understanding of chemical phenomena than solving standard text-based problems This helps students move beyond shallow problem-solving strategies [24], a finding also seen with other virtual laboratories and in other populations [e.g. 21].

In the activities considered here, students must determine both the identity (HCl, HF, etc) and concentration of an acid in an unknown solution, using a procedure known as titration. Students used two variants of this activity. In the non-game mode of the virtual laboratory (Fig. 1 top), students worked in pairs to identify unknown solutions and enter their answers into a web form that checked for accuracy and allowed three incorrect attempts before issuing a new unknown chemical solution. In the game mode of the virtual laboratory studied in this paper (Fig. 1 bottom), students first created an unknown solution for their opponent. The first student to determine the contents of the unknown created by their opponent won the game. In addition to competition, the game mode brings in the additional strategies of determining what chemical solution would be most difficult for an opponent to identify, and determining the procedure that would most quickly identify the contents of an unknown.

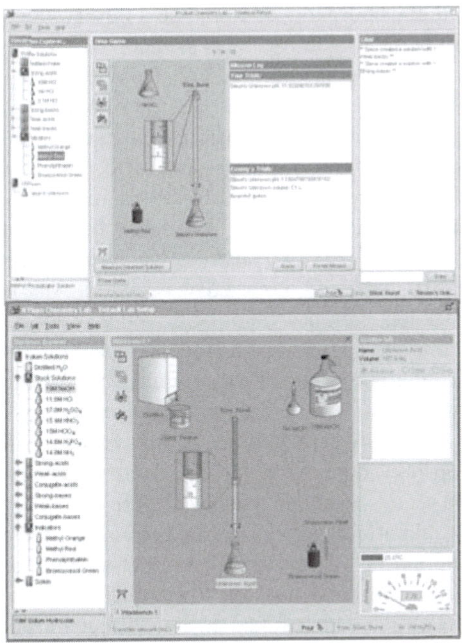

Fig. 1. The virtual laboratory for chemistry (top window represents the original version bottom window represents the game version)

Student behavior was coded as they used both versions of the virtual laboratory, by a pair of expert coders. The coders used software on a Google Android handheld computer, which implemented an observation protocol developed specifically for the process of coding behavior and affect during use of educational software, replicating the protocol in [1]. All coding was conducted by the third and fourth authors. These two coders were previously trained in coding behavior and affect by the first author and have achieved inter-rater reliability with the first author of 0.83 (first and third authors, behavior [cf. 2]) and 0.72 (first and fourth authors, affect) in previous research conducted with students using other learning environments. This degree of reliability is on par with kappas reported by past projects which have assessed the reliability of detecting naturally occurring emotional expressions [1, 4, 14, 19].

Observations were conducted in a computer laboratory at a private university in a city in the Northeastern United States, where 55 students used the Virtual Laboratory software as part of their regular undergraduate chemistry class. The activity lasted approximately 45 minutes, with students randomly assigned to the two conditions. Two class sections of students used the software, with students randomly assigned within class (i.e., each class had students in each condition). Before the class began, an ordering of observation was chosen based on the computer laboratory's layout, and was enforced using the hand-held observation software.

Each observation lasted up to twenty seconds, with observation time so far noted by the hand-held observation software. If affect and behavior were determined before twenty seconds elapsed, the coder moved to the next observation. Each observation was conducted using peripheral vision or side glances. That is, the observers stood diagonally behind the student being observed and avoided looking at the student directly [cf. 1, 3, 19], in order to make it less clear when an observation was occurring. This method of observing using peripheral vision was previously found to be highly successful for assessing student behavior and affect, achieving good inter-rater reliability [1, 2, 19]. To increase tractability of both coding and eventual analysis, if two distinct affective states were seen during a single observation, only the first state observed was coded. Similarly, if two distinct behaviors were seen during a single observation, only the first behavior observed was coded. Any behavior or affect of a student other than the student currently being observed was not coded.

The observers based their judgment of a student's state or behavior on the student's work context, actions, utterances, facial expressions, body language, and interactions with teachers or fellow students. These are, broadly, the same types of information used in previous methods for coding affect [e.g. 4], and in line with Planalp et al's [18] descriptive research on how humans generally identify affect using multiple cues in concert for maximum accuracy rather than attempting to select individual cues. The judgments of behavior and affect were based on a sub-set of the coding scheme used in [1]. Within an observation, each observer coded affect with reference to five categories: boredom, confusion, engaged concentration (the affect associated with the flow state [cf. 1]), frustration, and "?", which refers to any affect outside the coding scheme, including eureka, delight, and surprise. "?" also includes indeterminate behavior and cases where it was impossible to code affect, such as when a student went to the bathroom or the software crashed. Delight and surprise were removed from the earlier coding scheme due to the relative rarity of these affective states in prior research [e.g. 1, 6, 19]. Each observer coded behavior with reference to five categories: on-task solitary behavior, on-task conversation, off-task behavior, gaming the system, and "?". Working silently in the game was coded as on- task solitary behavior, even though the student was competing with another student.

During the period of observation, 700 observations were conducted across the students, at an average of 13.0 observations per student. Of the 700 observations, 46 behaviors were coded as "?", and 90 affective states were coded as "?". Observations labeled in this way were not analyzed, but were retained in sequences (e.g., in a sequence of three observations where observation two was coded "?", observation three was not considered to be immediately after observation one). An average of 131.7 seconds passed between observations.

3 Analysis and Results

3.1 Overall Frequency of Behaviors and Affective States

The frequency of each behavior coded, averaged within each student and then averaged across students, is given in Table 1. As can be seen, gaming was quite rare across students, occurring under 0.1% of the time. In fact, only one observation was noted as involving gaming the system, possibly due to the exploratory nature of the virtual laboratory, and the high cost of making errors in the game. Off-task behavior was also relatively uncommon within this population, occurring 6.3% of the time. However, on-task collaboration was quite common, accounting for 22.2% of student behavior. On-task solitary behavior accounted for 71.6% of student behavior.

The frequency of each affective state, averaged within each student and then averaged across students, is given in Table 2. The most common affective state was engaged concentration, occurring 81.6% of the time. The second most common affective state was confusion, occurring 14.1% of the time. Frustration and boredom were each relatively uncommon, respectively occurring 2.5% and 1.9% of the time.

The relative frequency of engaged concentration and confusion is consistent with past reports of the prevalence of affect during use of educational software across settings (laboratory and classroom), populations (undergraduate, high school, middle school), and educational software package [1, 5, 6, 15, 19], although frustration and boredom were less common than has been reported in these earlier studies. The lower incidence of these affective states and off-task behavior, compared to previous studies, is likely not due to observer effects, since many past studies of these constructs had similar numbers of observers and similar observation protocols.

There were no significant differences in the prevalence of any affective state or behavior between the two environments. As such, data from the two environments will be considered together throughout the remainder of the paper.

3.2 Transitions and Co-occurrences of Behaviors and Affective States

The transitions between affect and behavior, and co-occurrence between affect and behavior, were studied using D'Mello et al.'s [6] transition metric, ***L***. ***L*** provides an indication of the probability of a transition or co-occurrence above and beyond the base rate of each affective category or behavior. For instance, on-task solitary behavior was the most common behavior in the Chemistry Virtual Lab; therefore, this behavior is likely to be the most common behavior that follows or co-occurs with *any* affective state in these environments. ***L*** explicitly accounts for the base rate of each state when assessing how likely a transition is, given the probability that a transition between two states occurs, and given the base frequency of the destination state. ***L*** is computed as shown in equation 1:

$$L = \frac{\Pr(Next|Prev) - \Pr(Next)}{1 - \Pr(Next)} \quad (1)$$

A value of 1 means that the transition/co-occurrence will always occur, whereas a value of 0 means that the transition's likelihood is exactly what it would be if we were to predict the transition using only the base frequency of the destination state. Values

Table 1. Prevalence of each student behavior in the sample (averaged within students and then averaged across students). Observations labeled "?" are excluded from analysis.

	Gaming the System	Off-Task	On-Task Solitary	On-Task Conversation
Prevalence	<0.1%	6.3%	71.6%	22.2%

Table 2. Prevalence of each affective state in the sample (averaged within students and then averaged across students). Observations labeled "?" are excluded from analysis.

	Engaged Concentratio	Confusion	Frustration	Boredom
Prevalence	81.6%	14.1%	2.5%	1.9%

above 0 signify that the transition is more likely than expected (i.e., greater than the base frequency of the destination behavior or affective state), and values under 0 signify that the transition is less likely than expected (i.e., less than the base frequency of the destination behavior or affective state).

For a given transition or co-occurrence, we calculate a value for ***L*** for each student and then calculate the mean and standard error across students. We can then determine if a given transition is significantly more likely than chance (chance=0) using the two-tailed t-test for one sample. Note that the degrees of freedom for a two-tailed t-test for any given transition or co-occurrence is the number of students for whom equation 1 can be calculated, minus one ($df = N - 1$). Students who never displayed the preceding affective state or behavior give no evidence on transitions from that affective state or behavior. Similarly, it is not possible to calculate transition likelihood for students who always displayed the same following affective state or behavior.

In analyzing the affective states that precede, follow, and co-occur with each of the student behaviors studied, it was not possible to study gaming the system due to its low frequency. On-task solitary behavior was not explicitly studied, as it was the baseline behavior of use for these systems. Hence, we studied the relationship between off-task behavior and on-task collaboration, and the four affective states studied.

The full pattern of transitions and co-occurrence between affect and student behavior is shown in Table 3.

Table 3. Base-rate adjusted likelihood (average D'Mello's ***L*** across students) and standard deviation (in parentheses) of each behavior-affect transition (denoted by arrow) or co- occurence (denoted by dash-dash) within the data set. Statistically significant transitions (p<0.05) in boldface; marginally significant transitions (p<0.1) in italics.

Off Task→ Bored	**-0.04 (0.06)**	Off Task→ Confused	-0.04 (0.29)
Off Task→ Eng. Conc.	-0.20 (1.54)	Off Task→ Frustrated	0.07 (0.24)
OnTask Conv → Bored	-0.01 (0.06)	OnTask Conv → Confused	0.02 (0.27)
OnTask Conv → Eng. Conc.	0.10 (0.94)	**OnTask Conv → Frustrated**	**-0.01 (0.04)**
Bored → Off Task	-0.03 (0.16)	Confused → Off Task	-0.03 (0.14)
Eng. Conc. → Off Task	0.00 (0.10)	*Frustrated → Off Task*	*-0.04 (0.07)*
Bored → OnTask Conv	0.11 (0.66)	Confused → OnTask Conv	0.07 (0.54)
Eng. Conc. → OnTask Conv	-0.05 (0.26)	Frustrated → OnTask Conv	-0.05 (0.39)
Off Task -- Bored	**0.19 (0.37)**	**Off Task – Confused**	**-0.18 (0.26)**
Off Task -- Eng. Conc.	**-1.75 (1.67)**	*Off Task – Frustrated*	*-0.02 (0.06)*
OnTask Conv -- Bored	**-0.02 (0.05)**	**OnTask Conv – Confused**	**0.19 (0.32)**
OnTask Conv -- Eng. Conc.	*-0.78 (2.30)*	OnTask Conv – Frustrated	0.02 (0.10)

The pattern between boredom and off-task behavior was somewhat non-intuitive. First, boredom and off-task behavior co-occurred, $t(26) = 2.58$, two-tailed $p = 0.02$. However, a student who was bored was not more likely to go off-task in the next observation, $t(11) = -0.63$, two-tailed $p = 0.54$. But surprisingly, a student who was off-task was significantly *less* likely to be bored in the next observation, $t(23) = -3.05$, $p = 0.01$. This finding suggests that off-task behavior relieves boredom, in turn suggesting that off-task behavior may disrupt the "vicious cycles" of continual boredom that have been reported in [1, 6].

The dynamics between frustration and off-task behavior was also interesting. A student who was frustrated was marginally less likely to go off-task in the next observation, $t(11) = -2.03$, two-tailed $p = 0.07$. Off-task behavior and frustration also were less likely than chance to co-occur, $t(26) = -2.06$, two-tailed $p = 0.05$. There was not a statistically significant relationship between off-task behavior and future frustration, $t(23) = 1.51$, two-tailed $p = 0.15$.

No other affective states were significantly more or less likely than chance to precede or follow off-task behavior. However, both engaged concentration and confusion were significantly less likely when a student was off-task, respectively, $t(26) = -5.35$, two-tailed $p < 0.001$, $t(26) = -3.49$, two-tailed $p < 0.01$.

On-task conversation was not significantly preceded by any affective states. However, it was significantly less likely than chance to precede frustration, $t(42) = -2.11$, two-tailed $p = 0.04$. Hence, it appears that on-task conversation resolves problems that might cause future frustration.

In terms of co-occurrence, students were significantly more likely than chance to be confused while engaging in on-task conversation, $t(43) = 3.92$, two-tailed $p < 0.001$. We hypothesize that a confused student might seek help, increasing the likelihood of being on-task. Students were significantly less likely than chance to be bored while in on-task conversation, $t(43) = -2.92$, two-tailed $p = 0.01$. They were also significantly less likely to be in engaged concentration while in on-task conversation, $t(36) = -2.02$, two-tailed $p = 0.05$, a particularly striking finding given the higher probability of engaged concentration following on-task conversation. There was not a significant co-occurrence between on-task conversation and frustration, $t(43) = 1.10$, two-tailed $p = 0.28$.

4 Discussion and Conclusions

Within this paper, we have analyzed the affect which precedes, co-occurs with, and follows two forms of behavior that occur outside of interactive learning environments: off-task behavior, and on-task conversation. This analysis was carried out on field observation data from undergraduates using virtual laboratory software for chemistry.

Perhaps the most noteworthy finding is that off-task behavior co-occurs with boredom, but that boredom is significantly less likely than chance following off-task behavior. The complex relationship between boredom and off-task behavior seen here may explain why past research found that the overall prevalence of boredom does not significantly correlate with the overall frequency of extreme forms of off-task behavior [e.g. 12]. Overall prevalence may simply not be a sufficiently sensitive measure to catch the relationships between off-task behavior and affect.

Past theories of off-task behavior have frequently focused on its negative correlates, such as poorer learning [e.g. 3, 8, 11, 13], and skipping school and drop-out [e.g. 7, 23]. However, our findings suggest that off-task behavior may play a positive role in some situations, disrupting "vicious cycles," where a student who becomes bored is highly likely to remain bored [e.g. 1, 6], and helping some students regulate their boredom. A similar finding is obtained in [20], where frustrated students who go off-task were seen to demonstrate future engagement. Hence, off-task behavior, within reasonable limits, may actually be beneficial for affect and in turn perhaps even for learning. This finding accords with work by Kreijns [10] suggesting another positive effect of off-task behavior, improved relationships between students (and in turn improved collaboration).

We also find interesting relationships between on-task conversation and affect. In specific, on-task conversation is associated with less future probability of frustration (even when students are working solitarily). Much research on collaborative and individual learning attempts to determine which form of learning is most effective, and under which conditions. However, this finding confirms earlier reports that episodes of on-task conversation are a normal part of "individual" learning in classrooms [e.g. 3, 22], and goes further, suggesting that collaborative episodes during individual learning often lead to the types of affect and concentration that are associated with successful learning. It may be interesting to investigate, in future research, what the affective impacts are of periods of individual work during collaborative learning.

Overall, the findings presented here suggest that the interplay between student behavior and affect, within educational settings, is more complex than previously thought. This result warrants further fine-grained analysis of the effects of off-task behavior during learning, and the factors leading to and effects of on-task collaboration. By understanding these relationships, we may be able to design learning environments that better leverage the positive aspects of off-task behavior and on-task conversation, while minimizing the negative impacts of off-task behavior on learning.

Acknowledgements. The authors thank the Pittsburgh Science of Learning Center (National Science Foundation) via grant "Toward a Decade of PSLC Research", award number SBE-0836012. We would also like to thank Lisa Rossi, Carolyn Rosé, Ma. Mercedes Rodrigo, Sidney D'Mello, Vincent Aleven, and Timothy Nokes for helpful comments and suggestions.

References

1. Baker, R.S.d.J., D'Mello, S., Rodrigo, M.M.T., Graesser, A.C.: Better to be Frustrated than Bored: The Incidence, Persistence, and Impact of Learners' Cognitive-Affective States During Interactions with Three Different Computer-Based Learning Environments. International Journal of Human-Computer Studies 68(4), 223–241 (2010)
2. Baker, R.S.J.d., Corbett, A.T., Wagner, A.Z.: Human Classification of Low-Fidelity Replays of Student Actions. In: Proceedings of the Educational Data Mining Workshop at the 8th International Conference on Intelligent Tutoring Systems, pp. 29–36 (2009)

3. Baker, R.S., Corbett, A.T., Koedinger, K.R., Wagner, A.Z.: Off-Task Behavior in the Cognitive Tutor Classroom: When Students "Game the System". In: Proceedings of ACM CHI 2004: Computer-Human Interaction, pp. 383–390 (2004)
4. Bartel, C.A., Saavedra, R.: The Collective Construction of Work Group Moods. Administrative Science Quarterly 45(2), 197–231 (2000)
5. D'Mello, S., Graesser, A.: Modeling Cognitive-Affective Dynamics with Hidden Markov Models. In: Proceedings of the 32nd Annual Cognitive Science Society, pp. 2721–2726 (2010)
6. D'Mello, S.K., Taylor, R., Graesser, A.C.: Monitoring affective trajectories during complex learning. In: Proc. of the 29th Annual Cognitive Science Society, pp. 203–208 (2007)
7. Finn, J.D.: Withdrawing From School. Review of Educational Research 59(2), 117–142 (1989)
8. Karweit, N., Slavin, R.E.: Time-On-Task: Issues of Timing, Sampling, and Definition. Journal of Experimental Psychology 74(6), 844–851 (1982)
9. Kort, B., Reilly, R., Picard, R.: An affective model of the interplay between emotions and learning. In: Proceedings of the 2nd Int'l Conf. on Advanced Learning Technologies (2001)
10. Kreijns, K.: Sociable CSCL environments: Social affordances, sociability, and social presence. Unpublished Master's Thesis. Open University of the Netherlands, Heerlen, The Netherlands (2004)
11. Lahaderne, H.M.: Attitudinal and Intellectual Correlates of Attention: A Study of Four Sixth-Grade Classrooms. Journal of Educational Psychology 59(5), 320–324 (1968)
12. Larson, R.W., Richards, M.H.: Boredom in the Middle School Years: Blaming Schools Versus Blaming Students. American Journal of Education 99(4), 418–443 (1991)
13. Lee, S.W., Kelly, K.E., Nyre, J.E.: Preliminary Report on the Relation of Students' On Task Behavior With Completion of School Work. Psychological Reports 84, 267–272 (1999)
14. Litman, D.J., Forbes-Riley, K.: Predicting student emotions in computer-human tutoring dialogues. In: Proceedings of the 42nd Annual Meeting of the Association for Computational Linguistics, pp. 352–359 (2004)
15. McQuiggan, S.W., Robison, J.L., Lester, J.C.: Affective Transitions in Narrative-Centered Learning Environments. Educational Technology & Society 13(1), 40–53 (2010)
16. Nottelmann, E.D., Hill, K.T.: Test Anxiety and Off-Task Behavior in Evaluative Situations. Child Development 48(1), 225–231 (1977)
17. Pekrun, R., Goetz, T., Daniels, L.M., Stupnisky, R.H., Perry, R.P.: Boredom in Achievement Settings: Exploring Control-Value Antecedents and Performance Outcomes of a Neglected Emotion. Journal of Educational Psychology 102(3), 531–549 (2010)
18. Planalp, S., DeFrancisco, V.L., Rutherford, D.: Varieties of Cues to Emotion in Naturally Occurring Settings. Cognition and Emotion 10(2), 137–153 (1996)
19. Rodrigo, M.M.T., Rebolledo-Mendez, G., Baker, R.S.J.d., du Boulay, B., Sugay, J.O., Lim, S.A.L., Espejo-Lahoz, M.B., Luckin, R. The Effects of Motivational Modeling on Affect in an Intelligent Tutoring System. In: Proceedings of the International Conference on Computers in Education, pp. 57–64 (2008)
20. Sabourin, J., Rowe, J., Mott, B., Lester, J.: When Off-Task in On-Task: The Affective Role of Off-Task Behavior in Narrative-Centered Learning Environments. In: Biswas, G., Bull, S., Kay, J., Mitrovic, A. (eds.) AIED 2011. LNCS, vol. 6738, pp. 534–536. Springer, Heidelberg (2011)

21. Sao Pedro, M.A., Gobert, J.D., Raziuddin, J.J.: Comparing pedagogical approaches for the acquisition and long-term robustness of the control of variables strategy. In: Proceedings of the 9th International Conference of the Learning Sciences, pp. 1024–1031 (2010)
22. Schofield, J.W.: Computers and Classroom Culture. Cambridge University Press, Cambridge (1995)
23. Tobin, T.J., Sugai, G.M.: Using Sixth-Grade School Records to Predict School Violence, Chronic Discipline Problems, and High School Outcomes. Journal of Emotional and Behavioral Disorders 7(1), 40–53 (1999)
24. Yaron, D., Karabinos, M., Lange, D., Greeno, J.G., Leinhardt, G.: The ChemCollective: Virtual labs and online activities for introductory chemistry courses. Science 328, 584–585 (2010)

ikannotate – A Tool for Labelling, Transcription, and Annotation of Emotionally Coloured Speech

Ronald Böck[1], Ingo Siegert[1], Matthias Haase[2], Julia Lange[2], and Andreas Wendemuth[1]

[1] Otto von Guericke University, Dept. of Electrical Engineering and Information Technology, Universitätsplatz 2, 39106 Magdeburg, Germany
[2] Otto von Guericke University, Dept. of Psychosomatic Medicine and Psychotherapy, Leipziger Str. 44, 39120 Magdeburg, Germany
ronald.boeck@ovgu.de
http://www.cognitive-systems-magdeburg.de

Abstract. In speech recognition and emotion recognition from speech, qualitatively high transcription and annotation of given material is important. To analyse prosodic features, linguistics provides several transcription systems. Furthermore, in emotion labelling different methods are proposed and discussed. In this paper, we introduce the tool *ikannotate*, which combines prosodic information with emotion labelling. It allows the generation of a transcription of material directly annotated with prosodic features. Moreover, material can be emotionally labelled according to Basic Emotions, the Geneva Emotion Wheel, and Self Assessment Manikins. Finally, we present results of two usability tests observing the ability to identify emotions in labelling and comparing the transcription tool "Folker" with our application.

Keywords: Man-Machine-Interaction, Tool, Labelling, Transcription, Annotation.

1 Introduction

In emotion recognition from speech, data material is an important resource which influences the performance of a system directly. For this, in the past, several databases were recorded which are different in their characteristics. In the last few years, the focus switched from acted emotional material [2] to more realistic material, i.e., recordings that are done by naïve speakers and in non-ideal (noisy, realistic) conditions, e.g., [6, 19]. Whatever the differences in the material are, pre-processing is a significant step to utilise these databases in training and testing of automatic processing. In this paper, we do not deal with recording and signal pre-processing but with labelling, transcription, and annotation. The quality of these processes accounts for the quality of the material, which is used to train systems for recognising emotions in speech.

Transcription and annotation are related to each other. We define transcription as the process of generating a textual representation of the spoken utterances. The complexity of this task depends directly on the number of speakers

S. D´Mello et al. (Eds.): ACII 2011, Part I, LNCS 6974, pp. 25–34, 2011.

involved in the conversation, which vary between one in monologues [10], two in dialogues and typical Wizard-of-Oz (WOZ) experiments that are suitable to generate databases [6], to more than two in group conversations [19].

Annotation is a further kind of sub-symbolic pre-processing which is based on the transcribed material. In the nomenclature that is used in computer and engineering sciences, annotating a corpus is adding prosodic information to the utterances. Indeed, this directly depends on the annotation system (in linguistics it is also called transcription system). In linguistics various systems are available, e.g. codes for the human analysis of transcripts (CHAT) [8], semi-interpretative working transcript (HIAT) [4] as it is used in [12], and conversation analytic system of transcription (GAT) [16]. As in our research the focus is on non-acted material, which is recorded in WOZ scenarios, we decided to use the established GAT. This system is a common method in linguistics and social sciences (for detailed information cf. Sect. 3.2). Further advantages of GAT that lead to its application: (i) GAT makes a transcription available that provides a scheme of granularity, i.e., different levels of detail in transcription are build upon each other, which enable the user to refine the transcript if necessary (e.g., for special research questions), and (ii) GAT does not adopt theory orientated assumptions, so researchers with different theoretical background can use it [16].

As we are also interested in recognising emotions from speech, the recorded audio material has to be labelled with appropriate methods, i.e., tagging each utterance with marks, which correspond to emotional states of a user. According to the applied systematics, the utterances are marked either with Basic Emotion classes [3] or with a primitives-based concept [1]. Keeping in mind that emotional expressions vary in intensity and meaning very rapidly over time [11] we also observe the temporal progress of the emotion within a sentence. For further information of the utilised annotation methods see Sect. 2.

So far, transcription and annotation is done by using standard text editors or tools, which are focused on these specific tasks, e.g., "Folker" provided by the Institute for the German Language [15]. They provide a more comfortable handling of the process, but are intended for users who are familiar with the specifications of annotation systems. These applications are well suited for prosody and textual analyses, however they lack labelling opportunities. Moreover, the annotation of prosodic characteristics has to be done manually. In emotion recognition, the combination of these three processing steps is necessary. For this, it might be preferable to merge labelling, transcription, and annotation in one application. This is done in the *i*nterdisciplinary *k*nowledge-based *anno*tation *t*ool for *a*ided *t*ranscription of *e*motions (*ikannotate*) that implements a module for transcription and annotation according to GAT. Moreover, it can be used to label the transcribed material with different emotion labelling methods. And, it implements data preparation tools for emotion and speech recognition as well as GAT conform outputs as export functions. In the current version, *ikannotate* is focused on audio materials. Thus, it handles two types of recordings: (i) WAV or MP3 coded recordings of a whole session can be continuously processed and split afterwards; (ii) already split recordings can be handled sentence by sentence. *Ikannotate*'s modularity also enables extensibility to process material with multimodal signals, like audio-visual (video) or physio-biological data.

In the following, we describe general technical details of *ikannotate*: It is developed to handle different output formats, especially, XML and TXT files. The tool is written in QT4, which is a programming environment, based on C++ and therefore can be used with many different operating systems. We provide versions for Linux, Windows XP and higher, and MacOS.

The remainder of the paper is structured as follows: In Sect. 2, we discuss the emotion labelling methods combined with uncertainty as well as the module for temporal characteristics of emotions. In Sect. 3, we present the modules for transcription and annotation. Furthermore, general ideas of GAT's functionality and specifications are introduced. The output formats of *ikannotate* are introduced in Sect. 4 and the properties of additional tools (Sect. 5) are presented. Finally, results of usability tests are shown and discussed.

2 Labelling Component

2.1 Three Labelling Methods

So far, it is not clear which labelling method is suitable for emotion representation and recognition [3, 7, 13, 14]. Thus, we implemented three common methods in *ikannotate* and hence, we provide the opportunity to compare and investigate the labelling systems and their usability. Results of experiments dealing with this issue are presented in [18]. The utilised material was processed with *ikannotate*.

Basic Emotions. *Ikannotate* provides the possibility to label spoken utterances with Basic Emotions. For this, we implemented the model according to Ekman [5]. Due to possible differences in Human-Computer-Interaction (HCI) and Human-Human-Interaction (HHI) in characteristics of emotions, we extended the labelling system by *neutral*, because in HCI non-emotional parts can occur, and *other*, to provide the labellers with the opportunity to rate emotions that do not fit the given classes.

Geneva Emotion Wheel. One version of the Geneva Emotion Wheel (GEW) introduced by Scherer [13] is implemented. The advantages of this method include the natural way of labelling discrete categorical emotions represented by words and the possible mapping of these discrete labels into a 2-dimensional space (valance-dominance [13]) that is a sub-space of the valence-arousal-dominance space (VAD space) [9]. Additionally, it is possible to choose circles, which differ in size, for each emotion. This allows us to assign emotions with certain degrees of intensity, which are represented by expressive words. Prior to the study, the annotators are instructed to choose the emotion that fits their perception. Moreover, in the current release labellers can assign up to three labels (this value can be set by the experimenter) to each utterance, such that even mixed emotional states can be reflected by this method.

Self Assessment Manikins. The third method implements a kind of Self Assessment Manikins (SAM) [1]. This is a non-verbal emotion labelling system in a

3-dimensional space (VAD space [1, 7, 9]) and moreover suitable for self-ratings as well as external ratings. Each emotion is assigned to a point in VAD space given by a triple of integers. For instance, (5,5,1) for high valence, high arousal, and low dominance.

Detailed information of the modules' realisation and corresponding figures can be found on webpage: http://ikannotate.cognitive-systems-magdeburg.de/.

2.2 Temporal Characteristics of Emotion

As mentioned in the introduction, emotional expressions tend to vary in intensity rapidly over time. It is assumed that the emotional expression is not equally distributed over all words in a sentence, hence, a maximum of intensity could be found (assuming intensity is influenced by the method described in [14]).

We added a supplementary module to *ikannotate* that allows the labeller to define the maximum of emotion intensity in the expression. For convenience, users can adjust the intensity in units of words only in position and width, but not in height (cf. Fig. 1). We assume that the height is already coded in the assigned emotional label, especially in case of GEW and SAM.

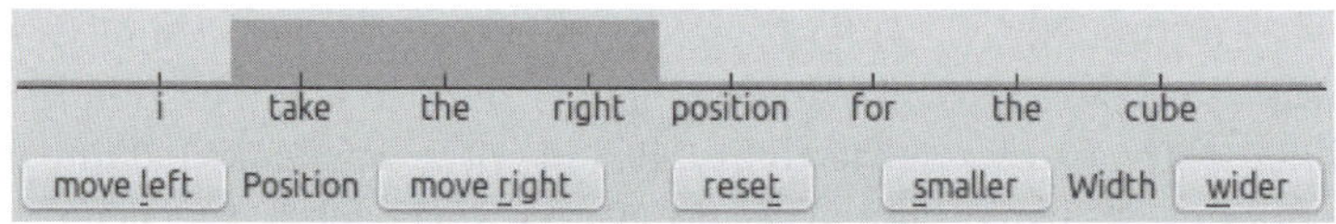

Fig. 1. Annotation module: Marking position of intensity maximum

2.3 Labelling of Uncertainty

Despite the variety of labelling methods, it is hard to assign the correct emotion to an utterance. Hence, each labelling process is afflicted with uncertainty. This can be in the assigned emotion itself, in the different meanings of an expression, or in the intensity. To avoid confusions in later analyses we provide an additional tool that implements indication of the degree of uncertainty of a user in current labels; hence, this is a self-rating.

The uncertainty values provide us with additional information about the labelling which can be used to combine given classifications. Moreover, this gives an indication of the quality of the assignment and a kind of ground truth marked with uncertainty values.

3 Transcription and Annotation

3.1 Transcription of Sentences

Transcription is so far a manual process that is necessary to extract well defined textual information from spoken utterances. This takes much effort and also much time. Nonetheless, a transcript is the basis of annotation as well as labelling and, for that reason, the ground truth of audio emotion recognition.

The transcription module of *ikannotate* (cf. Fig. 2) provides the opportunity to type in the utterance which is heard from the build-in audio player. Moreover, the transcriber can set a start and end time of each utterance to supply times utilised in audio material splitting. Once the processing of a sentence is finished, the current information is automatically stored on sentences level and saved in a corresponding XML file (see Sect. 4.1). Furthermore, it is possible to load already transcribed material and thus, we provide a sub-module that can be used to insert sentences missed in a previous transcription process.

Besides the pure textual transcription, additional information of the material like description of the recording environment, names of experimenters, etc. are captured [16, 17]. Moreover, the transcript contains comments to annotation conditions, which are common in this session, e.g., loudness, tempi, etc.

3.2 Adding Annotation Features

The annotation module of *ikannotate* is based on a conversation analytic system of transcription (GAT) [16] (cf. Fig. 2). This system tries to offer a standard for the prosodic annotation of spoken speech, which is already transcribed. The main ideas of GAT are derived by analysing German utterances. For detailed information and the corresponding nomenclature see [16, 17]. Even though it originates from German language, it is suitable for other languages as well. Indeed, our tool is not related to any language and hence more general. In the current release of *ikannotate*, two published versions of GAT are realised [16, 17]. According to the version, *ikannotate* distinguishes between basic and fine (GAT1 & 2) [16, 17] and minimal (only GAT2) [17] annotation.

As GAT's main focus is on prosodic annotation, the authors of GAT proposed to use standard text editors to process the material. Unfortunately, such output is hard to handle automatically. Further, as all categories are encoded directly into the same text, the coding process itself and the evaluation get very complex. Thus, we decided to separate GAT representation and data storage that has three advantages: (i) each annotation module is observed as a single category and therefore coded and stored separately; (ii) the GAT annotated utterance can be reproduced according to each module, for instance, the transcribed and annotated material can be presented and extracted in an issue-dependent way (cf. Sect. 5.1); (iii) due to modularity an annotator will not be confused by other prosodic categories because the annotated text is composed and syntax checked automatically.

As we employ the transcribed and annotated text for emotion labelling, we decided to work on sentence level. For all annotation modules, except processing structure, the user has to edit each sentence separately.

The processing structure describes the temporal sequence of the utterances, that is difficult to specify on sentence level. Hence, we decided to alleviate this as follows: In GAT, editing the processing structure is not handled in an intuitive way. Thus, we switched to score notation, which is contained in HIAT [4]. In this method, each speaker has his own (single) line and co-instantaneous spoken parts are presented stack-wise (cf. Fig. 3).

Fig. 2. Annotation module of *ikannotate* (GAT2)

Fig. 3. Score notation of two speakers

4 Output Formats

4.1 XML File Format

As already explained (cf. Sect. 3.2), the original and processed data are saved separately. We decided to store the transcribed, annotated, and labelled data in XML files, as this is a well defined and standardised data format that can be automatically processed and allows to structure the sentences by their type and person who uttered it.

The global structure of our XML file has two parts: a session description (session head) and the information for each sentence itself.

The session head contains all information according to the current session and the transcription head (cf. Sect. 3.1) as defined in GAT [17].

Every sentence is saved in a separate element that contains general as well as GAT information where each module is stored in a separate tag.

4.2 GAT Output

In the following, we discuss the output generated by *PsychCreator* (cf. Sect. 5.1), i.e. the GAT output. According to [16, 17], every GAT transcript begins with the transcription head (cf. Sect. 3.1) providing information of the following session, e.g. session name, names of participants and their roles, etc. Then, the current transcript is given in a formatted way. GAT defines that each line begins with a line number followed by three blanks, the speaker id, additional three blanks, and the annotated utterance. Due to *ikannotate*'s specifications, each sentence or utterance is printed in one line (cf. Ex. 1). Usually, no comments (/* */) are given in a GAT transcript; they are just inserted to explain the meaning of the signs.

Example 1.

01	S1	i (.) like <<dim>ikannotate>	/*short pause & to soften*/
02	S2	well meh .h too	/*exhalation & inhalation*/
03	S2	what do YOU think (.) about GAT	/*accent & short pause & accent*/
04	S1	it is (1.25s) fine for me	/*1.25s pause*/
05	S1	...	

5 Additional Tools

To extract information from stored XML files for speech processing and further analysis purposes, we created several tools, in addition. These are grouped into *PsychCreator* and *ASRCreator*.

5.1 PsychCreator

PsychCreator uses the XML material to generate a transcript according to GAT specifications [16, 17]. An example with few prosodic information is given in Ex. 1. Moreover, the user can select the information that should be extracted. The output can be controlled and adapted to the current issue.

In order to do this, we decided for three options: (i) the plain text, i.e., the text without any prosodic information, (ii) the full prosodic annotated text, and (iii) a text with user specific prosodic features. The generated output is saved as a TXT or RTF file in UTF-8 encoding to provide the opportunity to handle the file independent of the platform.

5.2 ASRCreator

Material that is processed with *ikannotate* should be ready to use for automatic speech recognition (ASR) and automatic emotion recognition from speech. Therefore, we developed a tool to generate files that are necessary to train models with the Hidden Markov Toolkit (HTK) provided by the University of Cambridge [20], which is common in ASR community. The main focus is on preparing so called master label files (MLFs) containing the corresponding labels of the utterances.

Moreover, we provide the possibility to split the audio material according to the start and end times, which are also marked by the annotators and labellers, respectively. Hence, these sub-sequences can be used for training and testing. The splitting can be skipped if already cut material is used (cf. Sect. 1).

6 Usability Tests

We tested *ikannotate* in the field of emotion labelling. For this, ten students, with no prior knowledge of emotion labelling, from different faculties, were asked to label an audio file with Basic Emotions, GEW, and SAM. For each method the same audio material, taken from a WOZ experiment, was used. After each trial, the students filled a questionnaire about the covered emotions in the material. Finally, they were asked whether *ikannotate* helps to identify emotions given in the audio files. The result is based on a one to seven scale where one means "totally disagree" and seven "totally agree". The means and standard deviation of answers are given in Table 1. Due to the small sample of ten students the standard deviation is large.

In addition, we conducted a study to compare the usability of the transcription module in *ikannotate* against "Folker" [15]. We used a sample of ten psychology students from our university, all German native speaker and laymen in transcription. The test phase was conducted as follows: After a short introduction into transcription in general, the users were randomly divided into one of two scenarios, separated by the number of students starting with a certain tool (cf. Table 2). After the test phase, all subjects were asked for their assessment of both tools by open questions. Results showed that subjects criticised the syntax control function of "Folker", because the information of the position of syntax faults is not given. In contrast, *ikannotate* offers an automatic fault protection function, that provides this information. Furthermore, *ikannotate* is assessed as more clearly laid out than "Folker". Moreover, "Folker" offers a function for displaying the course of the audio file, which the subjects missed in *ikannotate*. This function will be implemented in a future version of *ikannotate*.

Table 1. Means and standard deviation of helpfulness of the emotion labelling method (range one to seven)

	mean	standard deviation
Basic Emotion	3.70	1.64
GEW	5.00	1.41
SAM	4.50	1.90

Table 2. Comparison of experimental conditions

	trial 1	trial 2
scenario 1 - (6 of 10)	transcription of audio file 1 using "Folker"	transcription of audio file 2 using *ikannotate*
scenario 2 - (4 of 10)	transcription of audio file 1 using *ikannotate*	transcription of audio file 2 using "Folker"

7 Conclusion and Outlook

In this paper we introduced a tool that - to our knowledge - for the first time combines the processes labelling, transcription, and annotation in one single application. After conducting usability tests for transcription and emotion labelling using the *ikannotate* modules, we will utilise the data material for the training and testing of automatic emotion recognition. To train suitable models, which realise the recognition, pre-processed material is necessary. Our tool provides the opportunity to handle the pre-processing steps - even for laymen - and to generate outputs that can be further processed automatically.

In the next versions of *ikannotate* we will incorporate the course of the audio file to get a further improvement of handling. Furthermore, a video player and a module presenting physio-biological recording will be integrated. Hence, processing of multimodal material can be realised. Thus, in future, we plan to use *ikannotate* to transcribe speech, mark prosody, and assign emotional labels to utterances, which are recorded in our research groups. Hence, this material can be used to examine differences in uttered emotions, which might occur in HHI and HCI, cf. [18]. Further we will run several WOZ experiments to gather material for the analysis of emotions in the context of HCI.

Additional information like uncertainty values can be used to develop classifiers, i.e., as kind of expert systems, which handle and incorporate this information to deal with emotion and prosody recognition in a more human-like manner.

The current version of *ikannotate* is available at http://ikannotate.cognitive-systems-magdeburg.de/ and is licensed under Creative Common Licence (cc-by-nc-nd).

Acknowledgement. We acknowledge continued support by the Transregional Collaborative Research Centre SFB/TRR 62 "Companion-Technology for Cognitive Technical Systems" funded by the German Research Foundation (DFG). We also acknowledge the DFG for financing our computing cluster used for parts of this work.

References

[1] Bradley, M., Lang, P.: Measuring emotion: The self-assessment manikin and the semantic differential. Journal of Behavior Therapy and Experimental Psychiatry 25, 49–59 (1994)

[2] Burkhardt, F., Paeschke, A., Rolfes, M., Sendlmeier, W., Weiss, B.: A Database of German Emotional Speech. In: Proc. of the 5th Interspeech (2005)

[3] Douglas-Cowie, E., Campbell, N., Cowie, R., Roach, P.: Emotional speech: towards a new generation of databases. Speech Communication Special Issue Speech and Emotion 40, 33–60 (2003)

[4] Ehlich, K., Rehbein, J.: Erweiterte halbinterpretative Arbeitstranskriptionen (HIAT2): Intonation. Linguistische Berichte 59, 51–75 (1979)

[5] Ekman, P.: Are there basic emotions? Psychological Review 99, 550–553 (1992)

[6] Gnjatović, M., Rösner, D.: The NIMITEK Corpus of Affected Behavior in Human-Machine Interaction. In: Proc. of the Second International Workshop on Corpora for Research on Emotion and Affect (satellite of LREC 2008), Marrakech, Marocco (2008)
[7] Grimm, M., Kroschel, K., Mower, E., Narayanan, S.: Primitives-based evaluation and estimation of emotions in speech. Speech Communication 49(10-11), 787–800 (2007)
[8] MacWhinney, B.: The CHILDES Project: Tools for Analyzing Talk, 3rd edn. Lawrence Erlbaum Associates, Mahwah (2000)
[9] Mehrabian, A.: Pleasure-arousal-dominance: A general framework for describing and measuring individual differences in Temperament. Current Psychology 14(4), 261–292 (1996)
[10] Paul, D., Baker, J.: The Design for the Wall Street Journal-based CSR Corpus. In: Proc. of the Workshop on Speech and Natural Language, Stroudsburg, PA, USA, pp. 357–362 (1992)
[11] Picard, R.W.: Affective Computing. MIT Press, Cambridge, MA (2000)
[12] Rehbein, J.: Remarks on the empirical analysis of action and speech: The case of question sequences in classroom discourse. Journal of Pragmatics 8(1), 49–63 (1984)
[13] Scherer, K.: What are emotions? And how can they be measured? Social Science Information 44(4), 695–729 (2005)
[14] Scherer, S., Siegert, I., Bigalke, L., Meudt, S.: Developing an Expressive Speech Labeling Tool Incorporating the Temporal Characteristics of Emotion. In: Proc. of the 7th International Conference on Language Resources and Evaluation (2010)
[15] Schmidt, T., Schütte, W.: FOLKER: An Annotation Tool For Efficient Transcription of Natural, Multi-Party Interaction. In: Proc. of the 7th International Conference on Language Resources and Evaluation (2010)
[16] Selting, M., Auer, P., Barden, B., Bergmann, J., Couper-Kuhlen, E., Günthner, S., Meier, C., Quasthoff, U., Schlobinski, P., Uhmann, S.: Gesprächsanalytisches Transkriptionssystem (GAT). Linguistische Berichte 173, 91–122 (1998)
[17] Selting, M., Auer, P., Barth-Weingarten, D., Bergmann, J., Bergmann, P., Birkner, K., Couper-Kuhlen, E., Deppermann, A., Gilles, P., Günthner, S., Hartung, M., Kern, F., Mertzlufft, C., Meyer, C., Morek, M., Oberzaucher, F., Peters, J., Quasthoff, U., Schütte, W., Stukenbrock, A., Uhmann, S.: A system for transcribing talk-in-interaction: GAT 2. To appear in: Gesprächsforschung Online-Zeitschrift zur verbalen Interaktion 12 (2011)
[18] Siegert, I., Böck, R., Philippou-Hübner, D., Vlasenko, B., Wendemuth, A.: Appropriate Emotional Labeling of Non-Acted Speech Using Basic Emotions, Geneva Emotion Wheel and Self Assessment Manikins. In: Proc. IEEE Int. Conf. on Multimedia & Expo, Barcelona (2011)
[19] Strauss, P.M., Hoffmann, H., Minker, W., Neumann, H., Palm, G., Scherer, S., Traue, H., Weidenbacher, U.: The PIT corpus of German multi-party dialogues. In: Proc. of the Sixth International Language Resources and Evaluation (LREC 2008), Marrakech, Morocco (2008)
[20] Young, S., Evermann, G., Gales, M., Hain, T., Kershaw, D., Liu, X., Moore, G., Odell, J., Ollason, D., Povey, D., Valtchev, V., Woodland, P.: The HTK Book, version 3.4. Cambridge University Engineering Department (2009)

Being Happy, Healthy and Whole Watching Movies That Affect Our Emotions

Teresa Chambel[1], Eva Oliveira[2,1], and Pedro Martins[1]

[1] LaSIGE, University of Lisbon, 1749-016 Lisbon, Portugal
tc@di.fc.ul.pt, pedrofjfmartins@gmail.com
[2] DIGARC, Polytechnic Institute of Cávado and Ave 4750-810 Barcelos, Portugal
eoliveira@ipca.pt

Abstract. This paper discusses the power of emotions in our health, happiness and wholeness, and the emotional impact of movies. It presents iFelt, an interactive video application to classify, access, explore and visualize movies based on their emotional properties and impact.

Keywords: Happiness, Health, Wholeness, Emotions, Movies, Emotional Impact, Technology, Entertainment, Design, HCI, iFelt.

1 Introduction

Emotions permeate people's daily lives, influencing the way we think and act, our health, our happiness and our sense of well-being. Recent studies demonstrated that emotions constitute a central part in the cognitive and decision making processes. That positive emotions enhance cognitive capacities and creative problem solving tasks, as well as physical health; while negative emotions, which narrow the individual's repertoire of thought and action, have a valuable survival strategy. Emotions, which are globally distributed throughout body's nervous system and cells, also have the power to influence our immune system and DNA, and the world around us. Positive Psychology is a recent research field that aims at achieving a scientific understanding of happiness, positive emotions and longevity, and has its roots in the conviction that psychology should not only help disordered people but should instead promote the quality of life of ordinary people. They aim to help people lead not only pleasant, but engaging and meaningful lives. In a sense, they share their aim with that saying: "Happy, healthy and whole in body, mind and soul", an integrated perspective of well-being, where emotions seem to play a central role. One of the greatest strengths of video is its power to generate attitudes and emotions as no other medium can. And it is becoming more and more pervasive in our lives, making it pertinent to explore its valences in inducing and supporting our empowering emotions.

This paper addresses the power of emotions, in section 2. Section 3 discusses the emotional impact of watching videos and movies. Section 4 addresses related work. The iFelt system is presented in section 5, followed, in section 6, by a user study conducted to learn about the emotional impact of movies and the usability of iFelt. The paper ends in section 7, with conclusions and perspectives for future work.

S. D´Mello et al. (Eds.): ACII 2011, Part I, LNCS 6974, pp. 35–45, 2011.

2 The Power of Emotions

This section addresses the power of emotions in mental states, cognition, survival, health, happiness and wholeness. Although they are all somehow related, while contributing to our sense of well-being, we will present them in a structured way.

The Role of Positive and Negative Emotions: Many authors state that emotions are survival artifacts. They regulate biologic patterns to deal with specific environments, like hunger or fear [13], classifying things as being good or bad, or sometimes neutral [6]. However, positive emotions are not always beneficial and negative emotions are not always detrimental [11]. In evolutionary terms, it has been suggested that positive emotions are associated with opportunities and a strategy of approach, facilitating the use of internalized strategies; while negative emotions, which narrow the individual's repertoire of thought and action, have a valuable survival strategy. There is also extensive literature suggesting that it is as important to recognize our negative feelings as it is to recognize our positive feelings. For e.g., frustration or mild depression can signal that it is time to pursue a different goal.

in Health: It has been known for a long time that negative emotions are related to a higher prevalence and severity of disease, but how strong is the evidence for a link between positive emotions and health? There are a number of pathways (biological, cognitive, social...) through which positive emotions have direct and usually beneficial effects on physiological, hormonal and immune function which in turn influence health [11]. Davidson et. al., referenced in [11] demonstrated this effect obtained through meditation. Philippot et. al. [22] suggest interventions including the redirection of attention. In the early 1900's, Ed. Bach had already found and developed an approach to healing based on emotions. More recently, the new science of Epigenetics revealed that there are reserves of natural happiness within our DNA that can be controlled by us, by our emotions, beliefs and behavioral choices [3]. Also, people high in happiness or subjective well-being tend to have healthier lifestyles, more self-enhancing, productive, and more positive interpersonal experiences [11].

in Happiness and Wholeness. The Positive Psychology movement, launched in 1998 by Seligman [28], [29], [11], aims at achieving a scientific understanding of happiness, positive emotions and longevity, and effective interventions to make normal life more fulfilling for ordinary people, and not just for those with disorder or dysfunction, where the focus tended to be in psychology. It extends and has brought empirical support to the theories of the Humanistic approach, with overlaps with Existential psychology, and has influenced the more recent Coaching psychology. According to Seligman [29], happiness is related with three goals in life, to have: 1) a Pleasant life, feeling positive emotions; 2) a Good or Engaging life, based on being in flow, when time 'stops' while one engages in absorbing activities related with our higher strengths; and 3) a Meaningful life, using our signature strengths in service of something larger than ourselves. The sense of living a full life increases along the three and helps leading to health and longevity. At the crossroads of science and spirituality, authors like Braden and Lipton [3] argue that our reality code is based in the language of emotion and focused belief, giving our thought and ourselves power to change the conditions of healing within our bodies, and into the world around us. [10] defend that emotion is the indicator of whether we are blocking or allowing this flow towards the alignment with our true self, and a sense of wholeness.

3 Emotional Impact of Videos and Movies

By combining diverse symbol systems, such as pictures, texts, music and narration, video is a very rich media type, often engaging the viewer cognitively and emotionally, and having a great potential in the promotion of emotional experiences. Isen et. al. [12] attested this potential, evaluating the effect of positive affect in patients, inducted by ten-minute comedy films. Bardzell et al. [5] results suggest that emotional responses are complex but still implicated with video preferences and engagement, even in short Internet videos (more details in sec.4). The study of films as an emotion induction method has reports dated since 1916 [19], analyzing mental operations of film viewers and discussing how emotions guide the motivation of perception and the control of our attention by cinematographic narratives. According to [31], appraisal in film viewing can be seen as based on a set of illusions that are difficult to resist. It is difficult to escape the illusion of witnessing events in the fictional world, which along with two other factors explain the typically high intensity of emotion in the cinema: a certain willingness of the viewers to cooperate; and the self-amplification inherent in film-produced emotion. More recently, other researchers used films to induce emotions with different goals [8]. In media studies, the most common methods for eliciting emotions are images, music, or film based. [32] tested 11 induction methods and concluded that films were the best method to elicit emotions, positive and negative.

4 Related Work

We present a review of work that more closely relates with our iFelt system.

Models and Representations of Emotions. There is a diversity of perspectives on the emotional properties of video, regarding its content or the emotional impact it has on viewers. From the directors' point of view, there are a number of cinematographic techniques [2] to induce the emotional environment, like shots duration, lightning conditions, color and movements. From the viewer and content point of view, there are two main models of emotion: 1) The Dimensional Model [26] is based on a two dimensional spatial circumplex: arousal (intensity) and valence (polarity); 2) The Categorical Model defines emotions as discrete states that identify a certain behavior and experience. Ekman [7] identified six basic emotions based on facial expressions recognized across cultures: anger, disgust, fear, joy, sadness and surprise. There is a correspondence of these emotions in Russel's circumplex. The Appraisal Model is also categorical, defined as the evaluation of the interaction between someone and their goals, beliefs and the environment [27]. Plutchick [24] used both categorical and dimensional models and defined a 3D model (polarity, similarity, intensity) with eight primary emotions: anger, fear, sadness, disgust, surprise, anticipation, trust, and joy, represented around the center, in colors, with the intensity as the vertical dimension.

Emotional Classification of Movies and their Impact. Video content analyzes and classification deals with techniques to extract info from video, or users, to find meaningful segments. Some techniques use automatic processing, others are manual. The extraction of content-based emotional info expressed in videos has been based on low-level features like color, texture, lightning, motions, sounds, rhythm, lexicon, etc. inspired by cinema theorists tools [9], resulting from directors intention for felt emotions. The classification of movies by its actual affective impact has recently been the focus of some studies, using: biometric methods based on physiological signals, such as respiration, heart rate, blood pressure, electromyograms, and galvanic skin response; or recognition of facial emotional expressions [17]. Works have been recently developed to prove that films can be emotional inductors, helping psychologists in specific treatments [14], or to automatically index, search [30], or summarize [18] videos, according to the emotional impact, that tend to be significantly different among the viewers. [5] studied user emotions and engagement with internet videos, using physiological measures to assess valence and arousal, emotional self-reports, and prose reviews, concluding that emotion is implicated in video preferences.

Accessing and Visualizing Movies and Videos. IMDB (.com) provides info about actors, directors, genres, film ratings, etc. Others, like Netflix, also allow accessing and watching movies. YouTube is probably the most famous website to publish and watch videos, search, comment, share, and get recommendations. But none of these systems support emotional info, and they do not explore the visualization of video spaces much further then through lists. Film Finder [1] supported users to search and view films based on duration, genres, titles, actors and directors, using starfield graphics based on date and popularity. However, most visualization tools and apps do not address video. Among the exceptions, the most related to our work are: 1) the YouTube 2D view representing videos as circular scattered still images, allowing for visual neighborhood navigation based on similarity; and 2) Video Sphere (bestiario.org/research/videosphere), representing TED's videos around a 3D sphere connected by semantic links. In our previous works: we provided interactive 3D visualization and navigation of videos [25], to explore cultural and aesthetic properties of videos and videos spaces; and a 2D interactive system based on a physical particles system [16] to visualize and explore videos based on color dominance, rhythm and movement. These systems address video visualization but not emotions.

Eliciting and Visualizing Emotions. In this context, there are some recent works, but not so much on video. We Feel Fine (.org) harvests human feelings from weblogs, searching feelings after "I feel" and "I am feeling" and info about the author and local weather when it was written. The interface is based on a colored physical particles system, representing expressed feelings. Mappiness (.org.uk) maps happiness across space in UK, to better understand how people's feelings are affected by their current environment, including air pollution, noise, and green spaces, by prompting users a couple of times a day, on their iPhones. Synesketch (.krcadinac.com) is a textual emotion recognition and visualization software based on synesthesia, dynamically transferring text into animated visual patterns, using colored squares, and moving particles. The Emotionally}Vague (.com) project addresses the relation of body and emotion and how people feel emotions (e.g. body location and associated colors).

5 The iFelt System

iFelt is an interactive web video application that allows to catalog, access, explore and visualize emotional information about movies. It is being designed to explore the affective dimensions of movies in terms of their properties and in accordance with users' emotional profiles, choices and states, in two main components:

1. Emotional Movie Content Classification aims to provide video classification and indexing based on emotions, either expressed in the movies (objective emotions), or felt by the users (subjective emotions), as dominant emotions at the level of the movie or the movie scenes. Objective emotions are being classified with the aid of video low-level feature analysis, combined with audio and subtitles processing in our VIRUS research project [15]; while subjective emotions can be classified manually, or automatically recognized with biometric methods based on physiological signals, such as respiration, heart rate and galvanic skin response, employing digital signal processing and pattern recognition algorithms, inspired by statistical techniques used by [23]. This process and its results are thoroughly described in [21].

In the IFelt system, we started by using the categorical labels: happy, sadness, surprise, fear, anger and disgust, for the classification of both content and users' emotions, mainly due to the facts that: 1) the differentiations of a larger range of emotions by physiologic patterns is still limited; and 2) the Ekman's basic emotions are well known. In iFelt, emotions are detected or recognized along time, allowing to identify objective and subjective emotional scenes, along with the dominant emotion expressed or felt in each movie. Although work is already being done from both perspectives, in this first prototype, the focus was more directed towards the subjective perspective, where we consider three different views: 1) My view: represents videos classified by the emotions felt by the current user while watching each movie; 2) All Users view: computes the dominant emotions among those felt by all the viewers of each video; 3) The Directors view: represents the emotions that the movie's director, or possibly film expert, expects users to feel while watching it.

2. Emotional Movie Access and Exploration. This component aims to provide video access and visualization based on their emotional properties and users' emotions and profiles. The first prototype is focused on the subjective emotions perspective, to explore and evaluate the emotional paradigm, on top of which we will later add the other perspectives. The design options are thoroughly addressed in [20]. Here we shortly mention that our representation is based on colors, inspired in the model of Plutchik [24], representing anger, disgust, fear, sadness, surprise and happiness, by the colors pink, purple, green, blue, light blue, and yellow, and that we consistently adopt round shapes, and circular organizations inspired by the 2D Russel's circumplex [26]. Next, we will briefly highlight the main features of iFelt.

In the *Movie Space*, the user gets a view over the movies existing in iFelt, with info about their dominant emotions, in addition to the traditional info of title, etc. This can be the view of all the videos or a selection resulting from a previous search. From here, the user may navigate to any of the represented movies to watch it (Fig.1 a-b). In the current prototype, users can choose from: the 1) Emotional Wheel, where movies are represented by a colored circle, with their dominant emotion color, placed on the wheel accordingly in six emotional regions, and having the distance to the center representing the level of emotion dominance. Different versions were designed and tested, to increase the perceptiveness and effectiveness of this representation [20]; and the 2) Movie Title List, with an image and the title of the movie preceded by a colored circle representing the movie's dominant emotion (e.g. user profile Fig.1d).

In the *Movies Emotional Scenes Space*, users can view the scenes of the movies based on dominant emotions, by colored circles, with size reflecting dominance of emotion, and grouped by dominant colors. When the cursor is over one circle, the circles of the same movie in the different emotions are highlighted while the others dim (Fig.1c). When clicked, the user is directed to that individual movie, similar to Fig.1b), but presenting only the scenes with the selected emotion, as an emotional summary, e.g. scenes where most users felt sad. Both movie space and scenes space can be viewed from the three views: My, All Users (default) and Director's view.

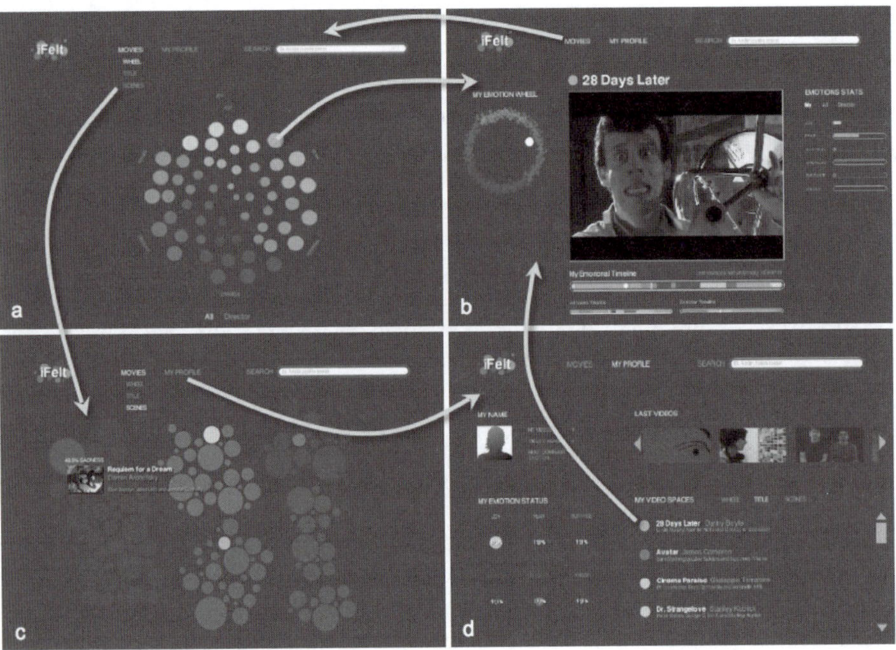

Fig. 1. iFelt: a) Movies Space (in movie wheel); b) Movie Profile; c) Emotional Scenes Space; d) User Profile (in TitleList)

At the *Individual Movie Level*, or Movie Profile, the movie can be watched, and there is info about its dominant emotions and emotional scenes, through: 1) The Most Dominant Emotion, as a big colored circle on top of the video; 2) The Dominant Emotions, in the current view, represented by the percentage of dominance of each emotion in the movie (bars to the right of the video, in Fig.1b); 3) The Emotional Timelines: the emotional scenes along time, below the video. The top timeline represents the emotions in the current view (mine, all users, or director's), while the bottom ones represents the other two, to help gain awareness. We explored their design to ease having one view as the dominant at each moment and to ease the comparison, when required [20]. These timelines also allow to access scenes based on their dominant emotions: by clicking the timeline in the chosen color; 4) The Current Emotion is represented: a) as a pointer traveling along the Timeline; and b) in a Circle of Emotions, as an animated white big dot moving to the current emotion.

From the *User Emotional profile*, the current users in iFelt can get info about movies classified from their own perspective or view: 1) My Personal Info: photo and name, most dominant emotion felt in the movies already classified from My perspective, and the date of the last classification (Fig.1d, top left); 2) My Dominant Felt Emotions: represented by colored circles, with size reflecting the % of felt emotion dominance in the movies classified by me (Fig.1d, bottom left); 3) My Last Classified Movies: in the representation in Fig.1d, top right, each movie is represented by an image of the movie, tainted with a color filter corresponding to the dominant emotion felt by me; 4) My Classified Movies Space: similar to the Movies Space, but presenting only my movies, classified through my felt emotions - in title list view in Fig.1d, bottom right; 5) My Classified Emotional Scenes: similar to the Emotional Scenes, but presenting my scenes (alternate with Movie Space, when selected).

6 User Study

This section presents the objectives, method and results of the user study conducted to 1) learn about emotional impact in Movie Watching; and 2) evaluate iFelt's usability. We performed an evaluation based mainly on semi-structured interviews, and user observation while they performed pre-defined tasks. After each task, users were confronted with usability questions and the opportunity to provide comments and suggestions. Finally, users were asked to answer to questions regarding their attitudes, awareness and preferences about the emotional impact of movies. We had 10 participants aged 21-56, 6 female, and computer literate. Results are presented next.

1. Emotional Impact in Movie Watching. We asked viewers a few questions that are presented in tables 1-3, along with the results. Questions Q1-Q3, in table 1, aimed at the awareness and attitudes. Viewers strongly agreed (4.6 in a 1-5 scale: totally disagree - totally agree) that watching a movie can fill one's soul, or make one sad (Q1). They quite often feel the need to watch movies (4.2 in Q3, in a 1-5 scale: never-often), and sometimes turn to movies to achieve a specific emotional state (3.1 in Q2).

Table 1. Awareness & Attitudes about Emotional Impact

Questions **agree: scale (1-5)**	**Std**	**Mean**
Q1. Do you agree that watching a movie can fill one's soul, or make one sad?	0.52	4.6
Q2. How often: you turn to movies to achieve a specific emotional state?	0.99	3.1
Q3. How often: you feel the need to watch movies?	0.63	4.2

Concerning the relation of genres and felt emotions (Q4-Q5 in table 2), we asked viewers what genres made them feel each of the emotions presented. We did not list the genres, to let them freely mention the most relevant. The most similar answers associated joy and happiness with comedy, sadness with drama, and scare/fear with terror movies. Next, action movies make most viewers feel energetic, what comedies does for fewer; most female feel depressed with drama, while most male feel depressed with romance; and disgust tends to come with terror movies, but also with those involving blood and documentaries (2M), and science (1F). Females get more inspired or motivated with romance, drama and action, while males get their inspiration and motivation from action and docs. Somehow opposite to the results on feeling depressed, romance makes some females feel joyful, happy, motivated and inspired, and 1 female and 1 male feel sad. As for the most wanted or preferred genre (Q5), females prefer drama and romance, while male prefer action, comedy and suspense.

To learn about preferred films and emotions, Q6-Q8 were asked as open questions (table 3). The most wanted emotion when selecting a movie (Q6) was surprise or suspense to half of the males and feeling good and fun to the others, while dreaming, inspiration or motivation were mentioned by half of the females, 2 mentioned related feelings: of making them think, wander and dream, and 1 mentioned happiness.

Table 2. Genres and Felt Emotions

Q4. What movie genre makes you feel:	Action	Drama	Romance	Comedy	Suspense	Terror	Bio	Doc.	Other
energetic	4F 2M			1F 1M	1M				
depressed		3F 1M	1F 3M			1F			
inspired	2F 1M	3F	2F	1M			1F	1M	1M horses
motivated	1F 2M	1F	2F	1F	1M			1M	1F politics
joyful happy			2F	4F 4M					
sad		6F 3M	1F 1M						
scared					1M	6F 3M			
disgusted						3F 2M		1M	1F science 1M blood
Q5. most wanted genre?	1F 1M	3F	3F	1F 1M	1M				1F advent

Table 3. Preferred Movies and Emotions (Fx & Mx: x=age)

	Q6. most wanted emotion	**Q7. a relevant movie in my life**	**Q8. main emotion felt**
disgust		Irreversible	M32
sadness		All About my Mother	M30
surprise, suspense	M30,32	Irreversible, Fight Club	M32, M23
		Rear Window	F56
fun, feeling good	M23, M25		
happiness	F21		
attraction		Interview with the Vampire	F21
wandering, imagination	F29,35	The Lion King	F29
dreaming, inspiration, motivation	F28,31,35	All The Invisible Chindren	F31
		Dead Poets Society	F28,35

When asked about a relevant movie in their lives (Q7-Q8), the movies and the associated main felt emotion align to a reasonable extent with the preferred emotions. Also interesting to note that in the imagination and motivation movies, answers were somehow more inspired: F29 "enjoyed wondering about the story", while F35, after watching the Dead Poets Society at 13, felt she "was going to conquer the world".

2. iFelt Usability Evaluation. The usability dimensions underlying the USE questionnaire (usesurvey.com): Usefulness (of emotional info and features in iFelt), Satisfaction (fun, good experience), and Ease of use, also present in the requirements and design rationale, informed the main objectives and structure of the evaluation of iFelt. Users found Movies Space very useful (U:4.5 on average in 1-5), satisfying (S:4.6) and easy to use (E:4.7). Overall usability of the Movie Profile was U:4.7, S:4.4,E:5; Scene Space had U:4.4, S:4.2, E:4.1, and the User Emotional Profile U:4.7, S:4.1,E:4.3. For a more thorough discussion of the design options, the tasks performed and the results of the usability evaluation of all the iFelt features refer to [20].

7 Conclusions and Perspectives

On the usability evaluation, iFelt was perceived as useful, satisfactory and easy to use. Most appreciated features included the possibility to access movies and scenes based on the emotions felt, and to access and compare their own emotional views with those of other users and directors, at the level of the movies and the scenes, and along emotional timelines [20]. On the user study on the emotional impact of movies, we observed that inquired viewers strongly agreed that watching a movie can fill one's soul or make one sad, they quite often feel the need to watch movies, and sometimes turn to movies to achieve a specific emotional state. Concerning the preferences and relation of emotions and movie genres, it was interesting to note that the difference between female and male answers somehow match some traits commonly associated with each genre, for e.g. in terms of romance vs action, or dreaming vs down to earth. This separation in genders emerged from the results, and although not generalizable, it is interesting to note the tendencies, and that they align for e.g. with [4] where females reported greater preference for happy-mood films than males, whereas males had greater preference for high-arousal films. It was also interesting to note some tendency in preferences towards emotions like surprise, fun, feeling good, happiness, and mostly, imagining, dreaming, inspiration and motivation. This is somehow aligned with the levels or goals related with leading a happy life [29]: increasing positive emotions is not enough, it requires engagement and meaning.

As future directions, we are considering to add the appraisal model in the emotion classification, in a manual perspective and, whenever possible, as part of an automatic process, that also needs to be tuned. This model gives a wider range of emotions, as those that emerged as important in our user study, also to be complemented with models of engagement and enjoyment. Other features include: extending the concept of movies summarizing, searching or recommending based on users current emotional states, profiles, or defined emotional criteria; to find movies by example: with emotional timelines similar to that of a given movie; and to include support for historical emotional info gathered along time, in the different perspectives. We also intend to do user studies with a wider range of viewers, including psychologists, movie experts, directors and actors (some already showed interest in knowing the emotional impact of movies), to increase our awareness in ways that might inform future design options in iFelt, and to learn how this tool may contribute to add to people's lives.

Acknowledgements. This work is partially supported by FCT through LaSIGE Multiannual Funding, PROTEC (SFRH/BD/49475/2009) & VIRUS project (PTDC/EIA-EIA/101012/2008).

References

1. Ahlberg, C., Truvé, S.: Tight coupling: Guiding user actions in a direct manipulation retrieval system. In: People and Computers: Proc. of HCI 1995, pp. 305–321 (1995)
2. Arijon, D.: Grammar of the film language. Focal Press (1976)
3. Baird, J., Nadel, L., Lipton, B.: Happiness Genes: Unlock the Positive Potential Hidden in Your DNA. New Page Books (2010)
4. Banerjee, S., Greene, K., Krcmar, M., Bagdasarov, Z., Ruginyte, D.: The role of gender and sensation seeking in film choice: Exploring mood and arousal. Journal of Media Psychology: Theories, Methods, and Applications 20(3), 97–105 (2008)
5. Bardzell, S., Bardzell, J., Pace, T.: Understanding Affective Interaction: Emotion, Engagement, and Internet Videos. In: Proc. of IEEE ACII, Amst., NL (September 10-12, 2009)
6. Damasio, A.: Descartes' Error. Harper Perennial (1995)
7. Ekman, P.: Are there basic emotions? Psychological Review 99(3), 550–553 (1992)
8. Gross, J., Levenson, R.: Emotion Elicitation Using Films. Cognition & Emotion 1(9) (1995)
9. Hanjalic, A., Xu, L.-Q.: Affective video content representation and modeling. IEEE Transactions on Multimedia 7(1) (2005)
10. Hicks, E., Hicks, J.: The Astonishing Power of Emotions: Let Your Feelings Be Your Guide. Hay House (2007)
11. Huppert, F.: Positive emotions and cognition: developmental, neuroscience and health perspectives. In: Forgas, J.P. (ed.) Hearts and Minds: Affective Influences on Social Cognition and Behavior, Psychology Press, New York (2006)
12. Isen, A.M., Daubman, K.A., Nowicki, G.P.: Positive affect facilitates creative problem solving. Journal of Personality and Social Psychology 52, 1122–1131 (1987)
13. James, W.: What is an Emotion? Mind 9(34), 188–205 (1884)
14. Kreibig, S., Wilhelm, F., Roth, W., Gross, J.: Cardiovascular, electrodermal, and respiratory response patterns to fear- and sadness-inducing films. Psychophysiology 44(5), 787–806 (2007)
15. Langlois, T., Chambel, T., Oliveira, E., Carvalho, P., Marques, G., Falcão, A.: VIRUS: Video Information Retrieval Using Subtitles. In: Proc.of Academic MindTrek 2010 (2010)
16. Martinho, J., Chambel, T.: ColorsInMotion: Interactive Visualization and Exploration of Video Spaces. In: Proc. of Academic MindTrek 2009, Tampere, Finland (September-October 2009)
17. Mauss, I., Robinson, M.: Measures of emotion: A review. Cognition & Emotion 23(2), 209–237 (2009)
18. Money, A., Agius, H.: Analysing user physiological responses for affective video summarization. Displays 30(2), 59–70 (2009)

19. Münsterberg, H.: The film: A psychological study: The silent photoplay in 1916. Dover Public, New York (1970)
20. Oliveira, E., Martins, P., Chambel, T.: iFelt: Accessing Movies Through Our Emotions. In: Proceedings of EuroiTV 2011, Lisbon, Portugal (June 29-July 1, 2011)
21. Oliveira, E., Benovoy, M., Ribeiro, N., Chambel, T.: Towards Emotional Interaction: Using Movies to Automatically Learn Users' Emotional States. In: Campos, P., Graham, N., Jorge, J., Nunes, N., Palanque, P., Winckler, M. (eds.) INTERACT 2011, Part I. LNCS, vol. 6946, pp. 152–161. Springer, Heidelberg (2011)
22. Philippot, P., Baeyens, C., Douilliez, C., Francart, B.: Cognitive regulation of emotion: Application to clinical disorders. In: Philippot, P., Feldman, R.S. (eds.) The Regulation of Emotion. Laurence Erlbaum Associates, New York (2004)
23. Picard, R., Vyzas, E., Healey, J. Toward Machine Emotional Intelligence: Analysis of Affective Physiological State. IEEE Trans. on Pattern Analysis & Machine Intel. (2001)
24. Plutchik, R.: Emotion: A psychoevolutionary synthesis. Harper & Row, New York (1980)
25. Rocha, T., Chambel, T.: VideoSpace: a 3D Video Experience. In: Proceedings of Artech 2008, 4th International Conference on Digital Arts, Porto, Portugal (November 2008)
26. Russell, J.: A circumflex model of affect. Journal of Personality and Social Psychology 39, 1161–1178 (1980)
27. Scherer, K.: What are emotions? and how can they be measured? Social Science Information 44(4), 695 (2005)
28. Seligman, M., Csikszentmihalyi, M.: Positive Psychology: An Introduction. American Psychologist 55(1), 5–14 (2000)
29. Seligman, M.: Martin Seligman on positive psychology, TED Talk (February 2004)
30. Soleymani, M., Chanel, C., Kierkels, J., Pun, T.: Affective Characterization of Movie Scenes Based on Content Analysis and Physiological Changes. In: Int. Symp. on MM (2008)
31. Tan, E.S.: Film-induced affect as a witness emotion. Poetics In Emotions and Cultural Products 23(1-2), 7–32 (1995)
32. Westermann, R., Spies, K., Stahl, G., Hesse, F.W.: Relative effectiveness and validity of mood induction procedures: a meta-analysis. Eur. Journal of Social Psychology 26(4), 557–580 (1996)

Investigating the Prosody and Voice Quality of Social Signals in Scenario Meetings

Marcela Charfuelan and Marc Schröder

DFKI GmbH, Language Technology Lab
Stuhlsatzenhausweg 3, D-66123 Saarbrücken, Germany and
Alt-Moabit 91c, D-10559, Berlin, Germany
{firstname.lastname}@dfki.de

Abstract. In this study we propose a methodology to investigate possible prosody and voice quality correlates of social signals, and test-run it on annotated naturalistic recordings of scenario meetings. The core method consists of computing a set of prosody and voice quality measures, followed by a Principal Components Analysis (PCA) and Support Vector Machine (SVM) classification to identify the core factors predicting the associated social signal or related annotation. We apply the methodology to controlled data and two types of annotations in the AMI meeting corpus that are relevant for social signalling: dialogue acts and speaker roles.

Keywords: Prosody, Voice quality, Vocal social signals, Acoustic measures, Acoustic correlates, Perceptual interpretation.

1 Introduction

The new research area of Social Signal Processing (SSP) is aimed at automatic understanding of social interactions through analysis of nonverbal behaviour. Social signals include (dis)-agreement, empathy, hostility, politeness, and any other stances towards others, and can be expressed through verbal and nonverbal means in different modalities [17]. One of the modalities through which social signals are supposedly expressed is *vocal nonverbal behaviour* – not *what* is said, but *how* it is said. This includes prosodic features such as pitch, energy and rhythm, as well as voice qualities such as harsh, creaky, tense, etc.

Most of recently reported works, related to the detection and classification of social signals, use only prosodic cues and in some cases in combinations with other cues. For example in [10] nonverbal prosodic and visual cues are used for predicting dominance and role-based status in scenario meetings. In [4] prosodic features have been used in combination with lexical and structural features for automatic detection of agreement in multiparty conversations. Prosodic features have been reported to discriminate quite well among dialogue acts [3] and voice quality features to discriminate quite well among emotions [11,12]. Furthermore in [9], both prosodic and voice quality features have been used to identify some groups of speech acts expressing specific functions, emotion or attitude.

S. D'Mello et al. (Eds.): ACII 2011, Part I, LNCS 6974, pp. 46–56, 2011.

This paper addresses the question whether we can observe, in corpora of spontaneous interactions, any systematic effects of social signals on measures of prosody and voice quality. If we are able to find such effects, we would like to know if prosody and voice quality carry redundant or complementary information, and whether the effects are perceptually interpretable. Our main goal is to develop a methodology for addressing these research questions, and to test-run it on a number of existing data sets. We start with controlled data which allow us to verify that the measures yield interpretations that are consistent with prior knowledge. We then proceed to apply the methodology to part of the Augmented Multi-party Interaction (AMI) meeting corpus, in which we investigate two types of existing annotations: dialogue acts and speaker roles. The paper is organised as follows. After outline the proposed methodology in Section 2, we describe in Section 3, the prosody and voice quality measures used in this study, as well as their perceptual interpretation. In Section 4 the methodology is test run on controlled data: the NECA database of voice quality and in Section 5, we present the application of the methodology to dialogue acts and roles in the AMI meeting corpus. Finally in Section 6 we draw conclusions and outline future work.

2 Outline of the Methodology

The starting point for the analysis is a collection of speech recordings with associated annotations, afterwards the following steps are performed. **(1) Acoustic measures extraction** and if necessary, perform a pre-processing of the data. With annotations of spontaneous data it might be necessary to reduce the variability of the data, we exemplify two possible pre-processing methods in the work with dialogue acts and roles in Section 5. **(2) Analysis of Variance**, we compute a simple Analysis of Variance (ANOVA) for each of the features. This is a simple first assessment of whether we find significant effects among the annotations under analysis. **(3) Principal Component Analysis (PCA)**, performed on the acoustic features. PCA is used as a technique to reduce redundancy among the acoustic measures and to identify salient effects. In order to find systematic differences, we look at the distribution of our annotated data along the PCs. Visually, this distribution can be shown as a scatter plot of observations on the first two PCs; numerically, we can give means and standard deviations for annotation classes on the different PCs. In order to relate this distribution to perceptual interpretations, we can attempt to interpret the "meaning" of each PC in terms of the acoustic features with high loadings on a given PC. **(4) Classification**, in order to assess the quantitative distinctiveness of the acoustic features, we train a classifier to predict the annotations from the acoustic features. We chose Support Vector Machine (SVM) as a classifier. We train separate classifiers to predict the annotations from prosody features alone, from voice quality features alone, and from all features. Comparing these numbers allows us to determine if the acoustic measures are complementary or redundant.

3 Acoustic Measures and Their Perceptual Correlates

Table 1 shows the prosody and voice quality (VQ) measures used in this study. Prosody measures have been extracted frame-based and averaged per utterance. VQ measures are extracted frame and utterance based. Frame-based VQ measures are rough spectral estimates of traditional voice quality parameters normally calculated in time domain. These measures were developed in [11] and tested successfully on classification of emotions under different levels of noise and reverberation. These measures are gradients (kind of normalisation by F0) instead of amplitud ratios and are calculated on the basis of frame-based raw measures like **formant frequencies:** F_1, F_2, F_3, F_4; **formant bandwidths:** B_1, B_2, B_3, B_4; **amplitude of the first two harmonics** at F0 and $2F0$: H_1, H_2; **frequency of spectrum peaks near formants**: F_{1p}, F_{2p}, F_{3p}; and **amplitude of spectrum peaks near formants**: A_{1p}, A_{2p}, A_{3p}. A tilde on some of the raw measures indicates that these measures have additionally included vocal tract influence compensation [11]. Utterance-based VQ measures were originally developed in [7] where various perceptual factors correlate with acoustic data from the Long Term Average Spectrum (LTAS) and fundamental frequency distribution. These measures are based on the calculation of long term average spectrum (LTAS) in three bands of frequency: 0-2kHz, 2-5kHz and 5-8kHz.

Table 1. Prosody and voice quality (VQ) measures used in this study

Type	Acoustic measure	Definition
Prosody	averageF0	Average fundamental frequency
	maxF0	Maximum F0
	minF0	Minimum F0
	rangeF0	maxF0 - minF0
	energy	Short term energy $\sum x^2$
	voicing rate	Number of voiced frames per time unit
VQ	**Frame-based [11]:**	
	OQG: Open Quotient Gradient	$(\tilde{H}_1 - \tilde{H}_2)/F0$
	GOG: Glottal Opening Gradient	$(\tilde{H}_1 - \tilde{A}_{1p})/(F_{1p} - F0)$
	SKG: Skewness Gradient	$(\tilde{H}_1 - \tilde{A}_{2p})/(F_{2p} - F0)$
	RCG: Rate of Closure Gradient	$(\tilde{H}_1 - \tilde{A}_{3p})/(F_{3p} - F0)$
	IC: Incompleteness of Closure	B_1/F_1
	Utterance-based [14,7]:	
	Hamm_effort	LTAS_{2-5k}
	Hamm_breathy	(LTAS_{0-2k} - LTAS_{2-5k}) - (LTAS_{2-5k} - LTAS_{5-8k})
	Hamm_head	(LTAS_{0-2k} - LTAS_{5-8k})
	Hamm_coarse	(LTAS_{0-2k} - LTAS_{2-5k})
	Hamm_unstable	(LTAS_{2-5k} - LTAS_{5-8k})
	slope_ltas1kHz	Least squared line fit of LTAS above 1 kHz in the log-frequency domain (dB/oct).

3.1 Perceptual Interpretation of Acoustic Measures

On the literature it is more common to find perceptual interpretations of traditional time domain voice quality measures. In the following we review the spectral effect and perceptual interpretation of traditional time domain voice quality measures and deduce the expected behaviour of their spectral domain counterparts.

Open quotient indicates the time during which the glottis is open and it is defined in the time domain as a fraction of the total glottal period. According to [16] the primary acoustic manifestation of a narrow glottal pulse, i.e. of a decrease in open time, is a reduction of the amplitude of the fundamental component in the source spectrum relative to adjacent harmonics . Thus the spectral effect of the open quotient can be determined by the difference $(\tilde{H}_1 - \tilde{H}_2)$ [16,6]. This means that a decrease in time domain open quotient corresponds also to a decrease in the spectral OQG. On the perceptual side, a very dominant H_1 has been widely found to be highly correlated with a breathy mode of phonation whereas a relatively strong H_2 can be correlated with tense or creaky voice [6].

Glottal opening and incompleteness of closure, glottal opening corresponds to the degree of opening over the entire glottal cycle. According to [16] the spectral effect of the glottal opening can be determined by the difference between the first harmonic and the amplitude of the first formant: $(\tilde{H}_1 - \tilde{A}_{1p})$. An increase in glottal opening correspond to a decrease in the amplitude of the first harmonic A_1 (increase in B_1) and therefore an increase of the spectral GOG and IC. On the perceptual side breathy voices have been associated with wide B_1 and tense voices with narrow B_1 [6], this means large values of GOG and IC for breathy voices and small values for tense voices.

Skewness and Rate of closure, skewness describes the abruptness (slope) of the glottal closure and the rate of closure the rate of decrease of flow at the instant of closure. [16] and [8] proposed that the amplitude of the third formant relative to that of the first harmonic $(H_1 - A_3)$ is a reasonably accurate indication of source spectral tilt, except if H_1 is weak. So for an increase in skewness and rate of closure we expect a decrease on the spectral SKG and RCG measures since the amplitude at middle and high frequencies increases relative to the amplitude at low frequencies. On the perceptual side, tense and creaky voices have been associated with high skewness or high speed quotient (SQ) and high rate of closure; on contrary breathy voices have been associated with low SQ [5].

Hamm_effort relates to vocal effort in a broad sense, *Hamm_breathy* will be expected larger for breathy voices than for creaky voices. *Hamm_head* is associated with head or chest register [7]. In [14] strong correlations of *Hamm_effort* have been found for the activation dimension of emotion. On the evaluation dimension, male speakers showed clear negative effects on the *Hamm_breathy* and *Hamm_coarse* for positive evaluation. On the power dimension, a negative correlation of power with *Hamm_unstable* has been found, i.e. higher power corresponds to a lower and more stable voice. Also in this study it has been found that higher activation corresponds to higher F0 median and range, larger F0 excursions and a flatter spectral slope, i.e, more high-frequency energy.

4 Test-Running the Methodology on Controlled Data: NECA Vocal Effort Database

We analyse three levels of vocal effort in the NECA database [15], having in mind that vocal effort describes a broad range of voice qualities [13]. With this relatively simple database we aim, not only to verify that the acoustic measures have the expected discriminatory power, but also to assert and exemplify the steps of the methodology proposed in this work. The NECA vocal effort database contains a full German diphone set for each of three levels of vocal effort ("soft", "modal" and "loud") and two speakers (one male, one female). Perception of the intended vocal effort was verified using stimuli generated using diphone synthesis voices built from the recordings [15]. Out of the original recordings, 100 short words per speaker and per vocal effort were used in this experiment (600 in total).

Analysis of Variance: The prosody and voice quality measures presented in Table 1 are extracted from the NECA database. After applying ANOVA on these measures it was found that most of the measures are significantly different among the three classes loud, modal and soft, at level 0.1% ($p<0.001$) except for: maxF0 ($p<0.01$) and averageF0 and minF0 ($p<0.3$).

Principal Component Analysis: Figure 1 shows the three vocal effort clusters, loud, modal and soft for male and female speakers, obtained after PCA of both prosody and voice quality acoustic measures. It can be seen that both the speaker gender and the intended vocal effort are very well separated on this two-dimensional solution. The first three more loaded measures in PC1 are: Hamm_breathy, Hamm_coarse and RCG; and in PC2 are: maxF0, averageF0 and Hamm_head. Together these two PCs explain 68% of the variance. PC1 represents voice quality measures. PC2 is related to the fundamental frequency

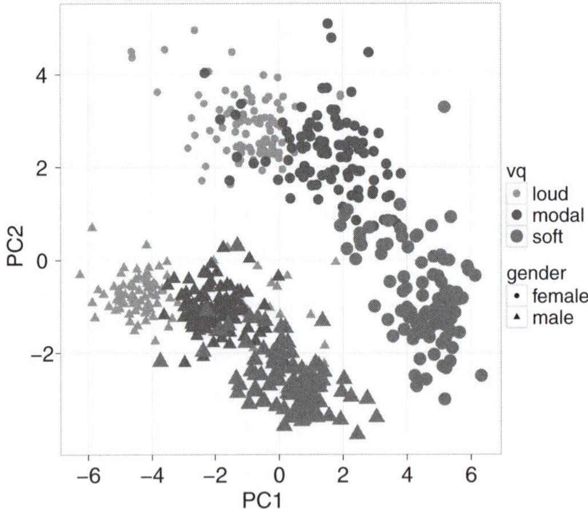

Fig. 1. NECA vocal effort PCA: variance explained PC1=45% and PC2=23%

and the relative amount of high-frequency energy in the spectrum. Taking into account the perceptual interpretation of voice quality measures presented in Section 3.1 and the acoustic measures extracted from the NECA database, it was verified that the tendencies of the following measures, in terms of soft and loud levels relative to modal vocal effort, are consistent:

Soft vocal effort, (including here perceptions like breathy, whisper, lax voices) high OQG, high GOG, high SKG, high RCG, high IC, low Hamm_effort, high Hamm_breathy, low F0, flatter slope_ltas1kHz.

Loud vocal effort, (including here perceptions like tense, creaky, fry, pressed voice) low OQG, low GOG, low SKG, low RCG, low IC, high Hamm_effort, low Hamm_breathy, high F0, steeper slope_ltas1kHz.

Classification: Three SVM models were trained with 60% of the NECA data using prosody and voice quality measures together and separately; 40% of the NECA data was used for testing. Table 2 shows the SVM average classification results for the annotation sets of the different data sets used in this study. The classification results for the three vocal effort levels in the NECA DB show that the voice quality measures produce a very good classification rate (90.8%) almost as good as using both prosody and voice quality measures (91.2%), which is the best classification rate for this database. The classification results obtained using just prosodic features is quite low in comparison to the others, maybe explained by the lack of significance on some of the prosodic measures.

Table 2. SVM classification rate for the data sets used in this study using both prosody and voice quality measures and the two type of measures separately

Measures	Vocal effort NECA DB	Dialogue act AMI-IDIAP meetings	Role AMI-IDIAP meetings
Prosody + Voice quality	**91.2**	**44.3**	41.8
Prosody	77.5	42.8	19.0
Voice quality	90.8	42.8	**45.8**
Chance level	33.3	25.0	25.0

5 Analysis of Meeting Data: AMI Meeting Corpus

The AMI Meeting Corpus is a multi-modal data set consisting of 100 hours of meeting recordings. Some of the meetings it contains are naturally occurring, and some are elicited, particularly using a scenario in which the participants play different roles. In this work elicited meetings are studied. In the scenario four participants play the roles: Project Manager (PM), Marketing Expert (ME), User Interface designer (UI) and Industrial Designer (ID) [1]. Nine meetings held at IDIAP Research institute (IS1000-IS1009, excluding IS1002) were selected from the AMI corpus, corresponding to 36 speakers (26 male and 10 female). The audio was taken from the individual headset. Table 3 presents the total number of dialogue act utterances extracted from these meetings and their distribution according to the dialogue act types studied in this work and speaker roles.

Table 3. Distribution of dialogue act utterances extracted from the meetings

DA vs. Role	PM	UI	ID	ME	Total
Assess	704	605	632	768	2709
Elicit	489	215	187	362	1253
Suggest	509	442	412	396	1759
Inform	1343	1538	1314	1470	5665
Total	3045	2800	2545	2996	11386

Table 4. Distribution of dialogue act utterances containing the word "control"

DA vs. Role	PM	UI	ID	ME	Total
Assess	10	11	2	8	31
Elicit	15	6	5	10	36
Suggest	22	18	10	18	68
Inform	55	58	33	92	238
Total	102	93	50	128	373

5.1 Dialogue Acts Analysis

Features extraction and pre-processing: We have selected four frequently annotated dialogue acts that seem to have a clearly different meaning: Inform, Suggest, Assess and Elicit (grouping different elicit types). Our objective is to analyse variation or patterns on the measures due to dialogue acts or roles, but the measures are also affected by other sources of variation like speaker gender, individual speaking style, various sources of noise including overlapping speech, outbursts such as laughter, as well as the intrinsic contextual variability. When applying PCA directly on the measures per dialogue act or per role, as we did for the controlled data in Section 4, we get only very weak effects. It seems that the large amount of uncontrolled variation masks any systematic effects that may be present in the data. Therefore, it is essential to reduce the variability of the data. In a first experiment to reduce the high variability of the data, the measures were averaged per dialogue act and speaker. This approach is comparable to the use of the Long-Term Average Spectrum (LTAS) as a means of "averaging out" the local effects of phonetic identity on the spectral distribution [7]. First of all the frame-based measures extracted from each dialogue act are averaged, resulting in one averaged frame-based measure per dialogue act. Then, all the dialogue act measures corresponding to a particular speaker in each sub-meeting are averaged.

Analysis of Variance: The analysis of variance corresponding to the averaged acoustic measures extracted from the four types of dialogue acts showed that the prosody measures and most of the voice quality measures allows to reject the null hypothesis that there is no significant difference among the dialogue act types. It seems that for this data the most relevant acoustic measures are the prosodic ones, significance level of 0.1 and 1%, although energy has a significance level of 5%. Three measures on the voice quality measures set: SKG, RCG and Hamm_unstable seem to be not significantly different.

Principal Component Analysis: Figure 2 (a) shows the projection of the averaged data onto a PC1-PC2 plane. It can be observed (indicated by an ellipse) that the first PC discriminates the Assess dialogue act from the others. The first three more loaded measures in PC1 are: Hamm_effort, Hamm_coarse and voicing rate; in PC2 are: RCG, GOG and SKG; and in PC3 are: averageF0, minF0 and

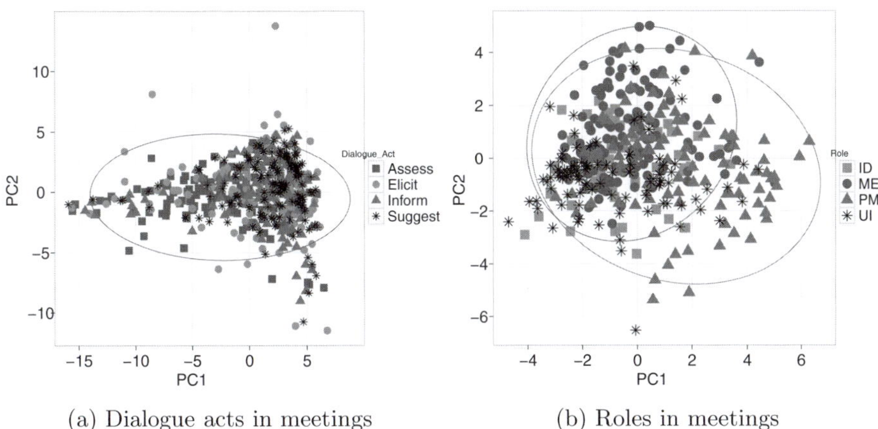

(a) Dialogue acts in meetings

(b) Roles in meetings

Fig. 2. AMI-IDIAP PCA: (a) Average data, variance explained PC1=49% and PC2=20%. (b) Single-word data, variance explained PC1=25% and PC2=18%.

maxF0. Analysing the mean acoustic values of these measures and referring to the perceptual correlates of Section 3.1, we observe that Hamm_effort for Assess has the highest value which indicates that Assess vocal effort is louder than the other DAs. The same loud vocal effort effect is observed for Hamm_coarse, and OQG, which have the lowest values among the DAs. AverageF0 and voicing rate present relatively small values which also suggest low activation. F0 was verified for both female and male data isolated, in both cases the lower effect for Assess DA was observed. The mean GOG value for Assess is not the expected for loud vocal effort, its value is higher than for the other DAs.

Classification: The classification of four types of dialogue acts in the AMI-IDIAP averaged data was performed speaker independent, with "leaving-one-speaker-out" cross validation and SVM. The classification results for dialogue acts are presented in Table 2. When both prosody and voice quality measures are used the average classification rate is 44.3%, no improvement was observed when using prosody or voice quality features separately obtaining in both cases an average classification rate of 42.8%. Among the DAs, Assess appears as best classified (76.4%) confirming the salient tendency observed in the PCA analysis. A relatively good classification was obtained as well for Inform (56.6%) although this DA did not present a salient tendency in the PCA analysis.

5.2 Speaker Roles Analysis

Features extraction and pre-processing: In an attempt to reduce the variability of the data, with respect to roles, averaging per speaker and role was applied but just weak effects were observed. So in a second experiment intended to reduce variability we control the phonetic content. That is, we used only the different occurrences of a single frequent word, "control". It would have been preferable to investigate a single vowel, but time-aligned phonetic labels are not yet available in the AMI corpus. Table 4 shows the distribution of dialogue acts that contain the word "control" per dialogue act type and speaker role.

Analysis of Variance: The analysis of variance showed that the null hypothesis can be rejected because most of the prosody and voice quality measures among role types are significantly different at level 0.1%. The prosody measures minF0 and voicing rate have a significance level of 5% and rangeF0 of 1%. The voice quality measure Hamm_head has a significance level of 1%, so it seems that the voice quality features are the most relevant acoustic features in this data set.

Principal Component Analysis: Figure 2 (b) shows the projection of the single-word data onto a PC1-PC2 plane. Clusters for ME and PM roles are apparent that differ (indicated by ellipses) from the general distribution. Gender distribution of ME and PM shows that these roles have more female participants than UI and ID, so that any joint deviation of ME and PM could potentially be attributed to speaker gender rather than speaker role; however, it can be seen from Figure 2 (b) that PM spreads more than average across PC2, whereas ME spreads more than average across PC1. This effect can not be explained merely by speaker gender, but seems specific for the speaker roles. The first three more loded features in PC1 are: Hamm_unstable, slope_ltas1kz and averageF0; in PC2: RCG, SKG and GOG; in PC3 Hamm_effort, Hamm_coarse and SKG. Analysing the mean acoustic values of these measures we observe that the main salient indicators of PM when comparing to the other roles are: a higher value of averageF0 and a lower value of GOG which suggest a loud vocal effort tendency employed by PM. Salient indicators of ME when comparing to the other roles are: higher values for GOG, SKG and RCG which suggest a soft vocal effort tendency employed by ME. The mean value of Hamm_unstable for ME seems to be in a modal range. The spectral slope above 1 kHz value for ME is relatively flat when comparing to the other roles, so this might also indicate a soft vocal effort tendency. Hamm_unstable and slope_ltas1kHz for PM contradict the loud pattern tendency though.

Classification: The classification of four roles in the AMI-IDIAP single-word data was also performed speaker independent, with "leaving-one-speaker-out" cross validation and SVM. The classification results for roles are presented in Table 2. In this case the best classification result is obtained when using just voice quality features (45.8%). When both prosody and voice quality measures are used the average classification rate is 41.8% and the classification rate drops to 19.0% when using just prosody measures. Among roles the best classification rates are for ME (61.72%) and PM (53.92%). The salient tendencies of ME and PM are confirmed with these results.

6 Conclusions

In this paper we have presented a methodology for investigating prosody and voice quality features of social signals in naturalistic recordings. We combine simple prosodic measures with measures from the literature that were reported to capture voice quality robustly, and use Principal Components Analysis and Support vector Machine classification to factor out redundancy and identify the strongest effects. The robustness of the measures and the methodology employed in this study have been verified with controlled data. We have verified that the results are consistent with perceptual impressions. The systematic differences found in the three sets of data are mainly concern with both prosody and voice quality measures. Using the methodology proposed in this paper it has been found that: "assess" dialogue acts were often spoken with a louder vocal effort than other dialogue acts; marketing experts often spoke with a softer voice than average, whereas project managers often spoke with a louder voice than average. So we would expect that when new databases with annotations for specific types of social signals become available in the future, the methodology can also be applied to these data sets, as it was the case for the analysis of dominance in some AMI-IDIAP meetings [2].

Future work will extend the set of acoustic measures to include other acoustic measures such as contour shapes and spectral measures. Another line of work will be to extend the methodology to be able not only to detect general effects on the data but more local effects, or salient acoustic events in a meeting.

Acknowledgements. The research leading to these results has received funding from the EU Programme FP7/2007-2013, under grant agreement no. 231287 (SSPNet).

References

1. Carletta, J., et al.: The ami meeting corpus: A pre-announcement. In: Renals, S., Bengio, S. (eds.) MLMI 2005. LNCS, vol. 3869, pp. 28–39. Springer, Heidelberg (2006)
2. Charfuelan, M., Schröder, M., Steiner, I.: Prosody and voice quality of vocal social signals: the case of dominance in scenario meetings. In: Proc. Interspeech, Makuhari, Japan (2010)
3. Fernandez, R., Picard, R.W.: Dialog act classification from prosodic features using support vector machines. In: Proc. Speech Prosody, Aix-en-Provence, France (2002)
4. Germesin, S., Wilson, T.: Agreement detection in multiparty conversation. In: Proc. ICMI-MLMI 2009, Cambridge, Massachusetts, USA (2009)
5. Gobl, C., Chasaide, A.N.: The role of voice quality in communicating emotion, mood and attitude. Speech Commun. 40(1-2), 189–212 (2003)
6. Gobl, C., Chasaide, A.N.: Voice source variation and its communicative functions. In: The Handbook of Phonetic Sciences, 2nd edn., pp. 378–423 (2010)
7. Hammarberg, B., Fritzell, B., Gauffin, J., Sundberg, J., Wedin, L.: Perceptual and acoustic correlates of abnormal voice quality. Acta Otolaryngologica (90) (1980)
8. Hanson, H.M.: Glottal characteristics of female speakers: Acoustic correlates. The Journal of the Acoustical Society of America 101(1), 466–481 (1997)
9. Ishi, C.T., Ishiguro, H., Hagita, N.: Evaluation of prosodic and voice quality features on automatic extraction of paralinguistic information. In: IEEE/RSJ International Conference on Intelligent Robots and Systems, Beijing, China (2006)

10. Jayagopi, D.B., Ba, S., Odobez, J., Gatica-Perez, D.: Predicting two facets of social verticality in meetings from five-minute time slices and nonverbal cues. In: Proc. 10th ICMI 2008, Chania, Crete, Greece, pp. 45–52 (2008)
11. Lugger, M., Yang, B., Wokurek, W.: Robust estimation of voice quality parameters under realworld disturbances. In: IEEE ICASSP, Toulouse, France (2006)
12. Monzo, C., Alías, F., Iriondo, I., Gonzalvo, X., Planet, S.: Discriminating expressive speech styles by voice quality parameterization. In: Proc. 16th Internat. Cong. of Phonetic Sciences (ICPhS), Saarbrücken, Germany (2007)
13. Nordstrom, K., Tzanetakis, G., Driessen, P.: Transforming perceived vocal effort and breathiness using adaptive pre-emphasis linear prediction. IEEE Transactions on Audio, Speech and Language Proscessing 16(6) (2008)
14. Schröder, M.: Speech and Emotion Research: An overview of research frameworks and a dimensional approach to emotional speech synthesis. Ph.D. thesis, PHONUS 7, Research Report of the Institute of Phonetics, Saarland University (2004)
15. Schröder, M., Grice, M.: Expressing vocal effort in concatenative synthesis. In: Proc. 15th Internat. Cong. of Phonetic Sciences (ICPhS), Barcelona, Spain (2003)
16. Stevens, K., Hanson, H.: Classification of glottal vibration from acoustic measurements. In: Vocal Fold Physiology: Voice Quality Control, ch. 9, no. 147-170 (1994)
17. Vinciarelli, A., Salamin, H., Pantic, M.: Social signal processing: Understanding social interactions through nonverbal behavior analysis. In: IEEE Computer Vision and Pattern Recognition Workshops, pp. 42–49 (2009)

Fast-FACS: A Computer-Assisted System to Increase Speed and Reliability of Manual FACS Coding

Fernando De la Torre[1], Tomas Simon[1], Zara Ambadar[2], and Jeffrey F. Cohn[1,2]

[1] Robotics Institute, Carnegie Mellon University, Pittsburgh, PA 15213, USA
[2] University of Pittsburgh, Pittsburgh, PA 15260, USA

Abstract. FACS (Facial Action Coding System) coding is the state of the art in manual measurement of facial actions. FACS coding, however, is labor intensive and difficult to standardize. A goal of automated FACS coding is to eliminate the need for manual coding and realize automatic recognition and analysis of facial actions. Success of this effort depends in part on access to reliably coded corpora; however, manual FACS coding remains expensive and slow. This paper proposes Fast-FACS, a computer vision aided system that improves speed and reliability of FACS coding. Three are the main novelties of the system: (1) to the best of our knowledge, this is the first paper to predict onsets and offsets from peaks, (2) use Active Appearance Models for computer assisted FACS coding, (3) learn an optimal metric to predict onsets and offsets from peaks. The system was tested in the RU-FACS database, which consists of natural facial behavior during a two-person interview. Fast-FACS reduced manual coding time by nearly 50% and demonstrated strong concurrent validity with manual FACS coding.

Keywords: Facial Action Coding System, Action Unit Recognition.

1 Introduction

FACS (Facial Action Coding System [1]) coding is the state of the art in manual measurement of facial action. FACS coding, however, is labor intensive and difficult to standardize across coders. A goal of automated FACS coding [2,3,4] is to eliminate the need for manual coding and realize automatic recognition and analysis of facial actions.Success of this effort depends on access to *reliably coded corpora* of FACS-coded images from well-chosen observational scenarios. Completing the necessary FACS coding for training and testing algorithms has been a rate-limiter. Manual FACS coding remains expensive and slow.

The inefficiency of current approaches for FACS coding is not inherent to FACS but to the failure to make use of technology to make coders more productive. This paper proposes an hybrid system, Fast-FACS, that combines automated facial image processing with manual coding to increase the speed and reliability of FACS coding. Figure 1 shows the main idea of the paper. The specific aims are to: (1) Reduce time and effort required for manual FACS coding by using novel computer vision and machine learning techniques. (2) Increase reliability of FACS coding by increasing the internal consistency of manual FACS coding. (3) Develop an intuitive graphical user interface that is comparable to commercially available packages in ease of use, while enabling fast reliable coding.

S. D'Mello et al. (Eds.): ACII 2011, Part I, LNCS 6974, pp. 57–66, 2011.

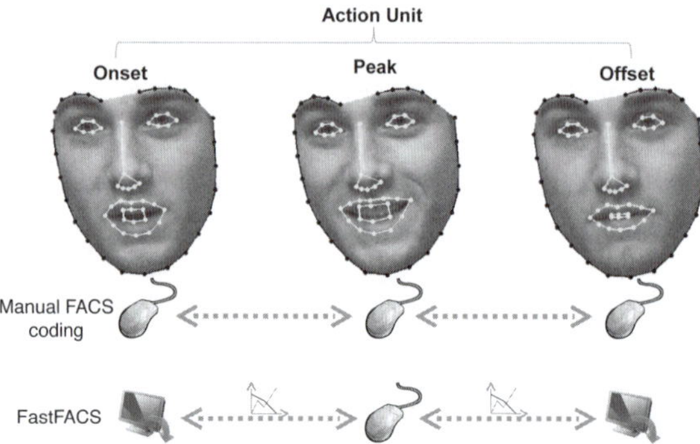

Fig. 1. FACS coding typically involves frame-by-frame inspection of the video, paying close attention to subtle cues such as wrinkles, bulges, and furrows. Left to right, evolution of an AU 12 (involved in smiling), from onset, peak, to offset. Using FastFACS only the peak needs to be labeled and the onset/offset are estimated automatically.

2 Previous Work

2.1 Facial Action Coding System (FACS)

FACS [1] is a comprehensive, anatomically-based system for measuring nearly all visually discernible facial movement. FACS describes facial activity on the basis of 44 unique action units (AUs), as well as several categories of head and eye positions and movements. Facial movement is thus described in terms of constituent components, or AUs. FACS is recognized as the most comprehensive and objective means for measuring facial movement currently available, and it has become the standard for facial measurement in behavioral research [5].

Human-observer-based methods like FACS are time consuming to learn and use, and they are difficult to standardize, especially across laboratories and over time. A goal of automated FACS coding [2,3,4] is to eliminate the need for manual coding and realize automatic recognition and analysis of facial actions. The success of this effort depends on access to reliably coded corpora of FACS-coded images from well-chosen observational scenarios, which entails extensive need for manual FACS-coding.

Currently, FACS coders typically proceed in either single or multiple passes through the video. When a single-pass procedure is used, they view the video and code the occurrences of all target AU in each frame. FACS coders view video at both regular video rate and in slow motion to detect often subtle changes in facial features, such as wrinkling of facial skin, that indicate the occurrence, timing, and intensity of facial AUs. AU intensity is coded on a 5-point ordinal intensity scale from trace to maximal intensity. FACS scoring produces a list of AUs, their intensity, and the video frames or times at which each began (i.e. onset), peaked (highest intensity observed), and ended (i.e., offset). Fig. 1 shows an example of onset, peak and offset of AU12, which raises the lip corners obliquely. Until now, manual FACS coding was slow and achieving reliability was challenging.

2.2 Automatic FACS Segmentation and Recognition from Video

Advances in computer vision over the past decades have yielded advances toward the goal of automatic FACS. That is, to eliminate the need for manual coding and realize automatic recognition and analysis of facial actions.

Two main streams on automatic analysis of facial expression consider emotion-specified expressions (e.g., happy or sad) and anatomically based facial actions (e.g., FACS). Most relevant to Fast-FACS is work that addresses the temporal segmentation of AUs into onset, offset, and peak. Pantic and Pantras [4] used a rule-based method to separate onset, apex and offset. Valstar and Pantic [6] combined Hidden Markov Models and Support Vector Machines to model the temporal dynamics of facial actions. They considered the onset, apex, and offset frames as different classes. Accuracy was measured as precision-recall in these classes. These approaches all used supervised learning with the goal of fully automated expression or AU coding.

More recently, two groups have proposed hybrid systems that make use of more unsupervised learning techniques to augment manual coding of AUs. Zhang et al. [7] proposed an active learning approach to improve speed and accuracy in AU labeling. In their approach, a sequence is labeled with an automatic system, and a user then is asked to label the frames that are considered ambiguous by the system. De la Torre et al. [8] proposed an unsupervised algorithm to segment facial behavior into AUs, an approach that achieved concurrent validity with manual FACS coding. Subsequently, we found that this unsupervised approach could achieve fast, accurate, robust coding of AU onsets and offsets when coupled with manual coding of AU peaks.

3 Fast-FACS

This section describes Fast-FACS, that uses advances in computer vision and machine learning to increase the efficiency and reliability of FACS coding.

3.1 Active Appearance Tracking

There exist a variety of methods for facial feature tracking. Over the last decade, appearance models have become increasingly prominent in computer vision and graphics. Parameterized Appearance Models (PAMs) have been proven useful for alignment, detection, tracking, and face synthesis [9,10,11]. In particular, Active Appearance Models (AAMs) have proven an excellent tool for detecting and aligning facial features. AAMs [9,11,10] typically fit their shape and appearance components to an image through a gradient descent, although other optimization approaches have been employed with similar results. Figure 1 shows how a person-dependent AAM [11,9] is able to track the facial features in a video segment that includes smiling (AU12). A person-dependent AAM is built by manually annotating about 3% of the video to use for training. The AAM is composed of 66 landmarks that deform to fit perturbations in facial features. To the best of our knowledge, the work described here is the first to use the results of AAMs in a hybrid system to improve the speed and reliability of FACS coding. The hybrid system augments the skill of highly trained FACS coders with computer vision and machine learning based video editing and estimation of AU onsets and offsets.

3.2 Peak, Onset, and Offset Coding

In the first step of Fast-FACS, the user annotates the peak of a facial action. The system then automatically estimates the remaining boundaries of the event, that is, the onset and offset (extent) of the AU. The estimation of the position of the onset and offset of a given event peak is based on a similarity measure defined on features derived from the AAM mesh of the tracked face and on the expected distribution of onset and offset durations (for a given AU) derived from a database of manually coded AUs.

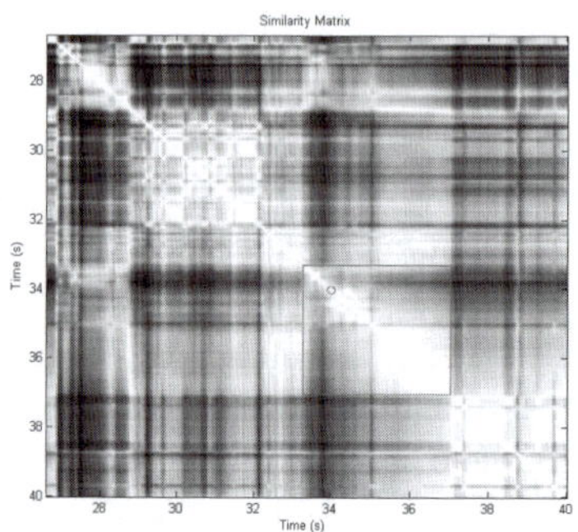

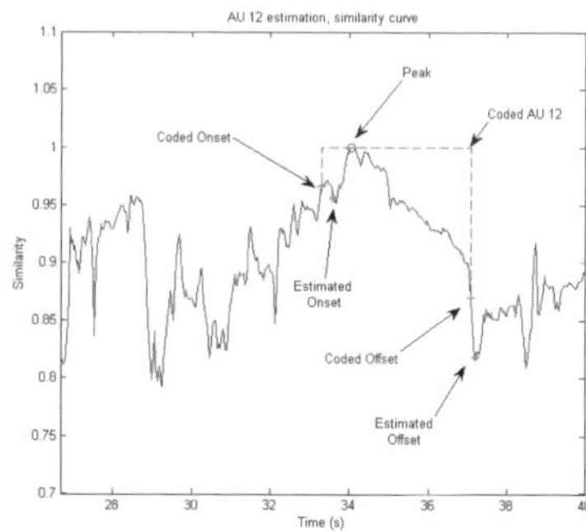

Fig. 2. Left) Similarity matrix for a video segment. The red rectangle denotes a specific AU 12 instance as coded manually. The red circle marks the user-labeled peak. Observe that the AU defines a region "bounded" by sharp edges in the similarity matrix. Right) Similarity curve for the marked peak (ie. $\mathbf{K}_{peak,j}$ for all j in a neighborhood). Note how the estimated onset and offset snap to local minima on the similarity curve.

We construct a symmetric affinity matrix $\mathbf{K} \in \Re^{n \times n}$, where each entry $k_{ij} \in [0, 1]$ represents the similarity between frames i and j, and n denotes the number of frames [8]. This similarity measure will be used to decide where best to partition the AU into onset, peak and offset sections.

To compute the similarity measure (a qualitative distance from the peak frame), k_{ij}, we use the 66 shape landmarks from the tracking. The particular distance measure will be addressed in section 3.3. The description of the feature extraction process follows: The AAM mesh is first interpolated to a finer resolution using B-Spline fitting in the region of interest (upper or lower face). The resulting mesh from frame i is aligned with respect to frame j using an affine transform intended to remove the rigid movement of the head while retaining the elastic deformations of facial actions. Once both frames are commonly referenced, the landmarks are stacked into vectors $\mathbf{f}_i$ and $\mathbf{f}_j$, and $k_{ij} = e^{\frac{-d(\mathbf{f}_i, \mathbf{f}_j)}{2\sigma^2}}$ where $d(\mathbf{f}_i, \mathbf{f}_j)$ measures distance.

Figure 2 shows the similarity curve for a video segment. The similarity measure is robust to changes in pose (rigid motion) as well as to changes in facial expression that do not affect the particular AU under study (non-rigid motion). Additionally, the measure need to be invariant with respect to each AU class. The distance between frames is computed with the Mahalanobis distance $d(\mathbf{f}_i, \mathbf{f}_j) = (\mathbf{f}_i - \mathbf{f}_j)^T \mathbf{A} (\mathbf{f}_i - \mathbf{f}_j)$. Next section describes a metric learning algorithm to learn $\mathbf{A}$.

3.3 Learning a Metric for Onset/Offset Detection

This section describes the procedure to learn a metric [12] for onset and offset estimation. Let d features of each frame i be stacked into a vector, $\mathbf{f}_i \in \Re^{d\times 1}$. $\mathbf{f}_i^p$ denotes a frame i within a close neighborhood of an AU peak frame, $\mathbf{f}_p$. Let $\mathbf{f}_k^{o(p)}$ denote a frame at or beyond the onset (or offset) of the same AU. The metric learning optimizes:

$$\min_{\mathbf{A}} \sum_{i,p} (\mathbf{f}_i^p - \mathbf{f}_p)^T \mathbf{A} (\mathbf{f}_i^p - \mathbf{f}_p) + C \sum_{k,p} \xi_{k,p}$$

$$s.t. \sqrt{(\mathbf{f}_k^{o(p)} - \mathbf{f}_p)^T \mathbf{A} (\mathbf{f}_k^{o(p)} - \mathbf{f}_p)} > th - \xi_{k,p} \ \forall k,p \ \ \mathbf{A} \succeq 0,\ \xi_{k,p} \geq 0 \qquad (1)$$

where $\mathbf{A} \in \Re^{n\times n}$ is a symmetric positive semi-definite matrix that minimizes the distance between frames neighboring the peak while ensuring that the distance between the peak and those frames at or beyond the onset and offset is greater than a given threshold th. Slack variables $\xi_{k,p}$ ensure that the constraints can be satisfied, while the parameter C adjusts the importance of the constraints in the minimization.

Eq. (1) can be solved with SDP approaches and we used the CVX package [13]. Restricting $\mathbf{A}$ to be diagonal is equivalent to individually weighting the features. While a full matrix could be used, in our experience diagonal and full matrices provide comparable performance, and we used this strategy for the experimental results.

3.4 Graphical User Interface (GUI)

There exist several commercial packages for manual event coding. These proprietary systems cannot be modified easily or all to accommodate user developed modules such as Fast-FACS and similar efficiencies. We have developed a GUI specifically for FACS coding with the goal of creating an open-source framework that makes it possible to add new features (such as onset and offset detection) in order to improve the speed and reliability of FACS coding.

Fig. 3 shows the GUI for Fast-FACS. As described above, the coder manually cods the AU peaks, assigning an AU identifier and related features of the event (intensity and laterality), as well as comments about the peak to indicate whether it is gradual, ambiguous or an instance of multiple peaks. Annotation other than labeling of the peaks is for the user's reference and not used in onset or offset estimation. Once the peaks have been labeled, the onset and the offset are automatically detected and the resulting events made available for the user's inspection. For FACS coders, it is usually difficult to determine the appropriate intensity level of a certain AU, meaning that they must go back to previous events to compare the relative intensity of an AU with other instances of that AU for a given person or multiple persons. Additionally, Fast-FACS has an option to view all instances of selected AU without having to view the intervening video. This efficiency further contributes to the increased productivity afforded by Fast-FACS. By being able to compare multiple instances of an AU, users (coders) can directly calibrate intensity without having to hold multiple instances in mind. With the *event navigation* menu the coder can quickly verify that the event has been correctly coded, as well as change the estimated onset and offset if required. Fig. 3 (right) shows some of these functionalities.

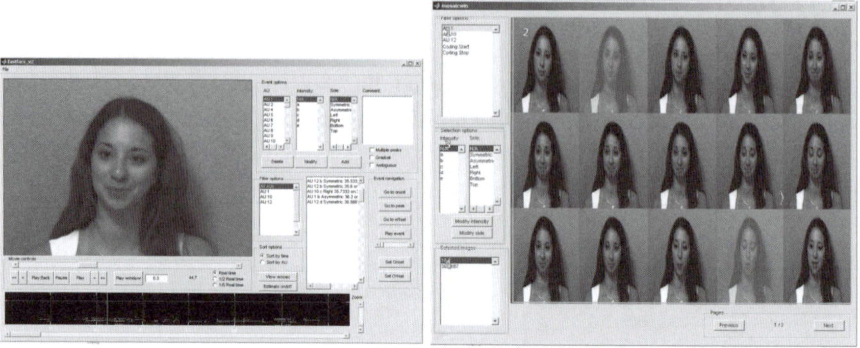

Fig. 3. Left) Fast-FACS main interface. Right) Details of mosaic window. 1.-AU list. 2.-Mosaic image. 3.-Intensity and side options. 4.-List of selected images. See PDF.

4 Experimental Evaluations

Fast-FACS enables computer-assisted coding of peaks and automatic coding of onsets and offsets. To evaluate Fast-FACS, at least three questions are relevant.

- How well does Fast-FACS compare with leading commercial software for manual coding of peaks? Inter-coder agreement should be comparable.
- Does automatic detection of onsets and offsets have concurrent validity with manual coding? Inter-system agreement for onsets and offsets should be comparable to inter-coder agreement of manual coding.
- Is Fast-FACS more efficient than manual coding? Does it substantially reduce the time required to complete FACS coding?

We conducted several experiments using a relatively challenging corpus of FACS coded video, the RU-FACS [14] video data-set. It consists of non-posed facial behavior of 100 participants who were observed for approximately 2.5 minutes. FACS-coded video from 34 participants was available to us. Of these, 5 had to be excluded due to excessive occlusion or errors in the digitized video, leaving data from 29 participants.

4.1 Inter-coder and Inter-system Agreement

Two sequences, S60 and S47, were selected at random from the RU-FACS database. The clips were 2 minutes 4 seconds and 2 minutes 50 seconds in duration, respectively. Each coder coded the two interviews using two software packages, Observer XT 7.0 [15], and Fast-FACS. AUs coded include AU 1, AU 2, AU 4, AU 10, AU 12, AU 15, and AU 20. Order of coding the clips was counter balanced across coders and across systems. Thus, for one subject, one coder used Fast-FACS first and Observer second, while the other coder began with Observer and then used Fast-FACS. The order was reversed for coding the other subject. Coding of the same clip was conducted several days apart to minimize possible familiarity effects. The time it took each coder to code peaks in Observer and Fast-FACS was recorded. In addition, onset and offset of each AU were coded in Observer, and the time it took to code onset and offset was also recorded. Onsets and offsets in Fast-FACS were not manually coded, rather automatically estimated.

In calculating inter-coder and inter-system agreement, a window of agreement of $\pm.5$ seconds (15 frames) was used. In FACS coding, it is a typically allowed margin of error [16]. Inter-coder agreement [17] refers to whether two coders using the same system agree. Concurrent validity refers to whether there is agreement between systems. Percent agreement was computed using percentage agreement Ekman & Friesen [18], and as a Kappa (k) [19]. Kappa is a more rigorous metric as it is controls for agreements due to chance. Agreement is reported for both all intensity levels and for intensity levels B and higher. In the original FACS manual, AU at trace levels were not coded, and reliability of A levels has not been reported in the literature.

Intra and inter-system agreement for AU peaks. For both percent agreement and kappa when labeling peaks of all intensities, agreement between systems (86% and 74% kappa) was comparable to inter-coder agreement using commercial software (84% and 70% kappa) . When considering intensities B or higher, agreement rose to 83% and 91%. Inter-coder agreement was comparable between commercial software and the Fast-FACS interface. Using commercial software, inter-coder agreement was 86% and kappa was 0.70; the corresponding results using Fast-FACS were agreement 84% and kappa 0.70. These results are for all intensity levels. When A-level (i.e. trace) inter-coder agreement increased.

Temporal agreement of manual coding of peak, onset and offset. This section evaluated the inter-coder differences of manual coding. Temporal agreement of manual coding for peak, onset and offset was evaluated in Fast-FACS and Observer. The same two clips from the RU-FACS [14] database were used. The temporal error was calculated only when there was agreement between the two coders within a $\pm.5$ sec window. Results for temporal error using Fast-FACS and Observer are shown separately in Table 1a (left) and Table 1b (right). Both systems achieved similar results. On average, temporal error for manual coding of peaks and onset are about ±2 frames. Temporal error for manual coding of offset was larger, on average ±10 frames in Observer and ±12 frames in Fast-FACS. Across AU, average agreement was within $10 - 12$ frames. This finding is consistent with what is known from the FACS literature. In general, onsets are relatively discrete, whereas offsets for many AU fade gradually and may be difficult to delimit [5]. Also, it appears that temporal error of manual coding is different for different AUs, with AU 10 and 12 showing larger temporal error and greater variability than other AUs, especially for offset coding.

4.2 Accuracy of Estimated Onsets and Offsets

To evaluate the accuracy of the onset and offset estimation, we used 29 subjects from the RU-FACS database. Leave-one-out cross-validation was used in the evaluation, using all subjects except the one currently under test to train the detection algorithm (i.e. metric learning 3.3) and repeating the training/testing phases for every subject in the database. The detected onsets and offsets for all subjects were then pooled and compared with those coded manually, taken as ground truth.

Table 1. Temporal error of manual peak, onset and offset in (a) Fast-FACS and (b) Observer. All units are in frames; M refers to mean, STD to standard deviation and N represents the number of samples.

(a) Fast-FACS

	Peak			Onset			Offset		
AU	M	SD	N	M	SD	N	M	SD	N
1	1.6	3.8	36	1.4	1.8	33	4.5	6.4	33
2	1.2	2.1	27	1.0	1.3	27	9.6	19.4	27
4	2.6	4.3	15	1.4	3.1	15	7.2	11.2	15
10	3.9	4.9	13	3.5	4.6	13	34.8	44.7	13
12	3.0	3.2	18	2.1	4.1	8	24.5	30.3	8
15	1.8	2.8	28	2.3	3.5	28	4.2	6.7	28
20	0.4	0.5	10	0.4	0.5	10	1.2	0.8	10
M	2.3			1.9			12.0		

(b) Observer

	Peak			Onset			Offset		
AU	M	SD	N	M	SD	N	M	SD	N
1	2.5	4.7	35	3.0	4.9	32	8.5	14.4	32
2	1.9	2.9	29	1.5	1.8	26	8.4	13.3	26
4	2.1	4.0	15	2.3	2.7	15	8.6	7.9	15
10	2.8	3.4	14	2.0	2.5	14	14.5	29.4	14
12	2.3	2.4	21	4.3	5.3	8	25.2	35.3	8
15	1.6	2.6	32	5.8	22.6	32	3.0	3.2	32
20	0.9	0.8	10	1.2	0.9	10	1.5	0.9	10
M	2.0			2.7			9.6		

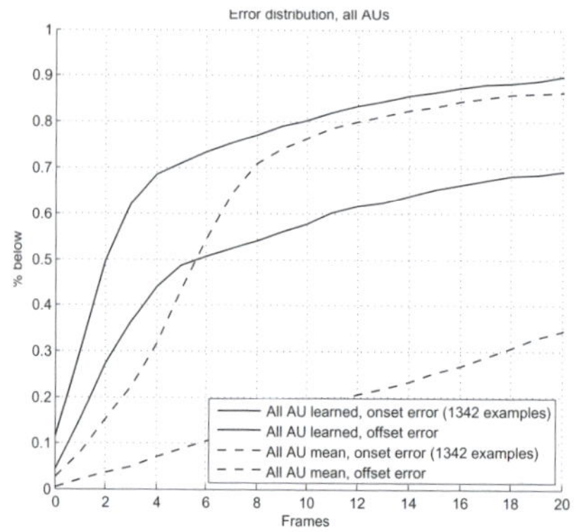

(a) Error distribution

		S60		S47	
		Manual	Fast-FACS	Manual	Fast-FACS
C1	Peak	189	147	163	135
	Onset/Offset	137	0.0	113	0.0
C2	Peak	114	64	64	72
	Onset/Offset	66	0.0	62	0.0
Mean	Peak	151.5	105.5	113.5	103.5
	Onset/Offset	101.5	0.0	87.5	0.0
	% On/Off over total	40% 253.0	0% 105.5	43% 200.0	0% 103.5

(b) Manual coding time

Fig. 4. Left) Error distribution for onset and offset estimation using the learned metric compared with estimating the mean onset and offset duration (for each AU). Graph shows the fraction of instances in the database for which the error committed when estimating the onset and offset from the coded peak was below a certain number of frames. Results are pooled for all AUs (1,2,4,10,12,15,20). Right) Time required to code peaks, onsets, and offsets using manual coding via Observer and Fast-FACS. Onset and offset coding in Fast-FACS is fully automated, thus requiring no coder time. Units are in seconds. C1 refers to coder 1. Images better seen in color.

As a baseline comparison and an intuition as to how much information the visual AAM features contribute to the estimation, Fig. 4 shows the performance of our system compared with a system that uses only the statistical distribution of AU onsets and offsets along time, and estimates the onset at the mean onset position (w.r.t. the peak) as found in the training data (similarly for offsets). Given that the temporal statistics of each AU can be different, these measures are taken for each AU separately. Note that for offsets especially, the visual features are key to an accurate estimation.

Figures 5a and 5b show the distribution of the errors committed for onsets of selected AUs, measured as the absolute difference in frames from the manually labeled onsets/offsets to those determined automatically, comparing the learned metric and

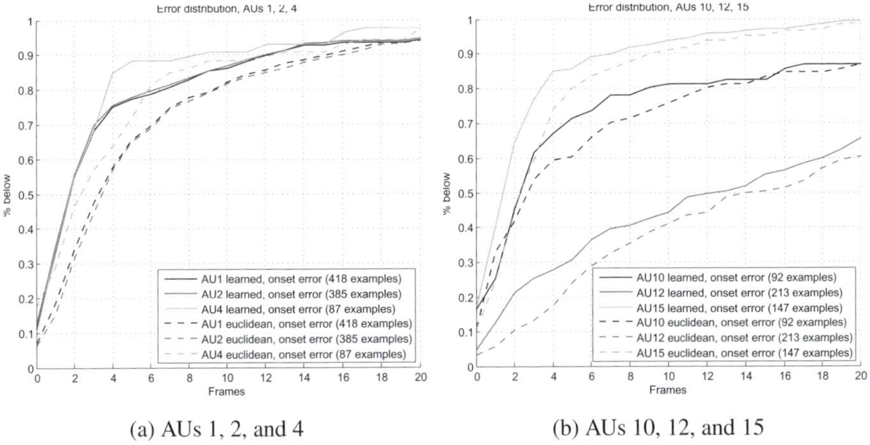

(a) AUs 1, 2, and 4

(b) AUs 10, 12, and 15

Fig. 5. Error distribution for onsets for (a) AUs 1, 2 and 4, (left) and (b) AUs 10, 12 and 15, comparing the learned metric with results obtained using Euclidean distance

Euclidean distance. Temporal error for onsets was relatively low. The mean error ranged from 3.8 to 13.1 for AUs 1,2,4,10 and 15. This is within the standard of acceptable error for manual coding. Inter-system agreement for offsets was lower and more variable. With the exception of AU 12, mean offset error ranged from 10.6 to 36.2 frames. Mean onset error for AU 12 was 32.13 frames, mean offset error 84 frames. Lower precision for offsets is consistent with the reliability of manual coding. Many AU fade slowly as the face relaxes, which attenuates the observable signal values of offsets. Indeed, only in some selected types of smiles (e.g., embarrassed), does one find fast offsets [20]. Perhaps the most important confound for AU 12 is mouth movement due to speech, which makes similarity based methods fail.

4.3 Efficiency of Fast-FACS

Fast-FACS reduced total coding time by one half or more. As shown in the table in Fig. 4 right, automatic coding of onsets and offsets was responsible for most of this decrease. However, it also appeared that efficiencies in the Fast-FACS GUI may have been a factor as well. Manual coding of peaks using Fast-FACS was faster in each case. Overall, the increased efficiency from the GUI and from automatic coding of onsets and offsets resulted in dramatically increased efficiency and productivity.

Acknowledgments. This work was partially supported by the U.S. NRL under Contract No. N00173-07-C-2040 and sponsored by the DHS. Any opinions, findings and conclusions or recommendations expressed in this material are those of the authors and do not necessarily reflect the views of the U.S. NRL or the DHS. Thanks to Joan Campoy for implementing the GUI of Fast-FACS.

References

1. Ekman, P., Friesen, W.: Facial Action Coding System: A technique for the measurement of facial movement. Consulting Psychologists Press, Palo Alto (1978)

2. Cohn, J.F., Kanade, T.: Use of automated facial image analysis for measurement of emotion expression. In: The Handbook of Emotion Elicitation and Assessment. Series in Affective Science. Oxford University Press, Oxford (2007)
3. Bartlett, M., Littlewort, G., Lainscsek, C., Fasel, I., Frank, M., Movellan, J.: Fully automatic facial action recognition in spontaneous behavior. In: 7th International Conference on Automatic Face and Gesture Recognition (2006)
4. Pantic, M., Patras, I.: Dynamics of Facial Expression: Recognition of Facial Actions and their Temporal Segments from Face Profile Image Sequences. IEEE Transactions on Systems, Man, and Cybernetics - Part B 36(2), 433–449 (2006)
5. Cohn, J.F., Ekman, P.: Measuring facial action by manual coding, facial EMG, and automatic facial image analysis. In: Harrigan, J.A., Rosenthal, R., Scherer, K. (eds.) Handbook of Nonverbal Behavior Research Methods in the Affective Sciences, NY, Oxford (2005)
6. Valstar, M., Pantic, M.: Combined support vector machines and hidden Markov models for modeling facial action temporal dynamics. In: Proceedings of IEEE Workshop on Human Computer Interaction. In conjunction with IEEE ICCV 2007, pp. 118–127 (2007)
7. Zhang, L., Tong, Y., Ji, Q.: Active image labeling and its application to facial action labeling. In: Forsyth, D., Torr, P., Zisserman, A. (eds.) ECCV 2008, Part II. LNCS, vol. 5303, pp. 706–719. Springer, Heidelberg (2008)
8. De la Torre, F., Campoy, J., Ambadar, Z., Cohn, J.F.: Temporal segmentation of facial behavior. In: International Conference on Computer Vision (2007)
9. De la Torre, F., Nguyen, M.: Parameterized kernel principal component analysis: Theory and applications to supervised and unsupervised image alignment. In: IEEE Computer Vision and Pattern Recognition (2008)
10. Cootes, T.F., Edwards, G.J., Taylor, C.J.: Active appearance models. In: Burkhardt, H., Neumann, B. (eds.) ECCV 1998, Part II. LNCS, vol. 1407, pp. 484–498. Springer, Heidelberg (1998)
11. Matthews, I., Baker, S.: Active appearance models revisited. International Journal of Computer Vision 60(2), 135–164 (2004)
12. Xing, E., Ng, A., Jordan, M., Russell, S.: Distance metric learning, with application to clustering with side-information. In: Advances in Neural Information Processing Systems, vol. 15, pp. 505–512. MIT Press, Cambridge (2003)
13. Grant, M., Boyd, S.: Cvx: Matlab software for disciplined convex programming (2008), `http://stanford.edu/~boyd/cvx`
14. Frank, M., Movellan, J., Bartlett, M., Littleworth, G.: RU-FACS-1 database, Machine Perception Laboratory, U.C. San Diego
15. Noldus information technology. Observer XT 10, The Netherlands (2011)
16. Sayette, M.A., Cohn, J.F., Wertz, J.M., Perrott, M., Parrott, D.J.: A psychometric evaluation of the facial action coding system for assessing spontaneous expression. Journal of Nonverbal Behavior (25), 167–186 (2007)
17. Cohn, J.F., Ambadar, Z., Ekman, P.: Observer-based measurement of facial expression with the Facial Action Coding System. In: Coan, J.A., Allen, J.J.B. (eds.) The Handbook of Emotion Elicitation and Assessment. Series in Affective Science. Oxford University Press, Oxford (2007)
18. Ekman, P., Friesen, W., Hager, J.: Facial action coding system: Research nexus. Network Research Information, Salt Lake City, UT (2002)
19. Fleiss, J.: Statistical methods for rates and proportions. Wiley, New York (1981)
20. Ambadar, Z., Cohn, J.F., Reed, L.: All smiles are not created equal: Morphology and timing of smiles perceived as amused, polite, and embarrassed/nervous. Journal of Nonverbal Behavior 33(1), 17–34 (2008)

A Computer Model of the Interpersonal Effect of Emotion Displayed in a Social Dilemma*

Celso M. de Melo[1], Peter Carnevale[2], Dimitrios Antos[3], and Jonathan Gratch[1]

[1] Institute for Creative Technologies, University of Southern California, 12015 Waterfront Drive, Building #4 Playa Vista, CA 90094-2536, USA
{demelo,gratch}@ict.usc.edu
[2] USC Marshall School of Business, Los Angeles, CA 90089-0808, USA
peter.carnevale@marshall.usc.edu
[3] Harvard University, 33 Oxford st., Maxwell-Dworkin 217, Cambridge, MA 02138, USA
antos@fas.harvard.edu

Abstract. The paper presents a computational model for decision-making in a social dilemma that takes into account the other party's emotion displays. The model is based on data collected in a series of recent studies where participants play the iterated prisoner's dilemma with agents that, even though following the same action strategy, show different emotion displays according to how the game unfolds. We collapse data from all these studies and fit, using maximum likelihood estimation, probabilistic models that predict likelihood of cooperation in the next round given different features. Model 1 predicts based on round outcome alone. Model 2 predicts based on outcome and emotion displays. Model 3 also predicts based on outcome and emotion but, considers contrast effects found in the empirical studies regarding the order with which participants play cooperators and non-cooperators. To evaluate the models, we replicate the original studies but, substitute the humans for the models. The results reveal that Model 3 best replicates human behavior in the original studies and Model 1 does the worst. The results, first, emphasize recent research about the importance of nonverbal cues in social dilemmas and, second, reinforce that people attend to contrast effects in their decision-making. Theoretically, the model provides further insight into how people behave in social dilemmas. Pragmatically, the model could be used to drive an agent that is engaged in a social dilemma with a human (or another agent).

Keywords: Emotion, Cooperation, Social Dilemma, Probabilistic Model.

1 Introduction

In multi-agent systems, agents frequently have to decide whether to pursue their own self-interest and collect a short-term reward or trust other agents to reach mutual

* This research supported by the Air Force Office of Scientific Research under grant FA9550-09-1-0507 and the National Science Foundation under grant IIS-0916858. The content does not necessarily reflect the position or the policy of the Government, and no official endorsement should be inferred.

S. D´Mello et al. (Eds.): ACII 2011, Part I, LNCS 6974, pp. 67–76, 2011.

cooperation and maximize joint long-term reward [1]. Initial solutions to such dilemmas were based on game-theoretic notions such as dominant strategies or Nash equilibria that prescribe the conditions under which it is rational to cooperate [2]. However, though appropriate for agent-agent encounters, these techniques are less so for human-agent encounters. Effectively, there is now considerable evidence that humans are not purely self-interested and do not always behave according to the predictions of game theory [3, 4]. Early research in the behavioral sciences has, in fact, shown many sources of cooperation in human-human interaction [5]: some people are simply inclined to cooperate [6]; group identity [7]; reciprocity [8]; monitoring and sanctioning [9]; and, verbal communication [10]. More recently, non-verbal displays have also been argued to impact emergence of cooperation [11, 12], in particular, facial displays of emotion (e.g., [13]).

In a pioneering set of studies [14-17], we have explored the interpersonal effect of emotion displays on emergence of cooperation between agents and humans in social dilemmas. In these studies participants play the iterated prisoner's dilemma with agents that, even though following the same strategy to choose their actions, convey different facial emotion displays according to the outcome of each round. In line with predictions from the behavioral sciences about the impact of non-verbal displays on decision-making [11, 12], the results indicate that people's decision to cooperate is influenced by emotion displays. For instance, people cooperate more with an agent which displays reflect an appreciation of cooperation (e.g., smile when both players cooperate) than one which displays reflect satisfaction with selfishness (e.g., smile when agent defects and participant cooperates). In line with the view that people respond emotionally to *relative* changes in their situations rather than the absolute consequences of their decisions [4], the results show that the order participants play the agents influences cooperation rates. For instance, people will cooperate more with an agent which displays reward cooperation *after* playing with one which displays reflect selfish interest, than if they were to play with the former agent first.

In this paper we develop a computer model of decision-making in a social dilemma that takes into account the other party's emotion displays and replicates findings from the literature on how people behave in social dilemmas. Such a model could be used to drive embodied agents - i.e., agents that have virtual bodies and can express through them like humans do [18] - when engaged in a social dilemma with humans. Effectively, it has been shown that people can treat embodied agents like people [19] and are capable of being influenced by them [20]. Moreover, since embodied agents can be used to learn about human-human interaction [21], such a model would allow us to get further insight on how people act in social dilemmas. Methodologically, we follow a novel approach: (1) Data from our empirical studies [14-17] is collapsed into a single database. Features represent aspects of the game, the outcome of the round and whether the participant cooperated in the next round (target); (2) Probabilistic models are fitted to the data using maximum likelihood estimation. Each model predicts likelihood of cooperation given a subset of the features (e.g., outcome and display in the current round). We explore models that predict based on outcome only, outcome and emotion, and outcome, emotion and contrast effects; (3) Regarding evaluation, even though we look at standard performance measures such as error rate, the focus is on the models' ability to replicate previous findings about how people behave in social dilemmas. To accomplish this, we "play" the models with different agents that display emotions, under the same configurations as in the empirical studies. Our results show that the best model replicates many of the findings about how people behave in social dilemmas and, overall, reinforce findings for the importance of attending to nonverbal signals and contrast effects in social dilemmas.

2 Background

This section describes three empirical studies we previously conducted where people are engaged in a social dilemma with agents that display emotions through the face.

Study 1. The first study [15, 16] follows a repeated-measures design where participants play 25 rounds of the iterated prisoner's dilemma with two agents that play the same strategy but show different emotion displays. The prisoner's dilemma game was recast as an investment game where participants can choose to invest either in Project Green (cooperation) or Project Blue (defection). The payoff matrix is shown in Table 1. The agents' action strategy is based on tit-for-tat [8]. The *expressively cooperative* agent displays reflect an appreciation of mutual cooperation (e.g., when both players cooperate it smiles). In line with the definition of selfish orientation [6], the *expressively individualistic* agent's displays reflect how valuable the outcome is to the agent, independently of the value to the participant (e.g., when the agent cooperates and the participant defects, it shows sadness). Table 2 summarizes the displays for both agents. Agent order was counter-balanced across participants. Fifty-one participants were recruited for this experiment.

Table 1. Payoff matrix for the social dilemma game

		Agent	
		Project Green	Project Blue
Participant	Project Green	Agent: 5 pts Participant: 5 pts	Agent: 7 pts Participant: 3 pts
	Project Blue	Agent: 3 pts Participant: 7 pts	Agent: 4 pts Participant: 4 pts

Table 2. Emotion displays for the agents in study 1

Expressively Cooperative		*Agent* Green	Blue
Participant	Green	Joy	Shame
	Blue	Anger	Sadness

Expressively Individualistic		*Agent* Green	Blue
Participant	Green	Neutral	Joy
	Blue	Sadness	Sadness

The results show that, as predicted, people's decision making is influenced by the emotion displays and people cooperate significantly more with the cooperative[1] agent. Additionally, the results reveal clear contrast effects: people cooperate more with the cooperative agent after playing with the individualistic agent, than the other way around. This contrast effect is in line with the well-known *black-hat/white-hat*

[1] When the context is clear we refer to the agents without the 'expressively' adverb.

(or *bad-cop/good-cop*) effect [22] that argues people cooperate more with a cooperative opponent if they're first matched with a tough opponent. In summary, the findings in this study are (see cooperation rates in Table 8 under 'Humans'):

F1.1 ***(a)*** *Participants cooperate significantly more with the cooperative than the individualistic agent;* ***(b)*** *but, this effect is mainly driven by the order where participants play with the individualistic agent first, followed by the cooperative agent.*

Study 2. The second study (unpublished) explores two new versions of the cooperative and individualistic agents that display the same type and quantity of emotions but, the displays are mapped differently to round outcomes. Table 3 summarizes these new agents. In this study we also compare the emotional agents to a no-emotion control agent. Three experiments were run: (1) cooperative vs. individualistic, with 39 participants; (2) cooperative vs. control, with 20 participants; (3) individualistic vs. control, with 37 participants. Otherwise, the design remained the same as study 1.

Table 3. Emotion displays for the agents in study 2

Expressively Cooperative		*Agent* Green	*Agent* Blue
Participant	Green	Joy	Sadness
	Blue	Sadness	Sadness

Expressively Individualistic		*Agent* Green	*Agent* Blue
Participant	Green	Sadness	Joy
	Blue	Sadness	Sadness

The results show the following (see cooperation rates in Table 8 under 'Humans'):

F2.1 *Participants tend to cooperate more with the cooperative agent than the individualistic agent, in all orders;*

F2.2 ***(a)*** *Participants tend to cooperate more with the cooperative than the control agent;* ***(b)*** *but, this effect is driven by the order where participants play with the control agent first;*

F2.3 *Participants do not cooperate differently with the individualistic and control agents.*

Study 3. The third study [17] compares (a variant of) the expressively cooperative agent with the *expressively competitive* agent. In line with the usual definition of competitive orientation [6], the competitive agent's displays reflect a goal of earning more points than the participant (e.g., when the agent defects and the participant cooperates, it smiles). Table 4 shows the emotion displays for these agents. In this study, we also compare the emotional agents to a no-emotion control agent. We ran 3 experiments: (1) cooperative vs. competitive, with 34 participants; (2) cooperative vs. control, with 38 participants; (3) individualistic vs. control, with 30 participants. The design remains the same as study 1, except that the payoff for the player that gets exploited (i.e., when it cooperates and the other defects) is reduced from 3 to 2 points.

Table 4. Emotion displays for the agents in study 3

Expressively Cooperative		*Agent* Green	*Agent* Blue
Participant	Green	Joy	Neutral
	Blue	Anger	Neutral

Expressively Competitive		*Agent* Green	*Agent* Blue
Participant	Green	Neutral	Joy
	Blue	Anger	Neutral

The results show the following (see cooperation rates in Table 8 under 'Humans'):

F3.1 ***(a)*** *When collapsing across orders, participants tend to cooperate more with the cooperative agent; however:* ***(b)*** *in the order cooperative → competitive, participants tend to cooperate more with the competitive agent;* ***(c)*** *in the order competitive → cooperative, participants cooperate significantly more with the cooperative agent;*

F3.2 ***(a)*** *Participants cooperate significantly more with the cooperative agent than the control agent;* ***(b)*** *but, this effect is mainly driven by the order where participants play with the control agent first;*

F3.3 *Participants do not cooperate differently with the competitive and control agents.*

3 Models

To develop a model for decision-making in social dilemmas, we follow a data-driven approach based on data collected in the aforementioned empirical studies.

Data and Features. The data consists of examples corresponding to each round each participant played in each study. Data corresponding to last rounds is ignored, since the goal is to predict whether the participant cooperates in the *next* round. In total, there are 12,432 examples. The feature set is the following:

(a) <u>Outcome of the Round</u>: whether the players cooperated or defected;
(b) <u>Emotion Display</u>: the agent's display following the outcome in that round;
(c) <u>First Game</u>: whether the example corresponds to a round in the first game;
(d) <u>Agent is cooperator</u>: 'true' if current agent is a cooperator;
(e) <u>Previous Agent is Cooperator</u>: 'true' if (eventual) previous agent is a cooperator;
(f) <u>Whether Participant Cooperates in the Next Round</u>: this is the target attribute.

Training, Validation and Test Sets. The data is first partitioned into a training (75%) and a test set (25%). The training set is further partitioned into 20 subsets to support 20-fold cross-validation. Every subset (including the test set) are created while making sure they have the same proportion of positive and negative examples in each of the three studies as in the whole dataset.

Models. Models consist of rules defining the probability of cooperation in the next round, given a subset of the features. We explore three different models, described below, that use different subsets of the features. Maximum likelihood estimation is used to fit the models to the data and estimate parameters. The training procedure does 20-fold cross-validation and the final model parameters correspond to the average over all training sets.

Model based on Outcome. The first model predicts likelihood of cooperation based only on outcome of the current round. Outcome is chosen as the first attribute as it ranks best according to the information gain metric (or Kullback–Leibler divergence). Thus, the model predicts probability of cooperation in the next round, given a certain outcome in this round. These probabilities are obtained by calculating the frequency the participant cooperated after each round, for each possible outcome. Table 5 shows the parameters (averaged over all training sets) for this model (under 'Model 1').

Model based on Outcome and Emotion Displays. The next model predicts likelihood of cooperation given outcome *and* the agent's display. This model's parameters are shown in Table 5 (under 'Model 2').

Model based on Outcome, Emotion Displays and Contrasts. Finally, the third model also tries to predict likelihood of cooperation based on outcome and emotion displays but, also takes into account the black-hat/white-hat contrast effects reported in our studies (see 'Background'). All the information required to represent these effects is in attributes (c), (d) and (e), i.e., attributes regarding whether the first and second agents are black-hats (non-cooperators) or white-hat (cooperators). However, these attributes are conceptually different than outcome and emotion displays, because they are *non-observable*. Effectively, they represent *inferences* participants make while playing the games. Nevertheless, notice these inferences *are* made, consciously or not, because otherwise there would have been no contrast effects. Still, for the time being, we do not attempt to model the mechanism by which participants make these inferences and simply assume that attributes (c), (d) and (e) are directly observable (but, see the 'Discussion' section for a way to address this in the future). In summary, the third model calculates, for each combination of the attributes (c), (d) and (e), probabilities given the outcome and agent's displays in the previous round (see Table 5 under 'Model 3'). Notice there is no prediction for the case where both the 1st and 2nd agents are white-hats because this was not explored in our studies.

Table 5. Parameters for the probabilistic models. Values represent probability of cooperation.

Outcome	Emotion	Model 1	Model 2	Model 3 BH *1st Game*	 WH *1st Game*	 BH→WH *2nd Game*	 WH→BH *2nd Game*	 BH→BH *2nd Game*
CC	joy	.67	.72		.64	.76		
	neutral		.62	.53			.71	.51
	sadness		.61	.61			.57	.54
DD	neutral	.22	.24	.22	.27	.30	.21	.26
	sadness		.20	.21	.20	.20	.17	.25
huCagD	joy	.29	.26	.30			.27	.16
	neutral		.26	.26	.15	.40	.19	.23
	sadness		.34		.35	.33		
	shame		.36		.27	.40		
huDagC	anger	.28	.27	.27	.28	.27	.37	.23
	neutral		.24	.22			.34	.19
	sadness		.31	.27	.30	.29	.34	.37

CC - mutual cooperation; *DD* - mutual defection; *huCagD* - human cooperates, agent defects; *huDagC* - human defects, agent cooperates; *BH* - Black-Hat (or non-cooperator); *WH* - White-Hat (or cooperator); *1st Game* refers to probabilities in the 1st game (with a BH or WH); *2nd Game* refers to probabilities in the second game (with a BH or WH) but, when the game was preceded by a specific first game (with another BH or WH)

Model Selection. Model selection is based on minimizing *error rate*, i.e., the percentage of incorrectly classified examples (averaged over all 20 validation sets). Table 6 shows the error rates for each model. The results show that error rates are significantly different ($F(2, 57)=28.207$, $p<.05$) and, *LSD* post-hoc tests reveal that: the error rate for Model 1 is higher than for Model 2 ($p=.100$); and, the error rate for

Model 2 is higher than for Model 3 (p=.000). Table 6 also reports several other standard measures (precision, recall, F1, etc.) and it is clear that Model 3 outperforms Model 2 which, in turn, outperforms Model 1. Table 7 reports the results over the test set. Error rate suggests, once again, that Model 3 is better than Model 2 and, in turn, Model 2 is better than Model 1. The remaining variables in Table 7 also generally support that Model 3 fares best and that Model 1 fares worst. Finally, *average log likelihood* measures the posterior probability of the (whole) dataset given the model, averaged over the number of examples (the closer to 0, the better). The results for the models are: Model 1, *-0.247*; Model 2, *-0.246*; and, Model 3, *-0.245*. Thus, the results suggest that the data was most likely to have been generated from Model 3 than any of the other models.

Table 6. Performance measures over validation sets

	Model 1		Model 2		Model 3			
	Mean	SD	Mean	SD	Mean	SD	F	Sig.
error	.382	.016	.373	.017	.345	.017	28.207	.000*
precision	.408	.024	.422	.025	.466	.025	29.842	.000*
recall	.407	.025	.423	.026	.466	.024	29.571	.000*
F1	.408	.025	.423	.026	.466	.024	29.575	.000*
true positives	61.332	4.935	63.717	5.298	70.134	4.958	16.147	.000*
false positives	88.885	4.434	87.196	4.582	80.339	4.785	19.342	.000*
true negatives	226.566	3.599	228.254	3.760	235.112	3.886	29.136	.000*
false negatives	89.069	4.618	86.684	4.526	80.267	4.583	19.798	.000*

* significant difference, p<.05

Table 7. Performance measures over the test set

model	error	precision	recall	F1	tp	fp	tn	fn
Model 1	.382	.411	.421	.416	422.86	606.99	1498.01	581.14
Model 2	.38	.414	.425	.419	426.72	605.25	1499.75	577.28
Model 3	.378	.417	.424	.421	425.85	595.55	1509.45	578.15

tp - true positives; fp - false positives; tn - true negatives; fn - false negatives

4 Evaluation

The results in the previous section suggest Model 3 was best and Model 1 worst at predicting how humans behave in these dilemma situations. However, in this section we explicitly test this by replicating our empirical studies [15-17] but, substituting humans for our probabilistic models. Aside from verifying the results from the previous section, this experiment allowed us to get insight into the mechanisms that explain *why* some models do better than others. To accomplish this, we ran each model 1000 times (500 times per order) for each experiment in our studies, and measured which findings (F1.1 to F3.3, see "Background") the models replicate. The cooperation rates and standard deviations for the original human data and the models are shown in Table 8. Two columns are shaded in this table, for each model: (1) the left column summarizes whether cooperation rates were significantly different (p<.05) and represent an effect size above a minimum threshold[2], which we set to 1.5 (corresponding to, at least, a small effect size). For instance, a '>' means the model cooperated significantly more with the agent on the left than the agent on the right and the effect size passed the threshold; (2) the right column shows a tick if the model successfully replicated the findings in the human data. Therefore, the more ticks a model has, the better it is at replicating findings. Overall, the percentage of findings each model replicated was: Model 1, *42.9%* (9 out of a maximum of 21 ticks); Model 2, *81.0%* (17 out of 21 ticks); and, Model 3, *95.2%* (20 out of 21 ticks).

5 Discussion

In this paper we propose a data-driven probabilistic model for decision-making in a social dilemma when the other party displays emotion. The evaluation reveals that the model is better at replicating findings about how humans behave in social dilemmas if, instead of considering round outcome alone, it also considers emotion displays. This result is in line with predictions in the behavioral sciences about the impact of non-verbal displays on decision-making [11, 12]. The results also show that considering (black-hat/white-hat) contrast effects further improves the ability to predict human behavior. This is in line with the view that people respond emotionally to *relative* changes in their situations rather than the absolute consequences of their decisions [4]. Theoretically, the model complements the findings in our original studies [14-17] by quantizing (through probabilities) the effect of emotion displays on decision-making in a social dilemma. For instance, Model 2 (see Table 5) suggests that, after the human is exploited by the agent (i.e., when the human cooperates and the agent defects), the human's likelihood of cooperating goes up from 26% to 36% if the agent displays shame as opposed to joy. Finally, pragmatically, the model can be used to drive an agent that is engaged in a social dilemma with another human (or agent) that shows emotion.

There is, naturally, much future work ahead: (1) error rates (Table 6 and 7) are still relatively high and this might reflect that important features that characterize how people decide in social dilemmas are being neglected. For instance, it is assumed that examples are independent and identically-distributed (i.i.d.), but this is not strictly accurate (e.g., people tend to defect towards the end independently of the agent they're playing with); (2) model 3 assumes it is known whether the other party is a black- or white-hat but, in fact, this information should be inferred. One way to address this is to use a Bayesian learning mechanism that increases the likelihood of the opponent being a black-hat according to the displays it shows for each outcome; (3) there are combinations of outcome and displays for which there are no examples in the database. To address this we need to run new experiments where participants face agents with the missing combinations of outcome and display; finally, (4) to further test the generalizability of the model, a new sample should be gathered with human participants and the results compared to the model's predictions.

---

[2] Because it's possible to get significance even for small differences if the sample size is large enough, it is important to require the effect size to be above a minimum threshold.

Table 8. Evaluation of the probabilistic models. Cooperation rates (standard deviations) are shown for the original empirical data (under 'Humans') and when running the models under each of the experimental configurations. The left-most shaded column summarizes the comparison between cooperation rates between the two agents in that configuration. The right-most shaded column is interpreted as follows: ✓ means the model replicates the findings in the human data; × means the model doesn't replicate the human data.

		Humans				**Model 1**				**Model 2**				**Model 3**			
Study 1	*Order*	*Cooperative*	*Individual.*			*Cooperative*	*Individual.*			*Cooperative*	*Individual.*			*Cooperative*	*Individual.*		
Coop	both	.37 (.28)	.27 (.23)	>	*F1.1a*	.33 (.14)	.33 (.14)	≈	×	.36 (.16)	.31 (.13)	>	✓	.35 (.16)	.31 (.14)	>	✓
Vs.	coop→indiv	.35 (.26)	.31 (.26)	≈	*F1.1b*	.32 (.14)	.33 (.14)	≈	✓	.37 (.17)	.30 (.12)	>	×	.31 (.14)	.32 (.15)	≈	✓
Indiv	indiv→coop	.39 (.30)	.23 (.19)	>	*F1.1b*	.33 (.14)	.33 (.14)	≈	×	.35 (.16)	.31 (.13)	>	✓	.39 (.17)	.30 (.12)	>	✓
Study 2		*Cooperative*	*Individual.*			*Cooperative*	*Individual.*			*Cooperative*	*Individual.*			*Cooperative*	*Individual.*		
Coop	both	.39 (.24)	.33 (.24)	>	*F2.1*	.33 (.14)	.33 (.14)	≈	×	.35 (.16)	.30 (.13)	>	✓	.35 (.16)	.30 (.13)	>	✓
Vs.	coop→indiv	.39 (.23)	.33 (.24)	>	*F2.1*	.33 (.14)	.32 (.14)	≈	×	.35 (.15)	.31 (.14)	>	✓	.33 (.14)	.29 (.13)	>	✓
Indiv	indiv→coop	.38 (.26)	.33 (.24)	>	*F2.1*	.33 (.15)	.33 (.13)	≈	×	.35 (.16)	.30 (.13)	>	✓	.38 (.18)	.31 (.13)	>	✓
		Cooperative	*Control*			*Cooperative*	*Control*			*Cooperative*	*Control*			*Cooperative*	*Control*		
Coop	both	.30 (.22)	.26 (.22)	>	*F2.2a*	.33 (.14)	.34 (.14)	≈	×	.36 (.16)	.31 (.12)	>	✓	.35 (.16)	.30 (.13)	>	✓
Vs.	coop→ctrl	.30 (.20)	.31 (.23)	≈	*F2.2b*	.32 (.14)	.33 (.14)	≈	✓	.36 (.15)	.30 (.12)	>	×	.34 (.14)	.33 (.15)	≈	✓
Ctrl	ctrl→coop	.31 (.27)	.13 (.15)	>	*F2.2b*	.34 (.15)	.35 (.15)	≈	×	.37 (.16)	.31 (.12)	>	✓	.37 (.17)	.27 (.11)	>	✓
		Individual.	*Control*			*Individual.*	*Control*			*Individual.*	*Control*			*Individual.*	*Control*		
Indiv	both	.33 (.15)	.30 (.19)	≈	*F2.3*	.33 (.14)	.33 (.14)	≈	✓	.32 (.13)	.31 (.13)	≈	✓	.30 (.12)	.28 (.11)	≈	✓
Vs.	indiv→ctrl	.35 (.15)	.31 (.19)	≈	*F2.3*	.32 (.14)	.34 (.14)	≈	✓	.31 (.13)	.30 (.13)	≈	✓	.30 (.13)	.29 (.11)	≈	✓
Ctrl	ctrl→indiv	.31 (.15)	.29 (.20)	≈	*F2.3*	.33 (.15)	.33 (.14)	≈	✓	.32 (.13)	.32 (.14)	≈	✓	.31 (.11)	.28 (.11)	>	×
Study 3		*Cooperative*	*Competitive*			*Cooperative*	*Competitive*			*Cooperative*	*Competitive*			*Cooperative*	*Competitive*		
Coop	both	.41 (.23)	.39 (.21)	≈	*F3.1a*	.34 (.15)	.34 (.15)	≈	✓	.36 (.15)	.33 (.13)	>	✓	.39 (.16)	.35 (.15)	>	✓
Vs.	coop→comp	.37 (.18)	.49 (.19)	<	*F3.1b*	.35 (.15)	.33 (.14)	≈	×	.36 (.15)	.32 (.14)	>	×	.33 (.13)	.38 (.16)	<	✓
Ctrl	comp→coop	.44 (.25)	.32 (.20)	>	*F3.1c*	.34 (.14)	.34 (.15)	≈	×	.37 (.16)	.33 (.13)	>	✓	.46 (.17)	.31 (.12)	>	✓
		Cooperative	*Control*			*Cooperative*	*Control*			*Cooperative*	*Control*			*Cooperative*	*Control*		
Coop	both	.34 (.17)	.24 (.14)	>	*F3.2a*	.34 (.14)	.34 (.15)	≈	×	.36 (.14)	.31 (.13)	>	✓	.38 (.16)	.31 (.14)	>	✓
Vs.	coop→ctrl	.24 (.09)	.21 (.12)	≈	*F3.2b*	.34 (.14)	.34 (.14)	≈	✓	.35 (.14)	.32 (.13)	>	×	.32 (.12)	.34 (.16)	≈	✓
Ctrl	ctrl→coop	.39 (.19)	.26 (.15)	>	*F3.2b*	.33 (.14)	.33 (.15)	≈	×	.36 (.14)	.31 (.13)	>	✓	.44 (.17)	.29 (.12)	>	✓
		Competitive	*Control*			*Competitive*	*Control*			*Competitive*	*Control*			*Competitive*	*Control*		
Comp	both	.23 (.11)	.23 (.17)	≈	*F3.3*	.35 (.15)	.34 (.14)	≈	✓	.33 (.13)	.31 (.13)	≈	✓	.29 (.11)	.29 (.11)	≈	✓
Vs.	comp→ctrl	.22 (.10)	.25 (.18)	≈	*F3.3*	.35 (.15)	.35 (.14)	≈	✓	.33 (.12)	.31 (.12)	≈	✓	.30 (.11)	.29 (.10)	≈	✓
Ctrl	ctrl→comp	.25 (.13)	.20 (.16)	≈	*F3.3*	.35 (.14)	.34 (.14)	≈	✓	.32 (.13)	.32 (.13)	≈	✓	.27 (.10)	.29 (.11)	≈	✓

References

1. Jennings, N.R., Sycara, K., Wooldridge, M.: A Roadmap of Agent Research and Development. Autonomous Agents and Multi-Agent Systems 1, 275–306 (1998)
2. Kraus, S.: Negotiation and Cooperation in Multi-Agent Environments. Artificial Intelligence 94(1-2), 79–98 (1997)
3. Tversky, A., Kahneman, D.: The framing of decisions and the psychology of choice. Science 211, 453–458 (1981)
4. Loewenstein, G., Lerner, J.: The role of affect in decision making. In: Davidson, R.J., Scherer, K.R., Goldsmith, H.H. (eds.) Handbook of Affective Sciences, pp. 619–642. Oxford University Press, Oxford (2003)
5. Kollock, P.: Social Dilemmas: The Anatomy of Cooperation. Annual Review of Sociology 24, 183–214 (1998)
6. McClintock, C.G., Liebrand, W.B.G.: Role of interdependence structure, individual value orientation, and another's strategy in social decision making: a transformational analysis. J. Pers. Soc. Psychol. 55(3), 396–409 (1988)
7. Kramer, R.M., Brewer, M.B.: Social group identity and the emergence of cooperation in resource conservation dilemmas. In: Wilke, H.A.M., Messick, D.M., Rutte, C. (eds.) Experimental Social Dilemmas, pp. 205–234. Verlag Peter Lang, Frankfurt (1986)
8. Axelrod, R.: The Evolution of Cooperation. Basic Books, New York (1984)
9. Yamagishi, T.: The provision of a sanctioning system as a public good. J. Pers. Soc. Psychol. 51, 110–116 (1986)
10. Jerdee, T.H., Rosen, B.: Effects of opportunity to communicate and visibility of individual decisions on behavior in the common interest. J. Appl. Soc. Psychol. 59, 712–716 (1974)
11. Boone, R., Buck, R.: Emotional expressivity and trustworthiness: The role of nonverbal behavior in the evolution of cooperation. J. of Nonverbal Behav. 27, 163–182 (2003)
12. Frank, R.H.: Passions within reason: The strategic role of the emotions. Norton, NY (1988)
13. Schug, J., Matsumoto, D., Horita, Y., Yamagishi, T., Bonnet, K.: Emotional expressivity as a signal of cooperation. Evolution and Human Behavior 31, 87–94 (2010)
14. de Melo, C., Zheng, L., Gratch, J.: Expression of Moral Emotions in Cooperating Agents. In: Ruttkay, Z., Kipp, M., Nijholt, A., Vilhjálmsson, H.H. (eds.) IVA 2009. LNCS, vol. 5773, pp. 301–307. Springer, Heidelberg (2009)
15. de Melo, C., Carnevale, P., Gratch, J.: The influence of Emotions in Embodied Agents on Human Decision-Making. In: Allbeck, J., et al. (eds.) IVA 2010. LNCS, vol. 6356, pp. 357–370. Springer, Heidelberg (2010)
16. de Melo, C., Carnevale, P., Gratch, J.: The Impact of Emotion Displays in Embodied Agents on Emergence of Cooperation with People. Submitted to J. Presence (submitted)
17. de Melo, C., Carnevale, P., Gratch, J.: Reverse Appraisal: Inferring from Emotion Displays who is the Cooperator and the Competitor in a Social Dilemma. In: Proc. of 33rd Annual Meeting of the Cognitive Science Society, pp. 396–401 (2011)
18. Gratch, J., Rickel, J., Andre, E., Badler, N., Cassell, J., Petajan, E.: Creating Interactive Virtual Humans: Some Assembly Required. IEEE Intelligent Systems 17(4), 54–63 (2002)
19. Reeves, B., Nass, C.: The Media Equation: How People Treat Computers, Television, and New Media Like Real People and Places. University of Chicago Press, Chicago (1996)
20. Blascovich, J.: Social influence within immersive virtual environments. In: Schroeder, R. (ed.) The Social Life of Avatars: Presence and Interaction in Shared Virtual Environments, pp. 127–145. Springer, London (2002)
21. Blascovich, J., Loomis, J., Beall, A.C., Swinth, K.R., Hoyt, C.L., Bailenson, J.N.: Immersive virtual environment technology as a methodological tool for social psychology. Psychological Inquiry 13, 103–124 (2002)
22. Hilty, J., Carnevale, P.: Black-Hat/White-Hat Strategy in Bilateral Negotiation. Organizational Behavior and Human Decision Processes 55, 444–469 (1993)

Agents with Emotional Intelligence for Storytelling

João Dias and Ana Paiva

INESC-ID and Instituto Superior Técnico, Technical University of Lisbon,
Tagus Park, Av. Prof. Cavaco Silva, 2780-990 Porto Salvo, Portugal
joao.dias@gaips.inesc-id.pt, ana.paiva@inesc-id.pt

Abstract. One core aspect of engaging narratives is the existence and development of social relations between the characters. However, creating agents for interactive storytelling and making them to be perceived as a close friend or a hated enemy by an user is an hard task. This paper addresses the problem of creating autonomous agents capable of establishing social relations with others in an interactive narrative. We present an innovative approach by looking at emotional intelligence and in particular to the skills of understanding and regulating emotions in others. To that end we propose a model for an agent architecture that has an explicit model of Social Relations and a Theory of Mind about others, and is able to plan about emotions of others and perform interpersonal emotion regulation in order to dynamically create relations with others. Some sample scenario are presented in order to illustrate the type of behaviour achieved by the model and the creation of social relations.

1 Introduction

People usually find emotional stories remarkably interesting [6], and this has been explored in narrative since its earliest days. Aristotle identified emotions as a core feature of classic tragedy: "A perfect tragedy should (...) imitate actions which excite pity and fear, this being the distinctive mark of tragic imitation" [2]. He also defined that the most relevant constituents in the tragedy or drama are the plot and the characters.

Thus, aiming at creating interactive storytelling systems, researchers in the autonomous agents community started by trying to create autonomous synthetic characters [18]. Their first problem was to make virtual non-real characters evoke emotions in viewers like human actors do in a dramatization, and appear to be alive in eyes of the viewers. Bates named this concept as believability[4]. However, with the goal of building increasingly engaging storytelling systems, one also needs to address the plot of the narrative. One core aspect of dramatic plots, which is capable of eliciting even stronger emotions is the existence and development of social relations between the characters. Ryan [20] states that dramatic narratives focus on evolving networks of human relations, and most of the actions in their plot correspond to either verbal communication or to physical actions that affect interpersonal relations.

S. D'Mello et al. (Eds.): ACII 2011, Part I, LNCS 6974, pp. 77–86, 2011.

Establishing social relations is thus critical if we want the user to interact with an agent in an interactive narrative, or role-playing game, where the relation between the two takes a preponderant role in the plot. Although one can build agents that are considered believable, making them to be perceived as a close friend or a hated enemy by an user, is certainly a more complex task. In order to do so, we need to explore mechanisms that mimic the way that relations between real people evolve. With this in mind, this paper addresses the following question:

> *How to create autonomous agents capable of dynamically creating social relations with others in an interactive narrative?*

The problem of creating social relations in autonomous agents has already been addressed in many different ways. Works such as of Prada [16] and Psychsim[17] are important landmarks. However, in here we present an innovative approach that draws inspiration from one particular type of social intelligence: emotional intelligence.

1.1 Emotional Intelligence

According to Salovey and Mayer [21], "Emotional intelligence refers to an ability to recognize the meanings of emotion and their relationships, and to reason and problem-solve on the basis of them". In other words, it corresponds to the understanding of the impact that emotions have on the self and on others, how emotions are created, and also being able to use this knowledge to regulate emotions on the self and in others. Continuing their research in Emotional Intelligence, Mayer and Salovey [9] put forward a four branch model that divides Emotional Intelligence in four main skills:

- **perceiving emotions in oneself and others -** has to do with the perception and expression of emotion through gestures, facial expressions, or other communication mechanisms.
- **using emotions to facilitate thought -** the second skill, focuses on using emotions to guide cognitive processes, such as learning and adaptation, attention and decision making.
- **understanding emotions -** the idea here is that emotions convey information. For instance, Anger indicates a possible intention of harming other. Therefore, understanding emotions involves understanding the meaning of emotions, together with the capacity to reason about those meanings.
- **managing emotions -** once a person understand emotions, it can manage one's own and other's emotions in order to promote social goals. For instance, one can go to see a movie when distressed in order to feel better, or do something pleasant to help a friend to overcome some bad mood.

Given the relevance of the fourth skill, there is an entire area of research in psychology that deals with the concept of managing emotions. Some psychologists refer it as Emotion Regulation, and we will use this same term throughout this document. The construct of Emotion Regulation first appeared in the developmental psychology literature [22], and then in the adult literature. According to Gross [7], "Emotion Regulation refers to the heterogeneous set of processes by which emotions themselves are regulated". These processes may dampen, intensify, maintain the intensity or even change the type of both positive and negative emotions. They may be automatic/unconscious or controlled/conscious. These processes may be intrinsic, when they involve regulating emotions in self (also called self-regulation), or extrinsic when they involve regulating emotions in others (also called interpersonal emotion regulation).

But how is emotional intelligence related to the development of social relations? Several studies [13,12] have shown that people who have higher emotional intelligence have more positive social interactions with peers. An additional study with german students also indicated that students with better scores in managing emotions in others were more liked and valued by the opposite sex[13]. Thus, it seems that the high emotionally intelligent individual is rather successful at establishing social relations with others.

Therefore, if we are able to understand how regulating emotions in others affects relations, and if we are able to model this capability we can hope to have better results at dynamically establishing relations with others.

2 Related Work

The problem of creating social relations in autonomous agents has already been addressed in many different ways. For instance Psychsim [17] is an environment for multi-agent simulation that employs a formal decision-theoretic approach using recursive models. This allows the agents to reason about the behavior and beliefs of other agents and to use communication to influence other agents beliefs about agents. Psychsim was used to model social-simulation scenarios that represent concepts such as social power, support, consistency and affinity. However, consistency and affinity are mainly used to help decide if the agent trusts the messages other agents send him and Psychsim does not model emotions and its influence on social relations.

Avatar arena[19] presents an agent model that can dynamically change social relationships between agents. The model is based on theories of cognitive consistency, such as Heider's Balance Theory [8], and is used for multi-party negotiation dialogues. Following Balance Theory, when an agent discovers a mismatch between his opinion about a concept and another agent's opinion about the same concept (e.g. he likes to talk about soccer and someone else does not), this causes the experience of a dissonance and triggers a change in the social distance to the other agent so that a balance is achieved again. Existing social relations, affective state and personality are then used to generate the dialog and negotiation between the agents. Nonetheless, the focus in Avatar arena is in the use of relations to directly influence the behaviour of the agents and it does not model behaviour that aims at explicitly changing those relations.

The SGD Model proposed by Prada [16] focus on modeling group dynamics between social agents. Amongst other things, it models relations of social power and of social attraction which are used to help build the dynamic of the group and resulting group behaviour. SGD divides agent interactions in two main categories: instrumental and socio-emotional. Instrumental interactions are task related (e.g. solving a cooperative problem) while socio-emotional are used to change the existing relations within a group. Similarly to Avatar arena, SGD model uses Heiders balance theory to determine that when an agent observes a positive socio-emotional interaction towards him, then his attraction for the performer of the interaction will increase.

Emotion regulation only got the attention of the autonomous agents research community very recently. For that reason, computational models of reasoning about emotions, and emotion regulation are at the moment (to our knowledge) just a few. One of them is Adam's Work. Adam [1] presents a very complete formalization of a cognitive logical model of emotions, which allows us to reason about, plan for and even explain an agent's emotions. Quite relevant to our work, is Adam's proposal for a formalization of coping behaviour, which can be used to regulate emotions in others. However, there is no explicit model for social relations (social behaviour is implicit in the rules defined), and the model does not consider strategies to worsen affect.

Boss and Lange [5] aim at developing IVAs with a Theory of Emotion Regulation (ToER), i.e, a Theory of Mind that models emotional states of others, and which allows them to reason about other's emotion regulation processes. Although the ToER model uses explicit interpersonal emotion regulation strategies,it was not designed with the goal of exploring the effect of emotion regulation in social relations. Thus, it also does not model social relations and explicit social goals. The ToER model shows us that in order to regulate emotions in others, we must build a theory of mind of others, which includes their emotional state.

3 Conceptual Model

In order to explain the proposed model we need to briefly overview the FAtiMA-PSI architecture as it was implemented on top of it[10]. This architecture was chosen because it provides a set of features necessary to address our research problem, such as the capability of generating and modeling emotions.

FAtiMA-PSI

FAtiMA-PSI follows OCC Theory of emotions [15] where emotions are seen as valenced (good or bad) reactions to events. Whenever an external event or action is perceived, both the knowledge base and autobiographic memory are updated. At the same time, the agent's motivational state is updated. For instance, if the agent finished an eating action, its need for energy will go down. FAtiMA-PSI models five drives: Energy, Integrity, Affiliation, Competence and Certainty. Whenever the motivational state is updated, the change on the drives is used to determine the desirability of an event. The determined desirability is used together with other appraisal variables to generate a wide range of emotions from Joy and Distress to Pity and Anger. The generated emotions are also stored in memory and associated to the events that triggered them.

After the appraisal phase, both reactive and deliberative components perform practical reasoning. The reactive layer uses simple and fast action rules that trigger action tendencies. Action tendencies define a character's reactions to particular emotional states (e.g. crying when very distressed). In addition, when the event is appraised, the deliberative level checks if any goal has become active, and determines the goal's utility based on its current drives. The utility of a goal depends on the impact of the goal on the drives and also on the current level of the drive [1]. The agent then tries to build a plan to achieve the most relevant goal. This is done using a continuous planner [3] that can be extended to incorporate planning about emotions.

Architecture for Emotionally Intelligent Agents

The aim of the model is to dynamically create believable social relations by endowing the agents with the capability of reasoning about and regulating emotions in others. Figure 1 shows the extensions to FAtiMA-PSI in order to do this. First of all, we need an explicit model of social relations, which is implemented by the social relations component. Furthermore, the appraisal process was divided into two separate processes, according to [14]. The first one, appraisal derivation, is responsible for evaluating the relevance of the event according to the agent's needs and determine a set of appraisal variables (e.g. desirability, desirability for others). The second process, affect derivation, takes the appraisal variables as input and generates the resulting emotions according to OCC Theory of emotions. This division facilitates the process of reasoning about emotions.

Having the capability of performing interpersonal emotion regulation requires us to model not only internal processes of the agent but also the processes of others. Similarly to Boss's and Psychsim's approach, the agent will need to create a model of other's emotional state, social relations, appraisal rules and action tendencies. These will constitute the Theory of Mind (ToM) component. Finally, the planner will then represent and reason about the emotional processes in order to achieve a set of high-level social goals, thus generating the agent's social behaviour.

Social Relations Component

The dynamics of social relations (which defines how social relations change with time) follows Heider's Balance theory [8]. Balance Theory hypothesis is that people avoid unstable cognitive configurations and that they mobilize their efforts to resolve it and change it to a stable state. For instance, if someone likes something you dislike, you tend to either start liking that thing or liking less the person. This principle is applied to the perception of events, similarly to SGD model. Suppose that the user (or another agent) has performed an action undesirable for the agent, such as insulting him. If the event was performed by

[1] To know more about how the goal utility is determined and how the drives are updated, please refer to [11].

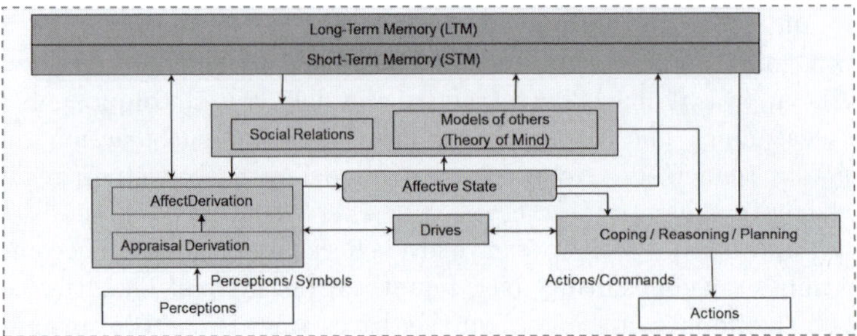

Fig. 1. Proposed Model for Agents with Interpersonal Emotion Regulation Skills

the user, then we assume that the user intended to perform that event and as such, the event is desirable to the user[2]. This corresponds to an unstable state.

However, differently from SGD model, events are not pre-classified as positive or negative. Instead, we use the result of the appraisal to determine whether a perceived event is positive or negative. Thus, whenever a new emotion caused by another agent is added to the emotional state, the social update component will analyze the valence and intensity of the emotion and update the corresponding relation proportionally in order to converge to a more stable state. Thus, positive emotions increase the interpersonal relation, while negative emotions decrease it. Stronger emotions cause bigger changes in the relationship.

Theory of Mind Component

The ToM component is responsible for storing and updating the knowledge that the agent has about other agents. It creates one ToM model for each existing agent that he perceives. So, if there are two other agents A and B, the ToM component creates a ToM Model for A that will store the knowledge that the agent has about A and another independent ToM Model for B. The ToM includes information about others' beliefs, memories, needs, emotions and social relations. When an event is perceived, the ToM component determines if others have perceived the same event (for instance, looking at which agents are near it). If so, it uses the event to simulate how others perceive, remember and appraise the event. Then, the result of each simulated processes is used to update the all the internal structures of the corresponding agent model (e.g. affective state, and social relations).

Reasoning and Planning about Emotions

In the proposed model, the planner was extended in order to be able to build plans of actions that aim at establishing emotions in others (or in self). With that aim, two special Meta-Operators were created to represent the processes of appraisal derivation and affect derivation (shown in Figure 2). Unlike normal operators, these operators have some semantics attached and may generate several instantiated operators.

[2] This is a simplification, since the user may have done the action unintentionally or may have been coerced to do so.

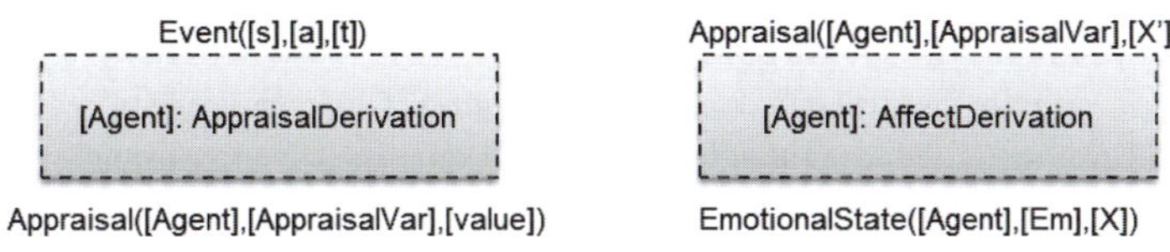

Fig. 2. Mapping Emotional Processes into special STRIPS Operators

Whenever a Meta-Operator is instantiated in order to achieve a precondition, it will use an internal function to generate the corresponding values for its own preconditions depending on its effects. For instance, if the goal is to make agent B Joyfull with intensity 3, the Meta-Operator AffectDerivation will be instantiated with $[Agent]/B$, $[Em]/Joy$, $[X]/3$ and it will apply the inverse function of the affect derivation function used in FAtiMA-PSI, in order to determine the set and values of appraisal variables that could make agent B experience a Joy emotion with at least intensity 3. In this example, the operator generated would have the precondition Appraisal(B,Desirability,3). This process of instantiation may possibly generate more than one operator. Following the previous example, when applied to the plan, the Meta-Operator AppraisalDerivation will try to find actions that are considered desirable with at least value 3 by agent B. This is done by simulating the effect that all possible actions can have in agent B drive's and determining the corresponding desirability. If more than one action satisfies this condition, several instantiations of the AppraisalDerivation operator will be generated (and added to different alternative plans), representing the alternative ways of achieving the desired appraisal variable.

Social Goals
The previously described components are used to define a set of high-level social goals which are responsible for the agent's social behaviour.

- **IncreaseRelation** - The IncreaseRelation goal becomes available for an agent A when he thinks that another agent B likes him less than he likes B. Following Balance Theory, the rationale is that agent A will try to make the relationship more consistent by increasing B's relation towards him. For this reason, the goal's success condition is for A to cause a positive emotion in B.
- **DecreaseRelation** - Becomes active when an agent A does not like another agent B, but thinks that B does like him. Similarly to the increase relation goal, this goal tries to create more consistent relations but this time by lowering B's relation toward A. To that end, the agent will try to cause a negative emotion in B.
- **RegulateNegativeEmotion** - The RegulateNegativeEmotion goal is activated when the agent thinks or perceives that another agent, which he likes, feels a negative emotion. The success condition of the goal is to make the target agent feel a positive emotion.

Once the goals become active, it does not necessarily mean that they will be selected and executed. Social goals are closely connected with the agent's need for affiliation (meaning that the stronger the need, the stronger the goals' importance). And a goal will only be selected for execution if it surpasses a predefined relevance. As such, the agent will perform social interactions more frequently and share emotions if its need for affiliation is high.

4 Scenarios

Two simple scenarios were created in order to show the development of social relations and illustrate the type of social behaviour that can be achieved by the model. In the scenario, the agents have a set of basic actions and goals, such as easting and resting, that can be executed to achieve the agents' needs: energy, integrity and affiliation. Additionally, the social goals defined above were added to the agents and a set of actions that influence other's needs were defined. Kicking others lowers their integrity, insulting or gloating has a negative impact on the target's affiliation and stealing food provides a way of influencing other's energy. As for positive actions, complimenting or hugging others increases their affiliation, healing improves integrity and giving food has an impact on energy.

Three agents were created with distinct initial social relations. Agent Luke likes John but dislikes Paul; John likes the other two agents; Paul dislikes Luke but is neutral to John. All of them are neutral to the user. Figure 3(a) shows an extract of the text-based result of the simulation, with the actions performed by the agents. One can see the different types of interaction according to the existing relations. Agent Luke does nice actions towards John (giving food) and bad actions towards Paul (insulting and taking food away).

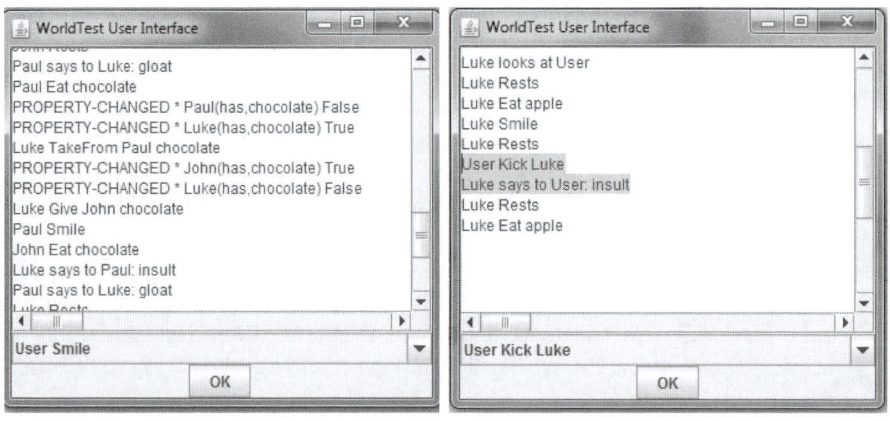

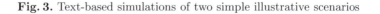

(a) Social interactions between agents (b) Luke interacts with the user

Fig. 3. Text-based simulations of two simple illustrative scenarios

It is important to point out the evolving dynamics of the behaviour presented. When performing interpersonal emotion regulation, the agent will use its model of appraisal to dynamically determine what are the actions that would elicit the desired emotion according to the target's current needs. Furthermore, the user's interaction can make the relation with the agent's evolve, thus changing their behaviour towards the user. As highlighted in Fig. 3(b), when the user kicks Luke, it will change its relation from neutral to negative, making the agent perform socially negative actions towards the user.

5 Summary and Future Work

This paper addresses the problem of endowing autonomous agents with the capability of dynamically creating social relations with others. To that end, we explore emotional intelligence skills and in particular the capability of regulating emotions in others. The agent architecture proposed has an explicit model of the existing socio-affective relations between agents and how they evolve according to experienced emotions, which follows Heider's balance theory. In order to perform interpersonal emotion regulation, the deliberative component models a set of meta-operators that represent the emotional processes. Using such operators, the planner is able to build a plan of actions to achieve a desired emotional state in others. A set of high-level social goals, which depend on existing affective relations, are then used to generate explicit social behaviour such as wanting to increase an agent's relation toward another.

We presented two small scenario that aim at illustrating the type of behaviour obtained with the very general social goals. We believe that the proposed model offers an flexible and general mechanism that can be used to try to establish social relations with others. We plan to create a more elaborate scenario where the user gets to play with several agents (with distinct relations) to complete a given quest. We will then assess if the proposed model can make the existing social relations more easily perceived by the user, and if the agents are able to establish stronger relations with the user.

Acknowledgements. This work was partially supported by European Community (EC) and by a scholarship (SFRH BD/19481/2004) granted by the Fundação para a Ciência e a Tecnologia (FCT). It is currently funded by the EU FP7 ICT-215554 project LIREC (LIving with Robots and IntEractive Companions). The authors are solely responsible for the content of this publication. It does not represent the opinion of the EC or the FCT, which are not responsible for any use that might be made of data appearing therein.

References

1. Adam, C.: Emotions: from psychological theories to logical formalization and implementation in a BDI agent. Phd thesis, Institut National Polytechnique de Toulouse (2007)
2. Aristotle: Poetics. Penguin, London (1996)

3. Aylett, R., Dias, J., Paiva, A.: An affectively driven planner for synthetic characters. In: Proceedings of International Conference on Automated Planning and Scheduling, ICAPS 2006, UK (2006)
4. Bates, J.: The role of emotion in believable agents. Communications of the ACM 37(7), 122–125 (1994)
5. Bosse, T., Lange, F.: Development of virtual agents with a theory of emotion regulation. In: Proceedings of the Eight IEEE/WIC/ACM International Conference on Intelligent Agent Technology, IAT 2008, pp. 461–468. IEEE Computer Society Press, Los Alamitos (2008)
6. Christophe, V., Rimé, B.: Exposure to the social sharing of emotion: Emotional impact, listeners responses and the secondary social sharing. European Journal of Social Psychology (27), 37–54 (1997)
7. Gross, J.: Emotion Regulation: conceptual foundations. In: Handbook of Emotion Regulation, pp. 3–24. The Guilford Press, NY (2007)
8. Heider, F.: The Psychology of Interpersonal Relations. Wiley, NY (1954)
9. Mayer, J., Caruso, D., Salovey, P.: Emotional intelligence meets traditional standards for an intelligence. Intelligence 27(4), 267–298 (1999)
10. Lim, M.Y., Dias, J., Aylett, R., Paiva, A.: Improving adaptiveness in autonomous characters. In: Prendinger, H., Lester, J.C., Ishizuka, M. (eds.) IVA 2008. LNCS (LNAI), vol. 5208, pp. 348–355. Springer, Heidelberg (2008)
11. Lim, M.Y., Dias, J., Aylett, R., Paiva, A.: Intelligent npcs for educational role play game. In: Workshop on Agents for Games and Simulation, in Autonomous Agents and Multi-Agent Systems, Budapest (2009)
12. Lopes, P., Salovey, P., Beers, M., Cote, S.: Emotion regulation abilities and the quality of social interaction. Emotion 5(1), 113–118 (2005)
13. Lopes, P.N., Salovey, P., Straus, R.: Emotional intelligence, personality and the perceived quality of social relationships. Personality and Individual Differences (35), 641–658 (2003)
14. Marsella, S., Gratch, J., Petta, P.: Computational Models of Emotion. In: A blueprint for an affectively competent agent: Cross-fertilization between Emotion Psychology, Affective Neuroscience, and Affective Computing. Oxford University Press, Oxford (2010)
15. Ortony, A., Clore, G., Collins, A.: The Cognitive Structure of Emotions. Cambridge University Press, Cambridge (1998)
16. Prada, R., Paiva, A.: Teaming up human with synthetic characters. Artificial Intelligence 173(1), 257–267 (2009)
17. Pynadath, D.: Psychsim: Agent-based modeling of social interactions and influence. In: ICCM, pp. 243–248 (2004)
18. Reilly, S., Bates, J.: Building emotional agents, cmu-cs-92-143. Technical report, School of Computer Science, Carnegie Mellon University (1992)
19. Rist, T., Schmitt, M.: Avatar arena: An attempt to apply socio-physiological concepts of cognitive consistency in avatar-avatar negotiation scenarios. In: Proc. of AISB 2002 Symposium on Animated Expressive Characters for Social Interactions, pp. 79–84 (2002)
20. Ryan, M.: Interactive narrative, plot types, and interpersonal relations, pp. 6–13 (2008)
21. Salovey, P., Mayer, J.: Emotional Intelligence. In: Imagination, Cognition and Personality, pp. 185–211 (1990)
22. Thompson, R.: Emotional regulation and emotional development. Educational Psychology Review (3), 269–307 (1991)

“That’s Aggravating, Very Aggravating”: Is It Possible to Classify Behaviors in Couple Interactions Using Automatically Derived Lexical Features?

Panayiotis G. Georgiou[1], Matthew P. Black[1], Adam C. Lammert[1], Brian R. Baucom[2], and Shrikanth S. Narayanan[1,2]

[1] Signal Analysis and Interpretation Laboratory (SAIL), Los Angeles, CA, USA
[2] Department of Psychology, Univ. of Southern California, Los Angeles, CA, USA
http://sail.usc.edu

Abstract. Psychology is often grounded in observational studies of human interaction behavior, and hence on human perception and judgment. There are many practical and theoretical challenges in observational practice. Technology holds the promise of mitigating some of these difficulties by assisting in the evaluation of higher level human behavior. In this work we attempt to address two questions: (1) Does the lexical channel contain the necessary information towards such an evaluation; and if yes (2) Can such information be captured by a noisy automated transcription process. We utilize a large corpus of couple interaction data, collected in the context of a longitudinal study of couple therapy. In the original study, each spouse was manually evaluated with several session-level behavioral codes (e.g., level of acceptance toward other spouse). Our results will show that both of our research questions can be answered positively and encourage future research into such assistive observational technologies.

Keywords: psychology, human behavior, observational studies, lexical features, categorization, couple therapy, behavioral signal processing, behavioral informatics, BSP.

1 Introduction

Human perceptual judgments form the basis for many kinds of psychological evaluations. Social therapies rely on a methodology involving careful observation and assessment of social, affective, and communicative behavior. While some of these judgments can be made in real-time during the interaction, oftentimes the interaction is recorded for offline hand coding of relevant observational events, especially for training purposes and research. In family studies research and practice, psychologists rely on a variety of established coding standards [8]. There are many examples of standardized coding schemes [4], all with the aim of producing accurate, consistent ratings of human behavior by human annotators.

S. D'Mello et al. (Eds.): ACII 2011, Part I, LNCS 6974, pp. 87–96, 2011.

This manual coding is a costly and time consuming process. First, a detailed coding manual must be created, which often requires several design iterations. Then, multiple coders, each of whom has his/her own biases and limitations, must be trained in a consistent manner. The process is mentally straining and the resulting human agreement is often quite low [8].

Given all of the practical challenges, there is clearly a strong motivation for finding technological solutions to manual coding. The ability to automatically estimate perceptual judgments and to predict the relevant behavioral codes could provide huge savings. This is one goal of human behavioral signal processing, which uses technology to extract human-centered information, including affect and emotions [6, 10].

In terms of designing a system for automatic coding, there are many possible signals to consider. These include video (e.g., gesture, body language), audio (e.g., acoustic properties of speech and other vocal cues), and transcripts (e.g., lexical features). Our working corpus – described below – offers us with access to all of these signals. It was collected in the context of a longitudinal study of couple therapy, where husband-wife pairs participated in spontaneous discussions about pertinent marital issues. The interaction sessions had been rated with a variety of high-level behavioral codes, including blame, acceptance, global negative and positive affect, as well as humor and sadness.

Recently published work from our group utilized audio features from this corpus to predict these high-level behavioral codes [1, 7]. In this paper, we investigate lexical features. We expect that lexical features contain rich information about these codes, and more broadly about the overall interactions. Towards establishing that we will pursue two goals:

1. to demonstrate that the specific behavioral codes sought by psychologists in couple interactions are expressed strongly through the lexical channel, and hence, lexical classification will be useful in this domain.
2. to show that despite the highly reverberant, noisy, spontaneous, emotional, and disfluent nature of the interactions, the automated lexical classification process from the audio signals can retain sufficient information towards extracting the behavioral codes.

Transcripts have proved useful in analyzing human social interactions [9]. Indeed, when coding manuals are used to help standardize a rating procedure, they are often very specific about the kind of phrasing and word choices, which are indicative of a particular behavioral code. The manuals used for generating our current corpus (see Section 2) are good examples. For instance, [3] states that "explicit blaming statements," such as "you made me do it," should warrant high ratings for the blame code. However it is unclear how context dependent is human interpretation of these transcripts, and hence how useful are shorter lexical units, so our first research goal will explore this question.

Obviously, automatic transcription is desirable since manually producing transcripts is laborious, albeit a very small fraction of the coding effort. Since the ultimate goal is not to produce a faithful reference transcript but to estimate behavioral codes, canonical automatic speech recognition (ASR) performance (e.g. word error rate) is not a suitable evaluation metric. We propose to proceed with our second research goal through probabilistic representations of ASR hypotheses but without a single reference transcript.

In Section 2 of this paper, we describe the couples' interaction corpus. Section 3 presents our methodology and results. In Section 4, we present discussion and future directions.

2 The Corpus

The corpus consists of audio and video, recorded during sessions of real couples interacting. The recordings were made in conjunction with a longitudinal study at the University of California, Los Angeles and at the University of Washington [2]. For the study, over 130 husband-wife pairs were recruited to receive couple therapy for a period of one year. Each couple was recorded three separate times: before therapy began, 26 weeks into therapy and two years after therapy had finished. During each session, the couples discussed a problem in their relationship. The couple spent ten minutes on a topic of the wife's choosing, as well as ten minutes on a topic chosen by the husband. These interactions took place with the therapist out of the room. The couples were married an average of 10.0 years (SD = 7.7), with the age of participants ranging from 22 to 72 years old. The median age for men was 43 years (SD = 8.8), and 42 years (SD = 8.7) for women. Participants were college-educated, on average, with a median of 17 years of education (SD = 8.7). The sample was 77% Caucasian, 8% African American, 5% Asian or Pacific Islander, 5% Latino/Latina, 1% Native American, and 4% Other [2].

Transcriptions were made of the audio recordings for each interaction that constituted the data used for this study. The speaker for each turn (husband or wife) was explicitly labeled. Efforts were made to keep the transcriptions as faithful to the audio as possible. An example fragment from one transcript can be seen in Table 1. It should be noted that nonverbal communication (e.g., laughing, throat clearing) was transcribed. However, names and proper nouns were de-identified for the sake of privacy. Unintelligible regions were also marked by the transcribers. Only 0.98 percent of the words were de-identified or marked unintelligible. In portions with overlapping speech, transcribers attempted to separate out words from each speaker. These portions were not explicitly marked.

For each session, both spouses were evaluated according to 33 codes, designed to rate an individual's interaction. The Social Support Interaction Rating System (SSIRS) measures both the emotional component of the interaction, as well as the topic of conversation. Its 20 codes are broken into four categories: affectivity, dominance/submission, features of the interaction, and topic definition [4]. The 13 codes in the Couples Interaction Rating System 2 (CIRS2) were specifically designed to capture perception relevant for conversations involving a problem in the relationship [3]. Three to four evaluators made their judgments after watching the video recording. All evaluators underwent training, in an effort to standardize the coding process. Ratings were expressed on an integer scale

Table 1. An example fragment from one transcript. In this particular interaction, the wife received a low rating for acceptance and a high rating for blame and negativity, and the husband received a low rating for humor and a high rating for positivity and sadness.

Partner	Transcript
H	WHAT DID I TELL YOU YOU CAN DO THAT AH AND EVERYTHING
W	BUT WHY DID YOU ASK THEN WHY DID TO ASK
H	AND DO IT MORE AND GET US INTO TROUBLE
W	YEAH WHY DID YOU ASK SEE MY QUESTION IS
H	MM HMMM
W	IF IF YOU TOLD ME THIS AND I AGREE I WOULD KEEP TRACK OF IT AND EVERYTHING
H	THAT'S THAT'S
W	**THAT'S AGGRAVATING VERY AGGRAVATING**
H	A BAD HABIT THAT
W	VERY AGGRAVATING
H	CAUSES YOU TO THINK THAT I DON'T TRUST YOU
W	THAT'S EXACTLY WHY THAT'S ABSOLUTELY THE WAY IT IS
H	AND IF I DON'T THE REASON FOR THAT IS AH
W	I DON'T CARE THE REASON YOU GET IT I GET IT TOO
H	THE REASON IS THE LONG TERM BAD PERFORMANCE
W	YEAH AND YOU KNOW WHY
H	MM HMMM
W	ALL YOU GET IS A NEGATIVE REACTION FROM ME

from 1 to 9. Here, we analyze a subset of codes which represent contrasting pairs with high inter-evaluator agreement. Codes which contrast conceptually do not necessarily contrast in rating, however. In particular, it is possible for an individual to receive similar scores on contrasting codes if each is displayed in a salient way. The codes considered in the paper include: level of *acceptance* and *blame* toward the other spouse, global *positive* and *negative*, as well as level of *sadness* and *humor*.

Further, for this work we chose to formulate the problem as a binary classification task, in which we wanted to automatically identify the two extremes of a particular code (e.g., high and low blame). To that end, we gathered 280 sessions, corresponding to the 70 highest and lowest ratings for both husband and wife. Each code was considered separately in this regard, resulting in six binary classification tasks. For all experiments in this study, we trained gender-independent models.

3 Methodology and Results

In this section we will present the mathematical methodology and results for addressing the two questions above. We start by providing the maximum likelihood classifier formulation and results on reference transcripts. Then we describe our available audio and the classification method on the automatically derived lexical features and results.

Our goal is to show the usefulness of lexical features in accurate prediction of the high-level behavioral ratings. For this first study we chose a simple classifier with unigram features. We expect that the frequencies of lexical terms (e.g., n-gram features) are crucially informative. As a first study we only deal with unigram features to minimize data sparsity issues that appear with higher order n-grams. More specifically, we make use of only the unigram frequencies of the individual being rated, while ignoring those of their spouse. Since information about one of the partners behaviors can arguably be highly dependent on the behavior of the other partner we intend to study that in future work.

3.1 Maximum Likelihood Classifier

In a maximum likelihood framework binary classification task we want to select the code that maximizes

$$p(\text{Code 0 or 1}|\text{Transcript}) = p(C_0 \text{ or } C_1|T) \tag{1}$$

Alternatively for $i = \{0, 1\}$:

$$C_i = \arg\max_{Ci} \frac{p(T|C_i)p(C_i)}{P(T)} \tag{2}$$

$$= \arg\max_{Ci} p(T|C_i)p(C_i) \tag{3}$$

For the purposes of this work as we described above we chose a balanced data set so $p(C_0) = p(C_1)$. Therefore the decision can be re-written as:

$$\frac{p(T|C_0)}{p(T|C_1)} = \begin{cases} > 1 \Leftrightarrow C_0 \text{ true} \\ < 1 \Leftrightarrow C_1 \text{ true} \\ = 1 \Leftrightarrow \text{no decision} \end{cases} \tag{4}$$

Given the use of unigrams

$$p(T|C_i) = \prod_{\forall w_j \in T} p(w_j|C_i) \tag{5}$$

where w_j is the jth word in the transcript. As we can see because of the product term, this estimator is very sensitive to data sparsity. For instance if we have no observations in the training data of w_j then $p(T|C_i)$ will be zero. To address this we use the commonly used technique of smoothing with statistics derived from generic data, often called *Universal Background Model* (UBM), here denoted by B:

$$p(T|C_i) = \prod_{\forall w_j \in T} [(1 - \lambda)\, p(w_j|C_i) + \lambda p(w_j|B)] \tag{6}$$

The background model also serves to boost the importance of lexically salient regions. As $\lambda \to 1$ only the words with significantly different probabilities within the two domains – and arguably more important – will contribute to the decision.

3.2 Classification on Reference Transcripts

For seeking our first research goal of establishing the usefulness of lexical information for behavioral code classification, we follow the process outlined in Fig. 1. Through a leave-one-couple-out process we train a maximum likelihood

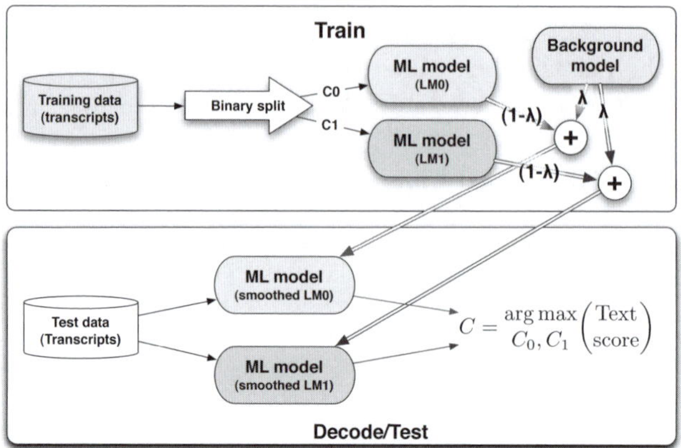

Fig. 1. Overview of the classification process from manually generated transcripts of the interactions

model of unigram probabilities for the two classes, and smooth it with a UBM. Each of these models can be used to score the test transcript.

As mentioned above we chose to work with the 280 sessions that had received the extreme behavior codes. Given that this sometimes may include the same couple twice this results in about 85 unique couples per code. For instance in *blame* the 100 sessions resulted in 89 couples. Model selection was done with leave-one-couple-out cross-validation, rather than leave-one-transcript-out, to avoid the possibility of some speakers appearing in both the training and test sets (e.g. *blame* resulted in 89 folds). For comparison purposes, we calculated the percentage correctly classified.

Table 2 shows the performance for the six codes. From the experimental results, it can be seen that regardless of λ lexical information support behavioral code prediction.

Separability by Human Experts and Machine. As can be seen by Table 2, the codes Humor and Sadness perform the worst amongst the six codes chosen. Fig. 2 provides insight as to why. As we can see, the human annotators had the least discrimination in those two codes with the positive (right) part of the distribution exhibiting a large spread. In fact one could argue that by looking at the data that Humor for instance did not exhibit a bi-modal distribution in the original

Table 2. Results of classification using reference transcripts for different λ

Results on reference transcript (% correct)											
code vs λ	**0.01**	**0.05**	**0.2**	**0.3**	**0.4**	**0.5**	**0.6**	**0.7**	**0.8**	**0.95**	**0.99**
acceptance	91.4	91.0	91.0	90.0	90.3	89.2	88.5	87.5	86.4	75.3	60.5
blame	91.0	91.4	91.8	91.0	90.3	89.2	89.2	88.5	88.2	78.1	63.4
humor	71.3	72.4	72.0	71.3	69.5	69.9	67.5	67.0	65.2	61.6	57.3
negative	83.8	84.9	86.7	86.7	86.4	85.7	86.0	86.0	85.3	74.9	60.2
positive	89.6	89.6	89.6	88.9	87.5	87.8	87.8	87.5	87.8	76.7	63.8
sadness	59.0	61.6	60.9	61.3	60.6	60.2	58.8	59.5	59.1	57.7	58.5

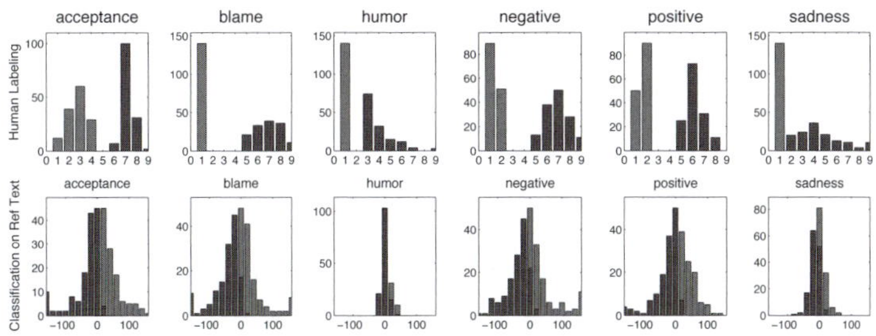

Fig. 2. *Distribution of data based on (top) the average ratings provided by multiple human experts and (bottom) the difference in log-likelihoods of the ML model for* $\lambda = 0.5$*. As can be seen codes where annotators had minimal separation also result in the greatest overlap by the ML model.*

annotations and that our choice of the top/bottom highest ratings may have been – for these two codes – a necessary but not necessarily the best choice.

3.3 Audio Segmentation

Prior to decoding the speech into words we need to separate the audio of the two participants. In this paper and in our previous work [1, 7], we decided to exploit the available transcriptions towards that task through forced alignment. The process employs *SailAlign* [5] that can be summarized as a recursive speech recognition and alignment of the ASR-output with reference transcript.

Although for our previous work this process offered the advantage of higher accuracy of word boundaries, it also has a higher rejection rate as words may be marked as un-aligned. Many times this can occur even if the word is in the middle of a continuous speech segment by the same speaker. Hence not all the spoken audio is used in the automated classification process. Of the original 569 sessions, 372 met both the threshold of 5 dB SNR and >55% aligned audio, which left us 62.8 hours of data across 104 unique couples. This reduction in data resulted in about 70% less data for the classification of section 3.4 compared to the transcript analysis in section 3.2.

This is clearly going to have some effect on the observed performance drop in the case of classification directly from audio. Note that all the transcripts are used in the classification from reference transcripts in order to set the upper bound of possible performance.

3.4 Classification on Audio Signal

For pursuing our second research goal of behavioral code classification from noisy automatically obtained speech transcriptions we follow the process outlined in Fig. 3. As before we train our models with smoothing from a UBM. In this case however we also create a class-independent ML model ($\mathrm{LM}_{\mathrm{ASR}}$) that can be used for the automatic speech recognition process. Note that the specific dataset has a very wide range of acoustic characteristics and as such our ASR

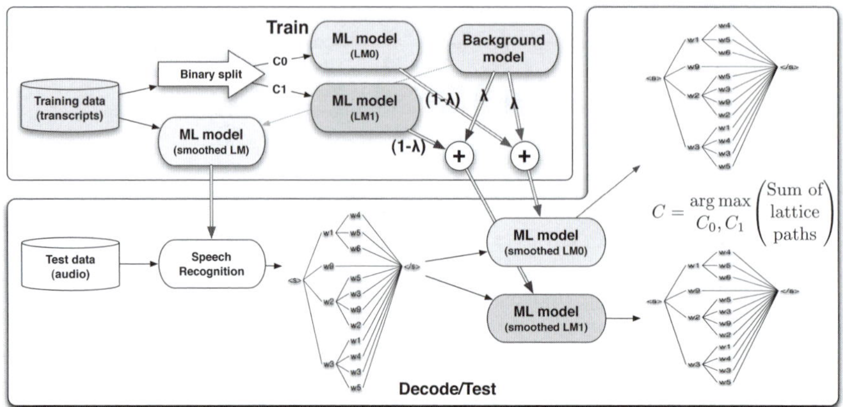

Fig. 3. Overview of the classification process without human transcripts through the use of ASR lattices

was not optimized for the domain, and online adaptation was switched off. We used OtoSense for our ASR (a SAIL implementation) and acoustic models based on WSJ and HUB4. LM_{ASR} similarly was not optimized in any fashion, except in including the training data and a background model, as it is only used for lattice pruning. The word error rate (WER) varied extremely with different sessions with most lying between a WER of 40-90%.

Our assumption towards establishing the procedure for implementing our second research goal is that the noise introduced through the ASR process is independent from the couple behaviors. We believe this assumption to be a valid one given that the acoustic mismatch includes reverberation, environment and sensing noise, and speaker-specific acoustic pattern mismatch.

Therefore at the test phase we decode and produce a lattice using the same ASR (acoustic models and LM_{ASR}) and then replace the language model scores in the lattice with the class LM values. The final step is to decode the two resulting lattices and find the score of the N-best paths. For the purposes of this paper we used N=100 (an unoptimized parameter).

Table 3 shows the performance for the six codes and for different values of λ. As we can see there is a significant degradation relative to the values in Table 2, however we can also note that for most codes the performance is significantly

Table 3. Results of classification using lexical analysis of audio for different λ

	Results through ASR lattices (% correct)										
code vs λ	**0.01**	**0.05**	**0.2**	**0.3**	**0.4**	**0.5**	**0.6**	**0.7**	**0.8**	**0.95**	**0.99**
acceptance	71.4	72.9	75.4	73.6	73.6	73.2	71.8	71.1	68.9	64.6	63.6
blame	75.0	76.8	77.9	78.6	78.2	77.9	76.8	76.4	73.9	67.5	63.9
humor	57.9	58.6	58.6	57.5	57.1	56.4	57.9	56.1	55.4	55.0	50.7
negative	64.3	66.1	69.6	71.1	70.4	69.3	69.3	67.9	65.7	60.7	58.9
positive	72.9	73.2	74.6	74.6	72.5	72.9	73.9	73.6	71.4	66.1	64.6
sadness	52.5	55.0	55.7	52.1	50.4	50.7	51.1	51.8	52.1	54.3	52.1

Table 4. The unigrams with most impact towards the correct classification of blame for one of the cross-validation folds

Most blaming words in terms of discriminative contribution				Least blaming words in terms of discriminative contribution			
Word	No Bl. (log prob)	Blame (log prob)	Δ	Word	No Bl. (log prob)	Blame (log prob)	Δ
YOU	-95.49	-85.88	-9.61	EXPECTS	-16.70	-17.84	1.14
YOUR	-51.24	-47.18	-4.06	CONSIDERATION	-16.11	-17.31	1.21
ME	-40.27	-37.74	-2.53	KNOW	-35.10	-36.62	1.53
TELL	-33.97	-32.46	-1.51	INABILITY	-16.76	-18.32	1.55
ACCEPT	-25.44	-23.99	-1.45	SESSION	-20.51	-22.07	1.56
CARING	-27.05	-25.91	-1.14	OF	-44.50	-46.26	1.76
KITCHEN	-21.22	-20.21	-1.02	ANTICIPATION	-22.22	-24.21	2.00
TOLD	-29.04	-28.19	-0.85	THINK	-35.70	-37.77	2.07
NOT	-40.32	-39.59	-0.73	WE	-29.39	-31.75	2.36
WHAT	-51.47	-50.77	-0.69	I	-99.92	-102.49	2.57
INTIMACY	-43.16	-42.53	-0.63	THAT	-91.30	-93.97	2.67
IT	-42.70	-42.18	-0.52	UM	-64.75	-70.76	6.01

better than chance (50%). Regardless of λ it is clear that Hypothesis 2 holds, even with a generic ASR and even with the data loss due to automated segmentation.

3.5 Lexical Significance

In a parallel analysis and in collaboration with our psychologist partners we also looked into whether specific words offered insights into specific behavioral codes. For instance Table 4 shows that specific words can carry a lot of insight towards the behavioral codes. As we can see the word YOU, which appeared 59 times, had the most contribution towards the blame decision, while the word UM (23 times) scored as the least blaming unigram ($\lambda = 0.4$). The mathematical analysis enables us to easily identify important terms that we will follow up with detailed experimental and psychological inquiry.

4 Discussion

Our goal in this work was to establish the usefulness of lexical features for the purpose of machine classification of human behavior in couple interactions. The answers to our first question clearly show that even a simple ML unigram based classifier can achieve good classification accuracy. The experiments related to our second research question established that despite the very large WER of the ASR, significant behavior information is contained in the noisy lattices.

In sum these experiments show that lexical information is an important information stream for the important task of automatic behavioral coding in couple interactions. There are a number of improvements toward improving automated classification that we plan on pursuing in our follow-up work.

First we want to address the relative importance of information within a specific data stream through salience detection. Currently as mentioned above lexically salient words are given more importance, however salience through acoustic information is not considered.

In addition we want to consider higher order n-gram streams. These can not be used directly with our current corpus due to data sparsity, so we plan to pursue techniques to address that including data mining for richer models, appropriate smoothing techniques (e.g. Kneser-Ney), and the fusion of the decision of different lexical classifiers (e.g. along salience sensitivity and n-gram order).

At the system level we want to investigate alternative classifiers. We already have initial results using a SVM classifier, but without using a UBM and noted that it under-performs the technique reported here. We intend to combine the smoothing with a SVM classifier in our future work.

Finally in our previous work [1] we presented an acoustics based classification framework. The fusion of the two information streams can potentially provide great benefits. In addition fusion can take place at various temporal resolutions from word level fusion to session level.

Acknowledgments. This research was supported in part by the National Science Foundation and the Viterbi Research Innovation Fund. Special thanks to the Couple Therapy research staff for sharing the data.

References

1. Black, M., Katsamanis, A., Lee, C.C., Lammert, A., Baucom, B.R., Christensen, A., Georgiou, P.G., Narayanan, S.: Automatic classification of married couples' behavior using audio features. In: Proc. Int'l. Conf. on Speech Communication and Technology (2010)
2. Christensen, A., Atkins, D., Berns, S., Wheeler, J., Baucom, D., Simpson, L.: Traditional versus integrative behavioral couple therapy for significantly and chronically distressed married couples. Journal of Consulting and Clinical Psychology 72(2), 176–191 (2004)
3. Heavey, C., Gill, D., Christensen, A.: Couples interaction rating system 2 (CIRS2). University of California, Los Angeles (2002), `http://christensenresearch.psych.ucla.edu/`
4. Jones, J., Christensen, A.: Couples interaction study: Social support interaction rating system. University of California, Los Angeles (1998), `http://christensenresearch.psych.ucla.edu/`
5. Katsamanis, A., Black, M.P., Georgiou, P.G., Goldstein, L., Narayanan, S.S.: SailAlign: Robust long speech-text alignment. In: Very-Large-Scale Phonetics Workshop (January 2011)
6. Lee, C., Narayanan, S.: Towards detecting emotions in spoken dialogs. IEEE Transactions on Speech and Audio Processing 13(2), 293–302 (2005)
7. Lee, C.C., Black, M., Katsamanis, A., , Lammert, A., Baucom, B.R., Christensen, A., Georgiou, P.G., Narayanan, S.: Quantification of prosodic entrainment in affective spontaneous spoken interactions of married couples. In: Proc. Int'l. Conf. on Speech Communication and Technology (2010)
8. Margolin, G., Oliver, P., Gordis, E., O'Hearn, H., Medina, A., Ghosh, C., Morland, L.: The nuts and bolts of behavioral observation of marital and family interaction. Clinical Child and Family Psychology Review 1(4), 195–213 (1998)
9. Ranganath, R., Jurafsky, D., McFarland, D.: It's not you, it's me: Detecting flirting and its misperception in speed-dates. In: EMNLP (2009)
10. Yildirim, S., Narayanan, S., Potamianos, A.: Detecting emotional state of a child in a conversational computer game. Computer Speech & Language (2010)

Predicting Facial Indicators of Confusion with Hidden Markov Models

Joseph F. Grafsgaard, Kristy Elizabeth Boyer, and James C. Lester

Department of Computer Science, North Carolina State University,
Raleigh, North Carolina, USA
{jfgrafsg,keboyer,lester}@ncsu.edu

Abstract. Affect plays a vital role in learning. During tutoring, particular affective states may benefit or detract from student learning. A key cognitive-affective state is confusion, which has been positively associated with effective learning. Although identifying episodes of confusion presents significant challenges, recent investigations have identified correlations between confusion and specific facial movements. This paper builds on those findings to create a predictive model of learner confusion during task-oriented human-human tutorial dialogue. The model leverages textual dialogue, task, and facial expression history to predict upcoming confusion within a hidden Markov modeling framework. Analysis of the model structure also reveals meaningful modes of interaction within the tutoring sessions. The results demonstrate that because of its predictive power and rich qualitative representation, the model holds promise for informing the design of affective-sensitive tutoring systems.

Keywords: Affect prediction, hidden Markov models, intelligent tutoring systems, tutorial dialogue.

1 Introduction

One-on-one human tutoring is highly effective for student learning [1]. Intelligent tutoring systems (ITSs) hold great promise for achieving this level of effectiveness, with many such systems producing significant learning gains [2,3]. Recent advances in ITS research such as modeling the strategies of expert human tutors [4] and examining learner emotions during tutoring [5] continue to enhance the effectiveness of ITSs. To date, a number of ITSs and tutorial dialogue systems have begun to address learner affect [6-8]. The emerging results highlight the importance of incorporating models of learner emotions into ITSs to provide students with more effective learning experiences.

Predicting student affect is an essential step toward identifying optimally effective behavior within affectively aware intelligent systems. A promising means for predicting student affect is through analyzing learners' facial expressions. Recent investigations have identified facial expression configurations that relate to learner emotions [5,9,10]. These results build on advances in human emotion modeling that are tied to particular cross-cultural facial expressions [11]. Compared to other modalities of affect detection, facial expressions may be a richer, more informative channel during learning [2,6]. Yet, the field is far from assembling a comprehensive catalogue of learner emotions and the facial expressions with which they correlate [5,12].

S. D'Mello et al. (Eds.): ACII 2011, Part I, LNCS 6974, pp. 97–106, 2011.

Although no comprehensive catalogue of learner emotions currently exists, there is widespread agreement that occurrences of *confusion* are highly relevant during learning [5,9,13]. While identifying episodes of confusion presents significant challenges, a promising approach leverages student facial expression. Numerous studies of the correlations between facial expressions and learner emotions have identified a link between confusion and the facial *action unit 4*, which is the "Brow Lowerer" movement, referred to as *AU4* [5,9,10,14]. The present work utilizes these findings to predict student confusion as evidenced by student AU4 during computer-mediated human-human tutoring.

The modeling approach presented in this paper represents the tutoring session (consisting of dialogue, task actions, and facial expressions) as a sequential set of observations. The goal is to predict unseen observations based on the prior observations. While a number of sequential modeling techniques may be appropriate for this task, a particularly promising framework is the hidden Markov model (HMM), which has been successfully used to model tutorial strategies within a tutorial dialogue corpus [15,16]. The present findings demonstrate that HMMs can learn a predictive model of *confusion*, as indicated by student AU4, from a corpus of human tutoring.

2 Related Work

Recent tutoring research has identified a set of cognitive-affective states that are particularly relevant to learning: *anxiety*, *boredom*, *confusion*, *curiosity*, *delight*, *eureka*, *flow*, and *frustration* [9,17]. These learner emotions appear to have different effects on learning and motivation [5,18]. For example, frustration seems to be a problematic cognitive-affective state, which promotes a negative "state of stuck" [7]. While frustration may have negative consequences, an even more detrimental state is boredom, which severely inhibits student learning [18]. In both cases, a paramount concern is the persistence of negative affective states, which can lead to a "vicious cycle" [5,8].

While the cognitive-affective state of confusion may at first glance appear to be negative, it has increasingly been shown to coincide with moments of learning [5,8]. The positive impact of confusion may be due to the associated concept of cognitive disequilibrium, which involves a moment of uncertain knowledge that is (ideally) subsequently revised to reach correct understanding [13]. Thus, confusion may function as an essential intermediary state on the path of deep learning [2,13]. This notion has been supported in studies across multiple learning environments [2,8,18].

Effectively incorporating affect in intelligent systems requires the capability to diagnose instances of learner emotion [19]. This diagnosis involves both detecting and understanding emotions, and recent years have seen increased research into both problems [2,5,20]. Facial expressions are a particularly meaningful channel for both learner affect detection and understanding [5,6,12]. With respect to affect detection, manual and automated recognition of facial expressions have been shown to improve predictive models [6,21,22]. With respect to affect understanding, specific facial configurations are known to be associated with learner affect. Confusion has been correlated with facial action unit 4 (AU4, "Brow Lowerer") in multiple studies, based on self, peer, and FACS-certified expert judgments of affective events [5,9,10].

A common thread in work on affect detection and understanding is the importance of identifying how learner affect follows from context. For this reason, a predictive model of affect holds great promise, not only for influencing the behavior of affectively aware ITSs, but also for informing a fundamental understanding of emotions during learning. This paper presents a predictive model of student confusion created using hidden Markov models (HMMs). The findings indicate that by leveraging dialogue, task, and facial expression history, HMMs can predict the presence of student AU4. These results have implications both for fundamental investigations of learner emotions, and for predicting affect during tutoring.

3 Corpus and Manual Annotations

A corpus of human-human tutorial dialogue was collected during a tutorial dialogue study [15]. Students solved an introductory computer programming problem and engaged in computer-mediated textual dialogue with a human tutor. The corpus consists of 48 dialogues annotated with dialogue acts (Table 1). Annotations also include information about student progress on the programming task [16].

Table 1. Dialogue act tags and frequency in corpus (*S* = student, *T* = tutor)

Act	Description	*S*	*T*
ASSESSING QUESTION	Task-specific query or feedback request	44	83
EXTRA DOMAIN	Unrelated to task	37	42
GROUNDING	Acknowledgement, thanks, greetings, etc.	57	38
LUKEWARM CONTENT FDBK	Partly positive/negative elaborated feedback	2	23
LUKEWARM FEEDBACK	Partly positive/negative task feedback	3	21
NEGATIVE CONTENT FDBK	Negative elaborated feedback	5	77
NEGATIVE FEEDBACK	Negative task feedback	10	10
POSITIVE CONTENT FDBK	Positive elaborated feedback	10	21
POSITIVE FEEDBACK	Positive task feedback	23	119
QUESTION	Conceptual or other query	31	24
STATEMENT	Declaration of factual information	55	320

Student facial video was collected during the tutoring sessions, but the videos were not shown to tutors. Fourteen of these videos were annotated with student displays of AU4 (Figure 1) using the Facial Action Coding System (FACS) [1] [14,23]. One certified FACS coder annotated all fourteen videos from start to finish, pausing at all observed instances of AU4. A second certified FACS coder annotated a subset of six videos. The continuous intervals of time were discretized into one-second intervals, on which intercoder agreement was κ=0.86 (Cohen's kappa). Annotated excerpts of the corpus are shown in Figure 2, which also displays the best-fit sequence of hidden states as identified by the HMM (Section 5.1).

Figure 3 shows the frequencies of AU4 corresponding to tutor and student dialogue acts. For tutor dialogue acts, an instance of AU4 is considered "corresponding" if it occurs within ten seconds after the tutor move; for student acts, ten seconds before the student move. These durations were empirically determined to account for student

[1] Manual annotation of facial action units is very labor intensive. Comprehensive FACS coding typically requires at least sixty hours per hour of video. Annotating a subset of AUs is faster, requiring approximately ten hours per hour of video.

Fig. 1. Student displays of AU4

Excerpt 1			
13:16:03	Tutor:	no, it's easier than that, you just have to make the middle if into an "else if" [NEGATIVE CONTENT FEEDBACK]	STATE 10
	Student:	CORRECT TASK ACTION AU4	STATE 6
13:16:31	Tutor:	does that make sense? [ASSESSING QUESTION AU4]	STATE 10
13:16:41	Tutor:	that way it only checks the 2nd conditional if the first one failed [STATEMENT]	STATE 8
13:17:20	Student:	it makes sense now that you explained it [...] [POSITIVE CONTENT FEEDBACK]	STATE 4
Excerpt 2			
14:52:18	Tutor:	no, before we start sorting [NEGATIVE CONTENT FEEDBACK AU4]	STATE 10
	Student:	CORRECT TASK ACTION AU4	STATE 6
14:52:27	Tutor:	so, before the first loop you can use i for this loop counter if you want to [STATEMENT AU4]	STATE 10
	Student:	MIXED PROGRESS TASK ACTION AU4	STATE 6
14:53:52	Student:	i try to keep them different so i don't confuse myself [STATEMENT]	STATE 7

Fig. 2. Excerpts from annotated tutoring session corpus, with most probable sequences of HMM hidden states (Section 5)

preparation of an utterance and reception of a tutor utterance. Of student utterances, LUKEWARM CONTENT FEEDBACK corresponds to the highest probability of student AU4. In this dialogue move students articulate partially correct knowledge. Of tutor utterances, the most likely to correspond to student AU4 is NEGATIVE FEEDBACK, in which the tutor states that the student has made a mistake but does not provide an explanation. Another dialogue move that has a relatively high probability of AU4 is student ASSESSING QUESTION, which constitutes a direct request for task-based feedback. Students generally make these requests when their confidence in a recent task action is low.

Task actions were labeled based on progress toward a correct solution to the programming problem at hand, at a between-dialogue-moves granularity. Each task action cluster was characterized as CORRECT, INCOMPLETE, INCORRECT, or MIXED PROGRESS (a mixture of correct, incomplete, and/or incorrect task actions). As shown

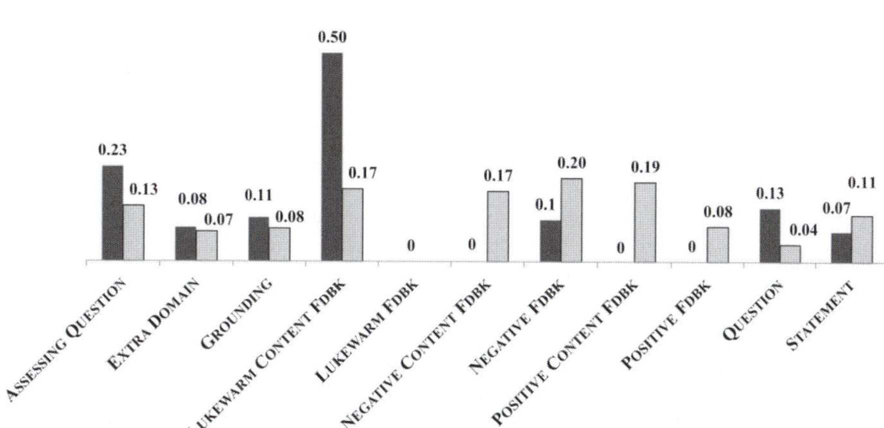

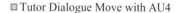

Fig. 3. Relative frequency of student and tutor dialogue moves with AU4

in Figure 4, students most frequently displayed AU4 during episodes of MIXED PROGRESS (37% of the time). Students were less likely (24%) to display AU4 during episodes of INCORRECT task action. As novices, these students were likely unaware of their mistakes when undertaking a completely incorrect task action. On the other hand, partially correct and partially incorrect task episodes indicate the student had sufficient knowledge to recognize that errors were present, and may have been experiencing constructive confusion toward reaching increased understanding.

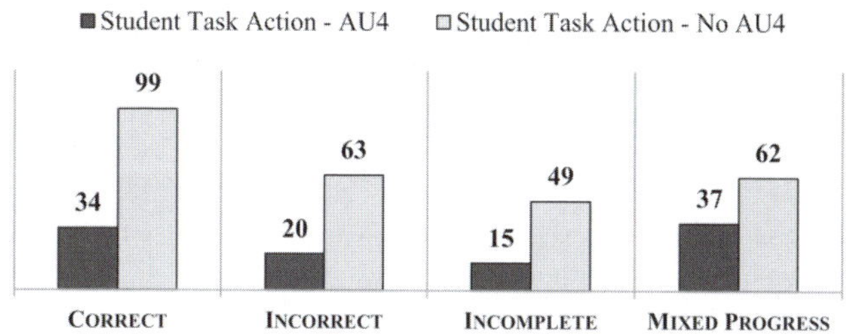

Fig. 4. Frequency of student task actions with AU4 present or absent

4 HMM Learning and Prediction of Student AU4

A hidden Markov model (HMM) is defined by an *initial probability distribution* across hidden states, *transition probabilities* among hidden states, and *emission probabilities* for each hidden state and observation symbol pair [24]. The hidden states represent the underlying probabilistic system that generates a given sequence of observed events. The initial state probability gives the possibility of beginning in any hidden state. Transition probabilities encode the likelihood of entering one hidden state from another. Emission probabilities encode the likelihood of producing a given observation from a particular hidden state. HMMs learn statistical dependencies between hidden states and the corresponding observations. The hidden state structure can then be analyzed to identify underlying trends. Using HMMs, it is possible to uncover a rich interplay between learner affect, tutorial dialogue and task context.

4.1 Model Learning

The observation sequences consist of annotated observations from the corpus, including dialogue moves by tutor or student, or student task action segments. Each of these observations also includes a tag for whether student AU4 was associated with that event. For example, the observation symbol sequence that corresponds to Excerpt 1 in Figure 2 is, [STUDENT NEGATIVE CONTENT FEEDBACK NOAU4, CORRECT TASK ACTION AU4, TUTOR ASSESSING QUESTION AU4, TUTOR STATEMENT NOAU4, STUDENT POSITIVE CONTENT FEEDBACK NOAU4].

The HMMs were learned within a leave-one-out framework. Within each fold, five random restarts of model parameters were performed to reduce the potential of model convergence at a local optimum. An additional outer training loop, ranging from two to twenty, was performed to identify the optimal number of hidden states. The best-fit model has eighteen hidden states, and its structure is discussed in detail in Section 5.

4.2 Prediction of AU4

The leave-one-out design resulted in fourteen training/testing folds, one for each tutoring session. Four of these sessions contained an observation symbol (combination of dialogue move and AU4 presence/absence) that occurred nowhere else in the data, so the learned model was not used to predict on these sessions. Predictive findings from the remaining ten test sessions are presented here, though an online predictive model used during tutoring could address this by learning across all possible symbols in the state space, regardless of absence in a particular session. The predictive accuracies of the HMMs are compared against a majority class baseline as well as a first-order observed Markov model (OMM) (Table 2).

Table 2. Comparison of predictive accuracy of classifiers; accuracies that are statistically significantly better than baseline are in bold (paired t-test, $p < 0.005$)

Classifier	Accuracy (across sessions)	Std. Dev. of Accuracy
HMM Train	**0.868**	0.021
HMM Test	**0.907**	0.059
OMM Train	0.186	0.013
OMM Test	0.557	0.284
Baseline	0.845	-

OMMs do not include hidden states, and thus condition the present state purely on the transition probability distribution from the previous state. The training set predictive accuracies indicate that HMMs fit the training data better than the other models. The predictive accuracy of the learned HMMs on the test set was higher on average than predictions on the training set, but not surprisingly, the standard deviation was also greater. Both the training and test predictions greatly outperformed the predictive accuracy of the OMMs, which were below baseline. This below-baseline performance of OMMs indicates that the presence or absence of AU4 at time t is not highly predictive of the presence or absence of AU4 at time $t+1$, which is an interesting discovery in this corpus. However, the additional stochastic structure provided by the HMM is able to predict AU4 significantly above baseline.

5 Discussion

The predictive accuracies of the HMMs suggest that these models hold great promise for learner affect prediction. On unseen test data, the HMMs predicted significantly better than an OMM and a (very high) majority class baseline. To gain more insight into how the HMM structure facilitates prediction of student AU4, this section examines and interprets the structure of the learned (best-fit) HMM.

5.1 Hidden State Structure

HMMs' predictive power is gained in part by the way these models can learn higher-order structure (in the form of hidden states) based on observation sequences. The model structure shown in Figure 5 illustrates this, with emission probability distributions displayed as bar graphs and transitions as edges. To facilitate discussion, the states were named after model learning through qualitative analysis. STATE 6, *Student Work with Confusion,* is dominated by student task actions with AU4 present. STATE 10, *Tutor Help*, emits a combination of tutor dialogue moves with AU4 present, and tutor feedback with no AU4. STATE 4, *Overcoming Confusion*, is dominated by tutor statements with AU4 present and student positive feedback. This state corresponds to tutor statements that are not consistent with students' prior knowledge. Interestingly, the state also generates student positive feedback, which may indicate that students moved past cognitive disequilibrium and into a state of understanding. STATE 16, *Conversational Grounding*, primarily encompasses non-task-oriented student and tutor dialogue moves, but also generates with small probability student negative feedback without AU4.

These emission probability distributions indicate ways in which the HMM abstracts from observation sequences to meaningful higher-order structure. Of equal importance are the transition probabilities between the hidden states. STATE 6 and STATE 10 are more likely to transition to each other than any other hidden states. This transition is illustrated in one sequence of events (Figure 2 Excerpt 1) in which the tutor provides negative content feedback followed by a student correct task action with confusion present (as evidenced by AU4). The tutor then asks an assessing question to gauge the student's understanding, which also coincides with a moment of confusion. The tutor further explains the computer programming concept with an instructional statement clarifying prior feedback. The student then takes a moment to reflect on the material and informs the tutor that the explanation was helpful. This example demonstrates the strong connection between *Student Work with Confusion*, STATE 6, and *Tutor Help*, STATE 10. Meaningful tutor feedback and instruction that induce confusion are produced in STATE 10, while STATE 6 corresponds with student tasks actions accompanied by confusion. Both states are highly relevant to learning.

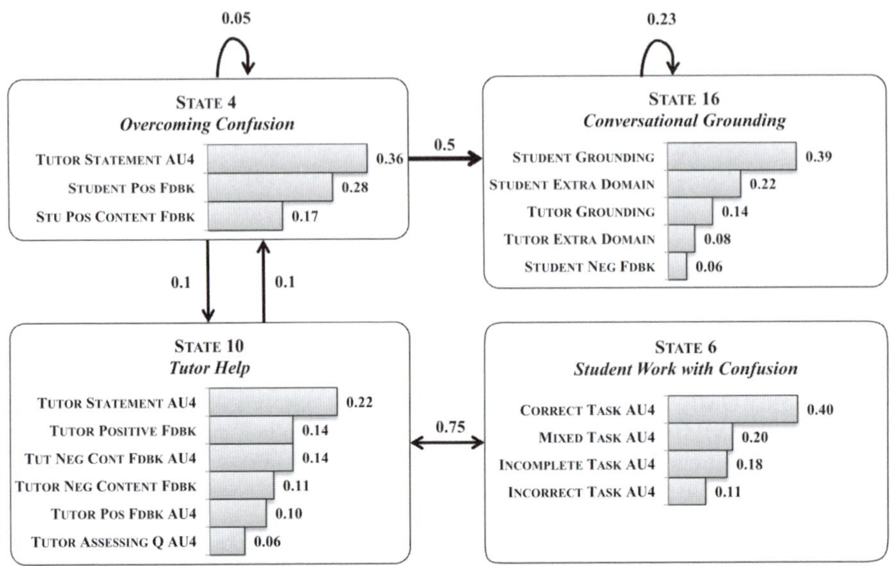

Fig. 5. Learned HMM structure: a subset of four hidden states is shown, with transition (arrow) and emission (bar chart) probabilities ≥ 0.05 indicated

The second example (Figure 2 Excerpt 2) further characterizes the interplay of State 6 and State 10, with the student progressing on the programming task (with AU4 present) while receiving tutor feedback and instruction. The excerpt begins with tutor negative content feedback on the student's current task progress, with student confusion indicated by AU4. The student then immediately completes the subtask, still showing AU4. The tutor continues instructing the student with a comment on a relevant programming concept (AU4 still present). The student then continues programming, with mixed progress (AU4 continues). After approximately a minute of working on the task, the student responds to the tutor statement with an explanation of the work performed. Thus, the student displays confusion until after the tutor completes instruction. Both excerpts seem to show effortful learning, with a combination of instruction during *Tutor Help* and task progress in *Student Work with Confusion*. Therefore, HMMs represent a promising approach to automatically learn semantically meaningful affect-rich models of tutorial interaction.

5.2 Limitations

There are two primary limitations that should be noted. First, manual annotation of facial expressions is very labor intensive, which constrained the number of sessions analyzed for learner affect. Automated techniques for FACS coding [14] are actively being investigated, although they are not currently as accurate as manual annotation [21,25]. Second, a learned HMM may potentially require large amounts of data to produce a predictive model generalizable enough to deploy within a larger population, as evidenced by the observation symbol sparsity that was encountered in this analysis. Further studies are necessary to evaluate the generalizability of predictive HMM models of learner affect and their use in online prediction during tutoring.

6 Conclusion

Learner affect plays a vital role in the success or failure of a tutorial interaction. In particular, the cognitive-affective state of confusion is highly relevant on the path to acquiring knowledge since confusion accompanies learning impasses during which students must resolve misconceptions that challenge their conceptual understanding. Predicting confusion is an important step toward understanding the effects of various ITS interventions and toward designing more effective strategies.

This paper has presented a novel predictive model of learner confusion that incorporates dialogue moves, task performance, and facial expression using hidden Markov models (HMMs). Such models may play an important role in the diagnosis of learner confusion for future systems. Additionally, analysis of the model structure identified meaningful transitions between affect-enriched states of tutor and student dialogue moves and student task progress. In future work, affect-predictive HMMs need to be further developed by incorporating data regarding a wider set of learner affective states. These future predictive models may be instrumental in diagnosing learner affect during interactions with intelligent tutoring systems.

Acknowledgements. This work is supported in part by the NC State University Department of Computer Science along with the National Science Foundation through Grants IIS-0812291, DRL-1007962 and the STARS Alliance Grant CNS-0739216. Any opinions, findings, conclusions, or recommendations expressed in this report are those of the participants, and do not necessarily represent the official views, opinions, or policy of the National Science Foundation.

References

1. Bloom, B.S.: The 2 Sigma Problem: The Search for Methods of Group Instruction as Effective as One-to-One Tutoring. Educational Researcher 13, 4–16 (1984)
2. D'Mello, S.K., Lehman, B., Sullins, J., Daigle, R., Combs, R., Vogt, K., Perkins, L., Graesser, A.C.: A Time For Emoting: When Affect-Sensitivity Is and Isn't Effective at Promoting Deep Learning. In: Aleven, V., Kay, J., Mostow, J. (eds.) ITS 2010, Part I. LNCS, vol. 6094, pp. 245–254. Springer, Heidelberg (2010)
3. Koedinger, K.R., Anderson, J.R., Hadley, W.H., Mark, M.A.: Intelligent Tutoring Goes To School in the Big City. Intl. Jl. of Artificial Intelligence in Education 8, 30–43 (1997)
4. D'Mello, S., Olney, A., Person, N.: Mining Collaborative Patterns in Tutorial Dialogues. Jl. of Educational Data Mining 2, 1–37 (2010)
5. D'Mello, S.K., Lehman, B., Person, N.: Monitoring Affect States During Effortful Problem Solving Activities. International Jl. of Artificial Intelligence in Education 20 (2010)
6. Arroyo, I., Cooper, D.G., Burleson, W., Woolf, B.P., Muldner, K., Christopherson, R.M.: Emotion Sensors Go To School. In: 14th International Conference on Artificial Intelligence in Education (2009)
7. Burleson, W.: Affective Learning Companions: Strategies for Empathetic Agents with Real-Time Multimodal Affective Sensing to Foster Meta-Cognitive and Meta-Affective Approaches to Learning, Motivation, and Perseverance. MIT Ph.D. thesis (2006)
8. McQuiggan, S.W., Robison, J.L., Lester, J.C.: Affective Transitions in Narrative-Centered Learning Environments. Educational Technology & Society 13, 40–53 (2010)

9. Craig, S.D., Graesser, A.C., Sullins, J., Gholson, B.: Affect and learning: an exploratory look into the role of affect in learning with AutoTutor. Jl. of Educational Media 29, 241–250 (2004)
10. McDaniel, B.T., D'Mello, S.K., King, B.G., Chipman, P., Tapp, K., Graesser, A.C.: Facial Features for Affective State Detection in Learning Environments. In: Proceedings of the 29th Annual Meeting of the Cognitive Science Society, pp. 467–472 (2007)
11. Russell, J.A., Bachorowski, J., Fernandez-Dols, J.: Facial and vocal expressions of emotion. Annual Review of Psychology 54, 329–349 (2003)
12. Afzal, S., Robinson, P.: Natural Affect Data - Collection & Annotation in a Learning Context. In: Proceedings of the International Conference on Affective Computing and Intelligent Interaction, pp. 1–7 (2009)
13. Graesser, A.C., Olde, B.A.: How does one know whether a person understands a device? The quality of the questions the person asks when the device breaks down. Jl. of Educational Psychology 95, 524–536 (2003)
14. Ekman, P., Friesen, W.V., Hager, J.C.: Facial Action Coding System. A Human Face, Salt Lake City, USA (2002)
15. Boyer, K.E., Ha, E.Y., Wallis, M., Phillips, R., Vouk, M., Lester, J.: Discovering Tutorial Dialogue Strategies with Hidden Markov Models. In: Proceedings of the 14th International Conference on Artificial Intelligence in Education, pp. 141–148 (2009)
16. Boyer, K.E., Phillips, R., Ingram, A., Ha, E.Y., Wallis, M.D., Vouk, M.A., Lester, J.C.: Characterizing the Effectiveness of Tutorial Dialogue with Hidden Markov Models. In: Aleven, V., Kay, J., Mostow, J. (eds.) ITS 2010. LNCS, vol. 6094, pp. 55–64. Springer, Heidelberg (2010)
17. D'Mello, S.K., Craig, S.D., Graesser, A.C.: Multi-Method Assessment of Affective Experience and Expression during Deep Learning. International Jl. of Learning Technology 4, 165–187 (2009)
18. Baker, R.S.J.d., D'Mello, S.K., Rodrigo, M.M.T., Graesser, A.C.: Better to Be Frustrated than Bored: The Incidence, Persistence, and Impact of Learners' Cognitive-Affective States during Interactions with Three Different Computer-Based Learning Environments. International Jl. of Human-Computer Studies 68, 223–241 (2010)
19. Picard, R.W., Papert, S., Bender, W., Blumberg, B., Breazeal, C., Cavallo, D., Machover, T., Resnick, M., Roy, D., Strohecker, C.: Affective Learning — A Manifesto. BT Technology Jl. 22, 253–269 (2004)
20. Woolf, B.P., Burleson, W., Arroyo, I., Dragon, T., Cooper, D.G., Picard, R.W.: Affect-aware tutors: recognising and responding to student affect. International Jl. of Learning Technology 4, 129–164 (2009)
21. Calvo, R.A., D'Mello, S.K.: Affect Detection: An Interdisciplinary Review of Models, Methods, and Their Applications. IEEE Transactions on Affective Computing 1, 18–37 (2010)
22. D'Mello, S.K., Graesser, A.: Multimodal Semi-Automated Affect Detection from Conversational Cues, Gross Body Language, and Facial Features. User Modeling and User-Adapted Interaction 20, 147–187 (2010)
23. Grafsgaard, J.F., Boyer, K.E., Phillips, R., Lester, J.C.: Modeling Confusion: Facial Expression, Task, and Discourse in Task-Oriented Tutorial Dialogue. In: Biswas, G., Bull, S., Kay, J., Mitrovic, A. (eds.) AIED 2011. LNCS, vol. 6738, pp. 98–105. Springer, Heidelberg (2011)
24. Rabiner, L.R.: A Tutorial on Hidden Markov Models and Selected Applications in Speech Recognition. Proceedings of the IEEE 77, 257–286 (1989)
25. Zeng, Z., Pantic, M., Roisman, G.I., Huang, T.S.: A Survey Of Affect Recognition Methods: Audio, Visual, and Spontaneous Expressions. IEEE Transactions on Pattern Analysis and Machine Intelligence 31, 39–58 (2009)

Recording Affect in the Field: Towards Methods and Metrics for Improving Ground Truth Labels

Jennifer Healey

Interaction and Experience Research, Intel Labs, Santa Clara, CA
jennifer.healey@intel.com

Abstract. One of the primary goals of affective computing is enabling computers to recognize human emotion. To do this we need accurately labeled affective data. This is challenging to obtain in real situations where affective events are not scripted and occur simultaneously with other activities and feelings. Affective labels also rely heavily on subject self-report for which can be problematic. This paper reports on methods for obtaining high quality emotion labels with reduced bias and variance and also shows that better training sets for machine learning algorithms can be created by combining multiple sources of evidence. During a 7 day, 13 participant field study we found that recognition accuracy for physiological activation improved from 63% to 79% with two sources of evidence and in an additional pilot study this improved to 100% accuracy for one subject over 10 days when context evidence was also included.

Keywords: Affective computing, emotional sensing, ambulatory assessment, ground truth, affective labels, physiology, smart phone, heart rate, galvanic skin response.

1 Introduction

Recording affect in the field allows for the capture of naturally occurring emotions, however, in order for such data to be truly useful it must be accurately labeled. In a laboratory setting it is easier to generate well labeled data sets: experience can be controlled, emotional responses can be primed, extensive recordings of events can be made and questionnaires can be used immediately following events to verify experience. In real life, emotions occur concurrently with other emotions and other "feelings" such as hunger, thirst, and pain. Emotions also occur during times when the participant is engaged in other physical and mental activities such as walking, talking or participating in a meeting. In her book on Affective Computing [3], Rosalind Picard describes the challenge of modeling emotion in the real world with a passage called "The Wheelchair Scenario" which describes how a person's overall disposition, general mood, immediate and gradually changing physical comfort all come into play in terms describing a person's emotional reactions to a series of events. This scenario is designed to illustrate many of the challenges of modeling emotion in real life, including the person's own successive time varying cognitive assessments of their own state, however, the book still has the advantage of a third person omniscient

S. D´Mello et al. (Eds.): ACII 2011, Part I, LNCS 6974, pp. 107–116, 2011.

perspective. In real experiments, we have do not have this absolute truth. Instead we must and rely on evidence such as the subject's own self report and whatever other evidence we can capture from sensors to get labels for these time-varying affective responses. This paper explores methods and metrics for obtaining high quality affective labels for emotional responses captured in the field. Our primary goal is to obtain the least ambiguous samples of emotion for training machine algorithms as well as collecting labels that are well understood by both the participants and the emotion research community.

We used smart phones to collect data because of their portability, widespread acceptance, journaling capabilities and their ability to serve as a hub for collecting sensor data. Smart phones allow users to make "in situ" ratings of emotional experience at any time, preferably as close to the emotional event as possible. They can also collect sensor data that can add to our understanding situation such as who the person is with and whether or not the person is moving, sitting standing, talking or participating in a meeting[1].

In addition to the "in situ" self-report ratings we also show the benefits of collecting retrospective labels from structured end of day interviews. Although it can be argued that retrospective assessments are subject to cognitive bias [11] and should be discredited, it could also be argued that in the moment annotations are also subject to a bias of passion, for example an irate person yelling "I'm not angry!" The fact is that the act of assigning a word label or quantity to an affective experience is an act of cognitive assessment, whether in situ or retrospective so in either case it could be argued that the "pure" affective experience is tainted. The advantage of the end of day assessment from a labeling perspective is that it allows a better relative comparison of affective events so that a daily ranking is possible. For example, in situ, a participant might rate several events on a scale as "7," extremely positive, however at the end of day, they might clearly articulate that one of these events was much more positive than the other two.

By collecting multiple sources of evidence, we can begin to triangulate affective ground truth to get the best possible labels for data collected in the field, in accordance with previously suggested guidelines for affective signal processing [4].

2 Related Work

There have been many attempts to capture accurate affective ground truth in the field. These have included pen and paper journaling [5] and more recently electronic journaling on PDAs and smart phones in conjunction with physiological and other types of sensors [1, 6, 7, 8, and 9]. In special situations such as driving, video has also been captured and used for evaluation by third party observers [10]. Previous work has also shown the challenges of recording affective ground truth, including: the variability of individual perception, the importance of cognitive assessment in the interpretation of emotion and the transformation of affective perceptions over time [1, 3, 11, 12, and 13]. Work in this area is still incomplete and as yet no unambiguous method of recording affective ground truth exists. The methods in this paper hope to contribute more empirical evidence toward finding the best way to annotate natural affective events in the field.

3 Background

The methods and metrics presented in this paper are improvements based on previous research in ambulatory affect monitoring [1]. The first improvements were changes in the metrics used for labeling emotion. In the first study, participants described their emotional experience in three ways: with emotion words, with free form text and by placing a mark in a two dimensional map of the arousal-valence space. Unfortunately, we found a wide variation of interpretation for both the emotion words and the arousal-valence space that made pooling the results problematic. A final analysis had to be made using an interpreted rating of each subject's results using human intermediaries to translate what each subject "meant" by their use of the emotion word. For the current study, we hoped to improve our process by using simplified rating system comprised of three seven point scales for describing each of the major axes of emotion proposed by Russell and Mehrabian [15]. Our hypothesis was that people outside the emotion research community would not have a preconceived understanding of these axes and that we could use a standardized training video to create a common understanding of these words across participants.

A second improvement was the introduction of the term "your normal" to describe the midpoint of the scale, "4". This method was introduced to address the problem of bias in the reported ratings. In the previous experiment, we found that ratings were skewed toward the "high energy" and "positive" corner of the arousal-valence space. We hypothesized several possible causes for this including: a misunderstanding of the arousal-valence space, a social masking towards wanting to be perceived as positive and high energy or a real self perception towards having a positive, high energy disposition. Some subjects reported that their rating was the sum both their current emotional reaction and their overall disposition, for example, one subject rated an episode that made them "angry" as "positive" because said they only felt angry temporarily and it was not so serious that it made them a negative person. We hypothesized that decoupling the axes and extensive training on the meaning of the axis labels would eliminate the first potential cause and that labeling "4" as "your normal" would allow the participants to self-normalize their real or masked "disposition bias" and rate only the deviation from "their normal" with the in situ rating score. To further eliminate bias, subjects encouraged to describe their disposition to the interviewer to help them feel "credited" for it, although this was not used in the analysis.

The third improvement was the triangulation of the in situ and end of day ratings. In the previous study, it was found that better quality labeled data sets were produced when the labels from two independent raters were combined and only the ratings where the two agreed were used. We hoped to replicate this result by triangulating two types of subject reported ratings: the "in situ" and "end of day" ratings from the structured interview. In this study, we combined these two ratings for all participants, for all data. Additionally, for three weeks of data we were able to have multiple independent raters assimilate data from these ratings in conjunction with text annotations, context data and end of week summaries. We show that these triangulated ratings generate higher performance using the same machine learning algorithm.

4 Study Design

The goal of the study was to collect naturally occurring physiological reactions to affective events in the field and to label these events as accurately as possible. The current study involved 13 participants (7 men and 6 women; ages 21-46 median age: 30) from a convenience sample of employees at a high tech company. Participants were recruited through e-mail and personal contacts. We asked people who were on heart or mood altering medications to exclude themselves from participation.

4.1 Study Protocol

The study involved seven days of affective journaling, the last five of which also included the participant wearing physiological sensors. The study began with a one hour training session on the affective journaling system, including thirty minutes of standardized videos describing the emotion axes and seven point scales. The first two days of the study were focused on the participants becoming familiar with the journaling process. Participants were asked to carry the smart phone throughout the day and annotate least ten emotion events per day. At the end of each day, participants met with interviewers to review their annotations. The interviewer then conducted a guided review of the participant's day and asked the participant to describe in detail the high and low emotional events of the day. During these sessions, the interviewer was available assess the participant's understanding of the emotion words and the seven point scales and answer any questions about the journaling system. On the morning of the third day, participants were given the physiological sensing system and activity monitoring systems to wear. The physiological monitoring system incorporated: a mobile phone journaling system, a wireless galvanic skin response sensor (GSR) and a wireless electrocardiogram (ECG) used for detecting heart rate and a physical activity monitoring system [1, 14]. Participants continued their emotion journaling and end-of-day interviews for an additional five days while wearing the sensing systems. Subjects were compensated up to $200 for their participation in the study which included nine hours of training and interviews, seven days of emotion journaling and five days of wearing and maintaining the physiological sensors. The $200 maximum compensation was pro-rated if the subject did not wear the sensors or complete the ten journal entries on a given day.

4.2 Journaling Training

The current study used a three axis emotion rating system based on Russell and Mehrabian's pleasure, arousal, and dominance axes [15], which were termed "pleasure," "activation" and "control." To create a common understanding of these axes across participants a series of short videos were created to describe each of the axes and to give an example of what a rating of "1" through "7" might mean on each of the axes. This was explained both for each of the axes individually and for each axis in conjunction with the other two. For example, to contrast control with respect to activation and valence, the following situations were described: going down a ski slope for an expert skier on a beautiful day under ideal conditions: high activation (7), positive valence (7), and high control (7). In contrast, riding a roller coaster for an enthusiast was described as: high activation (7), positive valence (7), and low control (1). Subjects were told these ratings applied for the personas described not necessarily how they would react to these situations. Subjects were further instructed to consider the "4" in the center of the rating system to be "their normal" and that ratings toward "1" or "7" should reflect deviations from their normal state, such as feeling more positive than normal, less activated than normal or more in control than normal. The goal of these instructions was to try to eliminate a baseline disposition bias by incorporating it into the "4" so that the rating would reflect only their perceived deviation from their normal or homeostatic state.

The rating guidance was followed by a walkthrough of how to use the journaling application on the mobile phone. This included explaining: how to click on the seven point scale for each of the emotion axes; how to record additional context information on the checklists including who they were with (pre-populated with a list of associates names' provided by the participant) and what they were doing (e.g. "in a meeting," "computer work," eating and talking) as well as how they were feeling physically (e.g. tired, sick, in pain, etc.) if these were relevant to their current state. The participants were also shown how to indicate on a timeline when they believe the emotion began and when it ended. This allowed participants to annotate emotional events that had occurred in the recent past at times when it was safe and appropriate for them to do so.

5 Analysis

To evaluate the new methods and metrics introduced in this study, two types of analysis were performed. The first analysis focused on the evaluating the in situ ratings for bias and skew. This was to confirm our hypothesis that a simplified rating system in conjunction with extensive journaling training would result in the reduction of reporting bias show a clear differentiation between the three axes of emotion.

The second analysis focused determining to what extent affective ground truth labels could be improved by triangulating different sources of evidence, in particular we performed analysis on the combination of "in situ" ratings and "end of day ratings" for high and low activation events. For this analysis we used 75 days of annotated physiological data from 11 subjects who recorded five days of data and 2 subjects who recorded ten days of data.

An extended analysis, incorporating text annotations, context information and end of week reviews, was performed on 15 days of data, five from one subject and ten from another. The data was assimilated by three independent raters who generated a seven-point activation score for each half hour of each day after reviewing all the available evidence.

5.1 Analysis of the Three Axis "In situ" Emotion Scores

The first analysis was designed to test for an improvement in the overall quality of the "in situ" ratings. In particular, we were hoping to find an elimination of bias in the rating metric and an increased independence of the three emotion axes.

5.1.1 Bias Analysis

To eliminate disposition bias, as part of the standardized training, we instructed the participants to rate as an emotional event a "4" if the event did not move them from "their normal." For example if an event was slightly positive, but had no other effect, participants were instructed rate the other two axes as "4" to reflect their normal (or homeostasis) even if they felt that they had a high activation, high control disposition. The analysis incorporated all seven days of ratings from the 11 subjects who participated for one week and the 12 days of ratings from the two subjects who collected the additional 5 days of physiological data for a grand total of weeks 812 rating annotations.

An analysis of the means of the scores along each of the three axes showed that bias was significantly reduced. For the 812 ratings, the mean scores were: 4.46 for the "Pleasure" axis; 4.21 for the "Activation" axis and 4.29 for the "Control" axis. These means are much closer to the unbiased mean of "4" than the means of the emotion words from our first experiment were to our expected values for them as shown in Figure 1. For example, in the first experiment "Calm" should have been close to the center and bottom, instead of being near the middle towards positive.

5.1.2 Axis Independence Analysis

We also performed a second analysis on the in situ ratings to determine the degree of independence of the axes. A high degree of independence would at least show that participants considered the axes differently and at best shed new insight into the actual degree of independence between these axes in the space of emotion. In a previous study using the International Affective Picture System (IAPS), a correlation was reported between the pleasure and arousal axes in that there were very few images that people found both "very negative" and "low arousal" [17]. However, this result may be reflective the fact that images and that it may be hard for an image to immediately create a "very negative, low arousal" event in the instant of looking at it. In our study of natural events we found many reports of "very negative, low arousal" events, but they were generally longer in duration (e.g. "boring meeting").

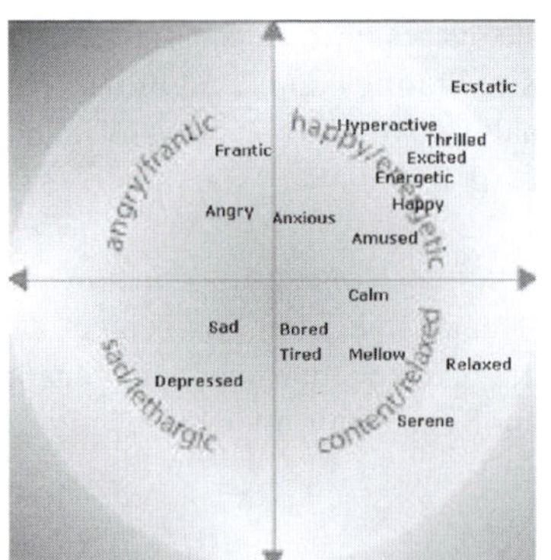

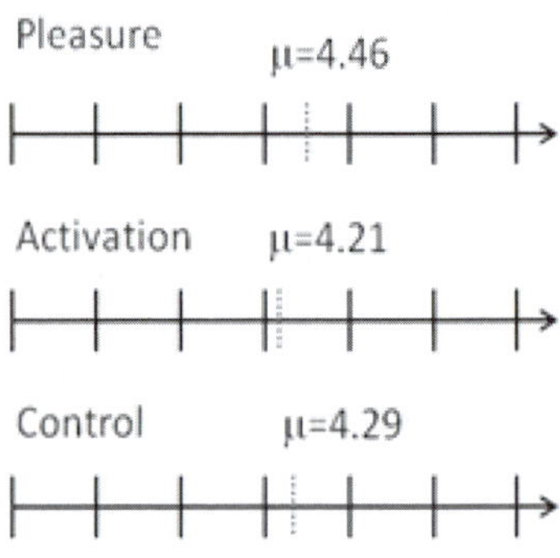

Fig 1. The emotion words from the previous experiment, placed at the location of their mean rating in the arousal valence space (left). The mean scores reflect a positive, high activation bias and a strong correlation of the two axes. A figure showing the mean score for the new rating system on a seven point scale (left) showing that the mean ratings were close to the desired mean of "4."

Using the same 812 subject ratings, we performed a correlation analysis for the three emotion axes. We found that the axes of "Activation" and "Control" were significantly correlated ($p<0.01$), but the "Pleasure" axis was not significantly correlated with either "Activation" ($p=0.15$) or "Control" ($p=.78$). On a per participant basis, 12 of 13 participants has a significant correlation ($p<0.05$) between "Activation" and "Control," 3 of 13 participants had a significant correlation between "Pleasure" and "Control" and 3 of 13 participants had a significant correlation between "Pleasure" and "Activation." The results of the analysis of the subject rating scores led to the conclusion that the emotion labels from this experiment were both less biased toward disposition and captured at least two independent axes of emotion.

5.2 Improving Ground Truth through Triangulation of "In situ" and "End of Day" Ratings

In our previous study we noted better performance of our machine learning algorithm when we selected only labeled segments in which both raters agreed on the quality of emotion experience [1]. In this analysis our goal was to determine if we could achieve a similar improvement by triangulating the "in situ" ratings with the ratings from the guided end of day interviews. In the end of day interviews it was often noted that some of the post hoc assessments did not agree with the "in situ" ratings. For example, one participant rated an event as a "2" on the in situ activation scale, but at the end of the day described this event as one of her highest activation periods. To find the most consistent set of affective labels, we eliminated in situ ratings where the end of day assessment conflicted with the in situ report. By using this kind of triangulation we are left with a more consistently labeled subset that can be used for training machine learning algorithms, resulting in higher recognition rates.

5.2.1 Modeling Physiology

For the time period indicated by the subject on the smart phone application, heart rate and galvanic skin response signals were extracted and the following features were calculated for both: mean (normalized both by beginning of period and by mean for the day), variance (normalized by variance for the day) and kurtosis. Additionally, a peak detector was applied to the GSR segment and features from maximum peak and valley were extracted as well as the orienting response frequency over the segment. These features were labeled with the "in situ" ratings from the subject.

5.2.2 "In situ" Only Rating Analysis

In the first analysis, we attempted to differentiate between low activation and high activation events. For this purpose the "in situ" ratings were binned into the following categories: "low" for ratings 1-3; neutral for "4;" and high for ratings "5-7." These bins were helped normalize the ratings scale since some participants tended to restrict their ratings to the range 3-5 whereas others chose to use 1, 4 and 7 for emotional events that seemed equivalent to the ones others had rater 3-5. Using the binned labels and the features from the associated data, we modeled a J48 decision tree classifier using the software package WEKA [18]. The result of classification using ten-fold cross-validation showed that using these features and labels, we could automatically recognize high and low activation states with 63% accuracy.

5.3 "In situ" and "End-of-Day" Combined Rating Analysis

The next analysis incorporated evidence from the end of day interviews to validate the in situ ratings. In the structured interviews, we asked the participants to report on the significant "high" and "low" activation events of the day. These periods were often more extended than those reported in the in situ ratings, for example entire half hours were remembered to be high arousal when the in situ ratings recorded only a five minute event, however these differences were not critical as we used the end of day results as a filter on the in situ ratings. We eliminated those samples where the in situ ratings conflicted with the end of day rating for the same period, for example if a period was rated "low activation" in situ but remembered as "high activation" the end of day it was excluded. The goal of this triangulation was to identify those experiences that were less ambiguous in their assessment, in the hope that these would provide the best training examples for our learning algorithm. Using the same physiological features and the same learning algorithm, the decision tree trained on the reduced set of combined labels achieved a recognition rate of 79% accuracy, an improvement over the 63% accuracy achieved before triangulation.

5.4 Extended Analysis: Assessing Evidence via Third Party Independent Raters

A substantial amount of additional context information was collected during the experiment. Since we have not yet developed an automatic process for extracting meaning from this data we used three independent human raters to assimilate evidence for 15 days worth of annotations with physiological data: five days from one subject and ten days from a second subject. The raters each scored every half hour period of each day using the same seven point activation scale that the participants used for the in situ ratings. They third parties considered all of the following when making their assessment: the in situ ratings; the entire end of day interview; text notes describing the context of the emotional experience; the activity of the participant (e.g. in a meeting, having lunch) and who the participant was with. The raters were allowed to use their own judgment in conjunction with this evidence to create the rating. The limitation of the data analyzed by this process was the length of time it took each rater to create this rating set.

For the analysis, the scores were binned into "low activation" (1-3), "neutral" (4), and "high activation" (5-7) for each half hour. The first triangulation was between the raters themselves. Only segments where at least 2 of the three raters agreed and where physiological data existed were kept. Using these labeled segments, a recognition rate of 67% was achieved on a balanced label set using one-third of the data for training using the J48 decision tree [18].

5.5 Extended Analysis: Combining Third Party and Subject Ratings

In a further extension of this analysis, the independent rater scores were triangulated with the end-of-day subject self report ratings. Only examples where the subjects in situ or end of day rating agreed with the majority rater agreement were kept. This resulted in insufficient data to model for the first participant, due to both missing physiological data and lower inter-rater agreement, however, for the second subject, fifty-four training examples were retained and used to train a J48 decision tree which was able to recognize high and low activation states with 100% accuracy using 10 fold cross validation[18].

6 Conclusions

These results indicate that triangulating multiple sources of affective ground truth information leads to a set of affective labels that correspond to more differentiated physiological features, as shown by the increase in recognition rates. In the quest to develop computers that can better automatically recognize human affect, it may be that we need to train our learning algorithms with natural affective examples that are validated by a triangulation of affective evidence. As more and more sensors become available on computers such as smart phones that we carry with us every day, the easier it will become to collect large databases of affective examples with multiple sources of evidence to help us reach the goal of developing individualized affective computing.

References

1. Healey, J., Nachman, L., Subramanian, S., Shahabdeen, J., Morris, M.E.: Out of the Lab and into the Fray: Towards Modeling Emotion in Everyday Life. In: Floréen, P., Krüger, A., Spasojevic, M. (eds.) Pervasive Computing. LNCS, vol. 6030, pp. 156–173. Springer, Heidelberg (2010)
2. Shimmer sensing platform, `http://shimmer-research.com/wordpress/?page_id=20`
3. Picard, R.: Affective Computing. MIT Press, Cambridge (1997)
4. van den Broek, E., Janssen, J.H., Westerink, J.H.D.M.: Guidelines for Affective Signal Processing (ASP): From Lab to Life. In: Proceedings of the International Conference on Affective Computing and Intelligent Interaction, September 10-12, vol. 1, pp. 217–222. IEEE, Los Alamitos (2009)
5. Oatley, K., Duncan, E.: The Experience of Emotion in Everyday Life: Cognition & Emotion, vol. 8(4), pp. 369–381. Psychology Press, San Diego (1994)
6. Morris, M., Guilak, F.: Mobile Heart Health: Project Highlights. IEEE Pervasive Computing 8(2), 57–61 (2009)
7. Fahrenberg, J., Myrtek, M. (eds.): Progress in Ambulatory Assessment. Hogrefe and Huber Publishers (2001)
8. Hofmann, S.G., Barlow, D.H.: Ambulatory psychophysiological monitoring: A potentially useful tool when treating panic relapse. Cognitive and Behavioral Practice 3(1), 53–61 (1996)
9. Westerink, J., Ouwerkerk, M., de Vries, G., de Waele, S., van den Eerenbeemd, J., van Boven, M.: Emotion measurement platform for daily life situations. In: Proceedings of the International Conference on Affective Computing and Intelligent Interaction, September 10-12, vol. 1, pp. 704–708. IEEE, Los Alamitos (2009)
10. Healey, J.A., Picard, R.W.: Detecting stress during real-world driving tasks using physiological sensors. IEEE Transactions on Intelligent Transportation Systems 6(2), 156–166 (2005)
11. Laird, J.D., Bresler, C.: The Process of Emotional Feeling: A Self-Perception theory. In: Clark, M. (ed.) Emotion: Review of Personality and Social Psychology, vol. 13, pp. 223–234 (1992)

12. Cooper, D.G., Arroyo, I., Park Woolf, B., Muldner, K., Burleson, W., Christopherson, R.: Sensors Model Student Self Concept in the Classroom. In: Proceedings 17th Intl. Conference on User Modeling Adaptation and Personalization and Trento, Italy, June 22-26, pp. 30–41 (2009)
13. Carroll, J.M., Russell, J.A.: Do facial expressions signal specific emotions? Judging emotion from the face in context. Journal of Personality and Social Psychology 70, 205–218 (1996)
14. Choudhury, T., Consolvo, S., Harrison, B., Hightower, J., LaMarca, A., LeGrand, L., Rahimi, A., Rea, A., Bordello, G., Hemingway, B., Klasnja, P., Koscher, K., Landay, J.A., Lester, J., Wyatt, D., Haehnel, D.: The Mobile Sensing Platform: An Embedded Activity Recognition System. IEEE Pervasive Computing 7(2), 32–41 (2008)
15. Russell, J.A., Mehrabian, A.: Evidence for a three-factor theory of emotions. Journal of Research in Personality 11, 273–294 (1977)
16. Morris, M.: Technologies for Heart and Mind: New Directions in Embedded Assesssment. Intel Technology Journal 11(1) (2007)
17. Lang, P.J., Greenwald, M.K., Bradley, M.M., Hamm, A.O.: Looking at pictures: affective, facial, visceral and behavioral reactions. Psychophysiology 20(3), 261–273 (1993)
18. Witten, I.H., Frank, E.: Data Mining: Practical Machine Learning Tools and Techniques with Java Implementations. Morgan Kaufmann, San Francisco (1999)

Using Individual Light Rigs to Control the Perception of a Virtual Character's Personality

Alexis Heloir[1], Kerstin H. Kipp[2], and Michael Kipp[1]

[1] DFKI, Embodied Agents Research Group, Germany
[2] Saarland University, Experimental Neuropsychology Unit, Germany
k.kipp@mx.uni-saarland.de

Abstract. We investigate how lighting can be used to influence how the personality of virtual characters is perceived. We propose a character-centric lighting system composed of three dynamic lights that can be configured using an interactive editor. To study the effect of character-centric lighting on observers, we created four lighting configurations derived from the photography and film literature. A user study with 32 subjects shows that the lighting setups do influence the perception of the characters' personality. We found lighting effects with regard to the perception of dominance. Moreover, we found that the personality perception of female characters seems to change more easily than for male characters.

Keywords: lighting, perception of personality, virtual characters.

1 Introduction

In order to be perceived as natural and engaging, virtual characters must convey affective and individual qualities such as personality, mood and emotional state. The expression of such attributes has traditionally been realized using bodily modalities: overall motion [1], gesture [2, 8, 11, 9], facial expression [3] or verbal content and prosody [11, 16]. However, a character's affective state and personality can also be expressed through environmental aspects like lighting, as is evident in paintings and movies. As a step towards a principled approach to exploiting the modality of lighting, we propose an interactive system for creating character-centric *lighting setups* (that we also call *light rigs*), and evaluate how this system influences the perception of a lit character's personality.

So far, little work has been done on studying how the environment could influence the perception of a virtual character's affective state and personality. Expressive environmental modalities that have been used include sound, camera position, on-surface textures, on-screen filters and lighting [6, 12, 5]. In painting and in the game industry, lighting is often used to emphasize a character's mood and emotion, guide visual interest and suggest a character's intentions. In these disciplines, successful lighting often violates the laws dictated by physically accurate illumination: for instance, a painter or a digital lighting artist might want to use an invisible spotlight which illuminates only one of many characters in order, for instance, to emphasize her status difference. If the lighting is successful, most viewers will recognize the artist's intention without being

S. D´Mello et al. (Eds.): ACII 2011, Part I, LNCS 6974, pp. 117–124, 2011.

irritated by the lighting inconsistencies: only experts will see that an added, invisible light source has been used. Designing a system that supports the creation of such effects in an interactive environment implies three research questions:

- **Effect:** Do specific lighting configurations cause a particular perception effect on characters? For instance, does bright lighting makes a character to be perceived as more agreeable?
- **Control:** What system allows us rigging up each character in a 3D scene with its own lighting setup? Lighting should remain constant with respect to the individual character, independent of the character's movement.
- **Acceptance:** Although reaching a desired effect may violate the physical rules of light, the lit characters should still integrate in an acceptable way within the environment. When does unnatural lighting become too obvious and irritating?

In this paper, we address the first two research questions by proposing a prototype of an individual lighting system (light rig) where a set of dynamic lights anchored to a character are created and used as a genuine expressive modality. We also validate our model by assessing a set of lighting setups commonly used in film and photography in a user study that shows how our lighting setups influence the perception of the characters personality.

2 Related Work

Only few research projects have addressed the problem of controlling the perception of a character's affective state and personality through the environment. These projects used modalities such as camera angle, pictograms and lighting. In the following, we provide a brief description of existing work.

Cameras, Image Mapping and Pictograms

Camera angle plays a crucial role in the building of the film language, and several projects have been dedicated to automated cinematography [4]. In psychology, studies have shown that camera angle has a significant influence on how juries assess a person's honesty in the context of criminal confessions [15]. The direct display of information about an agent's affect has been achieved using texture mapping on the character's mesh: for instance, Neviarouskaya et al. use heart-shaped pictogram textures to express the emotional state of SecondLife characters [12]. On-screen displays like text bubbles or floating billboards have been used to display speech, thoughts, or emotional state. Screen-space filters have also been used by de Melo et al. [5] to enhance rendering expressiveness in real time, for instance by manipulating picture light and contrast of the rendered output. In this work, we chose to focus solely on how lighting can be used to influence the perception of a virtual character's personality.

Lighting

Lighting has been used by de Melo et al. [6] as a genuine expressivity channel together with music and pictograms for expressing emotion and personality in a storytelling context. An empirical study showed that illumination had an influence on perceived emotion. However, this study did not focus on virtual humans but on dancing solids.

In follow-up work, de Melo et al. [5] use a more elaborated model combining lighting and screen-space filtering. An evolutionary model infers from user feedback the mapping between its parameterization and emotion categories defined in the OCC model of emotions [14]. However, because the lighting parameterizations obtained with this model are the result of a semi-automated evolutionary process that does not account for aesthetic principles, they can hardly be transferred to other applications. In our approach, the creation of lighting setups is theory-driven: our lighting configurations are derived from the lighting techniques commonly used in photography, film and gaming industry [10]. El-Nasr [7] presented the Expressive Lighting Engine (ELE), a dynamic lighting system that can be interfaced with modern video games and that is capable of adjusting scene lighting in real time to achieve aesthetic and communicative functions, including evoking emotions, directing visual focus, and providing visibility and depth. In this work, we focus on the perceived personality of the lit characters. Application designers who are dealing with virtual characters can therefore use the results of our studies as guidelines.

3 Individual Lighting Rigs

In our implementation, we use three dynamic lights per character. Lights are defined as directional lights, parameterized using a single direction vector defined according to the character's local frame of reference. Lights also cast shadows: they are bound to a shadowcaster shader that influences all the lit objects having a shadow generator shader enabled.

The design process for lighting can hardly be formalized; it is a manual process that requires a tight visual feedback loop. In order to help the designer crafting a successful lighting setup, we implemented an interactive editor, shown in Fig. 2. The editor provides interactive controls for every parameter of all the lights involved in the setup. The parameters are orientation, intensity, color and shadow hardness. Although such a tool can potentially generate an infinite set of lighting setups, we focused our empirical investigation on a few specific ones that are described in the next section.

4 Our Approach towards Lighting

In this study, we chose to evaluate the influence of four lighting setups defined by the position and intensity of their involved lights. These lighting configurations are taken from the film and photography literature [10] and are illustrated in Fig. 1.

A common general lighting technique in portrait photography, film and interactive drama is *three-point lighting*. In three-point lighting, there is the *key light*, the main source of light, the *fill light*, a low-intensity light filling the area on the character that otherwise would be too dark and the *back light*, separating the character from background by creating a light rim that crisply defines its edge. We used the following four specific three-point setups for our empirical investigation:

Broad Lighting (a): This lighting illuminates the larger portion of the face of a character. In this lighting, the area of the face that is highlighted must be larger than the area in shadow. We consider this lighting the default lighting.

Rembrandt Lighting (b): The general idea is to create a small upside-down triangle on the opposite side of the lit cheek on the subject's face. To create this pattern, it is necessary to move the main light source to the side and somewhat above eye level, casting a triangle of light on the subject's opposite cheek.

Butterfly Lighting (c): This lighting is also known as "glamour lighting" using a high frontal main and fill light, almost in imitation of a strong summer sun. The name butterfly comes from the distinctive butterfly-shaped shadow that appears beneath the nose and extends someway down the lips of the model.

From-Below Lighting (d): In this lighting setup, a light is placed below the shoulder level of the subject. This lighting casts strong shadows, giving the scene a dramatic tone.

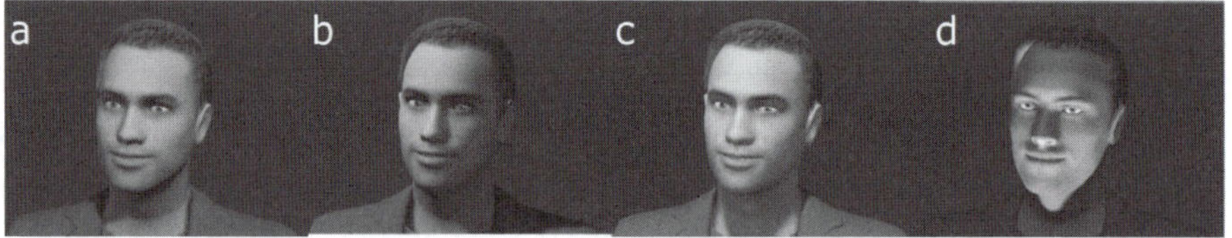

Fig. 1. Broadlighting(a), Rembrandt (b), butterfly (c), from below (d): the four lighting setups that we edited using our interactive authoring tool

5 User Study

To exploit individual lighting rigs effectively, one needs to know the precise effect that a particular lighting configuration, as described in Section 4, has in terms of personality perception. In a first user study, we aimed at identifying effects for a *single* agent.

5.1 Materials and Method

The experiment was conducted as an online questionnaire (in German) where selected participants were explicitly invited. The 36 participants were fluent German speakers, aged 25 to 68.

Ideally, the influence of the lighting rig system should be independent from the intrinsic characteristics of the lit characters: a gloomy lighting should evoke sadness for both a male and a female character. However, it has been shown that parameters like facial morphology [13] can significantly influence the perception of a character's personality. In order to assess how robust the lighting rig was against attributes like facial morphology or gender, we designed four declinations of a virtual agent by modulating two parameters, gender (male and female) and facial morphology (masculine and feminine). The resulting agents are shown in Fig. 2.

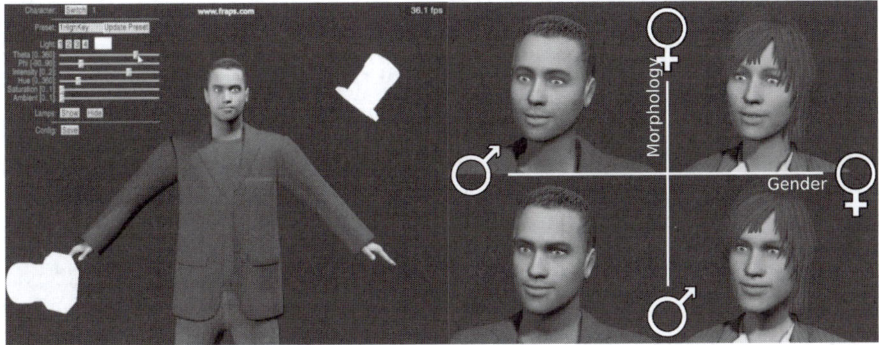

Fig. 2. (a) Our interactive authoring tool, (b) the four characters used in the study: Results show that morphology does not influence the perception of a character's personality whereas gender does

We used four different agents, all derived from two facial morphologies (A and B), rendered in two genders each (M and F): AM, AF, BM, BF. Each resulting character was lit with one of the four light setups described in Section 4: broad (BD), rembrandt (RT), from-below (FB) and butterfly (BF).

The test consisted of showing 16 screenshots of one of the four agents in one of the four light setups. We assessed personality perception by asking the subject to enter judgments along four dimensions D1 to D4. Each rating was done on a 7-point differential scale from -3 to +3. For the four dimensions we relied on research by Wiggins [17]. Every dimension had two opposing poles, specified as follows:

Table 1. The four dimensions used in the study and their corresponding adjectives

label	*left pole (-3)*	*right pole (+3)*
D1	cold, impolite	warm, polite
D2	arrogant, calculating	modest, guileless
D3	dominant, self-disciplined	timid, disorganized
D4	companionable, jovial	distant, shy

The rating scheme is based on work by Oosterhof et al. and Wiggins. Oosterhof et al. [13] showed that two orthogonal dimensions, valence and dominance are sufficient to categorize and describe face evaluation and that these dimensions can be approximated by judgments of trustworthiness and dominance. Wiggins [17] proposed a more comprehensive taxonomy of trait-descriptive terms in English: eight adjectival scales were developed as markers of the principal vectors of the interpersonal domain. We reduced the dimensions to four by collapsing two neighboring/similar dimensions to one.

5.2 Results

We analyzed 32 of the 36 participants. We took out 4 participants whose answers were almost always neutral. Our formal rejection criterion was a standard deviation < 1 across all replies (where 0 was the neutral reply).

To avoid an abundance of tests we declared the "broad" lighting condition the default lighting and compared the other three against it, to see if a difference emerged in these three pairings (BD-RT, BD-FB, BD-BF). For every pair we computed four ANOVAs, one for each question dimension, with the three factors face, gender and lighting (we also report mean value M). For brevity, we only report significant findings.

First of all, we found an effect for factor face in all tests. This was expected, as different facial appearances are interpreted differently in terms of personality, so we do not report these results in detail.

Rembrandt (BD-RT): We found effects for light and gender in the the BD-RT comparison. RT lighting makes the agent appear significantly more dominant/self-disciplined (dimension D3; M = -0.80) compared to BD (M = -0.25; F(1,31)=10.30, p<.01), independent of face and gender. RT also makes the agent to be perceived as more companiable/jovial, i.e. less distant/shy, (dimension D4; M = -0.54) compared to BD (M = -0.09; F(1,31)=8.21, p<.01). We found an additional gender effect: the male agent is perceived as more arrogant (dimension D2; M = -0.64; F(1,31)=10.87, p<.01) than the female one (M = 0.01). He was also found more dominant (dimension D3; M = -0.80) than the female agent (M = -0.25; F(1,31)=10.39, p<.01).

Butterfly (BD-BF): We found the same two gender effects as in DB-RT, also for dimensions D2 and D3. The male agent was judged more arrogant (M = -0.56; F(1,31)=14.29, p<.01) than the female one (M = 0.07). He was also found more dominant (M= -0.59; F(1,31)=5.37, p<.05) compared to the female version (M = -0.11), all independent of light and face.

From-Below (BD-FB): Here, we found a light-gender interaction for dimensions D2 (F(1,31)=8.30, p<.01) and D3 (F(1,31)=5.55, p<.05), the latter is shown in Fig. 3. Under From-Below lighting, a female agent was perceived more modest (D2; M = -0.67) and more timid (D3: M = -0.75) compared to BD (D2: M = 0.14; D3: M = 0.00). In contrast, the male agent was hardly affected by the change of lighting from BD (D2: M = -0.52; D3: M = -0.50) to FB (D2: M = -0.42; D 3: M = -0.45). A post-hoc analysis, using a Fisher LSD test, confirmed that changing lighting setup makes a significant difference for the female agent (D2: p < 0.05; D3: p < 0.05) but not for the male agent (D2: p = 0.77; D3: p = 0.90).

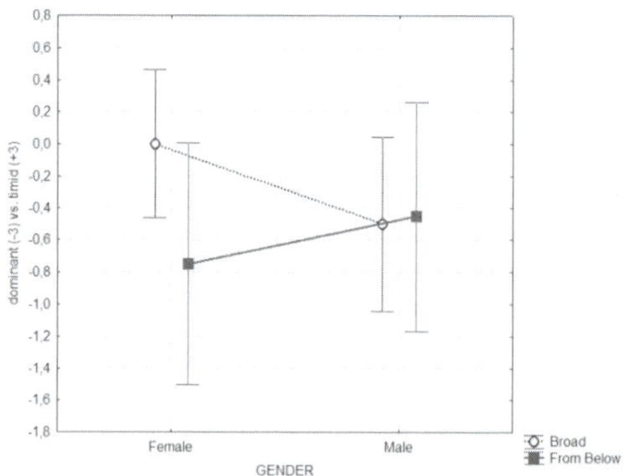

Fig. 3. The female agent is rated differently under BD vs. FB lighting, whereas the male agent is rated equally (dimension D3 for dominant vs. timid)

6 Discussion and Conclusion

The study showed that one lighting setup exhibited a significant effect for all characters, male and female: Rembrandt lighting (RT). Under RT lighting, agents are perceived as more *dominant and jovial* (D3 &D4). Only male characters were perceived as more arrogant under Butterfly lighting (BT), independent of facial morphology. In contrast, female characters lit with From-Below lighting (FB) were perceived as more modest and timid (D3), again, disregarding facial morphology.

More importantly, our results show that female characters are more susceptible to light changes in terms of personality perception. When comparing From-Below with the default lighting (Broad), we found that only the female agent was perceived differently, although both agents share facial morphologies. The fact that the effect of some lighting setups depends on the lit character's gender but not on its facial morphology may be explained by gender stereotypes almost universally observed: male subjects are commonly perceived as more dominant than female subjects. Even though we showed that lighting has indeed an effect on how the personality of virtual characters is perceived, none of the lighting configuration we assessed influenced the perception in the opposite direction of the commonly known stereotypes (e.g. male agent perceived as more modest and timid).

To sum up, we proposed a system for authoring character centric lighting rigs dedicated to modify the perception of a character's personality. This system is built upon a set of dynamic parameterizable lights anchored to an individual virtual character that can be modified with an interactive editor.

This system has been evaluated in a user study with 32 subjects. In this study, we assessed four lighting setups taken from the photography literature that we set up using our interactive editor. In order to rate the robustness of our model towards gender and morphology, we compared the effect of lighting on four different agents, derived from two facial models and two genders each.

We believe the system we proposed and the guidelines we derived from the empirical study could be used in interactive drama to make lighting a genuine expressive modality supporting the story. In future work, we plan to investigate how our system performs in dyadic configurations, for instance when agents are acting in a status game. We will also investigate how our system can be integrated into more complex environments. Most importantly, we have to empirically assess how much variety observers can tolerate while interacting with agents that are lit using different lighting setups, and at which point observers will be irritated by inconsistent lighting.

Acknowledgements. This research has been carried out within the framework of the Excellence Cluster *Multimodal Computing and Interaction* (MMCI) at Saarland University, funded by the German Research Foundation (DFG).

References

[1] Amaya, K., Bruderlin, A., Calvert, T.: Emotion from motion. In: Davis, W.A., Bartels, R. (eds.) Graphics Interface 1996, pp. 222–229. Canadian Human-Computer Communications Society (1996)

[2] Chi, D.M., Costa, M., Zhao, L., Badler, N.I.: Emote. In: Akeley, K. (ed.) Siggraph 2000, Computer Graphics Proceedings, pp. 173–182. ACM Press/ACM SIGGRAPH/Addison Wesley Longman (2000)
[3] Courgeon, M., Buisine, S., Martin, J.-C.: Impact of expressive wrinkles on perception of a virtual character's facial expressions of emotions. In: Ruttkay, Z., Kipp, M., Nijholt, A., Vilhjálmsson, H.H. (eds.) IVA 2009. LNCS, vol. 5773, pp. 201–214. Springer, Heidelberg (2009)
[4] Courty, N., Lamarche, F., Donikian, S., Marchand, É.: A cinematography system for virtual storytelling. In: Balet, O., Subsol, G., Torguet, P. (eds.) ICVS 2003. LNCS, vol. 2897, pp. 30–34. Springer, Heidelberg (2003)
[5] de Melo, C., Gratch, J.: Evolving expression of emotions in virtual humans using lights and pixels. In: Prendinger, H., Lester, J.C., Ishizuka, M. (eds.) IVA 2008. LNCS (LNAI), vol. 5208, pp. 484–485. Springer, Heidelberg (2008)
[6] de Melo, C., Paiva, A.: Environment expression: Telling stories through cameras, lights and music. In: Subsol, G. (ed.) ICVS-VirtStory 2005. LNCS, vol. 3805, pp. 129–132. Springer, Heidelberg (2005)
[7] Seif El-Nasr, M.: Intelligent lighting for game environments. Journal of Game Development 1(2), 17 (2005)
[8] Hartmann, B., Mancini, M., Pelachaud, C.: Implementing expressive gesture synthesis for embodied conversational agents. In: Gibet, S., Courty, N., Kamp, J.-F. (eds.) GW 2005. LNCS (LNAI), vol. 3881, pp. 188–199. Springer, Heidelberg (2006)
[9] Heloir, A., Kipp, M.: Realtime animation of interactive agents: Specification and realization. Applied Artificial Intelligence 24(6), 510–529 (2010)
[10] Millerson, G.: Lighting for Television and Film. Focal Press, Oxford (1999)
[11] Neff, M., Wang, Y., Abbott, R., Walker, M.: Evaluating the effect of gesture and language on personality perception in conversational agents. In: Allbeck, J., et al. (eds.) IVA 2010. LNCS, vol. 6356, pp. 222–235. Springer, Heidelberg (2010)
[12] Neviarouskaya, A., Prendinger, H., Ishizuka, M.: Emoheart: Conveying emotions in second life based on affect sensing from text. In: Advances in Human-Computer Interaction. Springer, Heidelberg (2010)
[13] Oosterhof, N., Todorov, A.: The functional basis of face evaluation. Proc. of the National Academy of Sciences of the United States of America (2008)
[14] Ortony, A., Clore, G., Collins, A.: The Cognitive Structure of Emotions. Cambridge University Press, Cambridge (1988)
[15] Ratcliff, J.J., Lassiter, G.D., Schmidt, H.C., Snyder, C.L.: Camera perspective bias in videotaped confessions: experimental evidence of its perceptual basis. Journal of Experimental Psychology: Applied 12, 197–206 (2006)
[16] Schröder, M.: Expressive speech synthesis: Past, present, and possible futures, affective information processing. In: Tao, J., Tan, T. (eds.) Affective Information Processing, pp. 111–126. Springer, Heidelberg (2009)
[17] Wiggins, J.S.: A psychological taxonomy of trait-descriptive terms: The interpersonal domain. Journal of Personality and Social Psychology 37, 395–412 (1979)

Call Center Stress Recognition with Person-Specific Models

Javier Hernandez, Rob R. Morris, and Rosalind W. Picard

Media Lab, Massachussets Institute of Technology, Cambridge, USA
{javierhr,rmorris,picard}@media.mit.edu

Abstract. Nine call center employees wore a skin conductance sensor on the wrist for a week at work and reported stress levels of each call. Although everyone had the same job profile, we found large differences in how individuals reported stress levels, with similarity from day to day within the same participant, but large differences across the participants. We examined two ways to address the individual differences to automatically recognize classes of stressful/non-stressful calls, namely modifying the loss function of Support Vector Machines (SVMs) to adapt to the varying priors, and giving more importance to training samples from the most similar people in terms of their skin conductance lability. We tested the methods on 1500 calls and achieved an accuracy across participants of 78.03% when trained and tested on different days from the same person, and of 73.41% when trained and tested on different people using the proposed adaptations to SVMs.

Keywords: Stress recognition, skin conductance, interpersonal variability, Support Vector Machines, Affective Computing.

1 Introduction

Chronic psychological stress carries a wide array of pathophysiological risks, including cardiovascular disease, cerebrovascular disease, diabetes, and immune deficiencies [8]. An important step in managing stress, before it becomes chronic, is recognizing precisely when and where it occurs. Technologies that automatically recognize stress can be extremely powerful, both diagnostically and therapeutically. As a diagnostic tool, technologies such as these could help individuals and clinicians gain insight into the conditions that consistently provoke maladaptive stress responses. As a therapeutic tool, these technologies could be used to automatically initiate stress-reduction interventions. In stressful work settings, such as a call center, these technologies could not only lead to more timely and reduced-cost interventions, but also to more productive environments where employees could better manage their workload, so that they could provide a better experience for customers.

While research on automated stress recognition has taken many different forms, the systems that have been proposed in the engineering literature typically contain two principle components: 1) a sensor-based architecture that records

S. D'Mello et al. (Eds.): ACII 2011, Part I, LNCS 6974, pp. 125–134, 2011.

relevant features and 2) a software-based system that makes predictions about an individual's current stress level. The sensing modalities can take many forms, including audio and visual modalities, but biosensors provide the most direct access into the physiological changes that accompany stress-induced changes [3].

While great strides have been made in real-life biosensing [13], the computational task of inferring stress levels from biosensor data is still a considerable challenge. There is often great variability in how people experience stress [10] and how they express it physiologically [11], and this interpersonal variability can stymie efforts to build a one-size-fits all stress recognition system. This work explores using data from each individual to help manage the problem of interpersonal variability. In particular, we modify the loss function of SVMs to encode a person's tendency to report stressful events, and give more importance to the training samples of the most similar participants. These changes were validated in a case study where skin conductance (SC) was monitored in nine call center employees during a one-week period of their regular work.

This paper is organized as follows. Section 2 reviews previous studies on the subject of this work. Section 3 provides details about the data collection. Section 4 presents the problem of interpersonal variability and proposes two complementary methods to address it. Section 5 explains the data preprocessing and experimental protocols. Section 6 provides results and analysis.

2 Background and Previous Work

2.1 Physiological Stress and Skin Conductance

Stress-induced changes can be monitored with biosensors, and a particular focus is often placed on the sympathetic nervous system, which is designed to mobilize the body's resources in response to a challenge or a threat. While most visceral organs are dually innervated by both the para- and sympathetic nervous systems, the eccrine sweat glands are thought to be solely controlled by the sympathetic nervous system [3]. Thus, skin conductance sensors that measure eccrine sweat gland activity are often used to monitor sympathetic nervous system activity.

A century of short-term lab measurements have shown that SC is subject to inter-person variability, with differences in age, gender, ethnicity, and hormonal cycles contributing to individual differences [3]. Furthermore, many researchers suggest that stable personality differences may contribute to differences in skin conductance lability - a psychophysiological trait characterized by high SC responsivity and slow habituation [12]. As early as 1950, researchers have seen links between SC lability and such personality characteristics as emotional expressiveness, and antagonism [5]. Moreover, individuals defined as SC labiles have been seen to show greater myocardial reactivity in response to stress [9]. When developing stress recognition algorithms that incorporate measures of SC, interpersonal sources of variance should be considered.

2.2 Automatic Stress Recognition

Several automatic stress recognition techniques have been explored in the research literature. In most cases, data are collected in the laboratory where variables that introduce noise are controlled or eliminated.

Researchers have explored a variety of classification methods, and techniques to reduce interpersonal variability. Barreto, Zhai and Adjouadi [1], for example, used SVMs to discriminate between stressful and non stressful responses in a laboratory setting. The SVMs outperformed other classification algorithms, obtaining an accuracy of 90.1%. Various physiological signals were used in the classification, including SC, blood volume pulse, pupil diameter (PD) and skin temperature (ST). To account for participant variability, they divided extracted features from each participant with their corresponding baseline features. In a separate study, Setz et. al. [14] used SC to automatically distinguish between cognitive load and psychosocial stress. In this case, Linear Discriminant Analysis (LDA) obtained 82.8% accuracy, outperforming SVMs. Setz et al. found that the average number of SC peaks, as well as their height distributions, were the most relevant features to the problem. To account for participant variability, distributions were computed for each participant independently. In another study, Shi et al. [15] discriminated between stressful and non-stressful responses under social, cognitive and physical stressors. They obtained 68% precision and 80% recall using SVMs with SC, electrocardiogram (ECG), respiration (R) and ST. The problem of participant variability was addressed by subtracting a person-specific parameter to the features of each participant. This parameter was estimated as the average feature of all-non-stressful events of the participant.

In an effort to automatically recognize stress in a real-life setting, Healey and Picard [6] monitored ECG, electromyogram, SC and R from people during a driving task. They used LDA to automatically discriminate between low (at rest), medium (city) and high (highways) levels of stress with 97% accuracy. In this case, the signals from each participant were normalized between zero and one, as proposed by [11].

All of these studies, except for Setz et. al. [14], used a combination of physiological signals, an approach that typically improves recognition accuracy. Nevertheless, some of the signals, such as PD and ECG, may not be easily recorded in real-life settings where comfortable and inconspicuous sensors are required to preserve natural behavior.

3 Study Design

Location and Participants. The study was conducted at a call center in Rhode Island, and was approved by the Institutional Review Board at the Massachusetts Institute of Technology. Nine call center employees (five females and four males) agreed to participate in the study. The employees all had the same job description and they all handled the same types of calls.

Throughout the course of one week, and only during work hours, participants wore a wristband biosensor and made self-report ratings at the end of each call they received. Besides those two, minimally invasive conditions, the participants went about their work as usual. Their day is primarily spent on the phone, and they handle high volumes of calls, many of which come from angry and frustrated customers.

Data Collection. Three sources of data were collected in this study: SC, self-report measures, and worker call logs. SC was collected at a sampling rate of 8 Hz, similar to [10] and [15], and was recorded from dry Ag-AgCl 1cm diameter electrodes on the wrist, using an early beta version of the Affectiva[1] Q^{TM}Sensor, a commercial sensor based on [13].

Throughout the study, participants were also asked to rate each call they received in terms of stress. Specifically, they were asked "How was the last call?" using a 7 point likert scale, with the endpoints labeled as "extremely good" indicating non-stressful and "extremely bad" indicating very stressful. While this question may not capture other types of stressors, it allowed for quick (1-2 seconds) and non-disruptive self-report ratings. The call center also provided break times and detailed call logs for each participant containing the start-time, end-time, and duration of every call our participants received.

A total of 1500 calls were included in our study, averaging 4.51 minutes in length. Calls that had missing stress ratings, or corrupted SC (due to beta hardware problems or motion artifacts), were excluded. Fig. 1 shows a one day example of collected raw data.

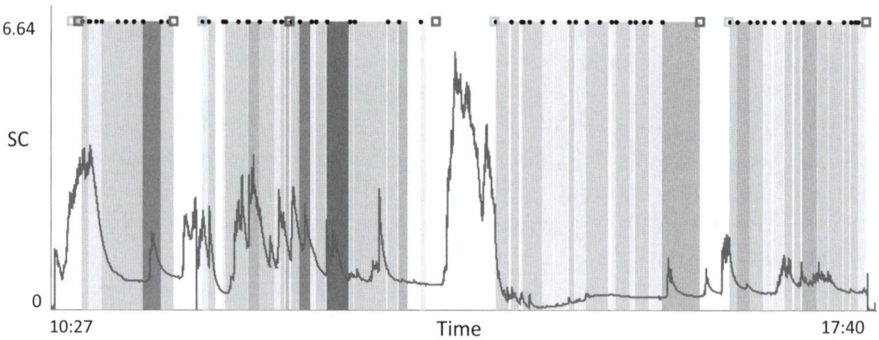

Fig. 1. Example of data from one participant that contain calls (*dots*), stress ratings (*darker areas* represent more stressful calls), and break times (*squares*)

4 Proposed Method

Throughout this paper, we shall focus on the problem of supervised classification. Let $\{(\mathbf{x}_i, y_i)\}_{i=1}^{n}$ be an i.i.d. training set, where $\mathbf{x}_i$ represents the feature vector of the sample i, and y_i its class label, where $y_i = \{-1, 1\}$. Let the class priors of this set be $P_+ = \frac{\#y=1}{n} = \frac{n_+}{n}$ and $P_- = \frac{n_-}{n}$. Similarly, we define the testing set as $\{(\overline{\mathbf{x}_i}, \overline{y_i})\}_{i=1}^{\overline{n}}$, and its priors $\overline{P_+}$, and $\overline{P_-}$.

[1] http://www.affectiva.com

We consider the problem where training data comes from the observation of a set of participants, and the testing data belongs to a new participant. This methodology introduces the common problem of participant variability, which usually violates the i.i.d. assumption and leads to an overall decrease in performance. To address the participant variability problem, we propose incorporating information of the testing participant into the loss function of SVMs.

Support Vector Machines [2] are considered state-of-the-art supervised classification algorithms, and their main goal is to find the hyperplane $\mathbf{w}$ that maximizes the margin between data samples belonging to two classes (e.g., stressful vs non-stressful responses). The standard formulation of SVMs is as follows:

$$\min_{\mathbf{w}} \quad \underbrace{\frac{1}{2}\|\mathbf{w}\|^2}_{regularization} \quad + \underbrace{\frac{C}{n}\left(\sum_{i \in \{y=+1\}}^{n_+} \xi_i + \sum_{j \in \{y=-1\}}^{n_-} \xi_j \right)}_{loss\ function} , \tag{1}$$

$$s.t. \;\; y_i(\mathbf{w}^T \mathbf{x}_i) \geq 1 - \xi_i \quad and \quad \xi_i \geq 0, \quad i = 1, 2, \dots n \tag{2}$$

where C is the misclassification cost, and ξ_i is the slack variable for the sample $\mathbf{x}_i$. For any new sample $\overline{\mathbf{x}}$, prediction is performed through $\overline{y} = \mathbf{w}^T \overline{\mathbf{x}}$.

4.1 Changing Class Priors

In the context of stress recognition, class priors indicate the probability to report stressful events. In equation 1, priors of the training data are directly integrated into the loss function, and will condition the predictions of the classifier. Since different people may report more or less stressful events, we propose modifying SVMs' loss function to encode the class priors of the testing participant.

A standard method to modify the class priors is the introduction of class weights (S_+ and S_-) for each type of misclassification error such as:

$$loss\ function \;=\frac{C}{n}\left(\sum_{i \in \{y=+1\}}^{n_+} S_+\xi_i + \sum_{j \in \{y=-1\}}^{n_-} S_-\xi_j \right) . \tag{3}$$

If $\frac{S_+}{S_-} = \frac{P_-}{P_+}$, the classifier will tend to equally predict positive and negative samples [7]. To predict with the same priors of the testing data, we propose to use $S_+ = \frac{\overline{P_+}}{P_+}$, and $S_- = \frac{\overline{P_-}}{P_-}$. These weights come from enforcing the testing class priors

$$\overline{P_+} = \frac{n_+ S_+}{n_- S_- + n_+ S_+} \quad and \quad \overline{P_-} = \frac{n_- S_-}{n_- S_- + n_+ S_+} , \tag{4}$$

while preserving the same magnitude of the misclassification error:

$$n_+ + n_- = S_+ n_+ + S_- n_- \; . \tag{5}$$

4.2 Selecting Training Samples

As described in Section 2, most of the approaches to address the interpersonal variability problem are based on feature transformations. Although these normalizations work well in practice, some participants may be less relevant than others to the classification because their display of physiologically responses is very different to the ones of the testing participant. Using a small set of unlabeled testing data, we propose finding the similarity of each training subject with the testing subject and use it during classification. We can encode this information as follows:

$$loss\ function = \frac{C}{n}\left(\sum_{p=1}^{r} v_p \sum_{i \in participant_p}^{n^p} \xi_i\right), \tag{6}$$

where r is the number of training participants, n^p is the number of samples of the participant p, and v_p defines the similarity of the participant p for classification, based on SC lability. In particular, we computed the average number of peaks (at least 0.05 μS of amplitude) per second and their height average for each training participant, and used k-Means clustering with $k = 2$ to divide the participants. Given a new testing participant, we computed the same information and assigned $v = 1$ to the participants of the closer cluster, and $v = 0$ to the participants of the furthest one.

5 Experimental Setting

Preprocessing. Prior to our analysis, stress ratings were normalized for each participant in order to use all of the scale and to attenuate subjectivity. Furthermore, since the call ratings were quite unbalanced (see Table 1), we transformed the problem to a binary case where calls defined as definitely non-stressful (rating of "extremely good") were grouped into the negative class, and the remaining calls were grouped into the positive class. Table 2 shows the average P_+ value of different days for each participant. As hypothesized, the tendency to report stressful events is very different between participants and similar for different days of the same person.

Table 1. Distribution of call ratings (1 - "extremely good" and 7 - "extremely bad")

Rating	1	2	3	4	5	6	7
Number of Calls	657	379	163	139	45	83	34

Exponential smoothing ($\alpha = 0.8$) was applied to the SC signals to reduce noise and motion artifacts. Skin conductance signals for each participant were also normalized between zero and one to reduce the overall variability of the group [11]. From each signal, we extracted the following features: duration, maximum and minimum values and their relative positions to the signal duration, mean, standard deviation, slope between the first and last signal values, number of zero crossings, and quantile thresholds to capture the distribution of peak heights as described in [14]. These features were normalized to have zero mean and unit standard deviation.

Table 2. Average and standard deviation (STD) of P_+ for the nine participants

Participant	1	2	3	4	5	6	7	8	9	Average	STD
Average (%)	97.06	86.63	78.88	75.51	66.35	56.77	34.76	28.73	10.93	59.51	29.05
STD (%)	2.69	10.89	10.06	14.80	5.45	11.68	2.93	31.01	2.86	10.26	8.96

Experiments. Two testing protocols were used for the analysis. The first protocol (A) used leave-one-day-out cross-validation to obtain the stress ratings of one participant. That is, we used all days of a participant's data to train the algorithm, except one day that was used for testing. The process was repeated until all days were used as testing data. We expect this protocol to give the best performance for this data set, because both training and testing data come from the same participant. In practice, however, this protocol scales badly because it requires annotated information for each new participant. The second protocol (B) used leave-one-participant-out cross-validation. Here, the algorithm was trained with data from eight participants to predict the stress levels of the remaining participant, and it was repeated until all of the participants had been part of the testing data. This is a more realistic but difficult protocol in which the distribution of the training data and the testing data are dissimilar due to interpersonal variance. We tested the proposed modifications in this protocol with the expectation that it would mitigate the variance while preserving scalability.

To perform classification, we used the publicly available LIBSVM library [4] that provides an efficient implementation of SVMs. We used the Radial Basis function as the kernel function to allow non-linear decision boundaries. For each training set, leave-one-participant/day-out was also used to find the parameters ($\log_2 C \in \{-3:2:5\}$) and $\log_2$ *kernel width* $\in \{-15:2:-1\}$) that maximized the following expression:

$$\frac{TN}{2(FN+FP+2TN)} + \frac{TP}{2(FN+FP+2TP)}, \tag{7}$$

where TP and TN are the number of correctly predicted stressful (true positives) and non-stressful (true negatives) calls respectively, and FN and FP correspond to the number of misclassified stressful (false negatives) and non-stressful (false positives) calls respectively. This expression enforces the same relevance to both classes independently of their class priors.

6 Results

Following the previous experimental settings, Fig. 2 shows the results for protocol A, protocol B, and improvements of protocol B - correcting class priors (CCP) and selecting training samples (STS). As expected, when no improvements were applied, protocol B showed consistently lower average performance than protocol A, 58.45% and 78.03% respectively. This finding confirms that participant variability is difficult to model even though our data was appropriately

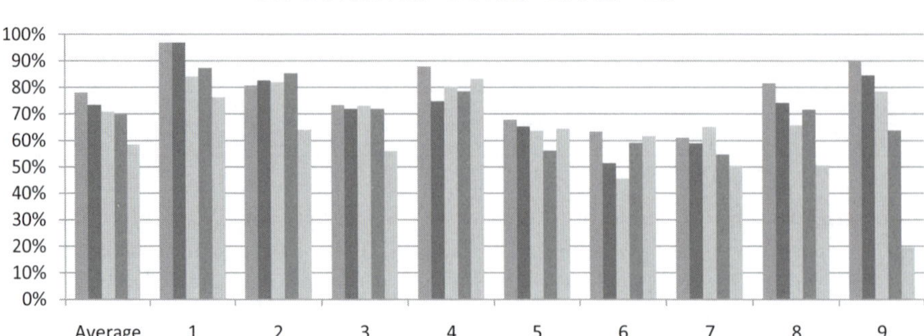

Fig. 2. Classification accuracy for each participant

normalized for all experiments. While CCP and STS individually increased the average accuracy to 69.83% and 70.91% respectively, the combination of the two improvements increased performance to 73.41%. Moreover, STS has the additional benefit of reducing the amount of training samples and therefore reducing the computational cost of the training phase. Closer inspection of Fig. 2 shows that the improvements did not increase performance for two out of the nine participants (4 and 6). No significant relationships could be made between the two participants, but a replication of similar experiments with a larger number of participants could shed light on this topic. To compare the overall performance, Fig. 3 (left) shows the Receiver Operating Characteristic (ROC) curves of protocol A, protocol B and B + STS + CCP. By observing the area under the curve (AUC), we can conclude that both improvements increased the overall accuracy.

Although accuracy has been used for most of the research papers to compare performance, it may not be the most adequate metric for real-life settings where class labels may be very unbalanced. For instance, accuracy values could be high if the algorithm predicted just the most likely class which could potentially

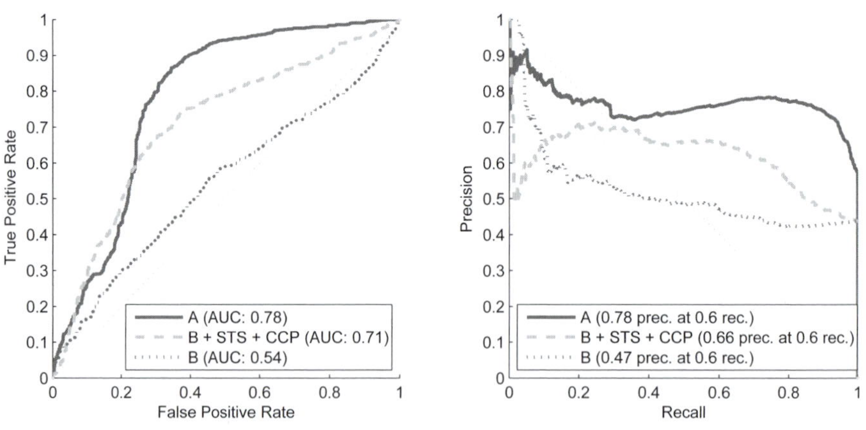

Fig. 3. ROCs and precision-recall curves

ignore the class of interest (e.g., stressful calls.) As a complementary metric, we use precision-recall curves (see Fig. 3, right.) To analyze this curve, we can study a real case application where the company wants to collect stressful calls to train their new employees. In this case, the company wants to know how many of the calls predicted as stressful by the classifier were also reported as stressful by the employees. For instance, if we optimize our methods to correctly detect stressful calls 60% of the time (i.e., recall = 0.6), the percentage of these detections that are also reported as stressful calls (precision) is 78.40% for protocol A, 65.84% for B + STS + CCP, and 46.82% for B alone. These results are in line with the results using accuracy and, therefore, we can conclude that the proposed methods partly address the participant variability problem.

7 Conclusions

This is one of the few research studies on stress recognition in an uncontrolled (real-life) setting. Unlike many other studies on workplace stress, we did not alter the working conditions to artificially create stressful scenarios. This naturalistic approach introduced undesired real-life variables (e.g., unbalanced reports, artifacts), many of which accentuated the problem of participant variability. In this context, we proposed two methods to account for individual differences in order to discriminate stressful vs. non-stressful calls of nine call-center employees.

The two improvements - correction of the class priors and the selection of training samples - rely on the use of data from the testing participant. In many cases, the recovery of testing class priors may be unfeasible or expensive but, in this case, simple questionnaires can be used to obtain that information. As we showed great similarity in participants' stress reports across days, we can also use one day of labeled monitoring to obtain the priors. As for the STS, we explored the use of SC lability to encode similarity between participants, a method that does not require any labeling. In the future, we intend to explore other similarity measures based on demographic characteristics (e.g., age, gender or ethnicity), and we intend to incorporate temporal models (e.g., Hidden Markov Models) to capture the dynamics of stress.

In this paper we have illustrated the benefits of using person-specific models for stress recognition in a call center setting, but the methods explored in this paper can generalize to many areas of Affective Computing. Indeed, participant variability is a common issue in many types of affect recognition applications, and new methods are sorely needed to help tackle this problem.

Acknowledgements. This work was supported in part by the MIT Media Lab Consortium. Javier Hernandez was supported by the Caja Madrid fellowship.

References

1. Barreto, A., Zhai, J., Adjouadi, M.: Non-intrusive physiological monitoring for automated stress detection in human-computer interaction. In: ICCV-HCI, pp. 29–38 (2007)

2. Boser, B.E., Guyon, I.M., Vapnik, V.N.: A training algorithm for optimal margin classifiers. In: 5th Annual ACM workshop on Computational Learning Theory, pp. 144–152. ACM Press, New York (1992)
3. Boucsein, W.: Electrodermal Activity. Plenum Press, New York (1992)
4. Chang, C.C., Lin, C.J.: LIBSVM: a library for support vector machines (2001), software `http://www.csie.ntu.edu.tw/~cjlin/libsvm`
5. Crider, A.: Personality and electrodermal response lability: an interpretation. Applied Psychophysiol Biofeedback 33(3), 141–148 (2008)
6. Healey, J.A., Picard, R.W.: Detecting stress during real-world driving tasks using physiological sensors. IEEE Trans. Intell. Transport. Syst. 6, 156–166 (2005)
7. Huang, Y.M., Du, S.X.: Weighted support vector machine for classification with uneven training class sizes. In: 4th International Conference on Machine Learning and Cybernetics, vol. 7, pp. 4365–4369. IEEE Press, Los Alamitos (2005)
8. Cacioppo, J.T., Tassinary, L.G., Berntson, G.G.: Handbook of Psychophysiology. Cambridge University Press, Cambridge (2000)
9. Kelsey, R.M.: Electrodermal lability and myocardial reactivity to stress. Psychophysiology 28(6), 619–631 (1991)
10. Lunn, D., Harper, S.: Using galvanic skin response measures to identify areas of frustration for older web 2.0 users. In: International Cross Disciplinary Conference on Web Accessibility, p. 34. ACM, New York (2010)
11. Lykken, D.T., Venables, P.H.: Direct measurement of skin conductance: A proposal for standarization. Psychophysiology 8(5), 656–672 (1971)
12. Mundy-Castle, A.C., McKiever, B.L.: The psychophysiological significance of the galvanic skin response. Experimental Psychology 46(1), 15–24 (1953)
13. Poh, M., Swenson, N., Picard, R.: A wearable sensor for unobtrusive, long-term assessment of electrodermal activity. IEEE Trans. Biomed. Eng. 57(5), 1243–1252 (2010)
14. Setz, C., Arnrich, B., Schumm, J., La Marca, R., Troster, G., Ehlert, U.: Discriminating stress from cognitive load using a wearable eda device. IEEE Transactions on Information Technology in Biomedicine 14(2), 410–417 (2010)
15. Shi, Y., Nguyen, M.H., Blitz, P., French, B., Fisk, S., De la Torre, F., Smailagic, A., Siewiorek, D.P., al' Absi, M., Ertin, E., Kamarck, T., Kumar, S.: Personalized stress detection from physiological measurements. In: International Symposium on Quality of Life Technology (2010)

Are You Friendly or Just Polite? – Analysis of Smiles in Spontaneous Face-to-Face Interactions

Mohammed Hoque[1], Louis-Philippe Morency[2], and Rosalind W. Picard[1]

[1] MIT Media Lab, Cambridge, MA 02139, USA
{mehoque,picard}@media.mit.edu
[2] Institute for Creative Technologies, University of Southern California, Marina del Ray, CA 90292, USA
morency@ict.usc.edu

Abstract. This work is part of a research effort to understand and characterize the morphological and dynamic features of polite and amused smiles. We analyzed a dataset consisting of young adults (n=61), interested in learning about banking services, who met with a professional banker face-to-face in a conference room while both participants' faces were unobtrusively recorded. We analyzed 258 instances of amused and polite smiles from this dataset, noting also if they were shared, which we defined as if the rise of one starts before the decay of another. Our analysis confirms previous findings showing longer durations of amused smiles while also suggesting new findings about symmetry of the smile dynamics. We found more symmetry in the velocities of the rise and decay of the amused smiles, and less symmetry in the polite smiles. We also found fastest decay velocity for polite but shared smiles.

Keywords: polite smiles, amused smiles, shared smiles, banking dataset, smile analysis.

1 Introduction

A smile is one of the simplest forms of expressions that is easy for humans to recognize. Several studies have reported success in developing computational models that can recognize smiles with fairly high accuracy [2]. Even though there has been a trend to equate smiles with the activation of lip corner pull (AU 12) and cheek raise (AU 6), several studies have attempted to disambiguate among different kinds of smiles (e.g., deliberate vs. genuine) by exploring their morphological and temporal patterns [1][5][8][9].

Being able to automate recognition of smiles has opened up new possibilities in areas such as conversational agents, customer service, and cognitive behavior modeling. However, a smile is a multi-faceted dynamic expression that can signal much more than "happy" – it can also indicate rapport, polite disagreement, sarcasm, frustration, pain and more. Even with one category of smile, there are ways to vary the dynamic and morphological properties of the smile to indicate the scale and sincerity of that expression. How are the properties of smiles different when they are shared vs. solo? Previously, these kinds of questions have been very difficult to answer,

S. D'Mello et al. (Eds.): ACII 2011, Part I, LNCS 6974, pp. 135–144, 2011.

especially since it is not trivial to collect large sets of labeled spontaneous expression data from quality-recorded natural conversational interactions.

In the past, Ambadar et al. [3] investigated morphological and dynamic properties of deliberate and genuine smiles. They collected data on a study where participants were brought to the lab to act various facial expressions. Between acting and data collection, the participants voluntarily looked at the experimenter and smiled. Those examples were then tagged by judges and were used to analyze the properties of deliberate and genuine smiles. In another study [4], Ochs et al. investigated the morphological and dynamic characteristics of amused, polite, and embarrassed smiles displayed by a virtual agent. A web platform was developed for users to provide smile descriptions (amused, polite and embarrassed) for a virtual agent. While these studies have been extremely useful to motivate the problem with initial exploratory results, none of them really address the issues of understanding those smiles in contextual face to face interactions when those smiles are shared and not shared.

In this study, we utilize a dataset collected by Kim et al. at MIT [10] [11], which contains spontaneous face-to face interactions in a banking environment, where smiles were labeled by both participants after the interaction. While the dataset is labeled for various expressions, for this study, we focus on understanding the differences between polite and amused smiles and how these change when smiles are shared or occur to just one participant. In particular, we focus more on understanding the difference in durations, occurrences, and dynamic properties of polite and amused smiles. The remaining part of the paper is organized as follows: Section 2 describes the dataset and experimental set up. Section 3 describes the research questions addressed in this paper, while Section 4 reports on the current findings. Section 5 provides discussions on the results and future work.

2 Spontaneous Face-to-Face Banking Dataset

This section describes how the data was collected and is largely an excerpt from the work of Kim [10]. In Kim et al.'s MIT study, young adults interested in learning about banking services were invited to meet with a professional banker in a conference room (Figure 1). The bankers provided information about two kinds of financial services just as they did at the retail branches where they worked during the day. The first service was to cash a $5 voucher from the participant as compensation for participating in the study. This part was designed to simulate a cashing a check scenario. The participants were recruited in the study with the incentive of getting $10 for their participation. However, after each arrived, the banker told him or her that they could only get $5 for now and would need to fill out additional paper work to claim their remaining $5. This manipulation was made to instill a slightly negative state in the customer in order to mitigate the "it's fun to be an experiment" phenomenon and also to approximate the real-world situation where a customer often goes to a bank feeling a little negative because of a need to fix a problem. After the experiment ended the participant received the rest of the money without additional paperwork.

The second service was for the banker to explain one of four financial services that a customer chose to learn more about. This part was designed to allow the customer to ask questions and receive information about the financial product just as they would in a real bank visit.

2.1 Participants

Two professional personal bankers were hired, each with over two years of career experience as a personal banker, to do what they usually do at work - explain financial services. One banker interacted with seventeen participants, while the other interacted with forty-four. Each experiment included one banker with one customer.

Before hiring, the bankers were asked if they would be willing and able to manipulate the type of facial expressions displayed during interaction with the customers. Each banker agreed to alter his facial expressions in three different ways, following these exact instructions.

- Manipulation 1 – Neutral facial expressions: Sustain neutral facial expressions over the entire interaction.
- Manipulation 2 – Always smiling: Sustain smiling over the entire interaction.
- Manipulation 3 – Complementary facial expressions, i.e., empathetic: Understand the customer's feeling and respond to it appropriately by smiling when the customer seems to feel good.

Throughout the experiment, the bankers interacted with the customer normally in addition to maintaining one of the three manipulations. This included greeting the customer, providing proper information, and thanking the customer for their time. The facial expressions and the voices of the banker and of the customer were unobtrusively recorded using a video camera from the moment they met and greeted to the end when the customer left. Customers were not told about the banker's facial expression manipulations and all the interactions appeared to proceed very naturally.

Forty one males and twenty females (n=61) who were interested in receiving information about different financial services were recruited through flyers. Before the experiment started, they were told that their face and voice data would be recorded as banks normally do for security reasons. However, they were not told that their facial expressions would be analyzed until after the study. Afterward, they were told about the need to analyze expressions and they were asked to help label them.

2.2 Experimental Setup

The experiment was conducted in a room equipped with a desk, two chairs, bank service advertising pamphlets and two cameras to make the appearance alike to a personal banking service section at banks (Figure 1). One camera was used to record the banker's facial expressions and the other was used to record the participant's facial expressions.

Prior to the participant entering the room the banker was told which expression manipulation to conduct. The participant was then allowed into the experiment room where they would interact with the banker and learn about specific financial services. At the end of the experimental interaction, which took about 10 minutes on average, both the banker and participant filled out 9-point Likert scale surveys evaluating the quality of the service based on the most comprehensive and popular instrument SERVQUAL [6] and the attitude of the banker.

Fig. 1. Experimental set up for banker and the customer interaction. The camera that is visible behind the banker is capturing the facial expressions of the customer. There is another camera, not visible in the image, behind the customer, capturing the facial expressions of the banker.

2.3 Facial Expressions Coding

After the banker and participant finished the surveys, they were debriefed and asked to label the video data for their facial expressions. After labeling their own video information, they labeled the videos containing the person they interacted with (e.g., banker coded customer & customer coded banker). Therefore, for each conversation, there are two videos containing the facial expressions of banker and customer.

Bankers and customers used custom labeling software to label their expressions and affective states. The label interface contained two parts: the upper part displayed the video and the lower part provided the entity for the banker and the participant to enter the time when a certain facial expression was observed and seven affective labels to select. These seven labels were: smile, concerned, caring, confused, upset, sorry, and neutral. If there was no proper label to choose from, the user could press "Other" and enter another label that they thought was appropriate for the expression. The labelers were instructed to stop playing the video and click on the label button when they saw a facial expression, and then to continue to play the video until they saw a change in the facial expression. On the right side of the user interface, there was a text box displaying the time and the labeling result and it was editable so that the user could annotate the reason for each facial expression, e.g. "smile – he made me laugh". The labelers were instructed to group every smile as either polite or amused. These extra labels were entered manually in the text box.

3 Research Questions

In this paper, we focus primarily on understanding the differences between polite and amused smiles. We anticipate that polite smiles in the context of our dataset are more likely to be social, masking and controlled smiles while the amused smiles in the context of our dataset are more likely to be genuine, and felt. In this study, we focus our attention towards exploring the differences between polite and amused smiles in face to face interactions.

We are primarily interested to explore three questions in this study. When people exhibit amused and polite smiles in a task-driven spontaneous face-to-face interactions:

1) Are there any differences in terms of durations between polite and amused smiles?
2) Do amused and polite smiles get shared by the conversation partner? Do people share them equally or does one type get shared more often?
3) Are there any differences in dynamic features between polite and amused smiles? How can we quantify the difference of dynamic?

We are interested to motivate and gain further insights on these questions because understanding those aspects of human communication can help develop models (e.g., virtual human) that can naturally mimic face-to-face interactions with other humans.

4 Experiments

To directly address our research questions, we performed a series of experiments. This section describes our experimental setup and results from our deep analysis.

4.1 Smile Annotation and Segmentation

In our study, we do not measure the dynamics of the bankers' smiles since they were manipulated; we only analyze the dynamics of the customers' smiles and whether or not their smiles occurred in conjunction with a banker smile or solo.

As mentioned in section 2, each customer video was labeled for polite and amused smiles by the banker and by the customer him/herself. We did not use the labels produced by the customers since, after looking at them and seeing huge variation in how the labels seemed to be applied, we realized different customers seemed to interpret the labels differently. Using the two banker's labels led to significantly more consistent labels as judged by outward appearance of the expressions. We therefore chose to use the labels produced by the bankers which are more likely to be consistent. Using a third party coder to code the smiling instances is an option that we are planning to implement in our future work. One significant advantage of using the banker's labels is that they are automatically taking conversational context into account when interpreting the smiles.

The labelers (bankers) indicated individual points in the video where they observed polite and amused smiles. Therefore, extra work was needed to be able to approximate the exact beginning and end points of each marked smile. Given the variability in the data, we manually annotated the beginning and end of each smile given the initial labels produced by the bankers. Through this process, we gathered 227 clips of amused smiles and 28 samples of polite smiles encompassing 61 participants playing the role of customers. We were also interested to find out which of those samples of smiling instances were also shared by the banker. Therefore, we separated the smiling instances of customers where the banker also self-labeled himself to be exhibiting the same kind of smiles (polite or amused).

4.2 Duration and Timing

The average duration of customers' shared polite, shared amused and unshared polite and unshared amused smiles are shown in Table 1.

Table 1. Comparison of durations for customers' polite and amused smiles

	Average duration	standard deviation
shared amused smiles (n=44)	6.1 sec.	4.6
non-shared amused smiles (n=183)	4.7 sec.	3.0
non-shared polite smiles (n=21)	3.7 sec.	1.2
shared polite smiles (n=10)	3.2 sec.	0.77

It is evident that the amused smiles are usually longer when shared as opposed to unshared. Comparatively, the durations of polite smiles are usually the same regardless of whether the smile is shared or not. The high standard deviation for un/shared amused smiles also indicates that the distribution of durations for amused smile is pretty widespread, as shown in Table 1.

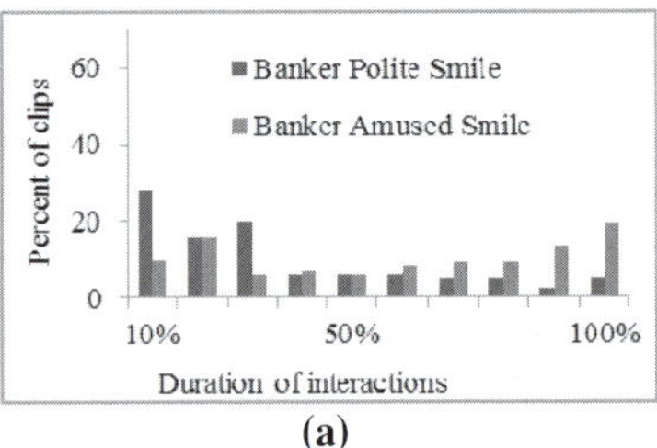

(a)

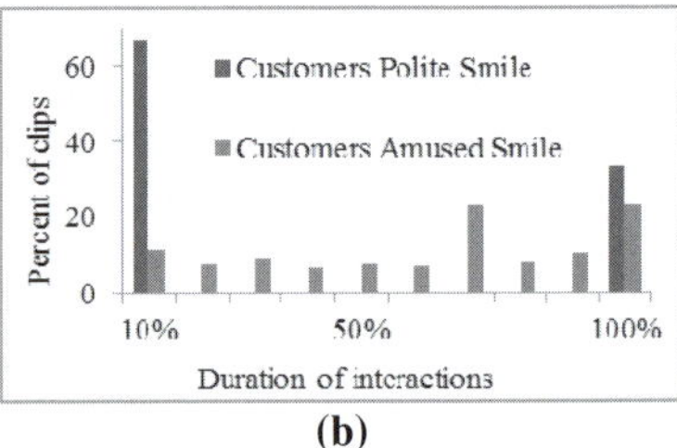

(b)

Fig. 2. Position of polite and amused smiles relative to the entire conversation. (a) Bankers yielded polite and amused smiles consistently throughout the interaction. (b) Customers yielded polite smiles only at the beginning and end of conversations, and amused smiles throughout the interaction.

We have also investigated the positions in respect to the entire conversations for amused and polite smiles, for both bankers and customers, as shown in Fig. 2. It is evident from Figure 2 that bankers seem to display polite and amused smiles throughout the interaction, whereas the customers seem to display polite smiles at the start and end of the conversations. On the other hand, about 1/3 of the 31 polite smiles were shared, while only about 1/5 of the 227 amused smiles were shared in these data.

4.3 Smile Dynamics: Rise, Sustain and Decay

Along with duration and position parameters, we were also interested to explore the dynamics of smile. We used the Sophisticated Highspeed Object Recognition Engine (SHORE) [7] API by Fraunhofer to detect the intensity/probability of smiles. The SHORE API provides a score between 0-100 for smiles by analyzing mouth widening, Zygomaticus muscles and other regions of the face in every frame, which creates a smile track per clip, as shown in Figure 3. We define three parameters to better analyze smile dynamics: rise, sustain and decay. Note that in our natural data, there was often not one clear "apex" or "peak" to the smile. Thus, we do not use the usual definition of onset time = "time to the highest peak", while, offset= "decay from that highest peak", because for spontaneous smiles, they often had a sustained region with multiple peaks, as in Fig. 3. Therefore, in this study, we refer to onset as rise time, offset as decay, and apex as sustain.

Careful observations indicated that the time stamps produced by the bankers were mostly the beginning of peak (L) of the smile without any further information on the rise and decay time as well as its sustain period.

The manual labeling process thus provided us with the beginning of rise times (R) and end of decay times (D). A visual example of where points L, R and R are more likely to be located is shown in Figure 3.

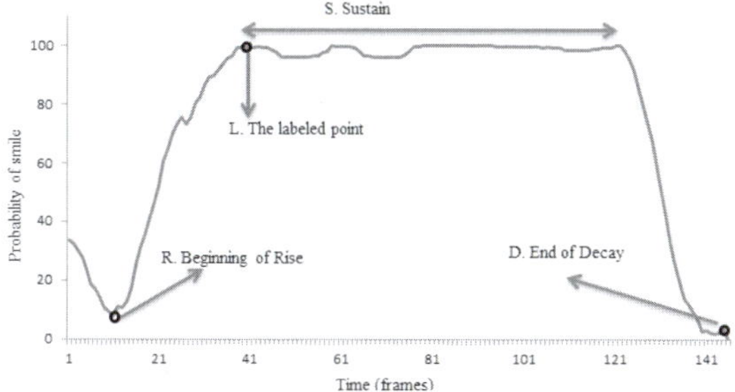

Fig. 3. A visual example of where points such as R (beginning of rise), D (end of decay) and S (sustain) could be located given the time stamp label, L, given by the labeler

Our task was to automatically identify the region, S, which defined the time frame when the participants are more likely to be holding their smiles. We automated an algorithm to identify the locations where the probability of smiling is the highest. Then it traverses left and right looking for deviations that are higher than a predetermined threshold to mark the start or end of the sustain period. For clips with multiple peaks spread over the signal, the algorithm is biased towards selecting an initial point that is closer to the point labeled by the labeler.

Figure 4 provides the comparison of sustain period among shared polite/amused smiles and unshared polite/amused smiles. In these data we see that amused smiles have a longer sustain period than polite smiles. Additionally, shared amused smiles have longer duration for sustain compared to unshared amused smiles, whereas the duration of sustain for both shared polite and unshared polite is almost the same. This finding appears to be consistent with the popular notion that shared joy multiplies joy, here manifest by the extended duration of an amused smile.

In addition to sustain, we also analyzed the rise and decay times of amused and polite smiles, as shown in Figure 5. It is evident for both amused and polite smiles, regardless of whether they are shared or not, the difference between rise time and decay time is not statistically significant, and they are somewhat symmetric. Given this result, we decided to look more closely at the velocity for both rise and decay.

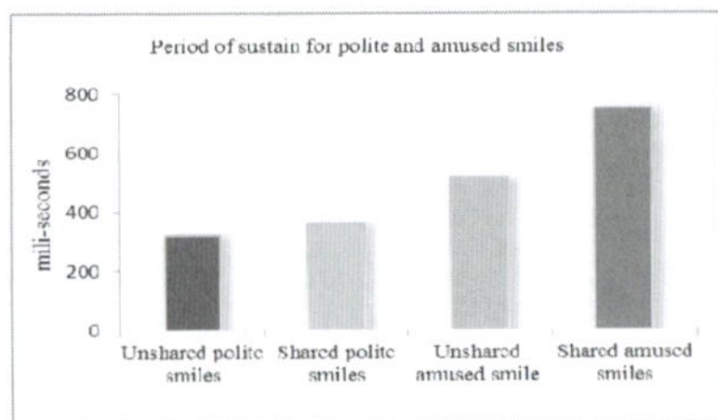

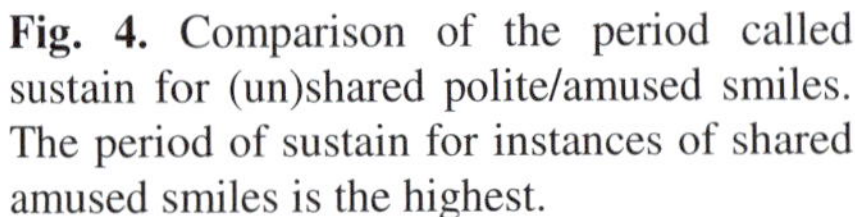

Fig. 4. Comparison of the period called sustain for (un)shared polite/amused smiles. The period of sustain for instances of shared amused smiles is the highest.

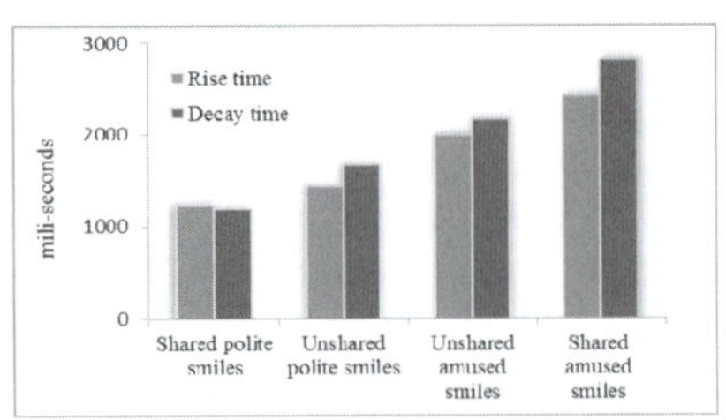

Fig 5. Comparison of rise, and decay time for (un)shared polite/amused smile instances. The ratio between rise time and decay time for all the categories seem very symmetrical.

4.4 Velocity of Rise, Sustain and Decay

We analyzed the velocity of rise and decay signals for polite and amused smiles when they are shared vs. not shared. The velocity of rise (Vr) and decay (Vd) were defined as displacement in y axis divided by the elapsed time.

$$\mathrm{Vr} = \frac{Y_s - Y_r}{T_s - T_r} \text{ and } \mathrm{Vd} = \frac{Y_d - Y_s}{T_d - T_s}$$

where Y_s, Y_r and Y_d represent the smile intensity at the middle of the sustain period, the beginning of rise and at the end of decay, respectively. T_s, T_r and T_d represent the time at the middle of sustain, at the beginning of rise and at the end of the decay, respectively.

As shown in Figure 6, our analysis suggests that the amused smiles have the most symmetric velocities of rise and decay, whether shared or unshared, $V_d \approx V_r$. However, for polite smiles, these velocities were more asymmetric. Shared polite smiles decayed the fastest: $V_r < V_d$ while the polite smiles that rose the fastest were unshared $V_r > V_d$. As shown in figure 5, for shared and unshared polite smile instances, the ratio between T_s - T_r (time difference between sustain and rise) and T_d - T_s (time difference between sustain and decay) remains almost same. It is the smile intensity (Y) that is contributing to the difference in velocities between shared polite and unshared polite instances.

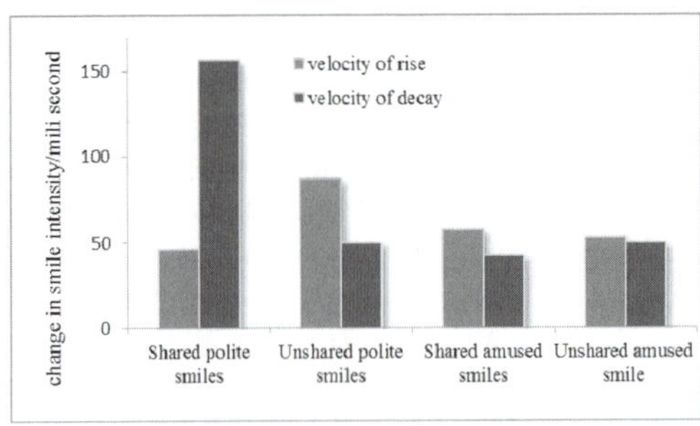

Fig. 6. Comparison of shared polite/amused smiles with unshared polite/amused smiles in terms of velocities

5 Discussion and Conclusions

In this study, we have investigated the phenomenon of polite and amused smiles in a new corpus of spontaneous face-to-face interactions. There were three key findings that have been reported in this paper. Our results suggested that duration of amused smiles are higher than the duration of polite smiles, which is consistent with what has been reported in the literature so far, although under different data gathering conditions. We additionally report that the duration of amused smiles are more likely to be higher when they are shared as opposed to solo. However, for polite smiles, the duration does not seem to change much regardless of whether the smile is shared or not (in fact, slightly higher duration when not shared).

In this spontaneous face-to-face banking dataset, we notice that when bankers labeled their polite and amused smiles during all the interactions, they seem to indicate that they have displayed polite and amused smiles consistently during the entire interaction, as shown in Fig. 2 (a). However, when the same banker labeled the corresponding customer video, he indicated the occurrences of polite smiles only in the beginning and end of the interactions, as shown in Fig. 2 (b). In other words, customers were viewed as less likely to share polite smiles with the bankers unless it happened at the beginning or end of the interactions. For amused smiles, the customers were more likely to share the smiles with the banker during the entire interaction. These data support a view that it is socially acceptable not to share a polite smile when it occurs in the middle of the discussion. Perhaps, we can argue that, in the context of a conversational agent, it may not be necessary or wise for the agent to mirror its user's smiles in every instance, but rather look for ones that are amused and "share" those.

One of the key findings in this paper is that amused smiles, whether shared or not, are more likely to be symmetrical in rise and decay velocities. We additionally report that the duration of amused smiles are more likely to be higher when they are shared as opposed to solo. However, for polite smiles, the duration does not seem to change much regardless of whether the smile is shared or not.

In this paper, we report subtle differences of dynamic and morphological features between polite and amused smiles in face to face interactions. Hopefully, the reported findings will further motivate the development of automated systems that can differentiate between polite and amused smiles under natural conditions.

Acknowledgments. The authors gratefully acknowledge Kyunghee Kim who designed the experiment and collected the data used in this paper as part of her MS thesis. The authors would also like to acknowledge the participants for their time helping with this study and agreeing to have their data shared with other researchers. This research was partially supported by the National Science Foundation (NSF) IIS Award HCC-0705647 and by MIT Media Lab consortium sponsors.

References

1. Cohn, J.F., Schmidt, K.L.: The timing of facial motion in posed and spontaneous smiles. International Journal of Wavelets, Multiresolution and Information Processing 2, 1–12 (2004)

2. Whitehill, J., Littlewort, G., Fasel, I., Bartlett, M., Movellan, J.: Towards Practical Smile Detection. Transactions on Pattern Analysis and Machine Intelligence, 2106–2111 (November 2009)
3. Ambadar, Z., Cohn, J.F., Reed, L.I.: All smiles are not created equal: Morphology and timing of smiles perceived as amused, polite, and embarrassed/nervous. Journal of Nonverbal Behavior 33(1), 17–34 (2009)
4. Ochs, M., Niewiadomski, R., Pelachaud, C.: How a virtual agent should smile? Morphological and Dynamic Characteristics of virtual agent's smiles. In: Allbeck, J., et al. (eds.) IVA 2010. LNCS, vol. 6356, pp. 427–440. Springer, Heidelberg (2010)
5. Hoque, M.E., Picard, R.W.: Acted vs. natural frustration and delight: Many people smile in natural frustration. In: 9th IEEE International Conference on Automatic Face and Gesture Recognition (FG 2011), Santa Barbara, USA, CA (March 2011)
6. Parasuraman, A., Zeithaml, V.A., Berry, L.L.: SERVQUAL: A multiple-iten scale for measuring consumer perceptions of service quality. Journal of Retailing 4, 12–39 (1988)
7. Kueblbeck, C., Ernst, A.: Face detection and tracking in video sequences using the modified census transformation. Journal on Image and Vision Computing 24(6), 564–572 (2006) ISSN 0262-8856
8. Krumhuber, E., Manstead, A.S.R., Kappas, A.: Temporal aspects of facial displays in person and expression perception: The effects of smile dynamics, head-tilt, and gender. Journal of Nonverbal Behavior 31, 39–56 (2007)
9. Valstar, M.F., Gunes, H., Pantic, M.: How to Distinguish Posed from Spontaneous Smiles using Geometric Features. In: Proceedings of ACM International Conference on Multimodal Interfaces (ICMI 2007), Nagoya, Japan, pp. 38–45 (November 2007)
10. Kim, K.: Affect Reflection Technology in Face-to-Face Service Encounters, MIT MS Thesis (September 2009)
11. Kim, K., Eckhardt, M., Bugg, N., Picard, R.W.: The Benefits of Synchronized Genuine Smiles in Face-to-Face Service Encounters. In: IEEE International Conference on Computational Science and Engineering, Vancouver, Canada, vol. 4, pp. 801–808 (2009)

Multiple Instance Learning for Classification of Human Behavior Observations

Athanasios Katsamanis, James Gibson,
Matthew P. Black, and Shrikanth S. Narayanan

University of Southern California
http://sail.usc.edu

Abstract. Analysis of audiovisual human behavior observations is a common practice in behavioral sciences. It is generally carried through by expert annotators who are asked to evaluate several aspects of the observations along various dimensions. This can be a tedious task. We propose that automatic classification of behavioral patterns in this context can be viewed as a multiple instance learning problem. In this paper, we analyze a corpus of married couples interacting about a problem in their relationship. We extract features from both the audio and the transcriptions and apply the Diverse Density-Support Vector Machine framework. Apart from attaining classification on the expert annotations, this framework also allows us to estimate salient regions of the complex interaction.

Keywords: multiple instance learning, support vector machines, machine learning, behavioral signal processing.

1 Introduction

Behavioral observation is a common practice for researchers and practitioners in psychology, such as in the study of marital and family interactions [1]. The research and therapeutic paradigm in this domain often involves the collection and analysis of audiovisual observations from the subject(s) in focus, e.g., couples or families. Meticulous evaluation of these observations is critical in this context and is usually performed by carefully trained experts. Guidelines for this evaluation are typically provided in the form of coding manuals, which are often customized for a particular domain; for example, the Social Support Interaction Rating System (SSIRS) was created to code interactions between married couples [2]. These manuals aim at standardizing and expediting the coding process, which unfortunately can still remain laborious, resource-consuming, and inconsistent [1].

In our recent work [3,4], we argued that the application of appropriate signal processing and machine learning techniques has the potential to both reduce the cost and increase the consistency of this coding process. We introduced a framework to automatically analyze interactions of married couples and extract audio-derived behavioral cues. These low- and intermediate-level descriptors were then

S. D'Mello et al. (Eds.): ACII 2011, Part I, LNCS 6974, pp. 145–154, 2011.

shown to be predictive of high-level behaviors as coded by trained evaluators. Building on this research, we are currently focusing on detecting salient portions of the voluminous, possibly redundant observations. This would enable us to better model the dynamics of the interaction by identifying regions of particular interest. In this direction, we formulate the automatic behavioral coding problem in a multiple instance learning setting and demonstrate the resulting benefits.

Multiple instance learning (MIL), in machine learning terms, can be regarded as a generalized supervised learning paradigm, in which only sets of examples, and not single examples themselves, are associated with labels. The examples are referred to as "instances," while the labeled sets are called "bags" [5]. Conventionally, a negatively labeled bag is assumed to contain *only* negative instances, while a positive bag should contain *at least one* positive instance. It is illustrative to consider the problem of object detection in images from this MIL perspective [6]. In most cases, image labels will only indicate whether an object exists or not in the image and will not provide information about its exact location. In MIL terminology, the image is the bag, and the various objects in the image are the instances. The image/bag will contain the requested object, i.e., be positively labeled, if at least one of the instances is indeed the requested object, i.e., is positive. Apart from object detection, MIL has been successfully applied in domains such as text and image classification [7,8,9], audio classification [10], and more recently in video analysis for action recognition [11].

In this paper, we argue that the MIL paradigm is well-suited for the automatic processing of behavioral observations, collected for the purpose of research in behavioral sciences like psychology. We properly adjust and employ the basic technique introduced in [8], which is known as Diverse Density Support Vector Machine and presented in detail in Sec. 2.2. In Sec. 2.3, we discuss the low-level lexical and intonation features that we extract from the corpus of married couple interactions (described in Sec. 2.1). In Sec. 3, we show significant improvement in predicting high-level behavioral codes using this MIL technique, which also has the advantage of simultaneously attaining saliency estimates for the observation sequences. We conclude in Sec. 4 with a discussion about ongoing work.

2 Proposed Approach

2.1 Corpus

Our current research focuses on a richly annotated audiovisual corpus that was collected as part of a longitudinal study on couple therapy at the University of California, Los Angeles and the University of Washington [12]. The study involved 134 seriously and chronically distressed married couples that received couple therapy for one year. The corpus comprises 574 ten-minute dyadic interactions (husband and wife), recorded at different times during the therapy period. During these sessions, the couple discussed a problem in their relationship with no therapist or research staff present. The recordings consist of a single channel of far-field audio and a split-screen video. No specific care was taken to standardize the recording conditions since the data were not intended for automatic processing. Word-level transcriptions for each session exist, which have allowed us to process the lexical content of the recordings without having to apply automatic speech recognition. A more detailed overview of the corpus can be found in [3].

For each session, both spouses were evaluated with 33 session-level codes from two coding manuals that were designed for this type of marital interaction. The Social Support Interaction Rating System (SSIRS) measures both the emotional features and the topic of the conversation [2]. The Couples Interaction Rating System (CIRS) was specifically designed for conversations involving a problem in the relationship [13]. Three to four trained evaluators coded each session, i.e., provided one set of 33 codes for each spouse, and all codes had written guidelines and were on an integer scale from 1 to 9.

Due to low inter-evaluator agreement for some codes [3], we only chose to analyze the six codes with the highest inter-evaluator agreement (correlation coefficient higher than 0.7): level of blame and level of acceptance expressed from one spouse to the other (taken from the CIRS), global positive affect, global negative affect, level of sadness, and use of humor (taken from the SSIRS). Furthermore, similarly to what was done in our previous work [3], we framed the learning problem as a binary classification task. That is, we only analyzed sessions that had mean scores (averaging across evaluators) that fell in the top 25% and bottom 25% of the score range, i.e., approximately 180 sessions per code. In contrast with our previous studies, we select the extremely scored sessions in a gender-independent manner. The session-level code values are hereafter referred to as "low" and "high." Thus, instead of trying to predict, for example, the numerical level of blame for a spouse in a given session, we are trying to predict whether the level of blame for that spouse is low or high. For this work, we will be using only observations from the coded spouse and not his/her partner.

2.2 MIL Using Diverse Density SVMs

Diverse Density Support Vector Machines (DD-SVMs) were originally introduced for image retrieval and classification [8]. We discuss how this approach can also be of merit for the problem of automatic analysis of behavioral observations. Let $B = \{B_1, \ldots, B_m\}$ be the set of sessions and $Y = \{y_1, \ldots, y_m\}$ be the corresponding set of session labels for one particular code; $y_i \in \{-1, 1\}$ is the ith session label (low or high). Based on the coding manuals [13,2], session-level behavioral evaluation is based on the presence/absence of one or more events that occur during the interaction. For example, the level of sadness for a spouse may be judged as high if he/she cries, and the level of acceptance is low if the spouse is consistently critical. Here, we assume that each session can be represented as a set of behavioral events/instances, e.g., crying, saying "It's your fault". More formally, $B_i = \{B_{i1}, \ldots, B_{iN_i}\}$. Since we do not have explicitly labeled instances in our corpus, we need to come up with a method to label instances and determine their relevance with respect to the six codes we are analyzing.

Diverse Density to Select Instance Prototypes. In the MIL paradigm, one can intuitively expect that the instance labels can be found by exploiting the entire set of instances and labeled bags. This can be accomplished by comparing the frequency count of an instance across the low vs. high sessions. For example, an instance that only appears in low-blame sessions can reasonably be regarded as low-blame, while an instance that appears uniformly in all sessions cannot be regarded as blame-salient. In practice, given that each instance is represented by a noisy feature vector, the direct implementation of the above idea will typically lead to poor performance. In addition, one has to take into consideration the fact that an instance may not appear identically in two different bags. The so-called "diverse density," which was introduced in [5], circumvents these difficulties by making proper assumptions on the probability distributions of both the instances and the bags. For a vector x in the instance feature space, diverse density is defined in [8] as:

$$DD(x) = \prod_{i=1}^{m} \left[\frac{1+y_i}{2} - y_i \prod_{j=1}^{N_i} (1 - e^{-||B_{ij}-x||^2}) \right], \tag{1}$$

where B_{ij} is the feature vector corresponding to a certain instance. Instances that are close to instances in the high-rated sessions ($y_i = 1$) and far from instances in the low-rated sessions ($y_i = -1$) have a high diverse density and are assumed to be more salient for high values of the code. Following [8], we can then find local maxima of the diverse density function to identify the so-called *instance prototypes*, i.e., salient instances for each code. By reversing the y_i labels, we can repeat the maximization process to identify the instance prototypes for the low values of each code.

Distance Metric to Compute Final Features. Having identified the set of instance prototypes $\{x_1^*, x_2^* \dots x_M^*\}$, we can then represent each session B_i by a vector of distances from each prototype [8]:

$$d(B_i) = \begin{pmatrix} \min_j ||B_{ij} - x_1^*|| \\ \min_j ||B_{ij} - x_2^*|| \\ \vdots \\ \min_j ||B_{ij} - x_M^*|| \end{pmatrix} \tag{2}$$

Given this feature vector for each session, supervised classification can be performed using conventional SVMs.

2.3 Feature Extraction

In this work, the instance was defined as a speaker turn, which simplified the fusion of lexical and audio features. We only used turns for which the temporal boundaries were reliably detected via a recursive speech-text alignment procedure [14].

Lexical Features. Lexical information in each instance is represented by a vector of normalized products of term/word frequencies with inverse document frequencies (*tfidf*) for a selected number of terms [15]. For a term t_k that appears n times in the document d_j, and in total appears in D_{t_k} of the D documents, its *tfidf* value in d_j is computed as follows [16]:

$$tfidf(t_k|d_j) = \begin{cases} n \log \frac{D-D_{t_k}}{D_{t_k}}, & D_{t_k} \neq D \\ 0, & D_{t_k} = D \end{cases} \tag{3}$$

In order to account for varying turn lengths, we further normalize the *tfidf* values, so the feature vector has unit norm [15]:

$$tfidf_n(t_k|d_j) = \frac{tfidf(t_k|d_j)}{\sqrt{\sum_{s=1}^{W} tfidf(t_s|d_j)^2}}, \tag{4}$$

where W is the number of turns in the instance. No stemming has been performed [15]. Term selection is achieved using the information gain, which has been found to perform better than other conventional feature selection techniques in text classification [17,18,19]. Information gain is a measure of the "usefulness", from an information theoretic viewpoint, with regards to the discriminative power of a feature. For the binary classification case, i.e., classes c_1 vs. c_2, the information gain G for a term t_k can be estimated as follows [17]:

$$\begin{aligned} G(t_k) &= -\sum_{i=1}^{2} Pr(c_i) \log Pr(c_i) \\ &+ Pr(t_k) \sum_{i=1}^{2} Pr(c_i|t_k) \log Pr(c_i|t_k) + Pr(\bar{t_k}) \sum_{i=1}^{2} Pr(c_i|\bar{t_k}) \log Pr(c_i|\bar{t_k}), \end{aligned} \tag{5}$$

where $\bar{t_k}$ represents the absence of the term t_k. Terms with lower information gain than a minimum threshold were ignored. The minimum threshold was set so that only 1% of the terms were kept. The first 10 selected terms for the whole corpus are given in Table 2.3, sorted by decreasing information gain for each behavior. Interestingly, fillers like "UM" and "MM" and "(LAUGH)" appear to have significant information gain for more than one behaviors.

Audio Features. For the representation of intonation extracted from the audio, we use a codebook-based approach. Intonation information in each turn is represented by a vector of normalized frequencies of "intonation" terms. These terms are defined by means of a pitch codebook. This is built on sequences of pitch values. Given the highly variable audio recording conditions and speaking styles, the codebook allows us to filter our data and only account for prototypical intonation patterns. The audio feature extraction algorithm mainly involves three steps:

Table 1. Terms with the highest information gain for discriminating between extreme behaviors

Behavior	Informative words
acceptance	UM, TOLD, NOTHING, MM, YES, EVERYTHING, ASK, MORE, (LAUGH), CAN'T
blame	NOTHING, EVERYTHING, YOUR, NO, SAID, ALWAYS, CAN'T, NEVER, MM, TOLD
humor	(LAUGH), TOPIC, GOOD, MISSING, COOL, TREAT, SEEMED, TRULY, ACCEPT, CASE
negative	TOLD, KIND, MM, MAYBE, NOTHING, UM, YOUR, NEVER, CAN'T, (LAUGH)
positive	UM, KIND, NOTHING, MM, GOOD, (LAUGH), TOLD, CAN'T, MEAN, WHY
sadness	ACTUALLY, ONCE, WEEK, GO, OKAY, STAND, CONSTANTLY, UP, ALREADY, WENT

1. **Pitch and Intensity Estimation.** Raw pitch values are extracted from the audio as described in [3] every 10ms. Non-speech segments are excluded by applying voice activity detection [20]. Pitch values are automatically corrected for spurious pitch-halving or doubling, and are then median-filtered and interpolated across unvoiced regions. Finally, pitch f_0 measurements are speaker-normalized [3], i.e., $\hat{f_0} = f_0 - f_{0\mu}$, where $f_{0\mu}$ is the mean speaker pitch, estimated over the whole session.
2. **Resampling and Buffering.** The pitch signals are low-pass filtered and resampled at 10Hz, i.e., we get one pitch value every 100ms. Each of these values roughly corresponds to the duration of a single phoneme. Since we expect informative intonation patterns to appear in a longer duration, approximately equal to the duration of at least two words, we group sequential values of pitch inside a window of 1sec duration, to create 10-sample pitch sequences. The window is shifted every 100ms.
3. **Clustering and Counting.** We cluster the resulting sequences using K-means. Each sequence is then represented by the center of the cluster in which it belongs. In analogy with the text representation, we consider the pitch cluster centers to be our intonation terms and we estimate their frequency of appearance in each turn.

The five most frequent occuring intonation terms are shown in Fig. 1.

3 Experiments

We compare the classification performance of the proposed approach with a conventional SVM-based classification scheme. All our experiments are performed using 10-fold cross-validation. The folds were determined in the set of couples

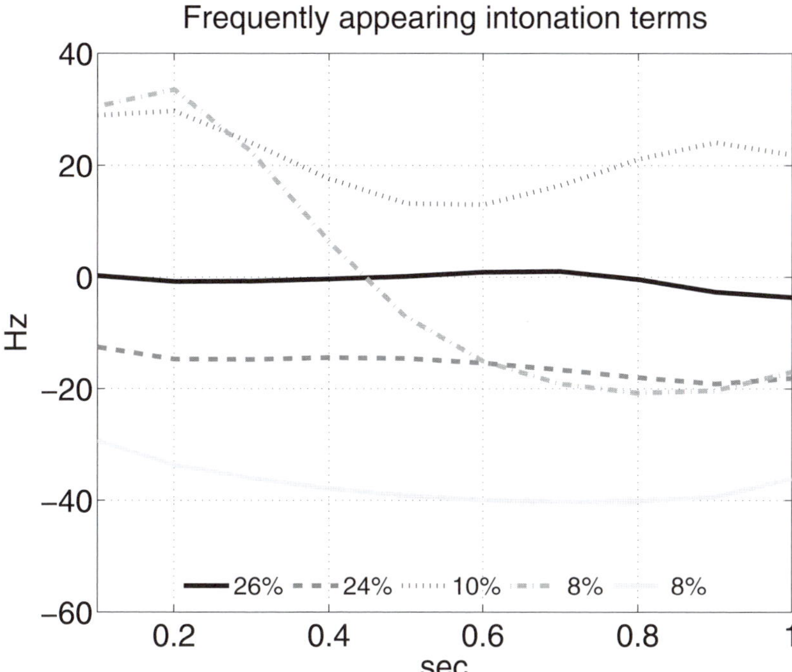

Fig. 1. The five most frequently appearing intonation terms are shown. Each term is defined as one of the 10 cluster centers to which 1-s long pitch sequence observations were clustered using k-means. The appearance frequency of each term is given as a percentage of the total number of pitch sequence observations.

and not in the set of sessions. In this way, we did not have any folds where a session from a training couple would appear in the testing set. Binary classification, i.e., "high" vs. "low", accuracy results are given as box plots in Fig. 2 for three cases, namely when using lexical features with a standard SVM, when using lexical features in the multiple instance learning scheme described earlier and when intonation features are also used in the same setup. Lexical and intonation features are extracted as described in Sec. 2.3. The leftmost box in each graph corresponds to the baseline, i.e., the standard SVM-based approach. The central line on each box is the median, while the diamonds represent the mean values. For the conventional SVM the session features were extracted over the whole session and not separately for each speaker turn. Based on the mean values and the overall distribution of the results for the 10 folds, there are two things that can be noted, namely overall performance is improved when switching to the MIL setup and the intonation features do not lead to further consistent accuracy improvements.

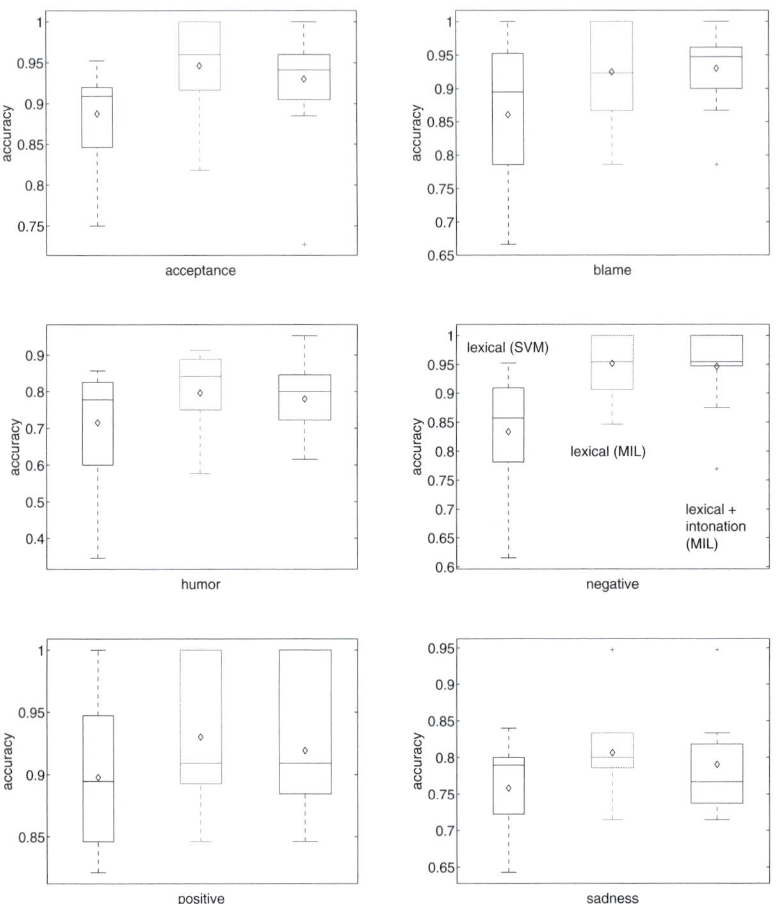

Fig. 2. Binary 10-fold cross-validated classification results for lexical and audio feature sets using conventional SVMs or Diverse Density SVMs for six behavioral codes. The central line on each box is the median, while the edges are the 25th and 75th percentiles. The diamonds correspond to the mean values. The whiskers extend to the most extreme fold accuracy values which are not considered outliers. Points that are smaller than $q_1 - 1.5(q_3 - q_1)$ or greater than $q_3 + 1.5(q_3 - q_1)$, where q_1 and q_3 are the 25th and 75th percentiles respectively, are considered to be outliers and are marked with crosses. The leftmost box in each graph corresponds to the conventional SVM classification with lexical features while the central and rightmost boxes illustrate the results of the MIL approach with lexical features only and joint lexical and intonation features respectively.

4 Conclusions and Future Work

We showed that the Multipe Instance Learning framework can be very useful for the automatic analysis of human behavioral observations. Our research focuses on a corpus of audiovisual recordings of marital interactions. Each interaction session is expected to comprise multiple instances of behavioral patterns not all of which are informative for the overall session-level behavioral evaluation of an interacting spouse. By means of the so-called diverse density we are able to identify salient instances that have significant discriminative power. Saliency is defined with reference to a specific discrimination task each time. We demonstrated improved performance when classification was only based on these salient instances.

In the future, we plan to further elaborate on the saliency estimation aspect of the proposed approach. Further, we would like to investigate alternative intonation and, in general, audio-based features that would help us more effectively exploit the corresponding information in the proposed scheme.

Acknowledgements. We are grateful to Brian Baucom and Andrew Christensen for giving us access to the couple therapy dataset. This research is partially supported from the National Science Foundation.

References

1. Margolin, G., Oliver, P.H., Gordis, E.B., O'Hearn, H.G., Medina, A.M., Ghosh, C.M., Morland, L.: The nuts and bolts of behavioral observation of marital and family interaction. Clinical Child and Family Psychology Review 1(4), 195–213 (1998)
2. Jones, J., Christensen, A.: Couples interaction study: Social support interaction rating system. University of California, Los Angeles (1998)
3. Black, M.P., Katsamanis, A., Lee, C.-C., Lammert, A.C., Baucom, B.R., Christensen, A., Georgiou, P.G., Narayanan, S.: Automatic classification of married couples' behavior using audio features. In: Proc. Int'l. Conf. on Speech Communication and Technology (2010)
4. Lee, C.-C., Black, M.P., Katsamanis, A., Lammert, A.C., Baucom, B.R., Christensen, A., Georgiou, P.G., Narayanan, S.: Quantification of prosodic entrainment in affective spontaneous spoken interactions of married couples. In: Proc. Int'l. Conf. on Speech Communication and Technology (2010)
5. Maron, O., Lozano-Pérez, T.: A framework for multiple instance learning. In: Proc. Advances in Neural Information Processing Systems (1998)
6. Viola, P., Platt, J.C., Zhang, C.: Multiple instance boosting for object detection. In: Proc. Advances in Neural Information Processing Systems (2006)
7. Andrews, S., Tsochantaridis, I., Hofmann, T.: Support vector machines for multiple instance learning. In: Proc. Advances in Neural Information Processing Systems (2003)
8. Chen, Y., Wang, J.Z.: Image categorization by learning and reasoning with regions. Journal of Machine Learning Research 5, 913–939 (2004)
9. Chen, Y., Bi, J., Wang, J.Z.: MILES: Multiple instance learning via embedded instance selection. IEEE Trans. Pattern Anal. Mach. Intell. 28, 1931–1947 (2006)

10. Lee, K., Ellis, D.P.W., Loui, A.C.: Detecting local semantic concepts in environmental sounds using Markov model based clustering. In: Proc. IEEE Int'l Conf. Acous., Speech, and Signal Processing (2010)
11. Satkin, S., Hebert, M.: Modeling the temporal extent of actions. In: Daniilidis, K., Maragos, P., Paragios, N. (eds.) ECCV 2010, Part I. LNCS, vol. 6311, pp. 536–548. Springer, Heidelberg (2010)
12. Christensen, A., Atkins, D.C., Berns, S., Wheeler, J., Baucom, D.H., Simpson, L.E.: Traditional versus integrative behavioral couple therapy for significantly and chronically distressed married couples. Journal of Consulting and Clinical Psychology 72(2), 176–191 (2004)
13. Heavey, C., Gill, D., Christensen, A.: Couples interaction rating system 2 (CIRS2). University of California, Los Angeles (2002)
14. Katsamanis, A., Black, M., Georgiou, P., Goldstein, L., Narayanan, S.: SailAlign: Robust long speech-text alignment. In: Workshop on New Tools and Methods for Very-Large Scale Phonetics Research (2011)
15. Sebastiani, F.: Machine learning in automated text categorization. ACM Computing Surveys 34, 1–47 (2002)
16. Salton, G., Buckley, C.: Term-weighting approaches in automatic text retrieval. Information Processing and Management 24, 513–523 (1988)
17. Yang, Y., Pedersen, J.O.: A comparative study on feature selection in text categorization. In: Proc. Int'l. Conf. on Machine Learning (1997)
18. Forman, G.: An extensive empirical study of feature selection metrics for text classification. Journal of Machine Learning Research 3, 1289–1305 (2003)
19. Gabrilovich, E., Markovitch, S.: Text categorization with many redundant features: using aggressive feature selection to make SVMs competitive with C4.5. In: Proc. Int'l. Conf. on Machine Learning (2004)
20. Ghosh, P.K., Tsiartas, A., Narayanan, S.S.: Robust voice activity detection using long-term signal variability. IEEE Trans. Audio, Speech, and Language Processing (2010) (accepted)

Form as a Cue in the Automatic Recognition of Non-acted Affective Body Expressions

Andrea Kleinsmith[1] and Nadia Bianchi-Berthouze[2]

[1] Goldsmiths, University of London, London SE14 6NW, UK
[2] UCL Interaction Centre, UCL, London WC1E 6BT, UK
a.kleinsmith@gold.ac.uk, n.berthouze@ucl.ac.uk

Abstract. The advent of whole-body interactive technology has increased the importance of creating systems that take into account body expressions to determine the affective state of the user. In doing so, the role played by the form and motion information needs to be understood. Neuroscience studies have shown that biological motion is recognized by separate pathways in the brain. This paper investigates the contribution of body configuration (form) in the automatic recognition of non-acted affective dynamic expressions in a video game context. Sequences of static postures are automatically extracted from motion capture data and presented to the system which is a combination of an affective posture recognition module and a sequence classification rule to finalize the affective state of each sequence. Our results show that using form information only, the system recognition reaches performances very close to the agreement between observers who viewed the affective expressions as animations containing both form and temporal information.

Keywords: Affect recognition systems, affective whole-body posture, form information, temporal information.

1 Introduction

With the emergence of whole-body interactive technology, it is becoming crucial to create systems that make use of body expression cues to determine the affective and mental state of the user. Some work in this direction has been carried out on acted body expressions [1]-[5], [24] and in natural context situations [6]-[8]. Most of the systems aimed at classifying dynamic body expressions make use of a combination of temporal information and postural descriptors. While neuroscience studies have shown the existence of separate pathways to process temporal and postural information [9]-[11], few studies have investigated the contribution of postural information alone to the recognition of affect. Furthermore, these studies have focused mainly on acted expressions [6], [11]. In this paper we investigate the contribution of form information (i.e., postural configuration) in the automatic recognition of affect from *non-acted* body expressions. Rather than looking at body expressions as a sequence of changes of postural configuration, the temporal information is discarded and only the form information of each posture (i.e., a static instance of an expression) in the sequence is maintained.

S. D´Mello et al. (Eds.): ACII 2011, Part I, LNCS 6974, pp. 155–164, 2011.

The remainder of the paper is organized as follows. A brief review of related work is presented in Section 2. The affective posture recognition system is described in Section 3. Section 4 explains the approach taken to test the system. The low-level posture description is explained in Section 5. In Section 6, the system is tested and the results are reported and evaluated. A discussion is provided in Section 7.

2 Related Work

Research findings indicate that form information can be instrumental in the recognition of biological motion [12], [13]. Indeed, a neuropsychological study by McLeod et al [14] found that a brain-damaged patient who was unable to detect moving stimuli, referred to as "motion blind", was still able to detect human form information from biological motion [12]. The importance of form information in recognizing biological motion has also been examined through several neuroscience studies. According to Giese and Poggio [15] and Vaina et al [16] there are two separate pathways in the brain for recognizing biological information, one for form information and one for motion information. Lange and Lappe [17] make even stronger claims by stating that *"...a model that analyses global form information and then integrates the form information temporally..."* can better explain results from psychophysical experiments of biological motion perception. They argue that the temporal information could be superfluous except when necessary to solve the task.

A study by Atkinson and colleagues [9] determined that both form and motion signals are assessed for affect perception from the body. Participants viewed clips of people acting out specific emotions and displaying affect through everyday actions such as bending and walking, in either full-light or patch-light. The clips were shown upright and upside-down, forward-moving and reversed. Results showed that for all conditions, affect could be recognized at above chance levels. However, recognition rates were significantly lower for the upside-down, reversed, patch- light displays, indicating a difficulty in recognizing a human form when the information is presented in a non-human-like configuration. The authors conclude that these results indicate the importance of form-related, configurational cues of posture for recognizing emotion. Through a systematic approach to identify the motor behavior features that were critical to determine the emotions conveyed by different gait patterns, the work by Omlor and Giese [10] and its more comprehensive follow up study [11] also suggest the existence of emotion specific spatio-temporal motor primitives that characterize human gait. All three studies were carried out on acted expressions.

Kleinsmith et al [6] explored this concept in non-acted static expressions to show that automatic affect recognition systems grounded only on form information could recognize affective states conveyed from single non-acted postures representing the most expressive instant of an affective movement in a video game context at a level comparable to human observers. In this paper, we extend this work to consider dynamic expressions (defined here as sequences of postures) and examine how form alone (i.e., no temporal information) can inform the recognition process. Furthermore, different from our previous work, the posture sequences are not manually chosen. This examination aims to show how form and motion should be better integrated in

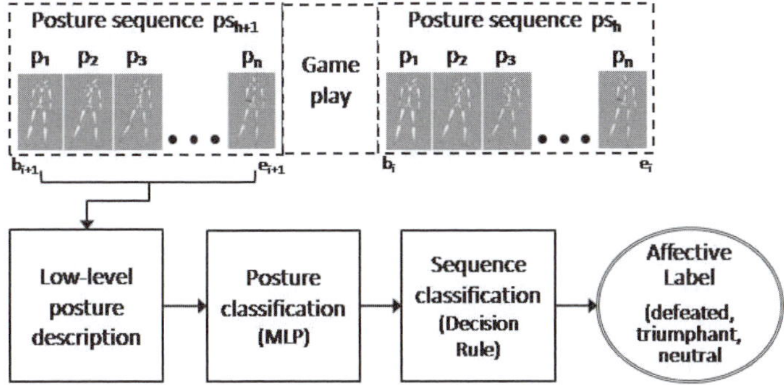

Fig. 1. The affective posture recognition system. A vector of low-level posture features is computed for each posture p_i in a posture sequence ps_h. Each vector is sent to the MLP. A decision rule is applied to an entire sequence of the MLP output to determine the label for ps_h..

building such systems. While we acknowledge that the recognition of the player's affective state would benefit from multimodal recognition, the research question here is how much information sequences of static postures alone carry.

3 The Affective Posture Recognition System

We present here a system to recognize affect from non-acted subtle body expressions represented as a sequence of postures of a person playing a video game by using only the information about the configurations of the postures without considering the temporal information. The sequences considered for this study are selected from the period just after a point in the game was won or lost, termed the *replay window*. While the player may have experienced affective states throughout the entire gaming session, different types of actions (i.e., game play versus non-game play) may require different training and testing sets as the actions involved in actual game play have an effect on how affect is expressed.

The system builds on our previous work on the recognition of affect from single non-acted postures [6]. A motion capture system is used to record the sequences of postures from the players as discussed in Section 4. The system is implemented as a combination of an affective posture recognition module and a sequence classification rule to finalize the affective state of each sequence. Refer to Figure 1 to see the flow of the system (which has already been trained with a set of postures as explained in Section 4.1). A vector of low-level posture description features is computed for each posture p_i in a posture sequence ps_h. A posture sequence corresponds to a non-game play, or replay window. The number of postures in a sequence changes according to the duration of each reply window.

Each frame of motion capture data corresponds to a single posture extracted from the sequence and is used to build a description vector (termed *posture description*) describing the relationship between the joint rotations of that posture as described in Section 5. The posture description of each posture is then presented to a trained multi-layer perceptron (MLP)[1] and each individual posture within the sequence is evaluated. Given ps_h: $h = 1,\ldots,g$, the output of the MLP for p_i is a probability distribution for the set of labels $L = \{defeated;\ triumphant;\ neutral\}$ for each p_i of ps_h. For each ps_h, cumulative scores $L_{sum}(lj)$: $j = 1,\ldots,3$ are computed as

$$\mathrm{L_{sum}(l_j)} = \frac{1}{\mathrm{n}}\sum_{i=1}^{n} q_{ij} \tag{1}$$

where q_{ij} is the output score for posture p_i and label l_j (i.e., the probability that l_j is used to label p_i of a ps_h) and n is the number of postures with that label.

Next, a decision rule is applied to the normalized cumulative scores $L_{sum}(lj)$ of ps_h. The decision rule is employed as a way to combine the sequence of postures and assign l_j to the entire sequence instead of individual postures only (as is the case with the MLP). This is similar to the approach used by Ashraf et al [18] to automatically recognize pain from facial expressions. Given that the replay windows are generally very short, we assume that only one affective state is expressed in each ps_h, i.e., replay window, and that independently by the order of the postures in the sequence, the form alone provides strong information about the affective state of the player. The decision rule is defined as follows

$$\begin{array}{c}
\text{if(Lsum(}\textit{defeated}\text{)} < \text{threshold \&\& Lsum(}\textit{triumphant}\text{)} < \text{threshold)} \\
\{\text{sequence label} = \textit{neutral}\} \\
\text{else if(Lsum(}\textit{defeated}\text{)} > \text{Lsum(}\textit{triumphant}\text{))} \\
\{\text{sequence label} = \textit{defeated}\} \\
\text{else if(Lsum(}\textit{defeated}\text{)} < \text{Lsum(}\textit{triumphant}\text{))} \\
\{\text{sequence label} = \textit{triumphant}\}
\end{array} \tag{2}$$

where $L_{sum}(defeated)$ and $L_{sum}(triumphant)$ are the normalized cumulative scores for the defeated and triumphant affective state labels for ps_h. The *threshold* was experimentally defined by building receiver operator characteristic (ROC) curves using the normalized cumulative scores for $L_{sum}(defeated)$ and $L_{sum}(triumphant)$ after which the coordinates of the curves were assessed. The point at which the true positive rate and the false positive rate were close to equal for the *defeated* ROC curve was chosen as the *threshold* [18]. The affective state label of the posture sequence is the output of the decision rule.

4 Data Preparation

Ten players were recruited for participation (three females) ranging in age from approximately 20 to 40. All players had little to no experience playing with the Nintendo Wii as experienced players have been shown to be less expressive with their body postures when they play to win [19], [20]. The players were asked to play Wii tennis for at least 20 minutes and have their body motions recorded while wearing a

[1] An MLP was chosen over other methods because better results were obtained when tested on the same type of data [1].

Gypsy 5[2] motion capture suit. The players were unaware of the purpose of the study to ensure that any affective displays would be spontaneous and non-acted. Players were asked to come with a friend with whom they could interact during game play as it has been shown to increase affective output [21].

After collecting the motion capture information, the files were annotated by manually locating the start and end frames of the replay windows of each gaming session. As stated in Section 3, the posture sequences are taken from these replay windows and the number can vary for each gaming session. Furthermore, the length of the posture sequence may also vary, meaning that the number of postures within a sequence is not fixed. The replay windows were manually located by viewing the video and motion capture data simultaneously. The reason for manually identifying the replay windows was that if the automatic recognition system being proposed here was integrated into an existing software application, the application itself would be able to signal the periods under investigation. The output of the identification process was a contiguous section of motion capture data.

Two separate posture judgment surveys were conducted in order to build separate training and testing sets for use in evaluating the affective posture recognition system. Separate groups of observers were recruited for each survey. This method was implemented as a way to increase the reliability of the comparison between the performance of the system and the target agreement between observers.

The view taken in this study is that there is no inherent ground truth affective state label that can be attached to the postures captured. The players are not used to label their own postures due to the unreliability of post-task reported feelings and it is not feasible to stop the players during the gaming session to ask them their current affective state. Furthermore, because the complete affective state is expressed through a combination of modalities in a non-acted scenario, it is difficult for the players to be aware through which modality affect was expressed [22]. Thus, the approach used is to obtain outside observers' judgments of the postures. An online posture evaluation survey was conducted with computer avatar stimuli built using the selected set of postures. In order to reduce potential social and cultural bias, avatars were used instead of human photos to create a non-gender, non-culturally specific, faceless 'humanoid'. This allows for the focus to be placed on the information being conveyed by the affective expressions.

4.1 Building the Training Set

Training set postures were manually extracted in order to ensure that a variety of posture configurations were considered. To build the training set, three postures were taken for each of 20 replay windows, yielding 60 postures. Three postures spanning an entire replay window were used to represent the entire movement for training the automatic recognition model considering that most of the movements were short in duration and/or contained little movement. The three postures were chosen as: 1) a posture at the start of the replay window (as soon as game play stopped when a point was won or lost); 2) a posture in the middle of the movement itself; 3) the apex of the movement. A set of eight observers was recruited to judge the set of 60 postures. The

[2] http://www.animazoo.com

posture order was randomized for each observer who was asked to associate an affective state label to each posture one page at a time. For each posture, the label with the highest frequency of use was determined to be the ground truth label, yielding 10 *defeated*, 17 *triumphant* and 33 *neutral* postures. To create a more balanced training set, additional *defeated* (22) and *triumphant* (16) postures from a previous study [6] were added to create a final training set of 98 postures: 32 *defeated*, 33 *triumphant* and 33 *neutral*.

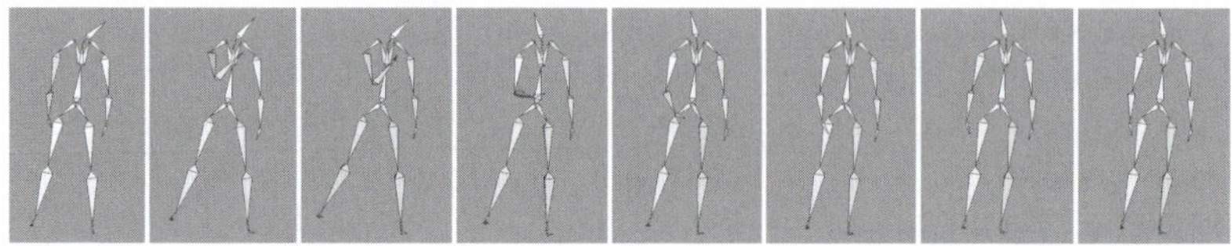

Fig. 2. A posture sequence example - posture frames automatically extracted from a replay window of a motion capture file

4.2 Building the Testing Set

To build a testing set for automatic recognition, posture sequences (Figure 2) were automatically extracted from the remaining replay windows (i.e., those not used to build the training set). Due to the high capture rate of the motion capture system (120 frames per second), the configuration of the body did not change significantly from one motion capture frame to the next. Therefore, it was not necessary to extract every posture within a replay window. Instead, every 40th posture (determined experimentally) was automatically extracted which still allowed for a variety of postures that represented the entire movement within a sequence. The automatic extraction yielded posture sequences ranging from two to 40 frames in length. 836 posture frames across 75 posture sequences were extracted.

A set of five observers (three females) was recruited for labelling the set of sequences. As opposed to labelling each individual posture within a sequence as was done for the training set preparation, the observers viewed each sequence in the testing set as an animated clip of a simplistic humanoid avatar and were asked to assign a unique label to the sequence. This approach was taken to set the target system performance as the level of agreement obtained by observers who considered both form and temporal information. We could have asked the observers to look at form only (i.e., to judge the set of postures without considering their order). However, this would have changed the objective of the study as it would have told us only whether the system was able to reach the same performance of the observers given the same task but it would not have told us the importance of form information.

The posture sequences and evaluation directions were emailed to the observers who agreed to take part. The entire task took approximately 1.5 hours to complete. The observers were instructed to take a break every 30 minutes in an effort to control for boredom. The set of posture sequences was randomly divided into four subsets, different for each observer. As with the training set, to determine the ground truth of a sequence in the testing set, the label with the highest frequency of use was chosen for each posture sequence. The within observers agreement was 66.67% with Fleiss' kappa reaching 0.162, indicating slight agreement. Possible reasons for the low consistency between the observers' judgments may be due to the subtlety of the posture sequences, the limited set of labels from which to choose or the small set of observers considered. There were 14 posture sequences with the defeated ground truth label, 8 triumphant, 39 neutral and 14 ties. In the case of ties, the ground truth was randomly selected between the two tied labels.

Table 1. Low level features and normalization range. The first value of the interval indicates the body-segment stretched outward or backward (according to the rotation considered), the second value indicates the body-segment stretched inward or forward, the 0 point indicates the neutral position (i.e. no rotation or bending of the joint). The last value indicates the range width.

Features	Z Rotation	X Rotation	Y Rotation
Hip	[-22,22] (44°)	[30,-55] (85°)	[-20,20]; (40°)
Knee	none	[55,-9] (64°)	none
Collar	[-4, 4] (8°)	[6,-3] (9°)	[-4,4] (8°)
Shoulder	[-170, 40] (50°)	[45,-110] (155°)	[-90,50] (140°)
Elbow	[-8, 135] (143°)	[8,-55] (63°)	[-1,90] (90°)
Wrist	[-55,55] (210°)	[45,-40] (85°)	[-90,90] (180°)
Torso	[35,-35] (70°)	[-15,55] (65°)	[-26,26] (52°)
Neck	[-15, 15] (30°)	[-18,18] (36°)	[-22,22] (44°)

5 Low-Level Posture Description

As proposed in [6], each posture stimulus is associated to a vector containing a low-level description of the posture. The description is built upon the 3D joint Euler rotations recorded by the motion capture system. The postures were recorded in the standard Biovision Hierarchy (BVH) format. Each rotation value was normalized to [0,1] by taking into account the fact that the maximum range of rotation differs for each joint and not all of the 360° rotations are feasible for the human body. The joints and corresponding ranges are listed in Table 1. For some of the joints, the range of one direction of the movement (e.g., forward) is greater than the range for the opposite direction of the movement (e.g., backward). Therefore, each portion of the range of movement (e.g., [30,0] = range of backward movement of the hip and (0,-55] = range of forward movement of the hip) was transformed independently to ensure that 0 remains the neutral position. To do this, each original value v was transformed as follows:

$$\text{if } v < 0, f = (v-b)/(e-b)]/2 \text{ else if } v > 0, f = 0.5+[(v-b)/(e-b)]/2 \quad (3)$$

where f is the normalized feature, v is the original value from the motion capture data, b is the start of the range, and e is the end of the range.

A further transformation was applied for non-directional rotation. The z and y rotations of the head, neck and torso features were considered non-directional, meaning that the head turned to the left was the same as the head turned to the right. This was accomplished with the following decision rule

$$\textit{if} \; (f \geq 0.5) \; \textit{then} \; f = 2(1\text{-}f), \; \textit{else} \; f = 2f \tag{4}$$

The ranges for each rotation were also determined on the basis of the data available taking into consideration the fact that rotations outside a certain range were possible but very improbable in the given context. By normalizing the rotation in the feasible range we would have risked to compress the values in a very limited space. Any rotation falling outside the set range is assigned respectively to 0 or 1. The z and y rotations for the knees were not considered given their low probability of being moved during the postures imposed by the video game. Only the x rotation (bending of the knees) was used in the models. The joints considered were: neck, collar, shoulders, elbows, wrists, torso, hips and knees.

6 Testing Results

The affective posture recognition system was trained with the training set of 98 postures described in Section 4.1 and tested with the testing set of 75 posture sequences described in Section 4.2. The percentage of correct automatic recognition achieved for the 75 posture sequences was 52%. It is noted that, as stated in Section 4.2, there were 14 posture sequences that were assigned two affective state labels with equal frequencies by the set of observers, thus the ground truth label was randomly determined between those two labels. Taking this into account and assessing correct recognition according to either of the two labels, the recognition rate increased to 57.33% which is well above chance level (33.33% considering three labels). This result indicates that form information appears to provide sufficient information to obtain a non-random classification of the set of affective states conveyed by the expressions (i.e., sequences of postures). Furthermore, as our main objective of this study, we can compare the results with the overall agreement level achieved by the observers (66.67%) obtained when classifying the expressions which consisted of both form and temporal information). The system performance reaches 86% of the observers' performance showing that form may indeed provide a strong source of information in building automatic recognition systems of affective expressions.

In order to better understand factors that may have affected the performance of the system we conducted a confidence rating task. A new observer was recruited to view the seven posture sequences for which the set of observers had assigned two affective state labels with equal frequencies, and were also misclassified by the system. The task was repeated three times over three days (i.e., three trials). For each trial the seven posture sequence clips were presented in a randomized order with a different label from the set of labels. The observer was asked to view the animated posture sequences and provide a confidence rating on a scale from 1 (not confident) to 5 (very confident) that the label corresponds to the expression portrayed by the sequence [23]. In the event of posture sequences with low confidence ratings (i.e., 1 or 2), the observer was asked to provide an alternative label from the remaining two.

The results indicated that some posture sequences seem to be ambiguous, partially due to the subtlety of natural, non-acted postures. For instance, two posture sequences received confidence ratings of 3 or above no matter which label was presented with the sequence. Because the sequences were taken automatically after every point played, it is possible that they were not affective, but also did not fit into the *neutral* category. It is also possible that the affective state expressed was not in the set of affective states considered. This can be an issue with classification according to discrete categories, indicating that a future implementation of the system may classify naturalistic affective body expressions in terms of levels of affective dimensions [6].

7 Discussion and Conclusions

The study aimed at investigating how much information form alone provides in the automatic recognition of dynamic body expressions. The recognition system achieved a recognition rate of 57.33% which is close to the human observer agreement target of 66.67%, which was obtained instead on the basis of both form and temporal information. The results are comparable and even higher than automatic recognition systems built by taking into consideration temporal information, (e.g., body movement and dance). This further supports the importance of considering form in the automatic description of affect from body expressions. For instance, the recognition system presented by Camurri et al [24] reached a low recognition rate of 36.5% (chance level = 25%), considering acted dance movements of basic emotions. Indeed, the system performance was considerably lower than the 56% agreement between the observers. The study by Kapur et al [25] also considers temporal information from acted dance movements of basic emotions. However, using several different automatic classifiers, they achieved higher recognition rates (62%-93%), but most were still below the observers' level of agreement (93%).

Overall our study demonstrated that for the subtle non-acted affective states considered, form is an important source of information for the recognition process resulting in quite a high recognition rate. However, further studies are necessary to fully understand the respective contribution of both form and temporal information.

References

1. Kleinsmith, A., de Silva, P.R., Bianchi-Berthouze, N.: Cross-cultural differences in recognizing affect from body posture. Interacting with Computers 18, 1371–1389 (2006)
2. Bianchi-Berthouze, N., Kleinsmith, A.: A categorical approach to affective gesture recognition. Connection Science special issue on Epigenetic Robotics - Modeling Cognitive Development in Robotic Systems 15, 259–269 (2003)
3. Meeren, H., van Heijnsbergen, C., de Gelder, B.: Rapid perceptual integration of facial expression and emotional body language. Proceedings of the National Academy of Sciences of the USA 102, 16518–16523 (2005)
4. Van den Stock, J., Righart, R., de Gelder, B.: Body expressions influence recognition of emotions in the face and voice. Emotion 7, 487–494 (2007)
5. Bernhardt, D., Robinson, P.: Detecting affect from non-stylised body motions. In: Paiva, A.C.R., Prada, R., Picard, R.W. (eds.) ACII 2007. LNCS, vol. 4738, pp. 59–70. Springer, Heidelberg (2007)
6. Kleinsmith, A., Bianchi-Berthouze, N., Steed, A.: Automatic Recognition of Non-Acted Affective Postures. IEEE Transactions on Systems, Man, and Cybernetics Part B (2011)

7. Kapoor, A., Picard, R.W., Ivanov, Y.: Probabilistic combination of multiple modalities to detect interest. In: 17th Int. Conf. Pattern Recog., pp. 969–972 (2004)
8. Kapoor, A., Burleson, W., Picard, R.W.: Automatic prediction of frustration. Int. J. Human-Comput. Stud. 65, 724–736 (2007)
9. Atkinson, A.P., Dittrich, W.H., Gemmell, A.J., Young, A.W.: Evidence for distinct contributions of form and motion information to the recognition of emotions from body gestures. Cognition 104, 59–72 (2007)
10. Omlor, L., Giese, M.A.: Extraction of spatio-temporal primitives of emotional body expressions. Neurocomputing 70, 1938–1942 (2007)
11. Roether, C., Omlor, L., Christensen, A., Giese, M.A.: Critical features for the perception of emotion from gait. Journal of Vision 8, 1–32 (2009)
12. Hirai, M., Hiraki, K.: The relative importance of spatial versus temporal structure in the perception of biological motion: An event-related potential study. Cognition 99, B15–B29 (2006)
13. Peelen, M.V., Wiggett, A.J., Downing, P.E.: Patterns of fMRI activity dissociate overlapping functional brain areas that respond to biological motion. Neuron. 49, 815–822 (2006)
14. McLeod, P., Dittrich, W., Driver, J., Perret, D., Zihl, J.: Preserved and impaired detection of structure from motion by a "motion-blind" patient. Visual Cognition 3, 363–392 (1996)
15. Giese, M.A., Poggio, T.: Neural mechanisms for the recognition of biological movements. Neuroscience 4, 179–191 (2003)
16. Vaina, L.M., Lemay, M., Bienfang, D.C., Choi, A.Y., Nakayama, K.: Intact biological motion and structure from motion perception in a patient with impaired motion mechanisms: A case study. Visual Neuroscience 5, 353–369 (1990)
17. Lange, J., Lappe, M.: The role of spatial and temporal information in biological motion perception. Advances in Cognitive Psychology 3, 419–428 (2007)
18. Ashraf, A., Lucey, S., Cohn, J., Chen, T., Prkachin, K., Solomon, P.: The painful face: Pain expression recognition using active appearance models. Image and Vision Computing 27, 1788–1796 (2009)
19. Bianchi-Berthouze, N., Kim, W.W., Patel, D.: Does body movement engage you more in digital game play? and why? In: Paiva, A.C.R., Prada, R., Picard, R.W. (eds.) ACII 2007. LNCS, vol. 4738, pp. 102–113. Springer, Heidelberg (2007)
20. Pasch, M., Bianchi-Berthouze, N., van Dijk, B., Nijholt, A.: Movement-based sports video games: Investigating motivation and gaming experience. Ent. Comp. 9, 169–180 (2009)
21. Ravaja, N., Saari, T., Turpeinen, M., Laarni, J., Salminen, M., Kivikangas, M.: Spatial presence and emotions during video game playing: Does it matter with whom you play? In: 8th Int. Workshop on Presence, London, pp. 32–333 (2005)
22. Russell, J.A., Feldman-Barrett, L.: Core affect, prototypical emotional episodes, and other things called emotion: Dissecting the elephant. J. Pers. Social Psychol. 76, 805–819 (1999)
23. Afzal, S., Robinson, P.: Natural affect data – collection and annotation in a learning context, vol. 3, pp. 22–28 (2009) ISBN: 978-1-4419-9625-1
24. Camurri, A., Mazzarino, B., Ricchetti, M., Timmers, R., Volpe, G.: Multimodal analysis of expressive gesture in music and dance performances. In: Camurri, A., Volpe, G. (eds.) GW 2003. LNCS (LNAI), vol. 2915, pp. 20–39. Springer, Heidelberg (2004)
25. Kapur, A., Kapur, A., Virji-Babul, N., Tzanetakis, G., Driessen, P.F.: Gesture-based affective computing on motion capture data. In: Tao, J., Tan, T., Picard, R.W. (eds.) ACII 2005. LNCS, vol. 3784, pp. 1–7. Springer, Heidelberg (2005)

Design of a Virtual Reality Based Adaptive Response Technology for Children with Autism Spectrum Disorder

Uttama Lahiri[1], Esubalew Bekele[2], Elizabeth Dohrmann[3], Zachary Warren[4], and Nilanjan Sarkar[1,2]

[1] Mechanical Engineering Department, Vanderbilt University, Nashville, TN, USA
[2] Electrical Engineering and Computer Sc., Vanderbilt University, Nashville, TN, USA
[3] Vanderbilt Kennedy Center, Vanderbilt University, Nashville, TN, USA
[4] Psychiatry Department, Vanderbilt University, Nashville, TN, USA

Abstract. Impairments in social communication skills are thought to be core deficits in children with autism spectrum disorder (ASD). In recent years, several assistive technologies, particularly Virtual Reality (VR), have been investigated to promote social interactions in this population. It is well-known that these children demonstrate atypical viewing patterns during social interactions and thus monitoring eye-gaze can be valuable to design intervention strategies. However, presently available VR-based systems are designed to chain learning via aspects of one's performance only permitting limited degree of individualization. Given the promise of VR-based social interaction and the usefulness of monitoring eye-gaze in real-time, a novel VR-based dynamic eye-tracking system is developed in this work. The developed system was tested through a small usability study with four adolescents with ASD. The results indicate the potential of the system to promote improved social task performance along with socially-appropriate mechanisms during VR-based social conversation tasks.

Keywords: Autism Spectrum Disorder, Virtual Reality, eye tracking, social communication, engagement.

1 Introduction

Autism Spectrum Disorder (ASD) is characterized by core deficits in social interaction and communication [1]. Children with ASD demonstrate difficulties in social judgment and in using face as a channel for social communication [2]. Thus social attention and its measurement is considered a major aspect in ASD intervention [3], which could involve acquiring and analyzing eye-gaze data [4]. Also, given the limitation on the availability of trained professional resources in ASD intervention, it is likely that emerging technology will play an important role in providing more accessible intensive individualized intervention [5]. We chose Virtual Reality (VR) technology since this possesses several strengths in terms of potential application for children with ASD, namely, malleability, controllability, replicability, modifiable sensory stimulation, and an ability to pragmatically individualize intervention approaches and reinforcement strategies [6].

S. D'Mello et al. (Eds.): ACII 2011, Part I, LNCS 6974, pp. 165–174, 2011.

Despite potential advantages, current VR environments as applied to assistive intervention for children with ASD [7] [8] are designed to chain learning via aspects of performance alone. In fact, a number of VR applications have investigated social skill training for children with ASD [7] [8]. These works were pioneering in establishing the usefulness of VR in ASD intervention. However, they monitored the partipants' performance and did not measure how long and where the individuals were looking during interaction and thus were not able to assess their engagement to the task. Recently Wilms et al. [9] demonstrated the feasibility of linking the gaze behavior of a virtual character with a human observer's gaze position during joint-attention tasks. Thus, the current VR environments as applied to assistive intervention for children with ASD are designed to chain learning via aspects of performance alone (i.e., correct, or incorrect) thereby limiting individualization of application. Even these recent systems that measure eye gaze do not adaptively respond to engagement predicted from one's viewing pattern and eye physiological indices. The viewing patterns (e.g., Fixation Duration (FD)), and eye physiological indices (e.g., Blink Rate (BR) and Pupil Diameter (PD)) of an individual can be indicative of one's engagement [10-12], and if properly considered during a VR-based interaction, may lead to a substantially realistic intervention.

The objective of this paper is to present the design and development of a VR-based engagement-sensitive system with adaptive response technology that can be applied to social communication task for children with ASD. We design the system to present VR-based social tasks of varying difficulty levels along with bidirectional interaction in the form of social conversations with virtual avatars coupled with the ability to monitor one's behavioral viewing and eye physiological indices in real-time. Based on the participant's behavioral viewing, eye physiological indices, and performance metric, the system adaptively and socially responds by using a rule-governed strategy generator. While not an intervention study, here we present the results of a usability study as a proof-of-concept of our designed system.

2 System Design

The VR-based engagement-sensitive system with adaptive response technology has three main subsystems: (i) a VR-based social communication task module, (ii) a real-time eye-gaze monitoring module, and (iii) an individualized adaptive response module utilizing a rule-governed intelligent engagement prediction mechanism.

2.1 VR-Based Social Communication Task Module

In this work, we use desktop VR applications. Vizard (www.worldviz.com), a commercially available VR design package, is used to develop the virtual environments and the assistive technology. In order to perform socially interactive tasks with children with ASD, we developed extensive social situations with context-relevant backgrounds, and avatars whose age and appearance resemble those of the participants' peers without trying to achieve exact similarities. Also, for effective bidirectional social communication between the avatars and the participants, we developed conversation threads. Our social communication task module comprises of task presentation and bidirectional conversation modules.

Task Presentation Module. We developed social task presentation modules with avatars narrating personal stories to the participants. These stories were based on diverse topics of interest to teenagers e.g., favorite sport, favorite film, etc. The voices for the avatars were gathered from teenagers from the regional area. The avatar can make pointing gestures and move dynamically in a context-relevant virtual environment. For example, when an avatar narrates his tour experience to a sea beach and introduces the participant to the rocky beach while narrating the rocks on the beach, the VR environment reflects the view of the beach (Fig. 1a). When the avatar narrates some of his favorite activities on the beach such as, tanning during the day, the VR world displays such a situation to the participant (Fig. 1b). Subsequently, when the avatar narrates his experience of the remarkable view of sunset he witnessed on the beach, the VR situation changes with a smooth transition of the background image to display such a situation to the participant (Fig. 1c). This helped us to expose the participants to realistic social situations relevant to the topic being narrated.

The avatar heads were created from 2D photographs of teenagers, which were then converted to 3D heads by '3DmeNow' software for compatibility with Vizard. One can view the avatars within our system from first-person perspective.

Fig. 1. Snapshot of avatar narrating his tour experience to a sea beach within VR environment

Bidirectional Conversation Module. The participant was asked to watch and listen to the avatar narrating a personal story during the VR-based task presentation. At the end of this task presentation, the participant was asked to extract a piece of information from the avatar using a bidirectional conversation module with varying levels of interaction difficulty (e.g., 'Easy', 'Medium', and 'High'). The bidirectional conversation module followed a menu-driven structure used by the interactive fiction community. The degree of interaction difficulty was controlled by requiring the number of questions a participant needed to ask in order to obtain a desired piece of information from the avatar and the nature of the conversation. In order to control the interaction difficulty, we chose three levels of conversation tasks, namely, Type 1, Type 2, and Type 3 tasks. In Type 1 conversation task, the participant was required to obtain a piece of information from the avatar that was directly narrated in the story and could be obtained by asking a minimum of 3 questions if the participant chose the right sequence of questions. In Type 2 conversation task, the participant was required to obtain a piece of information from the avatar that was not directly narrated in the story but was hinted during the narration and could be obtained by asking a minimum of 5 questions if the participant chose the right sequence of questions. Finally, in Type 3 conversation task, the participant was required to obtain a sensitive piece of information (e.g., the avatar's feeling about a situation in general or some personal details, etc.) from the avatar that was not discussed in the story and could be obtained by asking a minimum of 7 questions if the participant chose the right sequence of questions. If a participant could acquire the needed information in a particular level by asking the minimum number of questions for that interaction difficulty level, he/she achieved the highest performance score. On the other hand, if the participant could not choose the right questions in the right sequence, causing him/her to ask more questions to find the needed information, he/she would acquire a proportionately less performance score. After a certain number of attempts if the participant was still unable to obtain the right information, the system would terminate the task and provide a task of lesser challenge to the participant. In order to ensure consistency among the tasks, task in each level of difficulty was carefully designed in consultation with experienced clinicians such that the structure of conversation remains similar regardless of the topics.

Type 1 Conversation Task with Easy Level of Interaction Difficulty. For an easy scenario, a participant was required to ask 3 appropriate questions in right sequence to get the intended piece of information using the conversation-thread structure as shown in Fig. 2.

For example, after an avatar narrated his experience of a football game during the VR-based task presentation, the participant was asked to find the avatar's experience of his first football game that he played. If the participant first selected the choice 3 (from the top) of the menu (Fig. 3) to introduce (represented by block A in Fig. 2) himself to the avatar, the avatar responded by saying "Hi. I am Tom. Yes. I really love football, especially when I get to play!" If instead of selecting choice 3, the participant chose any other option, then the avatar responded as, "I'm sorry! Do I know you? Maybe we should introduce ourselves first." thereby serving the role of a facilitator. Then if the participant selected the choice 1 (from the top) of the menu (Fig. 3) to ask the avatar about the topic (represented by block B in Fig. 2) of the conversation (i.e., regarding the first time the avatar played a football game), the avatar responded by saying "Of course! I was in the second grade. Our P.E. teacher split our class into two small junior football teams." Finally, if the participant selected the choice 2 (from the top) of the menu to ask the avatar regarding his overall feeling (represented by block C in Fig. 2) of his first football game, the avatar ended the conversation by saying "Yes, it was a lot of fun to play with my classmates."

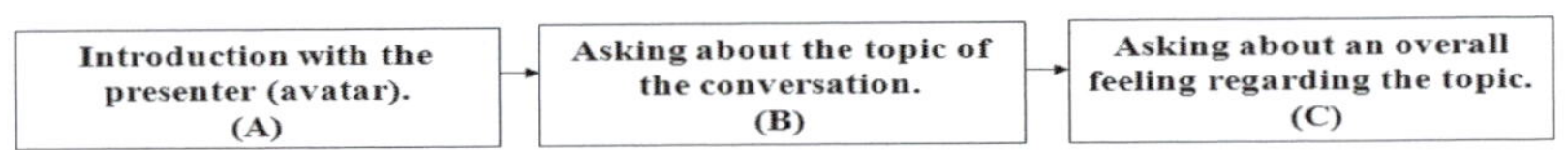
Introduction with the presenter (avatar). (A)
Asking about the topic of the conversation. (B)
Asking about an overall feeling regarding the topic. (C)

Fig. 2. Block Diagram of the Conversation Threads (Easy Level of Interaction Difficulty)

Type2 Conversation Task with Medium Level of Interaction Difficulty. For a scenario with a medium level of interaction difficulty, a participant was required to ask 5 questions in the right sequence to obtain the needed information from the avatar using a conversation-thread structure as shown in Fig. 4.

For example, after an avatar narrated her experience of her trip to a zoo with her friends during the VR-based task presentation, the participant was asked to find out some more details from the avatar about her experience at the zoo.

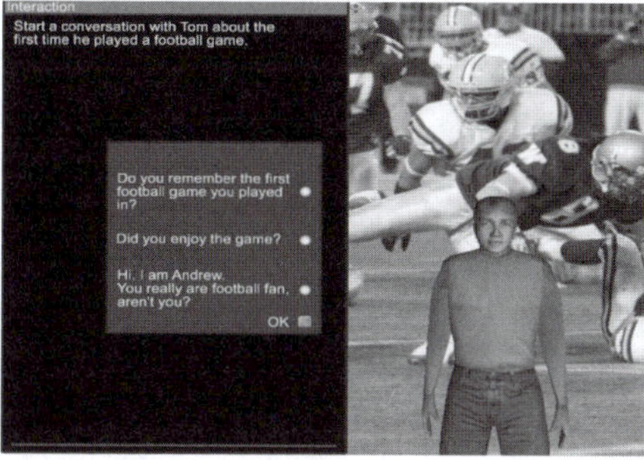

Fig. 3. Snapshot of a bidirectional conversation module (Easy Level of Interaction Difficulty)

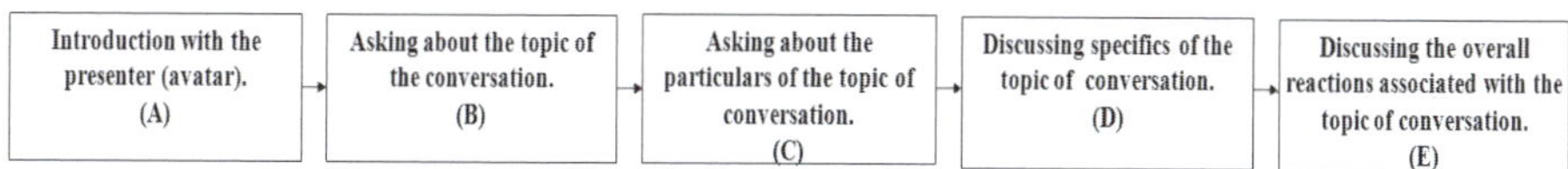

Fig. 4. Block Diagram of the Conversation Threads (Medium Level of Interaction Difficulty)

Type3 Conversation Task with High Level of Interaction Difficulty. For a scenario with a high level of interaction difficulty, a participant was required to ask 7 questions in the right sequence to obtain the needed information from the avatar using a conversation-thread structure as shown in Fig. 5.

For example, after an avatar narrated her experience of playing softball and her not liking the softball coach, the participant was asked to find out what the avatar actually felt for not liking the softball coach (i.e., 'sensitive' topic).

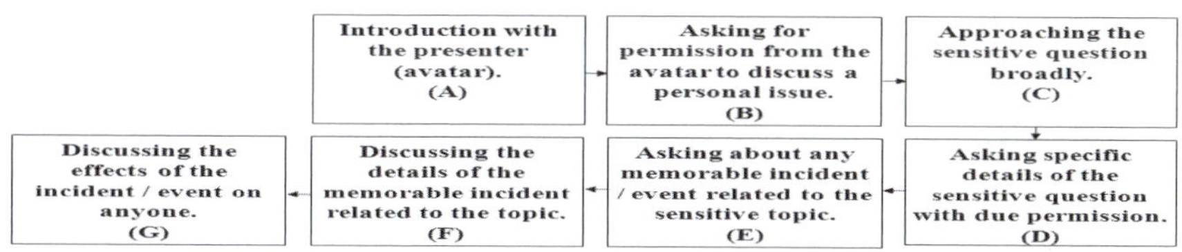

Fig. 5. Block Diagram of the Conversation Threads (High Level of Interaction Difficulty)

2.2 Real-Time Eye-Gaze Monitoring Module

The system captures eye data of a participant interacting with an avatar using eye-tracker goggles from Arrington Research Inc. This eye-tracker comes with some basic features acquiring capability for offline analysis and with a Video Capture Module with a refresh rate of 30 Hz to acquire a participant's gaze data using the 'Viewpoint' software. We designed the Viewpoint-Vizard handshake module, acquired the raw gaze data using Viewpoint, and transformed it to the Vizard compatible format using the handshake interface in a time synchronized manner. Subsequently, we applied signal processing techniques, such as windowing, thresholding, etc. to eliminate noise and extract the relevant features, such as, mean Pupil Diameter (PD_{Mean}), mean Blink Rate (BR_{Mean}), mean Fixation Duration (FD_{Mean}) at an interval of 33 ms.

2.3 Individualized Adaptive Response Module

Our goal was to switch tasks based on the composite effect of one's performance and engagement to the task. One's engagement to the VR-based social task was predicted based on objective metrics such as, dynamic viewing patterns characterized by Fixation Duration (FD) and two eye physiological indices - Blink Rate (BR), and Pupil Diameter (PD) – all of which have been shown to indicate engagement in other studies [10-12]. In order to discretize the engagement space, we assigned numeric values of 1, 2, and 3 (Tables 2a, 2b, and 2c) to these indices to quantify engagement in three levels – 'not engaged', 'moderately engaged' and 'highly engaged' respectively. If the cumulative sum of the engagement level obtained by real-time monitoring of FD, PD, and BR $\geq$ 6, then the engagement was considered as 'Good Enough', otherwise this was 'Not Good Enough'. If a participant scored $\geq$ 70% of the maximum score possible (e.g., 18, 30, and 42 for 'Type 1', 'Type 2', and 'Type 3' tasks representing the 'Easy', 'Medium', and 'High' difficulty level respectively with each relevant choice of bidirectional conversation options giving 6 points and an irrelevant choice causing a penalty of 3 points) in a task, then the performance was considered as 'Adequate', otherwise, this was considered as 'Inadequate'.

Table 2. Prediction of Engagement based on (a) Fixation Duration (FD), (b) Pupil Diameter (PD), and (c) Blink Rate (BR)

Fixation Duration	Value	Pupil Diameter	Value	Blink Rate	Value
$0\% \leq T \leq 50\%$	1	$PD_{Now} > PD_{Prev}$	1	$BR_{Now} > BR_{Prev}$	1
$50\% < T < 70\%$	2	$PD_{Prev} \geq PD_{Now} \geq 0.95PD_{Pre}$	2	$BR_{Prev} \geq BR_{Now} \geq 0.95BR_{Prev}$	2
$T \geq 70\%$	3	$PD_{Now} < 0.95PD_{Prev}$	3	$BR_{Now} < 0.95BR_{Prev}$	3

T : Percent FD towards Face region i.e., Face_ROI (during conversation) out of total FD.
PD_{Now}, PD_{Prev}:Pupil Diameter during present and previous situation respectively.
BR_{Now}, BR_{Prev}: Blink Rate during present and previous situation respectively.

This module fuses the information on the engagement (i.e., 'Good Enough' or, 'Not Good Enough') and the task performance (i.e., 'Adequate', or, 'Inadequate') to dynamically switch tasks of different difficulty levels by implementing an individualized task modification strategy (Table 3).

Table 3. Task Modification Strategy based on Composite Effect of Behavioral Viewing, Eye Physiology, and Performance

Case No.	Engagement	Task Performance	Overall Predicted Engagement
Case1	Good Enough	Adequate	Engaged
Case2	Good Enough	Inadequate	Not Engaged
Case3a/b	Not Good Enough	Adequate	Semi-Engaged
Case4	Not Good Enough	Inadequate	Not Engaged

In Case1, the strategy generator will increase task difficulty level. In Case2, task difficulty level will be reduced. In Case3a, the strategy generator will maintain tasks at the same level of difficulty and look out for an improvement in the next cycle. In case of no further improvement in the next cycle, task difficulty level will be reduced (Case 3b). In Case4, the task difficulty level will also be reduced. We implemented the dynamic task switching by a finite state machine representation [14] (Fig. 6).

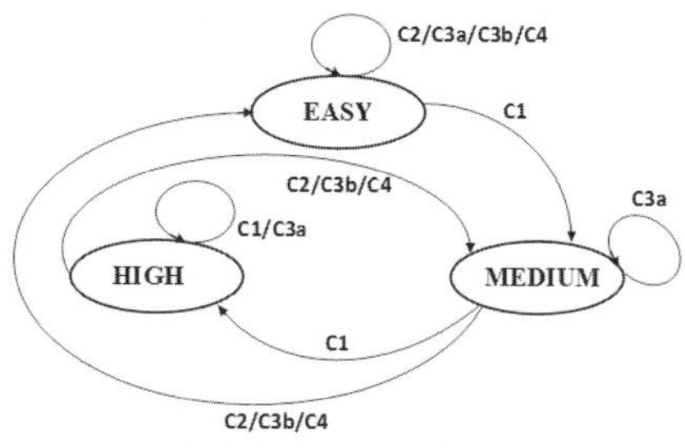

Fig. 6. State Machine Representation of Dynamic Decision Task Switching

3 Methods

3.1 Participants

Four adolescents with high-functioning ASD participated in this experiment. Their data on Peabody Picture Vocabulary Test (PPVT) [15], Social Responsive Scale (SRS) [16], Social Communication Questionnaire (SCQ) [17] Autism Diagnostic Observation Schedule (ADOS) [18], Autism Diagnostic Interview-Revised (ADI-R) [19] are presented in Table 4.

Table 4. Participant Characteristics

	Age (y)	PPVT	SRS	SCQ	ADOS	ADI-R
ASD1	17.58	134	80	12	13	49
ASD2	13.83	170	92	14	13	53
ASD3	18.25	97	63	17	9	49
ASD4	15.75	126	69	23	11	56

3.2 Procedure

Each participant participated in one session of VR-based social interaction task lasting for about 1 hour. During this visit, the participant sat comfortably on a height-adjustable chair and was asked to wear the eye-tracker goggles. They interacted with avatars narrating personal stories. They were asked to imagine that the avatars were their classmates at school giving presentations on several different topics. They were informed that after the presentations they would be required to interact with the avatar to find out some information from the avatar. They were also asked to try and make their classmate feel as comfortable as possible while listening to the presentation.

4 Results

We conducted a usability study to test whether the designed VR-based gaze-sensitive system with adaptive response technology functions as desired. Also, we tried to investigate whether the interaction with the system has the potential to impact the social task performance and behavioral viewing pattern of the participants with ASD.

4.1 Progression of VR-Based Social Communication Tasks

We analyzed the VR-based task progression for the participants across trials. ASD1 and ASD2 started at Medium difficulty level, and were able to achieve high difficulty level while interacting with our system (Fig. 7) with both of them interacting with 2 in Easy, 4 in Medium, and 3 in High difficulty levels. On the other hand, ASD3 started with Easy difficulty level and interacted with 7 VR-based social task trials with 2 in Easy, 2 in Medium, and 3 in High difficulty levels. ASD4 started with the High difficulty level and interacted with 4 VR-based social task trials in High difficulty level. Task switching ability of the system indicates the potential to individualize social communication training in the future.

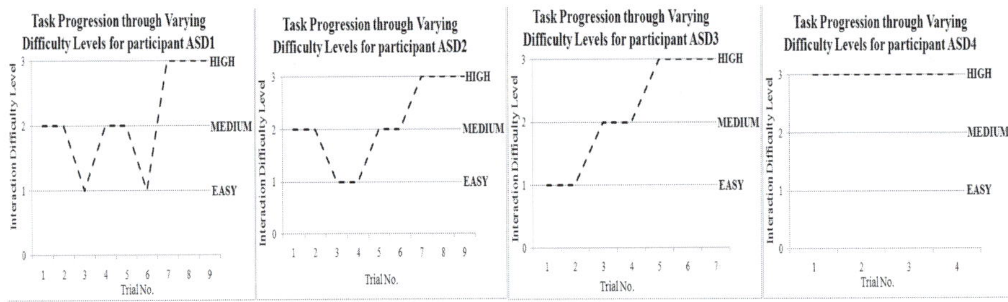

Fig. 7. VR-based Task Progression for ASD1, ASD2, ASD3, and ASD4 across trials. Interaction Difficulty Level=1: 'Easy'; Level=2: 'Medium'; Level=3: 'High'

4.2 Improvement in Behavioral Viewing Pattern

For effective social communication skills, one must not only achieve adequate task performance measures (e.g., obtaining the required information by asking the appropriate questions), but also carry out the conversation in a socially appropriate way (e.g., paying attention towards the face of the communicator during communication). We investigated to see whether there was any improvement in the behavioral viewing pattern of the participants while interacting with our VR-based engagement-sensitive system equipped with adaptive response technology.

Fig. 8 shows variation in the behavioral viewing pattern in terms of percent fixation duration towards the face region (Face_ROI) of the avatars of each participant across different trials. All participants demonstrated improvement in their behavioral viewing patterns in terms of greater attention towards the face of the communicator from trial1 to the last trial (trial9 for ASD1 and ASD2, trial7 for ASD3, and trial4 for ASD4). The mean percent fixation of all subsequent trials for each participant increased from their trial1 values by 26.58%. This data, although preliminary in nature, demonstrate that the feasibility of our system to impact the participants' looking patterns in a positive manner, i.e., they paid more attention to the avatars during conversation.

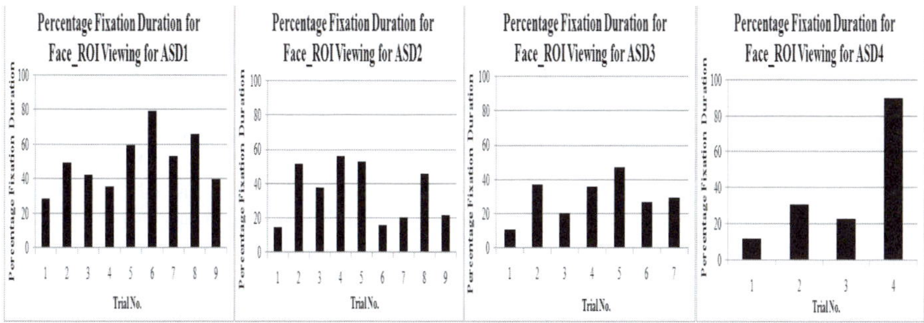

Fig. 8. Variation in Percent Fixation Duration while looking towards the face region (Face_ROI) of the avatar during the VR-based social communication task trials

5 Conclusion

In the present work we developed a VR-based engagement-sensitive system with adaptive response technology. In this paper we presented the system development and results of a small usability study to test the efficacy of the developed system as a first step to technology-assisted intervention. The developed system can detect subtle variations in one's eye-physiological features, and behavioral viewing pattern in real-time. Also it seamlessly integrates these pieces of information with the VR-platform to provide intelligent individualized adaptive response. Results of a usability study show the capability of the system to contribute to improving one's social task performance (e.g., ability of the participants to interact with VR-based social tasks with increased degree of difficulty) along with encouraging socially-appropriate mechanisms (e.g., improved attention towards the face of the communicator) to foster effective social communication skills among the participants with ASD. Such an integrated system has the potential to be incorporated into complex intervention paradigms aimed at improving functioning and quality of life for individuals with ASD.

Acknowledgments. The authors would like to acknowledge the National Science Foundation Grant 0967170 and the National Institute of Health Grant 1R01MH091102-01A1 that partially supported this research.

References

1. APA.: Diagnostic and statistical manual of mental disorders: DSM-IV-TR. American Psychiatric Association, Washington, DC (2000)
2. Kanner, L.: Autistic disturbances of affective contact. Nervous Child 2, 217–250 (1943)
3. Wieder, S., Greenspan, S.: Can Children with Autism Master the Core Deficits and Become Empathetic, Creative, and Reflective? The J. of Dev. and Learning Dis. 9 (2005)
4. Trepagnier, C.Y., Sebrechts, M.M., Finkelmeyer, A., Stewart, W., Woodford, J., Coleman, M.: Simulating social interaction to address deficits of autistic spectrum disorder in children. Cyberpsych. Behav. 9(2), 213–217 (2006)
5. Goodwin, M.S.: Enhancing and accelerating the pace of Autism Research and Treatment: The promise of developing Innovative Technology. Focus on Autism and other Developmental Disabilities 23, 125–128 (2008)
6. Strickland, D.: Virtual reality for the treatment of autism. In: Riva, G. (ed.) Virtual Reality in Neuropsychophysiology, pp. 81–86. IOS Press, Amsterdam (1997)
7. Parsons, S., Mitchell, P., Leonard, A.: The use and understanding of virtual environments by adolescents with autistic spectrum disorders. J. Autism. Dev. Disord. 34(4), 449–466 (2004)
8. Tartaro, A., Cassell, J.: Using Virtual Peer Technology as an Intervention for Children with Autism. In: Lazar, J. (ed.) Towards Universal Usability: Designing Computer Interfaces for Diverse User Populations, UK. John Wiley and Sons, Chichester (2007)
9. Wilms, M., Schilbach, L., Pfeiffer, U., Bente, G., Fink, G.R., Vogeley, K.: It's in your eyes using gaze-contingent stimuli to create truly interactive paradigms for social cognitive and affective neuroscience. Social Cognitive and Affective Neuroscience 5(1), 98–107 (2010)
10. NRC: Educating children with autism. National Academy Press, Washington, DC (2001)
11. Anderson, C.J., Colombo, J., Shaddy, D.J.: Visual Scanning and Pupillary Responses in Young Children with Autism Spectrum Disorder. J. of Clinical and Experimental Neuropsychology 28, 1238–1256 (2006)
12. Jensen, B., Keehn, B., Brenner, L., Marshall, S.P., Lincoln, A.J., Müller, R.A.: In-creased Eye-Blink Rate in Autism Spectrum Disorder May Reflect Dopaminergic Abnormalities. Intl. Society for Autism Research, Poster Presentation (2009)
13. Ruble, L.A., Robson, D.M.: Individual and environmental determinants of engagement in autism. J. of Aut. and Dev. Dis. 37(8), 1457–1468 (2006)
14. Booth, T.: Sequential Machines and Automata Theory. John Wiley and Sons, New York (1967)
15. Dunn, L.M., Dunn, L.M.: PPVT-III: Peabody Picture Vocabulary Test. Circle Pines. American Guidance Service, Minnesota (1997)
16. Constantino, J.N.: The Social Responsiveness Scale. W. Psych. Serv., California (2002)
17. Rutter, M., Bailey, A., Berument, S., Lord, C., Pickles, A.: Social Communication Questionnaire. Western Psychological Services, Los Angeles (2003a)
18. Lord, C., Risi, S., Lambrecht, L., Cook, E.H., Leventhal, B.L., DiLavore, P.C., Pickles, A., Rutter, M.: The Autism diagnostic observation schedule-generic: A standard measure of social and communication deficits associated with the spectrum of autism. J. of Autism and Dev. Dis. 30(3), 205–223 (2000)
19. Rutter, M., Couteur, A., Le, L.C.: Autism diagnostic interview revised WPS edition manual. W. Psych. Serv., Los Angeles (2003b)

Exploring the Relationship between Novice Programmer Confusion and Achievement

Diane Marie C. Lee[1], Ma. Mercedes T. Rodrigo[1], Ryan S.J.d. Baker[2], Jessica O. Sugay[1], and Andrei Coronel[1]

[1] Department of Information Systems and Computer Science, Ateneo de Manila University, Loyala Heights, Quezon City, Philippines
[2] Department of Social Science and Policy Studies, Worcester Polytechnic Institute, Worcester MA, USA
dianemarielee@gmail.com, {mrodrigo,jsugay,acoronel}@ateneo.edu, rsbaker@wpi.edu

Abstract. Using a discovery-with-models approach, we study the relationships between novice Java programmers' experiences of confusion and their achievement, as measured through their midterm examination scores. Two coders manually labeled samples of student compilation logs with whether they represent a student who was confused. From the labeled data, we built a model that we used to label the entire data set. We then analysed the relationship between patterns of confusion and non-confusion over time, and students' midterm scores. We found that, in accordance with prior findings, prolonged confusion is associated with poorer student achievement. However, confusion which is resolved is associated with statistically significantly better midterm performance than never being confused at all.

Keywords: Confusion, novice programmers, student affect, affective sequences, student achievement, Java, BlueJ.

1 Introduction

Learning to program is an emotional experience. According to interview-based reports in [13], when novice programmers begin reading problem specifications, a lack of comprehension of the instructions can lead to a feeling of disorientation. When they start to understand the problem, they can continue to feel lost, this time because they do not know how to begin the programming process. The first error they encounter can trigger strong negative emotions. Subsequent errors can lead to a sense of resignation and a reluctance to continue. Students also report different emotions based on their use of feedback while programming [13]. Students who effectively use feedback to guide their programming in some cases feel a constructive form of confusion that motivates them to systematically experiment with their code and converge to a solution. In contrast, students who

S. D´Mello et al. (Eds.): ACII 2011, Part I, LNCS 6974, pp. 175–184, 2011.

ignore or are unable to use feedback liken their experiences to running in a hamster wheel: They repeatedly try bug fixes with no reflection or understanding, eventually leading to a feeling of despair [13].

Recent studies illustrate the relationships between affective states and achievement in a variety of learning contexts. Craig et al. [6] found that, among students using an AutoTutor, an intelligent tutor for computer literacy, the affective states of confusion and flow [7] (called "engaged concentration" in [3]) were positively correlated with achievement. Boredom, regarded by Craig et al. [6] as the antithesis of flow, was negatively correlated with learning gains. Lagud and Rodrigo [15] found that high achieving students using Aplusix, an intelligent tutor for algebra, experienced significantly more flow than students with low achievement. Low-achieving students in the same study experienced the highest levels of boredom and, in contrast to [6], confusion.

In the context of learning to program, Rodrigo et al [19] found that boredom and confusion were again associated with lower achievement among students taking their first college-level programming course. Khan et al. [12] found that high levels of arousal regardless of valence – delight, rejoicing, even terror and restlessness – can lead to better debugging performance among students.

One of the limitations of these studies is that they examined these affective states in isolation, rather than as links in a cognitive-affective chain, cf. [10]. Researchers have therefore grown increasingly interested in studying affective dynamics, defined as the natural shifts in learners' affective states over time [8]. Studies by [3], [8], and [16], have found that certain affective states such as flow/engaged concentation, confusion, boredom, and frustration tend to persist over time. Confused students tend to stay confused; engaged students tend to stay engaged.

Affect and affective dynamics have also been shown to influence student achievement and key student behaviours that drive learning. Research by D'Mello et al [10] has found that students who are bored tend to get trapped in a "vicious cycle" of boredom, incorrect responses to problem solving questions, and negative feedback. Boredom has also been found to be an antecedent of gaming the system, a behaviour associated with significantly poorer learning, among students using simulation problem games and intelligent tutors [3]. By contrast, [10] found that the more positive affective state of curiosity leads to correct responses to problem solving questions, positive feedback, happiness, and continued curiosity. Confusion was found to have a dual nature. If a student is unable to work through confusion, the student is likely to give incorrect responses to questions, receive negative feedback and eventually experience frustration. If, on the other hand, confusion is resolved, the student's responses to questions will tend to be correct, the student will receive positive feedback and eventually transitions into a neutral affective state [10]. Some of D'Mello et al.'s [10] findings were corroborated by recent study by Rodrigo, Baker, and Nabos [20] that examined students using an intelligent tutor for scatterplots. They found that boredom was both persistent and detrimental to learning. Confusion could be positive if punctuated with periods of engaged concentration. Prolonged confusion, on the other hand, had a negative impact on student achievement.

Within this paper, we present a study that uses a discovery-with-models approach [2] to investigate novice programmer confusion and its impact on student overall achievement in a course. Two human coders manually labeled text replays [4] of excerpts of student compilation behaviour (termed "clips") as to whether they represented student confusion. From the labeled data, we built a machine-learned model of student confusion and used this model to label the entire dataset. We then aggregated student affect over time into sequences of confusion and non-confusion, and correlated each student's frequency of demonstrating these sequences with the student's midterm exam score.

2 Data Collection

The population under study consisted of 149 freshman and sophomore college students aged 15 to 17 from the Department of Information Systems and Computer Science (DISCS) of the Ateneo de Manila University during the School Year 2009-2010. These students are younger than the typical college freshman in other countries because the Philippines only has 10 years of mandatory basic education, two years less than basic education in other countries. These students were enrolled in five sections of CS21 A-Introduction to Computing I and were divided into five sections.

We collected the students' compilation logs during four practical lab sessions spread over two months. Laboratory sessions were held in two classrooms. Each student was assigned to a computer installed with a specially instrumented version of the BlueJ Interactive Development Environment (IDE) for Java (Figure 1) [11]. This version of BlueJ was connected to a SQLite database server. Upon each compilation, BlueJ saved a copy of the students' program and any compile-time error messages, on the server.

There were some lab sessions during which the data collection server was not running correctly. We were therefore only able to collect logs from 340 student-lab sessions, giving a total of 13,528 compilations.

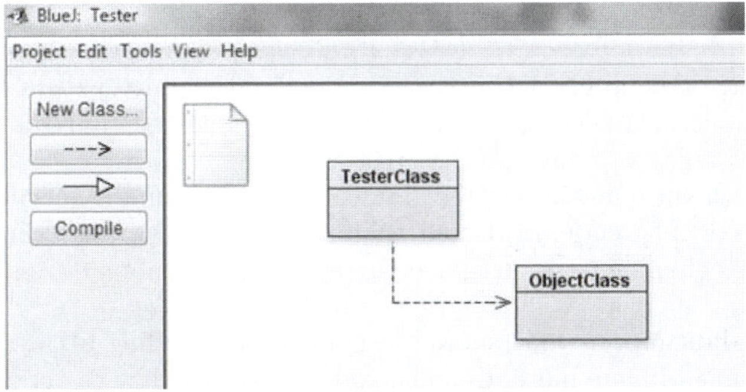

Fig. 1. Screenshot of the BlueJ IDE

3 Data Labeling

The first step in the labeling process was deciding the level of granularity at which the compilations were going to be examined. It was not possible, for example, to tell whether a student was confused from a single compilation. Neither did we want to judge student confusion based on an entire session's worth of compilations. If, later on, we were to design interventions for student confusion, we would like these interventions to be sensitive enough to detect confusion while the student is still writing the program and not after he or she has finished. We needed a sequence of compilation events to conduct data labeling but had to decide on the sequence length. We decided to group the compilations into clips of 8 compilations each where the number of compilations, 8, was chosen arbitrarily.

There were cases in which a Java program consisted of two or more Java classes. When a student compiled, all Java classes within the program were compiled and logged with the same time stamp. To generate the clips, we sorted all compilations first by student identifier, then by Java class name, then by time stamp. We then grouped the compilations with same student identifier and Java class into sets of up to 8 compilations. This produced a total of 2,386 clips which could be coded.

We attempted to sample 2 random clips per student-lab for labeling, which would have given 680 clips. However, some students only had a single clip for a specific lab (for example, due to requiring fewer than 16 compilations to complete a lab). We therefore coded a total of 664 clips.

A small application was written to display the clips in the form of low-fidelity text replays (Figure 2) [4], where human judgment is applied to pretty-prints of subsegments of log files. A previous study by Baker et al [4] showed that text replays enable coders to label student disengagement with greater efficiency than higher fidelity methods such as human observations and video replays, while maintaining good inter-rater reliability. This method of data labeling has also been used to study student meta-cognitive planning processes [17] and systematic experimentation behaviour patterns [21], again achieving good inter-rater reliability.

Once the application was completed, the two co-authors met to decide on criteria for labeling clips as "Confused","Not Confused" or "Bad Clip". The coders decided that the student's behavior implied confusion when

1. The same error appeared in the same general vicinity within the code for several consecutive compilations. The coders inferred that the student did not know what was causing the error and how to fix it.
2. An assortment of errors appeared in consecutive compilations and remained unresolved. The coders inferred that the student was experimenting with solutions, changing the actual error message but not addressing the real source of the error.
3. Code malformations that showed a poor understanding of Java constructs, e.g. "return outside method". The coders inferred that the student did not grasp even the basics of program construction, despite the availability of written aids such as Java code samples and explanatory slides.

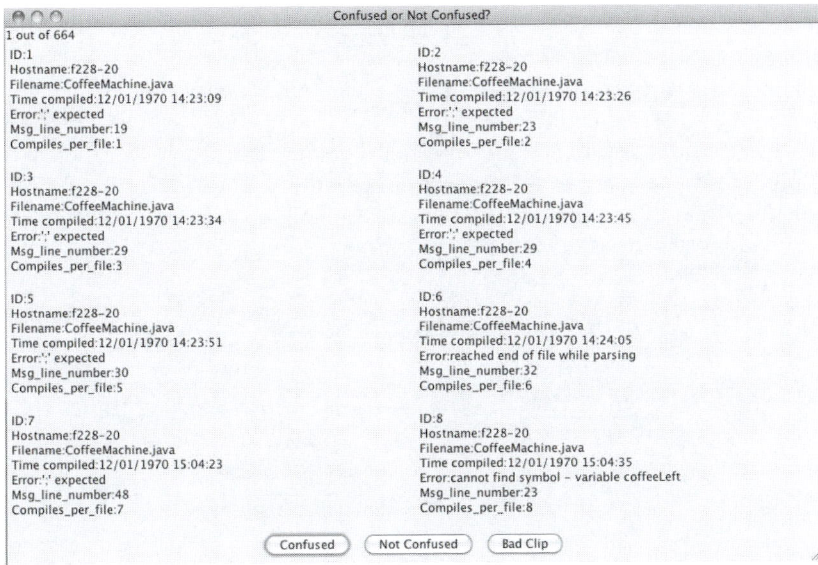

Fig. 2. Screen shot of the low-fidelity text replay playback program for a "confused" student

When a clip showed a student successfully resolving an error or an assortment of errors, it was labeled as "not confused." If a clip had compilations of programs other than the assigned laboratory exercise, e.g. instructor-supplied sample code or tester programs, it was labeled "bad clip."

Interrater reliability was acceptably high with Cohen's [5] Kappa = .77.

Given these labels, our next step was to build a detector to label the rest of the data. In order to do so, we filtered out all "bad clips" and all clips with less than 8 compilations. It was also necessary to filter out data from one of the five class sections due to a logging error. Finally, we removed all clips in which the two raters disagreed, for the purposes of building a model. We were left with 418 clips with which to build the model.

4 Model Construction and Data Relabeling

RapidMiner version 5.1 [1] was used to build a decision tree, using the J48 implementation of the C4.5 algorithm [18] (Figure 3), using the following feature set:

1. Average time between compilations
2. Maximum time between compilations
3. Average time between compilations with errors
4. Maximum time between compilations with errors
5. Number of compilations with errors
6. Number of pairs of consecutive compilations with the same error

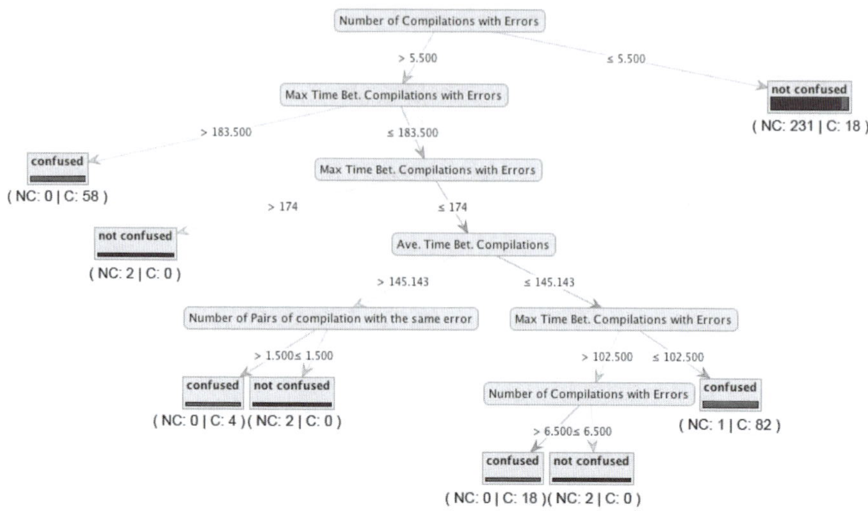

Fig. 3. Decision tree depicting the criteria for labeling a clip as confused or not confused

Student-level 10-fold cross-validation of the model resulted in an excellent Kappa of .86.

The model was implemented as a Java program. The program was then used to label all of the clips in the data set. Removing all bad clips, we generated three sets of confused-not confused sequences. The first set consisted of single states. The second set consisted of sequences of two consecutive states (2-step). The third and final set consisted of sequences of three consecutive states (3-step).

There were students who did not have any 2-step or 3-step sequences for any specific lab. Hence, the number of students in each set varied. We had 113 students in the 1-step set, 95 students in the 2-step set and 71 students in the 3-step set.

We counted the number of occurrences of each state or sequence per student within each set. The total number of sequences per student varied. We therefore normalized the data by dividing the number of occurrences of each state or sequence per student by the total number of occurrences for that student. We then correlated these percentages with the students' midterm examination scores. The midterm examination was composed of questions that tested students' programming comprehension. Students were given code fragments as well as whole programs. They were then asked questions about the code, including whether fragments would compile, what the output of a code fragment would be, or which part of the code performed a given action.

5 Results and Discussion

In terms of 1-step sequences, there was a marginally significant negative correlation between the incidence of confusion and student achievement (r= -.168;

Table 1. r-values of the incidence of 2-step sequences with midterm scores. Numbers in parenthesis are the p-values. Statistically significant correlations are in dark grey.

	Not Confused - Not Confused	Not Confused - Confused	Confused - Not Confused	Confused - Confused
Relationship with midterm	.064 (.539)	.139 (.180)	.144 (.163)	-.229 (.026)

p=.075). This indicates, rather unsurprisingly, that students who are confused in general tend to receive lower scores on the midterm exam.

The 2-step sequences (Table 1) show that confusion sustained over two clips is also negatively correlated with midterm scores (r=- .229; p=.026). No other 2-step sequences were significantly different than chance, suggesting that only sustained confusion impacts learning negatively to a significant degree.

Analysis of the 3-step sequences sheds further light on the relationship between confusion and learning. Confusion sustained over three consecutive clips, is again negatively correlated with midterm scores (CCC: r=-.337; p=.004). On the other hand, a student who over a 3-clip sequence starts out confused, resolves their confusion, and continues to be non-confused, then achieves higher midterm scores (CNN: r=.233, p=.05). This is consistent with D'Mello and Graesser's [9] cognitive disequilibrium model in which confusion has to be resolved through thought, reflection, and deep thinking to return the learner into a flow state. Unresolved confusion, on the other hand, leads to frustration and boredom.

Note that simply switching from confused to non-confused is not sufficient for positive learning; as shown in Table 2, other patterns of transition between confusion and non-confusion are not significantly associated with midterm performance; the key pattern for learning appears to be confusion which is resolved, and does not recur.

Also, in contrast to confusion which is resolved, never being confused at all is not significantly associated with midterm performance, r= -0.015, p=0.901. This finding is additional support for the hypothesis that some degree of confusion is beneficial for learning. Deep processing of the subject matter appears to require being confused, but resolving that confusion.

These findings shed additional light on the dual nature of confusion. Students experience confusion when confronted with new material or new problems they cannot immediately solve. At this point, confusion may spur students to work

Table 2. r-values of the incidence of 3-step sequences with midterm scores. Numbers in parenthesis are the p-values. Statistically significant correlations are in dark grey. N = Not Confused while C = Confused.

	NNN	NNC	NCN	NCC	CNN	CNC	CCN	CCC
Rel. with midterm	-.015 (.901)	.014 (.909)	.062 (.610)	-.046 (.704)	.233 (.05)	.163 (.174)	.052 (.665)	-.337 (.004)

through the problems and resolve them, returning eventually to a hopeful and enthusiastic state, as hypothesized in [14]. [9] consider this type of confusion to be productive. On the other hand students can become stuck in a state of hopeless – persistent – confusion, which does not lead to learning.

6 Conclusion

The purpose of this paper was to study the relationship between novice programmers' experience of confusion and their achievement as measured through their midterm examination scores. Using a discovery-with-models approach, we created a model of confusion using manually-labeled samples of student compilation logs. We then used this model to label the entire data set. From the labeled data set, we distilled students' patterns of transitions between being confused and not confused, and correlated these sequences' incidence with each student's midterm scores. We found that prolonged confusion has a negative impact on student achievement. Confusion which is resolved, however, is positively associated with midterm scores.

Overall, the findings of this study support D'Mello and Graesser's [9] model of cognitive disequilibrium, applicable to deep learning environments. The model proposes that confusion can be a useful affective state when it spurs learners to exert effort deliberately and purposefully to resolve cognitive conflict. If the learners are successful, they return to a state of flow [7]. If they are unsuccessful, though, they could become frustrated or bored, and may decide to disengage from the learning task altogether [9]. The model and these findings challenge educational designers to develop learning tasks that are complex enough to stimulate a constructive level of learner confusion while making scaffolding available to prevent hopelessness and disengagement.

As a response to these challenges, one important future use of this paper's model of confusion and the subsequent findings will be to support the incorporation of tools for automatically detecting novice programmer confusion, into computer science education environments. As the detector is based solely upon log files, it can be deployed at scale quite easily. These tools may enable educators to identify novices who are at academic risk and provide these students with the support they need to learn the material and persist in their studies. In addition, the detector could eventually be the basis of automated response to student confusion.

Acknowledgements. The authors thank the Department of Science and Technology's Philippine Council for Advanced Science and Technology Research and Development for the grant entitled "Development and Deployment of an Intelligent Affective Detector for the BlueJ Interactive Development Environment", and the Pittsburgh Science of Learning Center (National Science Foundation) via grant "Toward a Decade of PSLC Research", award number SBE-0836012. We thank Jose Alfredo de Vera, Hubert Ursua, Matthew C. Jadud and the Department of Information Systems and Computer Science of the Ateneo de

Manila University for their support. We thank Wimbie Sy and Clarissa Ramos for their contribution to the early part of this work. Finally, we thank the CS 21 A students of school year 2009-2010 for their participation in this study.

References

1. http://www.rapid-i.com
2. Baker, R.: Data mining for education. In: International Encyclopedia of Education, 3rd edn. Elsevier, Oxford (2010)
3. Baker, R., D'Mello, S., Rodrigo, M., Graesser, A.: Better to be frustrated than bored: The incidence and persistence of affect during interactions with three different computer-based learning environments. International Journal of Human-Computer Studies 68(4), 223–241 (2010)
4. Baker, R., Corbett, A., Wagner, A.: Human classification of low-fidelity replays of student actions. In: Proceedings of the Educational Data Mining Workshop at the 8th International Conference on Intelligent Tutoring Systems, pp. 29–36. Citeseer (2006)
5. Cohen, J.: A coefficient of agreement for nominal scales. Educational and Psychological Measurement (1960)
6. Craig, S., Graesser, A., Sullins, J., Gholson, B.: Affect and learning: an exploratory look into the role of affect in learning with AutoTutor. Journal of Educational Media 29, 241–250 (2004)
7. Csikszentmihalyi, M.: Flow: The psychology of optimal experience: Steps toward enhancing the quality of life. Harper Collins Publishers, New York (1991)
8. DMello, S., Taylor, R., Graesser, A.: Monitoring affective trajectories during complex learning. In: Proceedings of the 29th Annual Meeting of the Cognitive Science Society, pp. 203–208 (2007)
9. DMello, S., Graesser, A.: Dynamics of Cognitive-Affective States During Deep Learning. Paper under review
10. DMello, S., Person, N., Lehman, B.: Antecedent-consequent relationships and cyclical patterns between affective states and problem solving outcomes. In: Proceedings of AIED (2009)
11. Jadud, M., Henriksen, P.: Flexible, reusable tools for studying novice programmers. In: Proceedings of the Fifth International Workshop on Computing Education Research Workshop, pp. 37–42. ACM, New York (2009)
12. Khan, I., Brinkman, W., Hierons, R.: Do moods affect programmers debug performance? In: Cognition, Technology & Work, pp. 1–14
13. Kinnunen, P., Simon, B.: Experiencing programming assignments in CS1: the emotional toll. In: Proceedings of the Sixth International Workshop on Computing Education Research, pp. 77–86. ACM, New York (2010)
14. Kort, B., Reilly, R., Picard, R.: An affective model of interplay between emotions and learning. In: Proceedings of IEEE International Conference on Advanced Learning Technologies, pp. 6–8 (2001)
15. Lagud, M., Rodrigo, M.: The Affective and Learning Profiles of Students Using an Intelligent Tutoring System for Algebra. In: Aleven, V., Kay, J., Mostow, J. (eds.) ITS 2010, Part I. LNCS, vol. 6094, pp. 255–263. Springer, Heidelberg (2010)
16. McQuiggan, S., Robison, J., Lester, J.: Affective Transitions in Narrative-Centered Learning Environments. Subscription Prices and Ordering Information 13(1), 40–53 (2010)

17. Montalvo, O., Baker, R., Sao Pedro, M., Nakama, A., Gobert, J.: Identifying Students Inquiry Planning Using Machine Learning. In: Proceedings of the 3rd International Conference on Educational Data Mining, pp. 141–150 (2010)
18. Quinlan, J.: C4. 5: programs for machine learning. Morgan Kaufmann, San Francisco (1993)
19. Rodrigo, M., Mercedes, T., Baker, R., Jadud, M., Amarra, A., Dy, T., Espejo-Lahoz, M., Lim, S., Pascua, S., Sugay, J., et al.: Affective and behavioral predictors of novice programmer achievement. ACM SIGCSE Bulletin 41(3), 156–160 (2009)
20. Rodrigo, M., Baker, R., Nabos, J.: The Relationships Between Sequences of Affective States and Learner Achievement. In: Proceedings of the 18th International Conference on Computers in Education, pp. 56–60 (2010)
21. Sao Pedro, M., Baker, R., Montalvo, O., Nakama, A., Gobert, J.: Using Text Replay Tagging to Produce Detectors of Systematic Experimentation Behavior Patterns. In: Proceedings of the 3rd International Conference on Educational Data Mining, pp. 181–190 (2010)

Semi-Coupled Hidden Markov Model with State-Based Alignment Strategy for Audio-Visual Emotion Recognition

Jen-Chun Lin, Chung-Hsien Wu, and Wen-Li Wei

Department of Computer Science and Information Engineering, National Cheng Kung University, Tainan, Taiwan, R.O.C.
{jenchunlin,chunghsienwu,lilijinjin}@gmail.com

Abstract. This paper presents an approach to bi-modal emotion recognition based on a semi-coupled hidden Markov model (SC-HMM). A simplified state-based bi-modal alignment strategy in SC-HMM is proposed to align the temporal relation of states between audio and visual streams. Based on this strategy, the proposed SC-HMM can alleviate the problem of data sparseness and achieve better statistical dependency between states of audio and visual HMMs in most real world scenarios. For performance evaluation, audio-visual signals with four emotional states (happy, neutral, angry and sad) were collected. Each of the invited seven subjects was asked to utter 30 types of sentences twice to generate emotional speech and facial expression for each emotion. Experimental results show the proposed bi-modal approach outperforms other fusion-based bi-modal emotion recognition methods.

Keywords: Emotion recognition, hidden Markov model, bi-modal approach.

1 Introduction

Emotions are important in human intelligence, rational decision making, social interaction, perception, memory, and more [1]. Understanding human emotional states is indispensable for day to day functioning. In human-computer interaction system, emotion recognition technology could provide harmonious interaction or heart to heart communication between computer and human being. Hence, creating an emotion perception and recognition system to our daily lives are expected. The challenging research field, "affective computing," introduced by Picard [1] aims at enabling computer to recognize, express, and have emotions. In previous work, various studies in emotion recognition were focused only on considering single facial or vocal modality. Based on psychological analysis [2], [3] human emotional states were transmitted by multiple channel process such as face [4], voice [5], and speech content [6] for communication. For this reason, exploring data fusion strategies between various channels will meet a token of emotional expression and therefore can improve recognition performance [7], [8].

The fusion operation reported in the literature can be classified into three major categories, including feature-level, decision-level, and model-level fusion, for audio-visual emotion recognition [7]. In feature-level fusion [9], facial and vocal

S. D´Mello et al. (Eds.): ACII 2011, Part I, LNCS 6974, pp. 185–194, 2011.

features were concatenated to construct the joint feature vectors and then modeled by a single classifier for emotion recognition. Although fusion at feature level can obtain the advantage of combining visual and audio cues, it will increase the dimensionality and may suffer from the problem of data sparseness. In terms of decision-level fusion [10], multiple signals can be modeled by its corresponding classifier first and then the recognition results are fused together to obtain the final result. The fusion-based method at the decision level, without increasing the dimensionality, can combine the various modalities by exploring the contributions of different emotion expressions. Since facial and vocal features are complementary to each other for emotion expression, the assumption of conditional independence among multiple modalities at decision level is inappropriate. Hence, the mutual correlation between visual and audio modalities should be considered. Contrary to decision-level, model-level fusion [11] emphasizes the information of mutual correlation among multiple signal streams and explores the temporal relation between the visual and audio streams.

Recently, more and more studies have paid attention to model-level fusion in data fusion approaches. Coupled hidden Markov model (C-HMM) as one of the popular model-level fusion approaches has been proposed and was successfully used in different fields such as hand gesture recognition [12], speech prosody recognition [13], audio-visual speech recognition [14], and speech animation [15]. In C-HMM, two component HMMs were linked through cross-time and cross-chain conditional probabilities. A state variable at time t is dependent on its preceding nodes of two HMMs at time $t-1$, which describes the temporal coupling relationship between two streams. This structure models the asynchrony of multiple modalities and preserves their natural correlations over time. In bi-modal audio-visual processing, however, the statistical dependency between audio and visual features were often not strong enough to be captured. For most real-world scenarios, the statistical dependency between two hidden states of the observation sequences is difficult to obtain from insufficient training samples for C-HMM training. Hence, it may suffer from the problem of data sparseness. To deal with this problem, a semi-coupled hidden Markov model (SC-HMM) with simplified state-based alignment strategy is developed in this paper.

In view of the preceding shortcomings, the proposed model has several desirable characteristics:

1) It can model better statistical dependence between states of audio and visual HMMs for most real-world scenarios.
2) It has low computational complexity than C-HMM.
3) It can alleviate the problem of data sparseness.

Fig.1 illustrates an overview of the proposed emotion recognition system. First, the input bi-modal signals are separated into audio and visual parts. Since endpoint detection based on speech is easier and more robust than mouth movement, the start and end points of a salient speech segment were determined first and then used to obtain the time-aligned salient visual segment. The extracted salient speech and visual segments are used to extract prosodic and facial features, respectively. Finally, using the prosodic and facial features, the proposed SC-HMM is employed for emotion recognition.

The rest of the paper is organized as follows: Section 2 briefly outlines the method for feature extraction. Section 3 provides a detailed description of the proposed SC-HMM. Section 4 provides experimental result and discussion. Section 5 gives the conclusion.

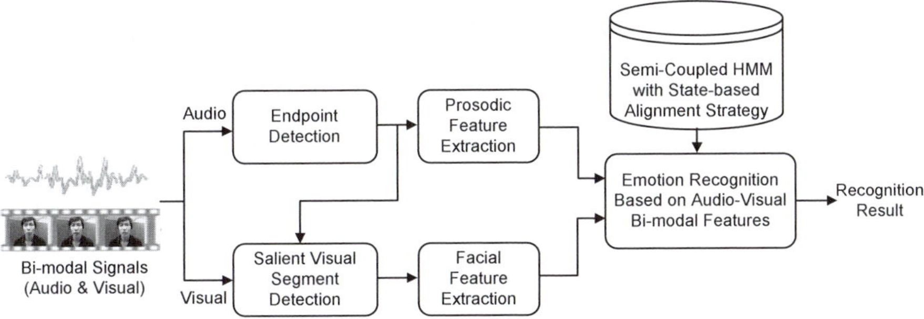

Fig. 1. System diagram of the proposed audio-visual emotion recognition

2 Feature Extraction

2.1 Facial Feature Extraction

Facial expression is one of the direct related cues to human emotions [2], [3]. In this paper, facial features containing five facial regions: eyebrow, eye, nose, mouth, and facial contour are considered. Face detection is performed based on the Adaboost cascade face detector proposed in [16] and can be used to provide initial facial position and reduce the time for error convergence in feature extraction. The active appearance model (AAM) [17] combines the two different characteristic features to effectively localize human facial features on a 2D visual image. The major structure of AAM can be divided into two statistical models, a shape model and an appearance model. It has achieved a great success on human face alignment even though the human faces may have non-rigid deformations. Hence, AAM has been widely used to extract facial feature points for facial expression recognition. In this paper, the AAM was used to extract the 68 labeled facial feature points from five facial regions for later motion trajectory calculation. The feature vector for each facial region consists of the set of motion trajectories which calculate the difference of facial feature points between the current frame t and its pervious frame t-1 in the same facial region.

2.2 Prosodic Feature Extraction

Recently, prosody has been proven to be the primary and classical indicators of a speaker's emotional state and it was widely and successfully used for emotion recognition [5], [7] based on speech signals. The pitch and energy have been reported to contribute the most to speech emotion recognition [7]. In addition, formants and speaking rate are also discussed frequently [5]. Although speaking rate is an important prosodic feature, speech recognition error resulting in incorrect detection of speaking rate will dramatically degrade the emotion recognition performance. Based on these analyses, three kinds of primary prosodic features are adopted, including pitch, energy and formants F1-F5 in each speech frame for emotion recognition. Endpoint detection of speech signals based on energy and zero-crossing rate is first used to extract the salient segment of speech signals. For prosodic feature extraction, the pitch detection tool "Praat" is used [18].

3 Semi-Coupled Hidden Markov Model

In this paper, SC-HMM is proposed for emotion recognition based on state-based alignment strategy for audio-visual bi-modal features. In C-HMM, while the frame-based cross-chain temporal relationship between two HMMs is completely considered, it may suffer from the problem of data sparseness and diminish the advantage of C-HMM. Unlike the C-HMM, the connections between two component HMMs in SC-HMM are chosen based on a simplified state-based alignment strategy which emphasizes on state level alignment rather than the frame level. Hence, the proposed SC-HMM can alleviate the problem of data sparseness and obtain better statistical dependency between states of audio and visual HMMs for most real-world scenarios.

3.1 Model Formulation

In this paper, the recognition task with four emotional states, happy, neutral, angry and sad, represented by $\{e_h, e_n, e_a, e_s\}$ are considered. The probability of two tightly coupled audio-visual observation sequences O^a and O^v given the parameter set $\Lambda = \{\lambda_{e_k}^a, \lambda_{e_k}^v\}$ is obtained using (1). e_k^* represents the emotional state with maximum probability of the audio-visual observation sequences O^a and O^v given the parameter set Λ of the SC-HMM.

$$e_k^* = \arg\max_{e_k \in \{e_h, e_n, e_a, e_s\}} P\left(O^a, O^v \mid \lambda_{e_k}^a, \lambda_{e_k}^v\right) \tag{1}$$

For SC-HMM with state sequence S^a and S^v for audio and visual HMMs respectively, the probability $P\left(O^a, O^v \mid \lambda_{e_k}^a, \lambda_{e_k}^v\right)$ can be further inferred by (2).

$$P\left(O^a, O^v \mid \lambda_{e_k}^a, \lambda_{e_k}^v\right) = \sum_{S^a, S^v} P\left(O^a, O^v, S^a, S^v \mid \lambda_{e_k}^a, \lambda_{e_k}^v\right) \tag{2}$$

where $P\left(O^a, O^v \mid \lambda_{e_k}^a, \lambda_{e_k}^v\right)$ can be approximated by selecting the optimal state sequence which maximizes the probability $P\left(O^a, O^v, S^a, S^v \mid \lambda_{e_k}^a, \lambda_{e_k}^v\right)$ as follows.

$$P\left(O^a, O^v \mid \lambda_{e_k}^a, \lambda_{e_k}^v\right) \approx \max_{S^a, S^v} P\left(O^a, O^v, S^a, S^v \mid \lambda_{e_k}^a, \lambda_{e_k}^v\right) \tag{3}$$

Given O^a and O^v and the corresponding audio and visual HMMs, the problem addressed in this paper is how to construct a useful structure linking the two component HMMs together. For SC-HMM, two component HMMs are modeled separately and their state sequences are related to each other for the same emotion state. The probability $P\left(O^a, O^v, S^a, S^v \mid \lambda_{e_k}^a, \lambda_{e_k}^v\right)$ can be further approximated by (4).

$$P\left(O^a, O^v, S^a, S^v \mid \lambda_{e_k}^a, \lambda_{e_k}^v\right) \approx P\left(O^a, S^a, S^v \mid \lambda_{e_k}^a\right) P\left(O^v, S^v, S^a \mid \lambda_{e_k}^v\right) \tag{4}$$

where $P\left(O^{a},S^{a},S^{v}\mid\lambda_{e_k}^{a}\right)$ can be divided into two parts using Bayes rule which consists of audio HMM output $P\left(O^{a},S^{a}\mid\lambda_{e_k}^{a}\right)$ and state alignment probability from audio to visual HMM $P\left(S^{v}\mid O^{a},S^{a},\lambda_{e_k}^{a}\right)$. Conversely, $P\left(O^{v},S^{v},S^{a}\mid\lambda_{e_k}^{v}\right)$ also can be divided into two parts which consists of visual HMM output $P\left(O^{v},S^{v}\mid\lambda_{e_k}^{v}\right)$ and the state alignment probability from visual to audio HMM $P\left(S^{a}\mid O^{v},S^{v},\lambda_{e_k}^{v}\right)$. Therefore, (4) can be re-written as (5)

$$\begin{aligned}&P\left(O^{a},O^{v},S^{a},S^{v}\mid\lambda_{e_k}^{a},\lambda_{e_k}^{v}\right)\\&\approx P\left(O^{a},S^{a}\mid\lambda_{e_k}^{a}\right)P\left(S^{v}\mid O^{a},S^{a},\lambda_{e_k}^{a}\right)P\left(S^{a}\mid O^{v},S^{v},\lambda_{e_k}^{v}\right)P\left(O^{v},S^{v}\mid\lambda_{e_k}^{v}\right)\end{aligned}\tag{5}$$

where the state alignment probabilities $P\left(S^{v}\mid O^{a},S^{a},\lambda_{e_k}^{a}\right)$ and $P\left(S^{a}\mid O^{v},S^{v},\lambda_{e_k}^{v}\right)$ are difficult to obtain, since they need a sufficient number of training data. Accordingly, these two alignment probabilities are approximated as $P\left(S^{v}\mid S^{a},\lambda_{e_k}^{a}\right)$ and $P\left(S^{a}\mid S^{v},\lambda_{e_k}^{v}\right)$ in (6), respectively, by simplifying the state alignment conditions.

$$\begin{aligned}&P\left(O^{a},O^{v},S^{a},S^{v}\mid\lambda_{e_k}^{a},\lambda_{e_k}^{v}\right)\\&\approx P\left(O^{a},S^{a}\mid\lambda_{e_k}^{a}\right)P\left(S^{v}\mid S^{a},\lambda_{e_k}^{a}\right)P\left(S^{a}\mid S^{v},\lambda_{e_k}^{v}\right)P\left(O^{v},S^{v}\mid\lambda_{e_k}^{v}\right)\end{aligned}\tag{6}$$

where $P\left(S^{v}\mid S^{a},\lambda_{e_k}^{a}\right)$ denotes the probability of visual state sequence S^v given that audio state sequence S^a has been decided by audio HMM $\lambda_{e_k}^{a}$ for the predicted emotional state. Conversely, $P\left(S^{a}\mid S^{v},\lambda_{e_k}^{v}\right)$ denotes the probability of audio state sequence S^a given that visual state sequence S^v has been decided by visual HMM $\lambda_{e_k}^{v}$ for the predicted emotional state.

Finally, we can combine (6) and (3) into (1) to obtain (7).

$$\begin{aligned}&e_k^{*}\approx\\&\underset{e_k\in\{e_h,e_n,e_a,e_s\}}{\arg\max}\left(\max_{S^a,S^v}P\left(O^{a},S^{a}\mid\lambda_{e_k}^{a}\right)P\left(S^{v}\mid S^{a},\lambda_{e_k}^{a}\right)P\left(S^{a}\mid S^{v},\lambda_{e_k}^{v}\right)P\left(O^{v},S^{v}\mid\lambda_{e_k}^{v}\right)\right)\end{aligned}\tag{7}$$

Clearly, the proposed method not only model the time series of audio and visual signals by individual HMM but also consider the state correlation between two component HMMs simultaneously to obtain an optimal recognition result.

In terms of training procedure (i.e. learning algorithm), the proposed SC-HMM consists of three parts:

1) Audio and visual HMMs were trained separately using the expectation-maximization (EM) algorithm.

2) The best state sequences of the audio and visual HMMs are obtained using the Viterbi algorithm, respectively.
3) The audio and visual state sequences are aligned based on the alignment strategy which was described in the Sub-section 3.2. Hence, the state alignment probabilities between audio HMM and visual HMM can be estimated over all training data.

An immediate advantage of this learning algorithm in SC-HMM over that for the C-HMM is computational efficiency and can alleviate the problem of insufficient data, while C-HMM attempts to optimize all the parameters "globally" by iteratively refining the parameters of the component HMMs and their coupling parameters.

In the test phase, the *n*-best output probabilities of state sequences of audio and visual HMMs in SC-HMM are first estimated, respectively. The state alignment probabilities are then considered to obtain the recognition result for each predicted emotional state. Finally the maximum probability of the predicted emotional state was selected as the final result (7).

3.2 State-Based Bi-modal Alignment Strategy

Fig. 2 illustrates the alignment strategy between the states of the audio and visual HMMs in the proposed SC-HMM. In Fig. 2, the upper and lower portions depict the input audio and visual observation sequences, respectively. The middle portion depicts the state alignment between two component HMMs. For the example shown in Fig. 2, the first state of audio HMM covers two audio frames with state boundary ASB_1. Assuming the audio and image data are synchronized, based on the state boundary ASB_1, the two frames in the first audio state can be aligned to the first two frames in the first visual state (i.e. $Count_{a1=>v1}=2$). Conversely, the first state of visual HMM covers three image frames based on state boundary VSB_1; the first two frames are aligned to first audio state (i.e. $Count_{v1=>a1}=2$), and the third frame is aligned to second audio state (i.e. $Count_{v1=>a2}=1$).

Based on the above description of the asymmetric alignment between audio and visual states, the alignment probability from the ith audio state to the jth visual state can be estimated by (8) given that the ith audio state sequence has been decided by audio HMM $\lambda_{e_k}^a$.

$$P\left(S_j^v \mid S_i^a, \lambda_{e_k}^a\right) = \frac{1}{N} \sum_{n=1}^{N} \frac{Count_{ai=>vj}^n}{N_{ai}^n} \tag{8}$$

where N_{ai}^n represents the number of frames of the ith audio state of the nth training data. $Count_{ai=>vj}^n$ denotes the number of frames of the ith audio state aligned to the jth visual state for the nth training data. N denotes the total number of training data. Conversely, the alignment probability from the jth visual state to the ith audio state $P\left(S_i^a \mid S_j^v, \lambda_{e_k}^v\right)$ can also be estimated by (9). Hence, the alignment probability between audio and visual states can be constructed in the training phase.

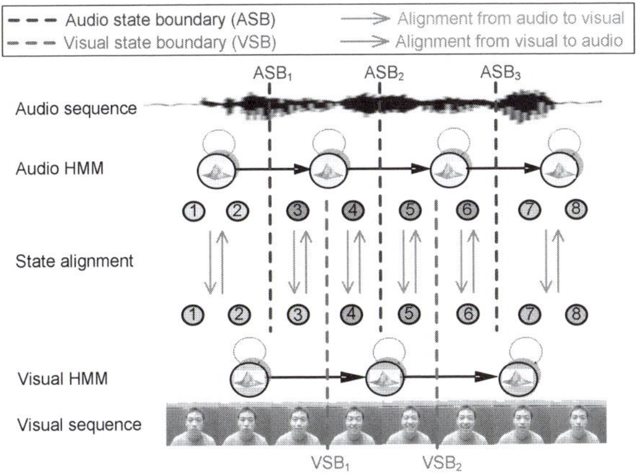

Fig. 2. State-based bi-modal alignment between audio and visual HMMs

$$P\left(S_i^a \mid S_j^v, \lambda_{e_k}^v\right) = \frac{1}{N}\sum_{n=1}^{N}\frac{Count_{vj=>ai}^n}{N_{vj}^n} \quad (9)$$

In the test phase, based on the audio and visual HMMs, the boundary of audio and visual states can be estimated, respectively. The constructed alignment probability can be further applied for linking the two component HMMs. The alignment probability from audio state sequence to visual state sequence of (7) can be re-written as (10).

$$P\left(S^v \mid S^a, \lambda_{e_k}^a\right) = \prod_{t=1}^{T} P\left(S_{j(t)}^v \mid S_{i(t)}^a, \lambda_{e_k}^a\right) \quad (10)$$

where $P\left(S_{j(t)}^v \mid S_{i(t)}^a, \lambda_{e_k}^a\right)$ denotes the alignment probability of the ith audio state aligned to the jth visual state at time t. Conversely, the alignment probability from visual state sequence to audio state sequence of (7) can also be re-written as (11).

$$P\left(S^a \mid S^v, \lambda_{e_k}^v\right) = \prod_{t=1}^{T} P\left(S_{i(t)}^a \mid S_{j(t)}^v, \lambda_{e_k}^v\right) \quad (11)$$

4 Experimental Result

For performance evaluation, four emotional states including neutrality (NEU), happiness (HAP), anger (ANG) and sadness (SAD) were considered. The recorded data was partitioned into two subsets, one for training and the other for testing. Seven subjects were asked to utter 30 types of sentences twice to generate emotional speech and facial expression for each emotion. For each subject, sentences with numbers 1-15 pronounced twice were used for training, and sentences with numbers 16-30 pronounced twice were used for testing. Hence, each emotional state contains 210 specific sentences for training and testing, respectively. In the experiments, the left-to-right HMM with eight states was employed. Table 1 lists and describes all the model abbreviations that were used in the experiments.

For the data format of the audio-visual database, the input images were captured with a Logitech QuickCam camera at a resolution of 320×240 pixels. The frame rate of recorded videos was 30 frames per second. Audio signals were sampled at 16 KHz and processed at a frame length of 33 ms. The recording was conducted in an office environment with a reasonable level of foreground and background noise, such as slight variation of subject's position, orientation, lighting conditions, white noise, and speech babble.

Table 1. List and description of abbreviations

Abbreviation	Description
FA	Facial HMM (uni-modal)
PR	Prosodic HMM (uni-modal)
FP	Facial-prosodic HMM (fusion at feature-level)
C-HMM	Coupled HMM (fusion at model-level)
SC-HMM	Semi-coupled HMM (fusion at model-level)

The recognition accuracy for uni-modal as well as for the bi-modal fusion approaches is shown in Table 2. In the experiment, happy and angry obtain better recognition accuracy compared to neutral and sad, since happy and angry have high discrimination for human emotional expression. For the average recognition rate as shown in Table 3, the facial model (FA) and prosodic model (PR) perform comparably to the feature-level fusion approach (FP). A reasonable explanation is that fusion at feature level will increase the dimensionality and may suffer from the problem of data sparseness. However, the performance of the FP is better than uni-modal approaches. It is therefore the advantage of combining audio and visual cues. Compared to FP, C-HMM improves approximately 10% recognition accuracy. The findings are in accordance with the previous analyses, that is, the information of mutual correlation among multiple modalities is of great help for emotion recognition.

In terms of model-level fusion, the results shown in Table 3 confirm that the proposed SC-HMM outperformed C-HMM. A reasonable explanation rests on the problem of data sparseness. In C-HMM, a state variable at frame t is dependent on its two predecessors (from two modalities) in previous frame $t-1$, which describes the temporal coupling relationship between two streams. The dependency between the hidden states is often too unreliable to capture the statistical dependency of the observation sequences. Probably the major reason for unreliable statistical dependency is due to the problem of data sparseness. To further support our contention, training data analyses were conducted and also shown in Table 4. In the experiment, the training data of different sizes were used and the testing data were fixed at 210 samples per emotional state.

Table 2. Recognition rates (%) of four emotional states for different approaches

Model \ Emotion	NEU	HAP	ANG	SAD
FA	59.0	81.9	74.3	53.8
PR	52.4	76.2	90.5	51.9
FP	62.4	81.9	78.1	61.0
C-HMM	66.7	91.9	90.5	72.9
SC-HMM	79.1	91.4	88.6	83.8

Table 3. Average emotion recognition rates (AERR) for different approaches

AERR (%) \ Model	FA	PR	FP	C-HMM	SC-HMM
AERR (%)	67.3	67.8	70.9	80.5	85.7

The results in Table 4 indicate that the SC-HMM can achieve better performance than C-HMM in insufficient training data condition. These findings show that the proposed SC-HMM with state-based alignment strategy can obtain stronger statistical dependency between two HMMs in data sparseness condition. The data sparseness problem has a significant effect on the recognition results of C-HMM. In terms of computational complexity, the C-HMM using "*N*-head" modified dynamic programming algorithm [19] can reduce the computational complexity from $O(TN^{2C})$ of the standard EM and Viterbi algorithms to $O(T(CN)^2)$ for C chains of N states apiece observing T data points. Compared to C-HMM with computational complexity of $O(T(CN)^2)$, the proposed SC-HMM can achieve $O(TCN^2)$. The lower computational complexity can significantly improve the efficiency of the system.

Table 4. Average recognition rates (%) for insufficient training data condition

Model \ Data	60	90	120
C-HMM	36.3	53.9	56.0
SC-HMM	59.3	66.9	71.7

5 Conclusion

This paper presented a new bi-modal fusion approach called SC-HMM to align the temporal relation of the states of two component HMMs based on the simplified state-based alignment strategy. Experimental results show that the proposed SC-HMM outperforms the uni-modal approaches and other existing fusion based approaches. It can also reach a good balance between performance and model complexity and hence the proposed SC-HMM is useful in different bi-modal applications for most real-world scenarios.

References

1. Picard, R.W.: Affective Computing. MIT Press, Cambridge (1997)
2. Mehrabian, A.: Communication without words. Psychol. Today 2(4), 53–56 (1968)
3. Ambady, N., Rosenthal, R.: Thin slices of expressive behavior as predictors of interpersonal consequences: A meta-analysis. Psychol. Bull. 111(2), 256–274 (1992)
4. Tian, Y.I., Kanade, T., Cohn, J.F.: Recognizing action units for facial expression analysis. IEEE Trans. Pattern Anal. Mach. Intell. 23(2), 97–115 (2001)
5. Wu, C.H., Yeh, J.F., Chuang, Z.J.: Emotion perception and recognition from speech. In: Affective Information Processing, ch. 6, pp. 93–110 (2009)
6. Wu, C.H., Chuang, Z.J., Lin, Y.C.: Emotion recognition from text using semantic labels and separable mixture models. ACM Transactions on Asian Language Information Processing 5, 165–182 (2006)
7. Zeng, Z., Pantic, M., Roisman, G.I., Huang, T.S.: A survey of affect recognition methods: audio, visual, and spontaneous expressions. IEEE Trans. Pattern Anal. Mach. Intell. 31(1), 39–58 (2009)
8. Wu, C.H., Liang, W.B.: Emotion recognition of affective speech based on multiple classifiers using acoustic-prosodic information and semantic labels. IEEE Trans. Affective Computing 2(1), 1–12 (2011)
9. Schuller, B., Muller, R., Hornler, B., Hothker, A., Konosu, H., Rigoll, G.: Audiovisual recognition of spontaneous interest within conversations. In: Proc. Ninth ACM Int'l. Conf. Multimodal Interfaces (ICMI 2007), pp. 30–37 (2007)
10. Metallinou, A., Lee, S., Narayanan, S.: Audio-visual emotion recognition using Gaussian mixture models for face and voice. In: Proc. Int'l. Symposium on Multimedia (ISM 2008), pp. 250–257 (2008)
11. Song, M., You, M., Li, N., Chen, C.: A robust multimodal approach for emotion recognition. Neurocomputing 71(10-12), 1913–1920 (2008)
12. Brand, M., Oliver, N., Pentland, A.: Coupled hidden Markov models for complex action recognition. In: Proc. Int'l. Conf. Computer Vision Pattern Recognition, pp. 994–999 (1997)
13. Ananthakrishnan, S., Narayanan, S.: An automatic prosody recognizer using a coupled multi-stream acoustic model and a syntactic-prosodic language model. In: Proc. 30th Int'l. Conf. Acoustics, Speech, and Signal Processing (ICASSP 2005), pp. 269–272 (2005)
14. Nefian, A.V., Liang, L., Pi, X., Liu, X., Mao, C., Murphy, K.: A coupled HMM for audio-visual speech recognition. In: Proc. 27th Int'l. Conf. Acoustics, Speech, and Signal Processing (ICASSP 2002), pp. 2013–2016 (2002)
15. Xie, L., Liu, Z.Q.: A coupled HMM approach to video-realistic speech animation. Pattern Recognition 40(8), 2325–2340 (2007)
16. Viola, P., Jones, M.: Rapid object detection using a boosted cascade of simple features. In: Proc. Int'l. Conf. Computer Vision Pattern Recognition, vol. 1, pp. 511–518 (2001)
17. Cootes, T.F., Edwards, G.J., Taylor, C.J.: Active appearance models. IEEE Trans. Pattern Anal. Mach. Intell. 23(6), 681–685 (2001)
18. Boersma, P., Weenink, D.: Praat: doing phonetics by computer (2007), `http://www.praat.org/`
19. Brand, M.: Coupled hidden Markov models for modeling interacting processes. MIT Media Lab Perceptual Computing / Learning and Common Sense Technical Report, Boston, MA, pp. 1–28 (1997)

Associating Textual Features with Visual Ones to Improve Affective Image Classification

Ningning Liu[1], Emmanuel Dellandréa[1], Bruno Tellez[2], and Liming Chen[1]

Université de Lyon, CNRS,
[1] Ecole Centrale de Lyon, LIRIS, UMR5205, F-69134, France
{ningning.liu,emmanuel.dellandrea,liming.chen}@ec-lyon.fr
[2] Université Lyon 1, LIRIS, UMR5205, F-69622, France
bruno.tellez@iut.univ-lyon1.fr

Abstract. Many images carry a strong emotional semantic. These last years, some investigations have been driven to automatically identify induced emotions that may arise in viewers when looking at images, based on low-level image properties. Since these features can only catch the image atmosphere, they may fail when the emotional semantic is carried by objects. Therefore additional information is needed, and we propose in this paper to make use of textual information describing the image, such as tags. Thus, we have developed two textual features to catch the text emotional meaning: one is based on the semantic distance matrix between the text and an emotional dictionary, and the other one carries the valence and arousal meanings of words. Experiments have been driven on two datasets to evaluate visual and textual features and their fusion. The results have shown that our textual features can improve the classification accuracy of affective images.

Keywords: textual feature, visual feature, affective image classification, fusion.

1 Introduction

Recently, with more and more photos that are published and shared online, providing effective methods to retrieve semantic information from images in huge collections has become inevitable. Currently, most of commercial systems use textual indexable labels to find the relevant images according to a given query. In order to avoid manual tagging, several content-based image retrieval (CBIR) and photo annotation systems have been proposed by using low level image visual features, such as color, shape and texture etc. [1]. However, these works remain on a cognitive level since they aim at automatically detecting the presence of particular objects in the image ("face", "animal", "bus", etc.) or identifying the type of scene ("landscape", "sunset", "indoor" etc.). Very few works deal with the affective level which can be described as identifying the emotion that is expected to arise in humans when looking at an image, or called affective image classification. Even though contributions in this emerging

S. D´Mello et al. (Eds.): ACII 2011, Part I, LNCS 6974, pp. 195–204, 2011.

research area remain rare, it gains more and more attention in the research community [2,3,4,8,17]. Indeed, many applications can benefit from this affective information, such as image retrieval systems, or more generally "intelligent" human/computer interfaces. Moreover, affective image classification is extremely challenging due to the semantic gap between the low-level features extracted from images and high-level concepts such as emotions that need to be identified. This research area, which is at its beginning stage [3], is at the crossroad between computer vision, pattern recognition, artificial intelligence, psychology, cognitive science, which makes it particularly interesting.

One of the initial works is from Colombo et al. [6], who developed expressive and emotional level features based on Itten's theory [7] and semiotic principles. They evaluated their retrieval performance on art images and commercial videos. Yanulevskaya et al. [9] proposed an emotion categorization approach for art works based on the assessment of local image statistics using support vector machines. Wang wei-ning et al. [10] firstly developed an orthogonal three-dimension emotional model using 12 pairs of emotional words, and then predicted the emotional factor using SVM regression based on three fuzzy histograms. Recently, Machajdik et al. [11] studied features for affective image classification including color, texture, composition, content features, and conducted experiments using IAPS dataset and two other small collected datasets.

All these works rely on visual features including color, shape, texture and composition, e.g. color harmony features based on Itten's color theory [6], fuzzy histograms based on Luminance Chroma Hue (LCH) color space [10], face counting and skin area, and aesthetic [11]. These visual features have generally been elaborated to catch the image atmosphere that plays a role of first importance in the emotion induced to viewers. However, these approaches may fail when the emotional semantic is carried by objects in images, such as a child crying for example, or a whale dying on a beautiful beach. Therefore additional information is needed, and we propose in this paper to make use of textual information describing the image that is often provided by photo management and sharing systems in the form of tags. Thus, we have developed two textual features designed to catch the emotional meaning of image tags. Moreover, we have proposed an approach based on the evidence theory to combine these textual features with visual ones with the goal to improve the affective image classification accuracy.

The contributions of the work presented in this paper can be summarized as follows:

- Proposition of two textual features to represent emotional semantics: one is based on a semantic distance matrix between the text and emotional dictionary; the other one carries the valence and arousal meanings expressed in the text.
- A combination method based on Dempster-Shafer's theory of evidence has been proposed to combine those textual features with visual ones.
- A discretization of the dimensional model of emotions has been considered for the classification of affective images that is well adapted to image collection navigation and visualization use cases.

– Different types of features, classifiers and fusion methods have been evaluated on two datasets.

The rest of this paper is organized as follows. Our textual features and four groups of visual features for representing emotion semantics are presented in section 2. Experiments are described in section 3. Finally, the conclusion and future works are drawn in section 4.

2 Features for Emotional Semantics

Feature extraction is a key issue for concept recognition in images, and particularly emotions. In this work, we propose to use two types of features to identify the emotion induced by an image: visual features to catch the global image atmosphere, and textual features to catch the emotional meanings of the text associated with the image (in the form of tags for example) that we expect to be helpful when the induced emotion is mainly due to the presence in the image of an object having a strong emotional connotation.

2.1 Textual Features

We propose in this section two new textual features that are designed to catch the emotional meaning of the text associated with an image. Indeed, most of photo management and sharing systems provide textual information for images, including a title, tags and sometimes a legend.

Method 1 (textM1): The basic idea is to calculate the semantic distance between the text associated with an image and an emotional dictionary based on path similarity, denoting how similar two word senses are, based on the shortest path that connects the senses in a taxonomy. Firstly, a dictionary has been built made of Kate Hevner's Adjective Circle, which consists of 66 single adjectives [13] such as exciting, happy, sad etc. After a preprocessing step (text cleaned by removing irrelevant words), the semantic distance matrix is computed between the text associated with the image and the dictionary by applying the path distance based on a WordsNet and using the Natural Language Toolkit [14]. At last, the semantic distance feature is build based on the words semantic distance matrix. It expresses the emotional meaning of the text according to the emotional dictionary. The procedure of Method 1 is detailed below.

Method 2 (textM2): The idea of is to directly measure the emotional ratings of valence and arousal dimensions by using the Affective Norms for English Words (ANEW) [15]. This set of words has been developed to provide a set of normative emotional ratings (including valence, arousal dimension) for a large number of words in English language. Thus, the semantic similarity between the image text and ANEW words is computed to measure the emotional meaning of the text according to the valence and arousal dimensions. The procedure for Method 2 is detailed below.

Method 1

Input: labels data W and dictionary $D = \{d_i\}$ with $|D| = d$
Output: text feature; $|f| = d, 0 < f_i < 1$.

- Preprocess the tags by using a stop-words filter.
- If image has no tags $W = 0$, return $f, f_i = 1/2$
- Do for each words $w_t \in W$:

1. If the path distance of w_t and d_i cannot be found, set $S(t,i) = 0$.
2. Calculate the path distance $dist(w_t, d_i)$, where $dist$ is a simple node counting in the path from w_t to d_i.
3. Calculate the path similarity as: $S(t,i) = 1/(dist(w_t, d_i) + 1)$,

- Calculate the feature f as: $f_i = \sum_t S(t,i)$, and normalize it to [0 1].

Method 2

Input: labels data W, dictionary D ratings of valence V and arousal A for each word in D. Ratings vary from 1 to 9. $|D| = |V| = |A| = d$.
Output: text feature; $|f| = 2, 0 < f_i < 9$.

- Preprocess the tags by using a stop-words filter.
- If image has no tags $W = 0$, return $f, f_i = 5$
- Do for each words $w_t \in W$:

1. If the path distance of w_t and d_i cannot be found, set $S(t,i) = 0$,
2. Calculate the path distance $dist(w_t, d_i)$, where $dist$ is a simple node counting in the path from w_t to d_i,
3. Calculate the path similarity as: $S(t,i) = 1/(dist(w_t, d_i) + 1)$,

- Calculate the distance vector $m_i = \sum_t S(t,i)$, and normalize it to [0 1],
- Calculate the feature f as: $f_1 = (1/d)\sum_i(m_i.V_i)$, and $f_2 = (1/d)\sum_i(m_i.A_i)$,

2.2 Visual Features

In order to catch the global image atmosphere that may have an important role in the emotion communicated by the image, we propose to use various visual features including information according to color, texture, shape and aesthetic. They are listed in Table 1.

3 Experiments and Results

3.1 Emotion Models

There are generally two approaches to model emotions: the discrete one and the dimensional one. The first model considers adjectives or nouns to specify the emotions, such as happiness, sadness, fear, anger, disgust and surprise. On the contrary, with the dimensional model, emotions are described according to one or several dimensions such as valence, arousal and control. The choice for an emotion model is generally guided by the application. We propose in this paper to use a kind of hybrid representation that is a discretization of the dimensional model made of valence and arousal dimensions. We believe that it is particularly well suitable for applications such as image indexation and retrieval since it allows characterizing images according to their valence and arousal independently

Table 1. Summary of the visual features used in this work

Category	Features (Short name)	#	Short Description
Color	Color moments (C_M)	144	Three central moments (mean, standard deviation and skewness) on HSV channels computed on a pyramidal representation of the image.
	Color histogram (C_H)	192	Histograms of 64 bins for each HSV channel that are concatenated.
	Color correlograms (C_C)	256	A three-dimensional table representing the spatial correlation of colors in an image.
Texture	Tamura (T_T)	3	Features from Tamura [16] including coarseness, contrast and directionality.
	Grey level Co-occurrence matrix (T_GCM)	16	Described by Haralick (1973): defined over an image to be the distribution of co-occurring values at a given offset.
	Local binary pattern (T_LBP)	256	A compact multi-scale texture descriptor analysis of textures with multiple scales.
Shape	Histogram of line orientations (S_HL)	12	Different orientations of lines detected by a Hough transform.
High level	Harmony (H_H)	1	Describes the color harmony of images based on Itten's color theory [8].
	Dynamism (H_D)	1	Ratio of oblique lines (which communicate dynamism and action) with respect to horizontal and vertical lines (which rather communicate calmness and relaxation) [8].
	Y. Ke (H_Ke)	5	Ke's aesthetic criteria including spatial distribution of edges, hue count, blur, contrast and brightness [19].
	R.Datta (H_Da)	44	Datta's aesthetic features (44 of 56) except those that are related to IRM (integrated region matching) technique [18].

which improves the applicability for navigation and visualization use cases [17]. Thus, six emotion classes are considered by discretizing each dimension into three levels: low, neutral and high. This model is illustrated in Figure 1.

3.2 Datasets

For testing and training, we have used two data sets. The International Affective Picture System (IAPS) [21] consists of 1182 documentary-style images characterized by three scores according to valence, arousal and dominance. We have considered another dataset that we called Mirflickr, which is a set of 1172 creative-style photographs extracted randomly from MIRFLICKR25000 Collection [22]. This collection supplies all original tag data provided by the Flickr users with an average total number of 8.94 tags per image. In order to obtain the ground truth for emotional semantic ratings, we have organized an annotation campaign within our laboratory. Thus, 20 people (researchers) have participated

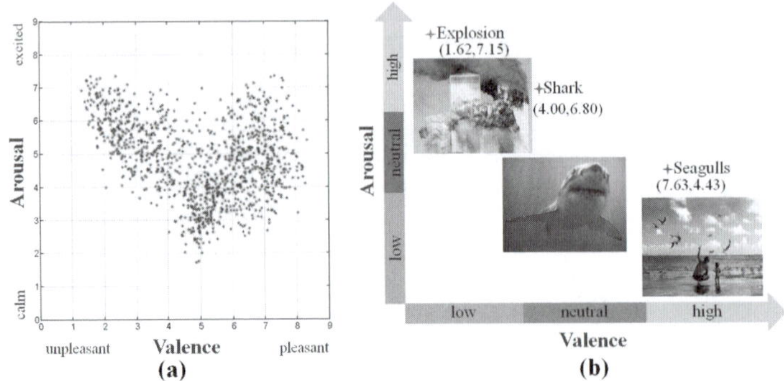

Fig. 1. The dimensional emotion model (a). This model includes two dimensions: valence (ranging from pleasant to unpleasant) and arousal (ranging from calm to excited). Each blue point represents an image from IAPS. (b) We build six classes by dividing valence and arousal dimension into three levels, such as low arousal (LA), neutral arousal (NA), high arousal (HA), low valence (LV), neutral valence (NV) and high valence (HV).

which has allowed obtaining an average of 10 annotations for each image. The image annotation consists in two rates according to the emotion communicated by the image in terms of valence (from negative to positive) and arousal (from passive to active). The description of the two data sets is given in Table 2.

Table 2. The description of the two data sets used in our experiments

Database	Size	Text	LV	NV	HV	LA	NA	HA
IAPS	1182	No tags	340	492	350	291	730	161
MirFlickr2000	1172	8.93/image	257	413	502	261	693	218

3.3 Experimental Setup

Experiment setup was done as follows: we built six Support Vector Machine (SVM) classifiers, each one being dedicated to an emotion class, and following a one-against-all strategy. A 5-fold cross-validation was conducted to obtain the results. Our objectives with these experiments were to evaluate: a) the performance of the different features on the two data sets; b) the performance of fusion strategies including max-score, min-score, mean-score, majority-voting and Evidence Theory on IAPS; c) the performance of the combination of visual features and textual features on Mirflickr2000 by using the Evidence Theory.

More specifically, in a) Libsvm tool was employed, and the input features were normalized to [0 1] to train a RBF kernel; in b) each feature set was used to train classifier c_n, which produces a measurement vector y^n as the degree of belief that the input belongs to different classes, then classifiers were trained based on adjusting the evidence of different classifiers by minimizing the MSE of training data according to [5]. Meanwhile a comparison with different types of combination approaches has been made, including: min-score: $z_k = min(y_k^1, y_k^2, ..., y_k^N)$, mean-score: $z_k = \frac{1}{N}\sum_{n=1}^{N} y_k^n$, max-score: $z_k = max(y_k^1, y_k^2, ..., y_k^N)$, majority-vote: $z_k = argmax(y_k^1, y_k^2, ..., y_k^N)$, where y_k^n represent the kth measurement of classifier c_n.

3.4 Results: Performance of Different Features

Figure 2 shows the performance of different features on the two data sets. For IAPS, it appears that texture features (LBP, Coocurrences, Tamura) are the most efficient ones among the visual features. However, for Mirflickr data set, which is composed of professional creative photographs, the aesthetic features from Datta [18] perform better on pleasant dimension and the color correlograms, color moment and aesthetic features is better on arousal dimension. This suggests that the aesthetic features are related to pleasant feelings particularly for photographs and colors affect arousal perception in a certain way. One can note that textual features do not perform as good as visual features, which may be explain by the fact that even if the text contains important information it is not sufficient and should be combined with visual ones, as it is evaluated in next experiment. Finally, the high-level features dynamism and harmony may first seem giving lower performance, but as they consist in a single value, their efficiency is in fact remarkable.

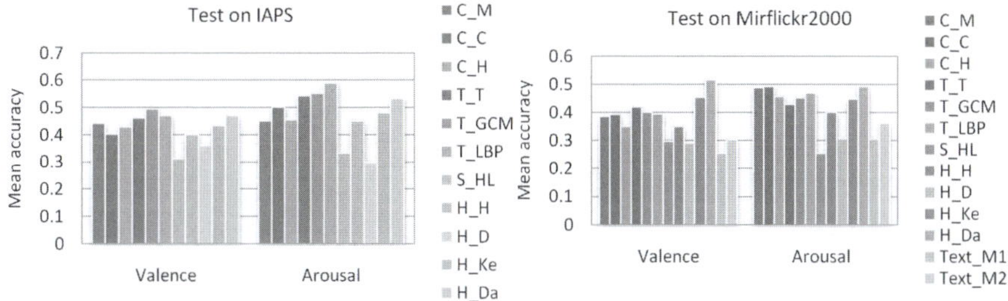

Fig. 2. The feature performance on two databases. Measurement is based on average classification accuracy: average of accuracy on each of the three emotion level categories.

3.5 Results: Performance of Different Combination Approaches on IAPS

The results for different combination methods using IAPS data set are given in Table 3. They show that the combination of classifiers based on the Evidence Theory with an average classification accuracy of 58% performs better than the other combination methods for affective image classification, which may be explained by its ability to handle knowledge that can be ambiguous, conflictual and uncertain that is particularly interesting when dealing with emotions.

Table 3. The performance of classifier combination techniques using IAPS. LV, NV and HV represent low, neutral, high level of valence and LA, NA and HA represent low, neutral, high level of arousal respectively. Results are given in percentage of average classification accuracy.

	Early-fusion(%)	Max-score(%)	Min-score(%)	Mean-score(%)	Majority vote(%)	Evidence theory(%)
LV	52.4	51.4	47.7	53.4	49.9	50.5
NV	51.3	53.2	51.6	52.3	51.0	55.3
HV	49.8	52.1	50.1	55.0	52.1	54.8
LA	60.6	61.7	57.2	62.7	58.7	62.7
NA	62.3	62.5	54.6	61.8	63.1	66.4
HA	53.7	54.1	52.1	50.9	53.6	58.3
Average	55.0	55.8	52.2	56.0	54.7	**58.0**

Table 4. The performance with different settings on Mirflickr2000 dataset by combining textual and visual features based on Evidence Theory. Text M1 and M2 refer to text feature method 1 and method 2, Color + Text M1 refer to visual classifiers that are trained based on color feature group and text classifier trained based on text M1 feature. The best performance in each panel is indicated in bold.

	LV(%)	NV(%)	HV(%)	LA(%)	NA(%)	HA(%)
Text M1	20.1	**36.2**	25.2	25.2	37.3	30.4
Text M2	**27.2**	35.5	**33.8**	**34.4**	**40.2**	**34.3**
Color	**39.5**	42.8	36.7	51.6	54.7	48.3
Color+Text M1	39.1	45.2	**38.1**	52.7	55.2	47.7
Color+Text M2	39.4	**52.8**	37.3	**56.6**	**57.1**	**50.5**
Texture	43.1	44.2	40.1	46.8	48.4	43.1
Texture+Text M1	44.2	42.2	42.3	50.1	52.0	46.7
Texture+Text M2	**45.3**	**46.8**	**44.3**	**51.3**	**55.5**	**50.9**
Shape	28.7	34.2	25.8	26.7	27.2	24.8
Shape+Text M1	29.7	34.6	29.5	29.1	36.5	30.7
Shape+Text M2	**31.5**	**38.4**	**33.7**	**37.3**	**41.8**	**36.4**
Highlevel	48.7	55.1	44.5	51.3	56.3	46.0
Highlevel+Text M1	49.4	53.4	45.2	54.6	52.3	47.4
Highlevel+Text M2	**52.1**	**56.2**	**47.7**	**55.7**	**58.7**	**54.6**
All visual	54.1	56.8	45.5	54.6	57.2	55.9
All visual+Text M1	55.4	57.2	44.1	56.8	58.4	56.1
All visual+Text M2	56.2	59.0	49.7	61.1	62.5	59.7
All visual+Text M1&M2	**59.5**	**62.2**	**50.2**	**63.8**	**63.7**	**62.5**

3.6 Results: Performance of Textual Features on Mirflickr2000

The results provided by different combination strategies using textual and visual features on Mirflickr data set are given in Table 4. These results show that the textual feature textM2 performs better than textM1 except for the neutral valence level. As pointed in section 3.4, textual feature did not outperform visual features when considered independently. However, the combination of textual and visual features improves the classification accuracy. Indeed, combination of high level features and textual features perform better on the valence dimension, and the color features combined with text features performs well on the arousal dimension. When combined with textual features, the performance of the shape feature group improves obviously. Moreover, the combination of all the visual features with textual features significantly improves the classification accuracy for all classes. These results show that by using the Evidence Theory as fusion method to combine visual features with our proposed textual features, the identification of the emotion that may arise in image viewers can greatly be improved compared to methods that only rely on visual information.

4 Conclusion

In this paper, we have proposed two textual features that have been designed to catch the emotional connotation of the text associated with images for the problem of affective image classification. Our motivation was to provide additional information to enrich visual features that can only catch the global atmosphere of images. This may be particularly useful when the emotion induced is mainly due to objects in the image, and not due to global image properties. Our experimental results have shown that the combination of visual features and our proposed textual features can significantly improve the classification accuracy. However, this supposes that a text is available for the images, in the form of tags or legend. Therefore our future research directions will include the proposition of strategies to overcome this difficulty using for example automatic image annotation approaches or by exploiting the text associated to similar images based on their visual content. Moreover, we will investigate solutions to exploit as much as possible text information when it is noisy and not completely reliable.

Acknowledgment. This work is partly supported by the french ANR under the project VideoSense ANR-09-CORD-026.

References

1. Smeulders, A.W.M., et al.: Content-based Image Retrieval: the end of the early years. IEEE Trans. PAMI 22(12), 1349–1380 (2000)
2. Zeng, Z., et al.: A survey of affect recognition methods: audio, visual and spontaneous expressions. IEEE Transactions PAMI 31(1), 39–58 (2009)

3. Wang, W., He, Q.: A survey on emotional semantic image retrieval. In: ICIP, pp. 117–120 (2008)
4. Wang, S., Wang, X.: Emotion semantics image retrieval: a brief overview. In: Tao, J., Tan, T., Picard, R.W. (eds.) ACII 2005. LNCS, vol. 3784, pp. 490–497. Springer, Heidelberg (2005)
5. Al-Ani, A., Deriche, M.: A new technique for combing multiple classifiers using the Dempster Shafer theory of evidence. J. Artif. Intell. Res. 17, 333–361 (2002)
6. Columbo, C., Del Bimbo, A., Pala, P.: Semantics in visual information retrieval. IEEE Multimedia 6(3), 38–53 (1999)
7. Itten, J.: The art of colour. Otto Maier Verlab, Ravensburg, Germany (1961)
8. Dellandréa, E., Liu, N., Chen, L.: Classification of affective semantics in images based on discrete and dimensional models of emotions. In: CBMI, pp. 99–104 (2010)
9. Yanulevskaya, V., et al.: Emotional valence categorization using holistic image features. In: ICIP, pp. 101–104 (2008)
10. Weining, W., Yinlin, Y., Shengming, J.: Image retrieval by emotional semantics: A study of emotional space and feature extraction. ICSMC 4, 3534–3539 (2006)
11. Machajdik, J., Hanbury, A.: Affective image classification using features inspired by psychology and art theory. ACM Multimedia (2010)
12. Wang, G., Hoiem, D., Forsyth, D.: Building text features for object image classification. In: CVPR, pp. 1367–1374 (2009)
13. Hevner, K.: Experimental studies of the elements of expression in music. American Journal of Psychology 48(2), 246–268 (1936)
14. Natural language toolkit, `http://www.nltk.org`
15. Bradley, M.M., Lang, P.J.: Affective norms for English words (ANEW). Tech. Rep C-1, GCR in Psychophysiology, University of Florida (1999)
16. Tamura, H., Mori, S., Yamawaki, T.: Textural features corresponding to visual perception. IEEE Transactions on SMC 8(6), 460–473 (1978)
17. Liu, N., Dellandréa, E., Tellez, B., Chen, L.: Evaluation of Features and Combination Approaches for the Classification of Emotional Semantics in Images. VISAPP (2011)
18. Datta, R., Li, J., Wang, J.Z.: Content-based image retrieval: approaches and trends of the new age. In: ACM Workshop MIR (2005)
19. Ke, Y., Tang, X., Jing, F.: The Design of High-Level Features for Photo Quality Assessment. In: CVPR (2006)
20. Dunker, P., Nowak, S., Begau, A., Lanz, C.: Content-based mood classification for photos and music. In: ACM MIR, pp. 97–104 (2008)
21. Lang, P.J., Bradley, M.M., Cuthbert, B.N.: The IAPS: Technical manual and affective ratings. Tech. Rep A-8., GCR in Psychophysiology, Unv. of Florida (2008)
22. Huiskes, M.J., Lew, M.S.: The MIR Flickr Retrieval Evaluation. In: ACM Multimedia Information Retrieval, MIR 2008 (2008)

3D Corpus of Spontaneous Complex Mental States

Marwa Mahmoud[1], Tadas Baltrušaitis[1], Peter Robinson[1], and Laurel D. Riek[2]

[1] Univeristy of Cambridge, United Kingdom
[2] University of Notre Dame, United States

Abstract. Hand-over-face gestures, a subset of emotional body language, are overlooked by automatic affect inference systems. We propose the use of hand-over-face gestures as a novel affect cue for automatic inference of cognitive mental states. Moreover, affect recognition systems rely on the existence of publicly available datasets, often the approach is only as good as the data. We present the collection and annotation methodology of a 3D multimodal corpus of 108 audio/video segments of natural complex mental states. The corpus includes spontaneous facial expressions and hand gestures labelled using crowd-sourcing and is publicly available.

1 Introduction

Human computer interaction could greatly benefit from automatic detection of affect from non-verbal cues such as facial expressions, non-verbal speech, head and hand gestures, and body posture. Unfortunately, the algorithms trained on currently available datasets might not generalise well to the real world situations in which such systems would be ultimately used. Our work is trying to fill this gap with a 3D multimodal corpus, which consists of elicited complex mental states. In addition, we are proposing hand-over-face gestures as a novel affect cue in affect recognition.

1.1 Motivation

There is now a move away from the automatic inference of the basic emotions proposed by Ekman [8] towards the inference of complex mental states such as attitudes, cognitive states, and intentions. The real world is dominated by neutral expressions [1] and complex mental states, with expressions of confusion, amusement, happiness, surprise, thinking, concentration, anger, worry, excitement, etc. being the most common ones [19]. This shift to incorporate complex mental states alongside basic emotions is necessary if one expects to build affect sensitive systems as part of a ubiquitous computing environment.

There is also a move towards analysing naturalistic rather than posed expressions, as there is evidence of differences between them [4]. In addition, even Action Unit [7] amplitude and timings differ in spontaneous and acted expressions [5]. These differences imply that recognition results reported on systems

S. D´Mello et al. (Eds.): ACII 2011, Part I, LNCS 6974, pp. 205–214, 2011.

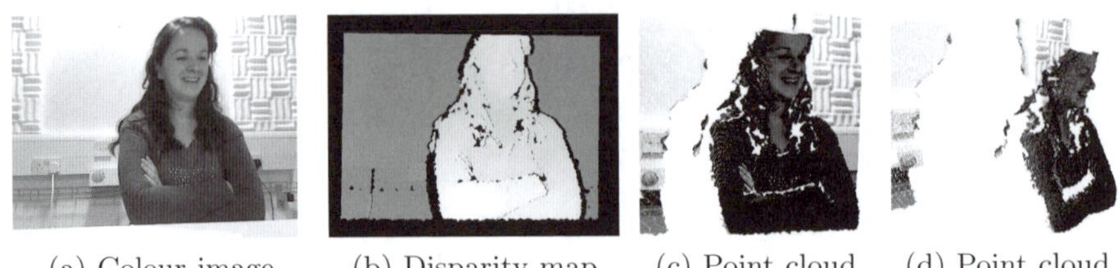

(a) Colour image (b) Disparity map (c) Point cloud (d) Point cloud

Fig. 1. Point cloud visualisation from two angles (c)&(d) combining colour image (a) and disparity (inverse depth) map (b) of an image captured using Kinect

trained and tested on acted expressions might not generalise to spontaneous ones. Furthermore, this means that systems trained on current posed datasets would not be able to perform in tasks requiring recognition of spontaneous affect.

Hand-over-face gestures, a subset of emotional body language, are overlooked by automatic affect inferencing systems. Many facial analysis systems are based on geometric or appearance facial feature extraction or tracking. As the face becomes occluded, facial features are either lost, corrupted or erroneously detected, resulting in an incorrect analysis of the person's facial expression. Only a few systems recognise facial expressions in the presence of partial face occlusion, either by estimation of lost facial points [3,22] or by excluding the occluded face area from the classification process [6]. In all these systems, face occlusions are a nuisance and are treated as noise, even though they carry useful information.

Moreover, current availability of affordable depth sensors (such as the Microsoft Kinect) is giving easy access to 3D data, which can be used to improve the results of expression and gesture tracking and analysis. An example of such data captured using Kinect can be seen in Figure 1.

These developments are hindered by the lack of publicly available corpora, making it difficult to compare or reproduce results. Researchers cannot easily evaluate their approaches without an appropriate benchmark dataset.

1.2 Contributions

In order to address the issues outlined, we have collected and annotated a corpus of naturalistic complex mental states. Our dataset consists of 108 videos of 12 mental states and is being made freely available to the research community. The annotations are based on emotion groups from the Baron-Cohen taxonomy [2] and are based on crowd-sourced labels.

Moreover, we have analysed hand-over-face gestures and their possible meaning in spontaneous expressions. By studying the videos in our corpus, we argue that these gestures are not only prevalent, but can also serve as affective cues.

1.3 Related Work

In Table 1 we list several publicly available databases for easy comparison with our corpus Cam3D. This list is not exhaustive, for a more detailed one see Zeng

Table 1. Overview of similar databases

Properties	Cam3D	MMI[16]	CK+[14]	SAL[15]	BU-4DFE[21]	FABO[11]
3D	Y	N	N	N	Y	N
Modalities	S/F/U	F	F	S/F	F	F/U
Spontaneity	S	P/S	P/S	S	P	P
Number of videos	108	2894	700	10h	606	210
Number of subjects	7	79	210	24	100	24
Number of states	12	6	6	N/A	6	6
Emotional description	B/C	B	B	D/C	B	B,C

Modalities: S:speech, F:face, U:upper body, Spontaneity: S:spontaneous, P:posed, Emotional description: B:basic, C:complex, D:dimensional

et al. [25]. When compared in terms of modality and spontaneity all available datasets concentrate on some factors we are trying to address, while ignoring the others. MMI and CK+ corpora do not have upper body or hand gestures, SAL corpus consists of emotionally coloured interaction but lacks segments of specific mental states, while the FABO dataset contains only posed data.

Several 3D datasets of still images [24] and videos [21] of posed basic emotions already exist. The resolution of the data acquired by their 3D sensors is much higher than that available from Microsoft Kinect, but it is unlikely that such high quality imaging will be available for everyday applications soon.

2 Corpus

Care must be taken when collecting a video corpus of naturally-evoked mental states to ensure the validity and usability of the data. In the following sections, we will discuss our elicitation methodology, data segmentation and annotation.

2.1 Methodology

Elicitation of affective states. Data collection was divided into two sessions: interaction with a computer program and interaction with another person. Most available corpora are of emotions collected from single individuals or human-computer interaction tasks. However, dyadic interactions between people elicit a wide range of spontaneous emotions in social contexts under fairly controlled conditions [18]. Eliciting the same mental states during both sessions provides a comparison between the non-verbal expressions and gestures in both scenarios, especially if the same participant, stimuli, and experimental environment conditions are employed, and also enriches the data collected with different versions of expressions for the same affective state.

Our desire to collect multi-modal data presented a further challenge. We were interested in upper body posture and gesture as well as facial expressions to investigate the significance of hand and body gestures as important cues in non-verbal communication. Recent experiments have shown the importance of body language, especially in conditions where it conflicts with facial expressions [10]. Participants were not asked to use any computer peripherals during data collection so that their hands were always free to express body language.

Our elicitation methodology operated in four steps:

1. Choose an initial group of mental states.
2. Design an experimental task to induce them and conduct a pilot study.
3. Revise the list of the mental states induced according to the pilot results.
4. Validate the elicitation methodology after collecting and labelling the data.

The first group of induced mental states were cognitive: *thinking, concentrating, unsure, confused* and *triumphant.* For elicitation, a set of riddles were displayed to participants on a computer screen. Participants answered the riddles verbally, with the option to give up if they did not know the answer. A second computer-based exercise was a voice-controlled computer maze. Participants were asked to traverse the maze via voice commands. In the dyadic interaction task, both participants were asked to listen to a set of riddles. They discussed their answers together and either responded or gave up and heard the answer from the speakers. In both tasks, the riddles' order was randomised to counter-balance any effect of the type of riddle on the results.

The second group of affective states were *frustrated* and *angry.* It was ethically difficult to elicit strong negative feelings in a dyadic interaction, so they were only elicited in the computer based session. During one attempt at the voice-controlled computer maze, the computer responded incorrectly to the participant's voice commands.

The third group included *bored* and *neutral.* It was also hard to elicit boredom intentionally in a dyadic interaction, so this was only attempted in the computer-based session by adding a 'voice calibration' task, where the participant was asked to repeat the words: left, right, up, down a large number of times according to instructions on the screen. Participants were also left alone for about three minutes after the whole computer task finished.

The last group included only *surprised.* In the computer-based session, the computer screen flickered suddenly in the middle of the 'voice calibration' task. In the dyadic interaction session, surprise was induced by flickering the lights of the room suddenly at the end of the session.

Experimental procedure. Data was collected in a standard experimental observation suite. A double mirror allowed experimenters to watch without disturbing the participants. In our experiment, a wizard-of-oz method was used for both the computer-based and dyadic interaction sessions. Participants knew at the beginning of the experiment that their video and audio were being recorded, but they did not know the actual purpose of the study. They were told that the experiment was for voice recognition and calibration. Not explaining the real objective of the experiment to participants in the first instance was essential for the data collection, to avoid having participants exaggerate or mask their expressions if they knew we were interested in their non-verbal behaviour.

(a) Dyadic task (b) Computer task (c) Examples of frames from Kinect and C2

Fig. 2. The layouts of the two parts of the data collection. P1 and P2 are the participants, C1 and C2 the HD cameras.

Participants. 16 participants (4 pilot and 12 non-pilot) were recruited through the university mailing lists and local message boards. The 12 non-pilot participants were 6 males and 6 females with age groups ranging from 24 to 50 years old (μ=27, σ=8). They were from diverse ethnic backgrounds including: Caucasian, Asian and Middle Eastern and with varied fields of work and study. All participants completed the two sessions: half the participants started with the computer-based task, while the other half started with the dyadic interaction task. Dyads were chosen randomly. Since cross-sex interactions elicit more non-verbal warmth and sexual interest than same-sex interactions [23], we chose same sex dyads to avoid this effect on the non-verbal expressions in the dyads. Half the participants (3 males, and 4 females) gave public consent for data distribution.

2.2 Data Acquisition

We used three different sensors for data collection: Microsoft Kinect sensors, HD cameras, and microphones in the HD cameras.

Figure 2a shows the layout for recording dyadic interactions. Two Kinect sensors and two HD cameras were used. The HD cameras each pointed at one participant and were used to record the voice of the other. In the case of the computer interaction task the camera layout is presented in Figure 2b. A Kinect sensor and an HD camera were facing the participant while one HD camera was positioned next to the participant and was facing away. The camera facing away was used to record the participant's voice.

Several computers were used to record the data from the different sensors, this required subsequent manual synchronisation.

The HD cameras provided 720 x 576 px resolution colour images at 25 frames per second. The recorded videos were later converted to 30 frames per second to simplify synchronisation with Kinect videos.

The Kinect sensor provides a colour image and a disparity map, which is the inverse of depth values, at 30 frames per second. The sensor uses structured infrared light and an infrared camera to calculate 640 x 480 px 11-bit disparity map. An additional camera provides a 640 x 480 colour image.

2.3 Segmentation and Annotation

After the initial data collection, the videos were segmented. Each segment showed a single event such as a change in facial expression, head and body posture movement or hand gesture. This increases the value of the annotation compared with cutting the whole video into equal length segments [1].

Video segments were chosen and annotated using ELAN [13]. From videos with public consent, a total of 451 segments were collected. The mean duration is 6 seconds (σ=1.2). For subsequent analysis, each video segment was annotated with the type of the task and interaction. In addition, we encoded hand-over-face gestures (if any) in terms of: hand shape, action, and facial region occluded. From the non-public videos recorded, only hand-over-face gestures (120 segments) were segmented and encoded to be included in subsequent hand gestures analysis.

Labelling was based on context-free observer judgment. Public segments were labelled by community crowd-sourcing, which is fast, cheap and can be as good as expert labelling [20]. The sound was low-pass filtered to remove the verbal content of speech. Video segments were displayed randomly through a web interface and participants were asked to give a 'word' describing the emotional state of the person in the video. Free-form input was used rather than menus in order not to influence the choice of label. In addition, an auto-complete list of mental states was displayed to avoid mis-spelling. The list was based on the Baron-Cohen taxonomy of emotions [2] as it is an exhaustive list of emotional states and synonyms (1150 words, divided into 24 emotion groups and 412 emotion concepts with 738 synonyms for the concepts). In total 2916 labels from 77 labellers were collected (μ=39). Non-public video segments were labelled by four experts in the field and segments with less than 75% agreement were excluded.

We decided to use categorical labels rather than continuous ones such as PAD (pleasure, arousal, dominance) scales because we used naive labellers. Dimensional representation is not intuitive and usually requires special training [25], which would be difficult when crowd-sourcing.

3 Data Analysis

3.1 Validation

Out of the 451 segmented videos we wanted to extract the ones that can reliably be described as belonging to one of the 24 emotion groups from the Baron-Cohen taxonomy. From the 2916 labels collected, 122 did not appear in the taxonomy so were not considered in the analysis. The remaining 2794 labels were grouped as belonging to one of the 24 groups plus *agreement*, *disagreement*, and *neutral*.

Because raters saw a random subset of videos not all of them received an equal number of labels. We did not consider the 16 segments that had fewer than 5 labels. To filter out non-emotional segments we chose only the videos that 60% or more of the raters agreed on. This resulted in 108 segments in total. As the average number of labels per video was 6 the chance of getting 60% agreement by chance is less than 0.1%. The most common label given to a video segment

Fig. 3. Example of still images from the dataset

was considered as the ground truth. Examples of still images from the labelled videos can be seen in Figure 3.

We validated the labelling of the selected videos using Fleiss's Kappa (κ) [9] measure of inter-rater reliability. The resulting $\kappa = 0.45$ indicates moderate agreement. This allows us to dismiss agreement by chance, and be confident in annotating the 108 segments with the emotional group chosen by the annotators.

Alternatively, if we were to choose a higher cutoff rate of 70% (56 videos) or 80% (40 videos), instead of 60% we would get $\kappa = 0.59$ and $\kappa = .67$ respectively, reaching substantial agreement. Although this would lead to fewer videos in our corpus, those videos might be seen as better representations of the mental states. We reflect this in our corpus by reporting the level of agreement per segment. Probabilistic systems can benefit from knowing the uncertainty in the ground truth and exploit that in classification.

Furthermore, we wanted to estimate inter-rater agreement for specific mental states in the resulting 108 segments. Expressions of basic emotions of *happy* ($\kappa = 0.64$) and *surprised* ($\kappa = 0.7$), had higher levels of agreement than complex mental states of *interested* ($\kappa = 0.32$), *unsure* ($\kappa = 0.52$), and *thinking* ($\kappa = 0.48$). For this analysis we only consider the expressions with no fewer than 5 representative videos.

We also wanted to see how successful certain elicitation methods were at generating certain naturalistic expressions of affect. Most of the affective displays came from the riddles both in computer and dyadic tasks. They were successful at eliciting *thinking* (26) and *unsure* (22), with some *happy* (14), *surprised* (3), *agreeing* (5), and *interested* (2). The longer and more complicated maze was successful at eliciting *interest* (4) and *thinking* (1). The third maze managed to elicit a broader range of expressions, including *surprised* (1), *sure* (1), *unsure* (1) and *happy* (3). This was somewhat surprising as we did not expect to elicit happiness in this task. There is some evidence [12] of people smiling during frustration which might explain perception of happiness by labellers.

3.2 Analysis of Hand-Over-Face Gestures

In *The Definitive Book of Body Language*, Pease and Pease [17] attempt to identify the meaning conveyed by different hand-over-face gestures. Although

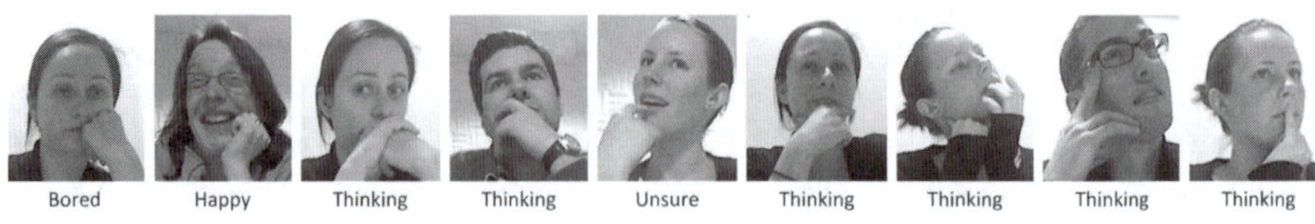

Fig. 4. Different hand shape, action and face region occluded are affective cues in interpreting different mental states

they suggest that different positions and actions of the hand occluding the face can imply different affective states, no quantitative analysis has been carried out. Using collected video segments, we have analysed hand-over-face gestures included in the videos in terms of the hand shape and its action relative to face regions. In the 451 initial public segments collected, hand-over-face gestures appeared in 20.8% of the segments (94 segments), with 16% in the computer-based session and 25% in the dyadic interaction session. Participants varied in how much they gestured, some had a lot of gestures while others only had a few.

Looking at the place of the hand on the face in this subset of the 94 hand-over-face segments, the hand covered upper face regions in 13% of the segments and lower face regions in 89% of them, with some videos having the hand overlapping both upper and lower face regions. This indicates that in naturalistic interactions hand-over-face gestures are very common and that hands usually cover lower face regions, especially chin, mouth and lower cheeks, more than upper face regions.

We analysed the annotated corpus of the 108 video segments in addition to the expert-labelled private segments. Total hand-over-face segments studied were 82. Figure 4 presents examples of labelled segments of hand-over-face gestures.

In the publicly labelled set, hand-over-face gestures appeared in 21% of the segments. Figure 5 shows the distribution of the mental states in each category of the encoded hand-over-face gestures. For example, index finger touching face appeared in 12 *thinking* segments and 2 *unsure* segments out of a total of 15 segments in this category. The mental states distribution indicates that passive hand-over-face gestures, like leaning on the closed or open hand, appear in different mental states, but not in cognitive mental states. On the other hand, actions like stroking, tapping and touching facial regions - especially with index finger - are all associated with cognitive mental states, namely *thinking* and *unsure*. Thus, hand shape and action on different face regions can be used as a novel cue in interpreting cognitive mental states.

4 Discussion

We have described the collection and annotation of a 3D multi-modal corpus of naturalistic complex mental states, consisting of 108 videos of 12 mental states. The annotations are based on crowd-sourced labels. Over six hours of data was collected, but only generated 108 segments of meaningful affective states, which highlights the challenge of collecting large naturalistic datasets. Analysing our

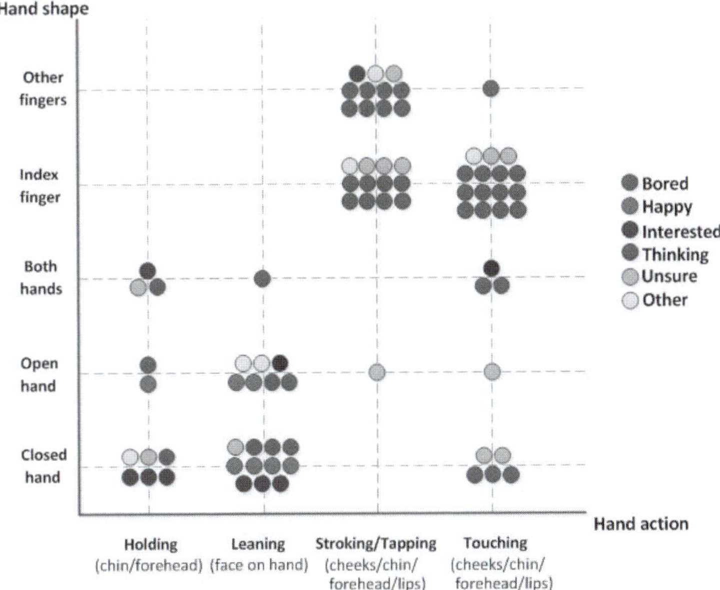

Fig. 5. Encoding of hand-over-face shape and action in different mental states. Note the significance of the index finger actions in cognitive mental states.

corpus, we noticed the potential of hand-over-face gestures as a novel modality in facial affect recognition. Our mental states elicitation methodology was successful; therefore, future work will include adding more data to our corpus. This will allow further exploration spontaneous gestures and hand-over-face cues. Furthermore, we are exploring the use of depth in automatic analysis of facial expressions, hand gestures and body postures.

Acknowledgment. We acknowledge funding support from Yousef Jameel Scholarships, EPSRC and Thales Research and Technology (UK). We would like to thank Lech Swirski and Andra Adams for their help in video recording and labelling.

References

1. Afzal, S., Robinson, P.: Natural affect data - collection & annotation in a learning context. In: ACII, pp. 1–7. IEEE, Los Alamitos (2009)
2. Baron-Cohen, S., Golan, O., Wheelwright, S., Hill, J.: Mind Reading: The Interactive Suide to Emotions (2004)
3. Bourel, F., Chibelushi, C., Low, A.: Robust facial expression recognition using a state-based model of spatially-localised facial dynamics. In: IEEE AFGR (2002)
4. Cowie, R.: Building the databases needed to understand rich, spontaneous human behaviour. In: AFGR, pp. 1–6. IEEE, Los Alamitos (2008)

5. Duchenne, G., Cuthbertson, R.: The mechanism of human facial expression. Cambridge Univ. Press, Cambridge (1990)
6. Ekenel, H., Stiefelhagen, R.: Block selection in the local appearance-based face recognition scheme. In: CVPRW, pp. 43–43. IEEE, Los Alamitos (2006)
7. Ekman, P., Friesen, W.: Manual for the Facial Action Coding System. Consulting Psychologists Press, Palo Alto (1977)
8. Ekman, P., Friesen, W.V., Ellsworth, P.: Emotion in the Human Face, 2nd edn. Cambridge University Press, Cambridge (1982)
9. Fleiss, J., Levin, B., Paik, M.: Statistical Methods for Rates and Proportions. Wiley, Chichester (2003)
10. de Gelder, B.: Why bodies? Twelve reasons for including bodily expressions in affective neuroscience. Phil. Trans. of the Royal Society B 364(1535), 3475 (2009)
11. Gunes, H., Piccardi, M.: A bimodal face and body gesture database for automatic analysis of human nonverbal affective behavior. In: ICPR, vol. 1, pp. 1148–1153. IEEE, Los Alamitos (2006)
12. Hoque, M.E., Picard, R.W.: Acted vs. natural frustration and delight: Many people smile in natural frustration. In: IEEE AFGR (2011)
13. Lausberg, H., Sloetjes, H.: Coding gestural behavior with the NEUROGES-ELAN system. Behavior research methods (2009), `http://www.lat-mpi.eu/tools/elan/`
14. Lucey, P., Cohn, J., Kanade, T., Saragih, J., Ambadar, Z., Matthews, I.: The extended Cohn-Kanade dataset (CK+): A complete dataset for action unit and emotion-specified expression. In: CVPRW, pp. 94–101. IEEE, Los Alamitos (2010)
15. McKeown, G., Valstar, M., Cowie, R., Pantic, M.: The SEMAINE corpus of emotionally coloured character interactions. In: ICME, pp. 1079–1084. IEEE, Los Alamitos (2010)
16. Pantic, M., Valstar, M., Rademaker, R., Maat, L.: Web-based database for facial expression analysis. In: IEEE Conf. Multimedia and Expo, p. 5. IEEE, Los Alamitos (2005)
17. Pease, A., Pease, B.: The definitive book of body language, Bantam (2006)
18. Roberts, N., Tsai, J., Coan, J.: Emotion elicitation using dyadic interaction tasks. In: Handbook of Emotion Elicitation and Assessment, pp. 106–123 (2007)
19. Rozin, P., Cohen, A.B.: High frequency of facial expressions corresponding to confusion, concentration, and worry in an analysis of naturally occurring facial expressions of Americans. Emotion 3(1), 68–(2003)
20. Snow, R., O'Connor, B., Jurafsky, D., Ng, A.: Cheap and fast-but is it good?: evaluating non-expert annotations for natural language tasks. In: Proc. of the Conf. on Empirical Methods in Natural Language Processing, pp. 254–263. Association for Computational Linguistics (2008)
21. Sun, Y., Yin, L.: Facial expression recognition based on 3D dynamic range model sequences. In: Forsyth, D., Torr, P., Zisserman, A. (eds.) ECCV 2008, Part II. LNCS, vol. 5303, pp. 58–71. Springer, Heidelberg (2008)
22. Tong, Y., Liao, W., Ji, Q.: Facial action unit recognition by exploiting their dynamic and semantic relationships. IEEE PAMI, 1683–1699 (2007)
23. Weitz, S.: Sex differences in nonverbal communication. Sex Roles 2, 175–184 (1976)
24. Yin, L., Wei, X., Sun, Y., Wang, J., Rosato, M.J.: A 3D facial expression database for facial behavior research. In: AFGR, pp. 211–216 (2006)
25. Zeng, Z., Pantic, M., Roisman, G.I., Huang, T.S.: A survey of affect recognition methods: Audio, visual, and spontaneous expressions. TPAMI 31(1), 39–58 (2009)

Evaluating the Communication of Emotion via Expressive Gesture Copying Behaviour in an Embodied Humanoid Agent

Maurizio Mancini[1], Ginevra Castellano[2], Christopher Peters[3], and Peter W. McOwan[2]

[1] InfoMus Lab, DIST, University of Genova, Italy
maurizio.mancini@dist.unige.it
[2] School of Electronic Engineering and Computer Science, Queen Mary University of London, United Kingdom
{ginevra.castellano,Peter.McOwan}@eecs.qmul.ac.uk
[3] Department of Computing and the Digital Environment, Coventry University, United Kingdom
christopher.peters@coventry.ac.uk

Abstract. We present an evaluation of copying behaviour in an embodied agent capable of processing expressivity characteristics of a user's movement and conveying aspects of it in real-time. The agent responds to affective cues from gestures performed by actors, producing synthesised gestures that exhibit similar expressive qualities. Thus, copying is performed only at the expressive level and information about other aspects of the gesture, such as the shape, is not retained. This research is significant to social interaction between agents and humans, for example, in cases where an agent wishes to show empathy with a conversational partner without an exact copying of their motions.

Keywords: Expressivity, gesture, emotion, copying behaviour, ECA.

1 Introduction

Several studies from psychology investigated relationships between emotion and movement qualities [4,21]. Nevertheless, automatic affect recognition from body movement remains an under-explored field [8], limiting the investigation of efficient and natural social interaction loops between agents and humans [18].

In previous work [9], expressive motion cues were proposed for communication in human-computer interaction, including *contraction index*, *velocity*, *acceleration* and *fluidity*. This paper contributes a perceptual experiment (Section 4) based on the automatic analysis, mapping and synthesis (Sections 3.1-3.3) of those cues from actors' upper-body motions and gestures to an embodied agent [17], in order to address the following questions:

- **Q1:** Are the proposed expressive motion cues, reproduced at the expressive level by an embodied agent, effective at communicating the same emotion conveyed by the original movement made by a human?

S. D´Mello et al. (Eds.): ACII 2011, Part I, LNCS 6974, pp. 215–224, 2011.

– **Q2:** How does the human perception of emotion change if specific expressivity parameters are not modulated from their 'neutral' values?

These questions are significant for providing important insights into the role of gestures' characteristics in the communication of affective content, important for informing the design of an agent capable of enabling an affective loop based on movement expressivity. The results of the experiment are described in Section 4.4 and implications for the aforementioned questions discussed in Section 4.5.

2 Related Work

Several studies have addressed affect recognition from the automatic analysis of body movement and postures. Studies on affect recognition from body movement include the work by Gunes and Piccardi [11], who developed a system for the recognition of acted affective states based on analysis of affective body displays and automatic detection of their temporal segments, and by Bernhardt et al. [2], Camurri et al. [7] and Castellano et al. [10], who proposed approaches to affect recognition based on the automatic analysis of movement expressivity. Examples of studies that addressed affect recognition from body posture include those of Sanghvi et al., who proposed a computational model to automatically analyse human postures and body motion to detect engagement of children playing chess with a robotic game companion [20], and of Bianchi-Berthouze and Kleinsmith [3], who proposed a model that can self-organise postural features into affective categories to give robots the ability to incrementally learn to recognise affective human postures through interaction with human partners.

Other studies have used embodied agents, either to investigate perception of emotion in individuals [15], or for reacting automatically to affective expressions of the user and systems providing low-level feedback, such as the generation or mimicry of non-verbal behaviour. Examples include the agent created by Maatman and colleagues [14], capable of generating rapport with human speakers by providing real-time non-verbal listening feedback, by Kopp et al. [13], who endowed their agent Max with the ability to imitate natural gestures performed by humans, and by Reidsma and colleagues [19], who designed a virtual rap dancer that invites users to participate in a dancing activity.

The experiment presented in this paper relates to previous studies on affect recognition from the automatic analysis of movement expressivity [7,10].

3 System Overview

The system (see [9] for more details) consists of two integrated software platforms: *EyesWeb XMI* [5] for motion tracking and movement expressivity processing (Section 3.1); and *Greta* [17], an Embodied Conversational Agent (ECA) with a humanoid appearance, capable of generating expressive behaviours (Section 3.2). The system architecture (Figure 1) integrates these two platforms with a module for mapping movement expressivity between a human and agent (Section 3.3).

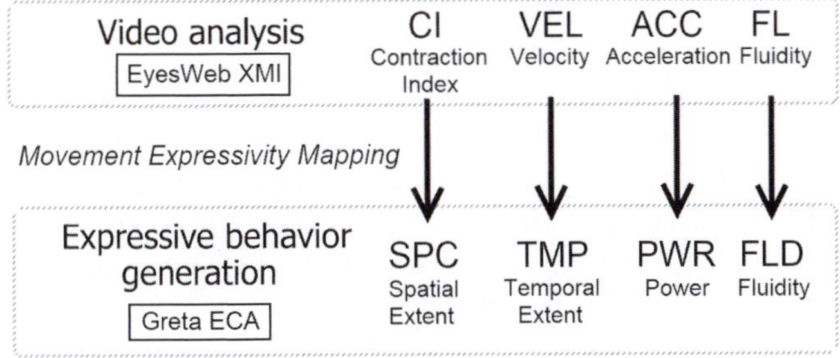

Fig. 1. The system's modules implementing the expressivity copying process

3.1 Video Analysis

Tracking of the full-body and the hands of the user is performed by the system using the EyesWeb Expressive Gesture Processing Library [6] to automatically extract the following low-level expressive motion cues:

Contraction Index - CI is a measure of the degree of contraction and expansion of the body, computed as the minimum bounding rectangle around it.

Velocity - VEL is calculated using the asymmetric backward numeric derivative, given the coordinates in a 2D plane of sampled points in a motion trajectory (here the barycentre of the coordinates of the user's right or left hand's).

Acceleration - ACC is calculated in the same way as Velocity. The asymmetric backward numeric derivative is applied to Velocity samples' x and y components.

Fluidity - FL is applied to the trajectory of the velocity of the hand's barycentre in a 2D plane. It is related the directness, or *Directness Index*, of the trajectory, indicating how direct or flexible it is [6].

3.2 Expressive Behaviour Generation

Hartmann et al. [12] have defined the expressivity of the Greta agent's behaviour over 6 dimensions. Here, 4 out of 6 dimensions varying in $[-1, 1]$ are modulated when expressive gestures are generated:

Spatial Extent - SPC determines the amplitude of gestures, contracting or expanding the agent's wrist end-effector positions according to the sectors illustrated in McNeill's diagram [16].

Temporal Extent - TMP refers to the global duration of gestures. It modifies the speed of execution of all gesture phases: preparation, hold, stroke and retraction.

Fluidity - FLD refers to the smoothness and continuity of movement (e.g., smooth/graceful versus sudden/jerky). It varies the continuity parameter of splines interpolating the agent's hands position.

Power - PWR makes the gesture look more strong/weak or tense/relaxed. It acts on stroke phase duration and agent's hand interpolation curves.

3.3 Movement Expressivity Mapping

The generation of expressive copying behaviour by the Greta agent is based on a movement expressivity mapping which is performed starting from the expressive motion cues automatically extracted during the video analysis. The Contraction Index is mapped onto the Spatial Extent, since they both provide a measure of the amplitude of movements; the Velocity onto the Temporal Extent, as they both refer to the speed of movements; the Acceleration onto the Power, as both are indicators of the acceleration of the movements; the Fluidity onto the Fluidity, as they both refer to the degree of the smoothness of movements.

Note, copying is performed only at the expressive level and information about other aspects of the gesture, such as the shape, is not retained.

4 Experiment

4.1 Overview

An experiment was performed to investigate the extent to which people can recognise the affective content expressed by the agent through the alteration of movement expressivity. It was designed to explore if and how the perception of emotion changes when the agent's expressivity parameters are altered while others remain static. The expressive copying behaviour was generated for the agent according to the process described in Section 3, to address the following:

- **Q1:** Are the proposed expressive motion cues, reproduced at the expressive level by the agent, effective at communicating the same emotion conveyed by the original movement?
- **Q2:** How does the perception of emotion change if some of the agent's expressivity parameters are not modulated from their 'neutral' values?

4.2 Materials

A set of gestures from an extract of videos of the GEMEP (GEneva Multimodal Emotion Portrayals) corpus, a corpus of acted emotional expressions [1], was analysed with EyesWeb XMI. Six videos of the corpus were considered, with three different emotions (*anger*, *joy*, *sadness*) expressed by two different actors observed by a frontal camera. The actors were free to choose the gestures they wished to conduct in each case.

As previously described in Section 3, the actor's expressive motion cues were extracted from the videos and reproduced by the Greta agent. Mapped values used in the experiment are reported in Table 1. Since the selected indicators of movement expressivity and the agent's expressivity parameters vary in different ranges, a rescaling of the former is performed based on maximum and minimum values of the indicators obtained by empirical observation.

For each video of the GEMEP corpus different types of gestures of the Greta agent were synthesised and recorded in videos according to the following specifications:

Table 1. EyesWeb motion cues and Greta's expressivity parameters

		EyesWeb motion cues				Greta's expressivity parameters			
	emotion	CI	VEL	ACC	FL	SPC	TMP	PWR	FLD
actor 1	anger	0.42	1.62	42.00	0.55	-0.04	0.18	1.00	0.55
	joy	0.27	2.73	22.41	0.53	1.00	1.00	0.06	0.00
	sadness	0.51	0.17	4.20	0.43	-0.50	-0.88	-0.80	-0.10
actor 2	anger	0.56	3.17	59.21	0.66	-0.41	1.00	1.00	0.66
	joy	0.30	0.60	13.92	0.49	1.00	-0.62	-0.53	0.50
	sadness	0.65	0.35	5.09	0.36	-0.83	-0.77	-0.83	0.36

Fig. 2. The *beat* performed by the Greta agent. Face has been obscured to ensure that it does not influence the perception of emotions from the participants.

1. Greta performs a *beat* gesture by modulating all the four expressivity parameters from their original neutral values. A beat gesture is a conversational gesture whose shape does not appear to convey any obvious emotional expression or meaning (see Figure 2). Six videos were created in this phase;
2. Greta performs a beat gesture by modulating three out of four expressivity parameters from their neutral values, disregarding at each step one of the four expressivity parameters (i.e., no expressivity control for one of the parameters); twenty-four videos were created in this phase;

Table 2 summarises the gestures considered in the experiments. All videos were modified to obscure the face of the agent in order to avoid influencing participants' judgements.

4.3 Procedure

Twelve students and researchers in computer science (10M:2F, average age: 29 years old) participated in the experiment. Each participant was asked to observe thirty-six videos over six conditions (C1 - C6; see Table 2). These consisted of six videos for each of the conditions C1 to C6, respectively.

A computer was used to show the participants the videos in a random order, different for each participant. Participants were told that they were participating in a study aiming to investigate the relationship between emotions and movement expressivity in an expressive virtual agent. Each participant was presented

Table 2. A total of 36 videos were used, 6 for each condition C1-C6. Gestures performed by actors featured in 6 videos (C1), while the remaining 30 videos contained synthesised gestures performed by the embodied agent (C2-C6).

Condition	Type of Movement	Performer
C1	Freely performed gestures	Actor
C2	Beat gesture: All expressivity parameters modulated	Embodied Agent
C3	Beat gesture: Fluidity not modulated	Embodied Agent
C4	Beat gesture: Power not modulated	Embodied Agent
C5	Beat gesture: Spatial Extent not modulated	Embodied Agent
C6	Beat gesture: Temporal not modulated	Embodied Agent

with the following instructions: "*You will be shown a set of videos in which a real person or a virtual agent performs one gesture. For each video you will be required to observe the body movements of the person or agent, and to evaluate which emotion(s) is/are being expressed*". Participants were asked to observe the gestures in the videos and to associate an emotion label (*anger*, *joy* or *sadness*) with each gesture using a slider: each emotion could be rated in a continuum scale of 1 to 100. Participants were allowed to watch each video as many times as they wanted and could select and rate all of the emotions they wanted or none.

4.4 Results

In order to investigate the effect of the type of movement on the participants' ratings, a one-way analysis of variance (ANOVA) with repeated measures was performed for each rated emotion (the dependent variable) when that specific emotion is expressed and in correspondence with different conditions of type of movement (the independent variable, with six levels: C1 to C6). Means and standard deviations for the one-way ANOVAs are reported in Table 3. Note that, in each one-way ANOVA, the focus is on the participants' ratings corresponding to the same emotion originally expressed by the actors.

Moreover, in order to identify specific differences among the ratings of emotions in correspondence with different conditions of type of movement, pairwise comparisons (Bonferroni corrected) were performed.

Anger: The one-way ANOVA for ratings of anger when anger is expressed by the actors showed a significant main effect of the type of movement [$F(5, 55) = 23.04$, $p < 0.001$][1]. Pairwise comparisons showed that ratings of anger when anger is expressed in correspondence with condition C1 are significantly higher than ratings of anger in correspondence with C2 ($MD = 43.13$, $p < 0.01$), C3

[1] In the case of sphericity violation, effects were Greenhouse-Geisser corrected (for readability reasons, the original degrees of freedom are reported throughout the results).

Table 3. Mean values and standard deviations of ratings of anger, joy and sadness for the different conditions (N = 12 in each condition, all ratings out of 100)

Condition		**Ratings of Anger**	**Ratings of Joy**	**Ratings of Sadness**
C1	Mean	82.00	30.63	46.29
	S.D.	13.40	17.46	26.69
C2	Mean	38.88	66.83	32.96
	S.D.	24.40	24.37	18.81
C3	Mean	41.92	58.75	28.13
	S.D.	23.75	24.94	15.64
C4	Mean	29.38	62.21	43.08
	S.D.	14.54	18.03	19.10
C5	Mean	45.83	39.50	37.17
	S.D.	23.90	17.43	15.24
C6	Mean	38.08	64.33	33.42
	S.D.	20.03	20.01	19.88

(MD = 40.08, $p < 0.01$), C4 (MD = 52.63, $p < 0.001$), C5 (MD = 36.17, $p < 0.01$), and C6 (MD = 43.92, $p < 0.001$).

Joy: The one-way ANOVA for ratings of joy when joy is expressed showed a significant main effect of the type of movement [$F(5, 55) = 11.40$, $p < 0.001$]. Pairwise comparisons highlighted significant differences between the ratings of joy in correspondence of different conditions for type of movement: C1-C2 (MD = -36.21, $p < 0.01$); C1-C4 (MD = -31.58, $p < 0.01$); C1-C6 (MD = -33.71, $p < 0.05$); C2-C5 (MD = 27.33, $p < 0.05$); C4-C5 (MD = 22.71, $p < 0.01$); C5-C6 (MD = -24.83, $p < 0.05$).

Sadness: The one-way ANOVA for ratings of sadness when sadness is expressed showed a significant main effect of the type of movement [$F(5, 55) = 3.34$, $p < 0.05$]. Pairwise comparisons highlighted no significant difference for ratings of sadness among all conditions for type of movement.

4.5 Discussion

The main objective of the experiments was to address two main questions. In the following, the results are discussed in relation to each of them.

Q1: Are the proposed expressive motion cues, reproduced at the expressive level by the agent, effective at communicating the same emotion conveyed by the original movement?

This question addresses the issue of evaluating whether the gestures performed by the Greta agent are associated with the same emotion expressed by the correspondent gestures performed by the actors.

First of all, in the case of anger, there is a significant difference between conditions C1 and C2 when anger is expressed by the actors (higher values in correspondence with C1 and greater than 50%, see Table 3). Values in correspondence with C2 are less than this, approaching 40%: We hypothesise that the type of gesture performed (i.e., the shape, in addition to the expressivity) plays an important role in emotion communication, although this is not the primary focus of this work.

For ratings of joy, there is a significant difference between C1 and C2 when joy is expressed by the actors (higher values for C2). Moreover, Table 3 shows that joy is given ratings greater than 50% for Condition 2 (66.83%), while ratings of joy for Condition 1 is 30.63%. These results suggest that, while joy is not recognised by the participants when the actors perform the gestures, the expressivity of the original movement reproduced in the Greta agent allows them to associate the original affective content with the synthesised gesture.

Finally, in the case of sadness, no significant difference was found when sadness is expressed by the actors. Ratings of sadness are higher for C1 (46.29 %) but they do not reach the 50% (see Table 3). This result suggests that the gesture and related expressivity chosen by the actors to express sadness might have been misleading for the participants. This may also be the reason why ratings of sadness for C2 are not very high (32.96%), but it may also be possible that the expressivity reproduced on the beat gesture performed by the agent did not evoke sadness in the participants.

Q2: How does the perception of emotion change if some of the agent's expressivity parameters are not modulated from their 'neutral' values?

This question refers to whether the percentage of the recognition of emotion by the participants decreases when some expressive motion cues are not modulated from their neutral values by the agent (conditions C3, C4, C5 and C6) in comparison with the case in which the agent performs the *beat* gesture modulating all expressivity parameters.

Results from the one-way ANOVAs for each emotion are of particular note in the case of joy: while for anger and sadness no significant difference between C2 and C3, C4, C5 and C6 was found, when joy is expressed by the actors pairwise comparisons highlighted a significant difference in the ratings of joy between C2 and C5. When the Spatial Extent is not modulated from its neutral value the recognition of joy by the participants decreases significantly. This result suggests that the degree of contraction and expansion is a relevant cue in the expression and recognition of joy, at least in the case of the sample of original and synthesised gestures that was considered in this study. Moreover, Table 3 shows that ratings of joy for C2 are also higher than those for C3, C4 and C6, suggesting that in the case of joy the choice of not modulating from their neutral values all motion cues results in an overall lower percentage of recognition of joy.

Overall, the results provide support for the proposed motion cues in the communication and expression of emotion in human-agent interaction.

5 Conclusion

In this paper we presented an evaluation study of a system for establishing an affective loop between a human user and an ECA: when the user performs an emotional gesture the embodied agent responds by copying the user's gesture expressivity. Results show that expressivity could convey the emotional content of the user's behaviour, i.e., if the agent's expressivity is not altered then emotional content cannot be conveyed effectively.

In the near future we aim to further enrich the agent's response: for example, by analysing the user's gesture expressivity, the agent could perform facial expressions that reflect the user's emotional state. We also aim to reverse the direction of our affective loop. For example, we could implement an embodied agent capable of influencing the user's quality of movement. If the agent perceives that the user's response is not the expected one it could perform gestures that exhibit, for example, faster or slower speeds.

Acknowledgements. We thank Tanja Bänziger and Klaus Scherer for the use of the GEMEP corpus, and Catherine Pelachaud and Antonio Camurri for their support. This work is partly supported by the EU FP7 project LIREC (LIving with Robots and IntEractive Companions; ICT-215554 2008-2012) and the EU FP7 project SIEMPRE (the project SIEMPRE acknowledges the financial support of the Future and Emerging Technologies FET programme within the Seventh Framework Programme for Research of the European Commission, under FET-Open grant number: 250026-2).

References

1. Banziger, T., Scherer, K.: Introducing the Geneva Multimodal Emotion Portrayal (GEMEP) Corpus. In: Scherer, K.R., Bänziger, T., Roesch, E.B. (eds.) Blueprint for Affective Computing: A Sourcebook. Oxford University Press, Oxford (2010)
2. Bernhardt, D., Robinson, P.: Detecting affect from non-stylised body motions. In: Paiva, A., Prada, R., Picard, R.W. (eds.) ACII 2007. LNCS, vol. 4738, pp. 59–70. Springer, Heidelberg (2007)
3. Bianchi-Berthouze, N., Kleinsmith, A.: A categorical approach to affective gesture recognition. Connection Science 15(4), 259–269 (2003)
4. Boone, R.T., Cunningham, J.G.: Children's Decoding of Emotion in Expressive Body Movement: The Development of Cue Attunement. Developmental Psychology 34(5), 1007–1016 (1998)
5. Camurri, A., Coletta, P., Varni, G., Ghisio, S.: Developing multimodal interactive systems with EyesWeb XMI. In: Proceedings of the 2007 Conference on New Interfaces for Musical Expression, pp. 305–308 (2007)
6. Camurri, A., Mazzarino, B., Volpe, G.: Analysis of expressive gesture: The Eyesweb Expressive Gesture Processing Library. In: Camurri, A., Volpe, G. (eds.) GW 2003. LNCS (LNAI), vol. 2915, pp. 460–467. Springer, Heidelberg (2004)
7. Camurri, A., Lagerlof, I., Volpe, G.: Recognizing emotion from dance movement: comparison of spectator recognition and automated techniques. International Journal of Human-Computer Studies 59(1-2), 213–225 (2003)

8. Castellano, G., Caridakis, G., Camurri, A., Karpouzis, K., Volpe, G., Kollias, S.: Body gesture and facial expression analysis for automatic affect recognition. In: Scherer, K.R., Bänziger, T., Roesch, E.B. (eds.) Blueprint for Affective Computing: A Sourcebook. Oxford University Press, Oxford (2010)
9. Castellano, G., Mancini, M.: Analysis of emotional gestures for the generation of expressive copying behaviour in an embodied agent. In: Dias, M.S., Gibet, S., Wanderley, M., Bastos, R. (eds.) GW 2007. LNCS (LNAI), vol. 5085, pp. 193–198. Springer, Heidelberg (2009)
10. Kleinsmith, A., Bianchi-Berthouze, N.: Recognising Human Emotions from Body Movement and Gesture Dynamics. In: Paiva, A., Prada, R., Picard, R.W. (eds.) ACII 2007. LNCS, vol. 4738, pp. 48–58. Springer, Heidelberg (2007)
11. Gunes, H., Piccardi, M.: Automatic temporal segment detection and affect recognition from face and body display. IEEE Transactions on Systems, Man and Cybernetics - Part B 39(1), 64–84 (2009)
12. Hartmann, B., Mancini, M., Buisine, S., Pelachaud, C.: Design and evaluation of expressive gesture synthesis for embodied conversational agents. In: Third International Joint Conference on Autonomous Agents & Multi-Agent Systems (AAMAS), Utretch (July 2005)
13. Kopp, S., Sowa, T., Wachsmuth, I.: Imitation games with an artificial agent: From mimicking to understanding shape-related iconic gestures. In: Camurri, A., Volpe, G. (eds.) GW 2003. LNCS (LNAI), vol. 2915, pp. 436–447. Springer, Heidelberg (2004)
14. Maatman, R.M., Gratch, J., Marsella, S.: Natural behavior of a listening agent. In: Panayiotopoulos, T., Gratch, J., Aylett, R.S., Ballin, D., Olivier, P., Rist, T. (eds.) IVA 2005. LNCS (LNAI), vol. 3661, pp. 25–36. Springer, Heidelberg (2005)
15. McDonnell, R., Joerg, S., McHugh, J., Newell, F., O'Sullivan, C.: Investigating the role of body shape on the perception of emotion. ACM Transactions on Applied Perception 6(3), 14–25 (2009)
16. McNeill, D.: Hand and mind: what gestures reveal about thought. University of Chicago Press, Chicago (1992)
17. Niewiadomski, R., Mancini, M., Hyniewska, S., Pelachaud, C.: Communicating emotional states with the Greta agent. In: Scherer, K.R., Bänziger, T., Roesch, E.B. (eds.) Blueprint for Affective Computing: A Sourcebook. Oxford University Press, Oxford (2010)
18. Petta, P., Pelachaud, C., Cowie, R. (eds.): Emotion-oriented systems: The Humaine handbook. Cognitive Technologies Series. Springer, Heidelberg (2011)
19. Reidsma, D., Nijholt, A., Poppe, R., Rienks, R., Hondorp, H.: Virtual rap dancer: Invitation to dance. In: CHI 2006 Extended Abstracts on Human Factors in Computing Systems, pp. 263–266. ACM, New York (2006)
20. Sanghvi, J., Castellano, G., Leite, I., Pereira, A., McOwan, P.W., Paiva, A.: Automatic analysis of affective postures and body motion to detect engagement with a game companion. In: ACM/IEEE International Conference on Human-Robot Interaction. ACM, Lausanne (2011)
21. Wallbott, H.G.: Bodily expression of emotion. European Journal of Social Psychology 28(6), 879–896 (1998)

Multi-score Learning for Affect Recognition: The Case of Body Postures

Hongying Meng[1], Andrea Kleinsmith[2], and Nadia Bianchi-Berthouze[1]

[1] UCL Interaction Centre, University College London, London, UK
[2] Goldsmiths, University of London, London, UK
h.meng@ucl.ac.uk, a.kleinsmith@gold.ac.uk, n.berthouze@ucl.ac.uk

Abstract. An important challenge in building automatic affective state recognition systems is establishing the ground truth. When the ground-truth is not available, observers are often used to label training and testing sets. Unfortunately, inter-rater reliability between observers tends to vary from fair to moderate when dealing with naturalistic expressions. Nevertheless, the most common approach used is to label each expression with the most frequent label assigned by the observers to that expression. In this paper, we propose a general pattern recognition framework that takes into account the variability between observers for automatic affect recognition. This leads to what we term a multi-score learning problem in which a single expression is associated with multiple values representing the scores of each available emotion label. We also propose several performance measurements and pattern recognition methods for this framework, and report the experimental results obtained when testing and comparing these methods on two affective posture datasets.

Keywords: Automatic emotion recognition, observer variability, affective computing, affective posture, pattern recognition, multi-labeling, multi-score learning.

1 Introduction

With the emergence of the affective computing field [17], various studies have been carried out to create systems that can recognize the affective states of their users by analyzing their vocal, facial [15] [23], and body expressions [9] and even their physiological changes [11]. An important challenge in building such automatic affective state recognition systems is establishing the ground truth, i.e., to label the training and testing sets necessary to build such systems. When the ground truth is not available, researchers recur to the use of perceptual studies where observers are asked to name the affective state conveyed by an expression (e.g., a body expression) and then use the most frequent label to label that expression. This approach assumes that a ground truth exists and that the automatic recognition system should behave as the majority of the observers.

S. D´Mello et al. (Eds.): ACII 2011, Part I, LNCS 6974, pp. 225–234, 2011.

As the field distances itself from acted datasets and begins to focus more on naturalistic expressions, unfortunately the subtlety of naturalistic expressions tends to lower the inter-rater reliability to fair or moderate levels [3]. This is particularly true for affective body expressions. For example, Kleinsmith *et al.* [9] used a random repeated sub-sampling method to assign ground truth labels to naturalistic postures according to groups of naïve observers. The results showed an average level of agreement of 67% between observers. This low level of agreement has also been observed for acted body expressions. Camurri *et al.* [2] examined the level to which groups of observers recognized the emotion portrayed in dance motions performed by professional dancers. The dancers' labels were considered the ground truth. 32 non-expert observers were asked to evaluate both the dance expression and its intensity and an average of 56% correct recognition was achieved. Another example is provided by Paterson et al.'s study [16] in which they also examined how well an actor's affective state may be recognized by a group of observers. Actors were motion captured while performing drinking and knocking motions according to 10 affective states. Human observers viewed the motions and judged the emotion displayed in a forced choice experimental design. The results showed that the overall recognition rate across the 10 emotions was a mere 30%.

Given the variability observed in these perception tasks (for both acted and non-acted datasets), it becomes important to take this variability into consideration. This problem has been addressed in more general terms by the machine learning community. Chittaranjan *et al.* [4] proposed to incorporate the annotator's knowledge into a machine learning framework for detecting psychological traits using multimodal data. They used the knowledge provided by the annotators, the annotations themselves and their confidences in the form of weights to estimate final class labels and then used these to train classifiers. Using this approach, the resulting classifiers outperformed classifiers that were trained using the most frequent label approach.

A different approach is taken by Fürnkranz and Hüllermeier [7]. They proposed to learn preferences rather than a set ground truth. In this case each sample is associated with a set of labels and their preferred value. A supervised learning of a ranking function is used to learn the complete ranking of all labels instead of only predicting the most likely label. The results show that even if the aim is only to predict the most preferred label, the learning process gains from taking into account the full ranking information. As the authors acknowledge, the problem with their approach is that it requires a large training dataset. Nicolaou *et al.* [14] treated the same problem as a regression task of predicting multi-dimensional output vectors given a specific set of input features. They proposed a novel output-associative relevance vector machine (RVM) regression framework that augments the traditional RVM regression by being able to learn non-linear input and output dependencies.

In line with these last two works, we propose a general framework for a pattern recognition problem that considers category labeling differences between observers which is described in the following section.

2 Multi-score Learning and Its Measurements

The scenario considered here is a pattern recognition problem in which there are multiple scores on the categories for a single sample. We call this problem multi-score learning. It should be noted that such a problem is different from typical machine learning problems with multiple outputs, such as multi-class learning, multi-label learning and multi-output learning. It is also different from typical regression models. Here, we describe multi-score learning with a detailed formulation of the problem, measurements and possible learning methods.

Let $X \subset R^d$ denote the d dimensional feature space of samples. Every sample $\mathbf{x} \in X$ has a multiple score vector $\mathbf{y}$ over C categories. All of these score vectors create a C dimensional score space $\{\mathbf{y} \in Y\}$. Because the scores have a maximum value, without losing generalization, we can assume that all the scores are within the interval $[0, 1]$, e.g. $Y \subset [0, 1]^C$. For a training dataset $\{(\mathbf{x}^i, \mathbf{y}^i), i = 1, 2, \cdots, N\}$, in which $\mathbf{x}^i = (x_1^i, x_2^i, \cdots, x_d^i)$ is a d dimensional feature vector and $\mathbf{y}^i = (y_1^i, y_2^i, \cdots, y_C^i)$ is its score, the machine learning task here is to find a function $h(\mathbf{x}) : X \rightarrow Y$ to predict the scores

$$\hat{\mathbf{y}} = h(\mathbf{x}) = (\hat{y}_1, \hat{y}_2, \cdots, \hat{y}_C), \, \hat{y}_j \in [0, 1] \tag{1}$$

for a given sample $\mathbf{x} = (x_1, x_2, \cdots, x_d)$.

In order to measure the performance of possible methods for multi-score learning, we define five measurements to compute the similarity between the true and predicted scores for all testing samples $\left\{(\mathbf{y}^i, \hat{\mathbf{y}}^i), i = 1, 2, \cdots, M\right\}$. These measurements give a full comparison between the true and predicted scores by considering their distance, similarity, ranking order and multi-class, multi-label classification performances.

Root Mean Square Error. Root Mean Square Error (RMSE) is a frequently-used measure of the differences between the values predicted by a model and the values actually observed from the object being modeled or estimated. The average RMSE over all the testing samples is computed as

$$\text{RMSE} = \frac{1}{M} \sum_{i=1}^{M} \sqrt{\frac{1}{C} \sum_{j=1}^{C} (y_j^i - \hat{y}_j^i)^2} \tag{2}$$

Cosine Similarity. Cosine Similarity is a measure of similarity between two vectors by measuring the cosine of the angle between them. The result of the Cosine function is equal to 1 when the angle is 0, and less than 1 when the angle is of any other value.

$$\cos(\theta) = \frac{\langle \mathbf{y}, \hat{\mathbf{y}} \rangle}{\|\mathbf{y}\|_2 \, \|\hat{\mathbf{y}}\|_2} = \frac{\sqrt{\sum_{j=1}^{C} y_j \hat{y}_j}}{\sqrt{\sum_{j=1}^{C} y_j^2} \sqrt{\sum_{j=1}^{C} \hat{y}_j^2}} \tag{3}$$

The average cosine similarity (ACS) on the testing dataset is computed as

$$\mathrm{ACS} = \frac{1}{M}\sum_{i=1}^{M}\frac{\left\langle \mathbf{y}^i, \hat{\mathbf{y}}^i \right\rangle}{\|\mathbf{y}^i\|_2 \left\|\hat{\mathbf{y}}^i\right\|_2} \tag{4}$$

Top Match Rate. Top match rate (TMR) evaluates how many times the top-ranked label is not the same as the top label of the sample. It is the same as the recognition error for multi-class classification.

$$\mathrm{TMR} = \frac{1}{M}\sum_{i=1}^{M}\mathbf{1}_{\left\{\underset{1\le j\le C}{\mathrm{argmax}}\mathbf{y}^i_j = \underset{1\le j\le C}{\mathrm{argmax}}\hat{\mathbf{y}}^i_j\right\}} \tag{5}$$

where $\mathbf{1}_A$ is a function on condition A.

$$\mathbf{1}_A = \begin{cases} 1, & A \text{ is true} \\ 0, & A \text{ is false} \end{cases} \tag{6}$$

Ranking Loss. The order of the predicted scores among C categories might be more important as it gives a relative comparison between these categories. The ranking loss (RL) measure considered here is based on an information retrieval application[19]. RL evaluates the average fraction of label pairs that are reverse ordered for the sample [24]. Assume that for sample $\mathbf{x}^i$, its real score $\mathbf{y}^i$ can be represented in order as $(y^i_{l_1} \ge y^i_{l_2} \ge \cdots \ge y^i_{l_C})$ and a predicted score $\hat{\mathbf{y}}^i$. With this inderstanding, the average RL function can be defined as

$$\mathrm{ARL} = \frac{1}{M}\sum_{i=1}^{M}\frac{\sum_{j=1}^{C}\sum_{k=j+1}^{C}\mathbf{1}_{\left\{\hat{y}^i_{l_j} < \hat{y}^i_{l_k}\right\}}}{C\times(C-1)/2} \tag{7}$$

Average Precision. In order to compare the overall recognition rate for multiple categories, average precision (AP) can be also considered. It is an important measurement for the average recognition rate for a multi-label classification problem. The problem is transferred into a multi-label classification task by thresholding($\ge \delta$) the true label into value "1" and "0". i.e. new labels $\mathbf{y}^i \in \{0,1\}^C$. AP measures the average fraction of labels ranked above a particular label l which has an actual value of "1" (e.g. $\mathbf{y}^i_l = 1$). The performance is perfect when the value is 1.

$$\mathrm{AP} = \frac{1}{M}\sum_{i=1}^{M}\frac{1}{\sum_{l=1}^{C}\mathbf{1}_{\{y^i_l=1\}}}\sum_{\substack{l=1\\ y^i_l=1}}^{C}\frac{\sum_{k=1}^{C}\mathbf{1}_{\{\hat{y}^i_k\ge\hat{y}^i_l, y^i_k=1\}}}{\sum_{k=1}^{C}\mathbf{1}_{\{\hat{y}^i_k\ge\hat{y}^i_l\}}} \tag{8}$$

3 Learning Methods for Multi-score Learning

There are many classification or regression methods that could be adapted to perform multi-score learning. The most popular methods are considered and applied here.

3.1 K-Nearest Neighbour

K-Nearest Neighbour (KNN) is a lazy learning method for classifying objects based on the closest training examples in the feature space. For sample $\mathbf{x}$, its predicted label $\hat{\mathbf{y}} = (\hat{y}_1, \hat{y}_2, \cdots, \hat{y}_C)$ can be computed as the average of the labels in its K neighbors $N(\mathbf{x}) \subset \{1, 2, \cdots, N\}$ in the N training samples. i.e.

$$\hat{y_j} = \frac{1}{K} \sum_{k=1}^{K} y_j^{i_k}, j = 1, 2, \cdots, C, i_k \in N(\mathbf{x}) \tag{9}$$

3.2 Regression

If we assume the dependent variables are independent from each other, we can use the general linear model (GLM), support vector regression (SVR) or partial least squares (PLS) methods.

General Linear Model. GLM [12] is a statistical linear model that has multivariate measurements $\mathbf{y}$. The feature vector $\mathbf{x}$ is usually assumed to follow a multivariate normal distribution. The components of $\mathbf{y}$ are assumed to be independent from each other. GLM is solved independently by solving a normal regression problem for each component .

Support Vector Regression. The SVR algorithm [6] is very similar to the support vector machine (SVM) algorithm, however it treats the data as a regression problem. The model produced by SVR depends only on a subset of the training data, because the cost function for building the model ignores any training data close to the model prediction.

Partial Least Squares. PLS regression is a statistical method that bears some relation to principal components regression. Instead of finding hyperplanes of maximum variance between the response and independent variables, it finds a linear regression model by projecting the predicted variables and the observable variables to a new space. Because both the X and Y spaces are projected to new spaces, PLS methods are known as bilinear factor models. Detailed information on the implementation of these methods can be found in [5] and [18].

3.3 Artificial Neural Networks

Artificial neural networks can be applied for multi-score learning without the assumption of independence between dependence variables. Two of these networks are introduced below.

Radial Basis Neural Network. A radial basis neural network (RBNN) [13] typically has three layers: an input layer, a hidden layer with a non-linear radial basis activation function and a linear output layer. The neurons in the hidden layer contain Gaussian transfer functions whose outputs are inversely proportional to the distance from the center of the neuron.

General Regression Neural Networks. A general regression neural network (GRNN) is a probabilistic neural network proposed by Donald F. Specht [21] in 1991. It needs only a fraction of the training samples that a back-propagation neural network needs [21]. The use of a probabilistic neural network is especially advantageous due to its ability to converge to the underlying function of the data with only a few training samples available. The additional knowledge needed to fit the data in a satisfying way is relatively small and can be achieved without additional input by the user.

3.4 Multi-task Learning

Multi-task learning (MTL) [1] is a method for learning sparse representations shared across multiple tasks. It is based on a novel non-convex regularizer which controls the number of learned features common across the tasks. The algorithm has a simple interpretation: it alternately performs a supervised and an unsupervised step. In the supervised step it learns task-specific functions, and in the unsupervised step it learns common-across-tasks sparse representations for these functions. MTL can be applied to multi-score learning by considering every component in $\mathbf{y}$ as a single task.

4 Multi-score Learning on Affective Posture: Results

Two posture datasets[1] were used to test our approach. Both datasets were collected using motion capture systems. Examples of postures from the two datasets can be seen in Figure 1. The first set contains 108 acted postures and each posture is described by a 24-dimensional feature vector. This vector describes the configuration of the posture in terms of distances between body joints and angles between body segments. Details on the data collection are provided in [10]. The second dataset contains 103 non-acted postures collected in a whole-body computer game scenario. For each posture, a 41-dimensional feature vector describing 3D rotational information for each body joint was extracted. Details on this dataset are provided in [9].

Each posture in both databases was labeled using non-expert observers and forced-choice surveys. For the acted dataset, 70 observers from 3 different cultures were asked to rate each posture in terms of 4 emotion labels (anger, fear, happiness and sadness). For the non-acted database, 8 observers made a series of 5 evaluations on the entire set of postures according to 4 affective state labels (concentrated, frustrated, triumphant and defeated). The results of the posture evaluation surveys for both the acted and non-acted datasets are shown in Figure 1. Each posture is represented by a pie chart showing the frequency of use of each label which was computed as the average over the number of observers who assigned that label to that posture. For details on the labeling process see [10] and [9] respectively. The agreement level for the acted dataset reached an average observer agreement of 85% (Cohen's kappa ranged between 0.75-0.84, i.e.,

[1] Available at: http://www.ucl.ac.uk/uclic/people/n_berthouze/research

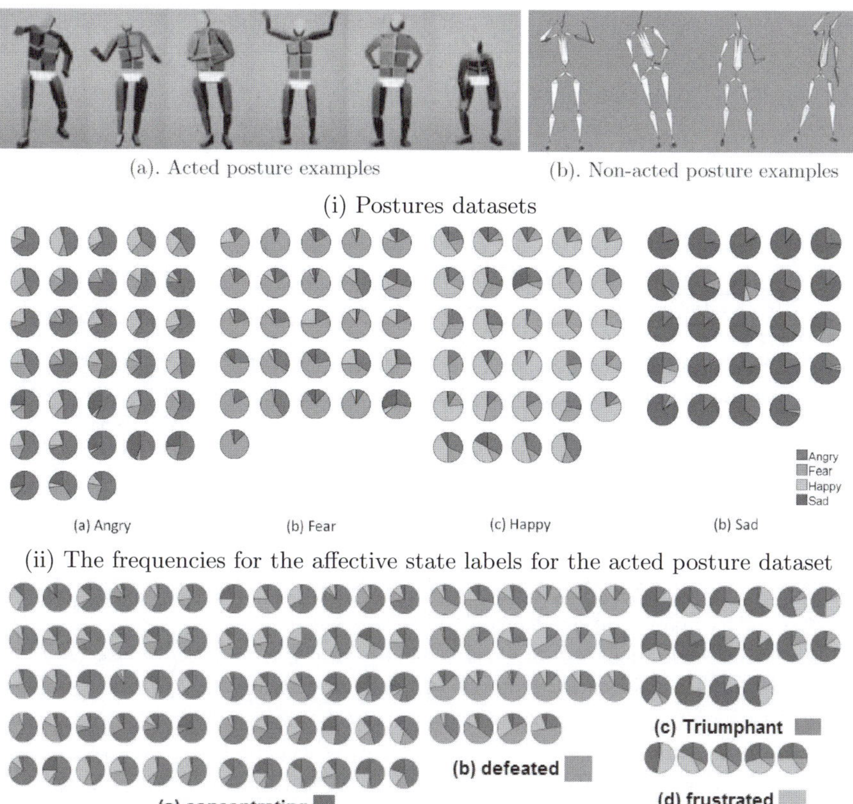

(iii) The frequencies for the affective state labels for the non-acted posture dataset

Fig. 1. (i) Postures examples. (ii) and (iii) represent the survey results for the two posture datasets. Each pie chart corresponds to the frequency of use for each affective state label for each posture image according to the observers. The pie charts are grouped according to the most frequent label indicated below each group.

substantial to almost perfect) [8]. The results for the non-acted dataset reached an average observer agreement of 67% (Cohen's kappa ranged between 0.30 to 0.62, i.e., fair to moderate), significantly lower than the acted dataset. For details on the relevance of the posture features see [10][9][20].

For each posture, its feature vector and pie chart were used for training the recognition system. In the testing, only the features vectors were input to the system and a pie-like label was produced for each posture representing the probability of each affective state. All the methods mentioned in Section 3 were used to test both the acted and non-acted posture datasets. A 10-fold cross-validation method and normalization were used to keep $\hat{\mathbf{y}} \in [0,1]^C$. $K = 5$ for KNN and $\delta = 0.25$ for AP were chosen for both datasets. The average values for 5 different performance measurements obtained by each method are shown in Table 1. In

Table 1. Performances for the 7 learning methods and the 5 evaluation measurements on both the acted (top) and non-acted (bottom) posture datasets

Acted Postures	KNN	GLM	SVR	PLS	RBN	GRNN	MTL
Root Mean Square Error (↓)	0.165	0.197	0.189	0.193	0.215	**0.161**	0.205
Cosine Similarity (↑)	**0.862**	0.814	0.836	0.822	0.771	0.852	0.807
Top Match Rate (↑)	0.635	0.601	0.595	0.602	0.522	**0.674**	0.619
Ranking Loss (↓)	0.164	0.239	0.223	0.244	0.287	**0.141**	0.269
Average Precision (↑)	**0.761**	0.687	0.717	0.699	0.663	0.756	0.683
Non-acted Postures	KNN	GLM	SVR	PLS	RBN	GRNN	MTL
Root Mean Square Error (↓)	0.141	0.161	**0.140**	**0.140**	0.145	0.143	0.139
Cosine Similarity (↑)	0.885	0.850	**0.892**	0.884	0.876	0.880	0.888
Top Match Rate (↑)	**0.702**	0.612	0.695	0.672	0.669	0.687	0.682
Ranking Loss (↓)	0.176	0.210	0.177	0.195	0.216	**0.152**	0.165
Average Precision (↑)	0.679	0.695	0.690	0.693	**0.734**	0.726	0.669

this Table, a "↓" indicates that smaller values correspond to higher performances, whereas a "↑" indicates that higher values correspond to higher performances. The best performances are shown in bold.

Among these five measurements, TMR(Top Match Rate) can be used for comparison with the top-label approach (i.e., most frequent label approach). Therefore, we also computed the performances of the KNN and SVM methods based on the top-label approach. For the non-acted dataset, the top-label approach for KNN and SVM reached 67.9% and 58.8% corect recognition rates, respectively. 59% was reported in [9] using a back propagation method. In Table 1, using the multi-score learning approach, TMR reached 70.2% with KNN and 69.5% with SVR, showing a clear improvement over the top-label approach and the human-observer agreement level (67%) if considered as a baseline. For the acted database, the top-label approach reached 63.9% and 54.1% with the KNN and SVM methods respectively. In comparison, TMR reached 67% with GRNN for multi-score learning. The results for the top-label approach using a multi-layer perception obtained higher recognition rates with performances between 63% and 77% for each separate culture group of observers [8].

The other 4 measurements shown in Table 1 provide information on the performances of each method over the distributions of all the affective states for all postures. For example, AP reached 76% correct recognition which is very close to the top-label approach performance (77%). AP of 76% means that the model can correctly predict 76% of top labels (i.e., the labels that have over 25% agreement between observers) for each posture regardless of whether the posture has only one, or more than one label with high observer agreement. In general, these measurements aim to provide a more complete description of the performance of each method. This framework allows for a more comprehensive evaluation of the methods and their properties with respect to the needs of the modeling problem.

5 Conclusions

Multi-score learning is a very common problem in affective computing applications. Agreement between observers is often not very high especially when dealing with naturalistic subtle expressions. This paper provides a framework for multi-score learning problems that take into account the variability between observers. The output scores provide more comprehensive information than single labels.

Overall, the performances of the various methods were very good and comparable to, if not higher than, the human observers' agreement levels and the top-label approach performances for both the acted and non-acted datasets. Furthermore, even when using TMR only, the results show better performance than the top-label approach for the non-acted posture dataset where the agreement between observers is quite low. Multi-score learning uses the complete label information instead of the majority agreed label to make the prediction more accurate and reliable. For TMR, multi-score learning uses a regression method to perform the classification task in which more detailed label information was used. From a learning method perspective, it can be seen that GRNN reliably obtained good performance on both datasets. The reason is that they not only provide non-linear regressions for each score, but also deal with the possible correlations between different categories.

The approach proposed here is also very general and modality independent. Therefore, it would be interesting to test the same approach for other modalities as well as with a fusion of modalities in cases where they may appear to disagree in the type of emotions they convey (e.g., a facial expression incongruent with its body expression). In this case, instead of the observers agreement, the problem of ground truth becomes one of the agreement between modalities. Furthermore, it would be interesting to investigate the benefits of each method with respect to the type of modality and the level of agreement that the data represent [22].

Acknowledgments. This work was supported by EPSRC grant EP/G043507/1: Pain rehabilitation: E/Motion-based automated coaching.

References

1. Argyriou, A., Evgeniou, T., Pontil, M.: Convex multi-task feature learning. Machine Learning 73, 243–272 (2008)
2. Camurri, A., Lagerlof, I., Volpe, G.: Recognizing emotion from dance movement: Comparison of spectator recognition and automated techniques. International Journal of Human-Computer Studies 59(1-2), 213–225 (2003)
3. Castellano, G., Karpouzis, K., Peters, C., Martin, J.-C. (eds.): Special Issue on Real-Time Affect Analysis and Interpretation: Closing the Affective Loop in Virtual Agents and Robots. Journal on Multimodal User Interfaces 3(1), 1–3 (2010)
4. Chittaranjan, G., Aran, O., Gatica-Perez, D.: Exploiting observers judgements for nonverbal group interaction. In: Proceedings of IEEE International Conference on Automatic Face and Gesture Recognition (FG 2011), Santa Barbara, CA, USA (March 2011)
5. Jong, S.: Simpls: An alternative approach to partial least squares regression. Chemometrics and Intelligent Laboratory Systems 18(3), 251–263 (1993)

6. Drucker, H., Burges, C., Kaufman, L., Smola, A., Vapnik, V.: Support vector regression machines. In: Advances in Neural Information Processing Systems, vol. 9, pp. 155–161 (1997)
7. Fürnkranz, J., Hüllermeier, E.: Pairwise preference learning and ranking. In: Lavrač, N., Gamberger, D., Todorovski, L., Blockeel, H. (eds.) ECML 2003. LNCS (LNAI), vol. 2837, pp. 145–156. Springer, Heidelberg (2003)
8. Kleinsmith, A.: Grounding Affect Recognition on a Low-Level Description of Body Posture. Ph.D. Thesis. University College London (2010)
9. Kleinsmith, A., Bianchi-Berthouze, N., Steed, A.: Automatic recognition of non-acted affective postures. IEEE Transactions on Systems, Man and Cybernetics, Part B 99, 1–12 (2011)
10. Kleinsmith, A., de Silva, P.R., Bianchi-Berthouze, N.: Cross-cultural differences in recognizing affect from body posture. Interacting with Computers 18(6), 1371–1389 (2006)
11. Mandryk, R.L., Inkpen, K.M., Calvert, T.W.: Using psychophysiological techniques to measure user experience with entertainment technologies. Behaviour & IT 25(2), 141–158 (2006)
12. Mardia, K.V., Kent, J.T., Bibby, J.M.: Multivariate Analysis. Academic Press, London (1980)
13. Moody, J., Darken, C.J.: Fast learning in networks of locally-tuned processing units. Neural Comput. 1(2), 281–294 (1989)
14. Nicolaou, M.A., Gunes, H., Pantic, M.: Output-associative rvm regression for dimensional and continuous emotion prediction. In: Proceedings of IEEE International Conference on Automatic Face and Gesture Recognition (FG 2011), Santa Barbara, CA, USA (March 2011)
15. Pantic, M., Rothkrantz, L.J.M.: Automatic analysis of facial expressions: The state of the art. IEEE Transactions on Pattern Analysis and Machine Intelligence 22, 1424–1445 (2000)
16. Paterson, H.M., Pollick, F.E., Sanford, A.J.: The role of velocity in affect discrimination. In: Proceedings of the 23rd Annual Conference of the Cognitive Science Society, pp. 756–761. Lawrence Erlbaum Associates, Mahwah (2001)
17. Picard, R.W.: Affective Computing. The MIT Press, Cambridge (1997)
18. Rosipal, R., Krämer, N.: Overview and recent advances in partial least squares. In: Saunders, C., Grobelnik, M., Gunn, S., Shawe-Taylor, J. (eds.) SLSFS 2005. LNCS, vol. 3940, pp. 34–51. Springer, Heidelberg (2006)
19. Salton, G.: Developments in automatic text retrieval. Science 253(5023), 974–980 (1991)
20. De Silva, P.R., Bianchi-Berthouze, N.: Modeling human affective postures:an information theoretic characterization of posture features. Computer Animation and Virtual Worlds 15(3-4), 269–276 (2004)
21. Specht, D.F.: A general regression neural network. IEEE Transactions on Neural Networks 2(6), 568–576 (1991)
22. Wagner, J., Andre, E., Lingenfelser, F., Kim, J., Vogt, T.: Exploring Fusion Methods for Multimodal Emotion Recognition with Missing Data. IEEE Transactions on Affective Computing 99, 1949–3045 (2011)
23. Zeng, Z., Pantic, M., Roisman, G.I., Huang, T.S.: A survey of affect recognition methods: Audio, visual, and spontaneous expressions. IEEE Trans. Pattern Anal. Mach. Intell. 31(1), 39–58 (2009)
24. Zhang, M., Zhou, Z.: ML-KNN: A lazy learning approach to multi-label learning. Pattern Recognition 40(7), 2038–2048 (2007)

Multi-modal Affect Induction for Affective Brain-Computer Interfaces

Christian Mühl[1], Egon L. van den Broek[1,3,4], Anne-Marie Brouwer[2], Femke Nijboer[1], Nelleke van Wouwe[2], and Dirk Heylen[1]

[1] Human Media Interaction, University of Twente, Enschede, The Netherlands
[2] TNO Behavioural and Societal Sciences, Soesterberg, The Netherlands
[3] Human-Centered Computing Consultancy, Vienna, Austria
[4] Karakter University Center, Radboud University Medical Center Nijmegen, The Netherlands

{cmuehl,nijboerf,d.k.j.Heylen}@ewi.utwente.nl,
{nelleke.vanwouwe,anne-marie.brouwer}@tno.nl,
vandenbroek@acm.org
http://hmi.ewi.utwente.nl/

Abstract. Reliable applications of affective brain-computer interfaces (aBCI) in realistic, multi-modal environments require a detailed understanding of the processes involved in emotions. To explore the modality-specific nature of affective responses, we studied neurophysiological responses (i.e., EEG) of 24 participants during visual, auditory, and audiovisual affect stimulation. The affect induction protocols were validated by participants' subjective ratings and physiological responses (i.e., ECG). Coherent with literature, we found modality-specific responses in the EEG: posterior alpha power decreases during visual stimulation and increases during auditory stimulation, anterior alpha power tends to decrease during auditory stimulation and to increase during visual stimulation. We discuss the implications of these results for multi-modal aBCI.

Keywords: affective brain-computer interfaces, emotion, ECG, EEG, visual, auditory, multi-modal.

1 Introduction

Affective computing aims to enrich the interaction with adaptive applications and devices by taking into account information about the user's affective state [21]. To date, several sources of information about the affective state have been successfully exploited, most prominently verbal and non-verbal behavior [27] and physiological signals from the peripheral nervous system [14]. With the advent of BCI, emotion assessment from neurophysiological activity gained prominence.

Affective brain-computer interfaces (aBCI) aim at emotion detection through real-time electroencephalographical (EEG) signal processing and classification. Research in aBCI has explored various paradigms and modalities to elicit emotions (e.g., visual, auditory, and tactile as well as self-induction). Multi-modal

S. D´Mello et al. (Eds.): ACII 2011, Part I, LNCS 6974, pp. 235–245, 2011.

emotion elicitation, however, has hardly been explored, although this is most prominent in real life (cf. [5]). To fill this knowledge gap in aBCI, the current study explores modality-specificity of EEG signals, using visual, auditory, and audio-visual affect induction protocols within a single experiment. We hypothesize that correlates of affect are (partially) modality-specific - they depend on the stimulation modality by which emotions are induced.

Functional neuroimaging studies provide evidence for stimulus-specific cognitive responses to affective stimulation. They show that correlates of affective responses can be found in core affective areas in the limbic system and associated frontal brain regions, but also in modality-specific areas associated with stimulus processing in general [15]. Emotional postures [10] and facial expressions [22] lead to a stronger activation of areas known to be involved in (visual) posture and face processing than their neutral counterparts. Similarly, affect-inducing sounds [8] activate auditory cortical regions stronger than neutral sounds, and auditorily induced affective states can be classified on the basis of the activations measured within these regions [7]. It should be noted that these responses are similar in their nature to purely cognitive responses, as observed during attentional orienting to a specific modality [25].

Most research on EEG responses toward affect uses visual affect induction by pictures. The late positive potential is a hallmark of visual affective correlates that is strongest over posterior cortical sites [11] and can be traced back to the activation of a network of visual cortices [23]. Unfortunately, in the realm of aBCI applications such time-domain based ERP correlates of affect are problematic, as they require averaging over many trials defined by clear stimulus onsets - something not available if affect is to be estimated during real-time interaction. Therefore, we and most other aBCI studies focus on features in the frequency domain, for which studies found indeed correlations during affective manipulations. Among other frequency bands, the power of the alpha band (8 - 13 Hz) - especially over posterior regions - was shown to respond to visual affective manipulation [1,2,9], which is of special interest as it also responds strongly to sensory manipulation in a modality-specific way [13,20].

Less is known about EEG correlates of auditory stimulation, as the activation of auditory areas is less easy to assess by EEG compared to that of visual areas [20]. However, magnetoencephalographic measurements have shown that alpha activity in the superior-temporal cortex correlates with auditory stimulus processing [13], and is supposed to be reflected in fronto-central EEG activity [12]. Consistent with this expectation, auditory-related cognitive processes were associated with differences in the amplitude of anterior and temporal alpha oscillations in the EEG [16]. A link between affective auditory manipulation and alpha band power was suggested by [2,19].

Summarizing, posterior alpha power has been associated with visual processing and with visual affective stimulation, whereas anterior alpha power has been linked to auditory processing and might be associated with affect. In general, alpha decreases during active processing, and increases otherwise [20]. To study the differentiation of posterior and anterior alpha power according to visual and auditory affective stimulation, respectively, we induce affective states differing in valence and arousal via visual, auditory, and audio-visual stimuli.

In accordance with the literature, we expect affect-related responses to pictures mainly for the alpha power over posterior cerebral regions. We define a region of interest (ROI) *pa* for parietal that comprises electrodes *P3,Pz,P4* and formulate our hypothesis for the expected response to the modality-specific affective stimulation: In the case of *visual affect induction*, alpha band power at *pa* is decreasing, as expected for increased visual processing. During *auditory affect induction*, alpha power at *pa* will increase, as expected for the inhibition of visual processing. During the *audio-visual induction*, however, a strong decrease of alpha at *pa* is expected.

Main effects of auditory affective stimulation might be anticipated in the activity over anterior cerebral regions. We define a ROI *fc* comprising the fronto-central electrodes of *FC1,Cz,FC2* and formulate the following hypotheses: In the case of *visual affect induction*, alpha band power at *fc* is increasing, as expected for decreased auditory processing. During *auditory affect induction*, alpha power at *fc* will decrease, as expected during increased auditory processing. During the *audio-visual induction*, a strong decrease of alpha at *fc* is expected.

To verify whether we manipulated emotional states as expected, we also recorded subjective ratings of the participants' emotional states and electrocardiographical (ECG) signals. We expect a decrease of heart rate during negative and arousing emotions [3,6].

2 Methods

2.1 Participants

Twelve female and twelve male participants (mean age: 27 years, standard deviation: 3.8 years) were recruited from a subject pool of the research group and via advertisement at the university campus. All participants, but one, were right-handed. Participants received a reimbursement of 6 Euro per hour or the alternative in course credits.

2.2 Apparatus

The stimuli were presented with "Presentation" software (Neurobehavioral systems) using a dedicated stimulus PC, which sent markers according to stimulus onset and offset to the EEG system (Biosemi ActiveTwo Mk II). The visual stimuli were presented on a 19" monitor (Samsung SyncMaster 940T). The auditory stimuli were presented via a pair of custom computer speakers (Philips) located at the left and right sides of the monitor. The distance between participants and monitor/speakers was about 90 cm.

To assess the neurophysiological responses, 32 active silver-chloride electrodes were placed according to the 10-20 system. Additionally, 4 electrodes were applied to the outer canthi of the eyes and above and below the left eye to derive horizontal EOG and vertical EOG, respectively. To record the electrocardiogram (ECG), active electrodes were attached with adhesive disks at the left, fifth intercostal space and 5 to 8 cm below. Additionally, participants' skin conductance, blood volume pulse, temperature, and respiration were recorded for later analysis. All signals were sampled with 512 Hz.

2.3 Stimuli

We used 50 pictures and 50 sounds validated for arousal and valence from the affective stimuli databases IAPS [17] and IADS [4]. For both stimulus modalities we selected 10 stimuli for each of 4 categories varying in valence (pleasant and unpleasant) and arousal (high and low). Additionally, a neutral class (i.e., low arousal, neutral valence) with 10 stimuli for each stimulus modality was constructed. Table 1[1] presents the mean arousal and valence values as reported in [17,4] for each condition (values in bold font). They were matched as good as possible between the emotion conditions, and between modalities. Footnote 1 includes the labels of the specific stimuli used. For the audio-visual conditions, visual and auditory stimuli of the same emotion conditions were paired with special attention to match the content of picture and sound (e.g., pairing of "aimed gun" picture and "gun shot" sound). The pictures and sounds of the unimodal conditions were paired in the order they are listed in Footnote 1.

Table 1. Mean (std) valence and arousal ratings for the stimuli of each emotion condition[1] computed from the **norm ratings** [17,4] and from *our participants' ratings*

Condition	Visual (IAPS)		Auditory (IADS)		Audio-visual	
	Valence	Arousal	Valence	Arousal	Valence	Arousal
(1) Unpleas.	**2.58(0.60)**	**5.24(0.54)**	**3.05(0.51)**	**5.81(0.43)**	-	-
low arousal	*1.99(0.79)*	*4.98(1.60)*	*2.84(0.81)*	*4.55(1.73)*	*2.28(0.78)*	*5.08(1.56)*
(2) Unpleas.	**2.26(0.34)**	**6.50(0.22)**	**2.70(0.51)**	**6.79(0.31)**	-	-
high arousal	*1.97(0.83)*	*5.73(1.84)*	*2.55(0.77)*	*5.32(1.64)*	*2.02(0.90)*	*5.82(1.61)*
(3) Pleasant	**7.53(0.44)**	**5.26(0.52)**	**7.09(0.43)**	**5.59(0.39)**	-	-
low arousal	*6.88(0.70)*	*5.24(1.45)*	*6.17(0.71)*	*4.97(1.50)*	*6.69(0.81)*	*5.37(1.50)*
(4) Pleasant	**7.37(0.31)**	**6.67(0.38)**	**7.19(0.44)**	**6.85(0.39)**	-	-
high arousal	*6.29(0.93)*	*5.50(1.60)*	*6.28(0.71)*	*5.67(1.62)*	*6.40(0.69)*	*5.92(1.65)*
(5) Neutral	**4.92(0.54)**	**5.00(0.51)**	**4.82(0.44)**	**5.42(0.42)**	-	-
low arousal	*4.52(0.64)*	*4.41(1.24)*	*4.86(0.60)*	*4.10(1.29)*	*4.54(0.60)*	*4.38(1.38)*

2.4 Design and Procedure

Before the start of the experiment, participants signed an informed consent form. Next, the sensors were placed. Before the start of the recording, the participants were shown the online view of their EEG to make them conscious of the influence of movement artifacts. They were instructed to restrict the movements to the

[1]
(1) IAPS:2141,2205,2278,3216,3230,3261,3300,9120,9253,8230; IADS:280,250,296,703,241,242,730,699,295,283
(2) IAPS:2352.2,2730,3030,6360,3068,6250,8485,9050,9910,9921; IADS:600,255,719,284,106,289,501,625,713,244
(3) IAPS:1811,2070,2208,2340,2550,4623,4676,5910,8120,8496; IADS:226,110,813,221,721,820,816,601,220,351
(4) IAPS:4660,5629,8030,8470,8180,8185,8186,8200,8400,8501; IADS:202,817,353,355,311,815,415,352,360,367
(5) IAPS:2220,2635,7560,2780,2810,3210,7620,7640,8211,9913; IADS:724,114,320,364,410,729,358,361,500,425.

breaks, and to watch and listen to the stimuli, while fixating the fixation cross at the centre of the screen.

Stimuli were presented in three separate modality blocks in a balanced order over all participants (Latin square design). Each modality block started with a baseline recording in which the participants looked at a black screen with a white fixation cross for 60 seconds. Between the modality blocks were breaks of approximately 2 minutes in which the signal quality was checked.

Each modality block consisted of the five emotion conditions (see Table 1) presented in a pseudo-randomized order, ensuring an approximate balancing of the order of emotion conditions within each modality condition over all subjects. Between the emotion blocks there were breaks of 20 seconds. Each emotion condition consisted of the presentation of the respective 10 stimuli, in a randomized order. Each stimulus was presented for about 6 seconds. Stimuli were separated by 2 seconds blank screens. Finally, all stimuli were presented again to the participants, to rate their affective experience on 9-point SAM scales of arousal, valence, and dominance as used in [4,17].

2.5 Data Processing and Analysis

After referencing to the common average, the EEG data was high-pass FIR filtered with a cut-off of 1 Hz and underwent a three-step artifact removal procedure: (1) it was visually screened to identify and remove segments of excessive EMG and bad channels, (2) eye artifacts were removed via the AAR toolbox in EEGlab, and finally (3) checked for residuals of the EOG. For the estimation of the power within the alpha frequency band, a FFT (Welch's method with 1 s overlapping Hamming-windows) was applied to each of the 15 blocks and their preceding baseline intervals for every participant separately. The resulting power values with a resolution of 1 Hz were averaged for the bins of 8 to 13 Hz for parietal and fronto-central regions. To approach normal distribution, the natural logarithm was computed, and baselining was performed by subtraction of the power of the preceding resting period. To compute heart rate (HR), the ECG signal was filtered by a 2-200 Hz bandpass 2-sided Butterworth filter and peak latencies extracted with the BIOSIG toolbox in Matlab. Next, the inter-beat intervals were converted to HR and averaged for each participant and each of the 15 stimulus blocks (3 modality $\times$ 5 emotional blocks). For the analysis of the effects of affect induction on ratings, HR, and alpha activity, repeated measures ANOVAs (rmANOVA) were conducted. Where appropriate, Greenhouse-Geisser corrected results are reported. As effect size measure we report the partial eta-squared η_p^2.

3 Results

3.1 Subjective Ratings

The affective manipulations yielded the expected differences in subjective ratings (see Figure 1). A 3(modality)$\times$5(emotion) rmANOVA on the valence ratings

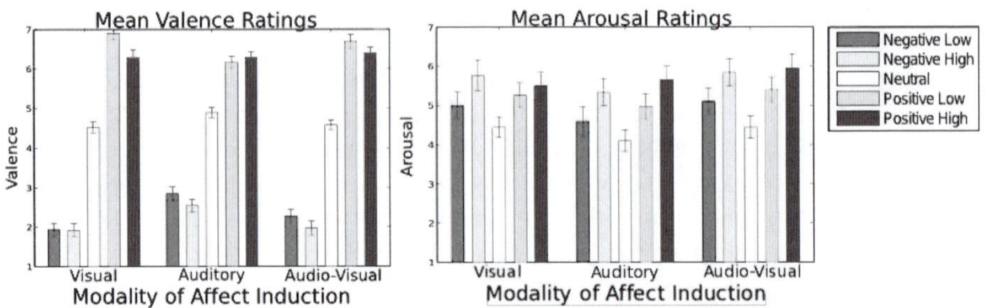

Fig. 1. The mean valence and arousal ratings for all 5 emotion conditions for visual, auditory, and audio-visual modality of induction (error bars: standard error of mean)

showed a main effect of both emotion (F(4,92) $= 246.100$,p < 0.001,$\eta_p^2 = 0.915$) and modality (F(2,46) $= 6.057$,p $= 0.005$,$\eta_p^2 = 0.208$). A 3(modality)×3(valence) rmANOVA on mean ratings of negative, neutral, and positive conditions, showed a main effect of valence (F(2,46) $= 264.100$, p < 0.001,$\eta_p^2 = 0.920$). Pairwise t-tests showed that the differences between negative, neutral, and positive conditions were highly significant. Furthermore, a main effect for modality (F(2,46) $= 7.078$, p $= 0.002$,$\eta_p^2 = 0.235$) reflected more positive ratings for states induced via the auditory modality compared to visual and audio-visual. An interaction effect indicates less extreme ratings for auditory stimuli (F(4,92) $= 14.813$, p < 0.001,$\eta_p^2 = 0.392$) and, hence, a weaker efficacy.

A similar pattern was found in a 3(modality)×5(emotion) rmANOVA on the arousal ratings, showing a main effect of emotion (F(4,92) $= 12.588$,p < 0.001,$\eta_p^2 = 0.354$), and of modality (F(2,46) $= 9.177$,p < 0.001,$\eta_p^2 = 0.285$). A 3(modality)×2(arousal) rmANOVA on mean ratings of low and high arousing conditions, showed a main effect of arousal (F(1,23) $= 27.180$, p < 0.001,$\eta_p^2 = 0.542$). A main effect for modality (F(2,46) $= 9.344$, p < 0.001,$\eta_p^2 = 0.289$) indicated, that auditorily induced affect was rated less arousing than visual, which in turn was rated as less arousing compared to audio-visual.

3.2 Heart Rate

The data of 3 participants was excluded from analysis, as ECG artifacts resulted in difficulties for adequate QRS-peak detection. The analysis of HR change relative to the resting baseline indicated differences resulting from the valence and arousal manipulations. A 3(modality)×5(emotion) rmANOVA showed main effects of modality (F(2,40) $= 6.063$, p $= 0.005$, $\eta_p^2 = 0.233$) and emotion (F(4,80) $= 4.878$, p $= 0.001$,$\eta_p^2 = 0.196$). A 3(modality)×3(valence) rmANOVA on low arousing negative, neutral, and positive conditions, showed a main effect of modality (F(2,40) $= 5.829$, p $= 0.006$,$\eta_p^2 = 0.228$) with significantly higher HR for the auditory conditions; as well as a main effect of valence (F(2,40) $= 5.641$, p $= 0.007$,$\eta_p^2 = 0.220$), with a lower HR for negative compared to neutral and positive valence. For arousal, a 3(modality)×2(arousal) rmANOVA on averaged

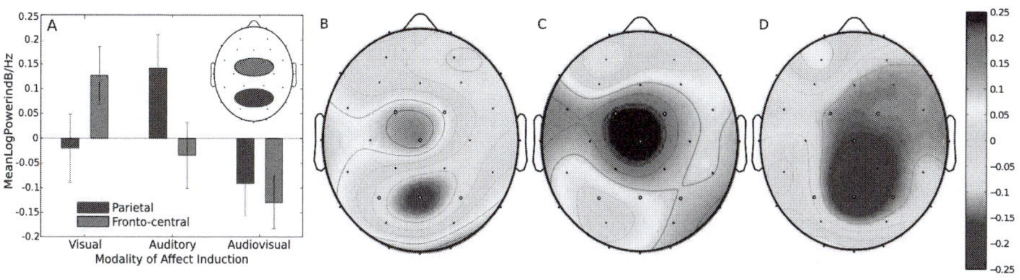

Fig. 2. The parietal and fronto-central alpha power (error bars: standard error of mean) during visual, auditory, and audio-visual affect (emotion – neutral), averaged over all subjects that entered the respective analyses (A); and the 2nd level contrasts of visual – auditory (B), visual – audio-visual (C), audio-visual – auditory affect (D), showing modality-specific responses averaged over all subjects

low versus high arousing emotion conditions, showed a main effect of modality (F(2,40) = 7.029, p = 0.002,η_p^2 = 0.260), with higher HR for the auditory conditions; and a main effect of arousal (F(1,20) = 5.360, p = 0.031,η_p^2 = 0.211), with a HR decrease for higher arousing stimuli.

3.3 EEG

For each ROI, the data of 4 cases was excluded according to the outlier criterium (1.5×interquartile range) to guarantee normality, which was potentially violated by the effects of residual artifacts on the alpha band power. To test the effect of modality-specific affective stimulation, we contrasted for all 3 modality conditions neutral against mean emotion response with a 3(modality) × 2(emotion) rmANOVA. We did so for the alpha power over the "visual" parietal *pa* and "auditory" fronto-central *fc* region (see Figure 2), separately. In accordance with our prediction for *pa*, we found an interaction effect between modality and emotion (F(2,38) = 3.373, p = 0.045, η_p^2 = 0.151). To specify the nature of the interaction, we computed the second-level emotion contrasts (emotion - neutral) for the visual, auditory, and audio-visual conditions. Pairwise t-tests confirmed the difference between audio-visual versus auditory affect (t = -2.651, p = 0.016, Figure 2D), and a trend for visual versus auditory affect (t = -2.093, p = 0.052, Figure 2B). Alpha power at *pa* decreases for visual and audio-visual affect, but increases for auditory affect. For *fc*, we found an interaction between modality and emotion (F(2,38) = 4.891, p = 0.013, η_p^2 = 0.205). As for the *pa*, we computed the second-level emotion contrasts for all conditions over the *fc*. Pairwise t-tests showed a significant difference between audio-visual versus visual affect (t = -3.155, p = 0.005, Figure 2B), and a trend for the visual versus auditory affect (t = -1.817, p = 0.085, Figure 2C). Alpha power at *fc* decreases for auditory and audio-visual affect, but increases during visual affect induction. A main effect of modality was observed for both regions (*pa*: F(2,38) = 3.821, p = 0.043, η_p^2 = 0.167; *fc*: F(2,38) = 6.110, p = 0.005, η_p^2 = 0.243), resulting from lower alpha power for general visual and audio-visual stimulation, compared to auditory stimulation (independent of affective conditions).

4 Discussion

In the current study, we explored neurophysiological responses to visual, auditory, and combined affective stimulation. We predicted, that parietal and fronto-central alpha power respond differently during visually and auditorily induced emotion.

The effects of valence and arousal on ratings and HR suggest that in general, the affect induction was successful. The affective stimulation had strong effects on the subjective experience of the participants. Despite our efforts to keep the emotional valence and arousal comparable over modalities, the ratings showed a slightly weaker efficacy of auditory stimuli to induce the affective states. This pattern was confirmed by the participants' HR. While arousal and valence contrasts showed the expected significant decreases of HR for arousing and negative stimuli [3,6], respectively, the overall HR change to stimulation was smallest for auditory, followed by visual, and strongest for audio-visual stimulation.

The observed responses of posterior (pa_α) and anterior (fc_α) alpha power (see Figure 2) match our expectations as formulated in the introduction. We found a lower pa_α for visual compared to auditory affective stimulation, especially when visual stimuli were paired with auditory stimuli. Complementary to pa_α, fc_α was lower for auditory compared to visual affective stimulation, especially when auditory stimuli were paired with visual stimuli. With regard to the literature on sensory processing [13,20], the effects might result from a decrease of alpha band power during "appropriate" stimulation (activation), and an increase during "inappropriate" stimulation (inhibition). The "appropriateness" is defined by the modality-specificity of the underlying cortices - the posterior visual cortices for ROI *pa* [20], and the temporal auditory cortices for ROI *fc* [12]. It should be noted, that the alpha increase to "inappropriate" stimulation seems more marked than the decrease during "appropriate" stimulation, stressing the inhibitory nature of the potential sensory gating process [13]. The relatively strong alpha decrease during audio-visual affective stimulation, might result from extra activation due to more intense processing of bimodal stimuli. Alternatively, it might be an additive effect resulting from an overlap of pa_α and fc_α due to volume conduction. Please note that these modality-specific effects were yielded after correcting emotion by neutral conditions for each modality, removing responses that are common to any visual or auditory stimulation, leaving the correlates of the affective response.

These results suggest that affective stimulation via different modalities has different, even opposing effects which can be observed in the EEG. These adhere to theories of modality-specific activation and inhibition of the respective, functionally specialized brain regions also involved in non-affective cognitive processes. Therefore, it is conceivable that these correlates are stimulus-specific cognitive consequences of affective stimulation, comparable to enhanced processing during attention [25], rather than primary correlates of affect. This is also in line with cognitive theories of emotion (e.g. the Component Process Theory [24]). These theories postulate the involvement of core affective processes such as affective self-monitoring (feeling) *and* of rather cognitive processes related to stimulus evaluation and behavior planning.

The complex response of the brain to emotional stimulation has consequences for those trying to detect affective user states from neurophysiological activity. Firstly, classifiers based on stimulus-specific neurophysiological responses, will be limited in their capability to generalize to affect evoked by other stimuli. Secondly, if these responses are of a general cognitive nature, also occurring in non-affective contexts, such classifiers are prone to confuse purely cognitive and affective events. The nature of the neurophysiological correlates enabling the successful detection of affective states should be taken into account when considering the application of such classifiers in real-world scenarios, to avoid threads to the reliability and validity of aBCIs.

The observed modality-specific responses might be of interest in their own right: assuming that a part of the response to affective manipulation can be attributed to the way (i.e. the type of stimulation) emotions are evoked, it might be possible to distinguish the origin of the affective response via neurophysiological activity. Another interesting consequence of the presumed cognitive nature of the responses is the discrimination of the attended modality in general, not only restricted to affect.

The current study also has its limitations. One is the creation of artificial multi-modal combinations of IADS and IAPS stimuli. The restricted choice of stimuli led to partial mismatches of the content, which could induce additional processes and correlates, such as mismatch negativity [18] or multi-sensory integration (cf. [5]). To prevent such effects, most often faces with accompanying speech are used. However, this limits the results of these studies for multi-modal affective processing. The results show, conveniently, that such effects are not likely to have occurred in the current study as for both modalities similar unimodal and multi-modal effects on the EEG signals were found. However, these effects are only two of many possible. Most likely very early and short processes or effects have occurred not reported in this study (e.g., [26]). Multi-sensory integration is a challenging endeavor on itself, its mapping on neurophysiology is relatively little explored, and the combination of these two factors with emotion is hardly touched upon, in particular in applied and ambulatory research.

5 Conclusion

Taken together, we have shown that neurophysiological correlates of affective responses measured by EEG are partially modality-specific: alpha band power over posterior and anterior regions differs in a systematic way between visual, auditory, and audio-visual stimulation. The responses in the alpha band suggest that visual processes are mainly reflected over parietal regions, while auditory processes are reflected over fronto-central regions. These results pose potential problems for generalization and specificity of affect classifiers relying on such modality-specific, rather cognitive neurophysiological effects. They also imply the possibility to detect the modality, visual or auditory or combined, through which the affective response was elicited. Further studies on the exploration and exploitation of the context-specificity of neurophysiological responses are needed.

Acknowledgments. The authors gratefully acknowledge the support of the BrainGain Smart Mix Programme of the Netherlands Ministry of Economic Affairs and the Netherlands Ministry of Education, Culture, and Science.

References

1. Aftanas, L.I., Reva, N.V., Varlamov, A.A., Pavlov, S.V., Makhnev, V.P.: Analysis of evoked eeg synchronization and desynchronization in conditions of emotional activation in humans: temporal and topographic characteristics. Neuroscience and Behavioral Physiology 34(8), 859–867 (2004)
2. Baumgartner, T., Esslen, M., Jancke, L.: From emotion perception to emotion experience: Emotions evoked by pictures and classical music. International Journal of Psychophysiology 60(1), 34–43 (2006)
3. Bradley, M.M., Lang, P.J.: Affective reactions to acoustic stimuli. Psychophysiology 37(2), 204–215 (2000)
4. Bradley, M.M., Lang, P.J.: The international affective digitized sounds (IADS-2): Affective ratings of sounds and instruction manual. Technical report, University of Florida, Center for Research in Psychophysiology, Gainesville, Fl, USA (2007)
5. Brefczynski-Lewis, J., Lowitszch, S., Parsons, M., Lemieux, S., Puce, A.: Audiovisual non-verbal dynamic faces elicit converging fMRI and ERP responses. Brain Topography 21(3-4), 193–206 (2009)
6. Codispoti, M., Ferrari, V., Bradley, M.M.: Repetitive picture processing: autonomic and cortical correlates. Brain Research 1068(1), 213–220 (2006)
7. Ethofer, T., Van De Ville, D., Scherer, K., Vuilleumier, P.: Decoding of emotional information in voice-sensitive cortices. Current Biology 19(12), 1028–1033 (2009)
8. Grandjean, D., Sander, D., Pourtois, G., Schwartz, S., Seghier, M.L., Scherer, K., Vuilleumier, P.: The voices of wrath: brain responses to angry prosody in meaningless speech. Nature Neuroscience 8(2), 145–146 (2005)
9. Guntekin, B., Basar, E.: Emotional face expressions are differentiated with brain oscillations. International Journal of Psychophysiology 64(1), 91–100 (2007)
10. Hadjikhani, N., de Gelder, B.: Seeing fearful body expressions activates the fusiform cortex and amygdala. Current Biology 13(24), 2201–2205 (2003)
11. Hajcak, G., MacNamara, A., Olvet, D.M.: Event-related potentials, emotion, and emotion regulation: An integrative review. Developmental Neuropsychology 35(2), 129–155 (2010)
12. Hari, R., Salmelin, R., Makela, J.P., Salenius, S., Helle, M.: MEG cortical rhythms. International Journal of Psychophysiology 26, 51–62 (1997)
13. Jensen, O., Mazaheri, A.: Shaping functional architecture by oscillatory alpha activity: gating by inhibition. Frontiers in Human Neuroscience 4 (2010)
14. Kim, J., André, E.: Emotion recognition based on physiological changes in music listening. IEEE Transactions on Pattern Analysis and Machine Intelligence 30(12), 2067–2083 (2008)
15. Kober, H., Feldman Barrett, L., Joseph, J., Bliss-Moreau, E., Lindquist, K., Wager, T.D.: Functional grouping and cortical-subcortical interactions in emotion: a meta-analysis of neuroimaging studies. NeuroImage 42(2), 998–1031 (2008)

16. Krause, C.M.: Cognition- and memory-related erd/ers responses in the auditory stimulus modality. Progress in brain research 159, 197–207 (2006)
17. Lang, P.J., Bradley, M.M., Cuthbert, B.N.: International affective picture system (IAPS): Technical manual and affective ratings. Technical report, University of Florida, Center for Research in Psychophysiology, Gainesville, Fl, USA (1999)
18. Näätänena, R., Paavilainen, P., Rinne, T., Alho, K.: The mismatch negativity (MMN) in basic research of central auditory processing: A review. Clinical Neurophysiology 118(12), 2544–2590 (2007)
19. Panksepp, J., Bernatzky, G.: Emotional sounds and the brain: the neuro-affective foundations of musical appreciation. Behavioral Processes 60, 133–155 (2002)
20. Pfurtscheller, G., Lopes da Silva, F.H.: Event-related EEG/MEG synchronization and desynchronization: basic principles. Clinical Neurophysiology 110(11), 1842–1857 (1999)
21. Picard, R.W.: Affective Computing. The MIT Press, Cambridge (1997)
22. Pourtois, G., Vuilleumier, P.: Dynamics of emotional effects on spatial attention in the human visual cortex. Progress in Brain Research, vol. 156, pp. 67–91. Elsevier, Amsterdam (2006)
23. Sabatinelli, D., Lang, P.J., Keil, A., Bradley, M.M.: Emotional perception: Correlation of functional MRI and event-related potentials. Cerebral Cortex 17(5), 1085–1091 (2007)
24. Sander, D., Grandjean, D., Scherer, K.R.: A systems approach to appraisal mechanisms in emotion. Neural Networks 18(4), 317–352 (2005)
25. Vuilleumier, P.: How brains beware: neural mechanisms of emotional attention. Trends in Cognitive Sciences 9(12), 585–594 (2005)
26. Wang, J., Nicol, T., Skoe, E., Sams, M., Kraus, N.: Emotion modulates early auditory response to speech. Journal of Cognitive Neuroscience 21(11), 2121–2128 (2009)
27. Zeng, Z., Pantic, M., Roisman, G.I., Huang, T.S.: A survey of affect recognition methods: Audio, visual, and spontaneous expressions. IEEE Transactions on Pattern Analysis and Machine Intelligence 31(1), 39–58 (2009)

Toward a Computational Framework of Suspense and Dramatic Arc

Brian O'Neill and Mark Riedl

School of Interactive Computing
Georgia Institute of Technology
{boneill,riedl}@cc.gatech.edu

Abstract. We propose a computational framework for the recognition of suspense and dramatic arc in stories. Suspense is an affective response to narrative structure that accompanies the reduction in quantity or quality of plans available to a protagonist faced with potential goal failure and/or harm. Our work is motivated by the recognition that computational systems are historically unable to reliably reason about aesthetic or affective qualities of story structures. Our proposed framework, Dramatis, reads a story, identifies potential failures in the plans and goals of the protagonist, and computes a suspense rating at various points in the story. To compute suspense, Dramatis searches for ways in which the protagonist can overcome the failure and produces a rating inversely proportional to the likelihood of the best approach to overcoming the failure. If applied to story generation, Dramatis could allow for the creation of stories with knowledge of suspense and dramatic arc.

Keywords: Affective computing, suspense, dramatic arc, narrative cognition.

1 Introduction

Narrative as entertainment, in the form of oral, written, or visual storytelling, plays a central role in many forms of entertainment media, including novels, movies, television, and theatre. One of the reasons for the prevalence of storytelling in human culture may be due to the way in which narrative is a cognitive tool for situated understanding [1, 2]. This narrative intelligence is central in the cognitive processes that we employ across a range of experiences, from entertainment contexts to active learning. Expert storytellers who craft narratives for entertainment – films, novels, games, etc. – often structure their narratives to elicit an emotional response from the viewer, reader, or player. The concept of the dramatic arc, identified by Aristotle [3], is one common pattern of emotional impact on an audience.

The construction of novel quality stories is a challenging task, even for humans. For more than 30 years, computer scientists have been trying to answer the question of whether, and how, intelligent computational systems can create stories from scratch. Computational story generation systems typically take one of two approaches. In a search-based approach, the system searches the space of possible stories to find the best story according to a heuristic. In the adaptation-based approach, systems take one or more existing stories, which are altered or recombined

S. D´Mello et al. (Eds.): ACII 2011, Part I, LNCS 6974, pp. 246–255, 2011.

into new narratives. See Gervás [4] for a summary of the history of story generation. We make the observation that, to date, story generation systems have been unreliable when it comes to creating novel stories with dramatic structure. Simply put, story generation systems do not have sufficient understanding of story aesthetics nor how story structure affects emotional change in an audience.

In this paper, we explore what it would take to make a story generation system be able to understand the concept of dramatic arc. There are many ways to produce dramatic arc in a story [5]. One such approach is to make stories suspenseful; Abbott describes suspense and surprise as the two things that "give narrative its life" [6]. Despite the importance and prevalence of suspense as a storytelling tool, there has been little investigation of computational techniques for generating or understanding suspense. The most relevant work has been in discourse generation: deciding what to tell and what to leave out when telling a pre-existing story [7]. However, the question of how to generate interesting stories from scratch remains open.

This paper describes preliminary work toward Dramatis: a framework for the detection of suspense, as part of dramatic arc. The proposed system "reads" elements of a story one at a time and generates a suspense response when appropriate. While we do not directly address the question of how to computationally generate suspenseful stories, our work on suspense detection will be used to heuristically guide search-based story generation processes. In the remainder of this paper, we discuss related work in narratology and computational approaches to suspense and narrative,. The next section describes Dramatis and walks the reader through an example using a recent film. Finally, we discuss why we believe this framework is plausible and describe future work in the implementation and testing of the framework.

2 Related Work

Suspense occurs in an audience – the reader or watcher of a narrative – when the audience perceives that a protagonist is faced with the possibility of an undesirable outcome. Gerrig and Bernardo suggest that one method used by authors to make readers feel suspense is to reduce the quantity and/or quality of plans available to the protagonist for avoiding an undesirable outcome [8]. They suggest that readers act as problem-solvers on behalf of the protagonist and when readers can only devise low-quality plans, or struggle to come up with any plans for a hero to escape the predicament, the perception of suspense will increase. In these studies, they found that readers reported higher suspense levels when story excerpts suggested potential escapes and then quickly eliminated them, thus reducing the quantity of available plans for the protagonist.

Branigan [5] suggests that suspense can occur when the audience knows more than the protagonist, particularly about the possibility of undesirable outcomes. He also points out that feelings of suspense can be intensified depending on the audience's affinity for the character in question. Suspense has also been described as a lack of closure within a narrative [6]; authors manipulate readers by appearing to satisfy the need for closure, only to take it away.

Readers continuously make inferences about aspects of the story which have not been explicitly stated [9]. These inferences can be divided into two classes. *Online*

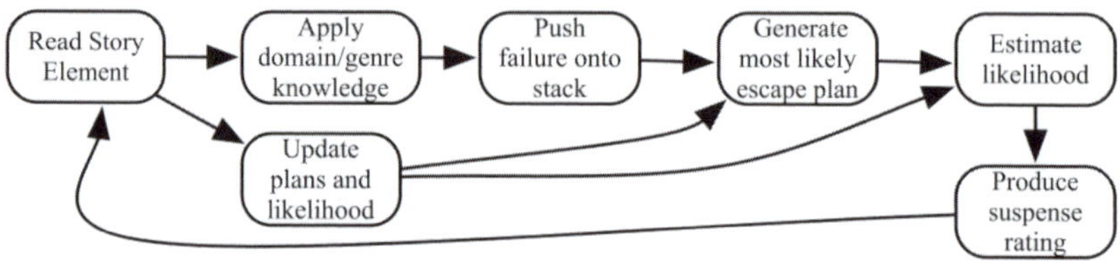

Fig. 1. This flowchart represents the process used by Dramatis to move from reading part of a story to producing a suspense rating

inferences can be made with little effort while reading, while *offline inferences* require that the audience is given time to reason. Online inferences include the recognition of causal antecedents and superordinate goals. Offline inferences include identifying subordinate goals, such as recognizing the lesser goals of a character or the plan of action used to achieve some state. Both classes of inference are important in recognizing when readers feel suspense.

The Suspenser system [7] computationally attempts to tell pre-existing stories in a suspenseful way. Suspenser tries excluding different sets of events from the discourse to maximize a suspense rating. The level of suspense of any telling of a story is measured by generating all possible plans a protagonist might have and taking the ratio of failed plans to successful plans. We are not seeking to modify existing stories, but rather detect suspenseful points in the discourse, as given. Additionally, in order to preserve cognitive plausibility our metric for suspense is not based on an exhaustive search of the plan-space.

3 Dramatis Framework

We present a framework for Dramatis: a suspense detection system based on the correlation between perceived likelihood of a protagonist's failure and the amount of suspense reported by the audience. Dramatis reads in elements of the story one at a time. The system attempts to predict failures in the protagonist's goals and plans, making predictions only when the pacing of the story affords time to engage in offline processing. Predictions are made using knowledge of the story domain and genre, and knowledge of the goals and plans of the characters in the story when available.

When a failure prediction is made, Dramatis must predict how likely it is that the failure will actually occur. Instead of exhaustively sampling the space of possible plans for those that fail and those that succeed, we invert the process by searching for the most likely plan that will avoid failure, which we call the *escape plan*. The system searches for the most likely escape plan and estimates the likelihood of the plan's success under the assumption that one only needs to find the best way to escape the failure given existing knowledge about the world. Dramatis uses the likelihood of successful escape to determine a suspense rating for the given point in the story; suspense is inversely proportional to the likelihood of failure escape. The system tracks the generated escape plan, and as the story progresses and new information is added, it recalculates the likelihood or regenerates the plan, if necessary. The flowchart in Figure 1 shows the complete suspense detection process. We highlight the key points of the framework below.

3.1 Reading a Story Element

Dramatis reads in story elements one at a time. We do not address any aspect of natural language understanding or computer vision necessary to literally read or view a creative artifact such as a story or film. Instead, the system will read in an annotated version of a story or film script, which is discretized into "time-slices." Each time-slice contains details about the characters involved in the current scene that are known to the audience (and may or may not be known to the protagonist), the location of the scene, symbolic representations of both the content of the dialogue, the actions performed by the characters and other non-agent items in the scene, the pacing of the scene (indicating whether the audience would have time to do offline processing), and non-diegetic information such as background music and camera angles used (as both of these are used by directors to manipulate audience emotion).

3.2 Searching for Failure

Dramatis searches for a failure when cued to do so by the most recently read time slice. This cue may come from non-diegetic information, such as ominous music or from new information about the narrative. When the audience is given new information that is not addressing an existing potential failure, Dramatis searches for a new potential failure that could disrupt the protagonist's pursuit of his goal. We have identified three cases. First, an opposing plan or goal is given as part of the time-slice. For example, a character being told he will be shot provides an opposing goal of that character's death. Second, the system applies relevant knowledge, such as domain and genre information, to determine a potential failure. This knowledge takes the form of scripts and schemas. For example, the knowledge that a character being poisoned typically leads to that character getting sick and then dying would be contained in a script. We do not explicitly search for this script; rather, it is retrieved from a collection of scripts indexed by character goals and elements present in the scene. Third, when Dramatis knows the protagonist's plan and the plans of an antagonist character, it may determine that these plans will require actions that are mutually exclusive, such that only one of the characters' plans can succeed. In this case, the other character's plan is stored as an opposing plan.

The scripts and plans retrieved during the search for failure are represented as plan networks [10]. Plan networks allow scripts to be represented as a set of possible sequences of discrete events. We have modified plan networks so that they contain explicit information about the causal relationships between the events listed. A causal relationship exists between two events when one event affects change on the world necessary for a later event to occur. Thus, each event in the script is described by a set of preconditions and effects where preconditions describe the state of the world that must exist before this event can occur and the effects describe how the world will be different after the event occurs. The preconditions and effects are given as a set of symbolic predicates that describe the world state. This approach to describing actions and their preconditions and effects is common in planning problems, but can easily be transferred to scripts as a form of meta-knowledge that enables an agent to reason about scripts and plans.

Dramatis may generate many hypothetical failures; the failure with the most negative utility – the one that would be most undesirable for the protagonist – is selected. Dramatis maintains a failure stack to track the obstacles to the protagonist's goals in the case that multiple failures arise. We make the simplifying assumption that the audience responds emotionally to the most immediate potential failures first.

3.3 Computing Likelihood of Escape

Once Dramatis has identified a new potential failure, it uses its knowledge of the protagonist's goal and the potential failure to search for an *escape plan* – a plan that enables the protagonist to avoid the undesirable outcome, while still allowing the protagonist to proceed toward his original goal. We generate an escape plan for the purpose of identifying the likelihood of the protagonist's escape, which is correlated with the suspense felt by a human audience.

Dramatis uses a form of Heuristic Search Planning (HSP) called set-additive HSP, which supports non-uniform action costs [11], to find an escape plan for the protagonist. HSP is a type of informed state-space search that uses a relaxed form of the planning problem to efficiently estimate the distance to a goal state. The distance to the goal state is the estimated sum of the action costs for reaching a goal state. To compute the escape plan, we use the current state of the story as the initial state, and the goal situation is any state in which any of causal relations in the script or plan identified during failure search becomes negated, so long as that negated state is not part of the final state of the script or plan – that is, the negated state should not assist in completing the script/plan. In this sense, the computation of the escape plan is a form of single-shot adversarial planning. The extent to which recursive adversarial planning is required has yet to be fully determined, however it is known that human processing of suspense is highly bound by time and effort.

Dramatis uses the likelihood of the first found escape plan as an indication of level of suspense. To ensure that the first complete plan found is also the most likely to succeed in averting the potential failure, we use likelihood of each action as action cost in set-additive HSP. Specifically, action cost is computed as a function of (a) the mental effort of retrieving the action from a computational memory, (b) the overall likelihood of that event succeeding given the state it will be executed in, and (c) the time remaining before the opposing plan/script is completed. MacLeod and Campbell [12] note that humans perceive events that can easily be retrieved from memory as being more likely to occur. When applied to the generation of escape plans, this suggests that actions more readily retrieved will be perceived as more likely to succeed. We intend to use a computational model of memory from which events are more easily retrieved when their elements, such as characters and objects involved or where the event occurs, are closely related to the same elements in recently mentioned events [13]. Using this approach, Dramatis can account for genre effects and for an audience's tendency to forget key details that have not been addressed recently. The overall likelihood of event success is calculated as a function of the state of the world. Humans learn these likelihoods through experience. An analogue in computational agents is a Q-function, a table look up of utility – in our case likelihood – given a state-action pair. In order to compute suspense, Dramatis must be bootstrapped with knowledge that would otherwise be learned over a lifetime of experiences. Finally, time is incorporated into the likelihood calculation based on the remaining steps in the opposing plan or script, based on the assumption that as the time available to avert a failure decreases, the quantity of available escape plans also decreases. Therefore, as the number of steps remaining decreases, the suspense level increases.

The system then applies the likelihood of the success of the escape plan to the computation of a suspense rating. Recall that as the likelihood of escape increases, suspense is expected to decrease. For each potential failure on the failure stack, Dramatis has found an escape plan and determined its likelihood. The suspense rating is proportional to the sum of the likelihoods of each escape plan, factoring in the affinity the audience feels for the protagonist, and the severity (in terms of negative utility) of the failures. Thus, because utility is negative, as likelihood goes down, suspense goes up. The likelihoods of escape plans for failures that are lower on the stack are discounted when calculating this rating. This final aspect exists in order to compute suspense with emphasis on the failure currently being faced, rather than older failures that may not be at the forefront of the story at the moment.

3.4 Updating Suspense

Once Dramatis has found an escape plan and calculated the suspense rating, it continues to the next time slice in the story. As it reads from this point, there are four possibilities for what occurs next: (1) The next step in the projected escape plan is executed; (2) The projected escape plan has been eliminated as an option by newly introduced information; (3) a different escape plan has been explicitly provided by the story and potentially acted upon; or (4) some different action occurs that does not fit with the projected escape plan, and may be part of some other escape plan.

In the first case, the projected escape plan appears to be correct. Dramatis keeps the projected escape plan and updates its estimate of the plan's likelihood of success with the knowledge that this step of the escape plan has been executed. The updated likelihood estimate leads to a new suspense level estimate. If the failure has now been completely avoided, it is removed from memory after the suspense level has been recalculated, and the system reverts to having no failure predicted.

In the second case, something has occurred to eliminate the current escape plan as an option. This might be because some new knowledge was provided, such as one of the escape plan prerequisites not being available. In this case, Dramatis uses its updated knowledge of the world to search for new escape plans using the same potential failure as before.

In the third case, some aspect of the newly read event specified the escape plan that the protagonist is going to use. This plan is stored, replacing the escape plan that was predicted in some earlier iteration. Dramatis then estimates the likelihood of success of this new plan, and determines the suspense level based on this new information.

In the final case, an action occurred that does not fit with the predicted escape plan, but is not direct conflict with that escape plan either. This action may be the first step of a different escape plan that the protagonist is using instead. Given this new action, Dramatis searches for an escape plan that is consistent with the new action. Dramatis calculates the likelihood of the new escape plan and recalculates the suspense level.

3.5 Knowledge Structure

Given this process for detecting suspense, what knowledge must the system have available to it, and what knowledge must it track throughout? From the outset, Dramatis must be provided with background knowledge. This knowledge includes domain knowledge for the purposes of planning, identifying potential failures, and estimating the likelihood of a plan's success. The domain knowledge comes in the form of scripts and action definitions. The scripts, represented as plan networks [10], are used for retrieving potential failures, while the action definitions inform the heuristic search planning.

Dramatis also tracks knowledge about the story through successive iterations. The system keeps track of character plans and goals, particularly those of the protagonist, whenever they are provided. Additionally, these goals include maintenance goals such as Avoid-Dying. Character plans and goals are used to predict possible failures and to identify conflicting plans. The system also tracks the potential failures that it predicts in the protagonist's plan. Finally, when the system predicts an escape plan from these failures, it is stored for later comparison. The system keeps track of whether its predicted escape plans are being used or being eliminated, as this will affect the audience suspense level.

3.6 Example

Consider the following example taken from the 2006 film *Casino Royale*[1]. In the film, the protagonist, James Bond, must play a high-stakes poker game in order to bankrupt international terrorist Le Chiffre and bring him to justice. Prior to the scene in question, the audience is aware of Bond's goal. At the beginning of the example, the following are known: (a) Le Chiffre intends to win this game and will kill Bond to do so if necessary, (b) Bond-ally Vesper is watching the poker game, and (c) Bond has a chip in his arm that allows British intelligence (MI6) to monitor his vital signs. Bond has the goal of winning the game as well as the maintenance goal of staying alive. In the preceding time slice, unbeknownst to Bond, his drink has been poisoned.

For the purposes of the example, the first time slice processed by Dramatis contains the following information: Bond drinks from his glass, Le Chiffre stares expectantly at Bond, and ominous music begins to play. The time slice also indicates time to think, affording time for offline inferences to be made. The music cues Dramatis to search for a potential failure and Dramatis retrieves a script about being poisoned. The poisoned script has the effect of harming Bond, which is antithetical to Bond's maintenance goal. Further, dying is the most dire possible failure state in terms of negative utility. With a potential failure found, Dramatis searches for escape plans as part of determining the audience suspense level. Suppose that the first escape plan generated is "Bond recognizes poison; Bond vomits poison." This plan prevents Bond's death and is determined to have a high likelihood of success. Dramatis thus computes a low suspense level based on this plan for overcoming the failure.

---

[1] *Casino Royale* is copyrighted by EON Productions, Columbia Pictures, Danjaq, and United Artists.

In time slice 2, Bond recognizes that he has been poisoned. The potential failure – Bond's death – has not changed and the escape plan found in the previous iteration seems to hold. As the scene continues, Bond leaves the poker game and goes to the bathroom to vomit, and Vesper notices Bond's departure and appears alarmed.

The next time slice in which Dramatis is afforded time to make offline inferences (Time Slice 5) reveals that Bond is staggering to his car, and still being affected by the poison, despite the earlier attempt to overcome the problem. The update loop rejects the previous escape plan and generates a new escape plan: "Go to doctor; Get help from doctor." Dramatis calculates the likelihood of this plan, finding it to be lower than the previous escape plan; the suspense level, therefore, increases.

In time slice 6, Bond pulls a medical kit and telephone out of his car, and activates the chip in his arm. Dramatis enters the update loop, and sees that Bond is acting on a different plan than the one predicted during the previous iteration. It generates a new escape plan: "Identify antidote; Bond takes antidote." Now that Dramatis knows about the medical kit, it finds this escape plan to be very likely. As the likelihood increased, the suspense level decreases.

In the seventh time slice, MI6 agents, monitoring his internal sensor, call to tell Bond that he will die in the next two minutes, and that they cannot identify an antidote. The escape plan remains intact, but this new information significantly decreases the estimate that the escape plan will succeed. Dramatis computes an increase in suspense. In time slice 8, Bond goes into cardiac arrest, resulting in the generation of a new escape plan: "Bond applies defibrillator; Bond restarts heart." With the new plan and the new information about the imminence of Bond's death, Dramatis finds this plan less likely, and the suspense level increases again.

Bond pushes the button on the defibrillator in the ninth time slice, but there is no effect. He keeps pushing the button, but to no avail. The pacing is such that there is no time for offline reasoning; Dramatis does not update until the next time slice, when it is revealed that a cord has become detached from the defibrillator. The previous escape plan is updated: "Bond re-attaches cord; Bond restarts heart."

In the subsequent time slice, Bond passes out before he can reattach the cord. Dramatis again sees that its most recent plan has been eliminated. It generates a new plan, which it calculates to be even less likely: "Someone sees Bond; They re-attach the cord; They restart his heart." As this is very unlikely (Dramatis has forgotten about Vesper due to the time that has passed since Dramatis was last aware of the character), the suspense becomes very high at this point.

Vesper appears at the car in the last time slice, as the audience hears Bond's heart start to fail. Dramatis recalculates the previous plan's likelihood with the knowledge that someone, Vesper, has appeared. With someone else actually present, the plan's likelihood of success increases, so the suspense level decreases. Finally, Bond wakes up, and the failure has been averted. From this point, Dramatis would search for possible failures in his plan to defeat and capture Le Chiffre.

4 Discussion and Future Work

We have proposed a framework, Dramatis, for the detection of suspense as part of dramatic arc in a story. The Dramatis approach to suspense is based on Gerrig and Bernardo's suggested approach to suspense – the reduction in quantity or quality of escape plans available to the protagonist, from the point of view of the reader [8]. In addition, we base our approach in the literature of narrative cognition and narratology. With this knowledge, we believe that Dramatis is a reasonable and cognitively plausible approach to the detection of suspense. The approach used by Dramatis to find the most likely escape plan to succeed is based on psychological studies of human perception of likelihood [12], as is our association of perceived likelihood with the level of suspense felt by a human audience [8]. Further, this search for plans is limited in depth and time in order to simulate the cognitive limits faced by human readers. Finally, Dramatis only conducts this search when a human audience would have sufficient time to reason.

We note some other potential benefits of our approach. First, the Dramatis framework accounts for suspense due to forgetting. It is often the case in narratives that clues about how a protagonist will escape are provided early – a gadget Bond receives from MI6, Vesper taking notice of Bond's condition, etc. – with the intention that the audience momentarily forgets. By linking escape plan generation to a computational model of memory based on concept activation [13] and priming [12], we believe we can reproduce event ordering effects on suspense ratings. Second, we believe we can account for genre effects; actions that are highly related to the genre will be more strongly activated than actions that are less associated with the genre.

Dramatis produces a set of suspense ratings for the points in a single story where the audience is given time to reason, or make offline inferences. The suspense ratings produced by Dramatis are relative to other points in the story and cannot be used to make comparisons across several stories. While the curves produced by Dramatis for two different stories can reasonably be compared, the exact numbers produced are not comparable across stories. Likewise, relative change in Dramatis suspense ratings can be compared to relative change in human suspense ratings. However, it is difficult to draw conclusions from comparing exact numbers between computational systems and humans, unless Dramatis has knowledge equivalent to human knowledge.

In the future, we plan to implement the Dramatis framework and apply the suspense detection process to annotated time-slice replications of actual stories and films other than the above example. Additionally, we intend to compare the suspense ratings produced by Dramatis to those given by a human audience as a means of validating the system output. We assert that it is not necessary that the ratings provided by Dramatis exactly match those of the human audience as long as the evaluation shows that the relative change in suspense levels are comparable.

As a practical application, we plan to apply Dramatis to the field of story generation. Story generation is the problem of finding a sequence of events that meets a given set of storytelling principles and aesthetic criteria, and can be told as a story. Search based story generation techniques such as [14], in particular, solve the story generation problem by adding and ordering events until the criteria are met. However, existing story generation systems have not been reliable at producing stories with dramatic structure, which can come from suspense, because of a lack of computational models of story aesthetics. Dramatis can be viewed as a domain-specific heuristic for story structure quality based on a computational model of perception of suspense. Thus, when applied to search-based story generation systems, we hypothesize that we can increase the overall subjective rating of computer-generated stories. To invoke Dramatis as a heuristic, one could provide an ideal target suspense curve. Dramatis would then "read" stories generated by a search-based story generation system and compute the mean error between Dramatis' resulting suspense curve and the ideal curve. While this "guess-and-check" method is not ideal, it provides a first step toward informing story generation systems about aesthetics and the cognitive principles of affect. The application of a model of dramatic arc and narrative aesthetics to story generation systems will lead to the creation of stories that are capable of eliciting emotional responses in human readers.

References

1. Bruner, J.: The Narrative Construction of Reality. Critical Inquiry 18, 1–21 (1991)
2. Gerrig, R.J.: Experiencing Narrative Worlds: On the Psychological Activities of Reading. Yale University Press, New Haven (1993)
3. Aristotle: The Poetics (T. Buckley trans.). Prometheus Books, Buffalo (1992); Original work published 350 B.C.E.
4. Gervás, P.: Computational Approaches to Storytelling and Creativity. AI Magazine 30(3), 49–62 (2009)
5. Branigan, E.: Narrative Comprehension and Film. Routledge, New York (1992)
6. Abbott, H.P.: The Cambridge Introduction to Narrative. Cambridge University Press, Cambridge (2008)
7. Cheong, Y.-G.: A Computational Model of Narrative Generation for Suspense. Doctoral dissertation, North Carolina State University (2007)
8. Gerrig, R.J., Bernardo, A.B.I.: Readers as Problem-Solvers in the Experience of Suspense. Poetics 22, 459–472 (1994)
9. Graesser, A.C., Singer, M., Trabasso, T.: Constructing Inferences During Narrative Text Comprehension. Psychological Review 101, 371–395 (1994)
10. Orkin, J.D.: Learning Plan Networks in Conversational Video Games. Masters of Science thesis, Massachusetts Institute of Technology (2007)
11. Keyder, E., Geffner, H.L.: Heuristics for Planning with Action Costs. In: Borrajo, D., Castillo, L., Corchado, J.M. (eds.) CAEPIA 2007. LNCS (LNAI), vol. 4788, pp. 140–149. Springer, Heidelberg (2007)
12. MacLeod, C., Campbell, L.: Memory Accessibility and Probability Judgments: An Experimental Evaluation of the Availability Heuristic. Journal of Personality and Social Psychology 63, 890–902 (1992)
13. Niehaus, J.: Cognitive Models of Discourse Comprehension for Narrative Generation. Doctoral dissertation, North Carolina State University (2009)
14. Riedl, M.O., Young, R.M.: Narrative Planning: Balancing Plot and Character. Journal of Artificial Intelligence Research 39, 217–267 (2010)

A Generic Emotional Contagion Computational Model

Gonçalo Pereira, Joana Dimas, Rui Prada, Pedro A. Santos, and Ana Paiva

INESC-ID and Instituto Superior Técnico and Universidade Técnica de Lisboa
Porto Salvo, Portugal
{goncalo.pereira,joana.dimas,rui.prada}@gaips.inesc-id.pt,
pasantos@math.ist.utl.pt, ana.paiva@inesc-id.pt

Abstract. This work describes a computational model designed for emotional contagion simulation in societies of agents, integrating the influence of interpersonal relationships and personality. It models the fundamental differences in individual susceptibilities to contagion based on the psychology study of Emotional Contagion Scale. The contagion process can also be biased by inter-individual relationships depending on the intimacy and power difference aspects of relationships between agents. Individuals' expressiveness in a group is influenced by both the extroversion personality trait and power difference.

Additionally, the computational model includes the process of mood decay, as usually observed in people, expanding its application domain beyond that of pure simulation, like games. In this paper we present simulation results that verify the basic emotional contagion behaviors. The possibility of more complex contagion dynamics depending on agent group relationships is also presented.

Keywords: emotional contagion, agents, personality, relationship.

1 Introduction

Throughout history emotions have been the focus of much interest, thought and research by many thinkers like Aristotle, Charles Darwin, Sigmund Freud and Walter Hess [15]. In computer science emotions have been researched for several decades, but their relevance was only widely projected by the seminal work of Picard[17]. The understanding and integration of affect in computer applications led to developments in areas such as videogames[20] and robot companions[4].

A scarcely explored and important process in agent believable simulations is Emotional Contagion (EC). It can be described as "the process through which we 'catch' other people's emotions" [10]. It is especially important in group situations where emotional states of individuals influence the behavior of others. Several examples of research inspired in processes of EC can be found in areas like Group Decision [14], Ambient Agents [3] and Interface Agents [16]. Further research into EC may have an important impact in several areas where believability of group behavior is important, such as games.

S. D´Mello et al. (Eds.): ACII 2011, Part I, LNCS 6974, pp. 256–266, 2011.

The goal of our work is to improve an existing computational model of EC by integrating the influence of interpersonal relationships and personality as found in social psychology literature. In the following section we review some previous work, next we present our EC model, followed by some tests based on our implementation, conclusions and future work.

2 Background

2.1 Emotional Contagion (EC)

Emotional processes such as EC deal with the concepts of emotion and mood. Both are used to describe how people feel, but are in fact different affective states regarding both duration and intensity. While emotions refer to emotional experiences that last from seconds to hours, moods can last from hours to weeks. Regarding intensity, moods are generally less intense. [15]

EC has been researched from different perspectives and there are many definitions [10]. However, one of the most insightful works [9] defined EC as:

> *"the tendency to automatically mimic and synchronize expressions, vocalizations, postures, and movements with those of another person's and, consequently, to converge emotionally."*

This definition is supported by two basic mechanisms:

Emotional mimicry/synchrony
A process by which "people automatically and continuously mimic and synchronize their movements with the facial expressions, voices, postures, movements, and instrumental behaviors of other people." [8]

Emotional experience / facial, vocal & postural feedback
Following the previous mechanism, "subjective emotional experience is affected, moment to moment, by the activation of feedback from facial, vocal, postural, and movement mimicry." [8]

These mechanisms are mostly primitive in the sense that they are automatically or unconsciously controlled. An example of the process is when a "source" person tells a friend about a happy event. The friend automatically synchronizes some of his own expressions by the mechanism of mimicry. The feedback mechanism is then activated and he experiences happiness as the "source" person felt.

The EC process is especially important in group dynamics and its effects have been presented in significant research. One in particular [1] shows the influence of EC at both the individual and group level on increased perceived task performance, increased cooperativeness and decreased conflict. Another effect of EC is emotion amplification (or "Emotion Contagion Spirals" [3] or "upward/downward spirals" [7,6]), based on a single emotional expression, other group members can be infected with the expressed emotion and also start expressing it. This creates an amplification of the initially expressed emotion in the complete group. Notice that this effect can be both a positive or a negative influence on the group and its goals [18].

2.2 Emotional Contagion Biases

Different individuals have different susceptibilities regarding the contagion of emotions. Understanding the existence of such differences, Doherty [5] created and validated the "Emotional Contagion Scale". It is a fifteen unidimensional scale that measures an individual's susceptibility to others regarding five basic emotions: love, happiness, fear, anger and sadness. This scale makes it possible to quantify an individual's tendency to be influenced by any expression of the five basic emotions into a set of five discrete values (one for the susceptibility to each emotion) each ranging from one (never susceptible) to four (always susceptible).

Beyond the individual inherent susceptibility, external factors such as interpersonal relationships, influence the contagion process. Kimura *et al.* [13] studied the effects of intimacy and power difference. In this work more intimate individuals showed greater contagion. In a relationship with a power difference between individuals, the one with more power was more susceptible to contagion. Identical results regarding the influence of power on EC had been previously obtained by Hsee *et al.* [11]. However, an older work by Snodgrass *et al.*[19] showed that subordinates were "more sensitive to the feelings" of their leaders. Our work follows the most recent research that indicates leaders as more susceptible.

Another EC influencing property is the expressiveness of individuals, which several factors can influence. Following previous work of Snodgrass *et al.*[19] on the susceptibility influence of power, it is indicates that one of the possible causes for the previous results is a greater expressiveness of the superiors, which in this case suggests superiors are usually more expressive. Another influence is that of personality which has been suggested, and only briefly investigated by Doherty [5]. Furthermore, Buck linked greater emotion transmission accuracy between individuals to extroversion.

3 Related Work

One of the few EC computational models developed was proposed by Bosse *et al.* [3] with the goal to simulate the occurrence of contagion spirals of negative emotions in ambient agents for virtual meeting support. Their "Emotion Contagion Spiral Model" is based on the characterization of a dyadic relationship. From the side of the emotion sender it is defined by its emotion level and its expressivity. On the receiver's side it is characterized by its emotion level and sensitivity to the sender. The strength of the communication channel between the two amplifies or reduces the communicated emotion. However, this work only models one emotion which is unrepresentative of humans where different emotions or combinations of them have different effects on people [15]. Additionally it does not enable the mapping of real data into agents and has a continuous simulation environment with an inevitable reach of equilibrium.

A different computational model of EC based on the EC scale (ECS) was proposed by Bispo *et al.* [2]. It models the mood of an individual (agent) which can be affected by emotional expressions from others. An individual is characterized by a "Current Mood" with values for five basic emotions (from ECS), an "emotional status" representing the individual's dispositional emotion and an "ECS Score" which determines its susceptibility. With this model the authors are able to simulate some EC patterns. However, the model continuously stimulates the agent, dismissing a mood decay as observed in humans and even implemented in agents. In the absence of another agent's expression the emotional status is used as a new emotional stimulus [12]. Furthermore, influences such as personality and interpersonal relationships are left out.

The existing computational models presented have several shortcomings. One is mostly focused on the collective emotional level rather than accurately reproducing the different emotions and their relationship with EC. Also, the second model despite having addressed a wider range of emotions, does not consider interpersonal influences on the contagion process or a decay of the mood status in individuals instead of a continuous stimulation process.

4 A Model for Emotional Contagion

Our computational model for EC builds upon the work of Bispo *et al.* [2] its conceptual map is presented in Figure 1. We maintain the central role of the EC scale and also acknowledge the EC effects at the level of mood contagion[1]. In our approach, we model the EC process at the individual agent level and group EC behaviors emerge from the interactions between agents. An agent can capture an "Emotional Expression" (EE) from the environment and filter it in the "Contagion Filter" to create a "Received Emotion"(RE) that is used to update its "Current Mood"(CM) by the "Mood Updater". When given a chance to express the agent decides on it with its "Emotional Expression Filter" and uses its "Current Emotion" (CE) to create a new EE.

An EE is used by an agent to interact with others in the same environment and is the basis of the model's dynamics. It is represented by the tuple $\langle t, i, o \rangle$. Element t specifies a type of emotion and can be one of the five emotions our model uses (inspired in ECS [5]): Love, Happiness, Sadness, Fear, Anger. While i represents the intensity of the associated emotion and is a positive real value, o identifies the transmitter of the expression.

4.1 Contagion Filter

In the "Contagion Filter" we transform an EE captured by the agent into a RE using two kinds of perception biases: susceptibility and contagion. The "Susceptibility Bias" probabilistically determines, based on the agent's individual ECS score and the type of the EE, if the agent is intrinsically affected or not. Each agent has its own ECS score for each emotion type given by the probabilistic function $ECS(t)$, where t is an emotion type. The susceptibility process is represented in Figure 1 by function $Suscept(t)$ (t is emotion type). It calculates a random value between 0 and 1 (with function $rnd(1)$ based on an uniform probability distribution) and compares it with the value of $ECS(t)$ for the received emotion type. Contagion occurs if $rnd(1) < ECS(t)$.

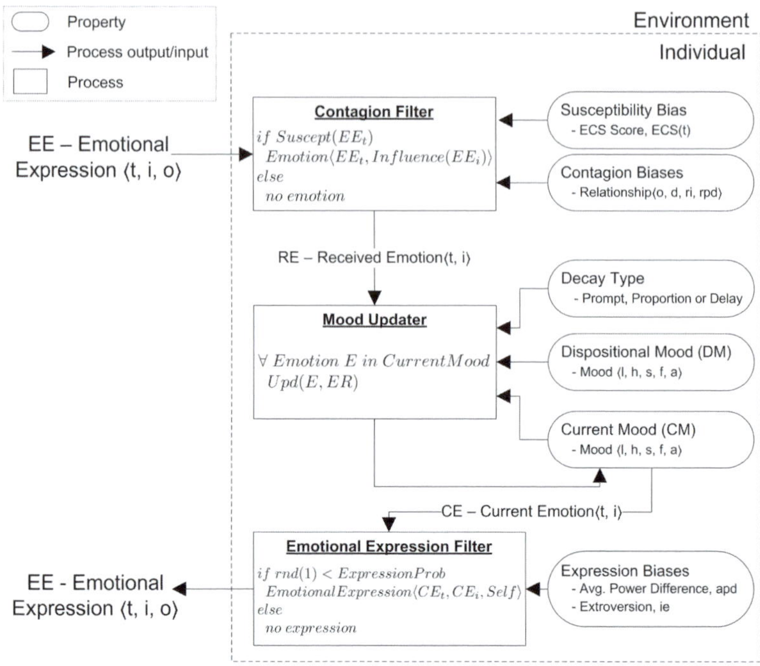

Fig. 1. Improved EC model diagram

Next are the "Contagion Biases" which determine how an expression received is influenced in terms of intensity, as some biases can make the perception more or less intense. The ones included are two relationship characteristics: intimacy[13] and power difference[13,11]. In our model we describe a relationship with the tuple $\langle o, d, ri, rpd\rangle$ where o and d map the origin and target of the relationship. Element ri represents the relationship intimacy property and ranges from 0 (not intimate) to 1 (very intimate). Element rpd represents the power difference characteristic and its value ranges from -1 (the agent is inferior) to 1 (the agent is superior). The influence these properties have on a received EE intensity is given by Equation (1). Intimacy has no effect if $ri = 0$ and a positive effect otherwise. Power difference has a negative effect for $rpd < 0$, no effect when $rpd = 0$ and a positive one for $rpd > 0$. Both properties have their maximum influence controlled by a percentage of the received intensity configured in the parameters i_range for intimacy and p_range for power difference.

$$Influence(EE_i) = EE_i(1 + ri * i\_range + rpd * p\_range) \quad (1)$$

As a result from the "Contagion Filter" a "Received Emotion" RE can be created. In our model an emotion is represented by the tuple $\langle t, i\rangle$ where t represents its type and i its intensity. If $Suscept(EE_t) = true$ the RE has the values $\langle EE_t, Influence(EE_i)\rangle$ otherwise no emotion is created. It is important to notice that emotions have a fixed maximum intensity.

4.2 Mood Updater

The agent's "Mood Updater" process uses the RE, CM, "Dispositional Mood" (DM) and a decay type to update the CM as given by Equation (2). In our model a mood is represented by the tuple $\langle l, h, s, f, a\rangle$ where l, h, s, f and a are represented by an emotion tuple. The CM represents the agent's current emotional status and the DM its dispositional one. An agent tends to its DM emotional status when unstimulated emotionally (no RE received).

If a RE is effectively received then the emotion in CM with a type corresponding to RE_t has its intensity updated by adding RE_i, emulating the emotional experience mechanism from EC. All the CM emotions, unaffected by RE, suffer a change in their intensity emulating an emotional decay. This change is formalized in the *Decay* function which interpolates between the intensity of the emotion in the CM and that of the same emotion type in DM. Our *Decay* function includes three types of decay: prompt (exponential), proportion (linear) or delay (logarithmic). These follow previous work[12] and let our system emulate different emotion decay patterns. An agent only uses one type for its decay.

$$\forall\, Emotion\ E\ in\ Mood\langle l, h, s, f, a\rangle$$
$$Upd(E, RE) = \begin{cases} E_i = E_i + RE_i, & \text{if } E_t \equiv RE_t \\ E_i = Decay(E_i, DM), & \text{otherwise} \end{cases} \tag{2}$$

4.3 Emotional Expression Filter

Finally, when an agent is given a chance to express himself emotionally, the "Emotional Expression Filter" based on "Expression Biases" decides probabilistically if it will express himself. If it does, it is based on the agent's CM. The expression biases considered are the power position of the agent in the group and its personality. These two biases are combined into a single probability value to decide on the expression as given by the Equation (4). The power difference influence is based on previous work [19] where an individual with a higher social power is more expressive. This is calculated by the Equation (3) as the average power difference (*apd*) from the N relationships the agent, representing its group power position.

$$apd = (\sum_{i=1}^{N} Ri_{rpd})/N \tag{3}$$

Regarding personality we only model the extroversion (*ie*) dimension, as it is the trait that influences the emotional expression the most. The higher the extroversion value the more expressive the agent is, a value of 0 makes it inexpressive and 1 the most expressive. The *e_range* parameter controls the maximum influence that *apd* can have in expression decision.

$$BiasedExpression = ie + apd * (1 - ie) * e\_range$$
$$ExpressionProb = \begin{cases} BiasedExpression, & \text{if } BiasedExpression \geq 0 \\ 0, & \text{if } BiasedExpression < 0 \end{cases} \tag{4}$$

As a result from the "Emotional Expression Filter" the agent creates an EE based on its CE for the other agents to capture. The CE is the highest valued emotion in the CM. The new EE is created with the values $\langle CE_t, CE_i * exp\_range, Self \rangle$, where exp_range represents the individual's expressiveness.

5 Model Simulations

In order to apply our model to different domains we must first verify the emergence of the basic EC behaviors added with our model (see the considered biases 2.2). To do so, we created a control scenario which predominantly creates an emotional spiral and compared it to the spiraling pattern of other scenarios (each exhibiting a different behavior). Each scenario was composed of a group of five agents to emulate a small group (similar to a RPG player's group that has several NPC companions). All agents had some common configurations: an ECS score of 2,75 (agents' susceptibility closer to "often" than "rarely" [5]), a prompt decay type(step of 0,3 due to discreet simulation), 0 intensity for all the emotions of CM and DM, a maximum emotion of 1000 (there is no fixed scale for emotion), an $e\_range = i\_range = p\_range$ of 0,5 and an exp_range of 0,2.

The simulation scenarios created were the following:

Control (Sc) all relationships have $ri = 0$ and $rpd = 0$. Agents with $ie = 0,5$;
Intimacy (Si) all relationships have $ri = 1$ and $rpd = 0$. Agents with $ie = 0,5$;
Power Difference (Spd) one agent is superior to all others having relationships of $ri = 0$ and $rpd = 1$ with them. The other agents have relationships with $ri = 0$ and $rpd = 0$. Agents with $ie = 0,5$;
Personality Low (Spl) all relationships have $ri = 0$ and $rpd = 0$. Agents with $ie = 0$;
Personality High (Sph) all relationships have $ri = 0$ and $rpd = 0$. Agents with $ie = 1$;

Each scenario was simulated 40 times and all the simulations had an identical predefined sequence. It started with an agent receiving an initial intensity of 50 (5% of the maximum emotion) for one of its CM emotions and then the agents would simulate the process of emotional expression/contagion for 100 turns. In each turn a single agent would be given the chance to express its current emotion for the group of agents, and if it did, the others who had been influenced would have the chance to express themselves in response.

The metrics used to evaluate the spiraling patterns of our simulations were:

Turn Maximum (TM) average turn time to reach maximum emotion;
Failed Spiral (FES) number of simulations which failed to create a spiral;
Average Contagion (AC) the average contagion value (RE_i) among all agents of the simulation;
Total Contagion (TC) the sum of all the contagion values (RE_i) that happened during the simulation;

Table 1. Simulation results and its standard deviations

	TM	σ	*AC*	σ	*TC*	σ	*AEC*	σ	*AER*	σ	*FES*
Sc	53,7	16,5	91,7	46,2	5033	2854	21,9	4,4	0,503	0,076	6
Si	37,2	14,6	206,4	33,7	11112	3873	22,0	5,1	0,504	0,083	0
Spd	66,4	17,8	54,8	43,2	2997	2548	21,1	6,2	0,497	0,144	10
Spl	-	-	-	-	-	-	-	-	-	-	40
Sph	15,5	2,1	175,9	3,3	27274	1736	66,7	4,5	1,000	0,000	0

Average Expression Count (*AEC*) the average number of times an agent generated an *EE*;

Average Expression Ratio (*AER*) the average ratio of *AEC* divided by the expressing chances.

The results of our simulations are shown in Table 1. When comparing scenarios *Si* and *Sc* we verify the expected (see 2.2) higher emotion contagion between individuals due to the agents' high intimacy relationships. This is shown by a quicker reach to maximum emotion (37,2 compared to 53,7) and much higher values for both average contagion (206,4 compared to 91,7) and total contagion (11112 compared to 5033). Intimacy reduces failed emotional spirals to zero since agents have increased emotion contagion between them.

Regarding *Spd* we can verify that the expected behavior of a single leader agent is more susceptible to contagion and more expressive with four other agents exhibiting the opposite behaviors. Due to a ratio of four subordinates to one leader we expected less emotional contagion, less emotional expressions and a slower spiraling effect. Regarding emotion contagion we indeed verified it, in both average contagion (54,8 compared to 91,7) and total contagion (2997 compared to 5033). The average expression ratio also decreased slightly (0,497 compared to 0,503) and a slower reach to maximum emotion (66,4 compared to 53,7) confirms a slow spiral. This scenario's symmetries are shown on high standard deviations for average contagion 54,8 $\sigma = 43,2$, total contagion 2997 $\sigma = 2548$ and average expression ratio 0,497 $\sigma = 0,144$. These symmetries destabilize the scenario regarding failed emotional spirals (10 compared to 6).

In the scenarios where we test the personality influence, we have a direct result for *Spl*. The very low value of extroversion does not enable any emotional spiral to emerge since individuals do not express enough to create one and agents quickly decay to their dispositional mood. Regarding the *Sph* scenario we observe that the highest extroversion (confirmed in the highest *AEC*=66,7) can have an even greater spiral amplification effect than intimacy. It is the quickest scenario to reach maximum emotion (15,5 compared to 53,7 in *Sc* and 37,2 in *Si*) and the one with the highest value of total contagion (27274).

Beyond the simulations done for patterns of basic behavior demonstration, the model can create more complex EC based dynamics. Such an example is shown in Figure 2 where a scenario with three agents (in order to make it visually simpler) was created. This simulation has a similar parameterization as

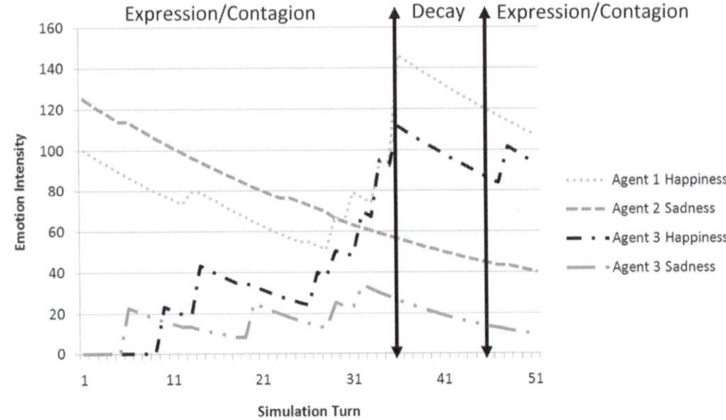

Fig. 2. An example of possible more complex dynamics

the Control scenario with the following differences: there is a relationship with $ri = 1$ and $rpd = 0$ between agents 1 and 3; agent 1 is initially happy with $CM\langle 0, 100, 0, 0, 0\rangle$; agent 2 is initially sad with $CM\langle 0, 0, 125, 0, 0\rangle$.

This simulation starts with 35 turns simulating the process of emotional expression/contagion then 10 turns of simple mood decay (no agent is given the chance to express) and again 5 turns of emotional expression/contagion. In the first part of the simulation we can observe that even though agent 2 has a stronger sadness emotion than agent 1, the intimacy relationship between 1 and 3 biases the EC process in favor of the happiness emotion from agent 1. The upward spiral of happiness continues until turn 35, where agents cease to interact and their emotional levels start decaying altogether. When agents restart to interact on turn 45 the spiraling effect of happiness continues.

6 Conclusions and Future Work

With the presented model we are able to create agents that simulate EC behavior patterns with interpersonal relationships and personality influence. Using our model, a variety of EC phenomenons in groups with intricate relationship networks and different individual characteristics can be simulated. Based on our simulations we verified the intended behaviors by observing the execution patterns throughout a set of individual and group metrics across different scenarios.

Nonetheless, this model can still be improved in a number of directions. One aspect is the manipulation of mixed emotions, instead of just choosing the most intense emotion as the current. The interference between emotions can also be taken into account on the update function, using either a linear model, for instance via a Markov matrix acting on the emotion tuple, or a non-linear one. Furthermore, the presented decay function may be used to create an EC dampening as emotional levels increase in the group.

In combining the influence of interpersonal relationships and personality with the agent's emotional decay, this model is a starting point to the application of EC beyond the area of pure simulation, such as games. A prototype game including it has already been developed and user tests are currently being performed.

Acknowledgments. This work was supported by FCT (INESC-ID multiannual funding) through the PIDDAC Program funds and by FCT scholarship SFRH / BD / 66663 / 2009 .

References

1. Barsade, S.: The Ripple Effect: Emotional Contagion and Its Influence on Group Behavior. Administrative Science Quarterly 47(4), 644–677 (2002)
2. Bispo, J., Paiva, A.: A model for Emotional Contagion Based on the Emotional Contagion Scale. In: 3rd International Conference on Affective Computing and Intelligent Interaction and Workshops, ACII 2009, pp. 1–6. IEEE, Los Alamitos (2009)
3. Bosse, T., Duell, R., Memon, Z., Treur, J., van der Wal, C.: A Multi-agent Model for Emotion Contagion Spirals Integrated within a Supporting Ambient Agent Model. In: Yang, J.-J., Yokoo, M., Ito, T., Jin, Z., Scerri, P. (eds.) PRIMA 2009. LNCS, vol. 5925, pp. 48–67. Springer, Heidelberg (2009)
4. Castellano, G., Leite, I., Pereira, A., Martinho, C., Paiva, A., McOwan, P.: It's all in the game: Towards an affect sensitive and context aware game companion. In: International Conference on Affective Computing and Intelligent Interaction (2009)
5. Doherty, R.: The emotional contagion scale: A measure of individual differences. Journal of Nonverbal Behavior 21(2), 131–154 (1997)
6. Fredrickson, B.: The role of positive emotions in positive psychology: The broaden-and-build theory of positive emotions. American Psychologist 56(3), 218–226 (2001)
7. Fredrickson, B., Joiner, T.: Positive emotions trigger upward spirals toward emotional well-being. Psychological Science 13(2), 172 (2002)
8. Hatfield, E., Cacioppo, J., Rapson, R.: Emotional contagion. Current Directions in Psychological Science 2, 96–99 (1993)
9. Hatfield, E., Cacioppo, J., Rapson, R.: Emotional contagion. Cambridge Univ. Pr., Cambridge (1994)
10. Hogg, M., Tindale, R.: Blackwell handbook of social psychology: Group processes, pp. 165–181. Wiley-Blackwell (2002)
11. Hsee, C., Hatfield, E., Carlson, J., Chemtob, C.: The effect of power on susceptibility to emotional contagion. Cognition & Emotion 4(4), 327–340 (1990)
12. Junseok, H., Chansun, J., Junhyung, P., Jihye, R., Ilju, K.: An artificial emotion model for visualizing emotion of characters. Proceedings of World Academy of Science: Engineering & Technology 50, 567–573 (2009)
13. Kimura, M., Daibo, I., Yogo, M.: The study of emotional contagion from the perspective of interpersonal relationships. Social Behavior and Personality: an International Journal 36(1), 27–42 (2008)

14. Marreiros, G., Ramos, C., Neves, J.: Dealing with emotional factors in agent based ubiquitous group decision. In: Enokido, T., Yan, L., Xiao, B., Kim, D.Y., Dai, Y.-S., Yang, L.T. (eds.) EUC-WS 2005. LNCS, vol. 3823, pp. 41–50. Springer, Heidelberg (2005)
15. Oatley, K., Keltner, D., Jenkins, J.: Understanding emotions. Wiley-Blackwell (2006)
16. Perera, N., Kennedy, G., Pearce, J.: Are you bored?: Maybe an interface agent can help? In: Proceedings of the 20th Australasian Conference on Computer-Human Interaction: Designing for Habitus and Habitat, pp. 49–56. ACM, New York (2008)
17. Picard, R.: Affective computing. The MIT Press, Cambridge (2000)
18. Poggi, I.: Enthusiasm and Its Contagion: Nature and Function. In: Paiva, A.C.R., Prada, R., Picard, R.W. (eds.) ACII 2007. LNCS, vol. 4738, pp. 410–421. Springer, Heidelberg (2007)
19. Snodgrass, S.: Women's intuition: The effect of subordinate role on interpersonal sensitivity. Journal of Personality and Social Psychology 49(1), 146–155 (1985)
20. Sykes, J., Brown, S.: Affective gaming: measuring emotion through the gamepad. In: CHI 2003 Extended Abstracts on Human Factors in Computing Systems, pp. 732–733. ACM, New York (2003)

Generic Physiological Features as Predictors of Player Experience

Héctor Perez Martínez[1], Maurizio Garbarino[2], and Georgios N. Yannakakis[1]

[1] Center for Computer Games Research,
IT University of Copenhagen,
Rued Langgaards vej 7, 2300, Denmark
{hpma,yannakakis}@itu.dk

[2] IIT Unit Dipartimento di Elettronica ed Informazione,
Politecnico di Milano,
Piazza Leonardo Da Vinci 32,20133 Milano, Italy
garbarino@elet.polimi.it

Abstract. This paper examines the generality of features extracted from heart rate (HR) and skin conductance (SC) signals as predictors of self-reported player affect expressed as pairwise preferences. Artificial neural networks are trained to accurately map physiological features to expressed affect in two dissimilar and independent game surveys. The performance of the obtained affective models which are trained on one game is tested on the unseen physiological and self-reported data of the other game. Results in this early study suggest that there exist features of HR and SC such as average HR and one and two-step SC variation that are able to predict affective states across games of different genre and dissimilar game mechanics.

Keywords: generality, heart rate, skin conductance, affective modeling, preference learning, feature selection.

1 Introduction

One of the primary goals pursued by affective computing [1] is the creation of accurate computational models of user experience. Studies in psychophysiology [2], in particular, contribute to this aim by drawing the relationships between user physiological signals, context-based cues and affective and/or cognitive states derived from empirical data. Psychophysiology focuses on the collection of physiological data from a group of subjects performing a set of controlled tasks which are designed to elicit a palette of dissimilar user emotional responses. Key characteristics of the physiological data obtained are then mapped to expected, observed or reported affective user states to form the desired affective models. While the generality of physiology-based affective models across different tasks, groups of subjects and experimental protocols comprises a necessary step towards reliable affective interaction, research in psychophysiology has not yet focused on the generic attributes of particular physiological features.

This paper examines the hypothesis that there exist features extracted from physiological signals which can act as inputs of accurate computational models that are able

S. D'Mello et al. (Eds.): ACII 2011, Part I, LNCS 6974, pp. 267–276, 2011.

to predict affective states of players across dissimilar games. For this purpose artificial neural network (ANN) models are trained via *neuroevolutionary preference learning* [3] on the signals to predict affective states of players expressed as pairwise preferences. Automatic feature selection chooses a subset of the extracted features that maximise the prediction accuracy of the model.

To test the generality of physiology-based affective models across games we collected heart rate (HR) and skin conductance (SC) signals and self-reports of two independent groups of participants playing two dissimilar games. In particular, a prey/predator and a car racing game are used in the experiments presented in this paper. The models are trained on data from one game and tested on the data of the other game revealing statistical features of physiology that are generic predictors of affect across different games. The differences between the experimental protocols, the biofeedback devices, the experience questionnaires and, most importantly, the games themselves are expected to affect the validation accuracy of the models when presented to unseen data from a dissimilar game. However, results show that there exist key physiological features such as average HR and SC variation features that successfully predict dissimilar affective states across the two games.

2 Related Work

The field of psychophysiology [2] explores the relationship between emotions and physiological signals of participants on their daily lives or in a laboratory experiment in which different mental states are induced. Several tasks have been employed to elicit emotional responses in experiment participants including watching videos, reading and solving mathematical problems (see [4,5,6] for extensive reviews) but also playing video-games (e.g. [7,8]).

More recently, with the establishment of the new field of Affective Games [9,10], research on detecting affect in computer game players is rapidly growing in several directions including psychophysiology [11]. Generally, these studies apply the concepts and methodologies of traditional psychophysiology [12] to analyse the effect of different game aspects such as social experiences (e.g. playing with friends or strangers [13]), game events (e.g. killing an enemy [14]) and game features (e.g. camera viewpoint [3]) to the player's state.

For example, Rani et al. [15] explore the correlation between anxiety, engagement, boredom and frustration and several physiological signals (HR and SC among others) while playing Pong while Nacke and Lindley [16] investigate the correlations between flow, boredom and immersion, and jaw electromyography (EMG) and SC in a first person shooter. In this paper we do not focus on linear psychophysiological relationships but, instead, we apply machine learning to create non-linear models that approximate the function between a set of physiological signal attributes and self-reported affective states. While most studies in machine learning within psychophysiology ([17,18,7,19] among others) focus on the classification accuracies of different methods and disregard the particular models built, this paper analyses the effect of various physiological features in the prediction of affective states.

Mandryk et al. [13] use fuzzy rules to map HR, SC, respiration and EMG of the jaw muscles to an arousal-valence space and to levels of fun, boredom, challenge, excitement and frustration during a hockey computer game. Yannakakis et al. [20,21] model the fun pairwise preferences of children playing physical interactive games from HR and SC using neuro-evolution. In all aforementioned studies psychophysiological models are built and the relationship between physiology and emotion in computer games is examined but the generality of the reported physiological models in similar or different game genres is not further investigated.

In [3] models for a set of different affective states (e.g. frustration and fun) built on HR, SC and blood volume pulse (BVP) features and game context cues are tested in a different version of the game from the one they are trained on. This paper is novel in that models are trained and evaluated in games of dissimilar genres which allow one to identify features of physiology that are generic predictors of affect in games.

3 Data Collection

The two datasets used in this study were gathered via two independent experimental surveys in which a group of participants played a sequence of different variants of the same game during which a set of physiological signal data is collected. The players are asked to report their affective preferences about these game variants in a post-experience manner. This section provides an overview of the experiments highlighting the similarities and the differences between them. The reader is referred to [3,22] for a more detailed description of the games and the experimental protocols used.

3.1 Games

The two test beds used in the experiments are short single player games controlled with the arrow-keys (one-handed). In the first test-bed game, named Maze-Ball[1], the player controls a green ball in a 3D maze with the goal of picking up as many pellets as possible in 90 seconds while avoiding a group of enemies. The eight variants of the game correspond to different virtual camera profiles. The second test-bed game, TORCS[2], is an open source racing car simulator customized in the experiment reported in this paper to allow 3 minute-long races against a computer-controlled car opponent whose performance skills change across variants.

3.2 Participants

Thirty six subjects (80% males) aged from 21 to 47 years (mean and standard deviation of age equal 27.2 and 5.84, respectively) played Maze-Ball at the Center for Computer Games Research (IT University of Copenhagen) and 75 subjects (80% males) aged from 18 to 30 years (mean and standard deviation of age equal 23.40 and 4.12, respectively) played TORCS at the IIT Unit Dipartimento di Elettronica ed Informazione (Politecnico di Milano).

[1] `http://itu.dk/people/hpma/MazeBall.html`

[2] `http://torcs.sourceforge.net/`

3.3 Experimental Protocol

In the TORCS experiment subjects played 7 games and reported (at the end of each game) whether they liked more the game they just played than the previous one using a 2 alternative forced choice (2-AFC) questionnaire. On the other hand, Maze-Ball participants played 8 games grouped in pairs after completing a tutorial. After each pair, subjects had to report whether the first or the second game felt more *anxious*, *boring*, *challenging*, *exciting*, *frustrating*, *fun* and *relaxing* or whether the affective state was felt equally in both games or in neither of them (4-AFC).

The final TORCS dataset contains 450 samples (pairs) and the Maze-Ball datasets contain, respectively, 97, 92, 90, 90, 86, 83 and 54 for challenge, fun, frustration, relaxation, anxiety, excitement and boredom after removing the unclear (equal or neither) preferences.

3.4 Physiological Signals and Extracted Features

Skin conductance, s, and blood volume pulse are collected at 32Hz from the Maze-Ball participants using the IOM biofeedback device. Skin conductance signal is collected at 256Hz and blood volume pulse at 2048Hz from the TORCS participants using the ProComp Infiniti hardware (signal artifacts are removed and the signals are filtered and re-sampled at 64Hz — see [22]). In both datasets, the heart rate signal, h, is inferred by the BVP signal (see [3] for details) and the magnitude (SM), m, and the duration (SD), d, of signal variation have been derived from SC [23].

The following set of features is extracted from the last 60 seconds of each signal ($\alpha \in \{h, s, m, d\}$) inspired by previous studies on physiological feature extraction [21,22]:

- average ($E\{\alpha\}$) and variance ($\sigma^2\{\alpha\}$) of the signal;
- initial (α_{in}) and final (α_{last}) recording and difference between them (Δ^α);
- minimum ($min\{\alpha\}$) and maximum ($max\{\alpha\}$) signal recording and difference between them (D^α);
- time when maximum ($t_{max}\{\alpha\}$) and minimum ($t_{min}\{\alpha\}$) samples were recorded and difference between those times (D_t^α);
- average first and second absolute differences ($\delta_{|1|}^\alpha$ and $\delta_{|2|}^\alpha$, respectively);
- Pearson's correlation coefficient (R_α) between raw α recordings and the time t at which data were recorded;
- autocorrelation (lag equals the sampling rate of α) of the signal (ρ^α);

All features are normalized to the [0,1] interval using standard min-max normalization.

4 Method

The computational models of affect constructed and compared in this paper are trained on self-reported pairwise preferences. The inputs of the ANN models are selected automatically from the set of the above-mentioned statistical features using *sequential forward feature selection* (SFS). Feature selection is essential in scenarios where the available features do not have a clear relationship and, thus, impact to the prediction of the target output (i.e. it is not easy to decide *a priori* which features are useful and which are irrelevant for the prediction). Moreover the computational cost of testing all available feature sets is combinatorial and exhaustive search might not be computationally feasible in large feature sets. Under these conditions, FS is critical for finding an appropriate set of model input features that can yield highly accurate predictors [24]. Additionally, we would like our models to be dependent on as few features as possible to make it easier to analyze and to make it more useful for incorporation into future implementations of real-time applications.

4.1 Sequential Forward Feature Selection

SFS is a bottom-up search procedure where one feature is added at a time to the current feature set. The feature to be added is selected from the subset of the remaining features such that the new feature set generates the maximum value of the fitness function over all candidate features for addition. The fitness function used in this paper is given by the average cross validation performance of the ANN model on unseen folds of data.

4.2 Neuroevolutionary Preference Learning

We apply preference learning [25] to build affective models that predict users' self-reported emotional preferences based on the subsets of features selected by the FS algorithm. In this study, the models are implemented as single layer perceptrons (SLPs) that are trained via neuroevolutionary preference learning (as in[3]) to map the selected features to a predictor of the reported pairwise emotional preferences. Note that the pairwise preference relationship of the training data is known (e.g. game A is preferred to game B) but the value of the target output is not (i.e. the magnitude of the preference is unknown). Thus, any gradient-based optimization algorithm is inapplicable to the training problem since the error function under optimization is not differentiable.

The expressivity of SLPs allows us to analyse the impact of each one of the selected features to the reported affective preferences. For instance, when a feature with a corresponding high connection weight value increases from one game to another, the magnitude of the predicted preference is increased or decreased depending on the sign of the weight value. On the other hand, weight connections with low values have a small impact on the prediction of preferences.

5 Experiments

In this section we test the generality of the psychophysiological models which are trained on one dataset and evaluated on the other. The performance of the models has been evaluated using cross-validation (10 and 3 folds when training on TORCS and Maze-Ball, respectively, which produces validation sets of acceptable size for all datasets while keeping the total number of runs low). Consequently each run produces a subset of features and a set of ANN models built on those features (1 per fold) that are tested on the unseen dataset. The baseline prediction for pairwise preferences depends on the distribution of reported preferences between different pairs of variants.

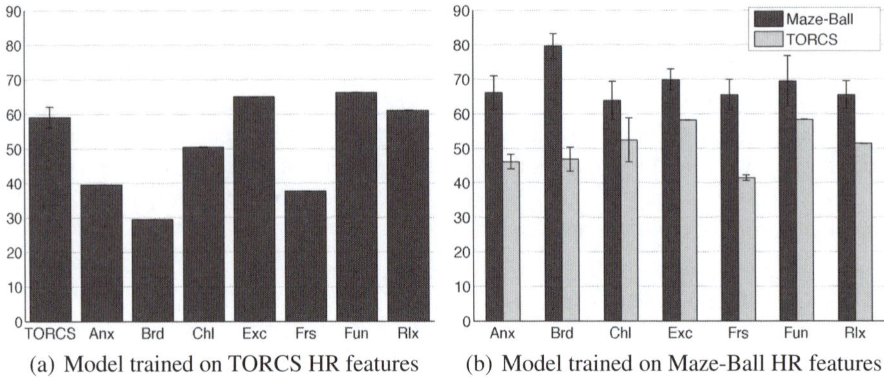

(a) Model trained on TORCS HR features (b) Model trained on Maze-Ball HR features

Fig. 1. Average cross-validation and standard error of performance on the training dataset and corresponding average accuracy on the testing datasets of the best FS run out of 10. Anx, Brd, Chl, Exc, Frs, and Rlx represent, respectively, anxiety, boredom, challenge, excitement, frustration and relaxation.

We approximate this baseline with the average accuracy of 100 SLPs — initialized with random weights and different number of randomly selected features — which lies between 45% and 55%. In the remaining of this paper, accuracies (and their standard error) on unseen data outside the 45-55% interval are considered to be significantly different from baseline. Note that, generally, a model that predicts correctly X% (e.g. 45%) of preference samples yields a prediction accuracy of 100-X% (e.g. 55%) if those preferences are inverted.

5.1 Heart Rate Features

To find the heart rate features that can predict preferences across the two games, FS runs 10 times on each dataset and the resulting models are tested on the unseen dataset. Figure 1 depicts the accuracies of the ANN models yielding the highest cross-validation accuracy on the training dataset.

TORCS data as training set. The best ANN models trained on data obtained from TORCS are able to yield prediction performances above the baseline for all affective states of Maze-Ball excluding challenge (see Fig. 1(a)). Average and minimum HR are the only two features that form the input of these ANN models, both connected with high positive weights. The ANN models yield a prediction accuracy of 65.06%, 66.30% and 61.11% for excitement, fun and relaxation and 60.47%, 70.37% and 62.22% for the inverse of anxiety, boredom and frustration, respectively, while reaching a 59.11% average cross-validation performance on TORCS preferences. These accuracies are comparable to the training performances reached when training models on the Maze-Ball set (see Figure 1(b)). These results suggest that average and minimum HR (both indicators of sympathetic arousal) are good predictors of preferences in TORCS but also efficient predictors of most affective states examined in Maze-Ball. Unsurprisingly, higher

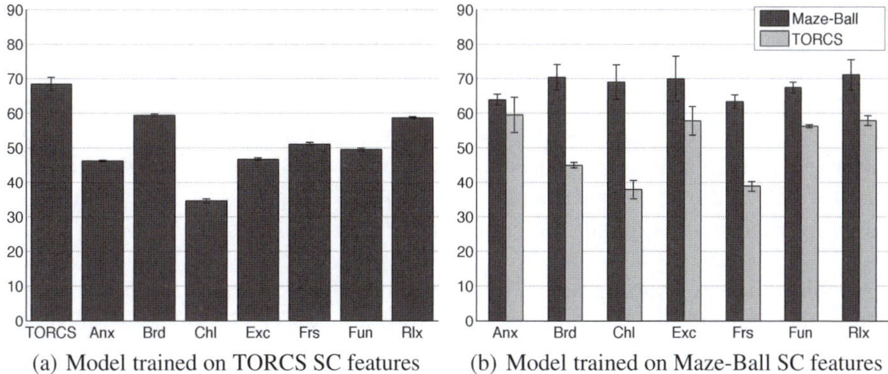

(a) Model trained on TORCS SC features (b) Model trained on Maze-Ball SC features

Fig. 2. Average cross-validation and standard error of performance on the training dataset and corresponding average accuracy on the testing datasets of the best FS run out of 10. Anx, Brd, Chl, Exc, Frs, and Rlx represent, respectively, anxiety, boredom, challenge, excitement, frustration and relaxation.

values of these features indicate higher preference for TORCS games but also predict heightened fun, excitement and relaxation and lower anxiety, boredom and frustration in Maze-Ball.

Maze-Ball data as training set. The highest performing models built on excitement (69.89%) and fun (69.46%) predict preferences in TORCS with accuracies comparable to the models trained directly on that dataset (58.22% and 58.37%, respectively). The excitement model contains solely average HR while the fun model's input contains two features: $E\{h\}$ (positive weight) and $\sigma^2\{h\}$ (negative weight).

The inverse of TORCS preferences are predicted with a performance of 58.44% by the model built on Maze-Ball frustration. The minimum and average HR features are present once again in the model accompanied by the difference between the times when maximum and minimum are recorded; all three features are connected with a negative weight. Finally, the models trained on anxiety, challenge and relaxation do not appear to be able to predict TORCS players' preferences with accuracies higher than the baseline.

Findings from this set of experiments suggest that HR features such as minimum HR, average HR and HR variance are selected to predict affective states in the Maze-Ball game but are also good predictors of TORCS preference. Specifically, it appears that heightened average HR suggests higher excitement and fun and lower frustration in Maze-Ball but also predicts higher preference in TORCS.

5.2 Skin Conductance Features

To find skin conductance features that can predict accurately preferences across games (as in the HR experiments), FS runs 10 times on each dataset and the resulting models are tested on the unseen dataset. Figure 2 shows the accuracies of the ANN models with the highest cross-validation accuracy on their training dataset.

TORCS data as training set. The highest performing subset of features (See Figure 2(a)) contains the second absolute difference of SC (positive weight), the second absolute difference of SD (positive weight) and the maximum SC (positive weight). While the second absolute differences on SC and SD are indicators of skin conductance variability, the maximum SC is an indicator of heightened arousal. This ANN model trained on TORCS data is able to predict well Maze-Ball boredom (59.44%), relaxation (58.6%) and inverse of challenge (65.36%) indicating the influence of the three aforementioned features in the prediction of these affective states in Maze-Ball.

Maze-Ball data as training set. The best ANN models obtained generate performances that range from 64.44% in predicting frustration to 71.11% in predicting relaxation in Maze-Ball. These models' validation performances in TORCS are rather close to the baseline for most affective states: 59.56%, 45.04%, 62.07%, 57.78%, 58.15%, 56.30% and 57.93% for anxiety, boredom, challenge (inverse), excitement, frustration (inverse), fun and relaxation respectively (see Figure 2(b)).

The ANN of the anxiety model contains the average SC and the first absolute difference of the SC signal. Both are connected with a positive weight to the model predicting TORCS preferences with 64.67% accuracy. This result suggests that heightened sympathetic arousal (increased average SC) and high SC variation are linked to preference in TORCS and anxiety in Maze-Ball.

The Maze-Ball challenge model, which did not show a prediction accuracy better than baseline on TORCS when trained on HR features, predicts the inverse of TORCS preferences well (62.07%). The input vector of that ANN model contains the second absolute differences of SM and SC (negative weights), the first absolute difference of SD (negative weights), the maximum SC (positive weight), the average SD (positive weight) and the time when maximum is recorded (negative weight) as inputs. It, therefore, appears that lower SC variation, higher SC and shorter times to reach maximum SC contribute to higher predicted challenge in Maze-Ball and lower predicted preference in TORCS.

The reported frustration ANN model trained on Maze-Ball data predicts the inverse of TORCS preferences with 61.11% accuracy and contains the first absolute difference of SC (negative wight), the SD variance (negative weight) and the autocorrelation of SC signal (positive weight). Maze-Ball frustration and TORCS inverted preference appear to be increased when there is lower SC variation but also when the SC signal's level of randomness is lower (higher autocorrelation).

The fun, excitement and relaxation models present lower TORCS validation accuracies while the boredom model does not even reach a performance which is significantly different from baseline performance. None of the above models contains either the first or the second absolute difference of SC indicating the importance of these features for predicting TORCS preferences.

6 Conclusions

This paper investigated the generality of affective preference models built on physiological features using two dissimilar games as test-beds. More specifically, the paper explores the existence of heart rate and skin conductance signal features that predict reported player affective states across dissimilar games. Results obtained show a strong dependency between the subsets of features used as inputs to a computational affective model and its prediction accuracy on different datasets highlighting the impact of automatic feature selection in the process of creating these models.

This initial study shows that average and minimum heart rate, indicators of sympathetic activity, can yield good estimators of player reported experiences across different games. Similar results have already been reported in a physical interactive environment in which average heart rate is picked as a predictor of reported fun in those games [20]. Observing the results obtained through the SC experiments, it appears that the 1 and 2-step differences of the SC signal — corresponding to the level of fluctuation existent in the SC signal — are good predictors of affective states across both games tested.

This explorative study on the generality of physiology-based preference models covers two physiological signals, a limited set of statistical features and a limited number of games. Future work includes an extended study on more physiological signals such as BVP and features such as those derived from heart rate variability (average inter beat interval among others) as well as models fusing inputs from different physiological signals and models combining physiology with generic game context features. Furthermore, more complex models such as multi-layer perceptrons will be employed and explored since those might be able to better approximate the mapping between game-independent physiological features and reported affective states.

References

1. Picard, R.: Affective computing. The MIT press, Cambridge (2000)
2. Cacioppo, J., Tassinary, L., Berntson, G.: Psychophysiological science. In: Handbook of Psychophysiology, vol. 2, pp. 3–23 (2000)
3. Yannakakis, G., Martínez, H., Jhala, A.: Towards affective camera control in games. User Modeling and User-Adapted Interaction 20, 313–340 (2010), doi:10.1007/s11257-010-9078-0
4. Andreassi, J.: Psychophysiology: Human Behavior and Physiological Response (2000)
5. Cacioppo, J., Berntson, G., Larsen, J., Poehlmann, K., Ito, T., et al.: The psychophysiology of emotion. In: Handbook of Emotions, pp. 119–142 (1993)
6. Calvo, R., D'Mello, S.: Affect detection: An interdisciplinary review of models, methods, and their applications. IEEE Transactions on Affective Computing, 18–37 (2010)
7. Rani, P., Liu, C., Sarkar, N., Vanman, E.: An empirical study of machine learning techniques for affect recognition in human–robot interaction. Pattern Analysis & Applications 9(1), 58–69 (2006)
8. Fernandez, R., Picard, R.: Signal processing for recognition of human frustration. In: Proceedings of the 1998 IEEE International Conference on Acoustics, Speech and Signal Processing, 1998, vol. 6, pp. 3773–3776. IEEE, Los Alamitos (1998)
9. Gilleade, K., Dix, A., Allanson, J.: Affective videogames and modes of affective gaming: assist me, challenge me, emote me. In: Proc. DIGRA 2005 (2005)
10. Hudlicka, E.: Affective game engines: motivation and requirements. In: Proceedings of the 4th International Conference on Foundations of Digital Games, pp. 299–306. ACM, New York (2009)
11. Kivikangas, J., Ekman, I., Chanel, G., Jarvela, S., Salminen, M., Cowley, B., Henttonen, P., Ravaja, N.: Review on psychophysiological methods in game research. In: Proc. of 1st Nordic DiGRA

12. Fairclough, S.: Psychophysiological inference and physiological computer games. In: ACE Workshop-Brainplay, vol. 7 (2007)
13. Mandryk, R., Atkins, M.: A fuzzy physiological approach for continuously modeling emotion during interaction with play technologies. International Journal of Human-Computer Studies 65(4), 329–347 (2007)
14. Ravaja, N., Saari, T., Laarni, J., Kallinen, K., Salminen, M., Holopainen, J., Järvinen, A.: The psychophysiology of video gaming: Phasic emotional responses to game events. In: Proceedings of the DiGRA Conference Changing Views: Worlds in play
15. Rani, P., Sarkar, N., Liu, C.: Maintaining optimal challenge in computer games through real-time physiological feedback. In: Proceedings of the 11th International Conference on Human Computer Interaction, pp. 184–192 (2005)
16. Nacke, L., Lindley, C.: Flow and immersion in first-person shooters: measuring the player's gameplay experience. In: Proceedings of the 2008 Conference on Future Play: Research, Play, Share, pp. 81–88. ACM, New York (2008)
17. Picard, R., Vyzas, E., Healey, J.: Toward machine emotional intelligence: Analysis of affective physiological state. IEEE Transactions on Pattern Analysis and Machine Intelligence, 1175–1191 (2001)
18. Nasoz, F., Alvarez, K., Lisetti, C., Finkelstein, N.: Emotion recognition from physiological signals using wireless sensors for presence technologies. Cognition, Technology & Work 6(1), 4–14 (2004)
19. McQuiggan, S., Lee, S., Lester, J.: Early prediction of student frustration. In: Paiva, A.C.R., Prada, R., Picard, R.W. (eds.) ACII 2007. LNCS, vol. 4738, pp. 698–709. Springer, Heidelberg (2007)
20. Yannakakis, G.N., Hallam, J., Lund, H.H.: Entertainment capture through heart rate activity in physical interactive playgrounds. User Modeling and User-Adapted Interaction 18(1), 207–243 (2008)
21. Yannakakis, G.N., Hallam, J.: Entertainment Modeling through Physiology in Physical Play. International Journal of Human-Computer Studies 66, 741–755 (2008)
22. Tognetti, S., Garbarino, M., Bonanno, A., Matteucci, M., Bonarini, A.: Enjoyment recognition from physiological data in a car racing game. In: Proceedings of the 3rd International Workshop on Affective Interaction in Natural Environments, pp. 3–8. ACM, New York (2010)
23. Tognetti, S., Garbarino, M., Bonarini, A., Matteucci, M.: Modeling enjoyment preference from physiological responses in a car racing game. In: 2010 IEEE Symposium on Computational Intelligence and Games (CIG), pp. 321–328. IEEE, Los Alamitos (2010)
24. Martínez, H.P., Yannakakis, G.N.: Genetic search feature selection for affective modeling: a case study on reported preferences. In: Proceedings of the 3rd International Workshop on Affective Interaction in Natural Environments, pp. 15–20. ACM, New York (2010)
25. Fürnkranz, J., Hüllermeier, E.: Preference learning. Künstliche Intelligenz 19(1), 60–61 (2005)

Guess What? A Game for Affective Annotation of Video Using Crowd Sourcing

Laurel D. Riek[1], Maria F. O'Connor[2], and Peter Robinson[2]

[1] Department of Computer Science and Engineering, University of Notre Dame, USA
[2] Computer Laboratory, University of Cambridge, UK
lriek@cse.nd.edu

Abstract. One of the most time consuming and laborious problems facing researchers in Affective Computing is annotation of data, particularly with the recent adoption of multimodal data. Other fields, such as Computer Vision, Language Processing and Information Retrieval have successfully used crowd sourcing (or human computation) games to label their data sets. Inspired by their work, we have developed a Facebook game called *Guess What?* for labeling multimodal, affective video data. This paper describes the game and an initial evaluation of it for social context labeling. In our experiment, 33 participants used the game to label 154 video/question pairs over the course of a few days, and their overall inter-rater reliability was good (Krippendorff's $\alpha = .70$). We believe this game will be a useful resource for other researchers and ultimately plan to make *Guess What?* open source and available to anyone who is interested.

Keywords: social context annotation, emotion annotation, video annotation, human computation, crowd sourcing.

1 Introduction

One of the most substantial problems researchers in Affective Computing face is data labeling. Beyond the length of time the standard video production process takes (collecting, segmenting, converting), the labeling process is one of the most time-consuming and expensive parts of the research lifecycle [24].

With the recent move as a community toward using multimodal data [6,17,20], labeling time is further increased. Researchers may wish to label several aspects of activity, such as facial expressions, gesture, posture, speech, and prosody; as well as more holistic attributes, such as overall mood, social roles, situational context, and social norms [19].

In the Computer Vision community, von Ahn [1] pioneered the field of Human Computation (HC), or crowd sourcing, to help with image data labeling. The premise of HC games is to have thousands of non-experts play a fun game while unwittingly labeling large corpora of data. For image labeling, HC is a well-validated technique, and yields results comparable to those of trained expert labelers [15].

S. D'Mello et al. (Eds.): ACII 2011, Part I, LNCS 6974, pp. 277–285, 2011.

This approach has also been effectively used in Human Language Technology for textual data labeling [11,22], in Information Retrieval for improving search [14,7], and in Speech for prosody labeling [23].

Many of these efforts have yielded similarly positive, comparable results to those found in the Computer Vision literature regarding the efficacy of non-expert labelers. Hsueh et al. [11] suggest that for some labeling tasks, such as a sentiment analysis, even if the HC data is noisy it still provides very useful data for modeling. This is also the consensus of Sheng et al. [21] for Data Mining tasks.

Inspired by these findings, we developed an HC game called *Guess What?* for labeling multimodal, affective video data. This paper describes an overview of the game, in terms of its implementation details, scoring mechanism, and game play. We also describe a pilot evaluation of the game, where we use it to macro-label social context in amateur You Tube videos.

We believe this game will be a useful resource to other researchers and ultimately plan to make *Guess What?* open source and available to anyone who is interested.

2 The Game

2.1 Overview

Guess What? is a Facebook game in which players are shown a video clip and are then asked a question about it. The objective of the game is to earn points. A player earns a small number of points for each question answered, but in order to do well, they need to guess what answer most other people would give.

Figure 1 shows some example screen shots from the game for macro-labeling the social context of scenes, which we used during our initial evaluation of the game.

2.2 Game Play and Scoring

Players first receive a neutral audio/visual test to make sure their system is properly configured. Following this, they can either play a round of the game or view the high scores list.

In a round of the game, the player will will be shown a video (which can be of any length), and either a fixed-choice or open-response question. *Guess What* automatically adjusts its layout and scoring mechanism to accommodate whatever mix of video and question types the researcher specifies in their initialization.

After players answer a question, they are given a score. Two scoring mechanisms are used in the game. If a question is fixed-choice, the player is awarded points based on the percentage of other players who chose the same answer as them. For open-response questions, players receive 25 points for a new answer which the system has never been seen before, 75 points for other answers, and 100 points for the answer which has been chosen most often. Both scoring mechanisms favour players who consistently answer "correctly" as judged by all other users.

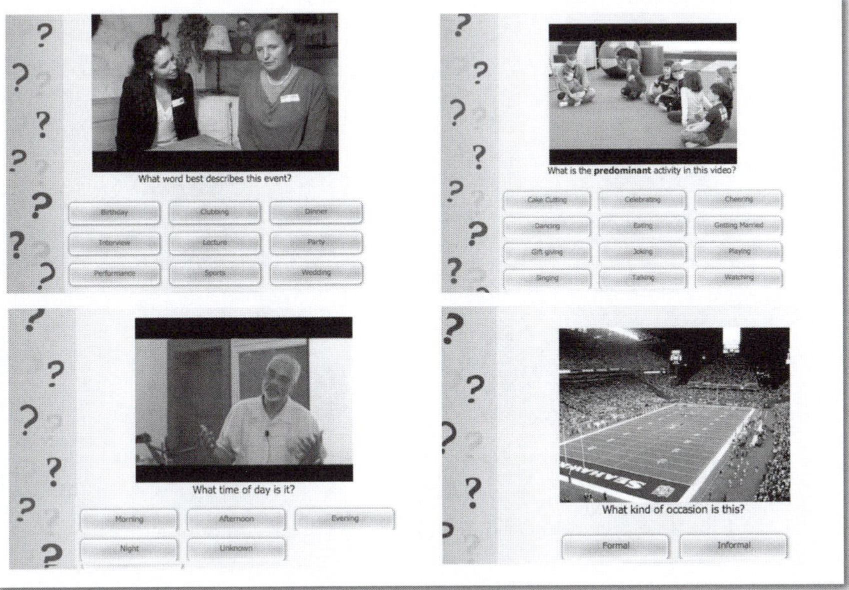

Fig. 1. Some sample screen shots from the *Guess What?* game. These are macro-level questions for labelling social context, but the game is easily configurable to also allow for micro-level annotation of video.

2.3 Implementation Details

As a crowd sourcing game, *Guess What* needs to reach the largest audience possible. This suggests two technical requirements - the game should run with minimal user effort (i.e., no downloading of plug-ins) and should be scalable to a large number of users.

For these reasons, *Guess What* is built using a java servelet backend with an HTML/Javascript user interface running on Google App Engine. App Engine is a request-driven, cloud-based application engine. As the application only consumes resources when required by a user, the cost of scaling is linear. A general overview of the server architecture is visible in Figure 2.

Google App Engine provides an object datastore, rather than a traditional relational database. All Videos and Questions are uploaded here. Researchers first need to provide a list of video URLs to App Engine, then use a web interface to run a servlet which reads this file and creates a blank datastore filled with video objects created using these URLs. Questions are also uploaded via a web interface.

When deciding what video a user will see, *Guess What* queries the datastore for the set of least-labelled videos coupled with ones the user has never seen. It then randomly selects one of these. This ensures both that a user who plays for

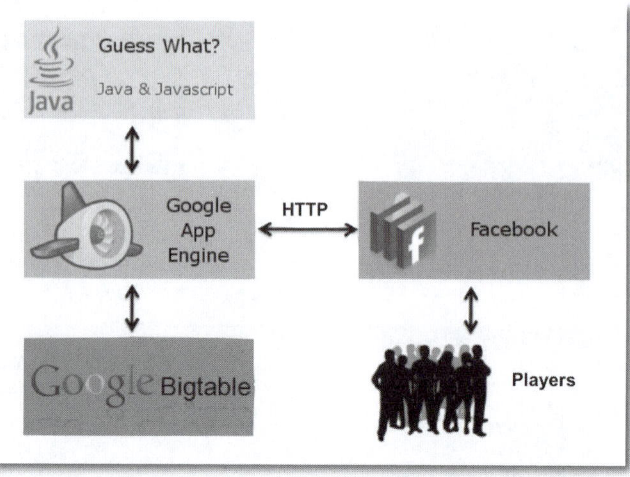

Fig. 2. A general overview of the game's server architecture

a long time will not see a repeating sequence of videos, and that labels will be assigned uniformly to the entire dataset.

For our initial deployment, we opted to deploy the game as a Facebook app. This was so we could utilize the Facebook authentication mechanism, as well as to allow people to easily share the game with their friends. While this was a successful strategy for the pilot version of our game, we found many users uncomfortable with Facebook's privacy settings for apps, so for our next deployment of the game we will switch to something else.

3 Evaluation

3.1 Data

In other work, we are investigating machine learning algorithms that can detect social context in naturalistic multimodal video data, in order to aid affective inference [16,19]. Therefore, when evaluating *Guess What?*, we opted to use data that will also help generate tags for our training set.

To generate an initial corpus of data to use in our evaluation, we searched You Tube for a variety of easily classifiable social events, such as birthday parties, weddings, sporting events, etc. We looked for videos with varying lighting conditions, camera angles, and quality, as we want our algorithms to be able to deal with as naturalistic data as possible. Because we were creating a multimodal corpus, we also searched for videos containing people speaking in different languages, playing different styles and kinds of music, and especially looked for people from a variety of ethnic, racial, and cultural backgrounds. Finally, we selected videos that were approximately three minutes in length.

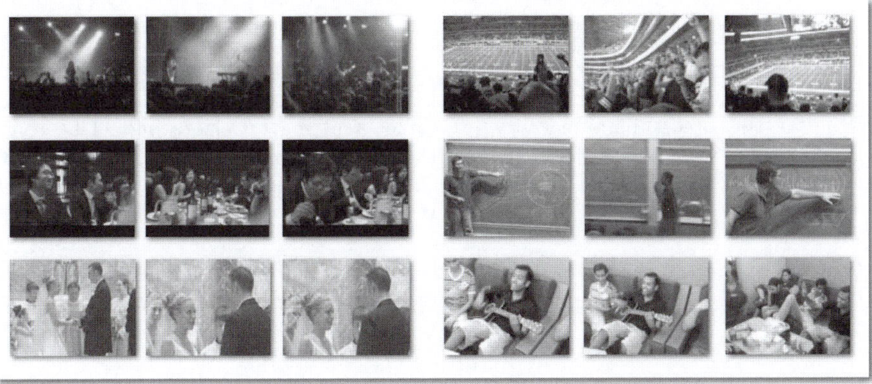

Fig. 3. Some sample video clips of social scenes used as stimuli in the game evaluation. The videos varied in the number of people, social context, and activity, as well as the video quality, colors, and lighting.

We ultimately selected 39 videos that fit these criteria. The videos contained events such as concerts, sporting events, interviews, dinners, lectures, birthday parties, etc. A sample of clips can be seen in Figure 3.

3.2 Labeling Pilot

In order to establish fixed-choice labels for our main experiment, we conducted a pilot study using the *Guess What?* game.

Participants were recruited via word-of-mouth, and were sampled from the same population as our main experiment. Six people participated in the pilot, three female and three male, and their ages ranged from 21 to 34. All pilot participants were native English speakers.

In the pilot, after giving consent to participate and undergoing a neutral audio/visual test, participants were shown the 39 stimuli videos in random order. After watching each video, participants were asked seven open-ended questions about their social context.

We developed these questions based on definitions of social context suggested by Philippot et al. [18] and Burke and Young [5]. The questions were:

- Do these people know one another?
- What type of event is this?
- How formal is this event?
- What are these people doing?
- What's the overall mood?
- What type of people are these?
- What time is it?

Following the pilot, we examined the responses per video and per question and selected the annotations with 66% or greater agreement among raters. To resolve

Table 1. The four social context questions used in our main experiment, and the choice of responses generated from the pilot study

Question	Labels
What is the predominant activity in this video?	Cake Cutting, Celebrating, Cheering, Dancing, Eating, Getting Married, Gift Giving, Joking, Playing, Singing, Talking, Watching
What word best describes this event?	Birthday, Clubbing, Dinner, Interview, Lecture, Party, Performance, Sports, Wedding
What would you estimate the time of day to be?	Morning, Afternoon, Evening, Night, Unknown
What kind of occasion is this?	Formal, Informal

emotion-related synonyms, we used the 24 emotion groups from the Baron-Cohen taxonomy [2,8]. For example, the labels "happy" and "joyful" would both be considered "happy". For other synonyms we used a thesaurus.

We decided to remove three of the questions from our main experiment, regarding subject relationship, person type, and overall mood. The relationship and person type questions caused some confusion among our pilot participants, particularly for some videos that depicted several different groups of people, for example at performances (e.g., the video shows both audience members and performers).

We removed the mood question because for nearly all the events we chose had a positive valence, so nearly all the pilot mood labels were synonyms of "Happy" (30/39 videos). The remaining nine videos were lectures and interviews, and the most common label given for them was "Serious". Thus, we did not see much point in collecting additional mood annotations for this dataset since they were already so well-labeled in the pilot.

We refined the remaining four questions to be more clear, and the final questions and labels used in the main experiment are shown in Table 1.

3.3 Main Experiment

For the main experiment, we recruited participants via Facebook and word-of-mouth. 33 people participated in our main experiment, 15 female and 17 male. Of those who chose to complete our optional demographics survey, ages ranged from 19 to 75, and all but one participant considered themselves fluent in English. Participants lived in the United Kingdom, United States, Ireland, Indonesia, and Germany.

After giving informed consent, participants took a neutral audio/visual test. They then had the option to give voluntary demographics information. Following this, they were presented one of the 39 videos in random order, with one of the four fixed-choice questions randomly assigned. (See Figure 1 for example screen shots from the experiment.) After submitting their answer, they were told their score and had the option to play again.

Participants could play as many times as they wanted, some played only once and some played well over 60 times, but on average participants played 22.29 times (s.d. = 22.74).

3.4 Results

For this evaluation we had one primary measure of interest, which was overall inter-rater reliability. We used Krippendorff's α, which is viewed as more reliable than other reliability measures when there are more than two raters [10]. Also, it is a robust measure capable of dealing with incomplete data, which one would expect when from crowd sourcing, and multiple nominal category levels, which for this experiment we had for each question (See Table 1.)

We used the SPSS macro developed by Hayes [9] for computing α. For this macro we provided all of our raw data, both labeled and missing, for the 33 participants labeling a possible 156 video/question pairs (39 videos x 4 questions).

Krippendorff's α was .702, which indicates fairly good reliability [13]. Krippendorf and Hayes suggest for most use of their measure, values between .667 and up are acceptable. Since this is a far more conservative measure than Fleiss' κ, we are confident for this experiment that we have good inter-rater reliability.

4 Discussion and Future Work

In this paper, we introduced our crowd sourcing game *Guess What*, and described an initial evaluation of it for macro-level labeling social context in videos. Based on our results and the positive feedback we received from participants, we believe this game will be a useful resource for other researchers and plan to make it open source and available to anyone who is interested.

In the future, we plan to experiment with using *Guess What?* for micro-level labeling [3], as well as allowing more fine-grained control to researchers on how questions are presented. For example, if questions were tied to particular subsets of videos, the game could be used in conjunction with machine learning algorithms which first crowd-sourced the high-level classifications then switched to a set of more fine-grained questions when a particular confidence level was reached.

We also plan to conduct a comparison between using *Guess What?* and performing traditional in-person experiments, as well as a comparison between trained and naïve labelers. For crowd-sourced multimodal affective data this sort of deeper methodological exploration is timely, as this is an important topic not just to the Affective Computing community, but to many other research communities as well (c.f. Bernstein et. al [4], and Kazai and Lease [12]).

Finally, we plan to extend our pilot and use *Guess What?* to macro- and micro- label a variety of aspects of social context, such as social norms, social roles, situational context, and cultural conventions [19]. Our first aim will be to determine broad social context by asking high-level questions relating to the setting, personal relationships, event and time. It may also be interesting to look at non-obvious data which can be collected using the game. For example, geolocation information could be used to compare answers from different cultural areas, and simple changes could allow the separate collection of labels associated with sound or vision only.

All of these extensions will help us to better label social context in video, which will ultimately be used to improve affective inference.

Acknowledgements. This work is supported by the Google Anita Borg Memorial Scholarship, the Neil Weisman Fund, and the Qualcomm Research Studentship in Computing.

We are grateful to James Neve for the substantial development effort he contributed to the original game. We would also like to thank Leszek Swirski and Heather Keith Freeman for their assistance.

References

1. von Ahn, L., Dabbish, L.: Labeling images with a computer game. In: Proceedings of the SIGCHI Conference on Human Factors in Computing Systems (CHI), pp. 319–326. ACM, New York (2004)
2. Baron-Cohen, S., Golan, O., Wheelwright, S., Hill, J.J.: Mind reading: the interactive guide to emotions (2004), `http://www.jkp.com/mindreading`
3. Bavelas, J., McGee, D., Phillips, B., Routledge, R.: Microanalysis of communication in psychotherapy. Human Systems 11(1), 47–66 (2000)
4. Bernstein, M., Chi, E., Chilton, L., Hartmann, B., Kittur, A., Miller, R.: Crowdsourcing and Human Computation: Systems, Studies and Platforms (May 2011), `http://crowdresearch.org/chi2011-workshop/` (last accessed April 15, 2011)
5. Burke, M.A., Young, P.: Norms, Customs, and Conventions. In: Benhabib, J., Bisin, A., Jackson, M. (eds.) Handbook for Social Economics. Elsevier, Amsterdam (2010)
6. Calvo, R., D'Mello, S.: Affect Detection: An Interdisciplinary Review of Models, Methods, and their Applications. IEEE Transactions on Affective Computing 1(1), 18–37 (2010)
7. Ganjisaffar, Y., Javanmardi, S., Lopes, C.: Leveraging crowdsourcing heuristics to improve search in wikipedia. In: Proceedings of the 5th International Symposium on Wikis and Open Collaboration, WikiSym 2009, pp. 27:1–27:2. ACM, New York (2009)
8. Golan, O., Baron-Cohen, S.: Systemizing empathy: Teaching adults with Asperger syndrome or high-functioning autism to recognize complex emotions using interactive multimedia. Development and Psychopathology 18(02), 591–617 (2006)
9. Hayes, A.: SPSS, SAS, and Mplus Macros and Code (2011), `http://www.afhayes.com/spss-sas-and-mplus-macros-and-code.html` (last accessed April 15, 2011)
10. Hayes, A.F., Krippendorff, K.: Answering the call for a standard reliability measure for coding data. Communication Methods and Measures (2007)

11. Hsueh, P.Y., Melville, P., Sindhwani, V.: Data quality from crowdsourcing: a study of annotation selection criteria. In: Proceedings of the NAACL HLT 2009 Workshop on Active Learning for Natural Language Processing, HLT 2009, pp. 27–35. Association for Computational Linguistics (2009)
12. Kazai, G., Lease, M.: TREC 2011 Crowdsourcing Track (November 2011), `https://sites.google.com/site/treccrowd2011` (last accessed April 15, 2011)
13. Krippendorff, K.: Content Analysis: An Introduction to Its Methodology. Sage Publications, Thousand Oaks (2004)
14. McCreadie, R., Macdonald, C., Ounis, I.: Crowdsourcing a news query classification dataset. In: Proceedings of the ACM SIGIR 2010 Workshop on Crowdsourcing for Search Evaluation (CSE 2010), pp. 31–38 (2010)
15. Nowak, S., Rüger, S.: How reliable are annotations via crowdsourcing: a study about inter-annotator agreement for multi-label image annotation. In: Proceedings of the International Conference on Multimedia Information Retrieval, pp. 557–566. ACM, New York (2010)
16. O'Connor, M.F.: Automatic Understanding of Social Scenes. Master's thesis, University of Cambridge (2011)
17. Pantic, M., Rothkrantz, L.: Toward an affect-sensitive multimodal human-computer interaction. Proceedings of the IEEE 91(9), 1370–1390 (2003)
18. Philippot, P., Feldman, R., Coats, E.: The social context of nonverbal behavior. Cambridge Univ. Pr., Cambridge (1999)
19. Riek, L.D., Robinson, P.: Challenges and opportunities in building socially intelligent machines. IEEE Signal Processing (2011)
20. Scherer, K., Banziger, T., Roesch, E.: A blueprint for affective computing: A sourcebook. Oxford University Press, Oxford (2010)
21. Sheng, V., Provost, F., Ipeirotis, P.: Get another label? improving data quality and data mining using multiple, noisy labelers. In: Proceeding of the 14th ACM SIGKDD International Conference on Knowledge Discovery and Data Mining, pp. 614–622. ACM, New York (2008)
22. Snow, R., O'Connor, B., Jurafsky, D., Ng, A.: Cheap and fast—but is it good?: evaluating non-expert annotations for natural language tasks. In: Proceedings of the Conference on Empirical Methods in Natural Language Processing, pp. 254–263. Association for Computational Linguistics (2008)
23. Tarasov, A., Delany, S., Cullen, C.: Using crowdsourcing for labelling emotional speech assets. In: W3C workshop on Emotion ML (2010)
24. Yan, R., Yang, J., Hauptmann, A.: Automatically labeling video data using multi-class active learning. In: 9th IEEE International Conference on Computer Vision, pp. 516–523. IEEE, Los Alamitos (2003)

Modeling Learner Affect with Theoretically Grounded Dynamic Bayesian Networks

Jennifer Sabourin, Bradford Mott, and James C. Lester

Department of Computer Science, North Carolina State University,
Raleigh, North Carolina, USA 27695
{jlrobiso,bwmott,lester}@ncsu.edu

Abstract. Evidence of the strong relationship between learning and emotion has fueled recent work in modeling affective states in intelligent tutoring systems. Many of these models are based on general models of affect without a specific focus on learner emotions. This paper presents work that investigates the benefits of using theoretical models of learner emotions to guide the development of Bayesian networks for prediction of student affect. Predictive models are empirically learned from data acquired from 260 students interacting with the game-based learning environment, CRYSTAL ISLAND. Results indicate the benefits of using theoretical models of learner emotions to inform predictive models. The most successful model, a dynamic Bayesian network, also highlights the importance of temporal information in predicting learner emotions. This work demonstrates the benefits of basing predictive models of learner emotions on theoretical foundations and has implications for how these models may be used to validate theoretical models of emotion.

Keywords: Affective modeling, Intelligent tutoring systems, Dynamic Bayesian networks.

1 Introduction

Affect has begun to play an increasingly important role in intelligent tutoring systems. The intelligent tutoring systems community has seen the emergence of work on affective student modeling [1], detecting frustration and stress [2,3], modeling agents' emotional states [4,5], detecting student motivation [6], and diagnosing and adapting to student self-efficacy [7]. All of this work seeks to increase the fidelity with which affective and motivational processes are understood and utilized in intelligent tutoring systems in an effort to increase the effectiveness of tutorial interactions and, ultimately, learning.

This level of emphasis on affect is not surprising given the effects it has been shown to have on learning outcomes. Student affective states impact problem-solving strategies, the level of engagement exhibited by the student, and the degree to which he or she is motivated to continue with the learning process [8,9]. All of these factors have the potential to impact both how students learn immediately and their learning behaviors in the future. Consequently, the ability to understand and model affective behaviors in learning environments has been a focus of recent work [1,10,11].

S. D´Mello et al. (Eds.): ACII 2011, Part I, LNCS 6974, pp. 286–295, 2011.

Correct prediction of students' affective states is an important first step in designing affect-sensitive learning systems. Knowledge of a student's current state is necessary to guide specialized feedback aimed at improving learning and motivation. However, the detection and modeling of affective behaviors in learning environments poses significant challenges. On the one hand, many current approaches to affect detection make use of a variety of physical sensors in order to make affective predictions (see Calvo et al. [12] for a review). Reliance on these types of sensors when building affect-sensitive learning environments severely limits how the systems can be delivered to students, reducing overall impact. On the other hand, systems that attempt to model emotion without the use of physiological sensors typically do so by incorporating theoretical models of emotion, such as appraisal theory, which is particularly well-suited for computational environments [4,13]. These models specify how individuals appraise events and actions along specific dimensions (e.g., desirability or cause) to arrive at emotional experiences. While there are a variety of appraisal-based theories of emotions, few models have been proposed that focus specifically on the emotions that typically occur during learning [9]. The lack of a widely accepted and validated model of learner emotions poses a challenge for the development of affect-detection systems using only contextual and goal-based features. This is especially true for learning environments where interpreting goals or measures of success or failure is non-trivial, such as exploratory environments or those focusing on ill-formed domains.

In this paper we investigate empirically derived models of student affect based on an appraisal-based theory of learner emotions that considers the different goals students may have during learning. Student self-reports of emotion were collected in an exploratory game-based learning environment, CRYSTAL ISLAND. Given the expected uncertainty of students' goals or appraisals, Bayesian techniques were used to develop models for prediction of student affect.

2 Background

As noted above, despite a large body of work, there is no single uniformly accepted theoretical model of emotion. However, appraisal theory (specifically the OCC model) has been typically favored by the affective computing community [9,12]. The OCC model proposes 22 emotions that occur as a result of an individual's appraisal of events, objects and the actions of others as well as oneself. Appraisal occurs across several dimensions including desirability, likelihood, control, and many others [13]. While this model has proven useful in several computing applications [1,4,5], it does not include many emotions that are believed to be important during learning situations [14,15].

Currently there are many theories and models of learner emotions, often called *achievement* emotions. Many models focus mainly on classifying emotions as they relate to the learning task. For example, the model proposed by Kort et al. considers four quadrants of emotions based on a dimension of learning and valence [8]. Alternatively, a model proposed by Csikszentmihalyi considers emotions along dimensions of individual skill and the challenge of the task, with high skill and high challenge corresponding to the optimal level of experience, a state termed *flow* [15]. While useful for classifying learner emotions, these theories do not take into account the many goals that students may have while learning.

Goal orientation is a term that has been used to describe a learner's primary focus when engaged in learning activities [16]. Students may either view learning in relation to performance or mastery. A performance approach would result in a student wishing to prove his competence and achieve better results than other students. A student with a mastery approach, however, views learning as an attempt to gain a skill, regardless of how her ability compares to others. This distinction between learning and performance goals forms the basis for the appraisal-based theory of learning emotions described by Elliot and Pekrun [17]. This model considers emotions in terms of learning and performance goals, along with evaluations of success and failure in these two categories. Additionally, they argue that certain individuals are more likely to focus on negative or positive valences of achievement emotions. For example, individuals with a positive (approach) disposition are more likely to experience positive feelings of enjoyment and pride, while those with negative (avoidance) dispositions are more likely to experience feelings of anxiety or shame [17]. This model of achievement emotions was used to inform the design of affect prediction models for the interactive learning environment, CRYSTAL ISLAND.

To date, many models of affect detection have been developed for use in computer-based learning environments. For instance, a model developed by D'Mello et al. considers facial expressions in terms of action units as well as students' posture and dialog acts to predict students' emotions as assessed by expert judges [11]. Similarly, Arroyo et al. have found benefit to multiple channels of physical evidence of affect [10]. By adding features such as facial expressions, skin conductivity, posture, and pressure they were able to account for much more variance over using contextual features of the tutoring environment alone. Conati and Maclaren have incorporated physical sensors into a complex model based on OCC theory [1]. Though they focus only on a subset of the emotions proposed by OCC they have used a dynamic Bayesian network to capture many of the complex phenomena associated with appraisal theories. This model estimates student goals based on personal traits and behaviors in the environment as well as evidence from physical feedback channels that further support the model's prediction. As in other environments the incorporation of physiological feedback data offered substantial improvement over models without this feature; however, the reliance on these sensors limits the ability to deploy the learning environments when sensors are unavailable or inappropriate.

The models explored in this paper extend previous work in the following ways. First, the models focus on incorporating features from learning-specific models of emotion in hopes of improving the accuracy of the predictive models. Second, the models are designed to achieve reasonable predictive accuracy without the use of physical sensors that would not be available during widespread distribution of the learning environment. Finally, the benefits of representing the dynamic nature of emotional experience will be demonstrated by comparing the performance of typical Bayesian networks with dynamic Bayesian networks.

3 Method

The predictive models of learner emotions were built using data from students' interactions with CRYSTAL ISLAND (Figure 1), a game-based learning environment being developed for the domain of microbiology that is aligned with the standard course of study for eighth grade science in North Carolina. CRYSTAL ISLAND features a science mystery set on a recently discovered volcanic island. Students play the role of the protagonist, Alex, who is attempting to discover the identity and source of an unidentified disease plaguing a newly established research station. The story opens by introducing the student to the island and the members of the research team for which her father serves as the lead scientist. As members of the research team fall ill, it is her task to discover the cause and the specific source of the outbreak. Typical game play involves navigating the island, manipulating objects, taking notes, viewing posters, operating lab equipment, and talking with non-player characters to gather clues about the disease's source. To progress through the mystery, a student must explore the world and interact with other characters while forming questions, generating hypotheses, collecting data, and testing hypotheses.

In order to empirically build and validate models of student affect, data from a study involving 296 eighth grade students from a rural North Carolina middle school was collected. After removing instances with incomplete data or logging errors, the remaining corpus included data from 260 students.

Pre-study materials were completed during the week prior to interacting with CRYSTAL ISLAND. The pre-study materials included a demographic survey, researcher-generated CRYSTAL ISLAND curriculum test, and several personality questionnaires. *Personality* was measured using the Big 5 Personality Questionnaire, which indexes student personality across five dimensions: openness, conscientiousness, extraversion, agreeableness and neuroticism [18]. *Goal orientation* was measured using a 2-dimensional taxonomy considering students' mastery or performance orientations along with their approach or avoidance tendencies [16]. Students' *affect regulation* tendencies were also measured using the Cognitive Emotion Regulation Questionnaire [19] though features from this survey were not included in the current models.

Fig. 1. CRYSTAL ISLAND environment **Fig. 2.** Self-report device

Students were given approximately 55 minutes to work on solving the mystery. Students' affect data was collected during the learning interactions through regular self-report prompts. Students were prompted every seven minutes to self-report their current mood and "status" through an in-game smartphone device (Figure 2). This report was described to students as being part of an experimental social network being developed for the island's research camp. Students selected one emotion from a set of seven options, which included *anxious*, *bored*, *confused*, *curious*, *excited*, *focused*, and *frustrated*. This set of cognitive-affective states is based on prior research identifying states that are relevant to learning [14, 17]. Each emotion label was accompanied by an emoticon to help illustrate the mood to students.[1] After selecting an emotion, students were instructed to type a few words about their current status in the game, similarly to how they might update their status in an online social network.

4 Results

In total, 1863 emotion self-reports were collected from 260 students, an average of 7.2 reports per student. These reports covered the range of available emotion choices with *focused* (22.4%) being the most frequent. Following this were reports of *curiosity* (18.6%), *frustration* (16.3%), *confusion* (16.1%), *excitement* (13.5%), *boredom* (8.5%) *and anxiety* (4.6%). Overall emotions with positive valence (*focused, curious,* and *excited)* accounted for 54.5% of emotion self-reports. These totals inform a baseline accuracy based on most frequent class against which the predictive models were compared: 22.4% for emotion prediction and 54.5% for valence prediction. These levels offer a more conservative estimate than a random model.

4.1 Predictive Modeling

Because of the inherent uncertainty in predicting student emotion, Bayesian networks were used to model the cognitive appraisal process. Bayesian networks are graphical models used to model processes under uncertainty by representing the relationship between variables in terms of a probability distribution [20]. In this study, each Bayesian network was specified using the GeNIe modeling environment developed by the Decision Systems Laboratory of the University of Pittsburgh (http://dsl.sis.pitt.edu). The variables and their dependencies were informed by the model of learner emotions described earlier. After the structure of the model had been specified, the parameters, or probability distributions of each dependency, were learned using the Expectation-Maximization (EM) algorithm provided within GeNIe. Each model was trained using 10-fold cross-validation, in which the model is trained on data from 90% of the students and is then tested for accuracy on the remaining 10%.

The models contained three types of variables:

(1) **Personal Attributes.** These static attributes were taken directly from students' scores on the personal surveys prior to the interaction. Included were all four attributes for goal orientation and three personality attributes expected to be relevant to the student's appraisal: *conscientiousness, openness*, and *agreeableness*.

[1] The emoticons were selected based on results from a validation study in which 18 graduate and undergraduate students rated the degree to which the emoticon images represented the desired emotional state.

(2) **Observable Environment Variables.** These dynamic attributes capture a snapshot of the student's activity in the learning environment up until the time of the self report. They provide a summary of important actions taken, such as *TestsRun, BooksViewed,* and *GoalsCompleted.* They also include information about how well the student is doing in the environment based on certain milestones, such as *SuccessfulTest* and *WorksheetChecks.*

(3) **Appraisal Variables.** The values of the appraisal variables are not directly observable in the environment. Instead they are the result of the student's cognitive appraisal of many factors. The selected appraisal variables and their relation to observable variables are informed by the model of learner emotions.

4.2 Bayesian Networks

In order to provide an additional baseline of comparison, a naïve Bayesian network was learned. A naïve Bayesian network operates under the "naïve" assumption that all variables are directly related to the outcome variable but are conditionally independent of each other [20]. The learned naïve Bayesian network achieved a predictive accuracy of 18.1% on emotion label and 51.2% on valence. This performance is less accurate than the most frequent label baseline model, but provides an additional baseline measure. By comparing carefully constructed Bayesian networks against the naïve assumption we can determine the degree to which affective models benefit from theoretically informed structure.

Next, a Bayesian network (Figure 3) was designed with the structure informed by the proposed relationships described within Elliot and Pekrun's model of learner emotions. The design of the structure focused on the appraisal of learning and performance goals and how these goals were being met based on the status of the game environment. For example, learning-focused activities such as book reading or note-taking are expected to impact how much a student's learning goals are being met, while performance appraisals are more likely related to achieving important milestones such as running a successful test. Meanwhile, goal focus and valence tendencies are considered to be dependent on their personal attributes as described by the model. For example, students with approach orientations are expected to have generally more positive temperaments and emotional experiences than students with avoidance orientations. Similarly, personality traits such as agreeableness and openness are expected to contribute to an individual's overall temperament.

After the structure was designed, the parameters of the model were learned using the EM algorithm. Evaluation of the model showed that the Bayesian network could predict the emotion label with 25.5% accuracy and could predict the valence of the emotional state with 66.8% accuracy (Table 1). Both of these predictions offer a significant gain over the most frequent baseline and the naïve Bayesian network ($p<0.05$). This improvement highlights the benefits of using a theoretical model of learner emotions to guide the model's structure.

However, the simple Bayesian network has no explicit representation of how emotions change over time. For instance, while poor performance at a task may merely be *frustrating* early in the interaction, for highly performance-oriented students this could turn into *anxiety* as more and more time passes. In order to capture the dynamic nature of emotions as they occur over time, the structure of the simple Bayesian network was used as the foundation of a series of dynamic Bayesian networks.

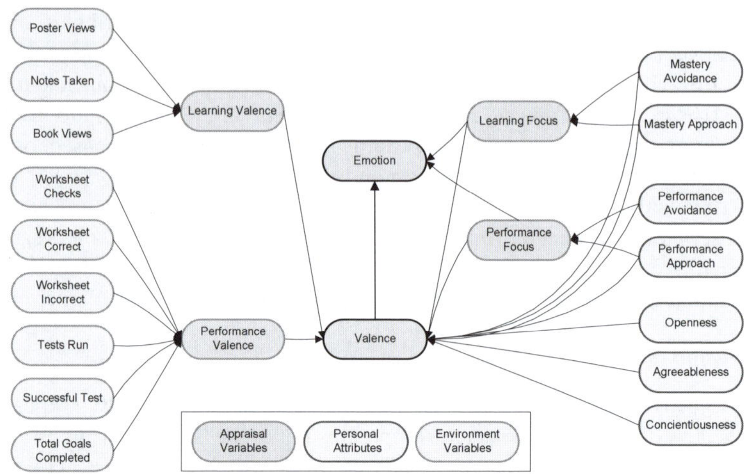

Fig. 3. Structure of static Bayesian network

Dynamic Bayesian networks extend Bayesian networks by representing changes of the phenomena modeled over time. In this way, observations at time t_n are able to inform observations at time t_{n+1} [20]. A variety of representations of the dynamic nature of appraisal and the resulting affective states were tested. Of these, the model with the highest accuracy was able to predict emotional state with 32.6% accuracy and valence with 72.6% accuracy. This model (Figure 4) included a dynamic link between both emotion and valence, where the values of these two variables at t_{n+1} are partially informed by the emotion and valence at time t_n.

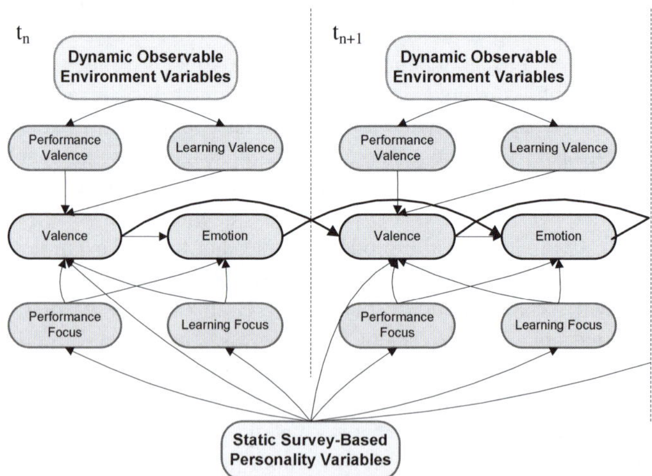

Fig. 4. Structure of dynamic Bayesian network

Table 1. Predictive accuracies

	Emotion Accuracy	Valence Accuracy
Baseline	22.4%	54.5%
Naïve Bayes	18.1%	51.2%
Bayes Net	25.5%	66.8%
Dynamic BN	32.6%	72.6%

Table 2. Predictive accuracy by emotion

Actual Emotion	**Correct Emotion Prediction**	**Correct Valence Prediction**
anxious	2%	60%
bored	18%	75%
confused	32%	59%
curious	38%	85%
excited	19%	79%
focused	52%	81%
frustrated	28%	56%

Table 3. Valence confusion matrix

Actual Valence	**Predicted Valence**	
	Positive	Negative
Positive	823	184
Negative	326	512

As expected, the predictive accuracy for *focused,* the most common self-report, was highest, with over half of the instances of *focused* being properly identified (Table 2). *Anxiety,* on the other hand, had the worst prediction with only 2% of instances being properly recognized. Positive affective states were recognized 81.7% of the time compared with 61.1% of negative affective states being correctly identified (Table 3). The predictive accuracies for specific emotions are particularly important for affect-sensitive learning systems that respond to detected emotions in light of recent work, which found that inappropriate responses can be detrimental to learners' emotional states [21].

5 Conclusion

This work presents Bayesian networks for predicting student affect with a structure informed by different models of learner emotions. By using empirical data to learn and validate the parameter of the models, it was found that the Elliot & Pekrun [17] model of learner emotions can successfully serve as the basis for computational models of learner emotions. The use of this model achieved performance beyond baseline measures as well as beyond a Bayesian network operating under a naïve assumption of the relationship of variables. This work also demonstrated a significant improvement in predictive power by extending the static model to a dynamic Bayesian network, which captured the changing nature of emotions across time. The models performed particularly well at recognizing positive emotional states. The negative affective states including *anxiety, boredom, confusion,* and *frustration* were often confused for each other. Improvements in predictions of these particular emotional states is an important area of future work for affective systems that intend to give feedback based on automated affect detection. Previous work has shown that experiencing these states has very different implications for students' behavior in the environment [22] and how affective feedback may be received [21]. While the performance of the current models could likely be improved through the use of biofeedback sensors, developing reasonably accurate models that do not require invasive and expensive physical equipment is an important direction for providing affective support that can be used on a broad scale.

These findings suggest many interesting lines of investigation. For example, future work is needed to determine whether the proposed model performs well in other intelligent learning environments. Specifically, CRYSTAL ISLAND differs from most learning scenarios in that it is an open-ended exploratory environment without a clearly defined problem space. Additionally, it will be interesting to explore other theoretical models of learner emotions to compare how well these translate into computational models. This approach may help to validate theoretical models of learner emotions. Finally, a more comprehensive set of learning-focused cognitive and affective states could provide additional power to affect-sensitive systems. For example, the current predictive models do not consider a "neutral" affective state, nor do they offer a clear distinction between traditionally cognitive states (e.g. *focused*) and affective states (e.g. *excited*). Representations that distinguish these states may improve predictive and responsive capabilities.

The findings suggest that theoretical models of learner emotions can provide valuable guidance in designing cognitively focused affect detection models. By focusing on modeling the cognitive appraisal process without the support of physical biofeedback sensors, we are able to avoid the costs associated with distributing these sensors to future students and may achieve a greater audience for our educational systems. Future work is needed to investigate how these models may generalize to other learning systems and other populations. Additionally, it will be important to determine what level of accuracy is needed for predictive models to inform affective feedback and ultimately lead to improved learning and motivation.

Acknowledgments. The authors wish to thank members of the IntelliMedia Group for their assistance, Omer Sturlovich and Pavel Turzo for use of their 3D model libraries, and Valve Software for access to the Source™ engine and SDK. This research was supported by the National Science Foundation under Grants REC-0632450, DRL-0822200, IIS-0812291, and CNS-0739216. This material is based upon work supported under a National Science Foundation Graduate Research Fellowship.

References

1. Conati, C., Maclaren, H.: Empirically Building and Evaluating a Probabilistic Model of User Affect. User Modeling and User-Adapted Interaction 19(3), 267–303 (2010)
2. Burleson, W.: Affective Learning Companions: Strategies for Empathetic Agents with Real-Time Multimodal Affective Sensing to Foster Meta-Cognitive and Meta-Affective Approaches to Learning, Motivation and Perseverance. PhD thesis, Massachusetts Institute of Technology (2006)
3. McQuiggan, S., Lee, S., Lester, J.: Early Prediction of Student Frustration. In: Paiva, A.C.R., Prada, R., Picard, R.W. (eds.) ACII 2007. LNCS, vol. 4738, pp. 698–709. Springer, Heidelberg (2007)
4. Marsella, S., Gratch, J.: EMA: A Process Model of Appraisal Dynamics. Cognitive Systems Research 10(1), 70–90 (2009)

5. Paiva, A., Dias, J., Sobral, D., Aylett, R., Sobreperez, P., Woods, S., Zoll, C., Hall, L.: Caring for Agents and Agents that Care: Building Empathetic Relations with Synthetic Agents. In: Proc. of the 3rd Intl. Joint Conf. on Autonomous Agents and Multiagent Systems, pp. 194–201 (2004)
6. de Vicente, A., Pain, H.: Informing the Detection of Students' Motivational State: An Empirical Study. In: Cerri, S.A., Gouardéres, G., Paraguaçu, F. (eds.) ITS 2002. LNCS, vol. 2363, pp. 933–943. Springer, Heidelberg (2002)
7. Beal, C., Lee, H.: Creating a Pedagogical Model That Uses Student Self Reports of Motivation and Mood yo Adapt ITS Instruction. In: AIED 2005 Workshop on Motivation and Affect in Educational Software (2005)
8. Kort, B., Reilly, R., Picard, R.: An Affective Model of Interplay Between Emotions and Learning: Reengineering Educational Pedagogy—Building a Learning Companion. In: Proc. IEEE Intl. Conf. on Advanced Learning Technology: Issues, Achievements and Challenges. IEEE Computer Society, Madison (2001)
9. Picard, R., Papert, S., Bender, W., Blumberg, B., Breazeal, C., Cavallo, D., Machover, T., Resnick, M., Roy, D., Strohecker, C.: Affective Learning – A Manifesto. BT Technology Journal, 22(4) (2004)
10. Arroyo, I., Cooper, D., Burleson, W., Woolf, B., Muldner, K., Christopherson, R.: Emotion Sensors Go to School. In: Proc. of the 14th Intl. Conf. on Artificial Intelligence in Education, pp. 17–24 (2009)
11. D'Mello, S., Graesser, A.: Multimodal Semi-Automated Affect Detection from Conversational Cues, Gross Body Language, and Facial Features. User Modeling and User-Adapted Interaction 20(2), 147–187 (2010)
12. Calvo, R., D'Mello, S.: Affect Detection: An Interdisciplinary Review of Models, Methods and Their Applications. IEEE Transactions on Affective Computing 1, 18–37 (2010)
13. Ortony, A., Clore, G., Collins, A.: The Cognitive Structure of Emotions. Cambridge University Press, Cambridge (1990)
14. Craig, S., Graesser, A., Sullins, J., Gholson, B.: Affect and Learning: An Exploratory Look Into the Role of Affect in Learning with AutoTutor. Journal of Educational Media 29, 241–250 (2004)
15. Csikszentmihalyi, M.: Finding Flow: The Psychology of Engagement with Everyday Life. Basic Books, New York (1997)
16. Elliot, A., McGregor, H.: A 2x2 Achievement Goal Framework. Journal of Personality and Social Psychology 80(3), 501–519 (2001)
17. Elliot, A., Pekrun, R.: Emotion in the Hierarchical Model of Aproach-Avoidance Achievement Motivation. In: Schutz, P., Pekrun, R. (eds.) Emotion in Education, pp. 57–74. Elsevier, London (2007)
18. McCrae, R., Costa, P.: Personality in Adulthood: A Five-Factor Theory Perspective, 2nd edn. Guilford Press, New York (1993)
19. Gernefski, N., Kraaij, V.: Cognitive Emotion Regulation Questionnaire: Development of a Short 18-Item Version (CERQ-Short). Personality and Individual Differences 41, 1045–1053 (2006)
20. Russell, S., Norvig, P.: Artificial Intelligence: A Modern Approach, 2nd edn. Pearson, London (2003)
21. Robison, J., McQuiggan, S., Lester, J.: Evaluating the Consequences of Affective Feedback in Intelligent Tutoring Systems. In: Proc. of the Intl. Conf. on Affective Computing and Intelligent Interaction, pp. 37-42 (2009)
22. Baker, R.S., D'Mello, S.K., Rodrigo, M.M.T., Graesser, A.C.: Better to Be Frustrated than Bored: The Incidence, Persistence, and Impact of Learners' Cognitive-Affective States during Interactions with Three Different Computer-Based Learning Environments. Intl. Journal of Human-Computer Studies 68(4), 223–241 (2010)

Evaluations of Piezo Actuated Haptic Stimulations

Katri Salminen[1], Veikko Surakka[1], Jani Lylykangas[1], Jussi Rantala[1], Pauli Laitinen[2], and Roope Raisamo[1]

[1] Kanslerinrinne 1, 33014 Tampereen yliopisto, Finland
{katri.salminen,veikko.surakka,jani.lylykangas,jussi.rantala, roope.raisamo}@cs.uta.fi
[2] Nokia Research Center, Itämerenkatu 11 – 133, 00180 Helsinki, Finland
Currently affiliated with Aito Interactive Inc.
pauli.laitinen@aito-interactive.com

Abstract. The present aim was to study emotion-related evaluations of piezo actuated haptic stimulations. We conducted three experiments where the presentation type (i.e., haptic only, haptic auditory, and auditory only) of the stimulus was varied. The participants' task was to rank which of the two sequentially presented stimuli was more pleasant and which was more arousing. All pairwise comparisons were created from 9 stimuli varied by rise time (i.e., 1, 3, and 10 ms) and amplitude (i.e., 2, 7, and 30 μm). The results showed that in general the haptic only and haptic auditory stimuli were ranked as more pleasant and arousing than the auditory only stimuli. In addition, the results suggest that the stimuli with long rise times can be seen as more applicable than the stimuli with short rise times as they were in general ranked as more pleasant and arousing.

Keywords: Haptics, piezo actuated feedback, touch screen, affective computing.

1 Introduction

Commercial applications and devices that stimulate the sense of touch have become increasingly popular, e.g., [3]. Also scientific community has grown interest in studying the effectiveness of haptic modality in human-technology interaction (HTI). The previous studies have mostly concentrated on mediating iconic cognitive information like the urgency of the incoming phone call or directional information to the participant, e.g., [7], [8], [20]. However, the emotion-related side of technology mediated haptics has been studied at a lesser degree. This is rather surprising as touch is known to be clearly related to social interaction and emotions, e.g., [9], [12], [13], [22]. People use the sense of touch when they aim to communicate, for example, affection or when they want to get someone's attention [16].

As noted by Haans and IJsselseijn [11] mediated social touch has an interesting potential in the field of HTI, but its significance needs to be empirically established first. First steps towards mapping the relationship between emotions and haptics have been taken only recently. In studies by Smith and MacLean [25] and Bailenson *et al.* [1] the aim was to study how well the participants could identify haptically presented

S. D'Mello et al. (Eds.): ACII 2011, Part I, LNCS 6974, pp. 296–305, 2011.

emotions. In their studies the task of a participant was to use a force-feedback device for creating a haptic message which would communicate a certain emotion from a list. The other participants' task was then to try to identify the emotion-related content of the message. The results of these studies indicate that computer mediated haptics can be used to communicate emotion-related information. However, based on these studies it is difficult to come to a conclusion on what kind of haptic stimulation as such might be experienced as emotion evoking.

Another approach has been to study how carefully controlled variations in stimulus parameters can affect the subjective experiences related to haptic stimuli. The dimensional theory of emotions suggests three dimensions that are pervasive in organizing human judgments of different stimuli. The dimensions are valence, arousal, and dominance, e.g., [4], [5], [19]. However, according to Lang *et al.* [19], it is possible to organize emotional responses by using only two of the dimensions, valence and arousal. Bradley and Lang [4] argue that valence and arousal represent primitive motivational parameters, and that the judgments of pleasure and arousal reflect in part this motivational imperative. Valence is related to the appetitive behavior and arousal to the intensity of that behavior.

To test possible emotion-related responses evoked by haptic stimuli the dimensional approach was chosen in a previous study [23]. A prototype with a rotating lead screw was used to present a set of stimuli varied by rotation style and burst length. The rotation style was either continuous (i.e., no breaks between the bursts) or discontinuous (i.e., short breaks between the bursts). The results showed that the continuous stimulations were rated as less pleasant and as more arousing than the discontinuous stimulations. In another study [24] Nokia 770 Internet Tablet produced piezo actuated stimuli varied by amplitude (2 and 30 μm), rise time (1 and 10 ms), and burst number (i.e., whether a single pulse consisting of amplitude and rise time was presented once or three times). The stimuli with three bursts and 30 μm amplitude were rated as more arousing than the stimuli with one burst and 2 μm amplitude. The stimuli with three bursts were also rated as less pleasant than the stimuli with one burst. Rise time had no effect on the ratings of the stimuli. The results presented above show that carefully controlled relatively simple haptic stimulations were associated with emotional experiences.

In recent years mobile phones equipped with touch screens have become increasingly popular. Traditionally used hardware buttons provide mechanical haptic feedback to the user when, for example, typing. Touch screen devices, however, have virtual buttons that lack the mechanical click familiar from the hardware buttons. It is known that users can benefit from artificially produced haptic feedback added to the virtual buttons. Previous studies [14], [17] with touch screen devices have shown that the presence of a haptic feedback makes typing faster, more accurate and more pleasant than typing without a haptic feedback. In fact, currently most devices with touch screen provide vibrotactile feedback to the user. Recently, some commercial touch screen products have started to provide piezo actuated haptic feedback. With piezo actuators one can create more high-fidelity and thus more realistic clicks for the virtual buttons than with conventionally used vibration motors [17]. There is evidence that the users prefer piezo actuated feedback in touch screen devices over vibrotactile feedback [17]. Piezo actuators can also be seen as a straightforward way to provide multimodal feedback. With one piezo actuator haptic, haptic auditory and auditory stimulations can be controlled more precisely than with a vibration motor. This can be an advantage in mobile contexts where the environment affects the users' ability to perceive feedback of the device. Typically a user can either only feel the haptic stimulation (e.g., noisy environments), or also hear the sounds produced by the piezo actuator (e.g., a quiet office). Situations where the touch screen provides feedback that the user can only hear are highly unusual (e.g., when the user has impaired sense of touch in the operating finger). However, when operating with the device in a silent environment other people sharing the space can only hear the feedback. Thus, the auditory qualities of the feedback should also be taken into consideration.

From HTI perspective, the emergence of piezo actuated touch screen devices raises an interesting question: what are the effects of piezo actuated feedback on the subjective experiences of the user? To find this out, haptic, haptic auditory and auditory stimulations should be compared when studying emotional responses to stimulations provided in touch screen environments. Previous neuroscientific findings have shown that auditory and tactile stimulations evoke responses partly in the same areas of the brain, e.g., [2], [10]. This indicates that haptic and auditory stimulations are processed at least partially in a similar manner in the central nervous system. Also, several studies have shown that auditory stimulation can modulate touch perception and vice versa. For example, in a study by Bresciani *et al.* [6] participant's task was to report how many tactile taps they perceived when presented simultaneously with auditory beeps. The number of beeps systematically modulated the number of tactile taps perceived regardless of the actual number of the taps. Ro *et al.* [21] found that when a near-threshold tactile stimulus was presented simultaneously with an auditory beep, the participants noticed the tactile stimulation more accurately than when it was presented alone. Taken together, previous findings showed that although auditory and tactile stimulations are partly processed by the same brain areas, they also have different modulatory effects to the perception of each other. This supports the idea that also emotional responses to haptic stimulation may be affected by the auditory component related to the stimulation. To map this issue further, emotional responses to haptic stimulation should be studied both separately as well as simultaneously with the auditory component.

2 Methods

2.1 Participants

The experiment was a between-subjects design. Fourteen voluntary participants (7 females, 7 males) participated in each experimental condition (i.e., haptic only, haptic auditory, and auditory only). So, the total number of the participants was 42. Their mean age was 24 years, range 18–35 years. Three of the participants were left-handed by their own report. A consent form was signed by all the participants.

2.2 Apparatus

A handheld prototype device based on the Nokia 770 Internet Tablet was used in the experiment. The device was equipped with a piezoelectric actuator solution. For more technical details, see [18]. The device was embedded firmly in an aluminum machined holder with a weight of approximately 3100 g. The holder did not vibrate when the stimulus was presented to the participant. Responses were given using a Bluetooth computer keyboard with two available response buttons.

2.3 Stimuli

All the stimuli (i.e., haptic only, haptic auditory, and auditory only) were created by controlling the driving voltage and thus the current of the piezo actuator. For the haptic stimuli controlling the drive current altered two parameters, amplitude and rise time (see Table 1). The stimuli were defined so that the full practical scale of these adjustable parameters could be utilized for production of single pulses. This way the amplitude (A) was the value of the haptic touch screen displacement and rise time (t) was the time when it reached the peak of the stimulus from the rest state. The total duration of a single pulse was rise time and non-changeable fall-time with an average of 2.1 ms. The minimum of the rise time (t_{min}) and the maximum of the amplitude (A_{max}) were set based on the full performance capability of the haptic device. Minimum value for the amplitude (A_{min}) was set based on the practical perceivable minimum amplitude, and maximum rise time (t_{max}) was set by practical limit of the tactile actuation system, as prolonged static strain was harmful for the piezo actuators. After the minimum and maximum values were defined, one set of values for both amplitude and rise time were set as an intermediate area to be A_{mid} and t_{mid}, respectively. For the auditory stimulations controlling the drive current resulted in variation of two parameters, audio volume (dB) and frequency (Hz). The haptic auditory stimulations were resulted from the variation of all above four parameters (i.e., amplitude, rise time, audio volume, and audio frequency).

Table 1. The parameters of the experimental stimuli

Stimulus	Drive current	Rise time		Amplitude		Audio volume	Frequency
	mA	level	ms	level	μm	dB	Hz
1	45.8	t_{min}	1	A_{min}	2	58.8	950
2	166.7	t_{min}	1	A_{mid}	7	68.5	950
3	206.2	t_{min}	1	A_{max}	30	68.1	950
4	2.2	t_{mid}	3	A_{min}	2	45	600
5	9.1	t_{mid}	3	A_{mid}	7	55.7	600
6	24.4	t_{mid}	3	A_{max}	30	61.1	590
7	1.1	t_{max}	10	A_{min}	2	47.1	200
8	1.4	t_{max}	10	A_{mid}	7	49.5	600
9	9.1	t_{max}	10	A_{max}	30	60.8	600

Creating the stimuli with the drive current resulted in a situation where the parameters of the audio output could not be controlled as precisely as the haptic output parameters. Thus, a 3 × 3 matrix of the experimental stimuli seen in Table 1 was formed by using three classes of both two controllable haptic parameters. From these 9 stimuli, all the possible combinations for presenting two different stimuli were created. Each of these 9 stimuli was presented as both the first and second stimulus in a pair. Thus, there were a total of 72 (i.e., 9 × 8) stimulus pairs.

2.4 Procedure

In the haptic only condition the participant's task was to rank which of the two stimuli presented sequentially was more pleasant and which was more arousing. The experiment was divided in two sessions. In session A the participant was instructed to rank the stimulus pairs based on their pleasantness and in session B based on their arousability. The order of the sessions was counterbalanced. In both sessions, a practice block preceded the experimental block. The stimuli in the practice block were different than the stimuli in the experimental blocks. In a practice trial, two stimuli separated by 1000 ms interval were presented at the participant's dominant hand's index finger. Immediately after the offset of the second stimulus, response instructions appeared on the screen and the participant was able to respond. The button '1' was to be pushed with the non-dominant hand's index finger if the first stimulus was more pleasant or more arousing, whereas the button '2' was to be pushed if the second stimulus was more pleasant or more arousing. The next trial was initiated automatically after 6200 ms delay. After finishing all the practice trials the experimental block began. The experimental block proceeded similarly to the practice block. In order to block the auditory component of the stimuli, the participant listened pink noise via hearing protector headset. Conducting the whole experiment took approximately 45 minutes. The experimental design and task of the haptic auditory and auditory only conditions were similar with the haptic only condition except for the following differences. In the haptic auditory condition both the haptic and auditory components and in the auditory only condition only the auditory components of the stimuli were presented to the participant.

2.5 Data Analysis

First, the overall frequencies of the "more pleasant" and "more arousing" rankings were calculated for each of the nine stimuli in each three experimental conditions separately. Then, as the experiment was between-subjects design a Kruskal–Wallis one-way analysis of variance by ranks was used to compare the rankings of each stimulus between the three experimental conditions. A Mann–Whitney *U* test was used for pairwise comparisons.

3 Results

For the rankings of the pleasantness, a 3 × 9 (experimental condition × stimulus) Kruskal-Wallis test showed that three stimuli were ranked differently between the experimental conditions (see Table 2). The results of the Mann-Whitney *U* test can be seen in Table 3.

Table 2. Overall means for the rankings of the stimulus pleasantness in each three experimental conditions, and test statistics for the between conditions Kruskal-Wallis analysis. The mean rank refers to the frequency of the ranking so that the mean rank 1 is the highest frequency of the ranking in each experimental condition, and 9 is the lowest.

Stimulus	Mean rank			X^2
	Haptic only	Haptic auditory	Auditory only	
2 µm 1 ms	9	7	7	3.3
2 µm 3 ms	2	2	1	2.6
2 µm 10 ms	4	1	3	5.3
7 µm 1 ms	1	8	9	17.2***
7 µm 3 ms	5	3	2	4.0
7 µm 10 ms	5	6	4	3.7
30 µm 1 ms	7	9	8	9.1**
30 µm 3 ms	3	4	6	3.6
30 µm 10 ms	8	5	5	7.2*

* $p < 0.05$, ** $p < 0.01$, and *** $p < 0.001$

Table 3. The Mann-Whitney *U* test statistics for the pairwise comparisons of each stimulus between all the experimental condition combinations. If the result was statistically significant, the condition where the stimulus has been ranked as more pleasant can be seen in column "more pleasant". In this column the haptic only condition is referred to as ho, the haptic auditory condition as ha, and the auditory only condition as ao.

Stimulus	Haptic only vs Haptic auditory		Haptic only vs Auditory only		Haptic auditory vs Auditory only	
	U	More pleasant	*U*	More pleasant	*U*	More pleasant
2 µm 1 ms	89	-	68.5	-	61.5	-
2 µm 3 ms	86	-	59	-	84	-
2 µm 10 ms	57	-	53.5	-	98	-
7 µm 1 ms	36**	ho	9***	ho	83	-
7 µm 3 ms	69	-	55.5	-	96	-
7 µm 10 ms	66	-	59.5	-	92	-
30 µm 1 ms	44*	ho	40**	ho	86	-
30 µm 3 ms	71.5	-	88.5	-	56	-
30 µm 10 ms	47*	ha	56.5	-	72	-

* $p < 0.05$, ** $p < 0.01$, and *** $p < 0.001$

For the rankings of the arousal, a 3 × 9 (experimental condition × stimulus) Kruskal-Wallis test showed that eight stimuli were ranked differently between the experimental conditions (see Table 4). The results of the Mann-Whitney *U* test can be seen in Table 5.

Table 4. Overall means for the rankings of the stimulus arousal in each three experimental conditions, and test statistics for the between experimental conditions Kruskal-Wallis analysis

Stimulus	Mean rank			X^2
	Haptic only	Haptic auditory	Auditory only	
2 µm 1 ms	9	9	6	20.0***
2 µm 3 ms	6	7	9	8.6*
2 µm 10 ms	4	3	4	14.4***
7 µm 1 ms	8	4	2	24.5***
7 µm 3 ms	7	8	8	6.5*
7 µm 10 ms	3	5	5	13.0**
30 µm 1 ms	1	1	1	4.1
30 µm 3 ms	2	3	3	6.7*
30 µm 10 ms	5	6	7	14.9***

* $p < 0.05$, ** $p < 0.01$, and *** $p < 0.001$

Table 5. The Mann-Whitney *U* test statistics for the pairwise comparisons of each stimulus between all the experimental condition combinations. The condition where the stimulus has been ranked as more arousing can be seen in column "more arousing".

Stimulus	Haptic only vs Haptic auditory		Haptic only vs Auditory only		Haptic auditory vs Auditory only	
	U	More arousing	*U*	More arousing	*U*	More arousing
2 µm 1 ms	65.5	-	11***	ao	26***	ao
2 µm 3 ms	78.5	-	39.5***	ho	52.5*	ha
2 µm 10 ms	94	-	30.5***	ho	26***	ha
7 µm 1 ms	26.5***	ha	1.5***	ao	43.5*	ao
7 µm 3 ms	54*	ho	48.5*	ho	96	-
7 µm 10 ms	47*	ho	22***	ho	74	-
30 µm 1 ms	61.5	-	60	-	96.5	-
30 µm 3 ms	81	-	40.5**	ho	66	-
30 µm 10 ms	65.5	-	18***	ho	44.5*	ha

* $p < 0.05$, ** $p < 0.01$, and *** $p < 0.001$

4 Discussion

The results showed that in general the stimuli were ranked in a relatively similar fashion in both the haptic only and haptic auditory conditions in terms of pleasantness and arousal. However, the variations in the output parameters (i.e., rise time and amplitude) brought out a few interesting differences to the rankings of the stimuli between the two conditions. When the rise time was short (i.e., 1 ms) the stimuli were ranked as significantly more pleasant in the haptic only than in the haptic auditory condition. On the other hand, the stimuli with long rise times (i.e., 3 and 10 ms) were ranked as significantly more arousing in the haptic only than in the haptic auditory condition especially with the amplitude of 7 µm. So, based on the results it seems that the effects of the haptic stimuli to the experienced pleasantness and arousal depended mostly on the rise time of the stimulation. The stimuli with short rise times were fast, and perhaps therefore when presented alone (i.e., without the auditory component) they were experienced as pleasant. On the other hand, the haptic only stimuli with longer rise times were in general connected to the elevated experience of arousal. This is an interesting result as it may have been expected intuitively that the stimuli with both the haptic and auditory components would have been experienced as more arousing than the haptic only stimuli.

When these results are compared to the auditory only condition, the following findings can be pointed out. Haptic only stimuli with short rise times were ranked as more pleasant than their auditory only counterparts. This finding indicates a possibility that the auditory component related to a stimulus with a short rise time can modulate subjective experience as less pleasant. Arousal rankings showed that the stimuli were in general ranked as more arousing in both the haptic only and haptic auditory conditions than in auditory only condition. This finding suggests that haptic component may modulate subjective experience of the stimulation as more arousing especially when the rise time is long. The result is in line with previous studies, e.g., [6], [21] which have shown that auditory and tactile stimulation can modulate the perception of each other.

An earlier study [24] showed that the experienced pleasantness and arousal of a piezo actuated haptic stimulation was affected when varying stimulus parameters (i.e., amplitude and rise time). For example, the stimuli with high amplitudes were rated as more arousing than the stimuli with low amplitudes. The current results show that the rankings of pleasantness and arousal of the piezo actuated stimulation were somewhat different when the presentation modality (i.e., haptic only, haptic auditory and auditory only) was varied. The differences obtained between the experimental conditions were related to the variations in the rise time of the stimulus. Thus, it seems that the rise time may be a central parameter affecting the subjective experience of the stimulus when operating in real user contexts. From an application point of view this raises an interesting question on whether the modality and parameters of an output signal should be selected individually for varying contexts.

In fact, many mobile phones have the technology to sense, for example, environmental noise and trembling. In an ideal case a mobile device could use this information to estimate the level of environmental distraction, and automatically select the most suitable feedback parameters for the present situation. In cases where the level of the environmental distraction is low (e.g., a silent office), the feedback is most likely noticeable as the user can easily feel and hear it. In silent environments also people around can hear the sounds produced by the device. In the light of the current results it would thus seem reasonable to use primarily pleasant haptic auditory feedback in such situations. The results suggest that in silent environments pleasant piezo actuated haptic auditory feedback should have long rise times. On the contrary, in contexts where the level of the environmental distraction is high (e.g., a noisy bus) the feedback is more likely to be left unnoticed. Given that in noisy environments the user cannot hear the sounds produced by the device, the feedback is most likely only felt. Thus, to ensure that the user can perceive the feedback, it would be reasonable to use primarily arousing haptic stimulations. According to the results, also for this purpose a feedback with long rise time would seem to be more applicable than the stimuli with short rise times.

A note of caution is related to the fact that in the current study piezo stimulation was controlled with one parameter, drive current. This is a relatively simple way to vary four output parameters of haptic and auditory stimulations (i.e., rise time, amplitude, audio frequency, and audio volume). The approach has been widely used in scientific research, e.g., [17]. The use of drive current results in a case where all four output parameters cannot be fully controlled. In the current study the haptic output parameters (i.e., rise time and amplitude) were in good control. But the variations in the audio output parameters (i.e., frequency and volume) could not be controlled as accurately. However, unlike auditory components of the stimulus, haptic components are almost always perceivable by the user. Therefore, accurate control of the haptic output can be seen as more important than the control of the auditory output.

Controlled masking noise is frequently used in experimental haptics research to block the auditory component of tactile stimulation, e.g., [15]. We used pink noise in haptic only condition to block the auditory component of the stimulus thus masking sound with a sound. This way the specific auditory components related to haptic stimulation could be fully isolated. Pink noise was fixed to be exactly the same in all the haptic only stimulus presentation conditions. As the noise was kept constant over all the stimuli the effect of auditory variation to the emotional experiences could be minimized. Also, in real user contexts feedback is provided via haptic modality alone only when sounds produced by the device cannot be heard due, for example, traffic noise. Thus, the pink noise provided a controlled way to imitate a background noise which often masks auditory component related to a piezo actuated feedback.

In summary, our results showed that the presentation modality affected the experienced pleasantness and arousal of a piezo actuated stimulation. From a theoretical point of view it can be pointed out that the haptic only and the haptic auditory stimuli were in general ranked as more pleasant and as more arousing than the auditory only stimuli. The dimensional theory of emotions suggests that pleasantness and arousal represent both the motivational parameters related to the general disposition to approach or avoid stimulation and the vigor of that tendency, e.g., [4], [5]. Thus, the results suggest that the regulation of this motivational tendency can be better with haptic only and haptic auditory stimuli than with audio alone. However, in spite of the obtained differences, from the application point of view the results suggests that for both quiet and noisy environments the stimuli with long rise times are more applicable than the stimuli with short rise times.

Acknowledgments. This research was funded by the Finnish Funding Agency for Technology and Innovation (Tekes), decision numbers 40120/08 and 40159/09.

References

1. Bailenson, J.N., Yee, N., Brave, S., Merget, D., Koslow, D.: Virtual Interpersonal Touch: Expressing and Recognizing Emotions through Haptic Devices. In: HCI, vol. 22, pp. 325–353 (2007)
2. Beauchamp, M.S.: See Me, Hear Me, Touch Me: Multisensory Integration in Lateral Occipital-Temporal Cortex. Current Opinion in Neurobiology 15, 145–153 (2005)
3. BMW (2009), `http://www.bmw.com/com/en/insights/technology_guide/articles/idrive.html`

4. Bradley, M., Lang, P.J.: Measuring Emotion: The Self-Assessment Manikin and the Semantic Differential. J. Beh. Therapy and Exp. Psych. 25, 49–59 (1994)
5. Bradley, M., Lang, P.J.: Affective Reactions to Acoustic Stimuli. Psychophysiology 37, 204–215 (2000)
6. Bresciani, J., Ernst, M.O., Drewing, K., Bouyer, G., Maury, V., Kherrad, A.: Feeling what You Hear: Auditory Signals Can Modulate Tactile Tap Perception. Exp. Brain Research 162, 172–180 (2005)
7. Brown, L.M., Brewster, S., Purchase, H.: A First Investigation into the Effectiveness of Tactons. In: Proc. Eurohaptics, pp. 167–176. IEEE Press, Los Alamitos (2005)
8. Brown, L.M., Kaaresoja, T.: Feel Who's Talking: Using Tactons for Mobile Phone Alerts. In: Proc. CHI, pp. 604–609. ACM Press, New York (2006)
9. Field, T.: Infant's Need for Touch. Human Development 45, 100–103 (2002)
10. Foxe, J.J., Morocz, I.A., Higgins, B.A., Murray, M.M., Javitt, D.C., Schroeder, C.E.: Multisensory Auditory–Somatosensory Interactions in Early Cortical Processing Revealed by High Density Electrical Mapping. Cogn. Brain Research 10, 77–83 (2000)
11. Haans, A., IJsselsteijn, W.: Mediated Social Touch: A Review of Current Research and Future Directions. Virtual Reality 9, 149–159 (2006)
12. Harlow, H.F.: The Nature of Love. American Psychologist 2, 673–685 (1958)
13. Hertenstein, M.J., Campos, J.J.: Emotion Regulation via Maternal Touch. Infancy 2, 549–566 (2001)
14. Hoggan, E., Brewster, S.A., Johnston, J.: Investigating the Effectiveness of Tactile Feedback for Mobile Touchscreens. In: Proc. CHI, pp. 1573–1582. ACM Press, New York (2008)
15. Jansson, G., Monaci, L.: Identification of Real Objects Under Conditions Similar to Those in Haptic Displays: Providing Spatially Distributed Information at the Contact Areas is More Important Than Increasing the Number of Areas. J. Virtual Reality 4, 243–249 (2006)
16. Jones, S., Yarbrough, A.: A Naturalistic Study of the Meanings of Touch. Communication Monographs 52, 19–56 (1985)
17. Koskinen, E., Kaaresoja, T., Laitinen, P.: Feel-good Touch: Finding the Most Pleasant Tactile Feedback for a Mobile Touch Screen Button. In: Proc. ICMI, pp. 297–304. ACM Press, New York (2008)
18. Laitinen, P., Mäenpää, J.: Enabling Mobile Haptic Design: Piezoelectric Actuator Technology Properties in Hand Held Devices. In: Proc. HAVE, pp. 40–43. IEEE Press, Los Alamitos (2006)
19. Lang, P.J., Greenwald, M.K., Bradley, M.M., Hamm, A.O.: Looking at Pictures: Affective, Facial, Visceral, and Behavioral Reactions. Psychophysiology 30, 261–273 (1993)
20. Lylykangas, J., Surakka, V., Rantala, J., Raisamo, R.: Providing Two-Dimensional Tactile Directional Information with One-Dimensional Movement. In: Proc. World Haptics, pp. 593–598. IEEE Press, Los Alamitos (2009)
21. Ro, T., Hsu, J., Yasar, N.E., Elmore, L.C., Beauchamp, M.S.: Sound Enhances Touch Perception. Exp. Brain Research 195, 135–143 (2009)
22. Rutter, M.: Developmental Catch-up and Deficit Following Adoption after Severe Global Early Privation. J. of Child Psych. Psychiatry 39, 465–476 (1998)
23. Salminen, K., Surakka, V., Lylykangas, J., Raisamo, J., Saarinen, R., Raisamo, R., Rantala, J., Evreinov, G.: Emotional and Behavioral Responses to Haptic Stimulation. In: Proc. CHI, pp. 1555–1562. ACM Press, New York (2008)
24. Salminen, K., Surakka, V., Rantala, J., Lylykangas, J., Laitinen, P., Raisamo, R.: Emotional Responses to Haptic Stimuli in Laboratory versus Travelling by Bus Contexts. In: Proc. ACII, pp. 387–393. IEEE Press, Los Alamitos (2009)
25. Smith, J., MacLean, K.: Communicating Emotion through a Haptic Link: Design Space and Methodology. Int. J. of Human-Computer Studies 65, 376–387 (2007)

The Relationship between Carelessness and Affect in a Cognitive Tutor

Maria Ofelia Clarissa Z. San Pedro[1], Ma. Mercedes T. Rodrigo[1], and Ryan S.J.d. Baker[2]

[1] Ateneo de Manila University, Loyola Heights, Quezon City, Philippines
[2] Worcester Polytechnic Institute, Worcester, MA, United States
sweetsp@gmail.com, mrodrigo@ateneo.edu, rsbaker@wpi.edu

Abstract. We study the relationship between student carelessness and affect among high-school students using a Cognitive Tutor for Scatterplots, using a machine-learned detector of carelessness and field observations of student affect. In line with previous research, we say a student is careless when he/she makes a mistake performing a task that he/she already knows. This construct is also known as slipping. Somewhat non-intuitively, we find that students exhibiting high levels of engaged concentration slip frequently. These findings imply that a student who is engaged in a task may be overconfident, impulsive or hurried, leading to more careless errors. On the other hand, students who display confusion or boredom make fewer careless errors. Further analysis over time suggests that confused and bored students have lower learning overall. Therefore, these students' mistakes stem from a genuine lack of knowledge rather than carelessness. The use of two versions of the tutor in this study, with and without an Embodied Conversational Agent (ECA), shows no significant difference in terms of the relationship between carelessness and affect.

Keywords: Carelessness, Slips, Engaged Concentration, Confusion, Boredom, Cognitive Tutors.

1 Introduction

Within learning, some students become careless, working unconscientiously [13] and making unintended errors [7]. This can happen when an individual is overconfident in carrying out a task [7], or carries out a task in an impulsive or in a hurried manner [13]. Carelessness is a common behavior among students, even among high-performing students [6, 7]. Carelessness not only reduces short-term performance, it can even lead to poorer overall academic performance among first year college students [17].

To study student carelessness in a fine-grained fashion within educational software, Baker, Corbett, and Aleven [2] created an automated detector of slips which operationalizes Clements' [7] definition of careless errors – errors committed on skills that a student knows (though slips may also occur for other reasons, such as shallow knowledge [3]). This model, which predicts carelessness from the features of student actions within the software (e.g. performance history on the associated skill, input

S. D'Mello et al. (Eds.): ACII 2011, Part I, LNCS 6974, pp. 306–315, 2011.

type, if action was a help request, time taken, etc.), proved to be robust enough to successfully transfer without degradation in predictive accuracy to intelligent tutor software with different design features, and between schools in different countries [18]. Recent research used this detector to study individual differences in carelessness, finding that students with strong mastery or performance goals tend to be more careless than students who lack strong goal orientation [12].

It has been hypothesized that a major factor driving carelessness is student affect, which accords with results showing links between affect and achievement goals [14]. Student affect has been shown to be associated with other disengaged student behaviors. For instance, boredom [5] was found to be associated with gaming the system, a disengaged behavior associated with poorer learning, where students systematically take advantage of regularities in the software's feedback and help to obtain answers and advance within the tutoring curriculum [4]. Within this paper, we study the relationship between student affect and carelessness, using two versions of Cognitive Tutor software for Scatterplot generation and interpretation [4], differing in the presence or absence of an Embodied Conversational Agent (ECA) which responds to student gaming behavior [4]. We detect the incidence of careless errors by analyzing interaction logs from high school students, based on previous work at modeling this construct [e.g. 2, 18]. The detectors created and validated for this tutor in [18] are applied to student data to obtain average estimates of what proportions of each student's errors were careless errors [18]. We combine these estimates with the proportions of each affective state exhibited by each student, gathered using quantitative field observations [16]. We then assess which affective states are associated with careless errors through correlational analysis, also examining whether these relationships change over time. Studying this relationship between carelessness and affect may lead to a deeper understanding of carelessness as a student behavior, thus allowing tutor design to better respond when the student is careless.

2 Methods

The study was conducted in a large, urban high school in Quezon City, Philippines (PH). The school had 5,368 students and 216 teachers [1]. The school's community is relatively poor where about half of the students' parents was unemployed and 70% of the households earned PhP10,000 (US$230.00) per month or less. Data were gathered from 126 first year high school students who used a Cognitive Tutor unit on Scatterplots [4]. The students, aged 12 to 14, used the tutor to solve as many problems as they could within 80 minutes. Data on student carelessness were distilled from the logs generated from tutor usage, while data on affective states from quantitative field observations used in [5, 16]. Students had not explicitly covered these topics in class prior to the study, and students viewed conceptual instructions via a PowerPoint presentation with voiceover and some simple animations before using the tutor. Each student took a nearly isomorphic pre-test and post-test, counterbalanced across conditions. An analysis of learning gains themselves is outside the scope of this paper.

2.1 The Scatterplot Tutor

Within the Scatterplot Tutor, the learner is given a problem scenario. He/she is also provided with data that he/she needs to plot in order to arrive at the solution. He/she is asked to identify the variables that each axis will represent. He/she must then provide an appropriate scale for each axis. He/she has to label the values of each variable along the axis and plot each of the points of the data set. Finally, he/she interprets the resultant graphs. The Scatterplot tutor provides contextual hints to guide the learner, feedback on correctness, and messages for errors. The skills of the learner is monitored and displayed through skill bars that depict his/her mastery of skills.

Sixty-four of the participants (Scooter group) were randomly assigned to use a version of the tutor with an embodied conversational agent, "Scooter the Tutor". Scooter was designed to both reduce the incentive to prevent gaming the system and to help students learn the material that they were avoiding by gaming, while affecting non-gaming students as minimally as possible. Scooter displays happiness and gives positive message when students do not game (regardless of the correctness of their answers), but shows dissatisfaction when students game, and provides supplementary exercises to help them learn material bypassed by gaming. The remaining 62 participants (NoScooter group) used a version of the Scatterplot Tutor without the conversational agent. The number of students assigned to the conditions in this study was unbalanced because of data gathering schedule disruptions caused by inclement weather.

2.2 Affect Observations

Each student's prevalence of each affective state was assessed using quantitative field observations. Each student was observed 24 times by a pair of trained expert coders, with an interval of 180 seconds between observations lasting 20 seconds. Observations were conducted using peripheral vision where the observer appeared to be looking at another student, so that the student being observed would not know that he/she is the one being observed, in order to reduce the degree to which affect is altered by the observation process. As in past research using this method, only the first observed affect was recorded, to minimize bias. The coding scheme included: boredom, confusion, delight, engaged concentration (flow in [10]), frustration, surprise and neutral. The observers' inter-rater reliability was found to be acceptable at Cohen's kappa (κ) of 0.54, a moderate level of agreement between raters. Cohen's kappa measures the proportion of agreement between two observers, with adjustments for the proportion that would be expected to occur by chance [9]. More details on the quantitative field observation method, including examples from the coding manual, can be found in [5].

2.3 Carelessness Detection

The incidence of carelessness within the Cognitive Tutor was traced with a model designed to assess "slips" [cf. 2], treated as an operationalization of carelessness in accordance with prior theory discussed in Section 1. This model, termed the Contextual Slip model, contextually estimates the probability that a specific action indicates a slip/carelessness, where a student knows a skill but answers incorrectly on a problem step which requires that skill. In this model, the estimates of the slip probability is dynamic, and depends on contextual aspects of the action, such as speed of action and history of the student's help-seeking from the tutor. The Contextual Slip model has been shown to be a statistically significant predictor of post-test performance measuring learning from a Cognitive Tutor for Genetics, even after controlling for assessment of each student's knowledge within the software [3].

The Contextual Slip model is based on Bayesian Knowledge Tracing (BKT) [7], a model used to estimate a student's latent knowledge based on his/her observable performance. In its original articulation, BKT is used within Cognitive Tutors to infer student knowledge by continually updating the estimated probability a student knows a skill every time the student gives a first response to a problem step regardless whether the response is correct or not. It uses four parameters – two learning parameters L_O (initial probability of knowing each skill) and T (probability of learning the skill at each opportunity to make use of a skill), together with two performance parameters G (probability that the student will give a correct answer despite not knowing a skill) and S (probability that the student will give an incorrect answer despite knowing the skill) – for each skill (estimated from data information in each skill). These parameters are invariant across the entire context of using the tutor. Using Bayesian analysis, BKT re-calculates the probability that the student knew the skill before the response (at time n-1), using the information from the response, then accounts for the possibility that the student learned the skill during the problem step, such that [8]:

$$P(L_n \mid Action_n) = P(L_{n-1} \mid Action_n) + ((1 - P(L_{n-1} \mid Action_n)) * P(T)) \ . \quad (1)$$

From this model, two detectors of Contextual Slip (one for the NoScooter group and one for the Scooter group) were produced from log files generated by the Cognitive Tutor software. A set of 26 transaction features identical to the set previously used in [2] to develop detectors of Contextual Slip for tutors in other domains was extracted and derived from the logs for each problem step. With the information from the logs, parameters needed for a baseline BKT model were fitted by employing brute-force search [cf. 3]. From this baseline model, estimates of whether the student knew the skill at each step were derived and used to label incorrect actions with the probability that the actions were slips, based on the student performance on successive opportunities to apply the rule [2]. As in [2], Bayesian equations were utilized in computing training labels for the Slip probabilities for each student action (A) at time N, using future information (two actions afterwards – N+1, N+2), in order to infer the true probability that a student's correctness at time N was due to knowing the skill, or due to a slip . The probability that the student knew the skill at time N can be calculated, given information about the actions at time N+1 and N+2 ($A_{N+1,N+2}$), and the other parameters of the Bayesian Knowledge Tracing model.

Models for Contextual Slip were then produced through Linear Regression to create models that could predict contextual slip without using data from the future. These models were used in the analyses in the remainder of the paper. The exact models used in these analyses (e.g. all parameters, weights and functional form) are given in [18].

3 Results

We assessed student carelessness using the slip detector from [18], as discussed in Section 2.3. For this analysis, we assessed carelessness of each student in each group (e.g. Scooter and NoScooter), by taking the average probability of carelessness (slip estimates) on each incorrect action the student made, as in [3]. The overall mean carelessness for students in the NoScooter environment was 0.09. The Scooter group had an overall mean carelessness of 0.14. The difference between the two conditions was significant, t(124) = 8.38, two-tailed p < 0.001. From the students' action logs, we also looked at each student's percentage of steps which were incorrect (careless and non-careless actions combined). For the NoScooter group, 46.55% of actions were incorrect. Although the Scooter group's percentage appeared slightly higher at 48.12%, the difference between groups was not significant, t(124) = -0.49, two-tailed p = 0.63. When we examined the incidence of affective states between the two conditions, we found no significant differences for any affective state; the largest difference found between conditions was for Engaged Concentration (Scooter students displayed this affect 37.17% of the time; NoScooter students displayed this affect 43.45% of the time; t(124) = 1.52, two-tailed p = 0.13).

We then studied the relationship between each student's proportion of carelessness and their proportion of each affective state, with correlational analyses conducted in SSPS, shown in Table 1. The results were somewhat surprising. Carelessness was negatively correlated with boredom in both interfaces, r=-0.29, p=0.02 for NoScooter group; r=-0.41, p=0.001 for Scooter group. Confusion was also negatively correlated with carelessness, r=-0.31, p=0.01 for NoScooter group; r=-0.21, p=0.09 for Scooter group. Carelessness was positively correlated with engaged concentration, r=0.47, p<0.001 for NoScooter group; r=0.49, p<0.001 for Scooter group. This indicated that more engaged students were careless more often, while less engaged students were careless less often. Carelessness and frustration were not significantly correlated in either condition, r=-0.06, p=0.66 for NoScooter group; r=-0.04, p=0.76 for Scooter group, which may be due to frustration's very rare occurrence among students. Hence, we focus the following analysis and discussion on carelessness's correlations with boredom, confusion and engaged concentration.

Table 1. Correlations of Carelessness and Affective State for Entire Tutor Usage. Statistically Significant Correlations in Bold.

	NoScooter group	Scooter group
Careless – Boredom	**-0.29 (p = 0.02)**	**-0.41 (p = 0.001)**
Careless – Confusion	**-0.31 (p = 0.01)**	-0.21 (p = 0.09)
Careless – Engaged Concentration	**+0.47 (p < 0.001)**	**+0.49 (p < 0.001)**
Careless – Frustration	-0.06 (p = 0.66)	-0.04 (p = 0.76)

Next, we examined the changes in carelessness and affect over time to see if there were significant differences in the relationship and occurrence of carelessness and affect as the student used the tutor. We did this by separating the observed affect during the student's tutor usage into two halves: the first 12 affect observations for each student (across both raters), and the remaining 12 observations per student. To split the estimates of carelessness into halves, each student's actions within the tutor was split by overall time (e.g. the split was by total time elapsed, rather than number of actions). We computed the average carelessness for incorrect actions during each half of each student's tutor usage. Figure 1 shows the student affect percentages and average estimates of carelessness in each half of the students' tutor usage in both NoScooter and Scooter groups.

Across time, the changes in the incidence of different affective states were consistent across conditions. In both conditions, students exhibited less confusion in the second half of their usage than the first half, $F(1,124) = 61.76$, $p < 0.001$. They also exhibited more engaged concentration over time, $F(1,124) = 40.26$, $p < 0.001$, and exhibited more boredom over time, $F(1,124) = 11.89$, $p = 0.001$. The changes in the proportion of these affective states over time were not significantly different between the NoScooter and Scooter conditions – for boredom $F(1,124) = 0.01$, $p = 0.93$, for confusion $F(1,124) = 0.79$, $p = 0.38$, and for engaged concentration $F(1,124) = 1.82$, $p = 0.18$.

Carelessness, on the other hand, showed a non-significant reduction over time in the NoScooter condition, $t(61) = 1.35$, two-tailed $p = 0.18$, and an non-significant increase in Scooter condition, $t(63) = -0.98$, two-tailed $p = 0.33$. This difference between conditions was statistically significant, $F(1,124) = 81.84$, $p < 0.001$. Overall, student errors (whether careless or not) significantly decreased over time in both conditions, $F(1,124) = 30.47$, $p < 0.001$. The changes over time were also not significantly different between the NoScooter and Scooter conditions, $F(1,124) = 0.31$, $p = 0.58$.

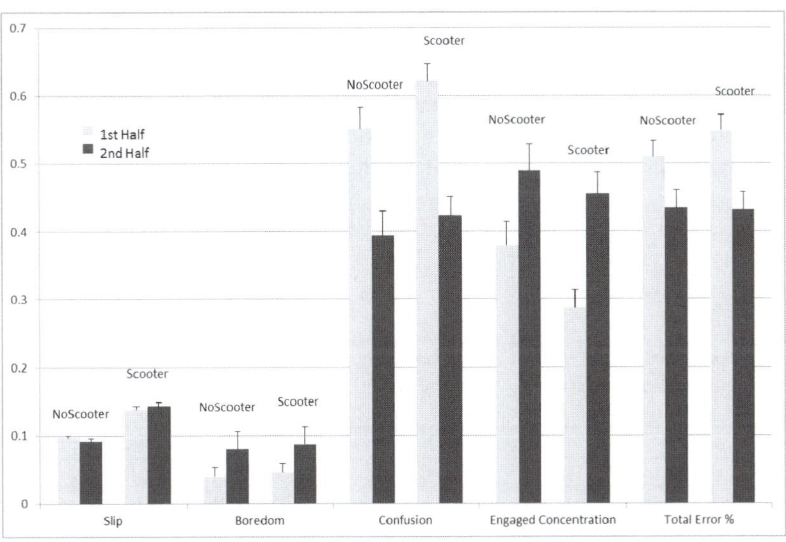

Fig. 1. Carelessness, Affect, Error, By Time of Tutor Usage

Table 2 shows the correlations between carelessness and the three most common affective states. During the first half of the tutor usage period, the correlations between carelessness and boredom trended negative in both groups, but were not significant, r = -0.08, p = 0.53 for NoScooter group; r = -0.10, p = 0.43 for Scooter group. During the second half, the correlations became significantly negative, r = -0.26, p < 0.001 for NoScooter group; r = -0.44, p < 0.001 for Scooter group. Steiger's Z-test [19], a standard test for comparing multiple correlations with no overlapping variables within a single population, was used to determine whether the correlation between carelessness and boredom was significantly different between the two time periods. The apparent difference in correlation was not significant for the NoScooter group, Z = 1.28, p = 0.20. However, the difference was statistically significant for the Scooter group, Z = 2.31, p = 0.02.

During the first half of the tutor usage period, the correlations between carelessness and confusion trended negative in both groups, but were not significant, r = -0.14, p = 0.28 for NoScooter group; r = -0.15, p = 0.24 for Scooter group. During the second half, the correlations became significantly negative, r = -0.28, p = 0.03 for NoScooter group; r = -0.36, p=0.004 for Scooter group. However, the difference in correlation between the time periods was not statistically significant for either group, Z = 0.89, p = 0.37 for NoScooter group; Z = 1.36, p = 0.17 for Scooter group.

During the first half of the tutor usage period, the correlations between carelessness and engaged concentration trended positive in both groups, but were not significant, r = 0.17, p = 0.20 for NoScooter group; r = 0.23, p = 0.07 for Scooter group. During the second half, the correlations became significantly positive, r = 0.46, p < 0.001 for NoScooter group; r = 0.64, p < 0.001 for Scooter group. The correlation between carelessness and engaged concentration was significantly different between the first half of tutor usage and the second half of tutor usage, for both groups, Z = -2.00, p = 0.05 for NoScooter group; Z = -3.23, p = 0.001 for Scooter group.

Finally, the correlations between carelessness and students' total error percentage were statistically significantly negative during the first half of the tutor usage period in both groups, r = -0.71, p < 0.001 for NoScooter group; r = -0.78, p < 0.001 for Scooter group. During the second half, the correlations remained significantly negative, r = -0.85, p < 0.001 for NoScooter group; r = -0.85, p < 0.001 for Scooter group. These correlations between the time periods were statistically significant for the NoScooter group, Z = 2.19, p = 0.03 but not statistically significant for the Scooter group, Z = 1.31, p = 0.19.

Table 2. Correlations Between Carelessness and Affect By Time Within Tutor Usage. Significant Correlations in Bold.

	Control	Experimental
Careless-Boredom (1st Half)	-0.08 (p = 0. 53)	-0.10 (p = 0.43)
Careless-Confusion (1st Half)	-0.14 (p = 0.28)	-0.15 (p = 0.24)
Careless-Engaged Concentration (1st Half)	+0.17 (p = 0.20)	+0.23 (p = 0.07)
Careless-Total Error Percentage (1st Half)	**-0.71 (p < 0.001)**	**-0.78 (p < 0.001)**
Careless-Boredom (2nd Half)	**-0.26 (p = 0.04)**	**-0.44 (p < 0.001)**
Careless-Confusion (2nd Half)	**-0.28 (p = 0.03)**	**-0.36 (p = 0.004)**
Careless-Engaged Concentration (2nd Half)	**+0.46 (p < 0.001)**	**+0.64 (p < 0.001)**
Careless-Total Error Percentage (2nd Half)	**-0.85 (p < 0.001)**	**-0.85 (p < 0.001)**

4 Discussion and Conclusion

In this paper, we studied the relationship between student carelessness and affective states within a Cognitive Tutor for Scatterplots, building off prior work in carelessness detection [2, 18] and observations of affective states [16]. Student carelessness, as represented by the presence of slips or careless errors, was estimated and detected per student using the Contextual Slip and Guess model by Baker et al. [2], implemented for this specific tutor by [18]. The detector inferred carelessness from the features of the individual student action [cf. 18]. The detector's assessment of each student's carelessness was then studied in conjunction with that student's proportion of each affective state.

Overall tutor usage showed that the more confused or bored a student is, the less likely errors are to be careless, likely due to the higher occurrence of non-careless errors stemming from poorer learning. The significant negative correlation between carelessness and boredom may be explained, at least in part, by earlier findings showing a negative relationship between boredom and strategies that lead to learning, constructs such as self-regulation and elaboration strategies, as well as effort [15]. In addition, boredom has previously been found to be correlated with poorer learning [10, 15]. As such, errors committed by students who were frequently bored may have stemmed from a lack of knowledge, which came in turn from a lack of interest in pursuing knowledge. This implies that these errors were not committed out of carelessness, where the student already knows the skill. The significant negative relationship between confusion and carelessness may be similarly explained by the students' lack of knowledge and his/her awareness of what he/she does not understand. Lack of knowledge is explicitly an implication that an error is not careless, within the model of carelessness used here [e.g. 2, 18]. On the other hand, the more a student displays the affective state of engaged concentration, the more likely he/she is to display carelessness, possibly due to overconfidence.

Examination of slip and affective state behavior over time and their respective correlations supported these assertions. The correlation between confusion and carelessness became significantly negative as students used the tutor more. However, confusion (as well as total errors – whether careless or not) decreased over time. Hence, the students who were struggling most and remained confused even after using the tutor for a substantial amount of time were less likely to become careless. The correlation between carelessness and engaged concentration became positive and significant during the second half of tutor usage, in both conditions. One possible interpretation for this is that a student who is engaged most of the time may succeed, become over-confident, and then commit careless errors. It is interesting to note that the connections between affect and carelessness were so much stronger in the second half of tutor usage than the first, across affective states. It is possible in this case that errors made during initial tutor usage in the Scooter condition were "honest" mistakes, born out of a genuine lack of knowledge and not out of carelessness. In the early part of their tutor usage, all students may have been learning the task, making it harder for an error to be careless.

Finally, these findings relate in interesting ways to recent work about carelessness on goal orientation [12]. In this work, carelessness was found to be positively correlated with academic efficacy and negatively correlated with disruptive behavior and self-presentation of low achievement [12]. In addition, carelessness was found to be higher among students with mastery or performance goals than among students manifesting neither type of goal orientation. These goal orientations were found to be related to learning and academic performance, such that mastery and performance goals lead to academic competence [11]. Hence, it unexpectedly seems that carelessness is more frequent among students displaying goal orientation and affect that are associated with positive learning.

The findings presented here also accord with results in Clements' [7] classic work on careless errors. Clements found that mathematically competent and confident children tend to make a greater proportion of careless errors than other children. In this current study, carelessness has a positive relationship with affect that has positive impacts on learning (engaged concentration [e.g. 10]) and a negative relationship to affect associated with negative effects on learning (boredom [e.g. 10, 15]) as well as affect stemming from difficulty learning the material (confusion).

In summary, these results illustrate the key role of affect in student carelessness, and suggest that adaptive responses to carelessness should take probable student affect into account.

Acknowledgments. This research was supported by the Philippines Department of Science and Technology Philippine Council for Advanced Science and Technology Research and Development under the project "Development of Affect-Sensitive Interfaces", and by the Pittsburgh Science of Learning Center (National Science Foundation) via grant "Toward a Decade of PSLC Research", award number SBE-0836012. We thank Mrs. Carmela Oracion, Jenilyn Agapito, Ivan Jacob Pesigan, Ma. Concepcion Repalam, Salvador Reyes, Ramon Rodriguez, the Ateneo Center for Educational Development, the Department of Information Systems and Computer Science of the Ateneo de Manila University and the faculty, staff, and students of Ramon Magsaysay Cubao High School for their support in this project.

References

1. Ateneo Center for Educational Development. Ramon Magsaysay Cubao High School: School Profile Report, Available from the Ateneo Center for Educational Development, Ateneo de Manila University, Loyola Heights, Quezon City, Philippines (2009)
2. Baker, R.S.J.d., Corbett, A.T., Aleven, V.: More Accurate Student Modeling through Contextual Estimation of Slip and Guess Probabilities in Bayesian Knowledge Tracing. In: Woolf, B.P., Aïmeur, E., Nkambou, R., Lajoie, S. (eds.) ITS 2008. LNCS, vol. 5091, pp. 406–415. Springer, Heidelberg (2008)
3. Baker, R.S.J.d., Corbett, A.T., Gowda, S.M., Wagner, A.Z., MacLaren, B.M., Kauffman, L.R., Mitchell, A.P., Giguere, S.: Contextual Slip and Prediction of Student Performance after Use of an Intelligent Tutor. In: 18th Annual Conference on User Modeling, Adaptation, and Personalization (2008)
4. Baker, R.S.J.d., Corbett, A.T., Koedinger, K.R., Evenson, S.E., Roll, I., Wagner, A.Z., Naim, M., Raspat, J., Baker, D.J., Beck, J.: Adapting to When Students Game an Intelligent Tutoring System. In: Ikeda, M., Ashley, K.D., Chan, T.-W. (eds.) ITS 2006. LNCS, vol. 4053, pp. 392–401. Springer, Heidelberg (2006)

5. Baker, R.S.J.d., D'Mello, S.K., Rodrigo, M.M.T., Graesser, A.C.: Better to Be Frustrated than Bored: The Incidence, Persistence, and Impact of Learners' Cognitive-Affective States during Interactions with Three Different Computer-Based Learning Environments. International Journal of Human-Computer Studies 68(4), 223–241 (2010)
6. Clements, M.A.: Analysing Children's Errors on Written Mathematical Tasks. Educational Studies in Mathematics, 1–21 (1982)
7. Clements, M.A.: Careless Errors Made by Sixth-Grade Children on Written Mathematical Tasks. Journal for Research in Mathematics Education 13(2), 136–144 (1982)
8. Corbett, A.T., Anderson, J.R.: Knowledge Tracing: Modeling the Acquisition of Procedural Knowledge. User Modeling and User-Adapted Interaction 4, 253–278 (1995)
9. Cohen, J.: A Coefficient of Agreement for Nominal Scales. Educational and Psychological Measurement 20, 37–46 (1960)
10. Craig, S.D., Graesser, A.C., Sullins, J., Gholson, B.: Affect and Learning: An Exploratory Look into the Role of Affect in Learning with AutoTutor. Journal of Educational Media 29(3), 241–250 (2004)
11. Harackiewicz, J.M., Barron, K.E., Tauer, J.M., Elliot, A.J.: Predicting Success in College: A Longitudinal Study of Achievement Goals and Ability Measures as Predictors of Interest and Performance from Freshman Year through Graduation. Journal of Educational Psychology 94(3), 562–575 (2002)
12. Hershkovitz, A., Wixon, M., Baker, R.S.J.d., Gobert, J., Sao Pedro, M.: Carelessness and Goal Orientation in a Science Microworld. In: Biswas, G., Bull, S., Kay, J., Mitrovic, A. (eds.) AIED 2011. LNCS, vol. 6738, pp. 462–465. Springer, Heidelberg (2011)
13. Maydeu-Olivares, A., D'Zurilla, T.J.: A Factor Analysis of the Social Problem-Solving Inventory Using Polychoric Correlations. European Journal of Psychological Assessment 11(2), 98–107 (1995)
14. Pekrun, R., Elliot, A.J., Maier, M.A.: Achievement Goals and Discrete Achievement Emotions: A Theoretical Model and Prospective Test. Journal of Educational Psychology 98(3), 583–597 (2006)
15. Pekrun, R., Goetz, T., Daniels, L.M., Stupnisky, R.H., Perry, R.P.: Boredom in Achievement Settings: Exploring Control-Value Antecedents and Performance Outcomes of a Neglected Emotion. Journal of Educational Psychology 102(2), 531–549 (2010)
16. Rodrigo, M.M.T., Baker, R.S.J.d., Nabos, J.Q.: The Relationships between Sequences of Affective States and Learner Achievements. In: 18th International Conference on Computers in Education (2010)
17. Rodriguez-Fornells, A., Maydeu-Olivares, A.: Impulsive/Careless Problem Solving Style as Predictor of Subsequent Academic Achievement. Personality and Individual Differences 28, 639–645 (2000)
18. San Pedro, M.O.C.Z., Baker, R.S.J.d., Rodrigo, M. M.T.: Detecting Carelessness through Contextual Estimation of Slip Probabilities among Students Using an Intelligent Tutor for Mathematics. In: Biswas, G., Bull, S., Kay, J., Mitrovic, A. (eds.) AIED 2011. LNCS, vol. 6738, pp. 304–311. Springer, Heidelberg (2011)
19. Steiger, J.H.: Tests for Comparing Elements of a Correlation Matrix. Psychological Bulletin 87, 245–251 (1980)

EmotionML – An Upcoming Standard for Representing Emotions and Related States

Marc Schröder[1], Paolo Baggia[2], Felix Burkhardt[3], Catherine Pelachaud[4], Christian Peter[5], and Enrico Zovato[2]

[1] DFKI GmbH, Saarbrücken, Germany
[2] Loquendo S.p.A., Torino, Italy
[3] Deutsche Telekom AG, Berlin, Germany
[4] Telecom ParisTech, Paris, France
[5] Fraunhofer IGD, Rostock, Germany
http://www.w3.org/TR/emotionml/

Abstract. The present paper describes the specification of Emotion Markup Language (EmotionML) 1.0, which is undergoing standardisation at the World Wide Web Consortium (W3C). The language aims to strike a balance between practical applicability and scientific well-foundedness. We briefly review the history of the process leading to the standardisation of EmotionML. We describe the syntax of EmotionML as well as the vocabularies that are made available to describe emotions in terms of categories, dimensions, appraisals and/or action tendencies. The paper concludes with a number of relevant aspects of emotion that are not covered by the current specification.

1 Introduction

Computerised systems, to the extent that they can recognise, simulate or otherwise process emotion-related information, need a representation format. If several components are to work collaboratively on the information, the format must be well-defined. In order to reach the best possible interoperability, a standard representation format should be used. This paper describes a long-running collaborative effort on defining and standardising an Emotion Markup Language.

The word "emotion" is used here in a very broad sense, covering both intense and weak states, short and long term, with and without event focus. This meaning is intended to reflect the understanding of the term "emotion" by the general public rather than any specific scientific theory.

The work started informally in 2006 as an "Emotion Annotation and Representation Language (EARL)" [23]. EARL tried to cover a lot in a short time, spanning the range from scientific descriptions of emotions, via use cases and requirements of technological applications, to the definition of an XML syntax.

Work then moved to the World Wide Web Consortium (W3C) in the form of two Incubator groups: first, the Emotion Incubator Group worked on use cases and requirements [18,17]; next, the Emotion Markup Language Incubator Group prioritised the requirements [1] and proposed elements of a syntax to

S. D'Mello et al. (Eds.): ACII 2011, Part I, LNCS 6974, pp. 316–325, 2011.

address them [19]. Three main use cases were identified: (1) manual annotation of data; (2) automatic recognition of emotion-related states from user behavior; and (3) generation of emotion-related system behavior.

This exploratory work was formalised in the "Recommendation Track" at W3C in 2009. A First Public Working Draft (FPWD) of EmotionML 1.0 was published in 2009, followed by a second Working Draft in 2010 [20]. The specification process consisted mainly in resolving the open issues in the second Incubator report, in making the syntactic choices compatible with other works in W3C and in the multimodal interaction working group, and in ensuring that the syntax was sufficiently simple to be usable in real-world settings.

A W3C workshop on EmotionML was organised in October 2010 (`http://www.w3.org/2010/10/emotionml/cfp.html`) to invite feedback on the draft specification from scientific experts as well as from potential users. The workshop provided highly relevant feedback and clarification, and played an important role in the definition of the full specification published as a Last Call Working Draft (LCWD) in spring 2011 [21]. The definition of a number of vocabularies for EmotionML was published as a separate W3C Working Draft [22].

2 Previous Work

The representation of emotions and related states has been part of several activities.

In the area of labelling schemes, maybe the most thorough attempt to propose an encompassing labelling scheme for emotion-related phenomena has been the work on the HUMAINE database [6]. The relevant concepts were identified, and made available as a set of configuration files for the video annotation tool Anvil [13]. A formal representation format was not proposed in this work.

Markup languages including emotion-related information were defined mainly in the context of research systems generating emotion-related behaviour of ECAs. The expressive richness is usually limited to a small set of emotion categories, possibly an intensity dimension, and in some cases a three-dimensional continuous representation of activation-evaluation-power space (see [24] for a review). For example, the Affective Presentation Markup Language APML [5] provides an attribute "affect" to encode an emotion category for an utterance (a "performative") or for a part of it:

```
<performative affect="afraid">
  Do I have to go to the dentist?
</performative>
```

An interesting contribution to the domain of computerised processing and representation of emotion-related concepts is A Layered Model of Affect, ALMA [10]. Following the OCC model [15], ALMA uses *appraisal* mechanisms to trigger emotions from events, objects and actions in the world. Emotions have an intensity varying over time. Each individual emotion influences mood as a longer-term affective state. ALMA uses an XML-based markup language named AffectML in two places: to represent the antecedents to emotion, i.e. the appraisals leading to emotions, or to represent the impact that emotions and moods have on a virtual agent's behaviour.

3 Syntax

The following snippet exemplifies the principles of the EmotionML syntax [21].

```
<sentence id="sent1">
  Do I have to go to the dentist?
</sentence>
<emotion xmlns="http://www.w3.org/2009/10/emotionml"
    category-set="http://www.w3.org/TR/emotion-voc/xml#everyday-categories">
  <category name="afraid" value="0.4"/>
  <reference role="expressedBy" uri="#sent1"/>
</emotion>
```

The following properties can be observed.

- The emotion annotation is self-contained within an '<emotion>' element;
- all emotion elements belong to a specific namespace;
- it is explicit in the example that emotion is represented in terms of categories;
- it is explicit from which category set the category label is chosen;
- the link to the annotated material is realised via a reference using a URI, and the reference has an explicit role.

We will now discuss the properties of the EmotionML syntax in some more detail.

3.1 Design Principles: Self-contained Emotion Annotation

EmotionML is conceived as a plug-in language, with the aim to be usable in many different contexts. Therefore, proper encapsulation is essential. All information concerning an individual emotion annotation is contained within a single '<emotion>' element. All emotion markup belongs to a unique XML namespace. EmotionML differs from many other markup languages in the sense that it does not *enclose* the annotated material. In order to link the emotion markup with the annotated material, either the reference mechanism in EmotionML or another mechanism external to EmotionML can be used.

Structurally, EmotionML uses element and attribute names to indicate the type of information being represented; attribute values provide the actual information. The use of attribute values (e.g., '<category name="joy"/>') was preferred over enclosed text (e.g., '<category>joy</category>') so that adding EmotionML to an XML node does not change that node's text content.

A top-level element '<emotionml>' enables the creation of stand-alone EmotionML documents, essentially grouping a number of emotion annotations together, but also providing document-level mechanisms for annotating global metadata and for defining emotion vocabularies (see below). It is thus possible to use EmotionML both as a standalone markup and as a plug-in annotation in different contexts.

3.2 Representations of Emotion

Emotions can be represented in terms of four types of descriptions taken from the scientific literature [24]: '<category>', '<dimension>', '<appraisal>' and '<action-tendency>'. An '<emotion>' element can contain one ore more of these descriptors; each descriptor must have a 'name' attribute and can have a 'value' attribute indicating the intensity of the respective descriptor. For '<dimension>', the 'value' attribute is mandatory, since a dimensional emotion description is always a position on one or more scales; for the other descriptions, it is possible to omit the 'value' to only make a binary statement about the presence of a given category, appraisal or action tendency.

The following example illustrates a number of possible uses of the core emotion representations.

```
<category name="affectionate"/>
<dimension name="valence" value="0.9"/>
<appraisal name="agent-self"/>
<action-tendency name="approach"/>
```

3.3 Mechanism for Referring to an Emotion Vocabulary

Since there is no single agreed vocabulary for each of the four types of emotion descriptions (see Section 4), EmotionML provides a mandatory mechanism for identifying the vocabulary used in a given '<emotion>'. The mechanism consists in attributes of '<emotion>' named 'category-set', 'dimension-set' etc., indicating which vocabulary of descriptors for annotating categories, dimensions, appraisals and action tendencies are used in that emotion annotation. These attributes contain a URI pointing to an XML representation of a vocabulary definition (see Section 4). In order to verify that an emotion annotation is valid, an EmotionML processor must retrieve the vocabulary definition and check that every 'name' of a corresponding descriptor is part of that vocabulary.

For example, the following annotation uses Mehrabian's PAD model [14] for representing a position in three-dimensional space.

```
<emotion dimension-set="http://www.w3.org/TR/emotion-voc/xml#pad-dimensions">
    <dimension name="arousal" value="0.3"/>   <!-- lower-than-average arousal -->
    <dimension name="pleasure" value="0.9"/>  <!-- very high positive valence -->
    <dimension name="dominance" value="0.8"/> <!-- relatively high potency    -->
</emotion>
```

3.4 Meta-information

Several types of meta-information can be represented in EmotionML.

First, each emotion descriptor (such as '<category>') can have a 'confidence' attribute to indicate the expected reliability of this piece of the annotation. This can reflect the confidence of a human annotator or the probability computed by a machine classifier. If several descriptors are used jointly within an '<emotion>', each descriptor has its own 'confidence' attribute. For example, it is possible to have high confidence in, say, the arousal dimension but be uncertain about the pleasure dimension:

```
<emotion dimension-set="http://www.w3.org/TR/emotion-voc/xml#pad-dimensions">
    <dimension name="arousal" value="0.7" confidence="0.9"/>
    <dimension name="pleasure" value="0.6" confidence="0.3"/>
</emotion>
```

Each '<emotion>' can have an 'expressed-through' attribute providing a list of modalities through which the emotion is expressed. Given the open-ended application domains for EmotionML, it is naturally difficult to provide a complete list of relevant modalities. The solution provided in EmotionML is to propose a list of human-centric modalities, such as 'gaze', 'face', 'voice', etc., and to allow arbitrary additional values. The following example represents a case where an emotion is recognised from, or to be generated in, face and voice:

```
<emotion category-set="http://www.w3.org/TR/emotion-voc/xml#everyday-categories"
         expressed-through="face voice">
    <category name="satisfaction"/>
</emotion>
```

For arbitrary additional metadata, EmotionML provides an '<info>' element which can contain arbitrary XML structures. The '<info>' element can occur as a child of '<emotion>' to provide local metadata, i.e. additional information about the specific emotion annotation; it can also occur in standalone EmotionML documents as a child of the root node '<emotionml>' to provide global metadata, i.e. information that is constant for all emotion annotations in the document. This can include information about sensor settings, annotator identities, situational context etc.

3.5 References to the "Rest of the World"

Emotion annotation is always about something. There is a subject "experiencing" (or simulating) the emotion. This can be a human, a virtual agent, a robot, etc. There is observable behaviour expressing the emotion, such as facial expressions, gestures, or vocal effects. With suitable measurement tools, this can also include physiological changes such as sweating or a change in heart rate or blood pressure. Emotions are often caused or triggered by an identifiable entity, such as a person, an object, an event, etc. More precisely, the appraisals leading to the emotion are triggered by that entity. And finally, emotions, or more precisely the emotion-related action tendencies, may be directed towards an entity, such as a person or an object.

EmotionML considers all of these external entities to be out of scope of the language itself; however, it provides a generic mechanism for referring to such entities. Each '<emotion>' can use one or more '<reference>' elements to point to arbitrary URIs. A '<reference>' has a 'role' attribute, which can have one of the following four values: 'expressedBy' (default), 'experiencedBy', 'triggeredBy', and 'targetedAt'. Using this mechanism, it is possible to point to arbitrary entities filling the above-mentioned four roles; all that is required is that these entities be identified by a URI.

3.6 Time

Time is relevant to EmotionML in the sense that it is necessary to represent the time during which an emotion annotation is applicable. In this sense, temporal specification complements the above-mentioned reference mechanism.

Representing time is an astonishingly complex issue. A number of different mechanisms are required to cover the range of possible use cases. First, it may be necessary to link to a time span in media, such as video or audio recordings. For this purpose, the '<reference role="expressedBy">' mechanism can use a so-called Media Fragment URI [25] to point to a time span within the media. Second, time may be represented on an absolute or relative scale. EmotionML follows EMMA [12] in representing time in these cases. Absolute time is represented in milliseconds since 1 January 1970, using the attributes 'start' and 'end'. A combination of the 'start' and 'duration' attributes can also be used to represent time intervals. Absolute times are useful for applications such as affective diaries, which record emotions throughout the day, and whose purpose it is to link back emotions to the situations in which they were encountered. Other applications require relative time, for example time since the start of a session. Here, the mechanism borrowed from EMMA is the combination of 'time-ref-uri' and 'offset-to-start'. The former provides a reference to the entity defining the meaning of time 0; the latter is time, in milliseconds, since that moment.

3.7 Representing Continuous Values and Dynamic Changes

As mentioned above, the emotion descriptors '<category>', '<dimension>', etc. can have a 'value' attribute to indicate the position on a scale corresponding to the respective descriptor. In the case of a dimension, the value indicates the position on that dimension, which is mandatory information for dimensions; in the case of categories, appraisals and action tendencies, the value can be optionally used to indicate the extent to which the respective item is present.

In all cases, the 'value' attribute contains a floating-point number between 0 and 1. The two end points of that scale represent the most extreme possible values, for example the lowest and highest possible positions on a dimension, or the complete absence of an emotion category vs. the most intense possible state of that category.

The 'value' attribute thus provides a fine-grained control of the position on a scale, which is constant throughout the temporal scope of the individual '<emotion>' annotation. It is also possible to represent changes over time of these scale values, using the '<trace>' element which can be a child of any '<category>', '<dimension>', '<appraisal>' or '<action-tendency>' element. This makes it possible to encode trace-type annotations of emotions as produced, e.g., by FeelTrace [4].

4 Vocabularies for EmotionML

As described above, EmotionML takes into account a number of key concepts from scientific emotion research [24]. Four types of descriptions are available: categories, dimensions, appraisals, and action tendencies. Depending on the tradition of emotion research and on the use case, it may be appropriate to use any single one of these representations; alternatively, it may also make sense to use *combinations* of descriptions to characterise more fully the various aspects of an emotional state that are observed: how an appraisal of triggers caused the emotion; how it can be characterised using a global description in terms of a category and/or a set of dimensions; and the potential actions the individual may be executing as a result. Insofar, EmotionML is a powerful representational device.

This description glosses over one important detail, however. Whereas emotion researchers may agree to some extent on the types of facets that play a role in the emotion process (such as appraisals, feeling, expression, etc.), there is no general consensus on the descriptive vocabularies that should be used. Which set of emotion *categories* is considered appropriate varies dramatically between the different traditions, and even within a tradition such as the Darwinian tradition of emotion research, there is no agreed set of emotion categories that should be considered as the most important ones (see e.g. [2]). Similarly, dimensional accounts of emotion do not agree on either the number or the names that should be given to the different dimensions.

For this reason, any attempt to enforce a closed set of descriptors for emotions would invariably draw heavy criticism from a range of research fields. Given that there is no consensus in the community, it is impossible to produce a consensus annotation in a standard markup language. The obvious alternative is to leave the choice of descriptors up to the users; however, this would dramatically limit interoperability.

The solution pursued in EmotionML is of a third kind. The notion of an 'emotion vocabulary' is introduced: any specific emotion annotation must be specific about the vocabulary that is being used in that annotation. This makes it possible to define in a clear way the terms that make sense in a given research tradition. Components can interoperate if the EmotionML markup that they produce and consume uses one or more emotion vocabularies that all components involved are able to handle.

The specification includes a mechanism for defining emotion vocabularies. It consists of a '`<vocabulary>`' element containing a number of '`<item>`' elements. A vocabulary has a '`type`' attribute, indicating whether it is a vocabulary for representing categories, dimensions, appraisals or action tendencies. A vocabulary item has a '`name`' attribute. Both the entire vocabulary and each individual item can have an '`<info>`' child to provide arbitrary metadata.

A W3C Working Draft [22] complements the specification to provide EmotionML with a set of emotion vocabularies taken from the scientific literature. When the user considers them suitable, these vocabularies rather than arbitrary other vocabularies should be used in order to promote interoperability. Whenever users have a need for a different vocabulary, however, they can simply define their own custom vocabulary and use it in the same way as the vocabularies listed in the document. This makes it possible to add any vocabularies from scientific research that are missing from the pre-defined set, as well as application-specific vocabularies.

In selecting emotion vocabularies, the group has applied the following criteria. The primary guiding principle has been to select vocabularies that are either commonly used in technological contexts, or represent current emotion models from the scientific literature. A further criterion is related to the difficulty to define mappings between categories, dimensions, appraisals and action tendencies. For this reason, groups of vocabularies were included for which some of these mappings are likely to be definable in the future.

The following vocabularies are defined. For categorical descriptions, the "big six" basic emotion vocabulary by Ekman [7], an everyday emotion vocabulary by Cowie et al. [3], and three sets of categories that lend themselves to mappings to appraisals, dimensions and action tendencies: the OCC categories [15], the categories used by Fontaine et al. [8], and the categories from the work by Frijda [9]. Three dimensional vocabularies are provided, the pleasure-arousal-dominance (PAD) vocabulary by Mehrabian [14], the four-dimensional vocabulary proposed by Fontaine et al. [8], and a vocabulary providing a single '`intensity`' dimension for such use cases that want to represent solely the intensity of an emotion without any statement regarding the nature of that emotion. For appraisal, three vocabularies are proposed: the OCC appraisals [15], Scherer's Stimulus Evaluation Checks [16], and the EMA appraisals [11]. Finally, for action tendencies, only a single vocabulary is currently listed, namely that proposed by Frijda [9].

While these vocabularies should provide users with a solid basis, it is likely that additional vocabularies or clarifications about the current vocabularies will be requested. Due to the rather informal nature of a non-Recommendation-track Working Draft, it is rather easy to provide future versions of the document that provide the additional information required.

5 Conclusion and Future Work

The EmotionML 1.0 specification addresses the majority of the requirements that arise from use cases. In a future call for implementations, the implementability of all features provided by the specification will be verified.

A number of important issues have been noted as important but too difficult to handle in the first version of EmotionML. Among these is a careful solution for representing *regulation* in EmotionML, i.e. the fact that an emotion was suppressed, simulated, masked by another emotion, etc. Another requirement that is not covered in EmotionML 1.0 is the use of ontologies to define the terms in an emotion vocabulary, to relate the terms to one another, and to define mappings between emotion vocabularies where possible. Another difficulty regards the specification of scales. Should it be discrete, continuous, unipolar or bipolar, etc.? Due to the difficulty of finding a consensus in the emotion community on best practice for scales, we have postponed a more detailed definition of scales.

Once that EmotionML 1.0 has reached its full maturity, these directions can be developed in future versions of EmotionML.

Acknowledgements. The preparation of this paper was supported by the W3C and the EU project ALIZ-E (IST-248116). Thanks to all who have provided input to this work, especially Roddy Cowie, Sylwia Hyniewska, and Jean-Claude Martin.

References

1. Burkhardt, F., Schröder, M.: Emotion markup language: Requirements with priorities. W3C incubator group report, World Wide Web Consortium (2008), http://www.w3.org/2005/Incubator/emotion/XGR-requirements-20080513/
2. Cowie, R., Cornelius, R.R.: Describing the emotional states that are expressed in speech. Speech Communication 40(1-2), 5–32 (2003)
3. Cowie, R., Douglas-Cowie, E., Appolloni, B., Taylor, J., Romano, A., Fellenz, W.: What a neural net needs to know about emotion words. In: Mastorakis, N. (ed.) Computational Intelligence and Applications, pp. 109–114. World Scientific & Engineering Society Press (1999)
4. Cowie, R., Douglas-Cowie, E., Savvidou, S., McMahon, E., Sawey, M., Schröder, M.: 'FEELTRACE': an instrument for recording perceived emotion in real time. In: Proc. ISCA Workshop on Speech and Emotion, Northern Ireland, pp. 19–24 (2000)
5. De Carolis, B., Pelachaud, C., Poggi, I., Steedman, M.: APML, a markup language for believable behavior generation. In: Prendinger, H., Ishizuka, M. (eds.) Life-Like Characters, pp. 65–85. Springer, New York (2004)
6. Douglas-Cowie, E., Cowie, R., Sneddon, I., Cox, C., Lowry, O., McRorie, M., Martin, J., Devillers, L., Abrilian, S., Batliner, A., Amir, N., Karpouzis, K.: The HUMAINE database: Addressing the collection and annotation of naturalistic and induced emotional data. In: Paiva, A.C.R., Prada, R., Picard, R.W. (eds.) ACII 2007. LNCS, vol. 4738, pp. 488–500. Springer, Heidelberg (2007), http://dx.doi.org/10.1007/978-3-540-74889-2_43
7. Ekman, P.: Universals and cultural differences in facial expressions of emotion. In: Cole, J. (ed.) Nebraska Symposium on Motivation, vol. 19, pp. 207–282. University of Nebraska Press (1972)
8. Fontaine, J.R., Scherer, K.R., Roesch, E.B., Ellsworth, P.C.: The world of emotions is not Two-Dimensional. Psychological Science 18(12), 1050–1057 (2007), doi:10.1111/j.1467-9280.2007.02024.x
9. Frijda, N.H.: The Emotions. Cambridge University Press, Cambridge (1986)
10. Gebhard, P.: ALMA - a layered model of affect. In: Proceedings of the Fourth International Joint Conference on Autonomous Agents and Multiagent Systems (AAMAS 2005), Utrecht (2005)

11. Gratch, J., Marsella, S.: A domain-independent framework for modeling emotion. Cognitive Systems Research 5(4), 269–306 (2004)
12. Johnston, M., Baggia, P., Burnett, D.C., Carter, J., Dahl, D.A., McCobb, G., Raggett, D.: EMMA: extensible MultiModal annotation markup language (February 2009), http://www.w3.org/TR/emma/
13. Kipp, M.: Anvil - a generic annotation tool for multimodal dialogue. In: Proc. Eurospeech, Aalborg, Denmark, pp. 1367–1370 (2001)
14. Mehrabian, A.: Pleasure-arousal-dominance: A general framework for describing and measuring individual differences in temperament. Current Psychology 14(4), 261–292 (1996), http://dx.doi.org/10.1007/BF02686918
15. Ortony, A., Clore, G.L., Collins, A.: The Cognitive Structure of Emotion. Cambridge University Press, Cambridge (1988)
16. Scherer, K.R.: Appraisal theory. In: Dalgleish, T., Power, M.J. (eds.) Handbook of Cognition & Emotion, pp. 637–663. John Wiley, New York (1999)
17. Schröder, M., Devillers, L., Karpouzis, K., Martin, J.-C., Pelachaud, C., Peter, C., Pirker, H., Schuller, B., Tao, J., Wilson, I.: What should a generic emotion markup language be able to represent? In: Paiva, A.C.R., Prada, R., Picard, R.W. (eds.) ACII 2007. LNCS, vol. 4738, pp. 440–451. Springer, Heidelberg (2007)
18. Schröder, M., Zovato, E., Pirker, H., Peter, C., Burkhardt, F.: W3C emotion incubator group final report. Tech. rep., World Wide Web Consortium (2007), http://www.w3.org/2005/Incubator/emotion/XGR-emotion-20070710
19. Schröder, M., Baggia, P., Burkhardt, F., Martin, J., Pelachaud, C., Peter, C., Schuller, B., Wilson, I., Zovato, E.: Elements of an EmotionML 1.0. W3C final incubator group report, World Wide Web Consortium (2008), http://www.w3.org/2005/Incubator/emotion/XGR-emotionml-20081120/
20. Schröder, M., Baggia, P., Burkhardt, F., Oltramari, A., Pelachaud, C., Peter, C., Zovato, E.: Emotion markup language (EmotionML) 1.0. W3C working draft, World Wide Web Consortium (July 2010), http://www.w3.org/TR/2010/WD-emotionml-20100729/
21. Schröder, M., Baggia, P., Burkhardt, F., Pelachaud, C., Peter, C., Zovato, E.: Emotion markup language (EmotionML) 1.0. W3C Last Call Working Draft, World Wide Web Consortium (April 2011), http://www.w3.org/TR/2011/WD-emotionml-20110407/
22. Schröder, M., Pelachaud, C., Ashimura, K., Baggia, P., Burkhardt, F., Oltramari, A., Peter, C., Zovato, E.: Vocabularies for EmotionML. W3C Working Draft, World Wide Web Consortium (April 2011), http://www.w3.org/TR/2011/WD-emotion-voc-20110407/
23. Schröder, M., Pirker, H., Lamolle, M.: First suggestions for an emotion annotation and representation language. In: Proceedings of LREC 2006 Workshop on Corpora for Research on Emotion and Affect, Genoa, Italy, pp. 88–92 (2006)
24. Schröder, M., Pirker, H., Lamolle, M., Burkhardt, F., Peter, C., Zovato, E.: Representing emotions and related states in technological systems. In: Petta, P., Cowie, R., Pelachaud, C. (eds.) Emotion-Oriented Systems – The Humaine Handbook, pp. 367–386. Springer, Heidelberg (2011)
25. Troncy, R., Mannens, E., Pfeiffer, S., van Deursen, D.: Media fragments URI 1.0. W3C last call working draft, World Wide Web Consortium (June 2010), http://www.w3.org/TR/1998/REC-xml-19980210

Emotion-Based Intrinsic Motivation for Reinforcement Learning Agents

Pedro Sequeira, Francisco S. Melo, and Ana Paiva

Instituto Superior Técnico
Universidade Técnica de Lisboa
INESC-ID
Av. Prof. Dr. Cavaco Silva
2744-016 Porto Salvo, Portugal
pedro.sequeira@gaips.inesc-id.pt,
{fmelo,ana.paiva}@inesc-id.pt

Abstract. In this paper, we propose an adaptation of four common appraisal dimensions that evaluate the relation of an agent with its environment into reward features within an *intrinsically motivated reinforcement learning* framework. We show that, by optimizing the relative weights of such features for a given environment, the agents attain a greater degree of fitness while overcoming some of their perceptual limitations. This optimization process resembles the evolutionary adaptive process that living organisms are subject to. We illustrate the application of our method in several simulated foraging scenarios.

Keywords: reinforcement learning, intrinsic motivation, appraisal.

1 Introduction

Emotions have often been regarded as detrimental to cognition by impairing rational decision-making. However, as the body of knowledge about the influence of emotions on humans and other animals grows, emotions are increasingly being regarded as a beneficial adaptive mechanism for decision-making [5,9]. Studies in animals and simple organisms showed that, throughout evolution, emotions might have provided animals with an ability to survive longer and procreate more [4,5]. This is done by means of associative learning processes that allow organisms to extend the range of stimuli perceived as hazardous or beneficial and focus their attention in important aspects of the environment while changing their behavior accordingly [4,5]. Emotions also play a fundamental role in learning, by eliciting physiological signals that bias our behavior toward maximizing reward and minimizing punishment [4]. Reinforcement learning mechanisms found in nature thus rely on emotional cues to indicate the advantages or adversity of an event. Without such mechanisms, animals could not know "*whether a behavior never performed by any of its ancestors should be repeated or not*" [5].

One way of explaining how emotions are generated according to one's relationship with the environment is by developing appraisal theories of emotion [7,9].

S. D´Mello et al. (Eds.): ACII 2011, Part I, LNCS 6974, pp. 326–336, 2011.

Appraisal theories posit that emotions are elicited by evaluations (appraisals) of events which characterize aspects of the situation in terms of its significance for the organism's well-being or goals [7]. In order to differentiate between emotional states, several theories propose a set of appraisal dimensions, each of which evaluates specific aspects of the subject-environment relationship.

Given the simplicity and usefulness of learning and emotional-processing skills in nature, we expect that these same mechanisms adapted to artificial agents may lead to more robust and adaptable agents. As such, in this paper we adopt the framework of intrinsically motivated reinforcement learning (IMRL) [16] and propose numerical counterparts for some common appraisal dimensions [7,9]. Each of the adopted dimensions evaluates a certain aspect of the agent-environment relation and is translated into a numerical feature that provides intrinsic reward to the agent in a reinforcement learning (RL) context. The specific way in which the agent interprets these features is optimized to the agent's environment, in a process that relates to the evolutionary environmental conditioning that organisms are subject to in nature. Our results show that the contributions from the different reward features in fact lead to distinct behaviors that allow agents to overcome certain shortcomings in particular environments and attain better performance. Moreover, we show that the absence of such emotion-based processing mechanism may have a significant negative impact on the agent's performance in some scenarios. Finally, we show that the proposed appraisal features can be used as general reward features for IMRL agents.

2 Background and Related Work

In the RL field there are only a few systems that make use of emotional processing. Examples include an emotional model for robots that combines the values of the robot's sensations, feelings and "hormones" to determine a dominant emotional state from a set of four basic emotions [8]. The agent learns state-behavior associations that are reinforced by emotions. In another approach, the agent's affective state is computed based on a statistical analysis of the reward it receives [3]. The results show that associating positive affective states with exploitation and negative affect with exploration strategies provides adaptive benefits for the agent. In [14], three basic emotions control the behavior strategy of an agent in an RL task: *Happiness* and *Sadness* are determined based on the amount of reward received by the agent, while *Fear* is used as a decision mechanism that prevents the agent from choosing low-valued actions. One other work proposes a model for *affective anticipatory reward* based on valence and arousal levels, which in turn influences decision-making in a risk-taking scenario [2]. Finally, in the *FLAME* model [6], RL is used to build associations of emotional states and objects and to predict the user's actions.

All aforementioned approaches rely on a set of discrete emotions that influence the learning and decision-making processes of the agent. In this paper, we propose an approach inspired in appraisal theories which, as seen in Section 1, stresses the importance of emotions in providing intrinsic cues for learning in dynamic environments. We propose a possible numerical translation of four appraisal dimensions to be used as features of intrinsic reward by an RL agent.

2.1 Intrinsically Motivated Learning

Reinforcement learning (RL) addresses the general problem of an agent faced with a sequential decision problem [18]. By a process of trial-and-error, the agent must learn a mapping that assigns perceptions to actions. Such mapping determines how the agent acts in each possible situation and is commonly known as a *policy*. In single agent scenarios, RL agents can be modeled using *partially observable Markov decision processes* (POMDPs). At every step, depending on its observation, the agent chooses an action a_t from a finite set of possible actions, $\mathcal{A}$, and transitions from state s_t to state s_{t+1} with probability $\mathsf{P}(s_{t+1} \mid s_t, a_t)$. It receives a reward $r(s_t, a_t)$ and makes a new observation z_{t+1} from a set of possible observations, $\mathcal{Z}$, with probability $\mathsf{O}(z_{t+1} \mid s_{t+1}, a_t)$, and the process repeats. The goal of the agent is to choose its actions so as to gather as much reward as possible, discounted by a positive discount factor $\gamma < 1$. Formally, this corresponds to maximizing the value

$$v = \mathbb{E}\left[\sum_t \gamma^t r(s_t, a_t)\right]. \tag{1}$$

The reward function r implicitly encodes the *task* that the agent must learn.

In typical RL scenarios, it is assumed that observations correspond to the actual states of the agent/environment [18]. When this is the case, it is possible to find a *policy* $\pi^* : \mathcal{Z} \to \mathcal{A}$ maximizing the value in (1). However, in many environments, the assumption that $z_t = s_t, \forall t$, is too restrictive, and policies mapping observations directly to actions (called *memoryless policies*) can have arbitrarily poor performance [15]. This means that the perceptual limitations of the agent in fact impair its ability to properly choose its actions. Moreover, computing the best memoryless policy is NP-hard in the worst case [10]. Several algorithmic approaches have been proposed to deal with partial observability in RL settings [1]. One important class of approaches builds into the agent *prior knowledge* that can, somehow, alleviate its perceptual limitations. Examples include approaches based on some form of *memory*. However, such approaches typically require specific learning algorithms tailored to leverage information from particular aspects of the agent's history [1].

Recently, a novel framework for *intrinsically motivated reinforcement learning* was proposed [16]. In this framework, a learning agent interacts with one among a set $\mathcal{E}$ of possible environments, and optimizes its policy with respect to one reward function r among a set $\mathcal{R}$ of possible rewards. An optimal reward function $r^* \in \mathcal{R}$ is such that the *expected fitness* of the agent with respect to a distribution over possible environments is maximized. This fitness is determined by some fitness function $\mathcal{F}$ that maps the history of the interaction of an agent with its environment into a numerical value that, in a sense, measures how well-adapted the agent is to its environment. In the IMRL framework, the learning

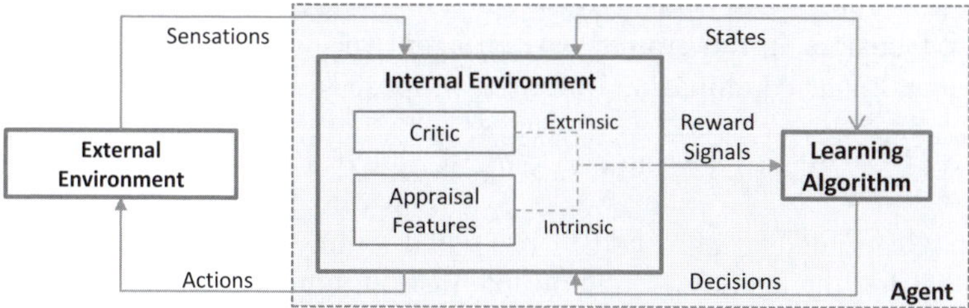

Fig. 1. Proposed framework for emotion-based intrinsic motivation; adapted from [16]

agent receives an *augmented* reward function that incorporates several reward components, herein referred as *reward features* and denoted by $\phi_i, i = 1, \ldots, N$. In this paper, we thus consider $\mathcal{R}$ as the set of all rewards of the form

$$r(s, a) = \sum_i \theta_i \phi_i(s, a), \tag{2}$$

where the weights θ_i determine the contribution of each reward-feature ϕ_i to the overall reward r that the agent must maximize throughout its lifetime. We refer to a *fitness-based reward signal* as a reward-feature r^{ext} that explicitly rewards fitness-maximizing states [16]. For ease of exposition, we henceforth refer to such feature as the *extrinsic reward*, which can be interpreted as corresponding to the fulfillment of some of the agent's basic needs. For example, if the agent is a predator, its task could be to find its prey and feed, and the extrinsic reward would correspond to the predator being satiated. The other reward-features constitute the *intrinsic reward*, which contrasts with the "original" extrinsic reward in that it does not necessarily relate to the task that the agent must accomplish. However, as shown in [16,17], intrinsic rewards can be an effective mechanism to endow the agent with useful information to overcome some of its perceptual limitations (such as memory) and enhance its performance. One important aspect that remains unexplored, however, is concerned with which information should be used to build these intrinsic rewards. In this paper we propose the use of simulated affective features inspired in common appraisal dimensions to build the intrinsic reward.

3 Emotionally Motivated Learning Agents

Figure 1 depicts the proposed framework for emotion-based intrinsically motivated learning, adapted from [16]. In this framework, we follow the perspective that certain affective states may encode useful information that guide an agent during learning and decision-making. In particular, we adopt four common appraisal dimensions: novelty, motivation, valence and control. Inspired by appraisal theories of emotion, we propose for each dimension a possible reward feature that evaluates certain aspects of the agent-environment relationship (corresponding to the internal environment in Fig. 1). These features map the result of appraisals into scalar values that somehow indicate the degree of activation of each dimension. In our framework, an agent receives a total reward r^{tot} calculated as a linear combination of all the proposed features,

$$r^{\text{tot}}(s,a) = \theta^{\mathfrak{n}}\mathfrak{n}(s,a) + \theta^{\mathfrak{m}}\mathfrak{m}(s,a) + \theta^{\mathfrak{c}}\mathfrak{c}(s,a) + \theta^{\mathfrak{v}}\mathfrak{v}(s,a) + \theta^{\text{ext}}r^{\text{ext}}(s,a), \quad (3)$$

where weights $\theta^{\mathfrak{n}}$, $\theta^{\mathfrak{m}}$, $\theta^{\mathfrak{c}}$, $\theta^{\mathfrak{v}}$ and θ^{ext} are scalar values between 0 and 1 which are initially set for the agent and remain fixed throughout its lifetime. A particular weight set $\boldsymbol{\theta} = [\theta^{\mathfrak{n}}, \theta^{\mathfrak{m}}, \theta^{\mathfrak{c}}, \theta^{\mathfrak{v}}, \theta^{\text{ext}}]$ corresponds to a built-in configuration for the agent that indicates which aspects of its relationship with the environment it gives more attention to. For example, a weight configuration $\boldsymbol{\theta} = [0, 0, 0, 0, 1]$ indicates that the agent is predisposed to value only extrinsic rewards while completely ignoring intrinsic motivation. Each particular weight configuration will yield different degrees of fitness depending on the environment where the learning takes place. Due to this fact, the weight set is optimized to maximize the agent's fitness according to the environment, which will also allow it to overcome some of its perceptual limitations. The optimal weight set is denoted by $\boldsymbol{\theta}^*$.

3.1 Affective Reward Features

Appraisal theories define a set of dimensions to generate affective states in response to events [7]. Our framework adopts four of the *major dimensions of appraisal* [7] that characterize many of the existing appraisal theories. We intentionally do not adapt common *social dimensions* as they are responsible for more complex emotions like shame or guilt that we do not explore here.

Appraisal theories characterize high-level psychological processes for the generation of emotions in humans. Some of the commonly proposed dimensions deal with complex concepts and mental representations such as beliefs, causal attribution or social norms [9,7]. However, in our learning framework, we are concerned with aspects of the agent-environment relationship capable of affecting the agent's behavior. Because of that, one of the main challenges is to map the evaluations made by the appraisal dimensions into low-level numerical features that can be used as intrinsic reward-features. Leventhal and Scherer [9] discuss the possibility of appraising events from the environment at three different levels of processing: sensory-motor, schematic and conceptual. This way, by considering the events at different levels, it is possible to explain emotions as an adaptive mechanism that develops from simple, reflex-like responses into more complex cognitive-emotional patterns through learning [9].

Considering this multi-level view of emotional appraisal, we now describe a possible mapping of the adapted appraisal dimensions into scalar values, corresponding to the reward features in the IMRL framework. We are not claiming these mappings to be the only ones possible. We propose low-level features that, in our framework, make similar evaluations to those expected from the respective appraisal dimensions. We henceforth denote by $n_t(s)$ the number of visits to state s up to time-step t, and by $n_t(s,a)$ the number of times that action a has been experienced in state s.

Novelty usually refers to the degree of familiarity of the perceived stimuli in relation to the agent's knowledge structures built so far [7,9]. Statistically, at a low-level, this is directly correlated to the number of visits to state-action pairs. Therefore, in our framework, this dimension is quantified as the reward-feature

$$\mathfrak{n}(s,a) = \frac{\lambda^{n_t(s,a)} + \lambda^{n_t(s)}}{2},$$

where λ is a positive constant such that $\lambda < 1$. λ can be seen as a "novelty rate", determining how the novelty dimension decays with experience.

Motivation asserts the *relevance* of a perceived event in terms of the agent's goals or needs [7,9]. As such, motivation increases as the agent approaches its perceived goals, and decreases otherwise. For the purposes of our model, we assume that, at each time-step t, the agent has access to an estimated distance, $\hat{d}(s_t, s^*)$, that returns an estimate of the number of actions needed to move from its current state s_t to a goal-state s^* where the reward is maximal. This distance estimate needs not be accurate, but should be coherent with the true values, *i.e.*, if $d(s_1, s^*) > d(s_2, s^*)$ then $\hat{d}(s_1, s^*) > \hat{d}(s_2, s^*)$, where $d(\cdot,\cdot)$ denotes the actual distance. This distance estimate is not computed from the model, but perceived by the agent. Motivation is thus translated in terms of the numerical value

$$\mathfrak{m}(s,a) = \frac{1}{1 + \hat{d}(s, s^*)}.$$

Control, depending on the level at which the appraisal is being made, indicates the *potential* of an agent in coping with the situation being evaluated [7,9] or the degree of *correctness/clarity* of the world-model that the organism has built of its own environment. Statistically, this is highly correlated with the number of visits to state-action pairs in a reverse manner to that of novelty. Therefore, for simplicity, we represent the amount of control as $\mathfrak{c}(s,a) = 1 - \mathfrak{n}(s,a)$. Because the agent becomes more familiarized with its environment overtime, the states, actions and even rewards that are not novel enhance the degree of *correctness* of its world-model.

Valence measures how pleasant a given situation is. It is a product of innate detectors or learned preferences/aversions that basically indicate whether a stimulus is "positive" or "negative" in terms of biological significance for the organism [7,9]. In our framework, we translate this as a measure of how much the current extrinsic reward r^{ext} contributes to the overall goal of the agent, which corresponds to the value

$$\mathfrak{v}(s,a) = \frac{r^{\text{ext}}(s,a)}{V^{\text{ext}}(s) - \gamma \sum_{s'} \mathsf{P}(s' \mid s,a) V^{\text{ext}}(s')},$$

where $V^{\text{ext}}(s)$ denotes the value (in terms of total discounted extrinsic reward) that the agent currently associates with state s. The expression for $\mathfrak{v}$ essentially follows the extrinsic reward-feature, but weighting it with respect to its contribution to the overall value that the agent expects to achieve[1].

[1] This expression is related to a well-known *shaping function* [12].

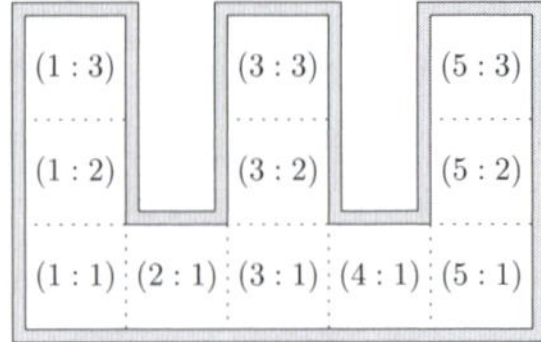

Fig. 2. The foraging environment used in the experiments. Each square marked by $(x : y)$ coordinates represents a possible location for the agent.

4 Experiments and Results

We designed a set of experiments in foraging environments inspired in [16] to illustrate the emergence of specific behaviors that overcome perceptual limitations of the agent and ultimately lead to a better fitness. In our experiments, the agent is a predator moving in the environment depicted in Fig. 2. At each time-step, the agent is able to observe its position in the environment and whether it is collocated with a prey. The agent has available 5 possible actions, $\{N, S, E, W, \text{Eat}\}$. The four directional actions move the agent deterministically to the adjacent cell in the corresponding direction; the Eat action consumes a prey if one is present at the agent's location, and does nothing otherwise. We use the Dyna-Q/prioritized sweeping algorithm [11] to learn a memoryless policy that treats observations of the agent as states. The agent follows an ε-greedy policy with decaying exploration rate $\varepsilon_t = \lambda^t$. We use a learning rate $\alpha = 0.3$, a novelty rate $\lambda = 1.0001$ and $\gamma = 0.9$. We ran four different experiments that differ in the particular distribution of preys and on the outcome of the agent's actions.

Exploration scenario: This scenario closely resembles the foraging scenario in [16]. At each time step, a prey can appear in any one the three end-of-corridor locations, $(1 : 3)$, $(3 : 3)$ or $(5 : 3)$. Whenever the agent eats a prey, it receives an extrinsic reward of 1. The prey disappears from its current location and randomly reappears in one of the two other locations.

Persistence scenario: In this scenario two preys are always available at $(1 : 3)$ and $(5 : 3)$. The prey in $(1 : 3)$ is a hare and corresponds to an extrinsic reward of 1. The prey in $(5 : 3)$ is a rabbit and corresponds to an extrinsic reward of 0.01. Every time the predator eats one of the preys, it returns to its initial position in $(3 : 3)$ and the prey is replaced in the corresponding location. We assume that eating is *automatic*: every time the predator is collocated with a prey automatically eats it. Additionally, in $(2 : 1)$ there is a fence that prevents the predator from moving from $(2 : 1)$ to $(1 : 1)$ in a single time-step. It will take the predator n successive E actions to "break" the fence for the nth time and move from $(2 : 1)$ to $(1 : 1)$. Every time that the fence is broken, it is rebuilt more solidly, requiring the agent to take $n+1$ actions to break it the next time[2].

[2] We note that the fence only prevents the agent from moving from $(2 : 1)$ to $(1 : 1)$, and not in the opposite direction.

Prey-season scenario: In this scenario only one of two kinds of prey is available at each time-step. In the "hare season", a hare is available in $(5:3)$ at every time-step. Every time the predator eats the hare it receives a reward of 1 and returns to its start location in $(3:3)$. In the "rabbit season", a rabbit is available in $(1:3)$, providing a reward of 0.1 when eaten. However, in each rabbit season, after eating 9 rabbits, a rabbit breeder shoots the predator whenever it tries to eat another, and our agent receives a punishment reward of -1, returning to the start position. Seasons switch every 10 000 steps.

Different rewards scenario: Finally, this is a rather simple scenario in which two preys are always available at $(1:3)$ (a rabbit, worth a reward of 0.1) and at $(5:3)$ (a hare, worth a reward of 1). Like with the previous scenarios, the agent returns to $(3:3)$ every time it eats a prey.

We note that, from the agent's perspective, the scenarios are non-Markovian, since the information about the location of the preys is not directly observable. This emulates some of the challenges that predators face in nature, where their observations do not provide all the necessary information for the best choice of action. The different scenarios were designed with two goals in mind: (i) to test whether the affective reward-features lead to distinct behaviors; and (ii) to determine if, by using them as intrinsic rewards, the agent improves its overall fitness. The weight vector $\boldsymbol{\theta} = [\theta^{\mathfrak{n}}, \theta^{\mathfrak{m}}, \theta^{\mathfrak{c}}, \theta^{\mathfrak{v}}, \theta^{\text{ext}}]$ is optimized for each environment to maximize the agent's fitness, using an adaptive sampling approach similar to the one in [16][3]. This optimization process is, in a sense, similar to the adaptive processes animals experience throughout their evolution.

Table 1. Agent fitness results for each scenario. The first column indicates the optimal weight set $\boldsymbol{\theta}^*$ obtained for each scenario. The column marked "Optimal" corresponds to the amount of fitness resulting from the optimized weight vector, while the "Extrinsic" column corresponds to the standard Dyna-Q agent ($\boldsymbol{\theta} = [0, 0, 0, 0, 1]$).

Scenario	$\boldsymbol{\theta}^* = [\theta^{\mathfrak{n}}, \theta^{\mathfrak{m}}, \theta^{\mathfrak{c}}, \theta^{\mathfrak{v}}, \theta^{\text{ext}}]$	Optimal	Extrinsic
Prey-season	$\boldsymbol{\theta}^* = [0.00, 0.00, 0.50, 0.00, 0.50]$	5 203.5	334.2
Exploration	$\boldsymbol{\theta}^* = [0.40, 0.00, 0.20, 0.00, 0.40]$	1 902.2	135.9
Persistence	$\boldsymbol{\theta}^* = [0.13, 0.29, 0.29, 0.00, 0.29]$	1 020.8	25.4
Dif. rewards	$\boldsymbol{\theta}^* = [0.00, 0.50, 0.00, 0.25, 0.25]$	87 925.7	87 890.8

Table 1 presents the obtained results of simulating the agent for 100 000 learning steps and correspond to averages of 100 independent Monte-Carlo trials. We present the optimal weight set $\boldsymbol{\theta}^*$ obtained for each scenario and the corresponding amount of fitness attained by the agent. For comparison purposes, we also present the fitness of a standard Dyna-Q agent receiving only extrinsic reward, which corresponds to the weight set $\boldsymbol{\theta} = [0, 0, 0, 0, 1]$. From the results

[3] Although more efficient methods are possible [13], we are not concerned with the computational efficiency of the process of reward optimization.

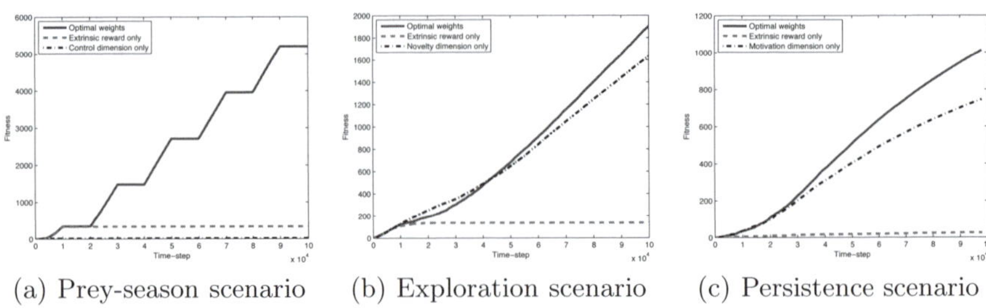

(a) Prey-season scenario (b) Exploration scenario (c) Persistence scenario

Fig. 3. Cumulative fitness attained in the prey-season, exploration and persistence scenarios. The results correspond to averages over 100 independent Monte-Carlo trials. We included the results for the optimal weight set, for an agent receiving only extrinsic reward, and for an agent receiving only the intrinsic reward component corresponding to the highest weight in the optimal weight set.

in the table, it is clear that our agent outperforms the standard Dyna-Q agent in all tested scenarios, supporting our claim that the features adapted from the emotional appraisal theories provide useful information that allows the agent to overcome some of its limitations. Our results also prompt several other interesting observations. Note, for example, that in the exploration scenario, the intrinsic reward arising from novelty is sufficient to significantly outperform the agent only pursuing extrinsic reward. These results are in accordance with those reported in [16,17] in a similar scenario. In general, depending on the scenario, the weight optimization procedure yields a distinct configuration that is related with specific aspects of the environment. This is also an important observation that supports our claim that different emotion-based features foster different behaviors. The prey-season scenario also provides a very interesting result: individually, neither the extrinsic reward or the control alone are sufficient for the agent to attain a significant performance. However, when combined, they lead to a boost in performance of at least one order of magnitude. This is due to the fact that each feature provides a different strategy: on one hand, the agent must consider extrinsic reward provided by the hares; on the other hand, it should choose more familiar actions during the rabbit season, as eating too much rabbits will result in negative reward. Fig. 3 depicts the learning performance of our agent in three of the test scenarios, against the performance of a "greedy" agent and an agent receiving reward only from one of the intrinsic features. This figure helps to further illustrate the behavior of our approach, showing that not having an emotional mechanism guiding the agent can severely impair its learning performance. It also shows that generally, a combination of the different proposed features is important to attain the best result, *i.e.*, it does not suffice receiving intrinsic reward from only one of the emotional features.

5 Discussion

In this paper we proposed a framework for generating intrinsic rewards for learning agents. The intrinsic reward is derived from four appraisal dimensions adapted from literature that map into reward-features. We modeled our agents within an IMRL framework and designed a series of experiments to test the validity of our approach. Our results show that the proposed affective features guide the agent in finding a right balance between different behavior strategies in order to attain the maximal fitness in each scenario. Our objective in this work was not to find general feature-weight configurations, but generic features that could be used to produce intrinsic reward. We believe that the success of this approach may be due to the fact that the reward-features, much like the appraisal dimensions they correspond to, characterize aspects of the agent's relationship with its environment. Because the features are embedded in the reward, they indirectly focus the agent in different aspects, bringing out attention to advantageous states while ignoring others that do not seem so favorable. In the future we would like to extend our framework to multiagent scenarios in order to test the appearance of socially-aware behaviors by the agents. This could be done by adding a social intrinsic reward-feature that evaluates whether certain behaviors by the agents are considerate in relation to the overall fitness of the population instead of considering only their own individual fitness.

Acknowledgments. This work was partially supported by the Portuguese Fundação para a Ciência e a Tecnologia (INESC-ID multiannual funding) through the PIDDAC Program funds. The first author acknowledges the PhD grant SFRH/BD/38681/2007 from the Fundação para a Ciência e a Tecnologia.

References

1. Aberdeen, D.: A (revised) survey of approximate methods for solving partially observable Markov decision processes. Technical report, NICTA (2003)
2. Ahn, H., Picard, R.: Affective cognitive learning and decision making: The role of emotions. In: EMCSR 2006: The 18th Europ. Meet. on Cyber. and Syst. Res. (2006)
3. Broekens, D.: Affect and learning: a computational analysis. Doctoral Thesis, Leiden University (2007)
4. Cardinal, R., Parkinson, J., Hall, J., Everitt, B.: Emotion and motivation: The role of the amygdala, ventral striatum, and prefrontal cortex. Neuroscience and Biobehavioral Reviews 26(3), 321–352 (2002)
5. Dawkins, M.: Animal minds and animal emotions. American Zoologist 40(6), 883–888 (2000)
6. El-Nasr, M., Yen, J., Ioerger, T.: FLAME - Fuzzy logic adaptive model of emotions. Auton. Agents and Multiagent Systems 3(3), 219–257 (2000)
7. Ellsworth, P., Scherer, K.: Appraisal processes in emotion. In: Handbook of Affective Sciences, pp. 572–595. Oxford University Press, Oxford (2003)
8. Gadanho, S., Hallam, J.: Robot learning driven by emotions. Adaptive Behavior 9(1), 42–64 (2001)

9. Leventhal, H., Scherer, K.: The relationship of emotion to cognition: A functional approach to a semantic controversy. Cognition & Emotion 1(1), 3–28 (1987)
10. Littman, M.: Memoryless policies: Theoretical limitations and practical results. From Animals to Animats 3, 238–245 (1994)
11. Moore, A., Atkeson, C.: Prioritized sweeping: Reinforcement learning with less data and less real time. Machine Learning 13, 103–130 (1993)
12. Ng, A., Harada, D., Russel, S.: Policy invariance under reward transformations: Theory and application to reward shaping. In: Proc. 16th Int. Conf. Machine Learning, pp. 278–287 (1999)
13. Niekum, S., Barto, A., Spector, L.: Genetic programming for reward function search. IEEE Trans. Autonomous Mental Development 2(2), 83–90 (2010)
14. Salichs, M., Malfaz, M.: Using emotions on autonomous agents. The role of Happiness, Sadness and Fear. In: AISB 2006: Adaption in Artificial and Biological Systems, pp. 157–164 (2006)
15. Singh, S., Jaakkola, T., Jordan, M.: Learning without state-estimation in partially observable Markovian decision processes. In: Proc. 11th Int. Conf. Machine Learning, pp. 284–292 (1994)
16. Singh, S., Lewis, R., Barto, A., Sorg, J.: Intrinsically motivated reinforcement learning: An evolutionary perspective. IEEE Trans. Autonomous Mental Development 2(2), 70–82 (2010)
17. Sorg, J., Singh, S., Lewis, R.: Internal rewards mitigate agent boundedness. In: Proc. 27th Int. Conf. Machine Learning, pp. 1007–1014 (2010)
18. Sutton, R., Barto, A.: Reinforcement Learning: An Introduction. MIT Press, Cambridge (1998)

The Good, the Bad and the Neutral: Affective Profile in Dialog System-User Communication

Marcin Skowron[1], Stefan Rank[1], Mathias Theunis[2], and Julian Sienkiewicz[3]

[1] Austrian Research Institite for Artificial Intelligence, Vienna, Austria
{marcin.skowron,stefan.rank}@ofai.at
[2] School of Humanities and Social Sciences, Jacobs University, Bremen, Germany
m.theunis@jacobs-university.de
[3] Faculty of Physics, Warsaw University of Technology, Warsaw, Poland
julas@if.pw.edu.pl

Abstract. We describe the use of affective profiles in a dialog system and its effect on participants' perception of conversational partners and experienced emotional changes in an experimental setting, as well as the mechanisms for realising three different affective profiles and for steering task-oriented follow-up dialogs. Experimental results show that the system's affective profile determines the rating of chatting enjoyment and user-system emotional connection to a large extent. Self-reported emotional changes experienced by participants during an interaction with the system are also strongly correlated with the type of applied profile. Perception of core capabilities of the system, realism and coherence of dialog, are only influenced to a limited extent.

Keywords: affective dialog system, affective profile, conversational agent, affective computing, HCI.

1 Introduction

Collective emotions play a pivotal role in creating, forming and breaking-up of online-communities. Recently, the study of these phenomena became an active interest for policy-makers, business professionals and multi-disciplinary research teams. One approach for studying collective emotions on the Internet focus on analysis of online discussions, such as blogs, newsgroups and Twitter-like posts[1] to understand the role of sentiment and other emotional factors for active Internet users. Using a complementary approach, we develop affective dialog systems to extend these analyses quantitatively, by engaging less active users, and qualitatively, by extending the interaction scope and engaging users in follow-up dialogs about introduced topics. The developed systems serve as testbed for studying affective human-computer interaction and for evaluating affective components in robust real-world interactions with a diverse set of users.

Previous experiments [20], focused on the evaluation of a precursor of the presented dialog system in a VR environment [9]. There, the system was responsible for managing verbal communication of a virtual agent, the Affect

[1] http://www.cyberemotions.eu/

S. D´Mello et al. (Eds.): ACII 2011, Part I, LNCS 6974, pp. 337–346, 2011.

Bartender. Results demonstrated that the system was capable of establishing an emotional connection, and further of conducting a realistic and enjoyable dialog. Obtained ratings did not differ from a Wizard-of-Oz (WOZ) setting. The experiments described below focuses on the role of a dialog system's affective profile and its effect on the communication with users and on their perception of the system capabilities. We aimed at evaluating the system in a setting typical for online, text-based communication platforms, i.e., web chat rooms. In this paper, we present the system architecture and the mechanisms used for affective profiles and character traits. We introduce the components for conducting task-oriented follow-up dialogs, i.e., dialogs about introduced "hot-topics" aiming at acquisition of data on users' affective responses and attitudes regarding these issues. After describing the interaction setting, we present the experimental procedure, characteristics of participants and discuss the system evaluation results.

2 Relevant Work

In interactions between humans and artificial agents, the capability to detect signs of human emotions and suitably react to them can enrich communication. For example, display of empathic emotional expressions enhanced users' performance [14], led to an increase in users' satisfaction [16] and improved the perception and assessment of virtual agents [11]. However, an agent with emotional facial expressions incongruous to the dialog situation is perceived more negatively compared to an agent that expresses no emotion [11]. In [4,10] applications of aspects of emotion detection and generation of personality traits were proposed for spoken and multi-modal dialog systems and ECA prototypes. Mello et al. [6] describe an intelligent tutoring system that integrates affect-sensing in order to classify emotions using facial expressions, body movements and conversational cues (i.e., correctness of an answer, verbosity, reaction and response time). Bee at al. [2] presents a Virtual Agent that senses affect from users' voice and applies affective, non-verbal cues for generating emotional mimicry and displaying envelope feedback and empathy.

In our approach, we focus predominantly on the text modality and on the fusion of results from natural language processing and affective dialog management. Further, we examine the effect of a dialog system's affective profile on users' perception of the system and its effect on users' communication style and their expressions of affective states. The developed system is applied to robust, online interactions with a variety of users and provides data that extends the scope of analysis of users' emotion driven responses to online and offline events. Relevant prior work for acquiring information from users through artificial conversational entities was mostly focused on extending a base of conversational systems' response candidates [17] or accumulating knowledge useful for the addition to the massive repository of common-sense, real-world knowledge [22].

Extending databases of contextual and episodic information is a potentially infinite task. As time progresses, external circumstances change and knowledge accumulates. However, other conversational components such as human emotions are comparatively stable and, at least to some degree, universal [5,7]. Because of their constant influence on human communication [12], they are immensely valuable for designing conversational systems. For instance, it has recently been demonstrated that affective mood influences the disclosure of personal information, both in real and virtual setups [8]. Such disclosure is an essential part of human relationship formation [1]. Conversational systems able to detect and respond to human affect therefore have the potential to improve HCI more than by accumulating knowledge bases—though both approaches are complementary.

3 Dialog System Architecture

The dialog system used in the experiments is equipped with three distinct affective profiles (positive, negative, neutral). The system is responsible for the management of text-based communication between an agent (the virtual bartender) and a user in an online web chat environment. The main objectives for the system in this interaction scenario are:

1. Realistic and coherent dialogs,
2. Conducive setting for communication (i.e. acquisition of large data sets),
3. Introducing and conducting task-oriented dialogs related to "hot topics" in order to acquire users' affective states and their stance towards the issues,
4. Maintaining a consistent affective profile (positive, negative, or neutral) throughout the whole communication with users.

The characteristic of online, real-time and unrestricted interactions with a wide range of users influenced the selection of methods and design decisions. We aimed at: (i) robustness regarding erroneous natural language input, (ii) responsiveness, (iii) extensibility regarding modification of used components and application scenarios. Below we provide an overview of the main system components and present mechanisms used for simulating affective profiles. For a detailed description of the system architecture refer to [18,20]. Changes, compared with our previous experiments [20], included the introduction of the Affective Profile Control Component (APCC) and extensions of the core system mechanisms for generating response candidates: Affect Listeners Dialog Scripting (ALDS) [18] and Affect Bartender AIML set (AB-AIML) [20]. We introduced a new component for modifying system responses to conform to a specific affective profile: Post-processing of System Responses. Fig.1 presents the top-level layers of the system architecture (communication, perception, control) and the interaction loop with the environment. Fig.2 shows an excerpt of the Perception Layer annotation for example inputs[2].

[2] The Perception Layer, cf. [19], annotates both, user utterances and system response candidates. DA- dialog act classes, SC- sentiment class (-1,0,1), NS/PS- neg./pos. sentiment (-5...-1, 1...5) [13], DR- drink instance, EM- exclamation mark, LC- categories in LIWC dictionary [15]. The ANEW classifier assigns valence (AV), arousal (AA), dominance (AD) between 1 and 9 [3].

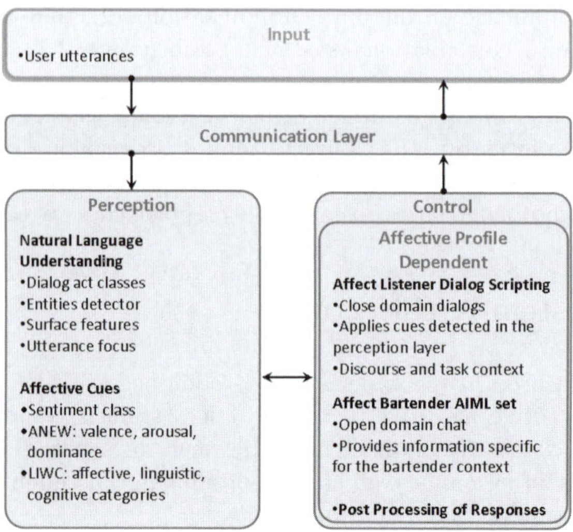

Fig. 1. Interaction loop and dialog system layers

Input	Perception Layer Output (excerpt)
You must be kidding! No more pina colada?	DA-Statement SC- -1 NS- -3 PS-1 DR-pina colada EM-1 LC-Social:Discrep:Certain AV-6.91 AA-5.27 AD-5.07
I really like being here! :=)	DA-Statement SC-1 NS- -1 PS-5 EE-smile LC-Affect:Posemo:CogMech AV-0.0 AV-0.0 AD-0.0
Didn't you forget to pay the bill last time??	DA-ynQuestion SC- -1 NS–3 PS-3 LC-Money:Work:Past:Negate AV-5.31 AA-4.64 AD-4.63

Fig. 2. Perception Layer – annotation example

3.1 Affective Profiles for a Dialog System

We define an *artificial affective profile* as a coarse-grained simulation of affective characteristics of an individual, corresponding to dominant, observable affective traits, that can be consistently demonstrated by a system during the course of its interactions with users. In this round of experiments, three distinct affective profiles were provided to the dialog system: positive, negative and neutral, limiting variations to baseline levels of positive and negative affectivity in personality [21]. Each affective profile aims at a consistent demonstration of character traits of the "Affect Bartender" system that could be described as, respectively:

- cooperative, emphatic, supporting, positively enhancing, focusing on similarities with a user,
- conflicting, confronting, focusing on differences with a user,
- professional, focused on job, not responding to expressions of affect.

Affective Profiles in Affect Listeners Dialog Scripting (ALDS). ALDS is an information state based dialog management component that uses a set of information cues provided by a perception layer to control dialog progression, cf. [18,19] for details on concept and implementation. The ALDS set used in previous experiments [20] was extended to offer the required, profile-dependent, variety of system response candidates and dialog scenarios. In particular, the following extensions were introduced:

- **affective variety:** new interaction scenarios and template-based response instructions that match the whole spectrum of the affective profiles,
- **affective responsiveness:** ALDS-based mechanism to select responses according to affective profiles and affective expressions detected in user utterances. E.g., positive - prefer similarity with users' expressions; negative - prefer dissimilarity.
- **dialog context:** analysis of local dialog context for initiating the task-oriented scenarios.

Further, new ALDS-based interaction scenarios were provided for conducting task-oriented dialogs with users, i.e., querying about users' initial responses and current stance towards selected topics of interest. The list of topics introduced to the discussion was selected based on their importance at the time of conducting the experiments (December 2010) for the participants (people of Polish nationality): (i) announcement of a tax increase for the year 2011, (ii) accusations about alleged bribery related to the Polish-Ukrainian winning bid for the organisation of 2012 European Soccer Championships, (iii) introduction of a smoking prohibition in public places.

For managing dialogs, ALDS scenarios depend on the discovery of particular cues in user utterances such as e.g., specific Dialog Act classes (Agreement, Rejection, yAnswer, whQuestion, etc.), LIWC categories or a positive or negative sentiment value. These influence dialog progression and enable the system to generate responses that match its affective profile. E.g., in the "hot-topics" part of a dialog, the positive affective profile relies on the assessment of the sentiment value (PS/NS from a Lexicon-Based Sentiment Classifier[13]) of a user response to a question "What was your first reaction when you heard about this?", when deciding on the suitable response, e.g. for ($PS+NS < 0$) - "You don't seem to be happy about this too. Can you tell me why does this news affect you?".

The initiation of a particular ALDS-based interaction scenario depends on dialog progression (i.e., number and type of message exchanges so far) and the local dialog context. The analysis of dialog context enables the system to avoid e.g., sudden changes of topic when there is sufficient evidence that such a change would break the dialog progression. In particular, new scenarios cannot be initiated when the system is already conducting other, task-oriented scenarios. Further, a new scenario cannot be started when the Dialog Act classes assigned to the last user's utterance includes categories such as: DA-ynQuestion, DA-whQuestion, DA-Order. Fig.3 presents an excerpt of an interaction log illustrating the change between task-specific parts of the dialog (here, ordering drinks

System: here you are! enjoy! [order served]
User: thank you
assessment of a dialog context: ability to start a new task oriented dialog
System: Have you heard that they want to raise the taxes in the next year? Do you think this decision was really necessary?
User: its annoying but i think its necessary
System: What was your first reaction when you heard about this?
User: angry
perception layer annotation (excerpt):LC-Affect:Negemo:Anger
SC- -1 NS- -3 PS-1 AV-2.85 AA-7.17 AD-5.55
System: You don't seem to be happy about this too. Can you tell me why does this news affect you?
User: because they promised not to rise it up
LC-CogMech:Cause:Social:They:Affect:CogMech:Negate **SC- -1 NS- -2 PS-1**
System: I feel very similar about it! It is a pleasure to talk with you. The next drink is on me :-)

Fig. 3. Dialog excerpt (positive profile) related to a hot-topic of discussion

and acquisition of current stance, initial response and affective states regarding tax increases).

Besides the "hot-topic" discussion part of a dialog, the profile-dependent, ALDS-based scenarios were also provided for "drinks and snacks ordering" and "hobby" scenarios, as well as for the ALDS-based system comments related to the user's affective states (based on LIWC categories and sentiment classification), each in three different versions matching the profiles.

Affective Profiles in AIML sets (AB-AIML). The AB-AIML set used in the previous round of experiments and described in more detail in [20] was extended to contain a variety of response templates suitable for the affective profiles. Based on an analysis of data from previous experiments, a sub-set of most frequently used templates was identified. This set included e.g., questions and comments about the user, messages used at the beginning and at the end of a dialog and confusion statements. In total, for the above presented categories, 133 response templates were provided: 40 positive, 55 negative and 38 neutral.

Affective Profile-Dependent Post-processing of System Responses. To achieve a consistent affective characteristic for all the responses generated by the system with a particular affective profile, we introduced profile-dependent post-processing of system responses. System response candidates are modified aiming at a specific affective profile. This is a crucial functionality that influences a majority of system-generated responses, for which no specific profile-dependent interaction scenarios or templates are present beforehand. The mechanism processes a response candidates and modifies (by adding or removing words) discovered positive or negative expressions, words and/or emoticons. For example, for the negative profile, the component removes text chunks that contain words, classified as "positive" (e.g., glad, happy, welcome, great, sir, please) from response candidates.

4 Experimental Method

For conducting experiments, a browser-based communication interface, resembling a typical web chat-room environment was developed: a user input field at the bottom of the screen and a log of communication above. Participants interacted with all three affective profiles in turn, once with each. To avoid ordering effects in the evaluation of systems, the actual sequence was randomly and evenly assigned and the list of evaluation statements was displayed to users before the start of the first interaction so that they could familiarize themselves with the statements to be rated. These statements were:

1. I enjoyed chatting with the conversational partner during the just completed interaction.
2. I found a kind of "emotional connection" between myself and the conversational partner.
3. I found the dialog with the conversational partner to be realistic.
4. I found the dialog to be coherent. In other words, the sequence of responses of the conversational partner made sense.
5. I noticed a positive emotional change in myself during the interaction.
6. I noticed a negative emotional change in myself during the interaction.
7. I would like to chat again with this particular conversational partner in the future.

During the experiments, after each experimental condition corresponding to a single affective profile, participants were asked to express their agreement or disagreement with the above presented statements on a five-point Likert scale (i.e., from 1 = *strongly disagree* to 5 = *strongly agree*). Participants interacted with the dialog system in an unsupervised manner and were aware that they talk with an artificial system. Interactions were always initiated by the system, i.e. the system provided the first utterance, and stopped after 7 minutes, with a suitable closing response followed by the display of the questionnaire. To further increase the number of system-user message exchanges compared to previous experiments [20], no artificial delays (e.g., a simulation of thinking or typing) were used in this experiment.

91 participants (33 female, 58 male), aged between 18 and 52, completed interactions in all three experimental settings resulting in 273 interaction logs. English, the language in which the experiments were conducted, was not their native language, but all participants who completed the set of interactions had at least average communication skills in this language.

5 Experimental Results

A repeated-measures analysis of variance (ANOVA) revealed the expected main effects of the dialog system's affective profile (positive, neutral, or negative) on all dependent measures: chatting enjoyment, subjective feeling of emotional connection, perception of dialog realism and coherence, participants self-reported positive or negative emotional change experienced during the interaction, as well as the willingness to chat again with a system that uses a particular type of affective profile (all Fs(2, 180) > 4.44, ps < .05). These effects were characterized by significant linear trends for all measures (all Fs(1, 90) > 6.60, ps < .05), reflecting the increasingly negative ratings of participants for progressively less positive affective profile of the system.

Pairwise comparisons with Bonferroni correction demonstrate significant differences on all measures between the positive and negative affective profiles (see Fig. 4). Additional differences are found between neutral and non-neutral profiles on some measures, such as enjoyment or desire to chat again.

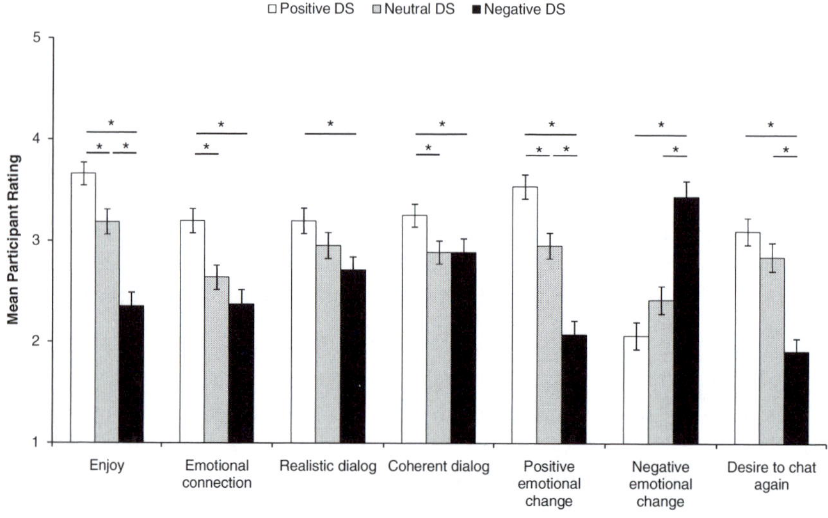

Fig. 4. Participant's mean ratings on all dependent variables, of their interactions with the dialog systems with three different affective profiles (positive, neutral, negative). An asterisk indicates a significant difference (at $p < .05$) between two types of affective profile used. Error bars represent 1 SE.

The effect sizes (i.e., the proportion of variance in measures (enjoyment, emotional connection, etc.) due to the differences in affective profile) vary. They are the lowest for dialog realism and coherence ($\eta_p^2 = .06$ and $\eta_p^2 = .05$, respectively), and biggest for enjoyment and the feeling of a positive emotional change ($\eta_p^2 = .31$ and $\eta_p^2 = .32$, respectively). In other words, the difference in dialog system profile does not have a large impact on how real or how coherent participants perceive it to be. However, it has a much bigger impact on the enjoyment of the conversation and on the positive emotional changes felt during the conversation.

6 Conclusions

In this paper, we have presented an implementation of affective profiles in a dialog system and its evaluation in an experiment with 91 participants.

The proposed components responsible for the realization of affective variety of system responses were integrated with a previously presented system architecture that has been evaluated in a VR setting, obtaining results on par with a WOZ setting regarding dialog realism, chatting enjoyment and participants' feeling of an emotional connection with the system. In the current experiment, participants conducted tests online, using only textual modality, in a setting typical for casual Internet activities. The presented experiments focused on the assessment of the effect of an affective profile and its influence on communication processes and system perception. The results demonstrate that the implemented affective profiles to a large extent determined the assessment of the users' emotional connection and enjoyment from the interaction with the dialog systems, while the perception of core capabilities of the system, i.e. dialog coherence and dialog realism, were only influenced to a limited extent. Further, the emotional changes experienced by the experiment participants during the online interactions were strongly correlated with the type of applied profile. The affective profile induced changes to various aspects of the conducted dialogs, e.g., communication style and the users' expressions of affective states.

Acknowledgments. The work reported in this paper is partially supported by the European Commission under grant agreements CyberEmotions (FP7-ICT-231323) and IRIS (FP7-ICT-231824). The Austrian Research Institute for AI is supported by the Austrian Federal Ministry for Transport, Innovation, and Technology.

References

1. Altman, I., Taylor, D.: Social penetration: The development of interpersonal relationships. Holt, Rinehart & Winston (1973)
2. Bee, N., André, E., Vogt, T., Gebhard, P.: First ideas on the use of affective cues in an empathic computer-based companion. In: AAMAS 2009 Workshop on Empathic Agents (2009)
3. Bradley, M., Lang, P.: Affective norms for english words (anew). Univ. of Florida (1999)
4. Cavazza, M., de la Cámara, R.S., Turunen, M., Gil, J.R., Hakulinen, J., Crook, N., Field, D.: how was your day?: an affective companion eca prototype. In: Proc. of the 11th Ann. Meeting of the SIG on Discourse and Dialogue, SIGDIAL 2010, pp. 277–280. Ass. for Computational Linguistics, Stroudsburg (2010)
5. Darwin, C.: The expression of the emotions in man and animal Murray (1872)
6. Dmello, S.K., Craig, S.D., Gholson, B., Franklin, S.: Integrating affect sensors in an intelligent tutoring system. In: Affective Interactions: The Computer in the Affective Loop Workshop at 2005 Intl. Conf. on Intelligent User Interfaces, 2005, pp. 7–13. AMC Press (2005)
7. Ekman, P., Friesen, W.V.: Constants across cultures in the face and emotion. J. of Personality and Social Psychology 17(2), 124–129 (1971)
8. Forgas, J.P.: Affective influences on self-disclosure: Mood effects on the intimacy and reciprocity of disclosing personal information. J. of Personality and Social Psychology 100(3), 449–461 (2011)

9. Gobron, S., Ahn, J., Quentin, S., Thalmann, D., Skowron, M., Rank, S., Paltoglou, G., Thelwall, M., Kappas, A.: 3d-emochatting: an interdisciplinary communication model for vr chatting. In Review Process (submitted)
10. Konstantopoulos, S.: An embodied dialogue system with personality and emotions. In: Proc. of the 2010 Workshop on Companionable Dialogue Systems, CDS 2010, pp. 31–36. Ass. for Computational Linguistics, Stroudsburg (2010)
11. Ochs, M., Pelachaud, C., Sadek, D.: An empathic virtual dialog agent to improve human-machine interaction (2008)
12. Osgood, C.E., Suci, G.J., Tannenbaum, P.H.: The measurement of meaning. Univ. of Illinois Press, Urbana (1957)
13. Paltoglou, G., Gobron, S., Skowron, M., Thelwall, M., Thalmann, D.: Sentiment analysis of informal textual communication in cyberspace. In: Proc. Engage 2010. Springer LNCS State-of-the-Art Survey, pp. 13–25 (2010)
14. Partala, T., Surakka, V.: The effects of affective interventions in human-computer interaction. Interacting with Computers 16(2), 295–309 (2004)
15. Pennebaker, J.W., Francis, M.E., Booth, R.K.: Linguistic Inquiry and Word Count: LIWC 2001. Erlbaum Publishers, Mahwah (2001)
16. Prendinger, H., Mori, J., Ishizuka, M.: Using human physiology to evaluate subtle expressivity of a virtual quizmaster in a mathematical game. Int. J. Hum.-Comput. Stud. 62(2), 231–245 (2005)
17. Schumaker, R.P., Liu, Y., Ginsburg, M., Chen, H.: Evaluating mass knowledge acquisition using the alice chatterbot: The az-alice dialog system. Int. J. of Man-Machine Studies 64(11), 1132–1140 (2006)
18. Skowron, M.: Affect listeners: Acquisition of affective states by means of conversational systems. In: Esposito, A., Campbell, N., Vogel, C., Hussain, A., Nijholt, A. (eds.) Second COST 2102. LNCS, vol. 5967, pp. 169–181. Springer, Heidelberg (2010)
19. Skowron, M., Paltoglou, G.: Affect bartender - affective cues and their application in a conversational agent. In: IEEE Symposium Series on Computational Intelligence 2011, Workshop on Affective Computational Intelligence. IEEE, Los Alamitos (2011)
20. Skowron, M., Pirker, H., Rank, S., Paltoglou, G., Ahn, J., Gobron, S.: No peanuts! affective cues for the virtual bartender. In: Proc. of the Florida Artificial Intelligence Research Society Conf. AAAI Press, Menlo Park (2011)
21. Watson, D., Tellegen, A.: Toward a consensual structure of mood. Psychological Bulletin 98(2), 219–235 (1985)
22. Witbrock, M., Baxter, D., Curtis, J., Schneider, D., Kahlert, R., Miraglia, P., Wagner, P., Panton, K., Matthews, G., Vizedom, A.: An interactive dialogue system for knowledge acquisition in cyc. In: Proc. of the IJCAI 2003 Workshop on Mixed-Initiative Intelligent Systems (2003)

Effect of Affective Profile on Communication Patterns and Affective Expressions in Interactions with a Dialog System

Marcin Skowron[1], Mathias Theunis[2], Stefan Rank[1], and Anna Borowiec[3]

[1] Austrian Research Institute for Artificial Intelligence, Vienna, Austria
{marcin.skowron,stefan.rank}@ofai.at
[2] School of Humanities and Social Sciences, Jacobs University, Bremen, Germany
m.theunis@jacobs-university.de
[3] Gemius SA, Warsaw, Poland
anna.borowiec@gemius.pl

Abstract. Interlocutors' affective profile and character traits play an important role in interactions. In the presented study, we apply a dialog system to investigate the effects of the affective profile on user-system communication patterns and users' expressions of affective states. We describe the data-set acquired from experiments with the affective dialog system, the tools used for its annotation and findings regarding the effect of affective profile on participants' communication style and affective expressions.

Keywords: affective profile, dialog system, affective computing, HCI.

1 Introduction

Emotionally driven online behavior is traceable in a wide range of human communication processes on the Internet. Here, the sum of individual emotions of a large number of users, with their interconnectivity and complex dynamics, influence the formation, evolution and breaking-up of online communities. Our research concentrates on dyadic communication as a fundamental building block for the modeling of more complex, multi-agent communication processes. Using artificial conversational entities, i.e. affective dialog systems, we investigate *the role of emotions* in online, real-time, natural-language-based communication.

In our current research we develop dialog systems and apply them to communicate with members of various e-communities to probe for affective states and background knowledge related to those states (Affect Listeners). These systems communicate with users in a predominantly textual modality, rely on integrated affective components for detecting textual expressions of the users' affective states, and use the acquired information to aid selection and generation of responses. Affect Listeners interact with users via a range of communication channels and interfaces (e.g., Internet Relay Chat (IRC), Jabber, online chat-site interface) and were already integrated as dialog management backbone of a virtual human, the

S. D´Mello et al. (Eds.): ACII 2011, Part I, LNCS 6974, pp. 347–356, 2011.

"Virtual Bartender", in a 3D environment [7]. Evaluation results showed that the system ratings for the dialog realism, participants' feeling of an emotional connection with an artificial conversational partner and of chatting enjoyment did not differ from these obtained in a Wizard-of-Oz (WOZ) setting [21].

This paper presents analysis of users communication recorded during new experiments with a revision of the dialog system, based on the "Affect Listeners" platform [19], in a setting typical for online, real-time, text-based communication (i.e., chat-rooms), equipped with three distinct affective profiles. *Artificial affective profile* is defined as a coarse-grained simulation of a personality, corresponding to dominant, extroverted character traits, that can be consistently demonstrated by a system during the course of its interactions with users. In this round of experiments, three distinct affective profiles were provided to the dialog system: positive, negative and neutral. Each affective profile aimed at a consistent demonstration of character traits of the "Affect Bartender" system that could be described as:

- cooperative, emphatic, supporting, positively enhancing, focusing on similarities with a user,
- conflicting, confronting, focusing on differences,
- professional, focused on job, not responding to affective expressions.

Findings related to the effect of affective profiles on the evaluation of the system and self-reported emotional changes experienced during the interaction are presented in[22]. In this paper, we focus on the effect of affective profiles on interaction patterns and participants' expressions of affective states. We consider a set of parameters such as: timing, textual expressions of affective states (as detected by Affective Norms for English Words dictionary (ANEW)[1], Lexicon Based Sentiment Classifier[16], Linguistic Inquiry and Word Count dictionary[17]), dialog act classes and surface features of the participants' communication style (e.g., wordiness, usage of emoticons).

2 Relevant Research

Prior study on the relationship between affective states and dialog patterns observed in the interactions with Intelligent Tutoring Systems, e.g. AutoTutor, was presented in [4]. The study focused on discovering the links between learning and emotions. It applied an emote-aloud procedure in which experiment participants verbalise their affective states experienced in the interaction with the tutoring system. The experimental results demonstrated significant correlations between accuracy of participants' answers and particular affective states, e.g. "confusion" indicating inaccurate answers, "eureka" as an indicator of students learning the material and "frustration" positively correlated with system's negative feedback and negatively correlated with a positive feedback. In our work, a different interaction setting is used, an online virtual bar. Communication content combines task-oriented dialogs specific to the interaction scenario and open domain dialogs regarding participants' attitude and affective responses to current issues of public debate, as well as their affective states expressed during interaction with the system. A further difference to an emote-aloud method: the presented analysis is based on an automated processing and annotation of the acquired dialog logs. In [2], models for utterance selection based on impoliteness that considers emotions, personality and social relations are presented. [13] describes a highly configurable system that generates utterances along the extroversion dimension and reports positive results regarding evaluation.

Taking into consideration limitations of the currently used experimental settings and the applied procedure, the motivation for our work is closer to the goals and visions presented recently e.g., by Picard [18] and Wilks [25]. In particular, the former postulates a change of the focus from comparing average statistics and self-report data across people experiencing emotions in labs to characterising patterns of data from individuals and clusters of similar individuals experiencing emotions in real life. The later stresses the importance of models of human-computer relationship forming a base for long-term interactions that should not be *inherently* tasks-based, e.g., lack of a stopping point to system conversation, role of politeness and users' preferences related to the a specific personality of a system, or its consistency in the long-term relationship.

3 Experimental Settings

3.1 Overview of Dialog System Architecture

The system architecture includes 3 main layers: perception, control and communication. The perception layer provides annotations for user utterances and system response candidates. It applies a set of natural language processing and affective processing tools and resources [20]. Based on the information cues provided by the perception layer, the control layer selects and, if necessary, modifies system response candidates. Further, the layer manages dialog progression taking into account the dialog context and the selected system's affective profile. The control layer uses an information state based dialog management component: Affect Listener Dialog Scripting (ALDS) [19] for the closed-domain and task-oriented parts of the dialog. For the open-domain chats, a template based mechanism and response generation instructions, Affect Bartender AIML set (AB-AIML) [20], are applied. The system's affective profile influences the selection of both ALDS scenarios and subsets of AB-AIML response instructions. To the remaining system response candidates for which no specific affective profile dependent interaction scenarios or system response instructions are provided, an automatic post-precessing is applied, i.e., addition, removal of positive or negative words. The mechanism aims at aligning the affective load, i.e. valence of system response candidates with the selected affective profile [22].

3.2 Characteristic of the Participants

The aim of the experiment was to study how affective profiles influence the perception of the system, communication patterns and participants' expressions of affective states. For this purpose invitations were sent to the panelists of a research panel[1]. This is a group of predominantly Polish users who expressed willingness to participate in various on-line surveys. During the study, respondents are in their "natural environment" - a place where they usually use the Internet, which is assumed to make them more receptive as well as spontaneous. For the majority of participants, English, the language in which the experiments were conducted, was not their native language, but all participants who completed the set of interactions had at least average communicative skills in this language. The usage of non-native languages in online interaction environments is a frequent phenomenon and provides the motivation for studying this type of communication. When filling out the registration form, an Internet user provides her demographic data (such as age, gender, education etc.).

Almost 70% of participants who completed the experiment are aged between 24 and 31 (inclusive) and over 90% of participants who completed the experiment are aged between 24 and 39 (inclusive). Over 95% of participants that completed the experiment access the Internet daily or almost daily. Over 70% of them are learning or studying.

3.3 Experimental Procedure

To avoid differences in the evaluation of systems related to the ordering of presentation of the different experimental conditions, the sequence of conditions was randomly and evenly assigned, and the list of evaluation statements was displayed to users before the start of the first interaction so that they could familiarize themselves with the statements to be rated. These statements were related to the following aspects of a completed interaction: chatting enjoyment, feeling of an "emotional connection" with the conversational partner, dialog realism and coherence. Further, participants were asked to report on emotional changes experienced during interaction (i.e., positive, negative) and willingness to chat again with the same partner. During the experiments, after each experimental condition corresponding to an affective profile, participants were asked to express their agreement or disagreement with each of the abovementioned aspects, using a five-point Likert scale from 'strongly disagree' to 'strongly agree'.

Participants completed experiments in an unsupervised manner and were aware that they talk with an artificial dialog system. Interactions were always initiated by an utterance from the system and stopped after 7 minutes, with a suitable closing response followed by the display of the questionnaire. No artificial delays (e.g., a simulation of thinking or typing) were used. System-user interactions were conducted with a web browser based communication interface, similar to popular online chat-rooms, implemented using Javascript and XML-RPC backends (AJAX).

4 Analysed Data-Set

Each participant performed three, seven minutes long interactions in a randomized order with three versions of the AffectBartender, introduced above. 91

[1] http://www.opinie.pl/

participants (33 female, 58 male), age between 18 and 42, completed interactions in all three experimental settings resulting in 273 interaction logs.

4.1 Applied Annotation Tools and Resources

The analysis of the presented data-set was conducted with a set of natural language processing and affective processing tools and resources, including: Support Vector Machine Based Dialog Act classifier, Lexicon Based Sentiment Classifier[16], Linguistic Inquiry and Word Count dictionary[17], ANEW dictionary based classifier [1]. Further, we analyzed timing information and surface features of participants communication style such as wordiness and usage of emoticons.

Dialog Act classifier. Dialog act classes are based on the annotation schema used in the NPS Chat Corpus [6]. The originally used taxonomy of DA classes (Accept, Bye, Clarify, Continuer, Emotion, Emphasis, Greet, No Answer, Other, Reject, Statement, Wh-Question, Yes Answer, Yes/No Question), was extended with an additional class "Order" (i.e. for ordering drinks). For this additional class 339 training instances were provided. The original NPS Chat class "System", irrelevant for the system-user dialogs, was excluded along with the set of corresponding training instances. For the presented taxonomy and training set, the Support Vector Machine Based DA classifier achieved 10-fold cross validation accuracy of 76.1%, improving the previously reported classification accuracy for the same data-set achieved with a Maximum Entropy based classifier - 71.2%[20].

Linguistic Inquiry and Word Count - LIWC. This lexical resource provides a classification of words along 64 linguistic, cognitive, and affective categories [17]. Among others, the resource provides 32 word categories for psychological processes (e.g., affective such as positive and negative emotions; cognitive such as insight and causation), 22 linguistic categories (e.g., adverbs, negations, swear words), 7 personal concern categories (e.g., home, work, leisure) 3 paralinguistic dimensions (fillers, assents), for almost 4500 words and word stems. For example, the word "compassion" is categorised in 3 categories: affective processes, positive emotion and social processes; the word "grief" in 4 categories: affective processes, negative emotion, sadness (psychological processes) and death (personal concern). In recent years, LIWC has been successfully applied in various psychological and psycholinguistic studies that included e.g., the investigation of linguistic style, the relations between language use and speaker personality [3].

Sentiment Classifier. Lexicon Based Sentiment classifier[16] provides information on: sentiment class (SC) i.e., negative {-1}, neutral {0}, and positive {1}. Further it assigns positive sentiment value (PS) {+1,...,+5} and negative sentiment value (NS) {-5, ..., -1} to user utterances and system response candidates. The initial scores for the input words are derived from two different emotional word-lists: The "General Inquirer" and "Linguistic Inquiry and Word Count" (LIWC) dictionary[2], the latter as enriched by [24]. The applied algorithm relies

[2] http://www.liwc.net

also on a detection of a range of linguistic features such as negation, capitalisation, intensifier, diminisher, etc., which modify the final sentiment score assigned to an input string. Higher absolute values indicate higher emotional content in that dimension and {-1,+1} indicate lack of emotion.

ANEW. Affective Norms for English Words dictionary is based on the assumption that emotion can be defined as a coincidence of values on a number of strategic dimensions [1]. It includes a set of 1,034 commonly used words, including verbs, nouns and adjectives. It provides information on emotional content of an input string, in three affective dimensions: valence, arousal and dominance, on the scale from 1 (very unpleasant, low arousal, low dominance/control) to 9 (very pleasant, high arousal, high dominance/control). For example "abuse" has the following mean score for the three presented affective dimensions (valence - 1.80, arousal - 6,83, dominance - 3.69).

4.2 Effects of Affective Profile on Users' Communication Style

Words and Timing. Repeated measures analyses of variance (ANOVAs) revealed an absence of effect of the affective profile on the number of utterances, words, and characters produced (all Fs(2, 180) < 1.78, $ps > .17$). Restriction in the duration of the interaction between participant and dialog system, as well as the constant responsiveness of the system across conditions most likely explain this result. Participants emitted a mean of 16 utterances ($SD = 7.4$) containing 5 words on average ($SD = 4.3$) during each interaction with the system. Furthermore, the affective profile neither had an effect on the response time (per utterance), $F(2, 180) = .62$, $p = .54$. Participants were equally fast in replying to system's utterances across all conditions.

Dialog Act and LIWC Spoken Categories classes. Omnibus repeated measures ANOVAs showed main effects of the dialog system affective profile on five Dialog Act classes: Statement, Emotion, ynQuestion, Continuer, and yAnswer (Fs(2, 180) > 3.98, $ps < .05$). Pairwise comparisons with Bonferroni correction (see Figure 1) show the expected presence of emotion in the positive compared to the neutral interaction, though the difference is not significant between the neutral an the negative condition[3]. Additionally, the positive profile elicited more statements, less polar questions and less continuations ("and" + text) compared to the negative profile. This higher number of statements and lower number of closed questions might indicate a more successful interaction (i.e., where the user tells more about him/herself and questions the system less), whereas the decrease in continuers remains open to interpretation. Through a similar analysis, a main effect of the affective profile on LIWC Assent class was found, $F(2, 180) = 8.39$, $p < .001$. Specifically, during interactions with the negative profile participants agreed (e.g., "ok", "yes", "yep") significantly less, compared with

[3] In all figures data are normalized with the number of utterances emitted by a user in a given interaction. Asterisks indicate significant differences at $p < .05$. Error bars indicate 1 standard error above and below the mean.

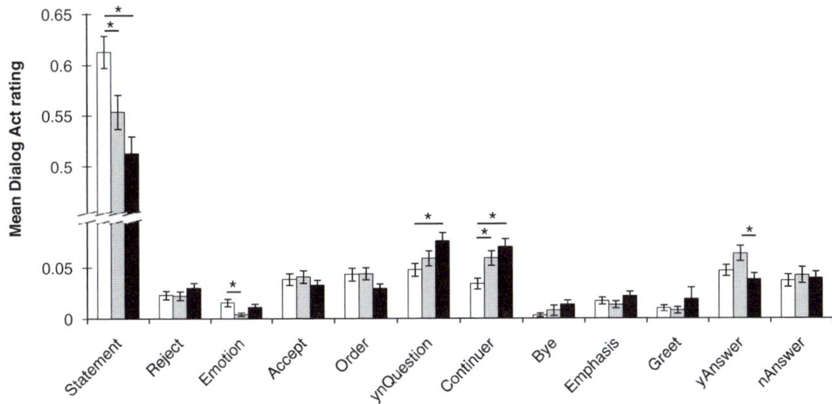

Fig. 1. Mean proportion of Dialog Act classes present in participant's utterances per condition. The Y-axis is broken due to the higher proportion of statements across all utterances, compared to all other classes. DS = Dialog System.

interactions with the two other profiles. No other significant effect was found on LIWC Spoken Categories classes (Fs(2, 180) $< .85$, $ps > .43$).

4.3 Effect of Affective Profile on Users' Expression of Affective States

After looking at formal aspects of speech, changes in users' affective states were examined through their utterances. [22] showed that user report significant affective changes after each interaction with an artificial affective profile. Investigations were therefore made upon subtle cues of influences of the affective profile on participant's emotions, exploiting the text produced. Based on previous research on emotional contagion [9], it was hypothesized that the dialog system's valence would linearly affect user's emotional state. In other terms, we expected to find changes toward a more negative emotional state in the user, elicited by exchanges with the dialog system's negative profile. The reverse effect was expected to be found in exchanges with the positive profile, and an absence of change was predicted for interactions with the neutral profile.

Emoticons, Sentiment Classifier, and ANEW lexicon. A first confirmation of the abovementioned hypothesis was found in a significant effect of the affective profile on user's production of positive emoticons, $F(2, 180) = 9.02$, $p < .001$. Pairwise comparisons reveal that users emitted significantly more positive emoticons while interacting with the positive affective profile, compared with interactions with the two other profiles. No effect was found concerning negative emoticons production, $F(2, 180) = 2.41$, $p = .09$. Furthermore, it was found that the dialog profile significantly affects the positive Sentiment Value found in users' utterances, $F(2, 180) = 15.08$, $p < .001$. As depicted in Figure 2 (Panel A), participants interacting with the negative profile produced text classified as significantly less positive compared with the two other conditions. No significant effect was found concerning the negative Sentiment Value, $F(2, 180) = .64$, $p = .53$. Additionally, the affective profile of the system was found to have a significant impact on valence, arousal, and dominance of user's utterances, based on ANEW ratings (Fs(2, 180) > 19.23, ps < .001). Compared with the two other conditions, when communicating with the negative profile, participants emitted utterances classified as significantly less positive, less activated, and less dominant (see Figure 2, Panel B).

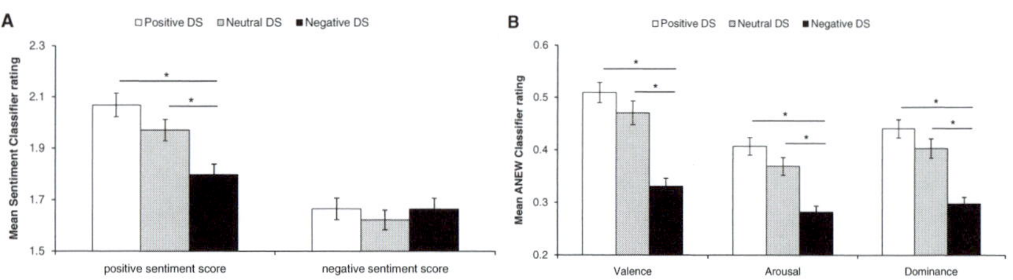

Fig. 2. Valence, arousal, and dominance ratings found in user exchanges with the dialog system (DS). Panel A shows the mean positive and negative Sentiment Classifier score per condition. Panel B shows the mean valence, arousal, and dominance scores based on the ANEW lexicon.

LIWC Psychosocial Processes classes. Finally, user's utterances were also analyzed using LIWC Psychosocial Processes classes. As hypothesized, the affective profile was found to have several significant effects on Affective Processes detected in text with LIWC's lexicon (Fs(2, 180) > 3.56, ps < .05). Multiple pairwise comparisons showed—among others—that, during interactions with the negative profile, users used significantly less positive emotion words (e.g., "love", "nice", "sweet"), more negative emotion words (e.g., "ugly", "nasty", "sad"), and more anger-related words (always compared with interactions with the two other profiles, positive and neutral).

5 Discussion and Outlook

Creating systems which adequately detect and respond to human emotions can have profound consequences. As research on emotional contagion showed [9], individuals tend to synchronize their affective states. When one interacts with a happy person, there is a higher probability that one will get happy as well [8], compared to the probability of getting upset or afraid. Social network analysis demonstrated that emotions not only spread from person to person, but throughout entire networks [10]. Moreover, it has now been clearly demonstrated that written text is affected by emotional states [23]. Research showed that emotional valence can accurately be detected in text [24], and linked to an individual's affective state [11]. Recent developments even evidenced the possibility to detect emotional categories from text (e.g., fear, anger, shame)[15]. Taking into account both streams of research, one showing that emotion is contagious, the other that it can be accurately detected, our approach has a high potential for enriching user's experience, and beyond. Combining an accurate detection of emotion in user text with an adequate emotional response from the system can enrich communication at a point close to human-human interaction [14]. Looking at the effect of such a design, the above described study presents an attempt at grasping the far-reaching implications of the development of an emotionally intelligent system. Effort now has to be put into increasing the level of compliance of the system architecture with psychological research [5], as well as taking into account the complex variations in user's affective experience [12]. Our future research includes further investigation of the effect of emotions in user-system interactions, e.g., social sharing of emotion, self-disclosure, both in the single and multiple users interaction environments.

Acknowledgments. The work reported in this paper is partially supported by the European Commission under grant agreements CyberEmotions (FP7-ICT-231323) and IRIS (FP7-ICT-231824). The Austrian Research Institute for AI is supported by the Austrian Federal Ministry for Transport, Innovation, and Technology.

References

1. Bradley, M.M., Lang, P.J.: Affective norms for english words (anew): Stimuli, instruction manual and affective ratings. Univ. of Florida (1999)
2. Campano, S., Sabouret, N.: A socio-emotional model of impoliteness for non-player characters. In: Proc. of the 8th Int. Conf. on Autonomous Agents and Multiagent Systems, AAMAS 2009, pp. 1123–1124. Int. Foundation for Autonomous Agents and Multiagent Systems, Richland (2009)
3. Chung, C.K., Pennebaker, J.W.: Revealing dimensions of thinking in open-ended self-descriptions: An automated meaning extraction method for natural language. J. of Research in Personality 42, 96–132 (2008)
4. D'Mello, S., Craig, S., Witherspoon, A., Sullins, J., McDaniel, B., Gholson, B., Graesser, A.: The relationship between affective states and dialog patterns during interactions with autotutor. In: Richards, G. (ed.) Proc. of World Conf. on E-Learning in Corporate, Government, Healthcare, and Higher Education 2005, pp. 2004–2011. AACE (October 2005)
5. Fontaine, J.R.J., Scherer, K.R., Roesch, E.B., Ellsworth, P.C.: The world of emotions is not two-dimensional. Psychological Science 18(12), 1050–1057 (2007)
6. Forsyth, E., Martell, C.: Lexical and discourse analysis of online chat dialog. In: Proc. of the First IEEE Int. Conf. on Semantic Computing, pp. 19–26 (2007)
7. Gobron, S., Ahn, J., Quentin, S., Thalmann, D., Skowron, M., Rank, S., Paltoglou, G., Thelwall, M., Kappas, A.: 3d-emochatting: an interdisciplinary communication model for vr chatting. In Review (submitted)

8. Hatfield, E., Cacioppo, J.T., Rapson, R.L.: Emotional contagion. Current Directions in Psychological Science 2(3), 96–99 (1993)
9. Hatfield, E., Cacioppo, J.T., Rapson, R.L.: Emotional Contagion. Cambridge Univ. Press, Cambridge (1994)
10. Hill, A.L., Rand, D.G., Nowak, M.A., Christakis, N.A.: Emotions as infectious diseases in a large social network: the sisa model. Proc. of the Royal Society B 277(1701), 3827–3835 (2010)
11. Kappas, A., Kuester, D., Theunis, M., Tsankova, E.: Cyberemotions: Subjective and physiological responses to reading online discussion forums. In: Society for Psychophysiological Research Abstracts for the Fiftieth Annual Meeting (2010)
12. Kuppens, P., Oravecz, Z., Tuerlinckx, F.: Feelings change: Accounting for individual differences in the temporal dynamics of affect. Journal of Personality and Social Psychology 99(6), 1042–1060 (2010)
13. Mairesse, F., Walker, M., Mehl, M., Moore, R.: Using linguistic cues for the automatic recognition of personality in conversation and text. J.of Artificial Intelligence Research 30, 457–500 (2007)
14. Mehrabian, A., Russell, J.A.: An Approach to Environmental Psychology. MIT Press, Cambridge (1974)
15. Neviarouskaya, A., Prendinger, H., Ishizuka, M.: Affect analysis model: novel rule-based approach to affect sensing from text. Natural Language Engineering 17(1), 95–135 (2011)
16. Paltoglou, G., Gobron, S., Skowron, M., Thelwall, M., Thalmann, D.: Sentiment analysis of informal textual communication in cyberspace. In: Proc. Engage 2010. Springer LNCS State-of-the-Art Survey, pp. 13–25 (2010)
17. Pennebaker, J.W., Francis, M.E., Booth, R.K.: Linguistic Inquiry and Word Count: LIWC 2001. Lawrence Erlbaum, Mahwah (2001)
18. Picard, R.W.: Emotion research by the people, for the people. Emotion Review 2 (2010)
19. Skowron, M.: Affect listeners. acquisition of affective states by means of conversational systems. In: Esposito, A., Campbell, N., Vogel, C., Hussain, A., Nijholt, A. (eds.) Second COST 2102. LNCS, vol. 5967, pp. 169–181. Springer, Heidelberg (2010)
20. Skowron, M., Paltoglou, G.: Affect bartender - affective cues and their application in a conversational agent. In: IEEE Symposium Series on Computational Intelligence 2011, Workshop on Affective Computational Intelligence. IEEE, Los Alamitos (2011)
21. Skowron, M., Pirker, H., Rank, S., Paltoglou, G., Ahn, J., Gobron, S.: No peanuts! affective cues for the virtual bartender. In: Proc. of the Florida Artificial Intelligence Research Society Conf. AAAI Press, Menlo Park (2011)
22. Skowron, M., Rank, S., Theunis, M., Sienkiewicz, J.: The good, the bad and the neutral: affective profile in dialog system-user communication. In: D'Mello, S., et al. (eds.) ACII 2011. Part I, LNCS, vol. 6974, pp. 337–346. Springer, Heidelberg (2011)
23. Tausczik, Y.R., Pennebaker, J.W.: The psychological meaning of words: Liwc and computerized text analysis methods. J. of Language and Social Psychology 29(1), 24–54 (2010)
24. Thelwall, M., Buckley, K., Paltoglou, G., Cai, D., Kappas, A.: Sentiment strength detection in short informal text. J. of the American Society for Information Science and Technology 61(12), 2544–2558 (2010)
25. Wilks, Y.: Is a companion a distinctive kind of relationship with a machine? In: Proc. of the 2010 Workshop on Companionable Dialogue Systems, Uppsala, Sweden, pp. 13–18. Association for Computational Linguistics (July 2010)

Persuasive Language and Virality in Social Networks

Carlo Strapparava, Marco Guerini, and Gözde Özbal

FBK-Irst
Via Sommarive 18
Povo, I-38100 Trento
{strappa,guerini,ozbal}@fbk.eu

Abstract. This paper aims to provide new insights on the concept of virality and on its structure - especially in social networks. We argue that: (a) virality is a phenomenon strictly connected to the nature of the content being spread (b) virality is a phenomenon with many affective responses, i.e. under this generic term several different effects of persuasive communication are comprised. To give ground to our claims, we provide initial experiments in a machine learning framework to show how various aspects of virality can be predicted according to content features. We further provide a class-based psycholinguistic analysis of the features salient for virality components.

1 Introduction

The effectiveness of a persuasive communication often depends on the nature of recipient-generated cognitive and affective responses. Analyzing and recognizing the impact of communication is of paramount importance in many theoretical and applied contexts.

For example, Persuasive NLP focuses on various techniques such as crowdsourcing [7] and corpus based methods [6] to address the various effects which persuasive communication can have in different contexts on different audiences.

In this context "virality" and data collected from social networks are burning topics for activities such as Viral Marketing - a set of marketing techniques using social networks to achieve various marketing objectives both in monitoring and promotion.

Buzz monitoring, for example, is the marketing technique for keeping track of consumer experiences with services and products. It involves checking and analyzing online sources such as forums, blogs, etc. in order to improve efficiency and reaction times. Moreover, identifying positive and negative customer affective responses (*white* and *black buzz*), can help to assess product and service demand, tackle crisis management, foster reputation online, etc. On the other side, as a promotional strategic goal, Viral Marketing campaigns can have to sustain *discussion* to get visibility for their product or to provoke *controversial* reactions to the brand (e.g. to strengthen the membership feeling). Many of the themes we have just sketched can be found in [12].

Generally speaking, virality refers to the tendency of a content to spread quickly in a community by word-of-mouth. In the spreading process there are several elements at play, e.g. the nature of the *spreader* and of the *audience*, the structure of the *network* through which the information is moving and the nature of the *content* itself. In this paper, we will mainly focus on the last point. First we will argue that virality hinges

S. D'Mello et al. (Eds.): ACII 2011, Part I, LNCS 6974, pp. 357–366, 2011.

on the nature of the content itself, and that it is a complex phenomenon which can be decomposed into several components. Then we will provide experiments, in a machine learning framework, showing how the various components of virality can be *separately* predicted using just the wording of the content being spread. Finally, we will provide a class-based analysis, from a psycholinguistic point of view, of the features salient for virality components.

2 Virality as a Content Dependent Phenomenon

Virality is a social phenomenon in which there are no "immune carriers". That is to say, a content is either viral or not. If a message is viral it will immediately spread, by no chance it will remain latent, waiting to awake. This means that although the study of epidemiology and information spreading in social networks is important, it does only partially account for content virality. Individuating the central nodes (i.e. the influencers) of a social network is certainly necessary if we want our content to spread quickly to a significant audience, but it will not grant its spreading to further nodes.

The book "The tipping point" [4], maintains that influencers have a central role in the spreading of a fashion or a product - even to further nodes - and this seems to contradict our idea. However, Gladwell's standpoint has also been criticized by some researchers [24]. Then, in our view, social network structure analysis accounts for *how* content spreads, rather than *why*; a similar claim is made in [22].

3 Virality as a Multifaceted Phenomenon

Traditional approaches based on "popularity metrics" (e.g. the number of *I_like*) are not sufficient to distinguish different affective responses within the community (see [5] for a discussion on the following concepts):

- *Virality*: generically it refers to the number of people who accessed a content in a given time interval.
- *Appreciation*: how much people like a given content, for example by clicking an *I_like* button.
- *Spreading*: how much people tend to share this content by forwarding it to other people.
- *Simple buzz*: how much people tend to comment a given content.
- *White buzz*: how much people tend to comment in a positive mood (e.g. "This is one of the best product I have ever bought").
- *Black buzz*: how much people tend to comment in a negative mood (e.g. "This product is a rip-off").
- *Raising discussion*: the ability to induce discussion among users.
- *Controversiality*: the ability to split audience affective responses (usually pro and against the given content).

4 Dataset and Virality Metrics

In this section, we will formalize some of the aforementioned phenomena using the Digg dataset described in [18]. This corpus allows us to define and analyze many of the above definitions in a unique framework. The formulae represent an initial attempt to model phenomena which have not been addressed before, and they can be refined as a future work.

Digg Dataset. Digg is a social bookmarking website where people can share, vote and comment "stories". Stories typically contain a `title`, a short textual description (`snippet`) and a link to the original web content. In this dataset the average length of the `title` is 7 words, the average length of `snippet` is 31 words. Users are allowed to publicly approve submitted stories with a process called "digging", and publicly approve or disapprove comments on submitted stories (called "DiggUp" and "DiggDown").

In Figure 1, an example of a Digg story is given. It has got 9,718 diggs, the `title` is "This Is Apple's Next iPhone" the `snippet` is "You are looking at Apple's next iPhone. It was found lost in a Bar in Redwood City, camouflaged to look like an iPhone 3GS. ..." The link to the original source is "gizmodo.com" and the user who submitted it is "turnipsun".

The data gathered from the site is a complete crawl spanning the months February, March and April 2009. Some statistics concerning the gathered data include: 1,195,808 submitted stories; 135,367 stories with at least one comments; 1,646,153 individual comments; 877,841 users who submitted a story/comment; 14,376,742 approvals (i.e. diggs).

Appreciation. Appreciation is connected to the number of diggs a story received. The formula for appreciation is:

$$A = ND \tag{A}$$

where ND represents the number of diggs for a given story.

Buzz and Spreading. Within the Digg community, the same story can be submitted only once. Therefore it is difficult to model the concept of spreading. In our view, the number of *different* users commenting on a story is a good hybrid measure to model buzz and spreading. The formula for Buzz and Spreading is:

$$BS = NUC \tag{BS}$$

where NUC is the number of different users commenting a story.

White and Black Buzz. To model black and white buzz, emotive feature annotation of Digg comments is required. The Digg corpus contains, for each comment, a `BinaryEmotion` field, which yields the results of an automatic classifications using a Lexicon-based approach; see [19] for further details. The `BinaryEmotion` field indicates whether the comment is considered as *positive*, *negative* or *neutral*. The formulae for White Buzz and for Black Buzz, using the `BinaryEmotion` field on the comment, are:

$$WB = (Positive > (Neutral + Negative)) \tag{WB}$$

$$BB = (Negative > (Neutral + Positive)) \tag{BB}$$

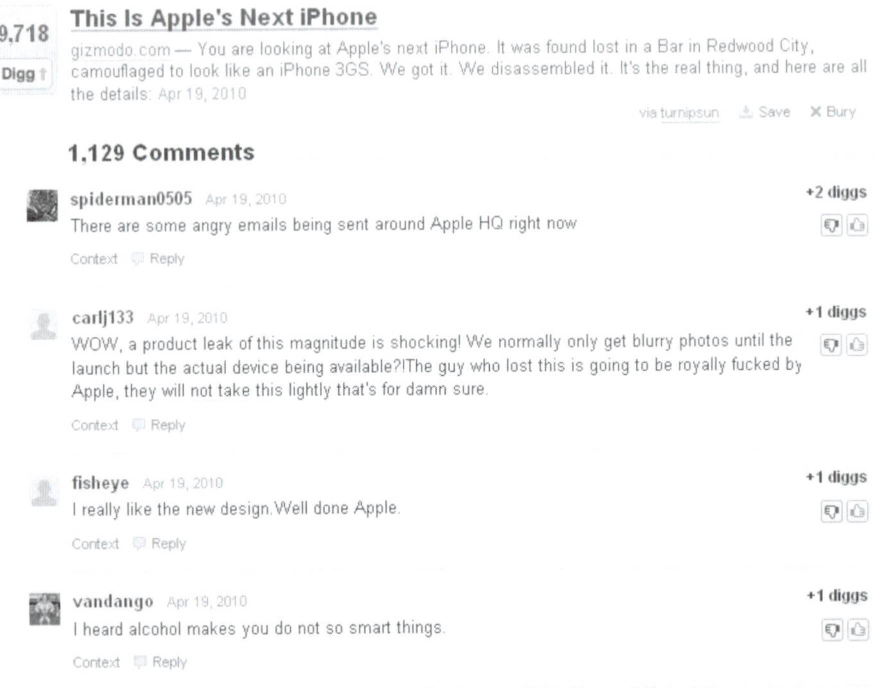

9,718
Digg
This Is Apple's Next iPhone
gizmodo.com — You are looking at Apple's next iPhone. It was found lost in a Bar in Redwood City, camouflaged to look like an iPhone 3GS. We got it. We disassembled it. It's the real thing, and here are all the details: Apr 19, 2010
via turnipsun Save Bury
1,129 Comments
spiderman0505 Apr 19, 2010
+2 diggs
There are some angry emails being sent around Apple HQ right now
Context Reply
carlj133 Apr 19, 2010
+1 diggs
WOW, a product leak of this magnitude is shocking! We normally only get blurry photos until the launch but the actual device being available?!The guy who lost this is going to be royally fucked by Apple, they will not take this lightly that's for damn sure.
Context Reply
fisheye Apr 19, 2010
+1 diggs
I really like the new design.Well done Apple.
Context Reply
vandango Apr 19, 2010
+1 diggs
I heard alcohol makes you do not so smart things.
Context Reply

Fig. 1. An example of Digg story

where *Negative*, *Neutral* and *Positive* indicate the number of comments for a given story, categorized as negative, neutral or positive, accordingly.

Raising-discussion. The number of comments alone do not state whether there has been a discussion among users about a story; we need to distinguish low level comments (i.e. *explicit* replies to other comments) from top level ones. The formula for raising discussion is:

$$RD = (NC_L/NC_T) * NUC \tag{RD}$$

where NC_T is the number of comments for a given story and NC_L is the number of (low-level) comments, i.e. comments which are replies to other comments.

Controversiality. The problem of opinion controversiality has received little attention, a notable exception being [3]. While their model comprises multiple classes (i.e. votes in a -3 to +3 scale), our model is binary: only "I like" (+1) or "I don't like" (-1) votes are allowed. Since stories cannot receive negative votes in Digg, we decided to consider the "diggsUp" and "diggsDown" of the associated comments. If the highest number of positive votes among comments is A and the highest number of negative votes is B, the formula for controversiality is:

$$C = min(A, B)/max(A, B) \tag{C}$$

$min(A, B)$ denotes the smaller value of A and B, and $max(A, B)$ denotes the larger of the two. This measure ranges from a minimum of 0 (total agreement, everybody who voted either liked or disliked the comments) to a maximum of 1 (highest controversiality, the sample votes splitted exactly into two).

5 Experiments

We conducted a series of preliminary experiments on the corpus in a machine learning framework to explore the feasibility of independently predicting the impact of stories according to the various metrics proposed. For every metric a specialized datasets was built.

For all the experiments we exploited Support Vector Machines (SVM) framework [23], in particular we used SVM-light under its default settings [10]. For every metric we conducted a binary classification experiment with ten-fold cross validation on the corresponding dataset. All datasets were balanced, i.e. 50% of evidently positive examples and 50% of evidently negative examples were collected. This accounts for a baseline of 0.5.

Dataset preprocessing. We focused only on the text present in the stories. As features we solely considered the words contained in the `title` and in the `snippet` of the story itself. To reduce data sparseness, we PoS-tagged all the collected words (using TreeTagger [21] and considering the PoS for nouns, verbs, adjectives and adverbs). We took into account lemmata instead of tokens. In the following experiments, we did not make any frequency cutoff or feature selection.

Appreciation. We considered as appreciated those stories which received more than 100 diggs (i.e. $A \geq 100$). In the DIGG dataset there are 16660 stories with this characteristic. Then, we randomly extracted an equal number of unappreciated stories (i.e. 0 or 1 digg) to obtain a dataset of 33320 instances.

Buzz. We considered as buzzed only stories which have a buzz score (BS) greater than or equal to 100. There are 3270 examples of buzzed stories, and we randomly extracted an equal number of non buzzed stories (i.e. 0 comments) to obtain a dataset of 6540 instances.

Controversiality. We considered as controversial stories only those which have a controversial score (C) ≥ 0.9. We collected 3315 examples of controversial stories, and we randomly extracted an equal number of non controversial stories to obtain a dataset of 6630 instances.

Raising-discussion. We considered as positive examples only the stories with a RD score > 50. Accordingly, we collected 3786 examples of stories raising discussion, and then we randomly extracted an equal number of negative examples to obtain a dataset of 7572 instances.

5.1 Discussion

As far as the performance is concerned, we can state that the simpler metrics (namely *buzz* and *appreciation*) have much higher F1 (see Table 1). This can be explained by

Table 1. Results for the classification tasks

	F1 measure
Appreciation	0.78
Buzz	0.81
Controversiality	0.70
Raising-Discussions	0.68

the fact that they represent simpler and more direct indicators of audience reaction to a given content. Still, also complex metrics (i.e. *raising-discussion* and *controversiality*) yield a good F1, which suggests that these phenomena can be automatically predicted as well, and that they are highly correlated to the content being spread.

White and Black Buzz. We considered WB and BB for stories with $NUC \geq 100$. According to the formulae, we found 254 stories raising white buzz, and 1499 stories raising black buzz. These examples are too few for a machine learning approach and, since the `BinaryEmotion` field is automatically calculated, results may not be very reliable. Nonetheless, we can do some qualitative remarks: it seems that a negative mood (black buzz) is predominant in the dataset. This predominance can be explained considering that DIGG does not allow "diggsDown" for stories. So people could be inclined to explicitly express (with comment) their dislike. Anyway this issue deserves further exploration.

6 Dominant Word Classes in Viral Texts

To explore the characteristics of viral texts, we used the method proposed in [17]. We calculate a score associated with a given class of words, as a measure of saliency for the given word class inside the collection of *appreciated*, *buzzed*, etc. texts.

Given a class of words $C = \{W_1, W_2, ..., W_N\}$, we define the class coverage in the texts collection A as the percentage of words from A belonging to the class C:

$$Coverage_A(C) = \frac{\sum_{W_i \in C} Frequency_A(W_i)}{Size_A} \quad \text{(COV)}$$

where $Frequency_A(W_i)$ represents the total number of occurrences of word W_i inside the corpus A, and $Size_A$ represents the total size (in words) of the corpus A. Similarly, we define the class C coverage for the whole corpus of Digg stories $\mathcal{D}$.

The *dominance score* of the class C in the given corpus A is then defined as the ratio between the coverage of the class in the examples set A with respect to the coverage of the same class in the corpus $\mathcal{D}$:

$$Dominance_A(C) = \frac{Coverage_A(C)}{Coverage_{\mathcal{D}}(C)} \quad \text{(DOM)}$$

A dominance score higher than 1 indicates a class that is dominant in collection A. A score lower than 1 indicates a class that is unlikely to appear in collection A. We use the classes of words as defined in the Linguistic Inquiry and Word Count (LIWC), which was developed for psycholinguistic analysis [20]. LIWC includes about 2,200 words and word stems grouped into about 70 broad categories relevant to psychological processes (e.g., EMOTION, COGNITION).

Sample words for relevant classes in our study are shown in Table 2. Table 3 shows the top ranked classes along with their dominance score. In the following we clustered these classes according to macro-categories that emerged from the analysis.

Emotion dimension. There are categories (e.g. DEATH) that are dominant in all the virality corpora. This indicates that in general tragic events (associated with negative emotions) tend to spread more in social networks. This finding on negative emotions related items is further supported in (i) Raising-discussion and Buzz by the cognitive process class INHIB, (ii) Raising-discussion and Controversiality by the correlation with the ANGER class (while other negative emotions are not relevant). On the other hand, positive emotions and positive concepts tend to be less "viral" in three classes out of four: POSEMO and OPTIM for Buzz and Raising-discussion, FRIENDS for Appreciation.

Certainty dimension. With regards to information presentation we observe a concordance among Buzz, Appreciation and Raising-discussion on positive linguistic processes (ASSENT), while for Controversiality there is a correlation with negative support of the information (NEGATE). Nonetheless, for appreciation we found a "mitigating" effect of the assent tendency due to the cognitive process class TENTAT.

Style dimension. With regard to the language "style" we see that, while swearing language is used both in Buzz and Raising-discussion, this is not the case for Appreciation and, surprisingly, Controversiality (where we could have expected more swearing due to flames).

Topic dimension. With regard to "topics" we found that religion is not dominant in Appreciation, but as it can have been expected, it is in Controversiality.

In general Buzz and Rasing-discussion are the sets with the higher overlapping of psycholinguistic classes and those with the higher number of relevant classes. This means that they tend to polarize on more dimensions. On the contrary Appreciation and Controversiality tend to overlap less with the other classes and to polarize on fewer psycolinguistic dimensions.

7 Related Work

Several researchers studied information flow, community building (and similar) on networks using Digg as a reference dataset [16,14,9,11,13,15,1]. However, the great majority considers only features related to the network itself or simple popularity metrics of stories (e.g. number of diggs, number of comments), without analyzing the correlations of these aspects with the actual content of the story spreading within the network.

A notable work using Digg datasets that begun to investigate some of the insight we proposed is [8]. It incorporates features, derived from sentiment analysis of comments, to predict the popularity of stories. Finally, the work presented in [2] is probably the closest to our approach. It uses *New York Times* articles to examine the relationship between the emotion evoked by content and virality, using semi-automated sentiment

Table 2. word categories along with some sample words

LABEL	*Sample words*
NEGATE	negat*, neither, never, nothing
SWEAR	damn, piss, fuck
FRIEND	buddy, friend, neighbor
POSEMO	love, nice, sweet
OPTIM	best, easy*, enthus*, hope, pride
ANGER	hate, kill, annoyed
TENTAT	maybe, perhaps, guess
INHIB	block, constrain, stop
HEAR	listen, hearing, talking, asking
RELIG	altar, church, mosque
DEATH	death, bury, coffin, kill, fatal
ASSENT	agree, OK, yes, alright

Table 3. Dominant word classes for virality dimensions

APPRECIATION		BUZZ		RAISING-DISCUSSION		CONTROVERSIAL
ASSENT 1.23	MONEY 0.90	DEATH 1.40	POSEMO 0.88	DEATH 1.40	FRIENDS 0.88	RELIG 1.17
DEATH 1.14	FRIENDS 0.88	ASSENT 1.26	OPTIM 0.80	ASSENT 1.27	POSEMO 0.86	DEATH 1.16
TENTAT 1.11	RELIG 0.86	SWEAR 1.19		SWEAR 1.18	OPTIM 0.80	NEGATE 1.12
		HEAR 1.15		HEAR 1.15		ANGER 1.12
		INHIB 1.10		INHIB 1.12		
				ANGER 1.11		

analysis to quantify the affectivity and emotionality of each article. The results suggest a strong relationship between affect and virality. Still their virality metric only consists of how many people emailed the article, an interesting but very limited metric (i.e. somehow representing a form of "narrowcasting").

8 Conclusions

In this paper, we argued that virality, in social networks, hinges on the nature of the viral content, rather than on the structure of the social network. We further argued that virality is a complex phenomenon which can be decomposed into several affective responses, namely *appreciation*, *spreading*, *buzz*, *raising discussion* and *controversiality*. We then provided machine learning experiments, which showed how the various viral phenomena can be *separately* predicted using just the wording of the content. Finally, we provided a psycholinguistic analysis of the features salient for the various viral phenomena.

As a future study we will deeply explore black and white buzz, possibly experimenting on other annotated datasets, and incorporating as features the emotions evoked by the stories (e.g. "fear", "joy", "anger"). Moreover, we are going to extract "viral" lexicons to be used in applicative scenarios, such as in generating messages for viral marketing campaigns.

Acknowledgements. The present work was partially supported by a Google Research Award.

References

1. Aaditeshwar Seth, J.Z., Cohen, R.: A multi-disciplinary approach for recommending weblog messages. In: The AAAI 2008 Workshop on Enhanced Messaging (2008)
2. Berger, J.A., Milkman, K.L.: Social Transmission, Emotion, and the Virality of Online Content. Social Science Research Network Working Paper Series (December 2009)
3. Carenini, G., Cheung, J.C.K.: Extractive vs. nlg-based abstractive summarization of evaluative text: the effect of corpus controversiality. In: Proceedings of the Fifth International Natural Language Generation Conference, INLG 2008, pp. 33–41. Association for Computational Linguistics, Morristown (2008)
4. Gladwell, M.: The Tipping Point: How Little Things Can Make a Big Difference. Little Brown, New York (2002)
5. Guerini, M., Strapparava, C., Özbal, G.: Exploring text virality in social networks. In: Proceedings of 5th International Conference on Weblogs and Social Media (ICWSM 2011). Barcelona, Spain (July 2011)
6. Guerini, M., Strapparava, C., Stock, O.: CORPS: A corpus of tagged political speeches for persuasive communication processing. Journal of Information Technology & Politics 5(1), 19–32 (2008)
7. Guerini, M., Strapparava, C., Stock, O.: Evaluation metrics for persuasive nlp with google adwords. In: LREC (2010)
8. Jamali, S.: Comment Mining, Popularity Prediction, and Social Network Analysis. Master's thesis, George Mason University, Fairfax, VA (2009)
9. Jamali, S., Rangwala, H.: Digging digg: Comment mining, popularity prediction, and social network analysis. In: Proceedings of International Conference on Web Information Systems and Mining (2009)
10. Joachims, T.: Text categorization with Support Vector Machines: learning with many relevant features. In: Nédellec, C., Rouveirol, C. (eds.) ECML 1998. LNCS, vol. 1398, pp. 137–142. Springer, Heidelberg (1998)
11. Khabiri, E., Hsu, C.F., Caverlee, J.: Analyzing and predicting community preference of socially generated metadata: A case study on comments in the digg community. In: ICWSM (2009)
12. Kirby, J., Mardsen, P. (eds.): Connected Marketing, the viral, buzz and Word of mouth revolution. Butterworth-Heinemann, Butterworths (2005)
13. Lerman, K.: Social Information Processing in News Aggregation. IEEE Internet Computing 11(6), 16–28 (2007), http://dx.doi.org/10.1109/MIC.2007.136
14. Lerman, K.: User participation in social media: Digg study. In: Proceedings of the 2007 IEEE/WIC/ACM International Conferences on Web Intelligence and Intelligent Agent Technology - Workshops, WI-IATW 2007, pp. 255–258. IEEE Computer Society, Washington, DC, USA (2007), http://portal.acm.org/citation.cfm?id=1339264.1339702
15. Lerman, K., Galstyan, A.: Analysis of social voting patterns on digg. In: Proceedings of the First Workshop on Online Social Networks, WOSP 2008, pp. 7–12. ACM, New York (2008), http://doi.acm.org/10.1145/1397735.1397738
16. Lerman, K., Ghosh, R.: Information contagion: an empirical study of the spread of news on digg and twitter social networks. In: Proceedings of 4th International Conference on Weblogs and Social Media, ICWSM 2010 (March 2010)

17. Mihalcea, R., Strapparava, C.: The lie detector: Explorations in the automatic recognition of deceptive language. In: Proceedings of the 47th Annual Meeting of the Association of Computational Linguistics (ACL 2009), Singapore, pp. 309–312 (August 2009)
18. Paltoglou, G., Thelwall, M., Buckley, K.: Online textual communications annotated with grades of emotion strength. In: Proceedings of the 3rd International Workshop of Emotion: Corpora for Research on Emotion and Affect, pp. 25–31 (2010)
19. Paltoglou, G., Gobron, S., Skowron, M., Thelwall, M., Thalmann, D.: Sentiment analysis of informal textual communication in cyberspace. In: Proceedings of ENGAGE 2010. LNCS, State-of-the-Art Survey, pp. 13–25 (2010)
20. Pennebaker, J., Francis, M.: Linguistic inquiry and word count: LIWC. Erlbaum Publishers, Mahwah (2001)
21. Schmid, H.: Probabilistic part-of-speech tagging using decision trees. In: Proceedings of the International Conference on New Methods in Language Processing (1994)
22. Szabo, G., Huberman, B.A.: Predicting the popularity of online content. Commun. ACM 53, 80–88 (2010), `http://doi.acm.org/10.1145/1787234.1787254`
23. Vapnik, V.: The Nature of Statistical Learning Theory. Springer, New York (1995)
24. Watts, D.J., Dodds, P.S.: Influentials, networks, and public opinion formation. Journal of Consumer Research 34(4), 441–458 (2007)

A Multimodal Database for Mimicry Analysis

Xiaofan Sun[1], Jeroen Lichtenauer[2], Michel Valstar[2], Anton Nijholt[1], and Maja Pantic[1,2]

[1] Human Media Interaction, University of Twente, Enschede, NL
{x.f.sun,a.nijholt}@ewi.utwente.nl
[2] Department of Computing, Imperial College, London, UK
{j.lichtenauer,michel.valstar,m.pantic}@imperial.ac.uk

Abstract. In this paper we introduce a multi-modal database for the analysis of human interaction, in particular mimicry, and elaborate on the theoretical hypotheses of the relationship between the occurrence of mimicry and human affect. The recorded experiments are designed to explore this relationship. The corpus is recorded with 18 synchronised audio and video sensors, and is annotated for many different phenomena, including dialogue acts, turn-taking, affect, head gestures, hand gestures, body movement and facial expression. Recordings were made of two experiments: a discussion on a political topic, and a role-playing game. 40 participants were recruited, all of whom self-reported their felt experiences. The corpus will be made available to the scientific community.

Keywords: Mimicry database, interaction scenario, synchronized multi-sensor recording, annotation, social signal processing, affective computing.

1 Introduction

To study the phenomena in social interactions between humans in more detail and to allow machine analysis of these social signals, researchers are in need of rich sets of labelled data of repeatable experiments, which should represent situation occurring in daily life [1], [2]. This data could then be used to develop and benchmark new methods for automatic detection and recognition of such behavioural cues. Having sufficient labelled/unlabelled data of mimicry episodes and detailed expressions is a prerequisite for automatically detecting and analyzing mimicry occurring in social interactions. Mimicry episodes are difficult to collect and detect mainly because they inherently involve the temporal interaction between two or more persons. They are unpredictable and relatively rare, which makes it difficult to elicit mimicry displays without deliberately designing recording scenarios. Good experiment scenarios are based on existing social psychology literature, increasing the chance of recording clear, salient, and high-quality cues that relate to displays of mimicry.

There is no doubt that mimicry occurs in the most basic interaction, which is a dyad. Mimicry can be expressed in both in auditory and visual channels. However, obtaining multi-modal sensor data that can be used for multi-modal analysis is a challenge in itself. The recording of different modalities requires different equipment,

S. D'Mello et al. (Eds.): ACII 2011, Part I, LNCS 6974, pp. 367–376, 2011.

and different equipment necessitates different expertise to develop, set up and operate [3], [4]. In summary, to create a database that will contribute to the research of mimicry, we need interdisciplinary knowledge, including social psychology and engineering, as well as methodological solutions to combine and fuse the sensory data from a diversity of multimodal equipment. This is probably the main reason that we currently lack such a mimicry database.

In addition, manual labelling of spontaneous mimicry is time consuming and requires trained annotators. It is also a subjective process, lacking strict guidelines how to perform the annotation. Thus, even if recordings are rich in expressions of spontaneous mimicry, there is no way of attaining a set of consistent and reliable labels. Due to these difficulties, nearly all of the existing databases are artificial and, to different extents, acted [5]. As a result, though mimicry has attracted increasing attention from researchers in different research fields, automatic mimicry analysis is not seriously addressed in current computer science and machine analysis.

Recently created databases containing emotional expressions in different modalities can be used as a reference for creating a mimicry database. These databases mostly consist of audio, video or audiovisual data [6], [7], [8], [9], [10]. Although many of these databases can be considered to contain naturalistic data, none of them were designed to capture episodes of mimicry. Another issue is that, because they were not designed to capture mimicry, there is no well-synchronized view of all partners in a conversation. This makes the automatic analysis and annotation of mimicry in these databases difficult, if not impossible.

One of the notable databases with spontaneous reactions is the Belfast database (BE) created by Cowie et al. [11]. Even though this database consists of spontaneous reactions in TV talk shows and is rich in body gestures and facial expressions, the context was less effective in evoking mimicry.

Some naturalistic or induced-spontaneous datasets of human-human or human-computer interactions might not contain a large number of explicit mimicry episodes. Nevertheless, they could be useful in training tools for the automatic detection of cues that do not directly indicate mimicry but could be relevant to e.g. human affect, which probably is a factor affecting mimicry. For example, the AMI meeting corpus [10] consists of 100 hours of meeting recordings in which people show a huge variety of spontaneous expressions. The data, mostly centred on the idea of enacting meetings, is related to mimicry of dominant and submissive nonverbal behaviours. Tiedens and Fragale [12] have demonstrated that people may react to others who display dominance with dominant displays of their own, and similarly respond to submissive behaviours with mutual submission. Both are referred to as postural mimicry.

The SEMAINE corpus [6] consists of recorded audio-visual conversations with annotation for five affective dimensions (arousal, valence, power, anticipation and intensity). It uses the Sensitive Artificial Listener (SAL) technique, described in [13] as "a specific type of induction technique that focuses on conversation between a human and an agent that either is or appears to be a machine and it is designed to capture a broad spectrum of emotional states". In the SEMAINE corpus, each participant has a conversation with four different emotionally coloured virtual agents, in which mimicry-relevant cues, such as emotional mimicry can probably be found.

Our proposed database intends to become a valuable resource for research of mimicry. This research, in turn, will allow conversational agents to improve their social interaction capabilities in face-to-face communication by recognising mimicry and responding appropriately by instantiating psychological theories through the use of nonverbal cues. From the automatic understanding of mimicry and other social signals, and prediction of how these signals might affect social situations, applications can be derived that can help people improve their social skills.

2 Mimicry Perception Conversation Recording

In this paper we describe a novel dataset called the MAHNOB HMI iBUG Mimicry database, or MHi-Mimicry-db for short, created to allow research in the automatic detection of mimicry. Our goal was to collect recordings of behaviour with as many occurrences as possible in which people are acting either identically and simultaneously or with a significant amount of resemblance and/or synchrony.

Besides collecting the expected (mimicry) behaviour, the data should also enable the analysis of those behaviours on a social interaction level. In order to explore the human perception correctly, the analysis of social interaction should at least include the relation between those behaviours, their function, and the intention behind them.

2.1 Interaction Scenario

As a general starting point in our database design, specific hypotheses in the field of social psychology determined what kind of scenarios would be suitable for our recordings. We chose to design our recording scenario such that the collected data allows us to test two hypotheses about mimicry that have been posed in the literature:

Hypothesis 1. Agreement-/Disagreement-Mimicry occurs in conversations when the participants agree with each other as well as when they do not agree with each other, with a higher frequency or amount of mirroring during agreement than during disagreement. Moreover, mimicry occurs in conversations in with there is the intention to gain acceptance from an interaction partner through conforming to that person's attitudes, opinions, and behaviours [14], [15], [16], [17], [18].

Hypothesis 2. Affiliation-Mimicry has the power to improve social interaction. That is: when individuals communicate, one partner who wants to affiliate with others may intentionally engage in more mirroring of them; in contrast, when they want to disaffiliate they intentionally engage in less mirroring [19], [20], [21], [22], [23], [24].

Based on the theoretical foundations of the above two mimicry hypotheses, we designed two conversational scenarios. The first scenario is a debate, and the second scenario is a role-playing game where one participant plays the role of a homeowner who wants to rent out a room, and the other participant plays the role of a student who is interested in renting the room.

2.2 Procedure

The recording includes two experiments. In Experiment A, participants were asked to choose a topic from a list. Participants were then asked to write down whether they agree or disagree with each statement of their chosen topic. The discussion is held between the participant and a confederate. Participants are led to believe that the confederate is a fellow naïve participant. Participants were asked to start the conversation by presenting their own stance on the topic, and then to discuss the topic with the other person, who may have different views about the topic.

Every topic has a list of statements regarding that topic associated with it. In the pre-recording assessment, the participants note their (dis)agreement with these statements. This is used as a reference for annotating, possibly masked, opinion or attitude. During the discussion participants and confederates express agreement and disagreement, and show a desire to convince the other person of their opinion.

In Experiment B, the intent was to simulate a situation where two participants want to get to know each other a bit better and need to disclose personal and possibly sensitive information about them in the process. Participants were given a communication assignment that requires self-disclosure and emotional discovery. Participant 1 played a role as a student in university who was looking for a room to rent urgently Participant 2 played a role as a person who owns an apartment and wants to rent one of the rooms to the other one.

Participants are not sure about their partner's preference at the beginning, so the hypothesis is that they will try to get more information from their partners first, only gradually showing more sensitive personal information to the other. Moreover, their conversation partners may not want to expose many details to them until s/he decides whether the participant is someone they like or not. However, they have the same goal, which is to share an apartment, so they have the tendency of affiliation.

To rule out mixed gender effects, experiments included either all male participants and confederates, or all female. After recording both sessions, participants finished a personality questionnaire and two separate experiment questionnaires, which were designed to measure the experienced affect and attitude during the two sessions.

2.3 Self-report of Participants

Nonconscious behavioural mimicry has been explained by the existence of a perception-behaviour link [26]; watching a person engage in certain behaviour activates that behavioural representation, which then makes the perceiver more likely to engage in that behaviour herself. Chartrand & Bargh [27] experimentally manipulated behavioural mimicry to explore the consequences for liking a person. They argued that perception of another person's behaviour automatically causes nonconscious mimicry, which in turn creates shared feelings of empathy and rapport. Perspective taking, or the ability to adopt and understand the perspective of others, is one component of empathy [28]. The ability to take the perspectives of others increases behavioural mimicry, suggesting that individuals who are able to affiliate with group members because of their ability to understand others also routinely use mimicry behaviour [29]. Few researchers use actual social interaction corpora to detect human postures to recognize mental states. In our experiments we considered that behaviour presentation in interaction is inherently linked to personality traits (confidence, nervousness, etc.) so personality questionnaires have been included.

28 male and 12 female students from Imperial College London (aged 18 to 40years) are participants. Each was paid 10 pounds for participating in the study,

which took about 1.5 hours. Two male confederates and one female confederate were from the iBUG group at Imperial College London. All participants were assigned to each other randomly. Four personality questionnaires were finished before attending the experiment. These were: 1) Big-Five Mini-Markers FNRS 0.2, 2) The Aggression Questionnaire including four subscales: physical aggression =.85), verbal aggression (= .72), anger (= .83), and hostility (= .77). 3), Interpersonal reactivity index consisting of four 7-item subscales, including Fantasy (FS), Perspective Taking (PT), Empathetic Concern (EC), and Personal Distress (PD), and 4) Self-Construal scale composed of 15 items made up the Independent self-construal subscale, and the remaining 15 items corresponded to the Interdependent self-construal subscale.

3 Synchronized Multi-sensor Recording Setup

The recordings were made under controlled laboratory conditions using 15 cameras and 3 microphones, to obtain the most favourable conditions possible for analysis of the observed behaviour. All sensory data was synchronized with extreme accuracy.

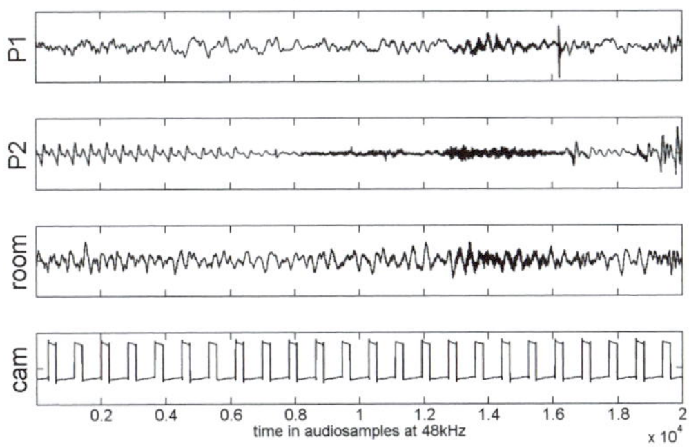

Fig. 1. 4 tracks recorded in parallel by the audio interface. From top to bottom: head microphones of participants 1 and 2, room microphone, and camera trigger.

3.1 Audio Channels

Three channels of sound were recorded using a MOTU $8pre_1$ eight-channel interface (Fig. 1). Channel 1 and 2 contain the signal from head-worn microphones, type AKG HC 577 L. Channel 3 contains the signal from an AKG C 1000 S MkIII room microphone. This channel can be used to obtain a noise estimate for noise reduction in the first two channels. Most of the noise originates from the building ventilation system, which was controlled remotely. The background noise cannot be assumed constant as the ventilation system was sometimes switched on or off during a recording.

3.2 Camera Views

Three types of cameras have been used: An Allied Vision Stingray F046B, monochrome camera, with a spatial resolution of 780x580 pixels; two Prosilica

GE1050C colour cameras, with spatial resolutions of 1024x1024 pixels; and 12 Prosilica GE1050 monochrome cameras, with spatial resolutions of 1024x1024 pixels. Different sets of cameras have been set up to record the face regions at two distance ranges: 'Far' corresponds to a distance range for upright poses and 'Near' corresponds to forward- leaning poses. The focal length and focus of the cameras have been optimized for the respective distance range. The best camera view to use for a facial analysis depends on a person's body pose in each moment. The cameras were intrinsically and extrinsically calibrated. See figure 2 for the camera views.

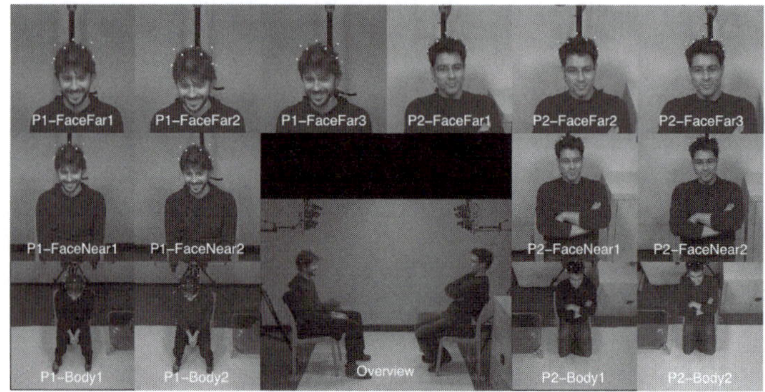

Fig. 2. Simultaneous views from all the cameras

3.3 Audio/Video Synchronization

The cameras are synchronized by hardware triggering [30], and configured to have exposure intervals around the same centre at 58 frames per second. To synchronize between audio and video, we recorded the camera trigger signal as a fourth signal, in parallel with the audio channels. Since the analogue inputs of the 8Pre are sampled using the same clock signal, an event in one of the channels can be directly related to a temporal location in all other channels. The camera trigger pulses can be easily detected and matched with all the captured video frames, using their respective frame number and/or time stamp. The final error of the synchronization is well below 20μs.

4 Annotation

The database has been segmented into speech acts, and annotated for a number of social signalling cues, as well as conscious and nonconscious higher-level behaviours.

4.1 Segmentation into Episodes of Interest

In our data, Experiment A includes two parts: presentation and discussion. In the presentation part, it is obvious that interviewees play a role as speakers while the interviewers listen all response from listeners is on the involvement or understanding level. For example, understanding can be expressed by nods. So it is natural that the range of nonverbal behaviour expressed by a listener is small, often limited to cues such as nodding, smiling, and certain mannerisms. On the contrary, in the discussion part, interviewers and interviewees both need to express an actual response, i.e. to give feedback on a communicative level. Even more interesting is that people often only mimic another's behaviour when they are playing the same role in interactions. In other words: people may not immediately mimic the speakers' behaviours while listening, and they may, instead, express a consensus response (since they are functioning on the involvement or understanding level). But when the former listener subsequently takes on the role of speaker, s/he often mimics their counterparts' behaviour that was expressed during the previous turn. This complies with one of the most important factors that can affect mimicry - similarity: The similarity of roles played in interactions. In Experiment B, the participants have complete similarity of conversational goal, which is to find a roommate successfully.

In summary, the analysis of relevance among mimicry and social interactions can be extended not only for recognizing human affect, but also for judging relationships (roles) and interaction management (turn-taking).

Annotation Steps:
Segmentation into episodes according to utterance tokens acquired from participants
Annotation of speakers and listeners
Annotation of behavioural cues for both participants separately
Annotation of mimicry

In our annotation tool, options for behavioural cues are predefined. After the annotation of episodes and behavioural cues, the tool can automatically compare whether the selected options are the same for both participants, from which the mimicry label (PRESENT/NOT PRESENT) is derived.

4.2 Annotation within Segments

For the episodes of interest, more detailed annotations are included, consisting of behavioural expression labels, mimicry/non mimicry labels, and social signal labels. In the interface of the annotation software, the first item that is provided concerns the behavioural expression labels: smile, head nod, headshake, body leaning away, and body leaning forward. When the video data is played, the annotator has to enter the time when a particular cue was observed, and choose a suitable label from the list. Cases where none of the available labels are appropriate for a certain expression are also taken into other account. Secondly, in order to learn more about the intent behind those behavioural expressions, for each behavioural expression the label of "conscious" and "unconscious" is also recorded. For unconscious behaviours, a SOCIAL SIGNAL EXPRESSION has to be chosen. This can be e.g. understanding, agreement, liking, confused, or uncertain. For conscious behaviour, a DESIRED GOAL has to be chosen. For example: to flatter others, to emphasize understanding, to express agreement, to share rapport/empathy, to increase acceptance. Since it is sometimes difficult, or even impossible, to specify a unique reason for mimicry, space is provided to include a comment.

Current annotation considers visual behaviour and participants' roles in each conversation. Further annotation will include the participants' affect and implied social signals relative to mimicry. It will be mainly based on the questionnaires taken during the experiments.

5 Overview and Availability

The MHi-Mimicry database is made freely available to the research community through a web-accessible interface (http://www.mahnob-db.eu/mimicry). The dataset consists of 54 recordings. Of these, 34 are of the discussions (Experiment A) and 20 recordings are of the role-playing game (Experiment B). The data contain imagery of 43 subjects (40 participants and 4 confederates). The durations of Experiment A are between 8 and 18 minutes, with an average of 15 minutes. The duration of Experiment B is between 4 and 18 minutes, with an average of 11 minutes. At the time of recording, all the participants ranged in age from 18 to 40 years. Of the participants 26% are female and 95% of the participants come from southern Europe.

All 18 sensor tracks are available in the database, as well as an audio-visual overview track that combines all views and the two audio tracks from the head-mounted microphones (Fig. 2). This overview track is intended for human inspection and labelling of the data. A large amount of metadata is stored in the database, and a search interface makes it possible for researchers to collect the data they require.

6 Conclusion and Future Work

This is the first accurately synchronized multimodal database of natural human-to-human interaction aimed at the study and automatic detection of mimicry. Although it is not the first database to address natural human-human interaction, the range of sensors, the multi-resolution synchronized views of both participants, and the high accuracy of the multi-sensor, multi-modal synchronization provides many new opportunities to study (automatic) human behaviour understanding in general. In the future, our work will mainly contribute to affective computing and human-machine interaction. In particular, we aim to contribute to (1) the understanding of how human mimicry works and subsequently, the development of automatic mimicry analyzers, (2) the improvement of the recognition of social and affective attitudes such as (dis)agreeing and (dis)liking through mimicry information, and (3) knowledge about the timing and the extent to which mimicry should occur in human-machine interaction by generating mimicry behaviour in agents. This technology would also strongly influence science and technology by, for example, providing a powerful new class of research tools for social science and anthropology. While the primary goal of such an effort would be to facilitate direct mediated communication between people, advances here will also facilitate interactions between humans and machines.

Acknowledgment. This work has been funded in part by the European Community's 7th Framework Programme [FP7/2007–2013] under the grant agreement no 231287 (SSPNet). The work of Jeroen Lichtenauer and Maja Pantic is further funded in part by the European Research Council under the ERC Starting Grant agreement no. ERC-2007-StG 203143 (MAHNOB). The work of Michel Valstar is also funded in part by EPSRC grant EP/H016988/1: Pain rehabilitation: E/Motion-based automated coaching.

References

1. Pantic, M., Gunes, H.: Automatic, dimensional and continuous emotion recognition. Int'l. Journal of Synthetic Emotion 1(1), 68–99 (2010)
2. Vinciarelli, A., Dielmann, A., Favre, S., Salamin, H.: A database of political debates for analysis of social interactions. In: IEEE Int'l. Conf. Affective Computing and Intelligent Interfaces, vol. 2, pp. 96–99 (2009)
3. Savran, A., Ciftci, K., Chanel, G., Mota, J., Viet, L.H., Sankur, B., Akarun, L., Caplier, A., Rombaut, M.: Emotion detection in the loop from brain signals and facial images. eNTERFACE report (2006)
4. Lichtenauer, J., Valstar, M., Jie, S., Pantic, M.: Cost-effective solution to synchronized audio-visual capture using multiple sensors. In: IEEE Int'l. Conf. Advanced Video and Signal Based Surveillance, pp. 324–329 (2009)
5. Gatica-Perez, D.: Automatic nonverbal analysis of social interaction in small groups: A review. Image and Vision Computing 27(12), 1775–1787 (2009)
6. McKeown, G., Valstar, M.F., Cowie, R., Pantic, M.: The SEMAINE corpus of emotionally coloured character interactions. In: IEEE Conf. Multimedia and Expo, pp. 1079–1084 (2010)
7. Littlewort, G., Bartlett, M.S., Fasel, I., Susskind, J., Movellan, J.: Dynamics of facial expression extracted automatically from video. In: IEEE Int'l. Computer Vision and Pattern Recognition Workshop, pp. 80–80 (2004)
8. Coan, J., Allen, J.: Handbook of Emotion Elicitation and Assessment. Oxford University Press, Oxford (2007)
9. Devillers, L., Vidrascu, L., Lamel, L.: Challenges in real life emotion annotation and machine learning based detection. Neural Networks 18(4), 407–422 (2005)
10. Carletta, J.: Unleashing the killer corpus: experiences in creating the multi-everything AMI meeting corpus. Language Resources and Evaluation 41(2), 181–190 (2007)
11. Athanaselis, T., Bakamidis, S., Dologlou, I., Cowie, R., Douglas-Cowie, E., Cox, C.: ASR for emotional speech: Clarifying the issues and enhancing performance. Neural Networks 18(4), 437–444 (2005)
12. Tiedens, L.Z., Fragale, A.R.: Power moves: Complementarity in dominant and submissive nonverbal behaviour. J. of Personality & Social Psychology 84(3), 558–568 (2003)
13. Douglas-Cowie, E., Cowie, R., Sneddon, I., Cox, C., Lowry, O., McRorie, M., Martin, J.C., Devillers, L., Abrilian, S., Batliner, A., Amir, N., Karpouzis, K.: The Humaine database: Addressing the collection and annotation of naturalistic and induced emotional data. In: Paiva, A.C.R., Prada, R., Picard, R.W. (eds.) ACII 2007. LNCS, vol. 4738, pp. 488–500. Springer, Heidelberg (2007)
14. Brass, M., Bekkering, H., Prinz, W.: Movement observation affects movement execution in a simple response task. Acta Psychologica 106(1-2), 3–22 (2001)
15. Catmur, C., Walsh, V., Heyes, C.: Sensorimotor learning configures the human mirror system. Current Biology 17(17), 1527–1531 (2007)
16. Estow, S., Jamieson, J.P., Yates, J.R.: Self-monitoring and mimicry of positive and negative social behaviors. J. of Research in Personality 41(2), 425–433 (2007)
17. Heider, J.D., Skowronski, J.J.: Ethnicity-based similarity and the chameleon effect. Austin State University (2008) (manuscript)
18. Van Swol, L.M.: The effects of nonverbal mirroring on perceived persuasiveness, agreement with an imitator, and reciprocity in a group discussion. Communication Research 30(4), 461–480 (2003)

19. Baaren van, R.B., Fockenberg, D.A., Holland, R.W., Janssen, L., van Knippenberg, A.: The moody chameleon: the effect of mood on non-conscious mimicry. Social Cognition 24(4), 426–437 (2006)
20. van Baaren, R.B., Holland, R.W., Steenaert, B., Van Knippenberg, A.: Mimicry for money: Behavioral consequences of imitation. J. of Experimental Social Psychology 39(4), 393–398 (2003)
21. van Baaren, R.B., Horgan, T.G., Chartrand, T.L., Dijkmans, M.: The forest, the trees and the chameleon: Context dependence and mimicry. J. of Personality and Social Psychology 86(3), 453–459 (2004)
22. Lakin, J.L.: Exclusion and nonconscious behavioral mimicry: The role of belongingness threat. Ph.D. dissertation (2003)
23. Lakin, J.L., Chartrand, T.L.: Exclusion and Nonconscious Behavioral Mimicry. In: The Social Outcast: Ostracism, Social Exclusion, Rejection, and Bullying, pp. 279–295. Psychology Press, New York (2005)
24. Maurer, R.E., Tindall, J.H.: Effect of postural congruence on client's perception of counselor empathy. Journal of Counseling Psychology 30, 158–163 (1983)
25. Bavelas, J.B., Black, A., Lemery, C.R., Mullett, J.: I show how you feel: Motor mimicry as a communicative act. J. of Personality and Social Psychology 50, 322–329 (1986)
26. Chartrand, T.L., Jefferis, V.E.: Consequences of automatic goal pursuit and the case of nonconscious mimicry, pp. 290–305. Psychology Press, Philadelphia (2003)
27. Chartrand, T.L., Maddux, W.W., Lakin, J.L.: Beyond the perception-behavior link: The ubiquitous utility and motivational moderators of nonconscious mimicry. In: Unintended Thought II: The New Unconscious, pp. 334–361. Oxford University Press, New York (2005)
28. MacDonald, G., Leary, M.R.: Why does social exclusion hurt? The relationship between social and physical pain. Psychological Bulletin 131, 202–223 (2005)
29. Lakin, J.L., Chartrand, T.L.: Using nonconscious behavioural mimicry to create affiliation and rapport. Psychology Science 14(4), 334–339 (2003)
30. Lichtenauer, J., Shen, J., Valstar, M.F., Pantic, M.: Cost-effective solution to synchronized audio-visual data capture using multiple sensors, Report, Imperial College London (2010)

Mood Recognition Based on Upper Body Posture and Movement Features

Michelle Thrasher[1], Marjolein D. Van der Zwaag[2], Nadia Bianchi-Berthouze[1], and Joyce H.D.M. Westerink[2]

[1] UCLIC, University College London, MPEB Gower Street, London WC1E6BT, UK
[2] Philips Research, High Tech Campus 34, 5656 AE Eindhoven, The Netherlands
{michelle.thrasher.09,n.berthouze}@ucl.ac.uk
{marjolein.van.der.zwaag,joyce.westerink}@philips.com

Abstract. While studying body postures in relation to mood is not a new concept, the majority of these studies rely on actors interpretations. This project investigated the temporal aspects of naturalistic body postures while users listened to mood inducing music. Video data was collected while participants listened to eight minutes of music during two sessions (happy and sad) in a within-subjects design. Subjectively reported mood scores validated that mood did differ significantly for valence and energy. Video analysis consisted of postural ratings for the head, shoulders, trunk, arms, and head and hand tapping. Results showed significant differences for the majority of these dimensions by mood. This study showed that certain body postures are indicative of certain mood states in a naturalistic setting.

Keywords: Affective body posture/movement, emotion recognition, body posture coding.

1 Introduction

Emotions are not just an important part of how we experience the world, but they also play a main role in how we communicate with others; pointed out as far back as Darwin. Both verbal and nonverbal communication channels are relied upon in our everyday interactions with others. While the linguistic channel mainly conveys the content of the message, nonverbal behaviors play a fundamental role in expressing the affective states, attitudes, and social dynamics of the communicators [5]. Within the affective computing field, the development of affective-sensitive systems has become a necessity, as our lives grow increasingly reliable on technology. One push has been to utilize these communication signals to interpret the emotional state of the user and, thus, build interactive systems around the affect of the user. Within the affective computing community, the channels to detect affect in users have undergone extensive research in order to understand how they can be incorporated and monitored by interactive systems. This project fits into a larger project utilizing music to induce a specific mood in the user. Philips Research has been exploring the development of an Affective Music Player (AMP) based on changes in certain physiological measures [4, 12]. The physiological channels have been explored, but the challenge with this

S. D´Mello et al. (Eds.): ACII 2011, Part I, LNCS 6974, pp. 377–386, 2011.

type of input is that it requires the user to wear numerous wired sensors in order to feed information into the system. Body movement could instead be another avenue of exploration. In [13] the authors automatically analyze body movement to modify real-time music performances. Their results show that participants could relate to the mapping of their affective expressions and the manipulation of the performance. Dahl and Friberg [14] explored how musician's emotional intention could be recognized from their body movements. The results showed that happy and anger performances were characterized by large movements with angry performances being faster and jerkier. Sad performances displayed small, slow, smooth and regular movements. Similar movement qualities were used in Mancini et al. [2] to visualize the expressive quality of a music performance through a virtual head.

In this paper, we will explore the possibility of using body posture and movement features to capture the affective state of the music listener, rather than the performer. This result will then be fed into an emotional closed loop system to direct the mood of the user within a working environment.

2 Coding Body Posture and Movement

This study is not the first to explore in details the relationship between postural features and affective state. In Argyles [1] book, Bodily Communication, he points out that despite there being a numerous amount of ways in which researchers have categorized posture and movement, there are a number of elements that are commonly used: Lean (forwards, backwards, sideways), Arms (Open, Closed, on hips), Head (lowered, raised, tilted sideways) and Legs (stretched, open, crossed). This listing was compiled from researching the current literature and pulling out the common themes found in the way researchers break the body down into significant regions of interest.

Mehrabian & Friar [9] also used a very interesting way to develop the scale used in their investigation of attitudes by a seated communicator via posture and position cues. Details on the development can be found in their paper, for now the important aspect of this study was the idea of utilizing information of a user directness of body orientation. The different dimensions included: eye contact, arm openness, distance, leg openness, hand and foot relaxation, backwards/sideways lean of torso, and leg, head, shoulder orientation. In a more detailed system, Wallbott [13] took a very eclectic approach to the coding of body movement and posture, relying mostly on the behavior really shown by the actors. They utilized trained observers to watch video sequences in which drama students portrayed the different emotionally charged scenarios. The observers were asked to freely record all of the body activity that they observed, with no restrictions on the limit available. Next, a second set of independent coders used those body activities recorded from the first set of observations to go back through all of the videos again. From here, reliability and agreement scores between the observers were calculated in order to get the final scale including only the features in which the agreement between observers reached a level above 75%.

As we can see from the descriptions of these coding systems, researchers have developed numerous ways in which the interpretation of body postures and body movements can be coded and analyzed. No two studies have focused on the same exact dimensions or measurements, but they all bring interesting perspectives on how the features can be extracted and coded. There are major similarities in regard to the inclusion of major body regions, which communicates the importance of the focus on these. In the method section, we will describe how the development of our coding system is based on the ideas observed within these systems. Since our investigation is quite specific it is important to note that it was developed from a multidisciplinary approach, which should lend to the wide applicability towards the understanding of body posture features.

3 Research Questions and Methodology

The majority of previous studies do not focus on naturalistic behaviors as they rely on actors portrayals. These dramatized postures would not be valid within an everyday working environment. They also lack longer term i.e., minutes to hours, temporal changes of body postures. Therefore, we studied the changes in postural features over time of naturalistic body postures while users listen to mood inducing music. The findings could then complement or substitute physiological measures to derive mood for the purpose of an affective music player or other affective closed-loop applications.

Data Collection. The video data was taken from an experiment examining the physiological reactions to mood inducing music. Therefore, the method of data collection that is applicable to this project will now be described. A full report on the data collection method can be found in van der Zwaag & Westerink [12]. Sixteen, eight women (mean age 27 years, SD 2 years) and eight men (mean age 29 years, SD 4 years), of the original 37 volunteers recruited from the Philips Research Laboratories were randomly selected for inclusion in this project. Two test sessions were run exactly one week apart from each other varying only by mood that was induced: Happy, Positive valence high energetic (PH) and Sad, Negative valence low energetic (NL). Mood induction was counterbalanced over session (first and second) and gender (male and female).

Materials. Mood was induced in the participants via music. As van der Zwaag & Westerink [12] report, music has been utilized to regulate mood in daily-life settings [11] as well as in laboratory environments [7]. Since music proves to be an extremely personal experience, the participants were asked to supply three songs that consistently made them feel good every time they listened to it [4]. The experimenter chose the music for the Sad condition. The Sad music was proven to induce a negative low energetic mood [6]. During both conditions, the music was played for a total of eight minutes. For the Happy music, the music was adjusted so that they all played for the same amount of time (2 minutes and 40 seconds).

Subjective mood was measured using the UWIST Mood Adjective Checklist [8] for three mood dimensions: valence (unpleasant to pleasant), energetic arousal (tired/without energy to awake/full energy), and calmness (restless/under tension to calm/relaxed). The UMACL contains eight bipolar items for each mood dimension, starting with "*right now I am feeling...*", and with answers ranging from 0: not at all to

4: very much. In order to ensure participants understood the checklist, it was shown to them prior to the study so clarification could be given before they started [8, 12]. Video data was recorded using a Sony Handy-cam HDR-SR7E 6.1 MPixel, AVCHD, and Full HD 1080. Three different angles were recorded (face, upper body, and side), but for the purpose of this study only the side video data was analyzed.

Procedure. Participants sat at a computer desk designed to resemble a normal working environment. The experiment was computerized so no verbal instructions were given, but presented on the screen in English. The habituation period then started, where participants watched a coral sea diving movie on the screen for eight minutes which served as a baseline period [10]. The UMACL questionnaire then followed [8]. After completion, the music, either PH (happy) or NL (sad), was presented to the participant. Participants were told there would be asked a series of questions relating to the music to ensure they focused on the music. Following the music phase, participants filled out the UMACL mood checklist. The second session differed from the first only in the mood that was being induced (PH or NL).

The effect of music on the UMACL mood scores was assessed via a repeated-measures MANOVA with Music (PH/ NL) as within subject factor on valence, energy, and calmness reaction scores. Mood reaction scores were calculated by subtracting the ratings obtained after the baseline period from the ratings obtained during the music mood induction. MANOVA results indicated that the PH and NL conditions were significantly different from each other ($F(3,34) = 33.33$, $p < .001$, $\eta^2 = .75$). Figure 1 (top-left) demonstrates that the reaction scores for the valence and energy were significantly higher in the PH compared to the NL condition (Valence: $F = 21.80$, $p < .001$, $\eta^2 = .60$, Energy $F = 31.35$, $p < .001$, $\eta^2 = .75$).

4 Data Analysis

Posture ratings. Several validated postural rating scales were merged in order to create a scale applicable to our investigation. The features that were extracted were consistently shown to be important indicators for mood. Wallbots categorical scale and Mehrabian orientation measures [9] were the two main scales that were combined to develop our final rating scale after a series of pilot testing. Table 1 reports the final scale used including inter-rater scores.

The inter-rater reliability of each feature was then tested for each postural and movement feature. Three trained observers used the created coding schemed to code four eight-minute sessions chosen randomly for condition (PH/NL) and gender of the participant ensuring that each postural feature was displayed. Training consisted of three different parts: pictorial representations of the different elements, a verbal explanation of the differences between the elements, and a practice coding session of a video. Careful consideration was taken to not explain the observers that mood was being induced via music. After each observer coded the sessions, the data was exported from The Observer XT (Noldus Information Technology) into Microsoft

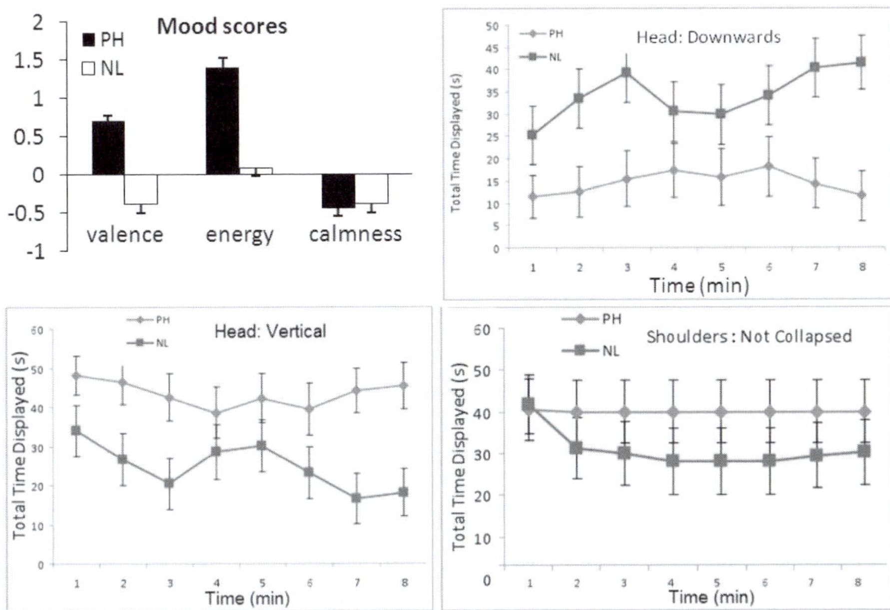

Fig. 1. Top-Left: Means and Standard Errors of the subjective mood reaction scores during mood induction. Graphs: head down (top-right), head vertical (bottom-left), and shoulders not collapsed (bottom-right) for PH/NL mood conditions.

Excel for further analysis. The data consisted of each postural feature in the coding scheme broken down into intervals of five seconds for the total eight-minute mood induction period. The interval time was chosen to be the shortest amount of time to control for human reaction rates and differences in judgments of the beginning of aselected posture. Each five second interval was then given a 0 or 1 rating for the absence or presence, respectively, of that particular postural feature for that time interval.

Intraclass correlations were then run using SPSS 17.0 to compare all three observers coding results against each other per feature. For example, head postures were compared between the three observers per five second intervals for the total eight minutes. The values for the first five second interval was discarded, because participants were all moving from interacting with the computer to passively listening to music. Due to the time consuming nature of coding the videos per feature, the inter-rater scores were also used to allow only one observer to code the videos. It was determined that if significant levels of agreement were reached between the three individual coders for each feature over a subset of videos, then one coder could confidently assess the rest of the data knowing the others would agree with their judgments. Therefore, give the high levels of agreement shown in Table 1, one trained observer coded the entirety of the videos included in the real analysis.

Table 1. Final rating scale including inter-rater agreement scores between three trained observers over four randomly selected videos

Posture Feature	Agreement	Posture Feature	Agreement
Arm Vertical	100%	Shoulder Collapsed	95.8%
Arm Frontal on Table	93.1%	Shoulder Not Collapsed	94.7%
Arms Crossed on Table	92.8%	Head Tapping	100%
Arms Crossed on Lap	93.0%	Head Not Tapping	100%
Head Downwards	86.2%	Hand Tapping	79.0%
Head Vertical	82.0%	Hand Tapping	79.0%
Hand Backwards	78.2%	----	----

5 Results

The total time each posture was displayed for each video was exported from Observer XT and analyzed using SPSS 17 for Windows. The level of significance was set at $p < .05$ (2-tailed). The pairwise comparisons were Bonferroni corrected. Effect size is expressed as η^2 values. All data was subjected to separate repeated-measures MANOVAs with Mood (Positive High Energetic/ Negative Low Energetic) and Time (eight 1-minute intervals) as within-subject factors for the head, shoulders, trunk, arm, and movement features. The significant univariate effects and results are described in Table 2. Head backwards, both shoulder dimensions, trunk upright, arm frontal on table, arm crossed on lap, and arm crossed on table did not show an significant main effect of Mood or Time (all $p > 0.05$), and will therefore not be further described. Multivariate tests revealed a main effect of the head features on mood ($F(1,15) = 16.25$, $p = .001$, $\eta^2 = .52$).

Head Downwards. The univariate effect of Mood, indicates that the downwards head posture (Figure 1, top-right) is displayed longer during negative low energetic mood than positive high energetic moods and is significant ($p < .001$). Subsequent pairwise comparisons between mood for each minute shows that the positive high energy and negative low energy moods are significantly different for all but the fourth minute with the head downwards being displayed longer in the NL mood ($p < .043$ except during the fourth minute where $p = .082$).

Head Vertical. The significant univariate effect of Mood ($p = .01$), indicates that the vertical head posture (Figure 1, bottom-left) is shown longer during positive high energetic mood than negative low energetic mood. Subsequent pairwise comparisons between mood for each minute shows that from the first minute onwards the positive high energetic and negative low energetic mood differ from each other with near significance ($p < .056$ except for the fourth minute where $p = .18$).

Shoulder Features. No significant multivariate effects were found. Univariate analysis showed that there is an interaction effect of Mood with Time for the shoulders being held in a collapsed position ($F(7,98) = 2.19$, $p = .042$, $\eta^2 = .1$). Subsequent pairwise comparisons showed that the first minute was significantly

Table 2. Overview of the significant results. NL = Negative valence/Low energetic, PH = Positive valence/High energetic

Feature	Direction of effect	Significantly different from (min.)
Head downwards	Longer in NL	4th minutes onwards
Head vertical	Longer in PE	1st minutes onwards
Trunk backwards	Longer in PE	4th minutes onwards
Trunk forwards	Longer in PE	5th minutes onwards
Head tapping	Longer in PE	1st minutes onwards
Hand tapping	Longer in PE	3rd minutes onwards

different from the rest during the negative low energy condition (all $p< .052$). The results also show that there is an interaction effect of Mood with Time for the shoulders not collapsed (Figure 1, bottom-right) ($F(7,98)= 2.19$, $p= .042$, $\eta^2= .14$). Subsequent pairwise comparisons showed that the first minute was significantly different from the rest during the negative low energy condition ($p< .052$ for all measures).

Trunk Features. The results show that there is a main effect of Time with the trunk being in the backwards position ($F(7,105)= 6.25$, $p< .001$, $\eta^2= .30$). Pairwise comparisons of each minute compared with all other minutes show that the trunk is held forwards significantly longer during the positive high energetic mood from the fourth minute onwards ($p< .05$). The results additionally show that there is a main effect of Time with the trunk being in the Forward position ($F(7,105)= 4.49$, $p< .001$, $\eta^2= .23$). Pairwise comparisons of each minute compared with all other minutes show that in both moods the trunk was significantly longer in a forward position from the fifth minute onwards (all $p< .05$). This indicates that regardless of the mood induction, the participants seem to adjust their postures over time.

Arm Features. Multivariate tests revealed no significant differences for Mood, Time, or Mood and Time interaction. Univariate effects show an interaction effect of Mood with Time for the arm being held in the vertical position ($F(7,105)= 2.78$, $p= .011$, $\eta^2= .16$). Pairwise comparisons show that the arm being held to a vertically up position towards the head changes over time and this change is different between the two mood (PH/NL) conditions. Subsequent pairwise comparisons did not show any significance ($p > .05$).

Head Tapping. Multivariate tests revealed significance for Mood ($F(1,15)= 12.60$, $p= .003$, $\eta^2 = .46$), time ($F(7,105)= 2.85$, $p< .001$, $\eta^2= .27$), and Mood with Time interaction ($F(7,105)= 2.33$, $p= .03$, $\eta^2= .134$) for head tapping. The univariate effect of Mood, indicated that head tapping is shown longer during positive high energetic mood than negative low energetic moods, is significant ($p= .003$). Pairwise comparisons between mood for each minute show that from the first minute onwards the positive energetic and the negative low energetic mood differ from each other with near significance (all $p< .05$, except for the 1st minute where $p= .06$) with the head tapping more in the PH mood. Also, a pairwise comparisons between mood for each minute shows that the positive high energy and negative low energy condition are significantly different for all eight minutes ($p< .061$).

Table 3. The significant correlation coefficients (p<.01; two tailed) for the comparison of the various body postures

	H.Down	H.Vertical	H.Back	T.Back	T.Vert.	Head
A. Vertical						
A. Frontal	-.381	.355		-.289		
A.xLap	.259	-.266				
AxTable		.296	.419			
T.Back					.526	.253
T.Forward						
Hand						-320

Hand Tapping. Multivariate tests display a main effect of mood (F(1,7)= 5.25, p= .037, η^2= .26) where hand tapping was shown significantly longer in the PH condition than the NL condition. A pairwise comparison between moods for each minute shows that from the third minute onwards the positive high energetic and the negative low energetic moods differ from each other with marginal significance with the hand tapping more in the PH mood (all p < .05 except for the first and second minute where p= .129, p= .135 respectively). Pairwise comparisons between each minute with all other minutes show that there is not a significant change over time (p> .05).

Correlation. An investigation into whether any of the postures correlate with each other was conducted by calculating Spearmans rho. This was done in order to see if postures were redundant in predicting the mood of the participant. Results did show that the features within separate posture regions are highly correlated within each other. The correlations between posture regions show nearly significant results, as shown in Table 3. These significant correlations confirm that a recognition system does not need to incorporate all features but solely the best differentiating features that do not correlate highly.

Mood prediction. In order to investigate whether we can predict the mood from certain postures, a logistic regression was performed with the postures that showed significance in the initial ANOVAS. This included: *head.down/ head.vertical/ shoulders.collapsed/ head.tap/ & hand.tap*. It must be noted that for the features with only two ratings (*hand.tapping/no.hand.tapping*) only one was utilized, since the other value was just the exact opposite. Running an initial regression data, it was found that the *shoulder.collapsed* posture was not significant and therefore was removed from the predictors. Additionally, it was decided to only run the regressional data for the last two minutes of the mood induction period because the ANOVAs showed that postures were only fully induced after six minutes of mood induction. Consequently, a logistic regression analysis, using method ENTER, was run on the data from the last two minutes of mood induction on the following variables: *head.down, head.vertical, head.tap, and hand.tap*. The overall prediction is 81.3%, i.e. 87.5% correct detection of the happy mood and 75% correct detection of the sad mood. Furthermore, all the included variables significantly contributed to this prediction (p<.05). Therefore, happy and sad moods can be detected correctly in 81% of the cases via head position and head and hand movements.

6 Discussion

The head has proven in numerous studies to have high importance in differentiating between moods. Participants in our study displayed the head in a vertical position longer during the happy mood than in the sad mood. The downward head posture was contrary, being displayed longer during the sad moods than happy moods. The results are consistent within the realm of the current literature with the head being held more laterally extended during more positive affective states. We also looked at the changes over time for the three head features. Both the head being held in a vertical and downward posture differentiate between moods from the first minute onwards, except during the fourth minute. We are still not sure what happened within the fourth minute, but the levels were very close to being significant. All in all, these results confirm and support the idea that the posture of the head is an extremely important feature of study and differentiates almost immediately between the two mood states.

The trunk feature showed only a main effect of time. From looking at the change over time per minute, the majority of participants started off in a more upright/forward position, but after the fourth minute onwards they displayed a backwards position more frequently. Argyle [1] related the forward lean of the trunk as being indicative of high interest levels and a backward lean to be associated with boredom. The trunk feature in our study seems to communicate this degree of arousal. Mehrabian [9] defined a more tense person as leaning forwards or upright and a more relaxed person as the opposite. Our results did not fall in line with the emotional expressivity of the trunk, but it did indicate the participant becoming comfortable within their environment.

Another interesting note relates to the previous study conducted with this data set in relation to the physiological measures. Essentially, the physiological responses start to differentiate between moods from the fourth minute onwards; which is when the trunk features changed from more tense to more relaxed [12]. The causality cannot be reliably pinpointed, but it is a very interesting observation and deems further research. Therefore, a distinction could then start to be made between the purposes of the different postural features. Some of the features could be utilized to understand the overall mood state of the user and other features could be utilized to understand the level of arousal of the user.

The tapping of the head had not been studied per se in the body movement literature, but was a logical inclusion since we were inducing mood with music. We received highly significant results for this dimensions, which indicates that this could be easily utilized to discriminate between happy and sad mood states. The tapping of the head was shown almost exclusively in the happy mood with significant differences starting after the first minute onwards. Along the same lines as the head tapping, the hand-tapping dimension was almost exclusively seen in the happy condition. Although the differentiation between the two moods was not made until the third minute, it is a significant predictor of mood. In relation to incorporating these two features within a recognition system, accelerometers being placed on the head/neck (e.g., ear buds or headphones) and on the hand region could easily allow their continuous measurement. The impact of these findings confirms the idea that the development of a system that focuses solely on the unobtrusive monitoring of body postures to identify affect could become a reality. The combination of this channel with other ones like physiology could also lend higher recognition accuracy.

References

1. Argyle, M.: Bodily communication. Taylor & Francis, Abington (1988)
2. Mancini, M., Bresin, R., Pelachaud, C.: A virtual head driven by music expressivity. IEEE Transaction on Audio, Speech, and Language Processing 15(6), 1833–1841 (2007)
3. Bernstein, N.: The Co-ordination and Regulation of Movements. Pergamo, Oxford (1967)
4. van den Broek, E., Janssen, J., Westerink, J.: Guidelines for Affective Signal Processing (ASP): from lab to life. In: Proceedings of Int. Conference on Affective Computing and Intelligent Interaction, pp. 1–6 (2009)
5. De Mello, S., Graesser, A.: Automatic detection of learner's affect from gross body language. Applied Artificial Intelligence 23(2), 123–150 (2009)
6. Gendolla, G., Kruken, J.: Informational mood impact on effort-related cardiovascular response: The diagnostic value of mood counts. Emotion 2(3), 251–262 (2002)
7. Gerrards-Hesse, A., Spies, K., Hesse, F.: Experimental inductions of emotional states and their effectiveness: A review. British Journal of Psychology 85(1), 55–78 (1994)
8. Matthews, G., Jones, D., Chamberlain, A.: Refining the measurement of mood: the UWIST Mood Adjective Checklist. British Journal of Psychology 81(1), 17–42 (1990)
9. Mehrabian, A., Friar, J.: Encoding of attitude by a seated communicator via posture and position cues. Journal of Consulting and Clinical Psychology 33(3), 330 (1969)
10. Piferi, R., Kline, K., Younger, J., Lawler, K.: An alternative approach for achieving cardiovascular baseline: Viewing an aquatic video. International Journal of Psychophysiology 37(2), 207–217 (2000)
11. Thayer, R.: The Origin of Everyday Moods: Managing Energy, Tension, and Stress (1996)
12. van der Zwaag, M.D., Westerink, J.H.D.M.: Physiological patterns during music mood induction (submitted, 2011)
13. Wallbott, H.: Bodily expression of emotion. European Journal of Social Psychology 28(6), 879–896 (1998)
14. Castellano, G., Bresin, R., Camurri, A., Volpe, G.: User-centered control of audio and visual expressive feedback by full-body movements. In: Paiva, A.C.R., Prada, R., Picard, R.W. (eds.) ACII 2007. LNCS, vol. 4738, pp. 501–510. Springer, Heidelberg (2007)
15. Dahl, S., Friberg, A.: Visual perception of expressiveness in musicians body movements. Music Perception 24(5), 433–454 (2007)

Emotional Aware Clustering on Micro-blogging Sources

Katerina Tsagkalidou[1], Vassiliki Koutsonikola[1], Athena Vakali[1], and Konstantinos Kafetsios[2]

[1] Department of Informatics
Aristotle University
54124 Thessaloniki, Greece
[2] Department of Psychology
University of Crete
GR74100 Rethymno, Greece

Abstract. Microblogging services have nowadays become a very popular communication tool among Internet users. Since millions of users share opinions on different aspects of life everyday, microblogging websites are considered as a credible source for exploring both factual and subjective information. This fact has inspired research in the area of automatic sentiment analysis. In this paper we propose an emotional aware clustering approach which performs sentiment analysis of users tweets on the basis of an emotional dictionary and groups tweets according to the degree they express a specific set of emotions. Experimental evaluations on datasets derived from Twitter prove the efficiency of the proposed approach.

Keywords: Microblogging services, sentiment analysis, web clustering.

1 Introduction

With the advent of Web 2.0 and social applications, millions of people broadcast their thoughts and opinions on a considerable variety of topics which are collectively called the *User Generated Content* (UGC) [10]. In particular, social networks and blogs provide an increasingly popular way of online communication by which users can interact and broadcast their personal thoughts. Therefore, these applications contain highly opinionated personal commentary and the new social media offer a unique look into people's emotion-laden reactions and attitudes.

In this paper we propose a method that employs a clustering technique in order to group users according to the affective content of opinions as expressed in a microblogging service and for this reason we have used datasets derived from the Twitter microblogging application. Our purpose was to test a tool that will automatically extract the affective orientation of users' posts and create groups of users that share common viewpoints towards a topic. Therefore, the affective element of people's attitudes, emotions and beliefs towards a specific topic could

S. D´Mello et al. (Eds.): ACII 2011, Part I, LNCS 6974, pp. 387–396, 2011.

be evaluated. Our method involves the creation of collections of users' posts that refer to specific topics and then based on an emotional dictionary we evaluated users' posts on the basis of a model of eight primary emotions [7]. Next, we applied a clustering algorithm which groups together users' tweets that present similar correlation to a set of primary emotions. Hence, we manage to categorize users tweets and therefore users according to their opinion in regard to a topic.

Given unique challenges in dealing with users' blog posts subjective manner of expression, appropriate pre-processing should be performed to result in suitable data structures for clustering analysis. The experimentation results show that the proposed framework managed to identify blog posts with similar evaluative or affective content towards a topic. To the authors' knowledge no emotional aware clustering approach has been proposed to analyze and identify users' emotions as expressed in blog posts.

The contribution of our work can thus be summarized to the following tasks:

- define the tweet-list, a convenient structure for further data analysis, to represent a user's blog post;
- create an extended emotional dictionary by enriching an opinion lexicon provided by the UMBC university[1] with synonymous words from WordNet;
- propose a similarity measure which evaluates the relation of a blog post to an emotion;
- propose a clustering framework to group blog posts according to the closeness they present to certain emotions.

2 Related Work

Typically, affective evaluations of internet content have been made through sentiment analysis. Sentiment Analysis (or Opinion Mining) is the computational study of opinion, sentiment and emotion of a text [10]. The research area of the sentiment analysis has significantly grown up mostly because of the web 2.0 technologies which have changed the way that people express their views and opinions in the web [12]. Most of the previous research work [14,9] proposed methods for the sentiment classification of product or movie reviews coming mostly from forums and blogs. Short messages from micro blogging sites, like Twitter, are different from reviews mainly because of their purpose and function. Reviews represent summarized thoughts of an author for a particular entity while tweets are more general, casual and abstract.

There is a number of interesting studies that have used the Twitter as a source for sentiment analysis. In [2], the authors found that the surveys' results about consumer confidence and political opinion correlate with sentiment word frequencies in tweets, and therefore they proposed text stream mining as a substitute for traditional polling. In [13], a machine learning algorithm was employed to compare multinomial naive Bayes, maximum entropy classifier, and a linear

[1] UMBC opinion lexicon: http://www.cs.umbc.edu/courses/331/spring10/2/hw/hw7/hw7/data/

support vector machine for the sentiment classification of tweets to positive and negative classes, while in [11], the classification based on the multinomial naive Bayes classifier that uses N-gram and POS-tags as features was evaluated. The above studies exhibited comparable accuracy on their test datasets, but they have certain differences concerning the features they used.

The method in [3] shows a methodology that demonstrates the temporal dynamics of sentiments in reaction to a live debate video. While viewers could only see opinions sequentially while watching, the proposed methodology offered a visual representation of tweets collection and provided the opportunity to understand the overall sentiment (positive and negative) of micro bloggers during the event. To accomplish this they proposed a method for an automatic collection of a corpus that has been used to train a sentiment classifier. The classifier also is based on the multinomial Naive Bayes classifier that uses N-gram and POS-tags as features.

In [1] a method was proposed which performs a sentiment analysis of tweets using an extended version of a well established psychometric instrument, the Profile of Mood States (POMS) and measures six individual dimensions of mood, Tension, Depression, Anger, Vigour, Fatigue, and Confusion. They extract a six-dimensional vector representing the tweet's mood and aggregate mood components on a daily scale comparing their results to the timeline of cultural, social, economic, and political events that took place in that defined period of time.

In this paper we adopted an approach following [7], that focuses on eight primary emotion dimensions: acceptance, fear, anger, joy, anticipation, sadness, disgust and surprise and their synonymous adjectives.This approach is based on the assumption that some basic emotional words which constitute the emotions representatives can determine the sentiment (or, at least some indication) of a sentence by analyzing how similar the sentence's words are with the emotion's representatives.

3 Problem Formulation

The main purpose of our analysis was to determine the orientation of an opinion expressed by web users in a blog post or else a tweet. Table 1 summarizes the basic symbols notation used in this paper.

Table 1. Basic Symbols Notation

Symbol	Definition
m, n, l, p	Number of tweets, tweet's words, primary emotions, emotion's representative words (respectively)
T	Tweets' set $\{t_1, \ldots, t_m\}$
TL_i	The set of words $\{w_1, \ldots, w_n\}$ contained in tweet t_i
E	The set of primary emotions $\{e_1, \ldots, e_l\}$
ER_i	The set of representative words $\{r_{i1}, \ldots, r_{ip}\}$ of the primary emotion e_i
ET_i	The set of emotional words $\{et_1, \ldots, et_d\}$ of tweet t_i

Let t_i denote a user tweet and $T = \{t_1, \ldots, t_m\}$ represents a set of m tweets that refer to a specific topic. Given that a tweet consists of words (140 at most) we define the notion of TWEET-LIST.

Definition 1 (THE TWEET-LIST). *The Tweet-List TL_i is a list used to represent the tweet t_i and it is defined as $TL_i = \{w_1, \ldots, w_n\}$: w_j is a word of t_i and $n \leq 140$.*

Example 1. If we assume that a user publishes the post "I really want a varsity-style jacket" then the respective Tweet-List will be $TL = \{I, really, want, a, varsity - style, jacket\}$.

In the proposed model our purpose is to group a set of tweets on the basis of their relation with specific primary emotions. Let $E_i = \{e_1, \ldots, e_l\}$ denote the set of l primary emotions and $ER_i = \{r_{i1}, \ldots, r_{ip}\}$ the set of p words which act as representatives of emotion e_i.

To calculate the similarity between a tweet t_i and a primary emotion e_j we define two types of similarities: the semantic similarity *Sema* and the sentiment similarity *Senti*.

For the estimation of the semantic similarity *Sema* between a tweet's word w_x and a primary emotion e_j we need to compute the semantic similarities *SeS* between the tweet's word and the emotion's representatives. In other words we need to define a measure that will capture semantic similarity between two words. Thus, we have to use external resources (i.e. web ontologies, thesauri, etc) and a mapping technique between the tweet and the emotion. In our work, we adopted the approach described in [15], due to its straightforward application to our data, according to which the semantic distance between two concepts is proportional to the path distance between them. For example, let w_x be a tweet's word and r_{yz} be the z-th representative of emotion e_y. Given that these are two words for which we want to find the semantic similarity, let $\overrightarrow{w_x}$ and $\overrightarrow{r_{yz}}$ be their corresponding mapping concepts via an ontology. Then, their *Semantic Similarity* SeS is calculated as:

$$SeS(w_x, r_{yz}) = \frac{2 \times depth(LCS)}{[depth(\overrightarrow{w_x}) + depth(\overrightarrow{r_{yz}})]} \tag{1}$$

where $depth(\overrightarrow{w_x})$ is the maximum path length from the root to $\overrightarrow{w_x}$ and LCS is the least common subsumer of $\overrightarrow{w_x}$ and $\overrightarrow{r_{yz}}$.

Then, the semantic similarity *Sema* between a tweet's word w_x and an emotion e_j is defined as the maximum *SeS* of the similarities between the word w_x and the emotion's representatives.

$$Sema(w_x, e_j) = max_{z=1,\ldots,p}(SeS(w_x, r_{jz})) \tag{2}$$

To compute the *Sentiment Score Senti* we have created an extended emotional dictionary, using two dictionaries provided by the University of Maryland. The first one contains 18.536 words and small phrases, as nouns, verbs, adjectives etc, scored with a value between $[-1, 1]$ that indicate their sentiment orientation. The second one contains the 55 most used sentislangs, like :-), :(, etc, scored into the same interval. We used the first dictionary as a seed word list and by looking on WordNet synsets, we derived all the synonyms and created an enriched opinion lexicon. We adopt the assumption of Esuli and Sebastiani [4] and we consider that if a synonymous word or phrase is found in WordNet, then it would have the same semantic meaning. So if a synonymous word exists then we add it into our lexicon assigning the same score value as the seed word. By this bootstrapping procedure we managed to create an extended emotional lexicon of 28.249 words and phrases.

Example 2. In the extended emotional lexicon the words "upstairs", "upstair", "up_the_stairs", ''on_a_higher_floor" are assigned the score value 0.625 while the words "overacting", "overact", "ham_it_up', "ham" the score value −0.75.

Thus, the *Sentiment Score* is directly extracted from the extended emotional lexicon and expresses a word's emotional intensity.

$$Senti(w_i) = FindScore(w_i, Emotional\ Lexicon) \tag{3}$$

Moreover, we define an *Emotional* word w_i as the word that presents an emotional intensity i.e. $Senti(w_i) \neq 0$. We then define the TWEET EMOTIONAL SET of tweet t_i, ET_i as the set of emotional words that belong to tweet t_i.

Definition 2 (THE TWEET-EMOTIONAL-SET). *The Tweet-Emotional-Set* ET_i *is defined as* $ET_i = \{w_j : w_j \in t_i, senti(w_j) \neq 0, 1 \leq j \leq n\}$

Both the semantic similarity *Sema* (Equation 2) and the *Sentiment Score Senti* (Equation 3) are combined in order to compute the total similarity $Sim(t_x, e_y)$ between a tweet t_x and a primary emotion e_y. The $Sim(t_x, e_y)$ considers both the relation of a tweet's words to a primary emotion's representatives and the emotional intensity of the tweet's words. It is defined as:

$$Sim(t_i, e_j) = \frac{\sum_{x=1,\ldots,n}(Sema(w_x, e_j) \cdot Senti(w_x))}{|ET_i|} \tag{4}$$

Lemma 1. *The similarity values Sim fluctuate in the interval* $[-1, 1]$.

Proof. Given that the *SeS* similarity (Equation 1) fluctuates in the interval $[0, 1]$, the definition of *Sema* (Equation 2) indicates the same fluctuation interval. Moreover, the *Senti* similarities (Equation 3) range in the interval $[-1, 1]$ and therefore the numerator in the *Sim* definition (Equation 4) varies in $[-n, n]$. Dividing with the number of the tweet's emotional words we result in the $[-1, 1]$ fluctuation interval for the *Sim* similarity.

At this point, we can define the EMOTION-AWARE CLUSTERING problem as follows:

*Problem 1 (*EMOTION-AWARE CLUSTERING). Given a set T of tweets, a set E of primary emotions and their representatives ER and an integer value k, find k subsets $C_1, C_2, \ldots, C_k$ of tweets which result in the maximization of the quantity $\sum_{x=1}^{k} \sum_{t_i, t_j \in C_x} Sim(t_i, t_j)$, $i = 1, \ldots, n$ and $j = 1, \ldots, n$.

4 The SentiTweetAlgo

The proposed clustering framework involves a three-step process which applies an emotional and semantic aware analysis on data retrieved from Twitter, based on a specific query/topic. At the first step, the preprocessing step, the data cleaning is performed which involves the removal of the tweets' words that are not semantically valid. Moreover, words that do not provide any useful information for our mining process, e.g. articles, numbers and links are removed. As a source of semantic information for terms concepts, we employ the lexicon WordNet [5], which stores english words in hierarchies, depending on their cognitive meaning.

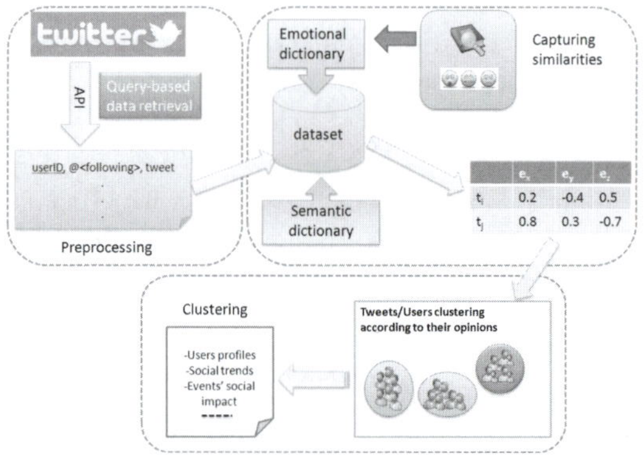

Fig. 1. The proposed framework

At the second step of the similarities capturing, the "clean tweets" derived from the previous step are evaluated in terms of a set of primary emotions. Given the semantic dictionary (Wordnet) and the extended emotional dictionary, which was created as described in Section 3, we calculate the relation of each tweet to a set of primary emotions. For this, we adopted an approach following [7], that focuses on eight primary emotion dimensions: acceptance, fear, anger, joy, anticipation, sadness, disgust and surprise and their synonymous adjectives. This approach is based on the assumption that some basic emotional words which constitute the emotions representatives can determine the sentiment (or, at least some indication) of a sentence by analyzing how similar the sentence's words are with the emotion's representatives. The model is in keeping with seminal activation-evaluative models of emotion [6] and has demonstrated to be particularly suited for computational and text analysis, with the emotions reliably discerned in asynchronous text.

Given the calculated relations between tweets and the eight primary emotions, we proceed to the third step of the algorithm, the clustering, where we apply the K-means clustering algorithm which assigns tweets (while the assignment could be extended to users) into k groups. K-means assigns tweets into groups in time linear on the number of tweets: O(m). Tweets of a group are characterized by similar expressions towards the set of primary emotions. For example, a cluster may contain those tweets that express fear and sadness about the earthquake in Fukushima, Japan. The analysis of the obtained clusters can be beneficial among others, in case of users' profile extraction and identification of social trends and social events' impact. Figure 1 presents the proposed clustering framework.

5 Experimentation

To evaluate the proposed approach we carried out experiments on various datasets derived from twitter (using the Twitter streaming api and a keyword-based filtering). A keyword-driven dataset collection normally results in better quality of data since chatty tweets without a specific meaning may be avoided. To this context, we have experimented with collections of tweets about topics that are expected to trigger different emotional behavior :"christmas" (for seasonal feelings), "lady gaga" (for idols followers) and "wikileaks" (for political opinions). Due to the lack of space we will present the results for the Christmas (of 65166 tweets) dataset which proved to contain quite emotional tweets. At the preprocessing phase tweets that contained no emotional words were removed resulting in a dataset with 63752. Thus, only 2% of the total tweets carried no emotional information. The experimental results presented below are indicative and were obtained for a number of clusters $k = 3$. This k value allows us to provide graphical representations of all clusters without exceeding the spatial restrictions.

Our main goal is to examine how well the proposed approach evaluates the tweets' emotional aspect, i.e. we want to examine the efficiency of our extended emotional dictionary and the proposed *Similarity Score Sim* (Equation 4). Thus, we proceed to a qualitative evaluation of the obtained clusters by examining the tweets assigned to each cluster in terms of the eight primary emotions.

To this context, Figure 2 depicts the number and the score of the tweets assigned to each cluster. Specifically, Figure 2(a) shows the distribution of tweets' scores in terms of the 8 primary emotions. As we can see this cluster contains tweets the majority of which is characterized by a positive score value for all of the emotions. On the contrary, Figure 2(b) depicts the second cluster whose members are tweets that denote negative score in terms of the emotions. Finally, Figure 2(c) includes the tweets with score near 0, which can be characterized as neutral tweets.

Next, we proceed to the creation of the clusters tag clouds (Figure 3) in order to provide an insight of the tweets content. Each tag cloud contains a set of the most frequent words that exist in the respective cluster's tweets. Thus, the first cluster (Figure3(a)) that contains positive tweets is represented by emotionally "strong" words such as *great, love, kiss* and *happy*. The second cluster (Figure 3(b)) is represented by words such as *separately, distance, working and little* which signify emotional negativeness. The third cluster (Figure 3(c)) contains words that do not exhibit a particular intensity.

Table 2 presents some sample tweets that exhibit high positive and negative scores in terms of the primary emotions. Our purpose is to examine whether the

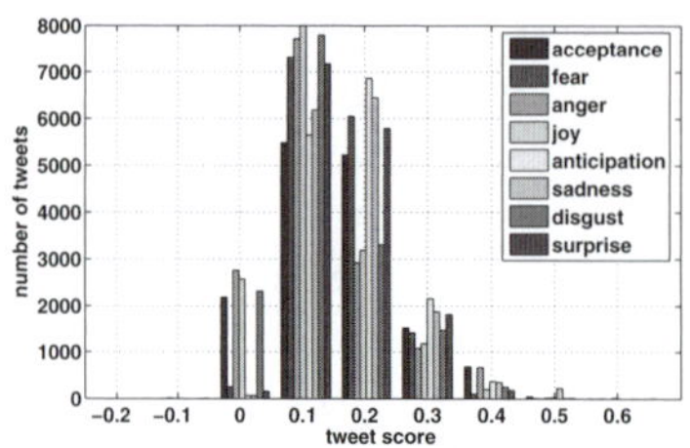

(a) Cluster with positive tweets' emotions

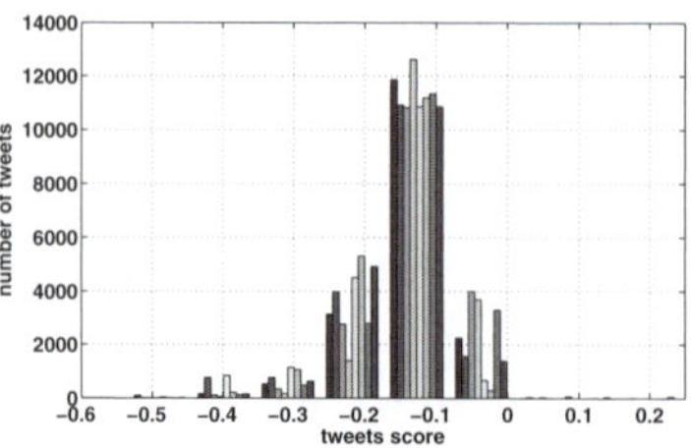

(b) Cluster with negative tweets' emotions

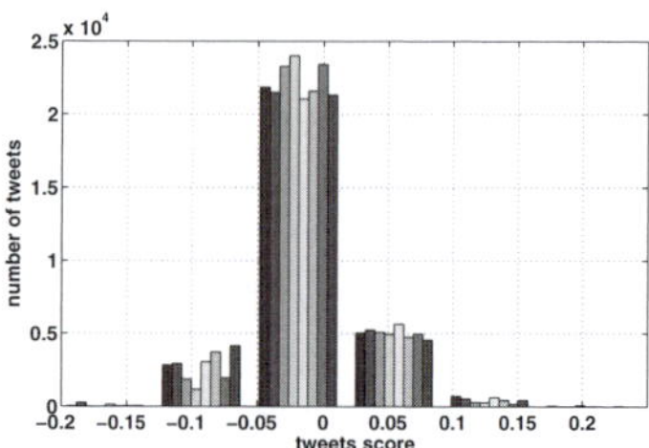

(c) Cluster with neutral tweets' emotions

Fig. 2. Tweets assignment to clusters

(a) Cluster with positive emotions

(b) Cluster with negative emotions

(c) Cluster with neutral emotions

Fig. 3. Clusters' tag clouds

Table 2. Sample tweets

Acceptance +	oh lovely christmas cake!?
Acceptance -	i really wish i understood christmas music goes annoying cheerful one week
Fear +	If I eat anymore chocolate oranges this Christmas I fear I will indeed become one!
Fear -	Who's brave enough to admit, that they secretly like to sing their favorite #Christmas songs, while driving alone in their car? Guilty ;)
Anger +	517/533 films on tv over Christmas will be repeats! Outrage!
Anger -	Investigation Reveals Christmas Cruelty Towards Reindeer
Joy +	At a Christmas concert supporting my niece. She is doing brilliantly.
Joy -	it is more that I hate people at Christmas. More than other times of the year that is
Anticipation +	merry christmas me! i've been listening the skillet tribute album and wow!! check it out! :)
Anticipation -	can't wait for new commercial merry christmas
Sadness +	sad i'm more excited "in darkness and light" box set than i am christmas
Sadness -	one thing i love christmas time
Disgust +	i hate christmas they suck
Disgust -	one thing i love christmas time
Surprise +	I love surprises I can't wait for Christmas!!!
Surprise -	At this boring work Christmas party and we gotta go back to work!!!!

extended emotional dictionary and the proposed similarity *Sim* manages to guide efficiently the clustering process. The tweets which are indicatively presented show that words inside the tweets that carry emotional information significantly affect the overall tweet *Sim* score. For example words such as *lovely, annoying, favorite, sad, hate* and *boring* considerably determine the tweet-emotion relation.

The above indicative (due to the lack of space) discussion clearly shows that the proposed approach can be used in order to automatically retrieve a set of tweets that share common emotions towards a topic. To guide more the clustering process and result for instance to a cluster with positive tweets scores in terms of specific emotions, we could execute the kmeans algorithm by providing a set of seeds, i.e. the initial cluster centers.

6 Conclusions and Future Work

The social web growth and the corresponding rise in available emotional text over the past years has led to an increased interest in sentiment analysis. In this paper we propose an emotional aware clustering approach which aims to group tweets, and therefore users, according to their opinions as expressed in a microblogging application. The results of the proposed framework can be very useful for the efficient extraction of users profiles and the identification of social trends and events' impact. They can also provide an unprecedented level of analytics for companies, politicians and other public services. As shown in [8] micro blogging services are a potentially rich source for companies to explore as part of their overall branding strategy. Customer perceptions and purchasing decisions appear increasingly influenced by social networking services, since these act as trusted sources of information, insights and opinions.

In the future we aim to improve the overall process incorporating other sentiment lexicons to enhance the data cleaning process and eliminate noise. This work could expand to explore the relative impact of positive and negative affect [6] in internet attitudinal material, employing more advanced linguistic techniques. Moreover, we plan to apply more advanced mining techniques that will result in more automatic and accurate identification of users emotions.

References

1. Bollen, J., Pepe, A., Mao, H.: Modeling public mood and emotion: Twitter sentiment and socio-economic phenomena. In: ICWSM 2011, arXiv: 0911.1583 (2011)
2. OĆonnor, B., Balasubramanyan, R., Routledge, B., Smith, N.: From Tweets to Polls: Linking Text Sentiment to Public Opinion Time Series. In: Int. AAAI Conf. on Weblogs and Social Media, Washington DC, pp. 122–129 (2010)
3. Diakopoulos, N., Shamma, D.: Characterizing Debate Performance via Aggregated Twitter Sentiment. In: ACM Conf. on Human Factors in Computing Systems (CHI), Atlanta Georgia, pp. 1195–1198 (2010)
4. Esuli, A., Sebastiani, F.: PageRanking WordNet Synsets: An Application on Opinion Mining. In: 45th Annual Meeting of the Association for Computational Linguistics (ACL 2007), Prague, CZ, pp. 424–431 (2007)
5. Fellbaum, C.: WordNet: An Electronic Lexical Database. MIT Press, Cambridge (1998)
6. Feldman Barrett, L., Russell, J.A.: Independence and bipolarity in the structure of affect. J. Personality and Social Psychology 74, 967–984 (1998)
7. Gill, A.J., French R.M., Gergle, D., Oberlander, J.: Identifying Emotional Characteristics from Short Blog Texts. In: 30th Annual Conf. of the Cognitive Science Society, Washington DC, pp. 2237–2242 (2008)
8. Jansen, B., Zhang, M., Sobel, K., Chowdury, A.: Micro-blogging as online word of mouth branding. In: 27th Int. Conf. Extended Abstracts on Human Factors in Computing Systems, Boston, pp. 3859–3864 (2009)
9. Hu, M., Liu, B.: Mining and Summarizing Customer Reviews.In: 10th ACM SIGKDD Int. Conference on Knowledge Discovery and Data Mining, Washington USA, pp. 168–177 (2004)
10. Liu, B.: In: Indurkhya, N., Damerau, F.J. (eds.) Handbook of Natural Language Processing, 2nd edn., Goshen, Connecticut, USA (2010)
11. Pak, A., Paroubek, P.: Twitter as a corpus for sentiment analysis and opinion mining. In: 7th Conf. on Int. Language Resources and Evaluation, Malta, pp. 1320–1326 (2010)
12. Pang, B., Lee, L.: Opinion Mining and Sentiment Analysis. Foundations and Trends in Information Retrieval 2(1-2), 1–135 (2008)
13. Parikh, R., Movassate, M.: Sentiment Analysis of User-Generated Twitter Updates using Various Classification Techniques
14. Turney, P.: Thumbs Up or Thumbs Down? Semantic Orientation Applied to Unsupervised Classification of Reviews. In: 40th Annual Meeting of the Association for Computational Linguistics, Philadephia, pp. 417–424 (2002)
15. Wu, Z., Palmer, M.: Verm semantics and lexical selection. In: 32nd Annual Meeting of the Association for Computational Linguistics, New Mexico, pp. 133–138 (1994)

A Phonetic Analysis of Natural Laughter, for Use in Automatic Laughter Processing Systems

Jérôme Urbain and Thierry Dutoit

Université de Mons - UMONS, Faculté Polytechnique de Mons, TCTS Lab
20 Place du Parc, 7000 Mons, Belgique
{jerome.urbain,thierry.dutoit}@umons.ac.be

Abstract. In this paper, we present the detailed phonetic annotation of the publicly available AVLaughterCycle database, which can readily be used for automatic laughter processing (analysis, classification, browsing, synthesis, etc.). The phonetic annotation is used here to analyze the database, as a first step. Unsurprisingly, we find that h-like phones and central vowels are the most frequent sounds in laughter. However, laughs can contain many other sounds. In particular, nareal fricatives (voiceless friction in the nostrils) are frequent both in inhalation and exhalation phases. We show that the airflow direction (inhaling or exhaling) changes significantly the duration of laughter sounds. Individual differences in the choice of phones and their duration are also examined. The paper is concluded with some perspectives the annotated database opens.

1 Motivation and Related Work

Laughter is an important emotional signal in human communication. During the last decades, it received growing attention from researchers. If we still do not understand exactly *why* we laugh, progress has been made in understanding *what* it brings us (enhanced mood, reduction of stress, and other health outcomes [2,14]) and in describing *how* we laugh (see [1,5,17,19]). This paper will focus on the last aspect, laughter description, with the aim of improving automatic laughter processing. In particular, we will mainly consider the acoustic aspects.

Bachorowski et al. [1] were the first to extensively report about the acoustic features of human laughter. They classified laughs in three broad groups: song-like, snort-like and grunt-like. They also labeled the syllables constituting these laughs as voiced or unvoiced. They analyzed several features (duration, pitch, formants) over syllables and whole laughs. They found that mainly central vowels are used in laughter and that the fundamental frequency can take extreme values compared to speech. More generally, laughter has been identified as a highly-variable phenomenon. Chafe [5] illustrates a variety of its shapes and sounds with the help of acoustic features (voicing, pitch, energy, etc.).

However, despite the numerous terms used in the literature to describe laughter (see the summary given by Trouvain [21]), there is currently no standard for laughter annotation. Phonetic transcriptions appear in a few laughter-related papers (see [7,16]) but, to our knowledge, no large laughter database has been

S. D´Mello et al. (Eds.): ACII 2011, Part I, LNCS 6974, pp. 397–406, 2011.

annotated that way. For example, the two most used natural laughter databases, the ICSI [9] and AMI [4] Meeting Corpora, do not include detailed laughter annotation (only the presence of laughter in a speech turn is indicated). The ICSI Meeting corpus contains around 72 hours of audio recordings from 75 meetings. The AMI Meeting Corpus consists of 100 hours of audiovisual recordings during meetings. Both databases contain a lot of spontaneous, conversational laughter (108 minutes in the 37 ICSI recordings used in [22]).

With the development of intelligent human-computer interfaces, the need for emotional speech understanding and synthesis has emerged. In consequence, interest for laughter processing increased. Several teams developed automatic laughter recognition systems. In [10,22], classifiers have been trained to discriminate between laughter and speech, using spectral and prosodic features. Reported Equal Error Rates (EER) were around 10%. The local decision was improved in [11] thanks to long-term features, lowering the EER to a few percent. Recently, Petridis and Pantic [15] combined audio and visual features to separate speech from voiced and unvoiced laughter with 75% of accuracy[1]. No method has been designed to automatically label laughs, classify them in finer categories than simply voiced or unvoiced, or segment long laughter episodes in laughter "bouts" (exhalation phases separated by inhalations).

A few researchers have also investigated laughter synthesis. Sundaram and Narayanan [18] modeled the energy envelope with a mass-spring analogy and synthesized the vowel sounds of laughter using linear prediction. Lasarcyk and Trouvain [13] compared synthesis by diphone concatenation and 3D modeling of the vocal tract. Unfortunately, in neither case the obtained laughs were perceived as natural by naive listeners. A recent online survey [6] confirmed that no laughter synthesis technique currently reaches a high degree of naturalness.

In a previous work, we have developed an avatar able to join in laughing with its conversational partner [24]. However, the laughs produced by the virtual agent were not synthesized but selected from an audiovisual laughter database, using acoustic similarities to the conversational partner's laughs.

We strongly believe that both automatic laughter recognition/characterization and synthesis would benefit from a detailed phonetic transcription of laughter. On the recognition side, transcriptions can help classifying laughs, on a simple phonetic basis or via features easily computed once the phonetic segmentation is available (syllabic rhythm, exhalation and inhalation phases, acoustic evolution over laughter syllables or bouts, etc.). On the synthesis side, transcription enables approaches similar to those used in speech synthesis: training a system with the individual phonetic units and then synthesizing any consistent phonetic sequence.

In this paper, we present the phonetic annotation of the AVLaughterCycle database [23], which currently is the only large (1 hour of laughs) spontaneous laughter database to include audio, video and phonetic transcriptions. In addition, we use these phonetic transcriptions to study some factors of variability – the

[1] Accuracy and Equal Error Rates cannot be directly compared. However, $1-EER$ is a measure of the accuracy; with no guarantee it is the best the system can achieve.

airflow direction and personal style –, which received few interest in previous works. The annotation process is explained in Section 2. Section 3 presents the most frequent phones[2] in exhalation and inhalation phases and shows differences in their duration. Section 4 focuses on individual differences in the phones used and in their durations. Finally, conclusions are given in Section 5. They include perspectives we consider with the large phonetically annotated database, which is the groundwork for further developments in the laughter processing field.

2 Annotation Scheme

We used the AVLaughterCycle database, which contains laughs from 24 subjects (9 females and 15 males) [23]. The female and male average ages were respectively 30 (standard deviation: 7.8) and 28 (standard deviation: 7.1). All subjects were participants of the eNTERFACE'09 Workshop in Genova (Italy). They came from various countries: Belgium (8), France (4), Italy (3), Canada (2), UK, Greece, Turkey, Kazakhstan, India, USA and South Korea (1 each). All subjects could speak English. Laughs were elicited with the help of a comedy video. The database consists of audio and video recordings, including facial motion tracking.

Laughs had previously been segmented on the basis of the audiovisual signal. In total, 1021 laughs have been segmented, for a total of 1 hour of spontaneous, hilarious laughs. The database and annotations are freely available on the website of the first author (`http://tcts.fpms.ac.be/~urbain`).

For the present work, one annotator labeled the 1021 laughs in phones in the Praat software [3]. Two annotation tracks have been used (see Figure 1). The first is used to transcribe the "phones"[3], according to the phonetic symbols defined by Ladefoged [12]. Diacritics (symbols added to a letter) have also been used to label voice quality (modal, creaky, breathy) or unusual ways of pronouncing a given phone (e.g. a voiceless vowel or a nasalized plosive), thereby leading to something that looks more like a narrow phonetic transcription of the database. Several sounds encountered in our data could not be found in the extended International Phonetic Alphabet. To describe them, similarly to previous works ([1,5]), the following labels have been added: hum, cackle, groan, snore, vocal fry and grunt. Examples are available on the website of the first author.

Since the respiratory dynamics are important to process laughter and since the acoustics of laughter are different when inhaling and exhaling, the airflow phases are transcribed on the second annotation track. The airflow phases were segmented using only the audio.

Unsurprisingly, we have noticed that the phones constituting a laugh are often perceived differently when listening to the laugh as a whole than when analyzing each of its phones separately. As a matter of fact, although laughter episodes exhibit no strong semantic contrast (as opposed to words), they still obey strong

[2] The phonological notion of "phoneme" is not clearly defined for laughter; we prefer to use the word "phone" for the acoustic units found in our database.

[3] Note that we used only audio for this transcription, while laughter segmentation was done on the basis of both audio and video.

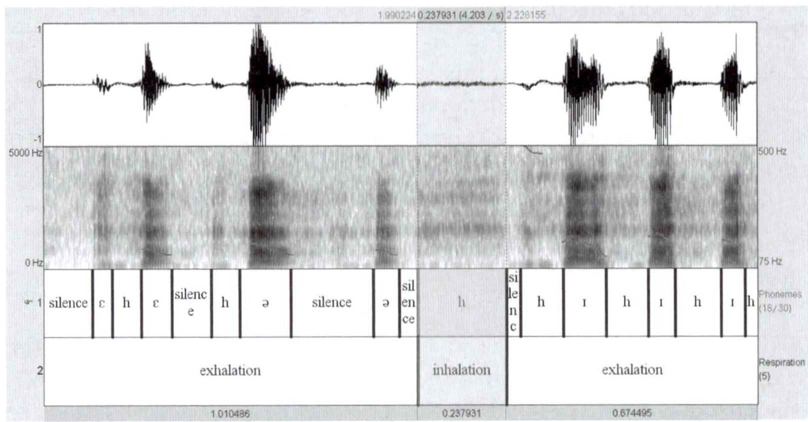

Fig. 1. Laughter annotation in Praat

phonotactic constraints (e.g. we will have the impression of *hahahaha* when actually listening to *haha-aha* because the first instance is more likely to happen). In addition, psychoacoustic effects are likely to influence our perception of continuous laughter, given its fast succession of sounds that can be highly contrasted in amplitude. In this work, we annotated laughter phones as they had been produced, rather than how they actually sounded, following a long tradition of articulatory phonetic transcription.

3 Laughter Phonetic Description

Out of the initial 1021 laughs, the 20 laughs involving speech and 4 short laughs labeled as only silence (i.e. they only had visual contributions) were discarded from our phonetic analysis, leaving 997 acoustic laughs. Excluding the silences outside acoustic laughs (as the laughs had been segmented with the help of visual cues, most of the times there are silences before the first phone and after the last phone), 17202 phones have been annotated: 15825 in exhalation phases and 1377 in inhalation phases. If we take diacritics into account[4], 196 phonetic labels appear in the database: 142 during exhalations and 54 during inhalations. This reinforces the idea that laughter is extremely variable.

For the sake of simplicity, the diacritics will not be considered in this paper. This reduces the number of labels to 124 (88 during exhalations, 36 during inhalations). The most frequent phonetic labels in exhalation and inhalation phases are respectively listed in Tables 1 and 2, with their average duration.

The outcomes of our annotation are mostly in line with previous findings ([1,17,19]). During exhalation phases, if we exclude silences that are extremely

[4] The following diacritics, showed here on the letter e, have been used: ẽ (nasalized), ḛ (creaky), e̤ (breathy), e̊ (voiceless), é (high tone).

Table 1. Most frequent phonetic labels in laughter exhalation phases

Label	Occurrences	Average duration (std)	Label	Occurrences	Average duration (std)
silence	4886	0.308s (0.427s)	ǀ	214	0.031s (0.032s)
h	2723	0.121s (0.068s)	x	176	0.228s (0.170s)
ə	1422	0.073s (0.044s)	ʌ	160	0.094s (0.066s)
ɐ	1373	0.082s (0.047s)	ħ	152	0.175s (0.085s)
ɦ̃̊	839	0.210s (0.134s)	ɦ	135	0.175s (0.114s)
ɪ	741	0.077s (0.039s)	ɵ	109	0.116s (0.058s)
cackle	704	0.034s (0.024s)	k	102	0.048s (0.051s)
hum	639	0.077s (0.042s)	t	81	0.073s (0.035s)
ɛ	370	0.076s (0.035s)	grunt	81	0.126s (0.104s)
ʔ	269	0.027s (0.016s)	ʉ	79	0.093s (0.090s)

Table 2. Most frequent phonetic labels in laughter inhalation phases

Label	Occurrences	Average duration (std)	Label	Occurrences	Average duration (std)
h	640	0.305s (0.133s)	s	38	0.340s (0.141s)
ə	172	0.095s (0.059s)	ħ	24	0.340s (0.154s)
ɦ̃̊	166	0.346s (0.170s)	t	23	0.049s (0.032s)
ɪ	108	0.097s (0.064s)	i	23	0.148s (0.058s)
ɦ	38	0.226s (0.121s)	ɛ	17	0.094s (0.039s)

frequent inside laughs, we obtained a large number of h-like phones (h, x, ɦ, ħ), and voiced parts are mainly central vowels (ə, ɐ, ɵ, ʉ). As stated in [5], but contested in [17], voiced segments can be abruptly ended by a glottal stop (ʔ).

We also found a lot of non-stereotypical laughter sounds. Nareal fricatives (ɦ̃̊) are frequently used, mostly in short laughs with a closed mouth, in which a voiceless airflow going through the nose accompanies a smile. In addition, we have occurrences of non central vowels (ɪ, ɛ, ʌ), which were not found by Bachorowski et al.'s formant frequency analyses [1]. Our data also contains numerous cackles, hum-like sounds (close to vowels, but with a closed mouth), and grunts. More surprising is the presence of a large number of dental clicks (ǀ) and plosives (t, k) that generally take place at the beginning of sudden exhalation phases.

During inhalation phases, the most used phones are similar. Deep breath sounds (h, ɦ̃̊, ɦ) are even more dominant. It can also be noticed that, except for t, the average duration of a phone is longer during inhalation phases than in exhalation phases. Student's *t-tests* show that the average duration in inhalation and exhalation is significantly different at a 99% confidence level ($p < 0.01$) for all the phones that appear in both Tables 1 and 2 (h, ə, ɦ̃̊, ɪ, ɦ and ħ) except for t (no difference) and ɛ ($p = 0.22$). Over the whole database, the average phone duration for exhalation and inhalation phases is respectively $0.165s$ ($std : 0.266s$) and $0.245s$ ($std : 0.159s$). The difference is significant at a 99% confidence level.

Table 3. Number of laughs with a given number of exhalation and inhalation phases

N	Number of laughs having N exhalations	Number of laughs having N inhalations
0	1	462
1	733	353
2	156	105
3	54	39
4	26	18
≥ 5	27	20

Regarding the airflow phases, 1551 exhalation phases and 943 inhalation phases have been annotated. The average duration of exhalation and inhalation phases is respectively $1.69s$ (std : $1.52s$) and $0.36s$ (std : $0.15s$). No correlation has been found between the duration of an exhalation phase and the duration of its surrounding inhalations (correlations < 0.1). Table 3 shows the number of laughs presenting a given number of exhalation and inhalation phases.

Most of the laughs have only one "bout" (i.e. exhalation segment separated by inhalations) [21]. The number of inhalation phases is lower than the number of exhalations, meaning that most laughs are not concluded by an audible inhalation. In fact, only 38% of the laughs are ended by an audible inhalation.

4 Interpersonal Differences

We have already stated that the AVLaughterCycle database as a whole contains a wide range of phones, and that these phones have variable durations, influenced by the airflow direction. We will now present some figures corroborating the impression that laughter exhibits individual patterns. We will see that there are more individual differences in the sounds produced than in the duration of the segments. Since the number of subjects and phones are large, we cannot give an exhaustive analysis in this paper and will concentrate on a few examples.

4.1 Phones Used

Subjects used different sets of phones while laughing. The number of phones used per laugher ranges from 2 to 59, with a mean (and median) of 32 (std : 14.4). There are large inter-individual differences in the choice of phones. Most laughers are quite consistent from one laugh to another, in accordance to Chafe's statement that users have their "favorite laugh" [5]. Figure 2 displays, for the 5 subjects who laughed the most and the 7 most used exhalation labels (except silence), the individual phone probabilities (i.e. the number of instances of phone X by subject Y, divided by the total number of phones produced by Y). We can see that subject 6 typically uses h and ɐ. His laugh is quite stereotypical. This is not the case for other subjects. Subject 20 produces much more nasal sounds (ɦ̃ and hum) than others. The choice of the vowel is another difference

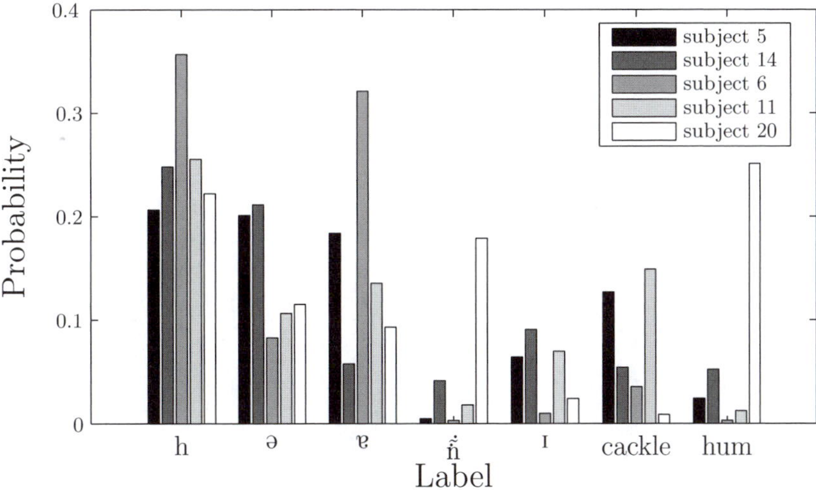

Fig. 2. Probabilities of the most used phones for the 5 subjects who laughed the most

between subjects: some laughers use up to 3 times more ə than ɐ, others do the opposite.

There are numerous other proofs of individual differences in the produced sounds that do not appear on the graph. For example, subject 14 is the only one to make a broad use of the phone m, which is present 23 times in her 48 laughs (generally at the end), while there are only 15 other instances of this phone in the database, produced by 11 different subjects. Subject 14 is also responsible for 87 of the 109 instances of the phone ɵ.

4.2 Phone and Airflow Phases Duration

The average duration of exhalation phones is similar for all subjects: slightly under 100ms for voiced phones, a bit larger for h-like sounds and nareal fricatives. There is a slightly larger individual variation for inhalation phones. Figure 3 represents the average duration of the 3 most frequent inhalation phones for all the subjects, with their corresponding standard deviations. No bar means that the subject did not produce the corresponding phone. We can see that there are some extreme values for all three phones, showing some individual influence over the length of inhalation phones.

Figure 4 shows the average durations (and standard deviations) of exhalation phases for all the subjects. We can notice some individual variability, but the large standard deviations prevent us from drawing strong conclusions. The average inhalation durations are similar for all the subjects. The large variability of the laughter phone and bout durations is in line with the findings in [1].

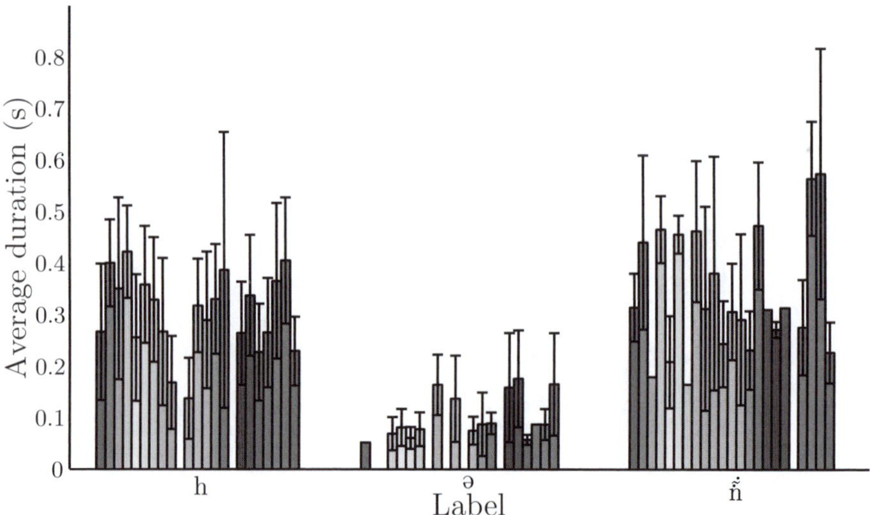

Fig. 3. Average duration of the most frequent inhalation phones, for all the subjects

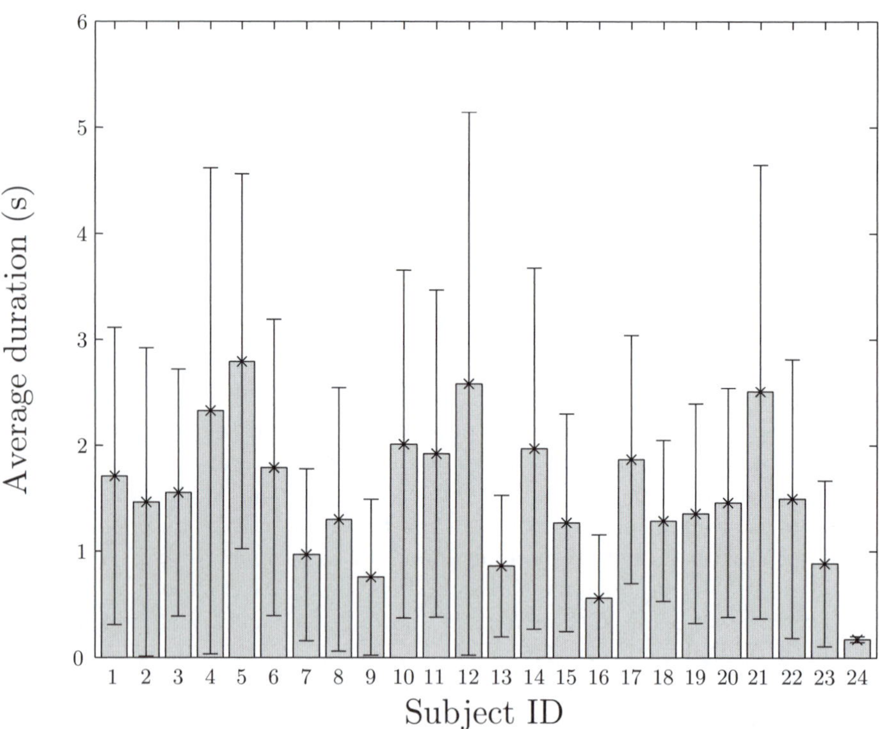

Fig. 4. Average duration of exhalation phases, for all the subjects

5 Conclusion and Further Work

In this paper, we have presented the phonetic annotation of a large laughter database. The AVLaughterCycle database and these annotations are freely available on the website of the first author (`http://tcts.fpms.ac.be/~urbain`).

This large, phonetically annotated database can be used for a broad range of purposes. First, it can serve to study and describe laughter, its variability, and factors responsible for these variations. We have started this type of analyses in this paper, showing that 1) the airflow direction influences the phone duration; 2) individuals have their own favorite subset of phones for laughing; 3) the duration of laughter units (phones and airflow phases) can also vary with individuals. More acoustic features (fundamental frequency, formants, etc.) could be extracted and compared over phones or individuals. We are currently working on robust fundamental frequency estimation for laughter.

Second, since there is currently no standard of annotating laughter, we hope that this paper will be an important step toward this type of agreement. Among the other available laughter databases (for example the ICSI [9] and AMI [4] Meeting corpora), the AVLaughterCycle is unique given its audiovisual data – including facial motion tracking – and annotation.

Manual phonetic annotation is extremely time-consuming. One of our objectives is to develop automatic laughter phonetic transcription, going beyond current laughter recognition systems that consider at most two categories [15].

Such a phonetic transcription is crucial to natural laughter synthesis, for which a phonetic description of laughter will make it possible to use efficient speech synthesis approaches (e.g. unit selection [8] or parametric synthesis [20]) to develop text-to-laughter (or more accurately, labels-to-laughter) synthesis.

Combining these approaches, we aim to improve our AVLaughterCycle application [24], which consists in enabling a virtual agent to detect its conversational partner's laugh and answer with an appropriate, human-like laugh.

All these aspects will be addressed within the European FP7 FET project ILHAIRE starting in September 2011. In this project, not only the computing aspects of how to recognize, characterize, generate and synthesize laughter will be studied, but also the psychological foundations of this important signal (to avoid inappropriate laughs sounding rude to the user) as well as cultural differences.

References

1. Bachorowski, J.A., Smoski, M.J., Owren, M.J.: The acoustic features of human laughter. Journal of the Acoustical Society of America 110, 1581–1597 (2007)
2. Bennett, M.P., Lengacher, C.: Humour and laughter may influence health. III. Laughter and Health Outcomes. Evidence-based Complementary and Alternative Medicine 5(1), 37–40 (2008)
3. Boersma, P., Weenink, D.: Praat: doing phonetics by computer (version 5.2.11) (computer program), `www.praat.org` (retrieved on January 20, 2011)
4. Carletta, J.: Unleashing the killer corpus: experiences in creating the multi-everything AMI Meeting Corpus. Language Resources and Evaluation Journal 41(2), 181–190 (2007)

5. Chafe, W.: The Importance of not being earnest. In: The Feeling Behind Laughter and Humor., paperback 2009 edn. Consciousness & Emotion Book Series, vol. 3. John Benjamins Publishing Company, Amsterdam (2007)
6. Cox, T.: Laughter's secrets: faking it – the results. New Scientist (July 27, 2010), `http://www.newscientist.com/article/dn19227-laughters-secrets-faking-it--the-results.html`
7. Esling, J.H.: States of the larynx in laughter. In: Proc. of the Interdisciplinary Workshop on the Phonetics of Laughter, Saarbrücken, Germany, pp. 15–20 (2007)
8. Hunt, A., Black, A.: Unit selection in a concatenative speech synthesis system using a large speech database. In: ICASSP, pp. 373–376. IEEE, Los Alamitos (1996)
9. Janin, A., Baron, D., Edwards, J., Ellis, D., Gelbart, D., Morgan, N., Peskin, B., Pfau, T., Shriberg, E., Stolcke, A., et al.: The ICSI meeting corpus. In: Proc. of ICASSP 2003, vol. 1, p. I–364. IEEE, Hong-Kong (2003)
10. Kennedy, L., Ellis, D.: Laughter detection in meetings. In: NIST ICASSP 2004 Meeting Recognition Workshop, Montreal, pp. 118–121 (2004)
11. Knox, M.T., Morgan, N., Mirghafori, N.: Getting the last laugh: automatic laughter segmentation in meetings. In: INTERSPEECH 2008, Brisbane, Australia (2008)
12. Ladefoged, P.: A course in phonetics, `http://hctv.humnet.ucla.edu/departments/linguistics/VowelsandConsonants/course/chapter1/chapter1.html` (consulted on January 20, 2011)
13. Lasarcyk, E., Trouvain, J.: Imitating conversational laughter with an articulatory speech synthesis. In: Proc. of the Interdisciplinary Workshop on the Phonetics of Laughter, Saarbrücken, Germany, pp. 43–48 (2007)
14. Mahony, D.L.: Is laughter the best medicine or any medicine at all? Eye on Psi. Chi. 4(3), 18–21 (2000)
15. Petridis, S., Pantic, M.: Is this joke really funny? Judging the mirth by audiovisual laughter analysis. In: Proc. of ICME 2009, New York, USA, pp. 1444–1447 (2009)
16. Pompino-Marschall, B., Kowal, S., O'Connell, D.C.: Some phonetic notes on emotion: laughter, interjections and weeping. In: Proc. of the Interdisciplinary Workshop on the Phonetics of Laughter, Saarbrücken, Germany, pp. 41–42 (2007)
17. Ruch, W., Ekman, P.: The expressive pattern of laughter. In: Kaszniak, A. (ed.) Emotion, Qualia and Consciousness. World Scientific Publishers, Tokyo (2001)
18. Sundaram, S., Narayanan, S.: Automatic acoustic synthesis of human-like laughter. Journal of the Acoustical Society of America 121(1), 527–535 (2007)
19. Szameitat, D.P., Alter, K., Szameitat, A.J., Wildgruber, D., Sterr, A., Darwin, C.J.: Acoustic profiles of distinct emotional expressions in laughter. The Journal of the Acoustical Society of America 126(1), 354–366 (2009)
20. Tokuda, K., Zen, H., Black, A.: An HMM-based speech synthesis system applied to english. In: 2002 IEEE TTS Workshop, Santa Monica, California (2002)
21. Trouvain, J.: Segmenting phonetic units in laughter. In: Proc. of the 15th International Congress of Phonetic Sciences, Barcelona, Spain, pp. 2793–2796 (2003)
22. Truong, K.P., van Leeuwen, D.A.: Evaluating automatic laughter segmentation in meetings using acoustic and acoustic-phonetic features. In: Proc. of the Interdisciplinary Workshop on the Phonetics of Laughter. Saarbrücken, Germany (2007)
23. Urbain, J., Bevacqua, E., Dutoit, T., Moinet, A., Niewiadomski, R., Pelachaud, C., Picart, B., Tilmanne, J., Wagner, J.: The AVLaughterCycle database. In: Proc. of LREC 2010, Valletta, Malta (2010)
24. Urbain, J., Niewiadomski, R., Bevacqua, E., Dutoit, T., Moinet, A., Pelachaud, C., Picart, B., Tilmanne, J., Wagner, J.: AVLaughterCycle: Enabling a virtual agent to join in laughing with a conversational partner using a similarity-driven audiovisual laughter animation. JMUI 4(1), 47–58 (2010), special Issue: eNTERFACE 2009

The Impact of Music on Affect during Anger Inducing Drives

Marjolein D. van der Zwaag[1], Stephen Fairclough[2], Elena Spiridon[2], and Joyce H.D.M. Westerink[1]

[1] Philips Research Laboratories, High Tech Campus 34, 5656 AE Eindhoven, The Netherlands
{marjolein.van.der.zwaag,joyce.westerink}@philips.com
[2] Liverpool John Moores University, Byromstreet, Liverpool, L3 3AF, United Kingdom
e.spiridon@2008.ljmu.ac.uk, s.fairclough@ljmu.ac.uk

Abstract. Driver anger could be potentially harmful for road safety and long-term health. Because of its mood inducing properties, music is assumed to be a potential medium that could prevent anger induction during driving. In the current study the influence of music on anger, mood, skin conductance, and systolic blood pressure was investigated during anger inducing scenarios in a driving simulator. 100 participants were split into five groups: four listened to different types of music (high / low energy in combination with both positive / negative valence) or a no music control. Results showed that anger induction was highest during high energy negative music compared to positive music irrespective of energy level. Systolic blood pressure and skin conductance levels were higher during high energy negative music and no music compared to low energy music. Music was demonstrated to mediate the state of anger and therefore can have positive health benefits in the long run.

Keywords: Anger, music, mood, blood pressure, skin conductance, simulated drive.

1 Introduction

The experience of anger is a relatively common emotion for many drivers [1,2]. The inconsiderate behavior of other road users coupled with natural sources of frustration such as being lost or encountering traffic jams may combine to induce negative emotional experiences while driving. Driver anger may stem principally from several sources: uncertainty due to the erratic behavior of others (e.g. a driver who brakes and slows down for no apparent reason), shock/surprise due to driver error (e.g. turning without signaling) or recklessness (e.g. high speeds, vehicles cutting across the path of one's own vehicle) and frustration due to obstacles (e.g. slow moving traffic, a diversion or being lost) [3].

The function of anger is to regulate body processes related to self-defense and social behaviors [4]. In concrete terms, this means that anger may serve a function to remove obstacles to task goals. Feelings of anger may be classified as 'unhealthy' emotions as these episodes are associated with increased cardiovascular reactivity and a heightened response from the sympathetic nervous system. This is not to say that

S. D'Mello et al. (Eds.): ACII 2011, Part I, LNCS 6974, pp. 407–416, 2011.

episodes of anger per se constitute a health risk, but rather that repeated exposure to increased anger and cardiovascular reactivity represents a form of "wear and tear" on the human body that may have a cumulative influence on health in the long-term [5].

Music is able to influence mood to a wide variety of states; from elation to relaxation or sadness [6]. The pleasurable effects of music might be asserted through affect. Hence, changing affect is mentioned as one of the most important functions of music. For example, music has shown to decrease anxiety in hospital environments [7], and reduced several negative emotions as a result of music therapy [6]. The changes in affect due to music have also been linked to physiological changes. For example, arousing music has been found to increase sympathetic nervous system activity shown in skin conductance [8]. Furthermore, music has been found to reduce skin conductance levels during sad low energy music [9,10].

Listening to music while driving is a common activity [11], which may influence behavior and mood states. Brodsky [12] described how listening to high tempo house music increased driving speed. It has additionally been found that listening to self-selected music compared to no music decreased stress while driving [13]. Furthermore, music compared to a no music situation lowered aggression during drives with time urgency [14]. People listen to music while driving because music influences affect and music distracts from the relative monotony of the driving task. The distraction of music might lead attention from negative events in the roadway environment thereby facilitating recovery from sources of anger or frustration. Music may affect the mood state of the individual by influencing the level of activation or by inducing positive or negative changes in mood valence.

The current study was designed to examine how the emotional properties of music (energy and valence) may impact on the psychophysiological status of an angry driver during a simulated journey. Thereby the current study follows the dimensional approach of mood into 2 (valence and energy) dimensions [15,16]. Five groups of participants completed a short journey under time pressure during which they encountered a number of obstacles, e.g. traffic jams. Four of the groups were presented with music, which could be described as: high energy / positive valence (i.e. activating, joyous music), low energy / positive valence (i.e. calming, relax music), high energy/ negative valence (i.e. activating, angry music), low energy/ negative valence (i.e. calming, sad music). A fifth group was included in the study as a control group who did not hear any music during the simulated journey.

2 Method

2.1 Participants

Each group of participants included 20 volunteers in total (10 males, 10 females) making 100 participants in total. The mean age of the participants was 21.2 years [s.d. = 4.7 years). Each participant received a £20 voucher for participation.

2.2 Design

The actual experiment consisted of two sessions. In the first session music was rated via the internet, at the convenience of the participants, and took approximately 60 minutes; note that also the control group completed this session. The purpose of this initial session was to personalize the music choice for those individuals in the four music groups: HE/PV = High Energy/ Positive Valence, LE/PV = Low Energy/ Positive Valence, HE/NV = High Energy/ Negative Valence, LE/NV = Low Energy/ Negative Valence. The second session took approximately 60 minutes in a laboratory and involved a baseline measurement, a mood induction, and driving in a simulated environment whilst wearing psychophysiological sensors.

2.3 Music Selection

Via an online questionnaire participants were asked to rate 80 songs (preselected on valence and energy levels using algorithms [17,18]) on their expressed valence (unpleasant to pleasant) and energy (without energy to energetic) levels on 7-point Likert scales. Participants were asked to listen to each song at different places within the song to get a good impression of the song. For each participant the 10 songs with the highest rating in their mood condition were selected: i.e., for a participant in the positive high energetic HE/PV condition songs with the highest scores on valence and energy were selected. The average valence (V) and energy (E) ratings of the selected song stimuli per music condition were the following: LE/PV V= 5.1, E=3.5, HE/PV V=6.7, E= 6.6, LE/NV V= 1.8, E = 1.3, HE/ NV V = 1.8, E = 5.1.

2.4 Anger Drive

To induce anger during the simulated drive the following manipulations were adapted from van der Hulst et al. [3]. In the first place, drivers experienced time pressure during the simulated journey in that they had to complete the drive within eight minutes. In addition, they were told there was a monetary incentive to complete the journey in time (an additional £10 bonus). However, participants could be fined for speeding (i.e. exceeding speed limit by 10% brought a £2 fine) and they were informed that they would lose 70% of their £20 remuneration if they crashed the car more than twice. During the drive, participants were exposed to a number of discrete obstacles, such as traffic lights that always turned red on their approach; drivers also encountered a number of vehicles that accelerated and decelerated in a sinusoidal pattern at a point with traffic coming in the opposite direction, preventing any attempt to overtake. The drivers also encountered two traffic jams that effectively prevented them from completing the journey on time. The first traffic jam was encountered early in the drive and lasted for approximately two minutes. The second traffic jam was encountered at the end of journey and lasted for approximately two-three minutes.

2.5 Dependent Variables

The STAXI [19] was used to verify anger induction. The UMACL [20] was used to assess valence, energy, and calmness of mood dimensions. The physiological measure of skin conductance was recorded continuously during the drive. Skin conductance measurements were conducted using dry finger electrodes, which were attached to Velcro strips. The electrodes were strapped around the index and middle finger of the non dominant hand [21]. Blood pressure was measured using a band around the upper arm. Blood pressure was measured after the baseline, after the induction, in the third minute, the sixth minute, and at the end of the drive.

2.6 Procedure

Prior to the experiment participants were randomly assigned to one of the five music conditions, and participants were not aware of their condition. The awareness that musical mood induction would take place could severely influence the results. The music selecting part took up to one hour prior to attendance at the laboratory. In the lab, after signing the informed consent, the participants were seated in the car chair and the physiological apparatus was attached. Next, a baseline period started in which the participants are asked to relax and watch an aquatic movie for eight minutes [22]. The data acquired during this time are used as baseline. Next, the participants were asked to listen to the music presented for six minutes. To make sure participants were paying attention to the music they were told questions about the music would be asked at the end of the experiment. After both the baseline period and the music listening the STAXI and UMACL were completed by the participants. Successively, participants were instructed on the driving task via instructions on paper; they were told that they had to bring children to school, in an eight minute drive. It was emphasized that it was important to arrive in time as the children had an exam, and they would not be allowed to start the exam when arriving late. The monetary penalties for traffic violations were made clear. When the participants did not have any further questions the drive started. During the drive music of one of the five groups was presented. After twelve minutes the drive was stopped and the STAXI and UMACL were presented. Last, a recovery period started in which the participants were presented the debriefing form and the monetary voucher. Participants were debriefed that the time pressure and driving violations did not affect their reward. Lastly, the physiological sensors were detached and the participants were thanked for their participation.

3 Results

All data were subjected to a univariate ANOVA model with Music (HE/PV, LE/PV, HE/NV, LE/NV) as within-subject factor in SPSS v.17 in order to test for between-group differences. Reaction scores for the UMACL and the STAXI were calculated by subtracting the scores obtained after the baseline from the scores obtained after the induction or task performance.

3.1 Subjective Self-report

The STAXI reaction scores obtained after the mood induction showed a significant main effect of Music [$F(4,95) = 5.02$, $p < .01$, $\eta^2 = 0.18$]. Post-hoc tests showed higher anger in the High Energy/ Negative Valence music condition compared to all other music types.

The analysis of STAXI reaction scores obtained after the drive also revealed a significant main effect for Music [$F(4,95) = 5.02$, $p < .01$, $\eta^2 = 0.18$]. Post-hoc tests revealed that subjective anger was significantly higher in the High Energy/ Negative

Valence music condition compared to either the High Energy/ Positive Valence or the Low Energy/ Positive Valence music types ($p<.05$). Mean values for the STAXI data are illustrated in Figure 1.

The analysis of the UMACL reaction scores obtained after the mood induction showed a significant main effect of Music [$F(12,285) = 9.37$, $p < .01$, $\eta^2 = 0.28$]. Univariate effects show significance for valence, energy, and calmness ($p < .001$). Post-hoc tests show higher valence levels in the positive compared to the negative music conditions. Furthermore, the no music condition had higher valence levels compared to the negative music conditions (all $p < .01$). Energy ratings are higher in the high energy music conditions compared to the low energy music conditions and the no music conditions (all $p < .01$).

The analysis of the UMACL reaction scores obtained after the simulated drive showed significant main effect of Music [$F(12,285) = 2.37$, $p < .01$, $\eta^2 = 0.09$]. No significant univariate main effects were found (valence $p = .11$, energy $p = .12$, calmness $p = .06$). Post-hoc test revealed that High Energy/ Positive Valence music induces higher valence levels than High and Low Energy / Negative Valence music (p = .04, LE/NV $p = .01$). Furthermore, Low Energy / Negative Valence music induces lower energy levels compared to High Energy / Positive and Negative Valence music (HE/PV $p = .04$, HE/NV $p = .02$). Calmness levels are lower during High Energy/ Negative Valence music compared to all other music types (HE/PV $p = .010$, LE/PV $p = .01$, LE/NV $p = 0.1$). Calmness averages were the following; HE/PV M= -1.16, LE/PV M= -1.06, HE/NV M= -1.89, LE/NV M= -1.08, NoMusic M = -1.34. See Figure 2 for the UMACL reaction scores.

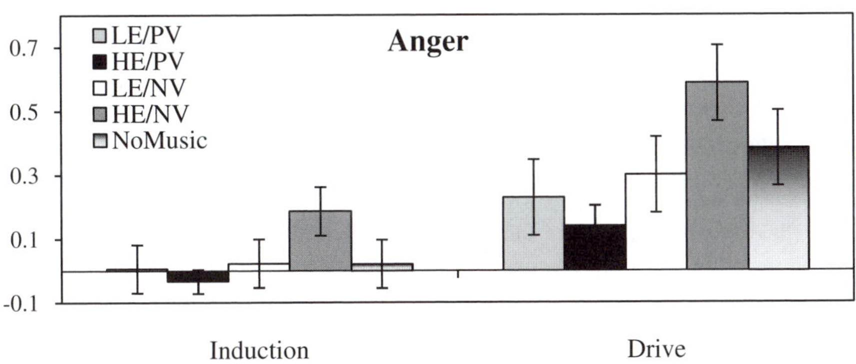

Fig. 1. The average STAXI reaction scores obtained after the mood induction and after the drive. Note: HE = High Energy, LE = Low Energy, PV= Positive Valence, NV = Negative Valence (Total N=100).

3.2 Autonomic Variables

The skin conductance level and systolic blood pressure data were averaged across the mood induction and the driving task and subjected to ANOVA analysis.

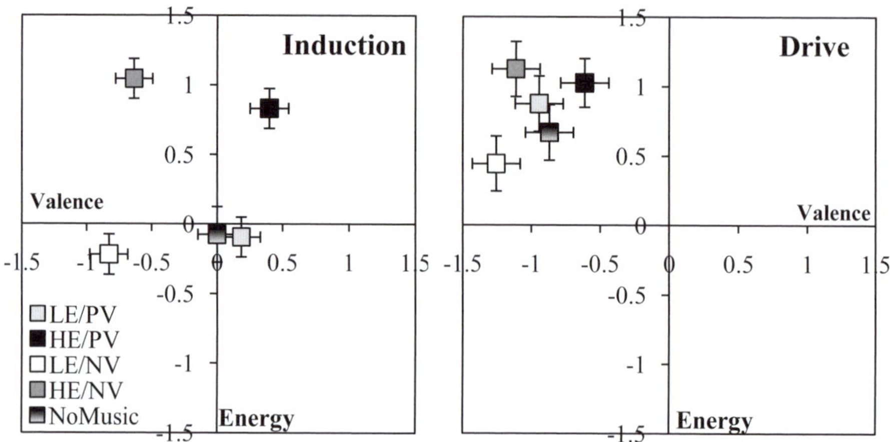

Fig. 2. The reaction scores of valence and energy obtained after the mood induction and after the drive. Note: HE = High Energy, LE = Low Energy, PV= Positive Valence, NV = Negative Valence (Total N=100).

Skin Conductance Level. The skin conductance level was measured continuously throughout the experiment. The data was corrected for the baseline measurement using a z-transformation. For this normalization the mean and standard deviation obtained during the baseline were taken. The normalized SCL values during the mood induction were subjected to an ANOVA with Music as between-subject variable and showed a main effect of Music [$F(4,94) = 2.71$, $p = .034$, $\eta^2 = 0.10$]. Post-hoc analysis shows that the High Energy Music conditions have higher normalized SCL values compared to the Low Energy Music conditions and the no music condition. The results of the ANOVA on the normalized SCL data obtained during the drive did not show a significant main effect of Music [$F(4,93) = .86$, $p = .49$, $\eta^2 = 0.36$]. To more specifically investigate the effect of the energy mood dimension on SCL, a repeated-measure ANOVA with Music Energy (LE / HE/ No) was conducted on the SCL during the drive. Results do not show a main effect of Music Energy [$F(2,95) = .28$, $p = .27$, $\eta^2 = 0.27$]. Pairwise comparisons show that the High Energy Music results in marginally higher SCL compared to the Low Energy Music ($p = .11$). See Figure 3 for the means normalized SCL values obtained during the drive.

Systolic Blood Pressure. Blood pressure was captured on several occasions during the simulated journey. The data from systolic blood pressure obtained during the simulated drive were baselined by subtracting the baseline values from that measured after the induction and during the drive, i.e. positive systolic reactivity indicate increased blood pressure during the drive. These systolic reactivity were subjected to separate ANOVA analyses. A main effect of Music was found on the systolic reactivity for the systolic data obtained at the end of the induction [$F(4,93) = 3.77$, $p < .01$, $\eta^2 = 0.14$]. Post-hoc comparisons show higher systolic reactivity in the no music condition and the HE/NV group compared to all other conditions (all $p < .02$), with the exception of the HE/NV and HE/PV conditions.

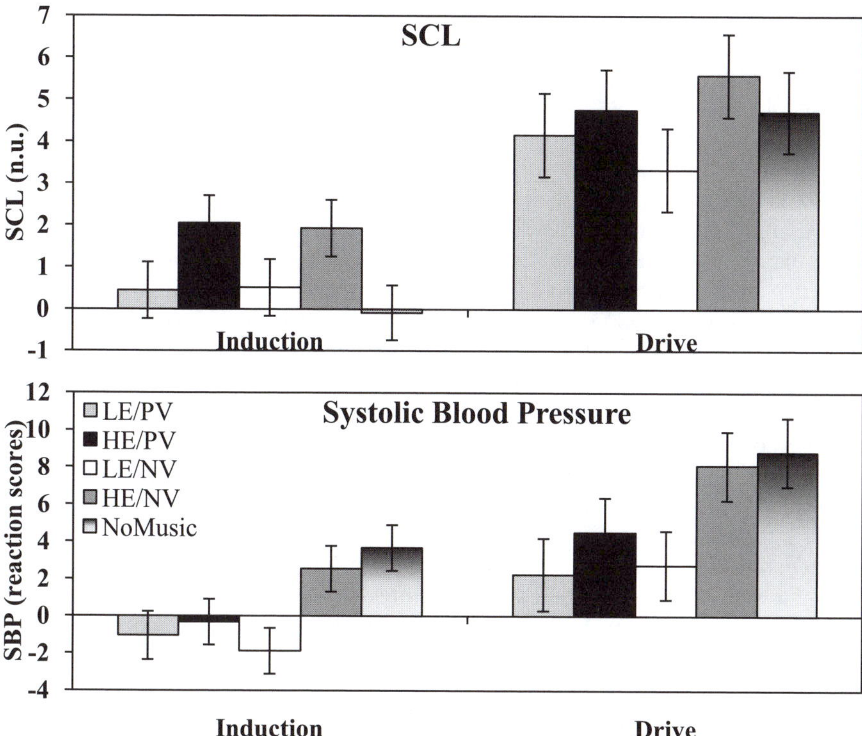

Fig. 3. The average SCL and systolic blood pressure reaction scores obtained during the mood induction and during the drive. Error bars represent standard errors. Note: HE = High Energy, LE = Low Energy, PV = Positive Valence, NV = Negative Valence.

The analysis of systolic blood pressure reactivity during the drive revealed a significant main effect for Music [$F(4,93) = 2.61$, $p < .041$, $\eta^2 = 0.11$]. Post-hoc tests revealed that systolic reactivity was significantly higher for both HE/NV and No Music drives compared to either LE/PV or LE/NV ($p < .05$). This effect is illustrated in Figure 3.

4 Discussion and Conclusion

Anger is a frequent occurring emotion while driving, which cannot only lead to unsocial driving behavior but also to health risks. Music is known to influence mood and listening to it is also a popular activity while driving. The current study was designed to assess the impact of four categories of music and a no music condition on psychophysiological and subjective markers of anger and mood while driving. The current study showed that different levels of anger were activated during the simulated drives with different types of music. The sympathetic nervous system activity of the systolic blood pressure showed the activating effect of anger on the body while listening to high energy negative valence music or no music. The skin conductance level shows most responsive to moods induced with high energy music. Hence, it is concluded that music can modulate the extent to which anger is induced while driving.

It should be noted that after mood induction through music each type of music occupied a different quadrant of the two-dimensional space representing valence and energy (Figure 2). However, valence and energy tend to interact. Hence LE/PV music elicits a higher mean energy than LE/NV music as positive valence tends to enhance the activating properties of the music; similarly HE/NV music has a lower energy level relative to HE/PV music as negative valence tends to blunt the activating properties of the music (Figure 2). So, whilst the four categories of music were distinct and personalized to the individual, it was impossible to make the valence and energy dimension of the music perfectly independent.

While driving, the induced moods all ended in the negative high energy quadrant implying successful induction of a high energy negative valence state as was intended with the anger drive. Even though the range of the induced moods decreased from induction to the drive, the moods induced by the different music types could still be discriminated in valence and energy levels. This result emphasizes the strong capacity of music to influence mood, even when music is only listened to in the background. An exception in the current situation is the low energy positive valence music: i.e., slightly lower energy and higher valence ratings were expected during the driving for this type of music. An explanation for this effect can be found in mood congruency principle; as low energetic positive valence mood is the most opposite state from anger (a high energetic negative valence state) this mood might have been perceived as incongruent to the situation and thereby seen as a negative stimulus. This finding reinforces an argument that the influence of music on moods should be interpreted from within the situational context [23].

With respect to the subjective measure of anger (STAXI) obtained during the mood induction, it was highest during the HE/NV music compared to all other music conditions. The experience of anger during the drive was also enhanced by HE/NV music and reduced by HE/PV music. The subjective anger also showed a trend to be reduced by HE/PV music relative to the no music condition. Both positive and negative categories of low energy music failed to make any substantial impact on subjective anger relative to the no music control condition, although the effects of music on the autonomic nervous system were subtle but present. It is possible that impact of the driving task tended to overshadow and obscure any autonomic changes due to the different categories of music.

Systolic reactivity is a variable that has been closely associated with beta-adrenergic response from the sympathetic nervous system [21]. The analysis of systolic reactivity revealed a significant increase during both the no music control condition and HE/NV music. The effect of the latter did not come as a surprise given the subjective results found. However, an elevation of systolic reactivity during the no music condition requires further explanation. It is proposed that systolic reactivity was enhanced for the no music control group because the music in other conditions (except for the HE/NV group) either enhanced the simulated driving experience or acted as a distraction from the irritating events on the road and the distressing effects of time pressure. Both categories of low energy music tended to reduce systolic reactivity relative to the no music condition (Figure 3), suggesting that beta-adrenergic activity was strongly influenced by the energy component of the music. This interpretation was supported by the trend observed in the normalized SCL data after mood induction, which is also considered as an index of activation, i.e. SCL was alternated for both high energy activation categories of music. The relation between subjective anger and mood and psychophysiological responses to mood could be further supported and explored by pattern recognition techniques [24,25].

On the basis of this study, we conclude that music may alter the subjective experience of anger and mediate the magnitude of the psychophysiological response to anger. It is proposed that music serves two effects in the context of the current study: firstly, music acts as an overt source of distraction from negative events in the environment and secondly, music exerts a subconscious effect on psychophysiology. People may use music to distract themselves from a monotonous situation (as in the traffic jam scenario) and to divert themselves from negative thoughts and feelings. It would appear that high energetic negative valence music tends to augment the latter, thus inflating subjective feelings of anger. With respect to psychophysiology, categories of music with low levels of energy (regardless of valence) appeared to reduce the sympathetic response to anger, which may be a positive adaptation in terms of long-term health.

The study has demonstrated that music can mediate the effects of anger in a simulated environment. These findings demonstrate the potential of music to manage mood states and to influence those covert psychophysiological states that accompany different mood states. It is suggested that the capability of music to influence physiology at a subconscious level has the potential to reduce the impact of negative emotion on health in the long term.

Acknowledgements. This work was funded by the 7th Framework Programme REFLECT Project of the European Union.

References

1. Mesken, J., Hagenzieker, M.P., Rothengatter, T., de Waard, D.: Frequency, determinants, and consequences of different drivers emotions: An on-the-road study using self-reports (observed) behaviour, and physiology. Transportation Research Part F 10, 458–475 (2007)
2. Underwood, G., Chapman, P., Wright, S., Crundall, D.: Anger while driving. Transportation Research Part F: Traffic Psychology and Behaviour 2, 55–68 (1999)
3. Van der Hulst, M., Meijman, T., Rothengatter, T.: Maintaining task set under fatigue: a study of time-on-task effects in simulated driving. Transportation Research Part F: Psychology and Behaviour 4, 103–118 (2001)
4. Lemerise, E.A., Dodge, K.A.: The development of Anger and hostile interactions. In: Lewis, M., Haviland-Jones, J.M., Feldman Barrett, L. (eds.) The Handbook of Emotions, 3rd edn. The Guilford Press, New York (2010)
5. Mauss, I.B., Cook, C.L., Gros, J.J.: Automatic emotion regulation during anger provocation. Journal of Experimental Social Psychology 43, 698–711 (2007)
6. Juslin, P.N., Sloboda, J.A. (eds.): Handbook of music and emotion: Theory, research, applications. Oxford University Press, New York (2010)

7. MacDonald, R.A.R., Mitchell, L., Dillon, T., Serpell, M.G., Davies, J.B., Ashley, E.A.: An empirical investigation of the anxiolytic and pain reducing effects of music. Psychology of Music 31, 187–203 (2003)
8. Rickard, N.: Intense emotional responses to music: a test of the physiological arousal hypotheses. Psychology of Music 32, 371–388 (2004)
9. Krumhansl, C.: An exploratory study of musical emotions and psychophysiology. Canadian Journal of Experimental Psychology 51, 336–353 (1997)
10. Salimpoor, V.N., Benovoy, M., Longo, G., Cooperstock, J.R., Zatorre, R.J.: The rewarding aspects of music listening are related to degree of emotional arousal. PLoSOne 4, e7487 (2009)
11. Dibben, N., Williamson, V.J.: An exploratory survey of in–vehicle music listening. Psychology of Music 35, 571–589 (2007)
12. Brodsky, W.: The effects of music tempo on simulated driving performance and vehicular control. Transportation Research Part F 4, 219–241 (2002)
13. Wiesenthal, D.L., Hennessy, D.A., Totten, B.: The influence of music on driver stress. Journal of Applied Social Psychology 30, 1709–1719 (2000)
14. Wiesenthal, D.L., Hennessy, D.A., Totten, B.: The influence of music on mild drivers aggression. Transportation Research Part F 6, 125–134 (2003)
15. Russell, J.A.: A circumplex model of affect. Journal of Personality and Social Psychology 39, 1161–1178 (1980)
16. Wilhelm, P., Schoebi, D.: Assessing mood in daily life. European Journal of Psychological Assessment 23, 258–267 (2007)
17. Skowronek, J., McKinney, M.F., van de Par, S.: Ground truth for automatic music mood classification. In: Proceedings of the 7th ISMIR, Victoria, Canada (2006)
18. Skowronek, J., McKinney, M.F., van der Par, S.: A Demonstrator for Automatic Music Mood Estimation. In: Proceedings of the 8th ISMIR, Vienna, Austria (2007)
19. Spielberger, C.D.: Manual for the State-Trait Anger Expression Inventory-2. Psychological Assessment Resources, Odessa (1999)
20. Matthews, G., Jones, D.M., Chamberlain, A.: Refining the measurement of mood: the UWIST mood adjective checklist. British Journal of Psychology 81, 17–42 (1990)
21. Cacioppo, J., Tassinary, L., Berntson, G.: Handbook of Psychophysiology. Cambridge University Press, Cambridge (2000)
22. Piferi, R.L., Kline, K.A., Younger, J., Lawler, K.A.: An alternative approach for achieving cardiovascular baseline: viewing an aquatic video. International Journal of Psychophysiology 37, 207–217 (2000)
23. DeNora, T.: Music in Everyday Life. Cambridge University Press, Cambridge (2000)
24. Picard, R.W., Vyzas, E., Healey, J.: Toward Machine Emotional Intelligence: Analysis of Affective Physiological State. IEEE Transactions on Pattern Analyses Machine Intelligence 23, 1175–1191 (2001)
25. Petta, P., Pelachaud, C., Cowie, R.: Emotion-Oriented Systems: The Humaine Handbook (Cognitive Technologies). Springer, Heidelberg (2011)

Unsupervised Temporal Segmentation of Talking Faces Using Visual Cues to Improve Emotion Recognition

Sudha Velusamy, Viswanath Gopalakrishnan, Bilva Navathe, Hariprasad Kannan, Balasubramanian Anand, and Anshul Sharma

SAIT India, Samsung India Software Operations, Bangalore, India

Abstract. The mouth region of human face possesses highly discriminative information regarding the expressions on the face. Facial expression analysis to infer the emotional state of a user becomes very challenging when the user talks, as most of the mouth actions while uttering certain words match with mouth shapes expressing various emotions. We introduce a novel unsupervised method to temporally segment talking faces[1] from the faces displaying only emotions, and use the knowledge of talking face segments to improve emotion recognition. The proposed method uses integrated gradient histogram of local binary patterns to represent mouth features suitably and identifies temporal segments of talking faces online by estimating the uncertainties of mouth movements over a period of time. The algorithm accurately identifies talking face segments on a real-world database where talking and emotion happens naturally. Also, the emotion recognition system, using talking face cues, showed considerable improvement in recognition accuracy.

Keywords: Talking faces, Temporal segmentation, Local Binary Pattern, Emotion recognition, Facial expression.

1 Introduction

Automatic emotion recognition is a key research component in the field of human computer interaction. Facial expression analysis also finds wide range of applications in video conferencing, gaming, surveillance, etc. Among the various facial features, the mouth region possesses highly discriminative information that is useful in inferring underlying emotions. However, in many real world scenarios where the user talks while expressing emotions, the mouth region in consecutive frames deforms into various shapes to produce the sounds. In other words, the shapes of the mouth while uttering various words might potentially mislead the inference of original emotion on the face. For example, Fig. 1 shows scenarios where emotions are displayed while a person is talking. Fig. 1(a-c) and (d-f) show sets of sample images for *Happy* and *Surprise* emotions, respectively.

[1] *Talking faces* refer to the faces that talk with or without any emotions, while *Emotion faces* (including neutral) refer to the faces that do not talk, but show some emotions.

S. D'Mello et al. (Eds.): ACII 2011, Part I, LNCS 6974, pp. 417–426, 2011.

Now we will analyze the example scenarios based on the Facial Action Coding System (FACS) system proposed by Ekman et al [1], and based on the method to infer emotions from facial action units (AUs) proposed by Velusamy et al [2]. In Fig. 1(a), the mouth AU on the face, AU12 (Lip corner puller), is a strong indicator that the emotion present on the face is *Happy*. However, in case of subsequent talking images shown in Fig. 1(b)&(c), the mouth shapes match with AU17 (Chin raiser) and AU26 (Jaw drop). This makes an emotion recognition system [2,3] to wrongly output *Sad* and *Surprise*, though the upper facial action AU6 (Cheek raiser) indicates *Happy* emotion. Likewise, in *Surprise* sequence present in Fig. 1(d-f), the mouth actions AU23 (Lip tightener) in Fig. 1(e) and AU20 (Lip stretcher) in Fig. 1(f) that occurred while talking tend to mislead the final emotions to be *Angry* and *Fear*.

From the above analysis, it is very evident that even though the upper half of the face holds cues to understand the displayed emotion, the lower AUs of mouth region mislead the emotion recognition mechanism for talking faces. Temporal information of such talking segments becomes a very crucial cue, as it can be used to improve the decision making rules of emotion recognition systems.

Research in automatic affect recognition has targeted identification of both basic emotions such as *Happy, Sad, Anger, Fear, Disgust, Surprise* and complex mental states like *Boredom, Thinking, etc* [3,4,5]. Efforts are being made to develop robust emotion recognition systems that can handle variations in illumination [6], variations in head pose [7] and facial occlusions [8]. Among the various features of a robust emotion detection system like handling illumination variation, head pose, facial occlusions etc., the feature of handling 'talking faces' is also a crucial component that is required to address more realistic scenarios.

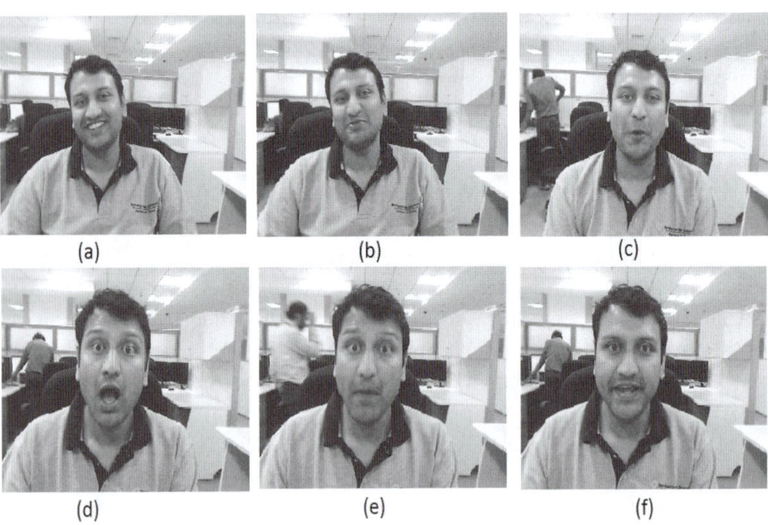

Fig. 1. Comparison of *'Emotion'* faces and *'Talking'* faces. (a) *Happy* without talking; (b-c) *Happy* while talking; (d) *Surprise* without talking; (e-f) *Surprise* with talking.

There are a few methods that target detection of lip activity from the context of lip reading or determining active speakers in a multi-person environment. For example, Zhao et al[9] proposed a method to infer the lip movements to improve speech recognition systems by learning specific mouth movements of commonly used phrases (e.g.,'Good Bye'). Identification of talking faces for lip activity detection in multi-user environment is discussed in [10,11,12]. Liu et al [10] applied Gaussian mixtures to model talking and silent frames, while [11] used optical flow information around the lip regions to detect the lip activity. Siatras et al[12] proposed to detect lip activity by measuring the increased mean value and standard deviation of grey scale intensity pixels over the lip region. However, the features used to model the lip regions in [11,12] can be sensitive to noise factors like illumination changes. Further more, the methods in [10,11,12] which target to determine the active speakers in a multi-person environment do not address the problem of temporally segmenting the lip activities of a single person as talking and non-talking.

As cited in [5] and to the best of our knowledge, [13] is the only work which addresses the problem of 'talking faces' in emotion recognition perspective. In [13], the method uses $MPEG-4$ facial animation parameters and Hidden Markov Model (HMM) based supervised training to model talking faces and six basic emotions. It considers talking face as a unique class apart from the six basic emotion classes and trains the talking face class using 28 video sequences from a private database. The method in [13] requires supervised training to detect talking faces and hence is dependent on the training data. Moreover, the method in [13] assumes no emotions during talking and considers 'Talking' as a separate class. The objective of the proposed method is to detect talking segments so that this information can be used to increase the accuracy of emotion recognition while talking. We would also like to point out that, though there are a few methods on temporal segmentation of facial behavior [14], unsupervised temporal segmentation of talking faces is a relatively unexplored topic.

We propose a method of detecting talking face segments in a video sequence by; *i*) estimating uncertainties involved in mouth or lip movements across the frames, and; *ii*) applying an unsupervised clustering method for online temporal segmentation. It becomes imperative to use visual cues in this regard as audio cues can also come from persons in range other than the target speaker and can mislead the detection. Moreover, the proposed work targets classifying talking and non-talking segments in which the non-talking segments can have different expressions with audio (e.g., *Laughter*) and hence visual cues have to be used in distinguishing between them. The method localizes the mouth regions, and encodes the movements into an Integrated Gradient Histogram (IGH) of Local Binary Pattern (LBP) values. The entropy of IGH is used to quantify the uncertainties that have been captured. The time series data of entropy values of sequence of frames is further clustered using online K-Means algorithm for online detection of talking mouth segments. Finally, we show the results of using talking face segmentation cues to improve the performance of emotion recognition systems. Section 2 describes various stages of the proposed method and the experiments. Results are detailed in section 3.

2 Proposed Method

Figure 2 shows the detailed flow diagram of the proposed method. Given an input sequence of video frames, the system detects primary face and localizes the pupils and nose. In our implementation we use Active Appearance Models (AAM) based method [15] to detect face, pupils and nose. The pupil information is used to rotate and scale normalize the face image, and nose location is used to crop out the mouth region in each frame for further processing. In our experiments, we maintain the distance between the pupils as 48 pixels to normalize the faces, crop the mouth region to the size of 56×46 pixels. The localized mouth region is represented using a novel feature descriptor and input to unsupervised temporal clustering method for online segmentation. The following subsections provide detailed explanation of these steps.

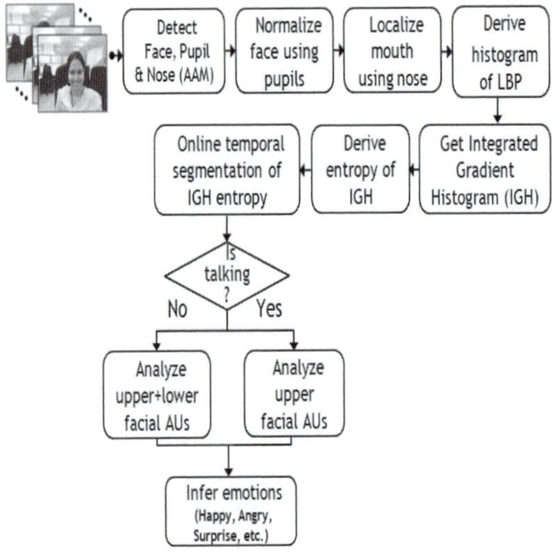

Fig. 2. Flow Diagram of the proposed method

2.1 Histogram of Local Binary Patterns

The cropped sequence of mouth images may have illumination variations and alignment errors across the frames and hence it is crucial to select a robust feature descriptor that can handle such conditions. In the proposed work, we use histogram of Local Binary Patterns(LBP) to represent the appearance details of mouth region. As cited in [16], LBP is a powerful feature used for texture classification. It is also proven to be an effective technique for face recognition and related applications [6]. We compute LBP image patterns for each of the cropped mouth images. We follow the method of using uniform LBP patterns (patterns with at most two bit wise transitions) [6], and derive a histogram (59 bins) of uniform LBP patterns.

2.2 Integrated Gradient Histogram

Main objective of the proposed work is to distinguish between a sequence of complex mouth movements that occur while talking and the smoother appearance changes between the onset and offset of emotions like *Smile*, *Surprise*. To discriminate between talking and non-talking segments, we have derived a method that encodes appearance changes over time in a single feature named Integrated Gradient Histogram (IGH). The procedure to calculate IGH is as follows. For each frame i, we compute gradient of LBP histograms using 2τ frames around the frame i. This captures the appearance changes over $2\tau + 1$ frames. Considering $2\tau + 1$ LBP histograms corresponding to each frame i, the gradient histograms are computed as,

$$H_n^i = H_i - H_{i+n}, -\tau \leq n \leq \tau, \ where \ n \neq 0 \tag{1}$$

H_n^i is the gradient histogram computed as an absolute difference of LBP histogram of ith frame and $(i+n)^{th}$ frame. The gradient histograms hold the mouth pattern changes along the temporal dimension. To encode the complete information regarding the appearance change over a segment of $2\tau + 1$ frames into a single feature, we calculate IGH as given in Equ.(2).

$$IGH_i = \sum_{n=-\tau, n\neq 0}^{n=\tau} H_n^i \tag{2}$$

Figure 3(a) shows the IGH values plotted for a frame in the middle of talking segment lasting 2 seconds, while Fig. 3(b) shows the IGH values plotted for a frame in the middle of *Happy* emotion segment lasting 2 seconds. From Fig. 3, it

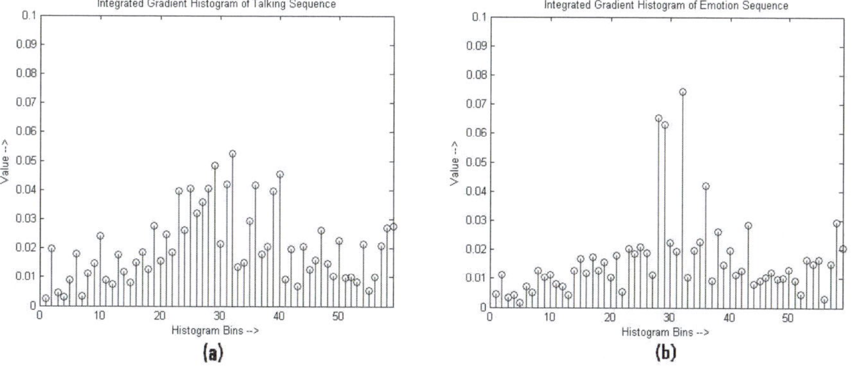

Fig. 3. Integrated Gradient Histograms for: (a) ***Talking*** segment; (b) ***Emotion*** segment

can be observed that a series of talking frames have more evenly distributed IGH values as compared to the frames displaying a single emotion. In other words, the uncertainty of information encoded in IGH is high for talking segments as compared to the emotion segments. To quantify the amount of uncertainty, we calculate entropy of the IGH corresponding to each frame. The entropy of IGH, $e(i)$, for each frame i is calculated as,

$$e(i) = -\sum_{k} p_k log(p_k), \tag{3}$$

where p_k is the probability of occurrences of IGH values at k^{th} bin. It has to be further noted that we need to normalize IGH to get the probabilities. The entropy values of IGH over different temporal segments will vary as a result of the gradient computation. Hence, the entropy values are normalized by adding the mean entropy difference between the original LBP histograms as a separate bin in the IGH. The temporal series data of entropy values evaluated from the IGH of every frame is used for unsupervised online segmentation of talking and non-talking faces.

2.3 Time Series Data Segmentation

The entropy values obtained for every frame of a video sequence form a time series data. Two class clustering of the entropy values indicating the talking and non-talking segments is our main objective. Buffering huge sequence of video frames before hand and clustering them as talking and non-talking segments is impractical in real-time systems. Hence in the proposed work, we apply an online, unsupervised method of time series data segmentation, which starts clustering soon after the first K ($K = 2$, talking and non-talking) IGH computations. No further assumptions are made regarding the range or initial values of data. Fig. 4 shows the segmentation results achieved by applying online K-means algorithm on an example sequential entropy data.

2.4 Methods to Improve Emotion Recognition

The problem of inferring emotions in the presence of occlusions over mouth region has been studied previously and solutions have been provided to improve the accuracy of emotion detection [20]. We also consider the mouth region as occluded whenever talking is detected. The logic behind this is that the emotion recognition accuracy can get inferior with the confusing visual data coming from mouth region when the individual is talking and hence it is better to disregard it. We follow the approach to described in [2] to map AUs to emotions but using only upper AUs whenever talking is detected. We experimentally show that such a simple approach also bring improvement in emotion recognition accuracy. These claims are demonstrated and analyzed in section 3.

Another direction to improve emotion recognition will be to use advanced strategies to interpret the emotion of talking mouth. Even though image features

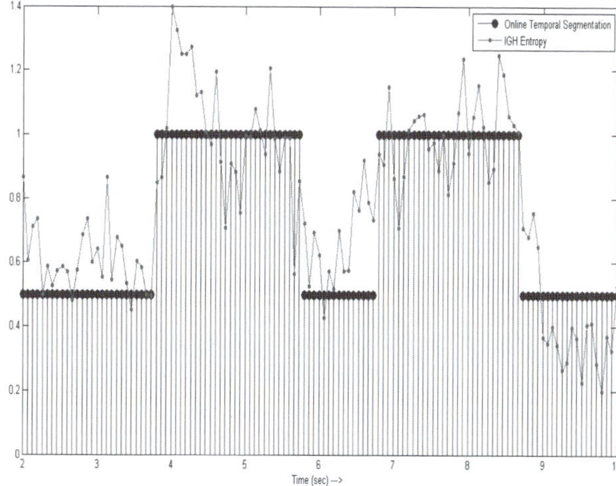

Fig. 4. Segmentation of sequential entropy data to talking and emotion segments. Higher values of entropy denote talking segment.

from a talking face are not easy to interpret, the mouth region still holds some cues to the current emotion. For example, we can discern between a happy talking face and a sad talking face using features like lip corners, whose relative positions and movement can distinguish certain emotions even while talking [18].

3 Experiments and Results

3.1 Database

Though there are many benchmark databases for facial expressions or emotions, the subjects in those databases do not talk while expressing the emotions. Hence, for our experiments and evaluation, we captured a set of 42 real-world videos by 7 people of Indian and Korean ethnicity, with indoor lighting and quiet office environment. People were asked to show the six basic emotions (*Happy, Sad, Anger, Fear, Disgust and Surprise*) while talking in between the emotions. The percentage of talking segments were approximately 50% of the whole data set. The videos were captured at the rate of 15 frames per second with the resolution of 640×480 and audio sampling rate of 8 kHz. The video frames were ground truth labeled for facial AUs according to FACS by 5 people who have been working with FACS based systems for a couple of years.

3.2 Results

As the proposed system detects talking faces using only visual modality, we evaluate its performance against a talk/voice detection system using audio modality. We also evaluate the performance of an emotion recognition system with and without the proposed method.

I. Comparison Results with Voice Activity Detection: Figure 5 shows the comparison results of the proposed method with a voice activity detection (VAD) algorithm [19] for an example test data extending for 11 seconds. The sampled images of the mouth of the test user are mapped to the time axis. Initially the user starts showing *Happy* emotion and then moves on to talking, where the detection outputs of VAD and the proposed method match closely. It can further be observed that there is a pause in talking (between 6th and 7th second) and the user shows *Exclamation*, which is a potential emotion to be detected. The proposed system detects emotion during this period while the VAD unit detects it as talking segment. Finally the user ends the experiment showing *Sad* emotion without any voice, where the proposed system and the VAD system match exactly. It can be concluded from this experiment that the proposed system is more suitable in the context of differentiating 'talking' faces from 'emotion' faces, as compared to voice based activity detection. It is evident from the above experiment that a VAD system cannot serve as an alternative to our proposed method as emotions like *Surprise* or *Happy* can have sounds in the form of *Exclamation* or *Laughter* that may get classified as talking. Likewise, there could be instances of multi-person environments where there is voice activity from other(s) while the target speaker does not speak, but displays some emotion that needs to be analyzed. Here, a VAD will again show voice activity which will mislead the emotion recognition system. Note that, under the ideal case of a single user giving out voice in the form of only talking, the proposed system is expected to give the same output as the VAD system.

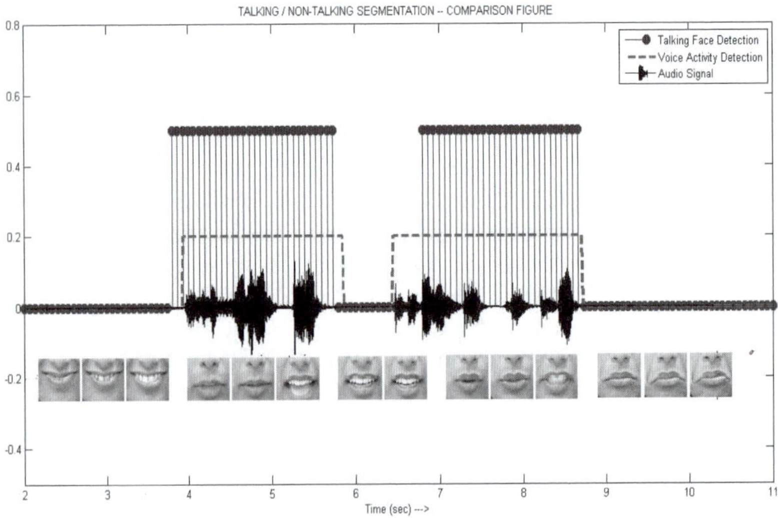

Fig. 5. Comparison of the proposed method with the Voice Activity Detection (VAD) [19]. Both the methods detect talking segments similarly, except at a segment between 6 and 7 seconds where the VAD detects voice during non-talking face segment.

Table 1. Emotion Recognition - Comparison Results

*	**Emotion Recognition Accuracy (%) of [2] without and with the proposed method**		
Emotion	**Without proposed method**	**With proposed method**	**Improvement**
Happy	59.30	79.40	20.10
Sad	57.50	74.55	17.05
Angry	58.30	83.50	25.20
Fear	63.70	82.20	18.50
Disgust	66.25	80.55	14.30
Surprise	67.70	81.00	13.30
Average	**62.125**	**80.200**	**18.075**

II. Comparison Results for Emotion Recognition: Table 1 shows the emotion recognition accuracy of [2] with and without the strategy of using the proposed talk detection method. The method present in [2] maps the combination of AUs to the six basic emotions as an example. We use ground truth AU labels as input to the above mentioned AU to emotion mapping system to avoid the detection errors associated with any practical AU detection system. The results presented in Table. 1 are for 42 videos of 6 basic emotions with talking segments. The second column shows percentage of detection accuracy of [2] without using the information of talking segments. The algorithm in [2] is then modified to use only upper facial AUs to infer emotions, when talking is detected, and the results are presented in the third column of Table 1. The last column explicitly shows the performance improvement for various emotions with the proposed method. It can be observed that, there is a significant improvement in detection accuracy irrespective of the emotion class. A more closer analysis says that there is a remarkable increase in accuracy for emotions like *Happy* and *Angry*, as mouth is a crucial feature in deciding the emotion class. The emotions like *Surprise* and *Disgust* show comparatively lesser improvement as the cues from upper facial AUs are strong enough for detecting these emotions.

4 Conclusions

We have proposed a novel unsupervised method to classify 'talking' faces from 'emotion' faces based on only visual cues. The proposed system does online clustering and hence can be used in real time systems. The information on talking segments obtained using the proposed system is used to change the strategy of emotion recognition and has resulted in an improved emotion detection accuracy.

References

1. Ekman, P., Friesen, W.V.: Facial action coding system: A technique for measurement of facial movements. Consulting Psychologists (1978)
2. Velusamy, S., Kannan, H., Anand, B., Navathe, B., Sharma, A.: A Method to Infer Emotions From Facial Action Units. In: IEEE International Conference on Acoustics, Speech and Signal Processing, ICASSP (2011)

3. Bartlett, M.S., Littlewort, G., Frank, M., Lainscsek, C., Fasel, I., Movellan, J.: Recognizing Facial Expression: Machine Learning and Application to Spontaneous Behavior. In: IEEE Conf. on Computer Vision and Pat. Recog., pp. 568–573 (2005)
4. Lien, J.J., Zlochower, A., Cohn, J.F., Kanade, T.: Automated Facial Expression Recognition Based on FACS Action Units. In: Proceedings of IEEE Int. Conference on Automatic Face and Gesture Recognition, pp. 390–395 (1998)
5. Kaliouby, R.: Mind-reading machines: the automated inference of complex mental states from video, Ph.D. Thesis, University of Cambridge (2005)
6. Ahonen, T., Hadid, A., Pietikainen, M.: Face Description with Local Binary Patterns: Application to Face Recognition. IEEE Transactions on Pattern Analysis and Machine Intelligence 28, 2037–2041 (2006)
7. Rudovic, O., Patras, I., Pantic, M.: Coupled Gaussian Process Regression for Pose-Invariant Facial Expression Recognition. In: Daniilidis, K., Maragos, P., Paragios, N. (eds.) ECCV 2010, Part II. LNCS, vol. 6312, pp. 350–363. Springer, Heidelberg (2010)
8. Buciu, I., Kotsia, I., Pitas, I.: Facial expression analysis under partial occlusion.: In: IEEE Int. Conf. on Acoustics, Speech, Signal Proc. (ICASSP), pp. 453–456 (2005)
9. Zhao, G., Barnard, M., Pietikainen, M.: Lipreading With Local Spatiotemporal Descriptors. IEEE Trans. Multimedia 11(7), 1254–1265 (2009)
10. Liu, P., Wang, Z.: Voice activity detection using visual information. In: Proc. of IEEE Int. Conf. on Acoustics, Speech, & Signal Proc. (ICASSP), pp. 609–612 (2004)
11. Bendris, M., Charlet, D., Chollet, G.: Lip activity detection for talking faces classification in TV-Content. In: International Conference on Machine Vision (2010)
12. Siatras, S., Nikolaidis, N., Krinidis, M., Pitas, I.: Visual Lip Activity Detection and Speaker Detection Using Mouth Region Intensities. IEEE Trans. Circuits and Systems for Video Technology 19(1), 133–137 (2009)
13. Montse, P., Bonafonte, A., Landabaso, J.L.: Emotion Recognition Based on MPEG4 Facial Animation Parameters. In: Proceedings of IEEE Intl. Conf. on Acoustics, Speech, and Signal Processing (ICASSP), pp. 3624–3627 (2002)
14. Zhou, F., De la Tore, F., Jeffrey, F.C.: Unsupervised Discovery of Facial Events. In: IEEE Conference on Computer Vision and Pattern Recognition, CVPR (2010)
15. Saragih, J., Lucey, S., Cohn, J.: Deformable Model Fitting by Regularized Landmark Mean-Shifts. Interl. Journal of Computer Vision 91(2), 200–215 (2011)
16. Ojala, T., Pietikainen, M., Harwood, D.: A comparative study of texture measures with classification based on feature distributions. Pattern Recogn., 51–59 (1996)
17. Alpaydin, E.: Introduction to Machine Learning. MIT Press, Cambridge (2004)
18. Hoque, M.E., Picard, R.W.: I See You (ICU): Towards Robust Recognition of Facial Expressions and Speech Prosody in Real Time. In: International Conference on Computer Vision and Pattern Recognition (CVPR), DEMO (2010)
19. Sohn, J., Sung, W.: A voice activity detector employing soft decision based noise spectrum adaptation. In: Proceedings of IEEE Int. Conference on Acoustics, Speech, Signal Processing (ICASSP), pp. 365–368 (1998)
20. Bourel, F., Chibelushi, C.C., Low, A.A.: Recognition of facial expressions in the presence of occlusion. In: Proc. of the Twelfth British Machine Vision Conference, vol. 1, pp. 213–222 (2001)

The Affective Experience of Handling Digital Fabrics: Tactile and Visual Cross-Modal Effects

Di Wu[1], Ting-I Wu[1,*], Harsimrat Singh[1], Stefano Padilla[2], Douglas Atkinson[3], Nadia Bianchi-Berthouze[1,**], Mike Chantler[2], and Sharon Baurley[3]

[1] UCLIC, University College London, Gower Street, London, UK
{ucjtdwu,ting-i.wu.09,h.singh,n.berthouze}@ucl.ac.uk
[2] School of Mathematical and Computer Sciences. Heriot-Watt University, Edinburgh, UK
{S.Padilla,M.J.Chantler}@hw.ac.uk
[3] Brunel Design, Brunel Universty, Uxbridge, London, UK
{douglas.atkinson,sharon.baurley}@brunel.ac.uk

Abstract. In the textile sector, emotions are often associated with both physical touch and manipulation of the product. Thus there is the need to recreate the affective experiences of touching and interacting with fabrics using commonly available internet technology. New digital interactive representations of fabrics simulating handling have been proposed with the idea of bringing the digital experience of fabrics closer to the reality. This study evaluates the contribution of handling real fabrics to viewing digital interactive animations of said fabrics and vice versa. A combination of self-report and physiological measures was used. Results showed that having previous physical handling experience of the fabrics significantly increased pleasure and engagement in the visual experience of the digital handling of the same fabrics. Two factors mediated these experiences: gender and interoceptive awareness. Significant results were not found for the opposite condition.

Keywords: Physiological Signals, Affective Interaction, Fabric Handling, Digital Fabric Handling, Touch, Cross-Modal transfer.

1 Introduction

In clothing retail stores, there is a 'selection process' that is based on the multi-sensorial experience of touching and seeing the cloth but also on the emotional experience deriving from these actions [1]. In the digital environment, where customers are unable to touch the fabrics, a mixture of pictures and words are the main methods of representing fabrics and remain the main method for consumers to create an opinion on those products. However, many investigators state that emotions are one of the most important parts of customers' experiences [2] and of their decision making processes [3]. Emotional experiences are much more subjective and ambiguous than the experience of the semantic properties of a fabric.

---

* Alphabetical order was used for the first two authors as they equally contributed to this study.
** Correspondent author.

S. D´Mello et al. (Eds.): ACII 2011, Part I, LNCS 6974, pp. 427–436, 2011.

Product experiences in the digital environment are currently significantly different from experiences in the real world. Despite the progressive development of technology and the widespread uptake of internet shopping, not many studies have been carried out to understand emotional experiences in the digital world. Moreover, most of these studies use vision as the only modality for product evaluation [4], [5]; while a few consider vision and touch separately [6]. Consequently, with the lack of tactile feedback on the internet, poor user experiences can be easily found in product evaluation [7], especially for products such as textiles, for which a sense of touch is thought to be essential for perceiving surface properties and evoking emotions.

The study[1] aims to evaluate the contribution made by the experience of handling the real fabric to the visual experience of digitally handling fabrics. Self-report and physiological measurements were used to capture people's emotional experience when they handle fabrics and when interacting with their digital representations.

2 Background: The Affective Experience of Handling Fabrics

With the increasing understanding of the existence of skin receptors dedicated to the perception of pleasant touch rather than involved in the discriminative role of touch [27], we are observing a growing interest in investigating the relationships between emotions and surface properties [1], [10], [28]. For example, Essick et al. [11] found that fabric materials that are soft or smooth were reported more pleasant than those that were stiff, rough, or coarse. This study showed that reliable pleasantness ratings could be obtained for different types of fabric materials. In a subsequent study, Essik et al [12] identified gender, site of skin contact, velocity and pressure as factors modulating the experience of being caressed by fabrics. Another study along similar lines concluded that feelings of pleasure will be produced when the texture is less rough than people's skin [13]. Furthermore, the use of differing gestures for assessing different semantic textile hand qualities may affect the hedonic experience of handling fabrics [29]. Moody *et al.* [1] cite a multiple finger pinch as the gesture that provides the maximum amount of haptic information when manipulating a textile.

The experience of touch has been also explored in relation to other modalities. It has been shown the visual and tactile experiences easily transfer between each other. For example pre-viewing (or pre-touching) an object facilitate the recognition of the object by only touching (or seeing) the object [14-15]. However, very little is still known on how the hedonic touch experience affects or is affected by the other sensorial experience [16]. A recent study [17] investigated the cross-modal interactions in affective processes between vision and touch. Their results show that pre-viewing a novel object has an effect on the hedonic experience of touching it afterwards but not vice-versa. The authors argue that the fact that the transfer between modalities occur only between vision and touch and not vice versa is because in their experiment participants were blindfolded during the touching condition. Hence, it is very possible that blindfolding might have increased anxiety and reduced the hedonic experience of interacting with a new object. Furthermore, in their experiment pre-touching a novel object had an effect on re-touching it but pre-seeing a novel object

[1] This work was supported by EPSRC grant EP/H007083/2: Digital SENSORIA.

did not have an effect on re-seeing it. The authors also point out that touch, being both an exteroceptive and as well as an interoceptive sense, *"may correlate with the somatic state that underlies affective processing ... hence touch might play a more important role than vision in affective information processing"*.

3 Experiment

The aim of this study is to evaluate whether pre-handling the physical fabrics could affect the emotional experiences of the use of interactive animations that simulate handling of fabrics and viceversa. To this purpose an experiment with two conditions was set up. In the first condition (called pre-physical condition), participants were asked to physically handle fabrics before seeing their digital handling. In the second condition (called pre-digital condition), participants were asked to look at the digital handling of fabrics before physically handling them. Given that in [17], it has been suggested that blindfolding may create anxiety when touching objects, participants were not blindfolded during the physical handling of the fabrics. This means that in the pre-physical condition, participants were also pre-seeing the physical fabric. This potential confound will be further discussed in the conclusion.

3.1 Protocol

Participants. Twenty-two healthy participants (12 males and 10 females) aged between 20 and 34 years old were recruited from the University College London. In order to remove the factor of cultural differences, only British nationals who were native English speakers were recruited. Of these, two were excluded because we were unable to collect physiological data from them due to problems with the skin conductance sensor. Of those that remained, ten female participants (M = 26.2 years, SD = 4.57 years) and ten male participants (M = 23.9 years, SD = 3.23 years) were randomly assigned to one of two conditions (n=10; each group comprising five males and five females to reduce the effect of gender differences.). Participants were measured for interoceptive awareness, i.e., a person's ability to sense their own bodily signals, such as their heartbeat. Previous studies indicated that people with good heartbeat perception tend to experience emotions more intensely than those with poor heartbeat perception [21][22].

Stimuli. Two sets of stimuli were used in the trials: a set of fabrics (Figure 1 (left)) and a set of interactive animations. The first set comprises six fabrics covering a range of roughness/smoothness and softness/hardness characteristics. These fabrics were selected by fashion design researchers. The second set comprises six interactive animations of the same fabrics. The reason to use interactive animations (rather than static pictures) for digitally representing the fabrics was twofold. It has been shown that users' perceptions of surface texture qualities such as roughness and directionality together with other material properties such as reflectance are improved when their relative viewpoint of the subject changes over time [8], [9]. Furthermore we have previously observed that users appear to become significantly more engaged when they perceive that they can directly control the pose of the surface or that they can deform a material (e.g. by ruffling or other manipulation). We have therefore developed a simple method of turning short video clips into interactive animations that we refer to as 'shoogles[2]'. The frames of the video are separated and loaded into an Adobe Flash movie or IOS app (to cater for both Apple and non-Apple systems) and the user can control the frame that is displayed simply by moving their finger or mouse across the animation.

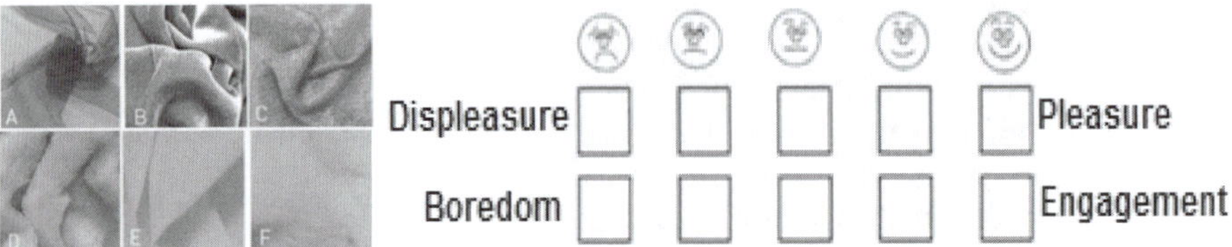

Fig. 1. (Left) Set of fabrics and (Right) self report-questionnaires

Measures. A four-item, five-point semantic differential self-report scale was designed for measuring users' affective experience (see Figure 1 (Right)). The engagement-boredom item was chosen because engagement is one of the crucial experiences to evaluate interactive technologies [18]. Physiological data were gathered from two sensors: a blood volume pulse detection sensor (HR/BVP Sensor) measuring heart rate (HR) and a skin conductance (SC Sensor) sensor measuring the resistance of the skin (electrodermal activity). Sensors were provided by the Thought Technologies ProComp unit, and signals were acquired with a sampling frequency of 256 Hz. The ProComp automatically calculated the HR signal using the inverse of the inter-beat intervals detected from the BVP sensor.

Procedure. Experiments were performed on an individual basis in a laboratory room. On arrival, each participant was given an information sheet which described the goal, the context and the duration of the experiment. Participants were also informed that they could stop the experiment whenever they wanted and then asked to sign the consent form. Sensors were attached to the participant's fingers on their non-dominant hand as they needed to rate attitude scale between trials. Participants were then sat at a desk and asked to avoid talking and to move as little as possible during the experiment. First, participants were asked to count their own heartbeat silently three times in order to identify each participant's interoceptive awareness. The heartbeat was measured at the same time with the BVP sensor.

Participants were instructed to concentrate on their body but not take their own pulse or try any other physical manipulations which might facilitate the detection of heartbeats. To reduce the chance of the participants memorizing numbers, each counting phase lasted different periods of time and participants were not told how long the intervals were. Additionally the order of counting phases for each participant was randomized in advance to counterbalance order effects.

---

[2] ***Shoogle:*** Lowland Scots: to rock backwards and forwards in small rapid movements. Information about the shoogle application is available at http://www.shoogleit.com and an iphone version is available at http://itunes.apple.com/uk/app/shoogleit-player/id427085804.

The main recording session took place upon completion of the heartbeat perception session. The participant was sat in front of the display. Before each trial (i.e., presentation of a stimulus), they were asked to relax and to fixate on a cross in the centre of a display for 10 seconds, during which the physiological signal baselines were collected. After this period the stimulus was presented. The participants in the "pre-physical" condition were first asked to handle the fabrics in front of them with multiple finger pinch with their dominant hand to feel the "*texture, stiffness, temperature, structure, friction, stretch and both sides of the fabrics*" [1]. The participant could see the fabric while touching it. After the physical handling of all the fabrics, the shoogles of the fabrics were shown to the participant. It was decided that the researchers rather than the participants would interact with the shoogle so as to remove a possible effect of touching the mouse or the display material. In the "pre-digital" condition, the participants were presented firstly with all the shoogles of the fabrics. After seeing all the shoogles they were asked to handle the physical fabrics. Also in this condition, the shoogles were controlled by the researcher. In each condition, the stimuli were presented twice in random order. After each presentation of either the digital or the physical stimulus (10 seconds on each trial), the participant was asked to fill in the self-report questionnaire.

3.2 Analysis

Assuming individual perceptions of fabric discriminative touch would not change over a short period of time, the stability of the results on different occasions was used to evaluate the reliability of the data collected from participants. By comparing the rating obtained for the two presentations of the same stimuli, data from 18 participants were considered to be valid since there were significant positive correlations between the two ratings in both conditions. For these participants, the correlation values were significant ($p < .05$) and greater than 0.70. Their values over the two repeated ratings were hence averaged for further analysis.

The physiological signals were separately analyzed for each participant. The first and last two seconds of each trial were discarded to avoid transitory bound problems since trials were continuously performed for each participant. The maximum value of heart rate was used in previous studies and considered as an appropriate feature to estimate the valence level of an emotion, especially in a short duration of recording time [23] whereas the mean value of skin conductivity is generally used to estimate the arousal level of an emotion [24]. Additionally, to compensate for variability between participants, the signals were normalised as indicated in equation (1). The maximum and minimum values were calculated with respect to the participants' trial's data and the average baseline was computed for each session.

$$\text{Normalized signal} = \frac{\text{raw\_signal} - \text{raw\_baseline\_average}}{\text{raw\_signal\_max} - \text{raw\_signal\_min}} \quad (1)$$

Individual heartbeat perception scores (HBP score) were calculated by averaging their scores for three heartbeat perception intervals, as shown in equation (2).

$$\text{HBP score} = \sum\left(1 - \frac{estimated\ heartbeats - actual\ heartbeats}{actual\ heartbeats}\right)/3 \quad (2)$$

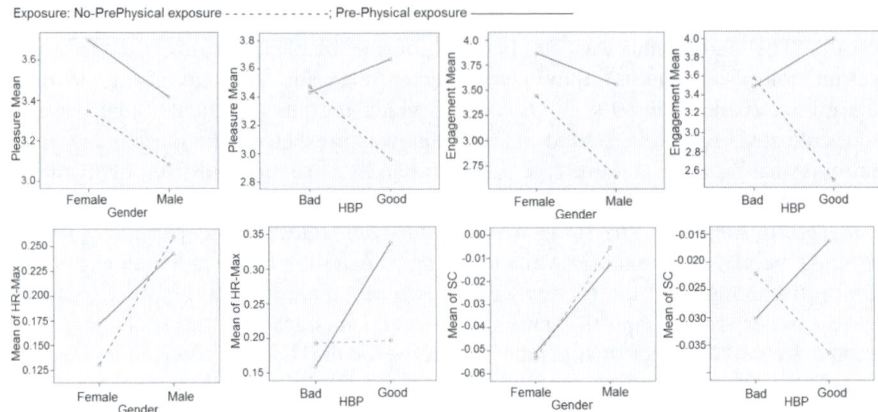

Fig. 2. Physical pre-handling: Exposure effect by gender and heartbeat perception (HBP)

Table 1. Effect of pre-physical handling on seeing the shoogle: MANOVA results

Self Report	Pleasure-Displeasure		Engagement-Boredom	
	F	p-value	F	p-value
Fabric	F(5,66) = 7.229	.000	F(5,66) = 10.162	.000
Exposure	F(1,66) = 7.725	.007	F(1,66) = 21.077	.000
Gender	F(1,66) = 8.338	.005	F(1,66) = 27.917	.000
Heartbeat perception	F(1,66) = 0.014	.905	F(1,66) = 1.104	.297
Exposure x Gender	F(1,66) = 8.247	.005	F(1,66) = 2.354	.130
Exposure x Heartbeat perc.	F(1,66) = 12.120	.001	F(1,66) = 29004	.000
Physiological signals	**HR-Max**		**SC-mean**	
	F	p-value	F	p-value
Fabric	F(5,66) = 0.200	.961	F(5,66) = 0.491	.781
Exposure	F(1,66) = 0.458	.501	F(1,66) = 0.450	.505
Gender	F(1,66) = 10.753	.002	F(1,66) = 8.266	.005
Heartbeat perception	F(1,66) = 7.557	.008	F(1,66) = 0.010	.920
Exposure x Gender	F(1,66) = 6.272	.015	F(1,66) = 4.184	.045
Exposure x Heartbeat perc.	F(1,66) = 5.878	.018	F(1,66) = 2.601	.112

A cut off score of 0.85 was selected since it was used in several studies [21-23]. The heartbeat perception task indicated that a total of five participants (two females, three males) were good heartbeat perceivers, and the rest were poor heartbeat perceivers.

4 Results

Effect of pre-handling of physical fabrics. The aim of this section is to investigate whether having previous handling experiences of the fabrics could increase the affective and engaging experience in the visual exposure to the same fabrics. We conducted a MANOVA test for a 6 (Fabric sample) × 2 (Exposure) × 2 (Gender) × 2 (Heartbeat perception) design with four independent variables. The exposure factor indicates whether people had pre-physical handling experience of the real fabric before viewing its interactive animation. Two types of dependent variables were considered: self report ratings and physiological responses.

A main effect of *Exposure, Fabric* and *Gender* was observed for both pleasure and engagement questionnaires (table 1, top). According to the post-hoc test (Bonferroni's method), participants in the pre-physical condition rated 'pleasure and engagement' significantly higher (see Figure 2, top). The interaction effects of *Exposure x Gender* were significant for both 'pleasure' and 'engagement' ratings ($p < .05$). Similar effects were observed for the interaction effects of *Exposure x Heartbeat* ($p < .05$). Through separate one-tailed independent *t* tests, interaction effects of exposure and gender (see Figure 2) were further explored. In both pleasure and engagement questionnaires, females in the pre-physical condition rated the experience of viewing the interactive animation significantly higher (Engagement: $t(58)=-1.884$, $p= .033$); Pleasure: $t(58)=-1.408$, $p=.082$, i.e., approaching significance). No significant results were found for male participants. In addition, as shown in Figure 1 (top), with pre-physical experience of the fabrics, good heartbeat perceivers only rated 'pleasure' and 'engagement' scores much higher than in the other conditions.

As shown in Table 1 (bottom), a main effect of *Gender* and *Heartbeat perception* is observed for HR-max (p-values < .05). Though the main effects of *exposure* were not significant for either physiological signals, the interaction effects of *exposure x Gender* and *Exposure x Heartbeat perception* were both significant for HR-max (all p-values < .05). Through separate independent 1-tailed *t* tests, the interactions of *exposure x gender* and by *Exposure x Heartbeat perception* were further analyzed. For both females and good heartbeat perceivers (figure 1 bottom), significantly higher values of HR-max were found in the pre-physical condition than without pre-physical handling experience (Female: $t(118)=-2.665$, $p = .045$; Good perceivers: $t(52)=-7.342$, $p=.000$). However, for males significantly lower values of HR-max were found in the pre-physical condition ($t(93)=2.401$, $p=.009$). For skin conductance (SC) only the effects of *Gender* and the interaction *Exposure x Gender* were observed ($p < .05$).

Effect of pre-seeing the digital fabric handling. The aim of this section is to investigate whether having prior seeing of the digital handling of the fabrics could increase the experience of handling the same physical fabrics. We conducted a MANOVA test for a 6 (Fabric sample) × 2 (Exposure) × 2 (Gender) × 2 (Heartbeat perception) design with four independent variables. The exposure factor indicates whether people had prior seeing experience of the digital handling of the fabric (shoogle) before physically handling the real fabric. Two types of dependent variables were considered: self report ratings and physiological responses. The main effect of *Fabric, Exposure and Gender* were observed for both 'pleasure' and 'engagement' questionnaires (table 2, top). The effect of *Heartbeat perception* was observed only for pleasure. The interaction effects of *Exposure x Gender and Exposure x Heartbeat perception* were significant for both 'pleasure' and 'engagement' ratings ($p = .019$). A main effect of *Exposure* for HR-max (p-values = .031) and a main effect of *Gender* for Sc (p-value = .042) are also observed. Even if there are very few significant effects, we can observe from Figure 3 that the pre-exposure to seeing the digital handling of the fabrics has produced lower ratings for female participants and for good heart beat perceiving participants for both pleasure and engagement

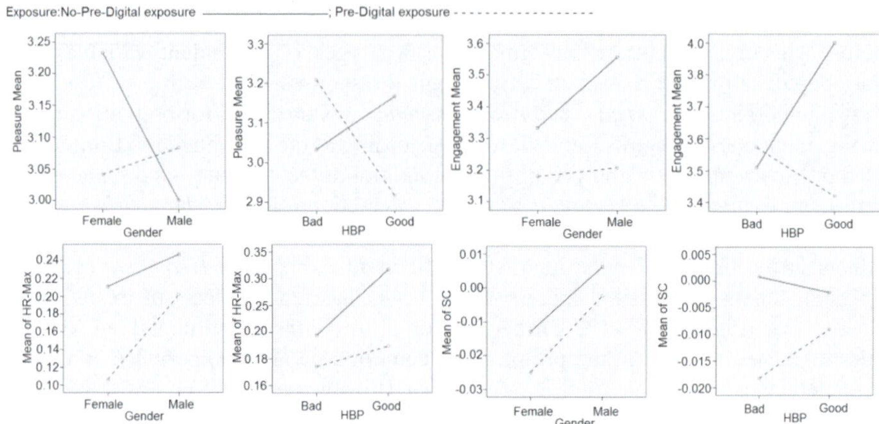

Fig. 3. Seeing digital handling: Exposure effect by gender and heartbeat perception (HBP)

questionnaires. Even if not statistically significant, we can instead observe that male have rated higher on the pleasure questionnaire after pre-exposure but still lower on the engagement questionnaire. Furthermore, both physiological signals show a decrease for all participants after pre-exposure to seeing the fabric digital handling.

Table 2. Effect of pre-seeing the shoogle on physical handling: MANOVA

Self Report	Pleasure-Displeasure		Engagement-Boredom	
	F	p-value	F	p-value
Fabric	F(5,66) = 17.368	.000	F(5,66) = 6.365	.000
Exposure	F(1,66) = 0.621	.433	F(1,66) = 2.887	.094
Gender	F(1,66) = 0.003	.955	F(1,66) = 0.254	.616
Heartbeat perception	F(1,66) = 0.652	.422	F(1,66) = 0.776	.381
Exposure x Gender	F(1,66) = 0.223	.638	F(1,66) = 0.758	.387
Exposure x Heartbeat perc.	F(1,66) = .0000	1.00	F(1,66) = 5.801	.019
Physiological signals	HR-Max		SC-mean	
	F	p-value	F	p-value
Fabric	F(5,66) = 0.168	.974	F(5,66) = 1.854	.114
Exposure	F(1,66) = 4.858	.031	F(1,66) = 0.411	.524
Gender	F(1,66) = 2.125	.150	F(1,66) = 4.313	.042
Heartbeat perception	F(1,66) = 3.849	.054	F(1,66) = 0.010	.921
Exposure x Gender	F(1,66) = 2.418	.125	F(1,66) = 0.055	.815
Exposure x Heartbeat perc.	F(1,66) = 0.769	.376	F(1,66) = 0.627	.431

5 Conclusions

This study investigated whether physically handling fabrics increased the positive experience of looking at the same fabrics being digitally handled, and vice versa. With respect to the former, the results showed that female participants and good heartbeat perceivers showed an increase in both self-reported ratings of their positive experience and heartbeat rate. The same effect was not observed for bad heartbeat perceivers and male participants, consistent with studies reporting a gender effect in the appreciation of handling of fabrics [12]. Whilst visual perception of the fabrics during touching could have been a confound, we argue that the effect is due to the tactile interaction with the fabric itself. The reason is twofold. First of all touch is an important sense when appreciating fabrics. Secondly, prior work [17] has shown that pre-seeing an object does not have an effect on the hedonic experience of re-seeing it. It may be that a participant that has previously touched the fabric imagine touching it whilst seeing it in the shoogle.

Prior observation of the fabrics being digitally handled did not have a significant effect on self-reports of engagement and pleasure. Although not significant, both ratings and physiological measures showed a decrease in female participants and good heart beat perceivers. This decrease in both ratings and physiological changes may indicate that engagement during observation of digital handling of the fabrics could not be carried over to the appreciation of the physical handling of the fabrics itself. This may be due to the researcher, rather than the participants, digitally handling the fabrics. But it is also possible that the expectation raised by only seeing the fabrics did not reflect the experience of touching it.

In our experiment, digital handling was performed by the researcher. In future work, we will assess whether the effects are enhanced by having participants perform the digital handling themselves. This will provide further understanding on the benefits that novel interfaces could gain by providing manual handling with haptic feedback even when this does not fully reflect the fabric texture. In fact, previous studies (see [30] for a review) have shown that the textural properties of a visually presented object were haptically perceived when the visual presentation was synchronously coordinated with touch feedback of an object of different texture.

References

1. Moody, W., Morgan, R., Dillon, P., Baber, C., Wing, A.: Factors underlying fabric perception. In: Proceedings of the Eurohaptics (2001)
2. Lin, T., Akimobo, M., Shigeo, M.: Using Subjective and Physiological Measures to Evaluate Audience-participating Movie Experience. In: AVI 2008, Napoli, Italy, pp. 28–30 (2008)
3. Clore, G., Palmer, J., Gratch, J.: Affective guidance of intelligent agents: How emotion controls cognition. Proceedings: Cognitive Systems Research 10, 21–30 (2009)
4. Laparra-Hernández, J., Belda-Lois, J.M., Medina, E., Campos, N., Poveda, R.: EMG and GSR signals for evaluating user's perception of different types of ceramic flooring. International Journal of Industrial Ergonomics 39(2), 326–332 (2009)
5. McDonagh, D., Bruseberg, A., Laslam, C.: Visual product evaluation: exploring users emotional relationships with product. Applied Ergonomics 33, 231–240 (2002)
6. Jansson-Boyd, C., Marlow, N.: Not only in the eye of the beholder: tactile information can affect aesthetic evaluation. Psychology of Aesthetics, Creativity, and the Arts 1(3), 170–173 (2007)
7. Citrin, A.V., Stem, D.E., Spangenberg, E.R., Clark, M.J.: Consumer need for tactile input: an internet retailing challenge. Journal of Business Research 56, 915–922 (2003)
8. Padilla, S., Drbohlav, O., Green, P.R., Spence, A., Chantler, M.J.: Perceived roughness of $1/f^{\beta}$ noise surfaces. Vision Research 48(17), 1791–1797 (2008)

9. Shah, P., Padilla, S., Green, P.R., Chantler, M.J.: Perceived Directionality of $1/f^{\beta}$ Noise Surfaces. In: Proceedings of 5th Symposium on Applied Perception in Graphics and Visualization (APGV), p. 203. ACM Press, New York (2008)
10. Chen, X., Shao, F., Barnes, C., Childs, T., Henson, B.: Exploring relationships between touch perception and surface physical properties. International Journal of Design 3(2), 67–77 (2009)
11. Essick, G.K., James, A., McGlone, F.P.: Psychophysical assessment of the affective components of non-painful touch. NeuroReport 10, 2083–2087 (1999)
12. Essick, G.K., McGlone, F., Dancer, C., Fabricant, D., Ragin, Y., Phillips, N., Jones, T., Guest, S.: Quantitative assessment of pleasant touch. Neuroscience & Biobehavioral Reviews 34(2), 192–203 (2010), Touch, Temperature, Pain/Itch and Pleasure
13. Barnes, C.J., Childs, T.H.C., Henson, B., Southee, C.H.: Surface finish and touch—a case study in a new human factors tribology. Wear 257(7-8), 740–750 (2004)
14. Easton, R.D., Green, A.J., Srinivas, K.: Transfer between vision and haptics: Memory for 2-D pattern and 3-D objects. Psychonomic Bulletin and Review 4, 403–410 (1997)
15. Reales, J.M., Ballesteros, S.: Implicit and explicit memory for visual and haptic objects: Cross-modal priming depends on structural descriptions. Journal of Experimental Psychology: Learning, Memory, and Cognition 15, 379–388 (1999)
16. Gallace, A., Spence, C.: The science of interpersonal touch: an overview. Neuroscience and Biobehavioral Reviews 34, 246–259 (2010)
17. Suzuku, T., Gyoba, J.: Visual and tactile cross-modal mere exposure effects. Cognition and Emotion 22(1), 147–154 (2008)
18. McCarthy, J., Wright, P., Wallace, J.: The experience of enchantment in human-computer interaction. Personal and Ubiquitous Computing 10, 278–369 (2006)
19. Lang, P.J.: The Emotion Probe: Studies of Motivation and Attention. American Psychologist 50(5), 285–372 (1995)
20. Agarwal, A., Meyer, A.: Beyond usability: evaluating emotional response as an integral part of user experience. In: Proceedings: CHI 2009 (2009)
21. Schandry, R.: Heart beat perception and emotional experience. Psychophysiology 18(4), 483–488 (1981)
22. Pollatos, O., Kirsch, W., Schandry, R.: On the relationship between interoceptive awareness, emotional experience, and brain processes. Cognitive Brain Research 25, 948–962 (2005)
23. Chanel, G., Kierkels, J.J.M., Soleymani, M., Pun, T.: Short-term emotion assessment in a recall paradigm. International Journal of Human-Computer Studies 67, 607–627 (2009)
24. Picard, R.W., Vyzas, E., Healey, J.: Toward machine emotional intelligence: Analysis of affective physiological state. IEEE Transactions on Pattern Analysis and Machine Intelligence, 1175–1191 (2001)
25. Kim, E.Y., Kim, S.-j., Koo, H.-j., Jeong, K.J., Kim, J.-I.: Emotion-Based Textile Indexing Using Colors and Texture. In: Wang, L., Jin, Y. (eds.) FSKD 2005. LNCS (LNAI), vol. 3613, pp. 1077–1080. Springer, Heidelberg (2005)
26. Kim, N.Y., Shin, Y., Kim, E.Y.: Emotion-Based Textile Indexing Using Neural Networks. In: Jacko, J.A. (ed.) HCI 2007, Part III. LNCS, vol. 4552, pp. 349–357. Springer, Heidelberg (2007)
27. Rolls, E.T., O'Doherty, J., et al.: Representations of Pleasant and Painful Touch in the Human Orbitofrontal and Cingulate Cortices. Cereb. Cortex 13(3), 308–317 (2003)
28. McGlone, F., Spence, C.: The cutaneous senses: Touch, temperature, pain/itch, and pleasure. Neuroscience and Biobehavioral Reviews 34, 145–147 (2010)
29. Nogueira, C., Cabeco-Silva, M.E., Schacher, L., Adolphe, D.: Textile Materials: Tactile Describers. Journal of Food Technology 7(3), 66–70 (2009)
30. Schutz-Bosbach, S., Tausche, P., Weiss, C.: Roughness perception during the rubber hand illusion. Brain and Cognition 70(1), 136–144 (2009)

Ranking vs. Preference: A Comparative Study of Self-reporting

Georgios N. Yannakakis[1] and John Hallam[2]

[1] Center for Computer Games Research, IT University of Copenhagen, Rued Langgaards Vej 7, Copenhagen S, Denmark
yannakakis@itu.dk

[2] Maersk Mc-Kinney Moller Institute, University of Southern Denmark, Campusvej 55, Odense, Denmark
john@mmmi.sdu.dk

Abstract. This paper introduces a comparative analysis between rating and pairwise self-reporting via questionnaires in user survey experiments. Two dissimilar game user survey experiments are employed in which the two questionnaire schemes are tested and compared for reliable affect annotation. The statistical analysis followed to test our hypotheses shows that even though the two self-reporting schemes are consistent there are significant *order of reporting* effects when subjects report via a rating questionnaire. The paper concludes with a discussion of the appropriateness of each self-reporting scheme under conditions drawn from the experimental results obtained.

1 Introduction

Self-reporting provides the most direct approach to user experience annotation and affect detection. Quantitative reports via questionnaires offer unique properties for constructing computational models of reported user states (affective or cognitive) and ease the analysis of subjective assessment in user studies. Even though beneficial for cognitive and affective capture and modeling, such reporting has several limitations such as self-deception, intrusiveness and subjectiveness. The appropriateness of the reporting scheme used for affect detection is therefore vital for the validity of the obtained analysis.

This paper examines the relationship between two popular self-reporting schemes in user studies: self-reporting via *ranking* (or scaling) and via *pairwise preference*. The two schemes are compared in two dissimilar game survey studies in which experiment participants are asked to post-report a set of affective states. For the comparison to be possible, pairwise preferences are inferred from the ranking values and compared to the direct pairwise preferences. The two hypotheses the two questionnaire schemes are tested against are:

- H1: There is an inconsistency between reported preferences and reported ranking. Ranking responses do not match reported preferences.
- H2: The order of post-experience reporting has an effect on both ranking and preference report schemes. Randomness exists in both self-report schemes.

S. D'Mello et al. (Eds.): ACII 2011, Part I, LNCS 6974, pp. 437–446, 2011.

The statistical analysis followed to test the above hypotheses suggests that while ranking and preferences are consistent (with variant degrees of consistency), pairwise preferences are more appropriate detectors of user states, eliminating the subjective notion of scaling and effects related to reporting order.

2 Self-reporting

This paper focuses on *forced* self-reports obtained via questionnaires. Such a self-report scheme constrains the participant to specific questionnaire items which could vary from simple tick boxes to multiple choice items while both the questions and the answers provided could vary from single words to sentences. Two types of forced self-reports that are described in more detail below, define the framework of investigations in this paper: self-reports via *ranking* (or scaling) and self-reports via *preferences*.

2.1 Ranking

The vast majority of psychometric and user studies have adopted a type of rating report to capture the subjective assessment of the experiment participants ([11] among others). The most popular approach to ranking reports is a form of a Likert scale [5] in which users are asked to rate an experience, an emotion or an interactive session. In most such studies Likert ratings are usually averaged across users before they are further analyzed. Such a practice has an impact on the ratings losing their subjective nature but also implies a knowledge of the scale that is beyond a relative rank order of data [11].

Among the limitations of ranking ordinal scales, Linn and Gronlund [6] indicate the existence of personal bias which may (among others) occur when the subject is consistently using only part of the scoring scale, logical errors due to the confusion of the distinct items of an ordinal scale and the ability to use numerical information within scales which is affected by the subject's internal cognitive processes, cultural background, temperament, and interests [13]. There is also a large body of work suggesting the presence of *primacy* and *recency* order effects in Likert questionnaires (see [2] among others).

The authors are not aware of a reliable statistical test that validates the reliability of a ranking questionnaire as a whole. Cronbach's alpha [4] (*inter alia*) is an estimate of internal consistency (or reliability) of sections of the questionnaire; Cohen's kappa [3] assesses rater agreement in nominal scales.

2.2 Preference

Reporting via pairwise preferences has recently attracted the interest of researchers in affective and cognitive modeling ([16,14,12] among others) since it minimizes the assumptions made about subjects' notions of highly subjective constructs such as emotions and allows a fair comparison between the answers of different subjects. Moreover, artifacts such as the subjective notion of ranking/scaling are eliminated and lead to the construction of generalisable and accurate computational models of affect via user preference modeling [14].

A preference questionnaire scheme may ask for the pairwise or multiple preference of participants or even ask them to provide a preferred order. In this paper we investigate pairwise preferences and are inspired by the seminal work of Scheffe [10] and Agresti [1] for the analysis of paired comparisons.

3 User Survey Case Studies

This section presents the main phases of the experimental procedure followed to obtain self-reported emotional or cognitive states of experiment participants via both ranking and preference schemes. The reader is referred to [16] for more details on the experimental protocol used. The section concludes with the presentation of the two case studies considered in this paper.

3.1 System Instrumentation

The interactive systems we investigated are instrumented based on controllable parameters identified by the designer. The selection of the parameters is based on their potential impact on the user's affective and cognitive states examined and thereby to the post-experience self-reporting. For instance, a controllable parameter in a game system could be the speed of the game.

For each parameter under investigation, a number of states (e.g. 'Low', 'High') are selected. The product of the number of states for each of the parameters defines the number of different system variants that will be examined. Given the proposed experimental design [16] each survey participant interacts with system variants in pairs (variant A and variant B) — differing in the levels/states of one or more of the selected controllable parameters — for a selected time window. To test for potential order effects each subject interacts with the aforementioned system variants in both orders. Each time a system variant is completed the subject is asked to rate a particular experience using both a ranking and a pairwise preference reporting scheme (described below).

3.2 Self-reported Post-Experience

For *ranking* questionnaires the question is expressed as: "The session felt E." where E is the emotional state (e.g. frustration) under investigation. Two ranking scales have been used in the experiments reported: a 20 point 0-10 scale, and a 1-5 scale. The 0-10 scale uses principles of the *funometer* [9]; subjects have to rate the experience in a thermometer-designed Likert scale. On the other hand, the answers in the 1-5 scale rating scheme are inspired by the game experience questionnaire (GEQ) [8]; numbers have following glosses: 1: *not at all*; 2: *slightly*, 3: *moderately*, 4: *fairly* and 5: *extremely*.

For pairwise *preference* questionnaires subjects are asked to fill in a questionnaire each time a pair of game sessions (variants) is finished. According to this scheme, the subject is asked to report whether the first variant felt more E than the second variant. Specifically, for each completed pair of system variants A and B, subjects report their preference regarding an emotional state, E, by selecting among the following 4-alternative forced choices (4-AFC): A [B] felt more E than B [A] (*cf.* 2-alternative forced choice); both felt equally E; neither of the two felt E.

One of the limitations of the experimental protocol proposed is post-experience. Users report emotional states *after* playing games, which might generate memory-dependencies in the reports. Effects such as order of play and game learnability might also be apparent and interconnected to memory. The experimental protocol, however, is designed to test for order of play effects which, in part, reveal memory (report consistency over different orders) and learnability effects, if any. Lack of significant order effect provides evidence that the experimental noise generated in this way is random. Statistical analysis of the effect of order on subjects' emotional judgement indicates the level of randomness in subjects' preferences. Randomness is apparent when the subject's expressed preferences are inconsistent for the pair (A, B) independently of the questionnaire-scheme used.

3.3 The Playware Case Study

The first case study presented concerns game play sessions followed by self-reporting sessions of children playing physical interactive games [16,17]. The game, called 'Bug-Smasher', designed using the Playware playground (interactive tiles) platform [7], is used here as the test-bed interactive system for investigating the relationship between self-reporting schemes. (The reader is referred to [16] for more details of Bug-Smasher).

Seventy six children, aged 8 to 10 years old, participated in the survey experiment. Each subject played a set of 90 second Bug-Smasher variants, differing with respect to two control parameters: the speed of the game and the spatial diversity of game opponents. Children were not interviewed but were asked to fill in a questionnaire, minimizing interviewing effects. Each subject was asked to rate each game via a 10-scale *funometer* [9] (in increments of 0.5) and after a pair of games were finished, to report a fun preference for the two games she played using a 2-AFC question, "which one of the two games was more fun?" The options offered for choice were "first" and "second".

3.4 The Maze-Ball Case Study

A screen-based computer game, named Maze-ball, is used for the second experiment reported in this paper. Maze-ball [18] is a three-dimensional predator/prey game. The goal of the player (ball) is to maximize her score by gathering as many tokens, scattered in the maze, as possible while avoiding being touched by a number of opponents in a predefined time window of 90 seconds. Further details about Maze-Ball and experimental design can be found in [18].

Thirty six subjects aged from 21 to 47 years participated to the experiment. Each subject played a predefined set of eight games for 90 seconds each; the games differ in the virtual camera profile embedded. For each completed game and pair of games A and B, subjects report their emotional preference using a 5-point Likert scale based on GEQ [8] followed by a 4-AFC pairwise preference protocol. The emotional states, E, examined comprise *fun*, *challenge*, *boredom*, *frustration*, *excitement*, *anxiety* and *relaxation*. The selection of these seven states is based on their relevance to computer game-playing and player experience.

3.5 Case Study Dissimilarities

The main dissimilarities between the two case studies are that in Playware 1) subjects are children (aged: 8 to 10), 2) a pen-and-paper (instead of a digital) questionnaire is used, 3) a rather broad ordinal scale from 1 to 10 is used for the rating scheme, 4) 2-AFC (instead of 4-AFC) is used for the preference scheme; 5) and subjects are asked only one question, about fun. Cognitive load during the reporting phase in the Playware experiment appears less due to the presence of only one question. Moreover, the broad rating scale used may allow for a better approximation of the level of reported fun.

Comparison of findings across the two case studies is not appropriate given the large number of dissimilarities in terms of gameplay interaction and experimental protocol. However, collectively, they provide two related but different studies of post-experience reporting in games and their analysis assists the understanding of the interplay between reported preferences and ranking across different schemes.

4 Results and Analysis

This section presents the results of the statistical analysis for testing our hypotheses in the two case studies. First, the statistics employed to test our research hypotheses H1 and H2 are outlined below.

4.1 H1 Test Statistic

To measure the degree of agreement between the rating and preference self-reports we calculate the correlation coefficients between them, obtained using $c(\mathbf{z}) = \sum_{i=1}^{N}\{z_i/N\}$ following the statistical analysis procedure for pairwise preference data introduced in [15]. N is the total number of incidents to correlate, and $z_i = +1$, if rating reports match preference reports and $z_i = -1$, if rating and preference reports are mismatched in the game pair i. In the calculation of $c(\mathbf{z})$ we only take into account *clear* preferences and ratings of participants. That is, we only consider game pairs in which both a clear preference (i.e. $A \succ B$ or $A \prec B$; 2-AFC) and a clear rating (i.e. $A > B$ or $A < B$) are expressed. The p-values of $c(\mathbf{z})$ are obtained via the binomial distribution.

4.2 H2 Test Statistics

To measure whether the order of play affects the player's judgement of rating or pairwise preference for affective states, we follow the order testing procedure described in [15], based on the number of times that the subject prefers the first (primacy effect) or the second (recency effect) game in both pairs. Briefly, the order test statistic is calculated as $r_o = (K - J)/\mathbf{N}$, where the subject prefers (either via ranking or preference) the first session in both pairs K times and, the second session in both pairs J times. The greater the absolute value of r_o the more the order of play tends to affect the subjects' judgement of interest. r_o is trinomially-distributed under the null hypothesis..

In addition to the r_o value we calculate the $r_c = (K + J)/\mathbf{N}$ test statistic, which yields a measure of reporting consistency with respect to order. The obtained r_c value lies between 0 (reporting is consistent) and 1 (reporting is inconsistent) and is binomially-distributed with mean 0.5 under the null hypothesis.

The order effects are calculated solely on clear preferences (i.e. when A $\succ$ B or A $\prec$ B) and ratings (i.e. when A $>$ B or A $<$ B) in both pairs played in both orders. The significance level used in this paper is 5%.

4.3 Playware

The total number of game pairs with valid reported data is 105 in the Playware experiment. To calculate the statistics we exclude the 35 game pairs in which an equal rating is reported. The correlation between reported rating and preference $c(\mathbf{z}) = 0.857$ (p-value $= 4.002 \cdot 10^{-10}$) indicates a statistically significant effect and rules out H1.

Order Effect Analysis. Statistical analysis of the subjects' answers shows that no significant order effect occurs ($r_o = -0.102$, p-value $= 0.224$) when preferences are reported, which rules out hypothesis H2. However, a significant effect of playing order on rating reports is found ($r_o = -0.3809$, p-value $= 0.0097$) which indicates a tendency to consistently rate the second game higher. The insignificant order effect for reported *preferences*, in part, demonstrates that effects such as a subject's possible preference for the very first game played and the interplay between reported fun and familiarity with the game are statistically insignificant. On the other hand, the significant order effect for reported ranking suggests that the order of play influences reporting when the ranking scheme is used.

The r_c values for ranking and preferences are 0.476 (p-value $= 0.124$) and 0.338 (p-value $= 0.009$), respectively, suggesting that only the preference reports appear to be consistent with respect to order.

Analysis & Conclusions. The first case study provides indications of inconsistency between rating and preference reports. While the two are statistically correlated ($c(\mathbf{z}) = 0.857$) there are several instances (16.6% of the data samples) in which preferences do not agree with their corresponding rating.

The inconsistency between the two report schemes may have occurred for a number of reasons including self-deception, cognitive load, question understanding in small children etc. A first analysis of the effect of order of game interaction shows that significant order effects exist only in reported ratings which in turn suggests existence of randomness when expressing rating choices for the game sessions attempted. Moreover, the consistency of reports with respect to order, r_c, appears to be significant for the preference reports only.

4.4 Maze-Ball

For the Maze-Ball case study we follow the same statistical analysis presented above for the Playware game. The total number of valid game pairs examined in the Maze-Ball survey is 56 and the matching correlation ($c(\mathbf{z})$) values between rating and preference reports for the Maze-Ball test-bed are depicted in Table 1.

It appears there is a varying degree of consistency between rating and preference reports depending on the affective state (question asked). Overall 2-AFC preference

Table 1. Maze-ball: Correlation coefficient values ($c(\mathbf{z})$) between rating and clear preferences (2-AFC), and order of play (r_o) and consistency (r_c) correlation coefficients for all investigated emotional states E. Significant effects appear in bold.

		r_o		r_c	
E	$c(\mathbf{z})$	Ranking	Preference	Ranking	Preference
Fun	**0.925**	**−0.375**	−0.150	0.375	0.450
Challenge	**0.733**	**0.300**	−0.222	0.500	0.444
Frustration	**0.878**	−0.083	−0.066	**0.250**	**0.187**
Anxiety	**0.619**	0.200	−0.222	**0.200**	0.444
Boredom	**0.666**	**−0.333**	−0.111	0.333	**0.111**
Excitement	**0.642**	−0.200	−0.117	**0.200**	**0.312**
Relaxation	**0.652**	**−0.250**	0.052	0.250	0.368
Total	**0.744**	−0.090	−0.112	**0.309**	**0.353**

reports appear to be consistent with rating reports. For the fun, frustration and challenge reports the two schemes are highly correlated (correlation higher than 0.7) whereas for the other four questionnaire items the correlation lies within the 0.6-0.7 interval; however, in all seven affective state questionnaire items, the correlation is statistically significant ruling out H1. These effects might be linked to the order of question items appearing in the questionnaire which is equivalent to the order the emotional states that appear in Table 1; the questions about excitement and relaxation, for instance, were the last two items in both questionnaires.

Order Effect Analysis. The statistical analysis presented in Table 1 shows that order of play does not affect the pairwise preferences of users. The insignificant order effects also, in part, demonstrate that effects such as a user's possible preference for the very first game played and the interplay between reported emotions and familiarity with the game are statistically insignificant. Even though not statistically significant, the correlation statistic values of Table 1 reveal a preference for the second game played for most questionnaire items (negative correlation values).

The H2 hypothesis is ruled-out: no effect exists in any preference questionnaire item while significant effects are observed in the fun, challenge, boredom and relaxation ranking questions. These effects may, in part, explain the low $c(\mathbf{z})$ values in boredom and relaxation but also be responsible for the level of inconsistency in fun and challenge. In general it appears that — excluding the anxiety state — $c(\mathbf{z})$ values (significant or not) are larger in the ranking scheme than in the preference questionnaire scheme. The total order effect is not significant for either questionnaire scheme, which does not allow any safe conclusions to be drawn when all questionnaire items are considered.

The r_c values in Table 1 demonstrate that both questionnaire schemes are consistent in frustration and excitement and no additional conclusions can be drawn for these two states. On the other hand, it appears as if the inconsistencies of anxiety preferences have an impact on the low $c(\mathbf{z})$ value of that state given that the r_c values are not significant. The order statistics computed including the equal preference (3-AFC) could provide a clearer picture of the relationship between order effects and questionnaire scheme inconsistencies and are left for future analysis due to space considerations.

Analysis & Conclusions. The statistical analysis for the Maze-Ball case study revealed two main effects: consistency (of varying degree) between ranking and preference reports in all 2-AFC questionnaire items and significant order effects for the ranking scheme.

Results related to the first effect suggest that even though for some question items (e.g. fun, frustration and challenge) the consistency is higher than others (e.g. anxiety, relaxation and boredom), the hypothesis H1 is ruled out for all emotional states in Maze-Ball. Nevertheless, as in Playware, there are questionnaire items for which the agreement between rating and preferences is far from exact (i.e. $c(\mathbf{z}) = 1.0$). For instance, correlation values between 0.6 and 0.7, observed in four out of seven question items of the Maze-ball questionnaire, are significant yet raise questions for the several mismatch instances present in the reports.

The second effect suggests that hypothesis H2 is ruled out. The analysis of order of reporting shows, in general, higher order test statistic values in ranking than in preferences and significant order effects in four emotional states when reported via a ranking scheme. Both indicate a potential higher degree of randomness reporting with ranking schemes for that case study.

Finally, note that the consistency of preferences indicated by the r_c statistic is more often significant for the 2-AFC answers derived from 4-AFC protocol, which is to be expected since 4-AFC explicitly accounts for cases of non-preference.

5 Discussion

This initial set of game case studies and the results obtained raise several questions with respect to the relationship between rating and preference self-reports and the particular game survey studies used to test our hypothesis. While a comparison between the two studies is not appropriate given their large set of dissimilarities, an initial analysis across both test cases will assist the design of additional user survey studies that could shed more light to self-reporting effects.

Most significant is the observation that while direct and derived preferences are generally well-correlated, mismatches occur rather frequently and rating questionnaires appear more susceptible to order-of-play effects than preference questionnaires. It is, therefore, interesting to ask *why reported preferences and ratings do not match exactly?* The two studies presented in this paper link the reporting order effect and the existence of randomness in reporting with the inconsistency between the two self-report schemes. The effect of play order is present in most user states examined. Unsurprisingly, these effects vary across different studies, questionnaire schemes and affective states. In both studies there is a general trend of preference for the second game played (recency order effect) with significant effects appearing only in the rating scheme. Moreover, the statistic measuring the degree of rating consistency suggests that randomness existent in ranking reports appears to be a critical factor for the inconsistency between the two reporting schemes. Preliminary results of a fairer calculation of the r_c values — including the equal option of preference and allowing for the equality of ranking reports — show that consistency is significant only in the preference scheme, which suggests a benefit of preferences for accurate subjective affective reporting and annotation.

A number of other points are worth noting; a study taking account of all of them exceeds the scope of the present paper, but the results reported here suggest that such a study may be worthwhile.

The experimental protocol favors expressed rating score. Rating questions were asked twice as often as preference questions were asked. Thus, subjects are expected to be familiar with the structure of the ranking scheme more than the preference scheme. The preference scheme is arguably simpler for the respondent, but requires increased short-term memory since at least two — instead of one in the ranking scheme — interaction sessions are necessary for comparison. Moreover, the rating scheme question comes first, straight after the experience, followed by the preference scheme. One would, therefore, expect that cognitive and short-term memory load and furthermore questionnaire completion times would be higher when preferences are reported. However, preliminary results from current game survey studies suggest that the time taken to complete a rating questionnaire is significantly higher than a preference questionnaire.

Questionnaire usability. Clearly, usability does not affect the results between the two report schemes since the interaction is the same for both: pen-n-paper in Playware, digital bullet-form questionnaire in Maze-Ball.

Amount of perceived information. The amount of information provided through the questionnaire is quite unlikely to have an effect on the findings. All questions, preference or rating, are asked in a similar fashion with very small differences — e.g. "I felt challenged" (rating) vs. "I felt more challenged in:" (preferences). The rating schemes used, however, have more available choice options than the preference schemes. For Playware, the options were 2 for preference and 20 for rating. On the other end, rating and preferences have 5 and 4 options, respectively, for Maze-Ball. The thermometer-like rating scheme of Playware appears to generate higher consistencies between preferences and rating but those consistencies are not apparent in all user expressed states of the Maze-Ball study. The thermometer type of ranking questionnaire and the 5-option game experience questionnaire (GEQ) [8] are used for their popularity in user and player experience research. A dedicated control experiment is required to explore the impact of the number of options of the questionnaire schemes on the consistency between expressed rating and preference. Four or three-option ranking questionnaires could possibly lead to reduced cognitive load of users and higher consistencies.

Self-report limitations. Well known limitations of self-reporting such as self-deception, high intrusiveness and learnability effects are applicable to both questionnaire schemes and, thereby, do not seem to have a particular impact on the comparison. While there is no clear way to identify such effects, controlling the order of games and questionnaire sessions, as proposed, alleviates in part such effects inherent in naive questionnaires. Other multimodal input sources, including biofeedback and additional context-based game metrics, could be used for further analysis but do not supplant the self-reports.

Acknowledgments. The authors would like to thank all subjects that participated in the experiments. Special thanks also goes to Héctor P. Martínez for his help in conducting the Maze-Ball user survey experiment. The research was supported, in part, by the FP7 ICT project SIREN (project no: 258453).

References

1. Agresti, A.: Analysis of ordinal paired comparison data. Journal of the Royal Statistical Society. Series C (Applied Statistics) 41(2), 287–297 (1992)
2. Chan, J.C.: Response-order effects in Likert-type scales. Educational and Psychological Measurement 51(3), 531–540 (1991)
3. Cohen, J.: A coefficient of agreement for nominal scales. Educational and Psychological Measurement 20, 37–46 (1960)
4. Cronbach, J.L.: Coefficient alpha and the internal structure of tests. Psychometrika 16(3), 297–334 (1951)
5. Likert, R.: A technique for the measurement of attitudes. Archives of Psychology 140, 1–55 (1932)
6. Linn, R., Gronlund, N.: Measurement and assessment in teaching. Prentice-Hall, Englewood Cliffs (2000)
7. Lund, H.H., Klitbo, T., Jessen, C.: Playware technology for physically activating play. Artificial Life and Robotics Journal 9(4), 165–174 (2005)
8. Poels, K., IJsselsteijn, W.: Development and validation of the game experience questionnaire. In: FUGA Workshop Mini-Symposium, Helsinki, Finland (2008)
9. Read, J., MacFarlane, S., Cassey, C.: Endurability, engagement and expectations. In: Proceedings of International Conference for Interaction Design and Children (2002)
10. Scheffe, H.: An analysis of variance for paired comparisons. Journal of the American Statistical Association 47(259), 381–400 (1952)
11. Stevens, S.S.: On the Theory of Scales of Measurement. Science 103(2684), 677–680 (1946)
12. Tognetti, S., Garbarino, M., Bonarini, A., Matteucci, M.: Modeling enjoyment preference from physiological responses in a car racing game. In: Proceedings of the IEEE Conference on Computational Intelligence and Games, Copenhagen, Denmark, August 18-21, pp. 321–328 (2010)
13. Viswanathan, M.: Measurement of individual differences in preference for numerical information. Journal of Applied Psychology 78(5), 741–752
14. Yannakakis, G.N.: Preference Learning for Affective Modeling. In: Proceedings of the Int. Conf. on Affective Computing and Intelligent Interaction, pp. 126–131. IEEE, Amsterdam (2009)
15. Yannakakis, G.N., Hallam, J.: Towards Optimizing Entertainment in Computer Games. Applied Artificial Intelligence 21, 933–971 (2007)
16. Yannakakis, G.N., Hallam, J., Lund, H.H.: Entertainment Capture through Heart Rate Activity in Physical Interactive Playgrounds. User Modeling and User-Adapted Interaction, Special Issue: Affective Modeling and Adaptation 18(1-2), 207–243 (2008)
17. Yannakakis, G.N., Maragoudakis, M., Hallam, J.: Preference Learning for Cognitive Modeling: A Case Study on Entertainment Preferences. IEEE Systems, Man and Cybernetics; Part A: Systems and Humans 39(6), 1165–1175 (2009)
18. Yannakakis, G.N., Martínez, H.P., Jhala, A.: Towards Affective Camera Control in Games. User Modeling and User-Adapted Interaction 20(4), 313–340 (2010)

Towards a Generic Framework for Automatic Measurements of Web Usability Using Affective Computing Techniques

Payam Aghaei Pour and Rafael A. Calvo

School of Electrical and Information Engineering, University of Sydney, Australia
{payama,rafa}@ee.usyd.edu.au

Abstract. We propose a generic framework for the automatic usability evaluation of web sites by combining traditional automatic usability methods with affective computing techniques. To evaluate a framework a pilot study was carried out where users (n=4) reported their affective states using dimensional and categorical models. Binary task completion, time, mouse clicks, and error rates as an indicator of web usability were automatically captured for each page. Results suggested that frustration experienced when error rates and time for the task were higher. Delight on the other hand was at the other side of the spectrum. In the case that usability measurements had almost same values (e.g. confusing or engaging pages), affective states may be a way to show the difference.

Keywords: affective computing, web usability, framework.

1 Introduction

In the last decade the web has become the main environment for individuals and organizations to publish ideas and information to a potentially large audience online. Making these web sites easy to use without the requirement for users to undertake specialized training is a key to success. Thus, measuring the usability of the web site has aroused a growing interest among researchers and developers. However, due to the costly nature of the usability evaluation most of the organizations either ignore it or postpone it until the final product is ready. But according to usability studies [1] the evaluation of the web application usability during the development process is also very important.

There are many methods of usability evaluation. Most of them require an evaluator to observe the user behavior during the interaction with the system [2]. Observing users behavior is an efficient method to find usability issues but the costs of finding test subjects, preparing test laboratories, performing the test, and analyzing the data often make it prohibitive [3].

Aforementioned issues have motivated researchers to investigate the possibility of automating the process of usability testing. Automation can be done in any of the three common phases of the test: capture, analysis, or critique [4]. However, capturing all aspects of user behavioral and mental states (i.e. goal, emotion) which is very

S. D´Mello et al. (Eds.): ACII 2011, Part I, LNCS 6974, pp. 447–456, 2011.

important in usability evaluation is not an easy task when evaluators and users are separated in space and time. Thus, almost all of the studies in the automating usability evaluation have either ignored the user mental states or just recorded it using online questionnaires. One of a few studies that incorporated multimodal information (e.g. eye tracking, video) to capture user behavior is proposed in [5]. They have described a multimodal tool for remote usability evaluations of web sites that captures and analyze data regarding the user behavior coming from various sources. Still the study around user affective experience is very scarce. Affective computing, the study of systems that can detect, interpret and respond to human affects [6], has recently open a new window for many HCI studies to expand their studies to include some aspect of human affects in the various contexts.

In this paper, we propose a generic framework for evaluating web usability not only by measuring usability features, but also by detection of users' affective response. The framework incorporates user's affective response with other objective usability measurements (e.g. task time, input rate, and etc) in order to identify usability issues automatically. The ultimate goal of this study is to measure the affective component of users' satisfaction, mostly rated by filling long questionnaires, by affective computing techniques.

In a pilot study, a sample system based on the proposed framework was developed to evaluate the framework. The goal of the pilot study was to show that the framework is capable to find usability problems of a content delivering system. The analysis of the data is included in this paper.

2 Background

Many studies have shown that human cognitive processes tend to engage emotions [7]. Accordingly, researchers in the field of human-computer interaction (HCI) have recently been investigating the ways of modeling the affect of users in computer systems [8-12]. Affective computing as an interdisciplinary field that spans computer science, cognitive science, and psychology is the study of systems that can detect, interpret and respond to human affects [6].

Usability has been a central activity in the field of HCI for the last two decades. Usability has different interpretations but maybe the most common one presented in ISO 9241-11, standard related to definition of usability [13]. In this standard, usability is defined as "the effectiveness, efficiency, and satisfaction with which specified users can achieve goals in particular environments". Effectiveness is defined as the accuracy and completeness to achieve goals. Measures of effectiveness include, for example, binary task completion and error rates [14]. Efficiency is defined as resources used in achieving the task goals effectively. Efficiency measurements are usually task completion times and input rate [14]. Finally, subjective satisfaction is defined as the user's comfort and positive attitudes toward the use of the system. Satisfaction is typically measured using questionnaires asking users about their preference, ease-of-use and attitudes towards interface or contents [14].

Affective response of the users cannot be an exclusive determinant of satisfaction since satisfaction is a positive user's attitude toward the use of the system [13] and current psychological models of attitudes define attitude on the basis of three components, cognition, emotion, and behavior (e.g. [15]). This suggests that the user evaluation of satisfaction is determined by an evaluation of their affective response, the cognitive evaluation of the system based on their goals, and behavioral tendencies. Therefore, finding some correlations between subjective report of satisfaction and other usability measurements such as effectiveness and efficiency is not out of expectation [14, 16]. Furthermore, there are some studies suggesting that it would be more useful to measure and understand customer happiness and anger (emotional response) rather than satisfaction [17]. Despite these evidences of close relation between affects and usability, usability community has not taken into account the importance of affect in their studies. Therefore, it would be a great advantage to evaluate user affective responses (e.g. frustration and engagement) besides other usability measurements [18].

3 Measuring Usability

In a review by Hornbæk [14], published in the core HCI journals and proceedings, he reviewed 180 studies in usability and described practical methods for measuring usability. He organized his review around three aspects of usability measurements: effectiveness, efficiency, and satisfaction. 78% of these studies either reported some measurements of effectiveness or at least controlled it. Some researchers questioned the reliability of studies that ignore any measurements of effectiveness [19]. Among the studies that measured effectiveness, the two most assessed factors were binary task completion (13%) and error rates (26%). Binary task completion indicates the number of tasks where users failed to finish within a set time or the number of tasks where users gave up. Error rates quantify the number of errors users make either during the process of completing tasks or in the solution to the tasks.

A further 81% of the reviewed studies measured efficiency or controlled it. Among those that measured efficiency, 57% of them measured task completion time and 7% of them measured input rate as an indicator for resources needed to complete the task. Task completion time indicates the time users take to complete a task and input rate indicates rate of input users have to use to accomplish a task, for example mouse or keyboard.

Satisfaction measurements are the least measured factor in the studies reviewed by Hornbæk. Only 62% of the studies have some level of subjective satisfaction measurements. This can be due to the intrusive and time consuming nature of satisfaction evaluation, since users need to fill long questionnaires or participate in focus groups. Another issue with measuring satisfaction is that there are few standard questionnaires available and only 7% of the studies used standard questionnaires which makes comparison of studies very complicated. Attitude towards interface, asking users to specify their attitudes towards the interface, is the most common measured feature. Popular attitudes are: fun, liking, annoyance, control, learnability, anxiety, complexity, and engagement. These affective states (or similar ones) have been the focus of affective computing researchers [8, 20-22], who are trying to find automated detection techniques.

4 Proposed Framework

Our proposed framework for performing usability testing is based on automatically capturing of objective usability measurements and user's affects. Objective usability measurements can be extracted from usage log which can be captured in each of three layers: client side, proxy, or server side [3]. Each method has its own advantages and disadvantages. For example, client side recording provides the possibility of capturing more accurate and comprehensive usage data from both browser and web page; however special software is needed to be installed in the client computer which may cause loss of many potential users [3]. Server side logging on the other hand makes the interaction for end user simpler, but for capturing more accurate data web pages are needed to be changed. For web sites that contain other objects than plain HTML (e.g. flash, java applets), the server side logging has a benefit that enables recording of events from these objects. However, browser cache and shared IP address are two limitations of this design [3]. The third automatic capturing method is based on proxy model. This method has many fans due to clear separation of concerns. Any modifications required can be done on the proxy leaving client and server intact. In addition, any web site can be monitored without any substantial changes in the content. However, capturing data from plug-in components such as java applets and flash is hardly possible [3]. Also, monitoring secure connections (e.g. Secure Sockets Layer (SSL)) is not feasible in the proxy model.

We proposed our framework based on proxy model similar to the method proposed in [23]. However, other models can also be used without major changes to the framework. The framework is composed of 4 main components (i.e. Task Definition, Web Proxy, Affect Detection, and Data Analyzer) as shown in Fig. 1.

- Component 1 – Task Definition

The first step in the framework is to define the tasks that are needed to be monitored for usability testing. A task is defined as a sequence of actions performed by users to accomplish a specific goal. This task model is provided by system developers or designers who are aware of the purpose of the system. For example a task for an online shopping web site can be defined as buying a product. This task has expected scenario like: search or browse product, check out, enter shipping address, pay for product, and finalize. The expected time for each task is also given for future analysis. This model can be used in the process of task detection from actual user behavior in the log files.

- Component 2 – Users Interaction Capture (Web Proxy)

This component is responsible to capture user interaction with the web site by sitting between client and server side. The possible captured data could be: mouse movements, mouse clicks, spent time on each page, page loaded, keystrokes, etc. Afterwards, the captured data are sent to data analyzer component for further analysis.

- Component 3 – Affect Detection

Users affect can be detected from multiple modalities. Video can be captured by user's webcam and streamed to the system. Other modalities such as physiological signals also can be acquired by special devices and be sent over network connections. Affect detection component is responsible to collect various signals coming from multiple sources and make a decision on what affect user might have had during interaction with each page. The result can either be in dimensional (valence/arousal) or categorical (e.g. confusion, delight, frustration) model. In the next step, detected affective state is sent to data analyzer component for further analysis.

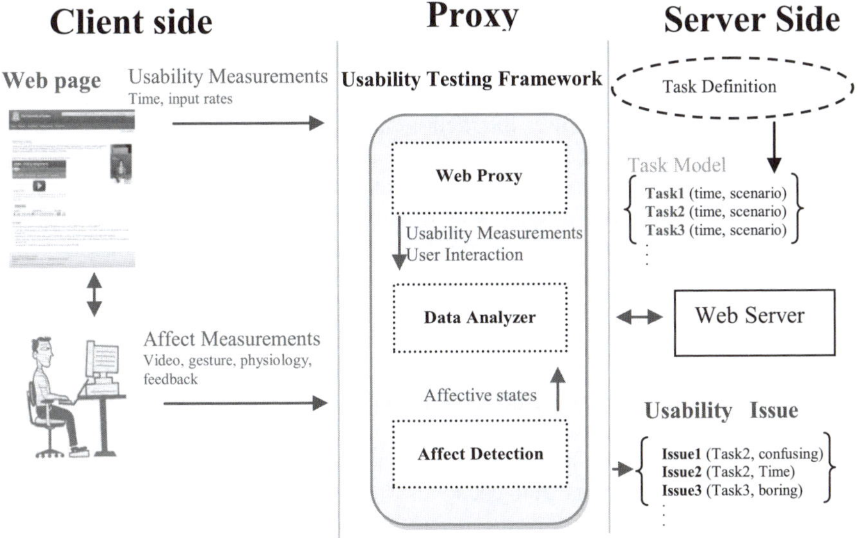

Fig. 1. The generic framework for automatic measurements of web usability

- Component 4 – Data Analyzer

This component is the core of the framework. Here all data captured in the components 2 and 3 are analyzed and the possible usability issues are reported to the server. First, performed tasks are extracted by comparing user inactions and the task model. Then, usability measurements and affective responses of each page are computed. These data are used to identify three measurements of usability testing: effectiveness, efficiency, and satisfaction regarding each page. Usability problems will be generated by automatic analysis of these data.

5 Method and Data

In order to validate our framework, a pilot evaluation was carried out. In this experiment, we collected usability and affective data from 4 subjects, all postgraduate students from The University of Sydney, while they were interacting with an online tutorial in iWrite system [24]. The experiment typically took 45 minutes for each subject. The online tutorials in iWrite system include activities and explanations of good writing strategies in the types of genres that engineering students normally engage with them. To remove the effect of user behavior in this experiment, subjects were instructed to follow the exact given path. Since user's behavior is controlled, affective response can also reflect user's satisfaction level. Therefore, in the rest of the paper we can consider affective responses as an indication of low or high satisfaction. In this pilot study we also considered self-report as an affective judgment, instead of automatic affect recognition. Moreover instead of the proxy model proposed in the framework, a server side capturing model was selected since the exercise pages were written in Flash. This change will not affect the framework evaluation because the usage data that were captured at server can also be recorded in the proxy. The only limitation was that proxy could not capture flash events so we decided to change web pages and flash codes to make the logging of both page and flash components possible.

Binary task completion and time as an indicator of effectiveness were recorded for each page. Also, mouse clicks and error rates as an indicator of efficiency were captured and calculated from user interaction data. For affect evaluation, immediately after each page users should rate their emotional experience in both two dimensional model of valence/arousal and categorical model by choosing one affective state from the category of six provided affects. The affective states were: frustration, confusion, engagement, delight, boredom, and neutral. Frustration was defined as dissatisfaction or annoyance. Confusion was defined as a noticeable lack of understanding, whereas engagement was a state of interest that results from involvement in an activity. Delight was a high degree of satisfaction. Boredom was defined as being weary or restless through lack of interest. Neutral was defined as no apparent emotion or feeling. These affective states are believed to occur during cognitive tasks [8, 10]. Fig. 2 presents the annotation page shown to the users. For annotation of valence and arousal Emocard [25], a sixteen cartoon-like faces, half male and half female, each representing distinct emotions were used.

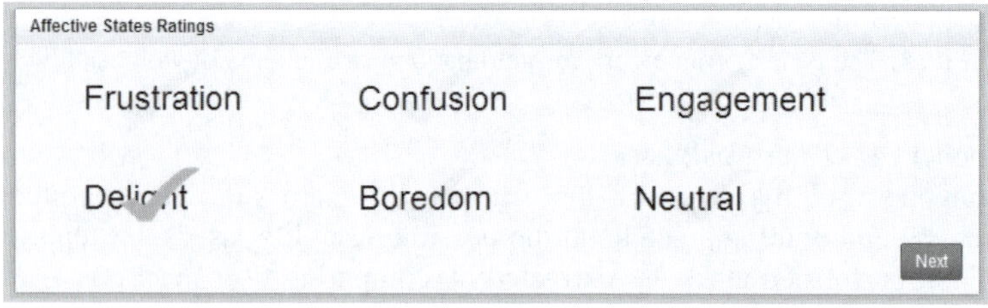

Fig. 2. Six affective states user can select as categorical affective model

The online tutorial used in this experiment was on the topic of how to write a *paragraph* including 3 sub categories named *the topic, the body,* and *the conclusion.* Users had to read a total of 41 pages including the exercises and examples and report their affective experience at the end of each page. Fig. 3 reflects the proportional values and 95% confidence interval for the affective states reported by all users. As depicted in the Fig. 3, engagement was the majority of reported affective state. This suggests the method we used for annotation may not affect the flow of the actual task.

6 Primary Results and Discussion

As discussed earlier, users annotated their emotions on both dimensional and categorical models. To find the empirical mapping of affective states with two dimensional model of valence/arousal, we rescaled the dimensional model from -1 to 1 for both valence and arousal axis. Then for each affective state, the average for all values of valence and arousal were computed. Fig. 4 shows the mapping of these two models in our experiment. As it was expected, delight and engagement fallen in the positive valence and relatively average arousal while frustration and confusion mapped in the negative side with relatively higher arousal. Boredom fallen into the low arousal side which is in par with our expectation.

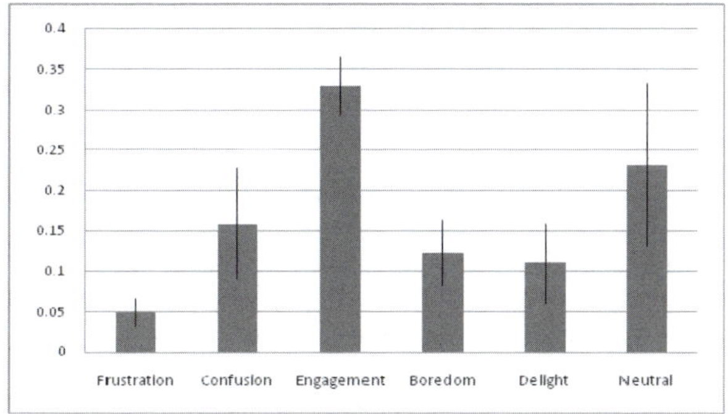

Fig. 3. Proportional values with 95% confidence interval for affective states reported by all users

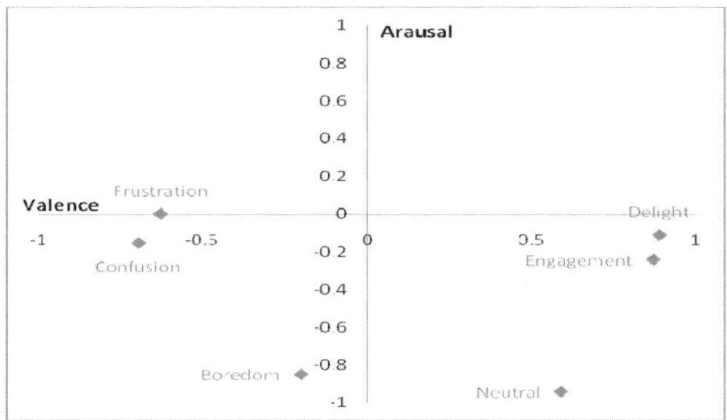

Fig. 4. Mapping of 6 affective states used in this experiment with the dimensional model of emotions in the scale of -1 to 1. (e.g. [-1,-1] indicates calm-unpleasant and [1, 1] indicates excited-pleasant). Affective states were: frustration, confusion, boredom, neutral, engagement, and delight.

To investigate the relationship between user affective states and web site effectiveness, we calculated the error rates as an indicator of effectiveness measurement. The results were compared with affective states users given for each page. Table 1 shows the average of errors users made where specific affective state reported. Errors include both interface error (i.e. number of mouse clicks that are not related to accomplish the task), and exercise error (i.e. number of error users made to find the right answer to the questions). The exercise error can be caused by poor interactive user interface or poor content. It is not easy to separate usability of content from user interface, thus we combined the errors from both interface errors and exercise error together in column 2 of Table 1.

Table 1. Affective states and average number of errors users made during interaction with the system. Average errors were computed by averaging number of errors made by users on entire pages where a specific affect was reported.

Affect	Error (interface + exercise)	Average Interface Error	Average Exercise Error
Frustration	5.5	1.75	3.75
Confusion	1.65	0.96	0.69
Engagement	1.04	0.39	0.65
Neutral	0.71	0.56	0.15
Boredom	0.55	0.45	0.1
Delight	0.39	0.28	0.11

As many studies in usability suggest that users satisfaction has some relation with other objective usability measurements [14], our data also confirm this relation. For example, frustration was reported when the users made the highest number of errors and delight was reported when user interface and exercises were straight forward so fewer errors have occurred. Interestingly, when users were engaged with system also made few errors which are mostly exercise error. This could be because they were trying to solve the exercises and errors were related to their misunderstanding of concept instead of poor interactive user interface or poor available content. Our data suggest that only depending on the number of errors as an indicator for usability issues can be sometimes misleading. For example: the error rates for affective state of engagement are higher than boredom but obviously we cannot consider exercises that make users feel more engaged as potential usability issue.

In the next step, we computed the task time as an indicator of the web page efficiency. Less time users spent on a particular task can suggest that either the design of the user interface were straightforward or the task was so simple to perform. The third dimension, user's affective states, can explain the difference of these two situations. As Table 2 shows, frustration and confusion have the highest spent time on the tasks while neutral and delight have the lowest. This complies with our expectation and also with usability studies that compared subjective satisfaction with other usability measurements [14].

Table 2. Affective states and average task time users spent during interaction with the system. Average time was computed by averaging spent time on entire pages where a specific affect was reported.

Affect	Average Task Time (sec)
Frustration	75
Confusion	46
Engagement	42
Boredom	38
Delight	31
Neutral	28

Interestingly, engagement has also relatively high average of task time. So only depending on task-time as a measurement of usability cannot distinguish the situations between confusing task and engaging one. However, by providing the information on affective response of the users this situation can be identified. System designers may want to provide more help for the tasks that made users confused or change UI and work flow of these tasks.

7 Conclusion and Future Work

In this study, a framework for automatic detection of web usability problems was proposed. To evaluate our framework, a pilot experiment carried out. In the experiment we used server side logging techniques. Binary task completion, time, mouse clicks, and error rates were captured and calculated from log files. In addition, users rated their affects after interaction with each page in both dimensional and categorical model. Analysis of the data showed a degree of relation between affective states and average number of errors made by users. For confusion and engagement that the average error was almost the same, affective response can be a better indication of user satisfaction level. Also, we find the same relation between affects and spent time on the task. While confusion and engagement had almost same spending time, engaging tasks will not consider as usability issue.

For future we are planning to include physiological signals such as heart rate, skin conductivity, and respiratory rhythm for automatic detection of affective states. The other possible modality for affect detection is face and posture analysis of the users, as many studies have already reported promising results in affect detection using these modalities. In our research lab we are currently developing a system for identification of user's attention, which can potentially be used as an input for our framework.

References

1. Cato, J.: User-centered web design. Pearson Education, London (2001)
2. Nielsen, J.: Usability engineering. Morgan Kaufmann, San Francisco (1993)
3. Paternò, F., Santoro, C.: Remote Usability Evaluation: Discussion of a General Framework and Experiences from Research with a Specific Tool. Maturing Usability, 197–221 (2008)
4. Ivory, M.Y., Hearst, M.A.: The state of the art in automating usability evaluation of user interfaces. ACM Computing Surveys (CSUR) 33, 470–516 (2001)
5. Paternò, F., Piruzza, A., Santoro, C.: Remote Web usability evaluation exploiting multimodal information on user behavior. In: Computer-Aided Design of User Interfaces V, pp. 287–298 (2007)
6. Picard, R.: Affective computing. The MIT Press, Cambridge (1997)
7. Dolan, R.J.: Emotion, cognition, and behavior. Science 298, 1191 (2002)
8. Aghaei Pour, P., Hussain, M., AlZoubi, O., D'Mello, S., Calvo, R.: The Impact of System Feedback on Learners Affective and Physiological States, pp. 264–273. Springer, Heidelberg (2010)

9. Klein, J., Moon, Y., Picard, R.: This computer responds to user frustration: Theory, design, and results. Interacting with Computers 14, 119–140 (2002)
10. D'Mello, S., Craig, S., Gholson, B., Franklin, S., Picard, R., Graesser, A.: Integrating affect sensors in an intelligent tutoring system, pp. 7–13 (2005)
11. Bianchi-Berthouze, N., Lisetti, C.L.: Modeling multimodal expression of user's affective subjective experience. User Modeling and User-Adapted Interaction 12, 49–84 (2002)
12. Calvo, R.A., D'Mello, S.: Affect detection: An interdisciplinary review of models, methods, and their applications. IEEE Transactions on Affective Computing, 18–37 (2010)
13. Iso, I.: 9241-11. Ergonomic requirements for office work with visual display terminals (VDT's). Part 11 (1997)
14. Hornbæk, K.: Current practice in measuring usability: Challenges to usability studies and research. International Journal of Human-Computer Studies 64, 79–102 (2006)
15. Petty, R.E., Fabrigar, L.R., Wegener, D.T.: Emotional factors in attitudes and persuasion (2003)
16. Sauro, J., Kindlund, E.: A method to standardize usability metrics into a single score, pp. 401–409. ACM, New York (2005)
17. Edwardson, M.: Measuring consumer emotions in service encounters: an exploratory analysis. Australasian Journal of Market Research 6, 34–48 (1998)
18. Partala, T., Kangaskorte, R.: The Combined Walkthrough: Measuring Behavioral, Affective, and Cognitive Information in Usability Testing. Journal of Usability Studies 5, 21–33 (2009)
19. Frøkjær, E., Hertzum, M., Hornbæk, K.: Measuring usability: are effectiveness, efficiency, and satisfaction really correlated?, pp. 345–352. ACM, New York (2000)
20. D'Mello, S., Graesser, A., Picard, R.: Toward an affect-sensitive AutoTutor. IEEE Intelligent Systems 22, 53–61 (2007)
21. Arroyo, I., Cooper, D., Burleson, W., Woolf, B., Muldner, K., Christopherson, R.: Emotion Sensors go to School (2009)
22. Calvo, R.A., D'Mello, S.K.: Affect Detection: An Interdisciplinary Review of Models, Methods, and their Applications. IEEE Transactions on Affective Computing 1, 18–37 (2010)
23. Vargas, A., Weffers, H., da Rocha, H.V.: A method for remote and semi-automatic usability evaluation of web-based applications through users behavior analysis, p. 19. ACM, New York (2010)
24. Calvo, R.A., O'Rourke, S.T., Jones, J., Yacef, K., Reimann, P.: Collaborative Writing Support Tools on the Cloud. IEEE Transactions on Learning Technologies 4, 88–97 (2011)
25. Desmet, P.: Emotion through expression; designing mobile telephones with an emotional fit. Report of Modeling the Evaluation Structure of KANSEI 3, 103–110 (2000)

Simulating Affective Behaviours : An Approach Based on the COR Theory

Sabrina Campano, Etienne de Sevin, Vincent Corruble, and Nicolas Sabouret

Université Pierre et Marie Curie, Laboratoire d'Informatique de Paris 6
4, place Jussieu, 75005 Paris, France
{sabrina.campano,etienne.de-sevin,vincent.corruble,
nicolas.sabouret}@lip6.fr

Abstract. The expression of emotion is usually considered an important step towards the believability of a virtual agent. However, current models based on emotion categories face important challenges in their attempts to model the influence of emotions on agents' behaviour. To adress this problem, we propose an architecture based on the COnservation of Resources theory (COR) which aims at producing affective behaviours in various scenarios. In this paper we explain the principle of such a model, how it is implemented and can be evaluated.

Keywords: affect, emotion, virtual agent, simulation, behaviour.

1 Introduction

In this article we are interested in how virtual agents can display behaviours in a simulation. More precisely, our context is the use of virtual agents in credible situations, which requires to model behaviours close to those of human beings. For example, virtual characters in a video game must behave in a credible manner in order to support player's immersion. According to [1], emotions are important to enhance virtual agents' believability. This is why we focus this paper on the definition of an architecture handling *affective behaviours.*

Many situations are associated with emotions. Escape from a danger is often qualified with emotional terms, but they could also apply to other situations like waiting in line. If someone jumps a queue, a typical response to this sign of disrespect is "an emotion of *moralistic anger* directed against the wrongdoer" [17]. But those in the line may not react to this intrusion in order to avoid an "*embarassing confrontation*" [12]. Emotions are also related to behaviours that are not depicted specifically as emotional. [18] showed that human observers can perceive emotions in simple robot's behaviours like avoiding obstacles, collecting ore, and collecting energy. More generally, an affective behaviour can be defined as a behaviour descriptible with emotional terms. The WordNet-Affect thesaurus [21] contains a set of vocabulary linked to emotions. In this paper, we consider that an affective behaviour is a behaviour that can be described with terms included in the WordNet-Affect thesaurus.

S. D´Mello et al. (Eds.): ACII 2011, Part I, LNCS 6974, pp. 457–466, 2011.

Several architectures have been proposed to take into account the influence of emotions on behaviour [2] [7], however, they show limitations for our purpose. For example, it is necessary to associate a set of behaviours with an emotion category, and this parsing is difficult to achieve. Another approach could be used : selecting those behaviours without using emotion categories, but in a way that is coherent enough so that agents exhibit affective behaviours as defined above. To do so, we propose an architecture for the selection of affective behaviours without using emotion categories. We hypothesize that a human observer will describe with emotional terms agents' behaviours produced by our architecture, even though it does not manipulate emotions.

After describing some related work, we present in this paper the core architecture of our model. The description of resources and how they fulfill an agent's needs is explained, along with the selection process for resource-oriented behaviours. We also list evaluation procedures intended to be used on future results. Finally, we discuss the proposed model.

2 Related Work

In affective computing community, we often use emotion categories as an artefact for programming affective behaviours. But this approach can be challenged : actually, emotions might not be *natural kinds* [11], and there seems to be no consensus on the number of existing emotions, neither on their role or consequences on cognition and behaviour [6,19]. Nevertheless, several theories propose a list of emotion categories based on different criteria [8,9,5].

[8] identifies two types of *core affect* dimensions which are valence, i.e. how good or bad a feeling is, and arousal, and points out that any additional differenciation is based on contextual differences made upon various non-emotional processes. In a study on culture and categorization of emotions [10], the author lists emotion words for which there is no equivalence from a language to another, revealing that emotion categories are culture specific, and that even the categories of *fear* and *anger* are not universal. [9] distinguishes among six basic emotions, grounded on the hypothesis of universal facial expressions, and on distinctive patterns of physiological changes during emotional episodes. But if autonomic specificity seems to have solid support [4], these studies do not prove the existence of emotions, but the existence of a correlation between an autonomic response and an emotional interpretation of this response by the subject. These approaches were discussed in [20]. The OCC model [5], popular within computational science, accounts for 22 emotions. It is able to determine which emotion category could be associated to an agent based on classification criteria. However it is not intended to select behaviours, because "the same behavior can result from very different emotions" and "very different behaviors can result from the same emotion". Besides, behaviours might be a part of one's emotional experience [14], more precisely they might be a part of the criteria used to infer emotion categories. According to [11], if no set of clearly defined emotional patterns has been found, it is because emotions are concepts instead of being

distinct entities of our affective system. Human beings experience emotions in the same manner as they experience colors, they use their knowledge to label their perceptions with categories.

The classification of emotion is a difficult task that may rely upon different criteria. Emotion categories seem complicated to use for the simulation of affective behaviours, because emotion theories are dedicated more to appraisals rather than on the link between emotion and behaviour. This drives us to look for an other approach than emotion categories. The question is : what components an affective architecture generating behaviours labelled as "emotional" must have ? Our hypothesis is that the theory of conservation of resources by psychologist S.E. Hobfoll [13] offers an interesting lead. In this theory, the drive for the acquisition and protection of resources is at the core of the dynamics which explains the stress or well-being of an individual, and is even able to predict it. The concept of resource refers to many types of elements : social ones such as self esteem or caring for others, material ones such as a car, or physiological ones such as energy. The main principle is that individuals strive to protect their resources, and to acquire new ones, and this can be easily linked to behaviours. In our opinion, this model is adaptable to many simulation scenarios to display affective behaviours, while overcoming some difficulties encountered in models based on emotion categories to generate behaviours. For example, instead of being associated with emotion categories, behaviours can be associated to resource types : in order to acquire a ticket for a musical event an agent has to buy it, in order to acquire a social interaction, it has to talk to an other agent.

As the model of conservation of resources seems suitable for the production of affective behaviours, we propose a model based on this theory.

3 Proposed Model

3.1 Principle of the Model

In this model, each agent's behaviour is intended to acquire or protect a resource. An agent's well-being depends on its needs for resources, whose type can be material, social, or intellectual, i.e., respectively, cars, verbal interactions, or books. Resources in the environment allow to compensate an agent's needs. A decrease in a need is considered as a reward, and an increase is considered as a cost. Hence agents seek to acquire resources to decrease their needs, and to avoid resource losses that would increase their needs. The need level for a resource type is dynamic, and changes either automatically, either as an effect of environment events. For example the need for food increases over time until the agent acquires food, whereas the need for a cell phone decreases if an agent receives a cell phone as a gift from an another agent. The output of the architecture is the display of the behaviour executed by an agent, that might be interpreted as "emotional" by a human observer (see figure 1). A running example involving agents queuing in a waiting line will be used along the paper in order to explain model details.

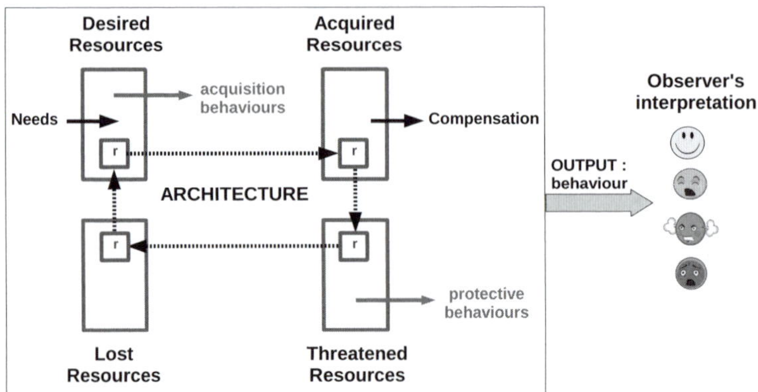

Fig. 1. General Architecture : state of resources activate behaviours. The display of the selected behaviour might be interpreted as "emotional" by an observer.

3.2 Definitions

Resources: let R be the set of resource instances of the simulation environment. Each resource $r \in R$ has a given type denoted as $type(r)$. This type allows to define which set of behaviours are associated to this resource. For example all resources of "Position" type in a waiting line can be acquired with the behaviour "Move to position". Each resource in the simulation environment is a type instance, including agents. Behaviours are executable only on instances. A type also determine which instances in the environment can fulfill an agent's needs. For example if an agent has a need for a "Ticket Counter" type of resource, then all instances in the environment with the type "Ticket Counter" will be desired resources for this agent.

Needs and Compensations: each agent has a set of *needs* $N_i(t)$, which contains needs for resource types. "Train Ticket" or "Position in Waiting Line" are examples of need types. Let i be an agent, $\forall type \in N_i(t)$, $\mu_i^{type}(t) \in [0, 1]$ is the need value of i for a resource type at time t. When an agent losses or acquires a resource, its need for the type of this resource is updated with the *compensation* value of the resource. $\forall r \in R$, $C_i^r \in [0, 1]$ is the compensation value of r over $\mu_i^{type(r)}(t)$. For example, in order to model an agent that queues in front of a ticket office, in our approach we will set a need for the resource type "Position" in the waiting line. Each instance of this type in the waiting line will have a compensation over agent's need for "Position", with the compensation of the first position instance higher than the compensation of the last position instance of the waiting line. An agent will chose to acquire the best position according to its own needs and other agents' needs, influenced by its individual parameters (see section 4.2). When an agent moves forward in the queue, the agent which is behind knows that a position is available in front of him. He can move on the new position, that entails the following consequences : (i) he will lose its current position and the compensation associated to this position, (ii) he will gain a new position and the compensation associated to this position. The agent takes the new position only if it offers a higher compensation than the previous position. Hence, an agent may jump the queue in order to obtain a greater compensation.

Behaviours: an agent can trigger behaviours for resource acquisition or for resource protection. Let $B_i(t)$ the set of behaviours that can be performed by an agent i at time t. A behaviour $b \in B_i(t)$ has effects over resources during and after its realization for a given set of agents denoted as $patients(b)$. An effect is a change in the state of a resource for an agent. When an agent i begins the execution of an acquisition behaviour towards a resource, if another agent j has this resource as *acquired*, then it becomes *threatened* for j. For example, if an agent i wants to execute the behaviour "Move to Position" to acquire the position p of an agent j in a waiting line, the consequences of this behaviour is that p will be moved to the *threatened* state for j. If i achieves the execution of its behaviour, then p is *lost* for j and *acquired* for i. $\forall b \in B_i(t)$, $\forall j \in patients(b)$, we denote the following effects :

- $R_b^+(j)$: resource instances that behaviour b makes *acquired* for j ;
- $R_b^\sim(j)$: resource instances that behaviour b makes *threatened* for j;
- $R_b^o(j)$: resource instances that behaviour b makes *protected* for j;
- $R_b^-(j)$: resource instances that behaviour b makes *lost* by j;

3.3 Architecture

An agent's affective architecture is composed of affective sets. The presence of a resource in one of these sets, i.e. the resource state, is a key factor influencing agent's behaviour. A *desired* resource activates acquisition behaviours, while a *threatened* resource activates protective behaviours.

Let A the set of agents and R the set of resources in a simulation, with $A \subset R$. $\forall i \in A$, we denote the following affective sets :

- $DR_i(t)$, the resource instances desired by i at time t;
- $AR_i(t)$, the acquired resource instances of i at time t;
- $TR_i(t)$, the threatened resource instances of i at time t;
- $LR_i(t)$, the resource instances at time t that i has lost .

During the simulation, addition and removal of resources in affective sets, as well as behaviour selection, are handled by the Affective Controller. This module takes into account resources perceived in agent's environment, behaviours executed by other agents, events (for example a fire), and agent's needs level. Each behaviour selected by this module has the purpose to acquire or protect a resource. To perform behaviour selection, an utility value is associated to each behaviour $b \in B_i(t)$, taking into account the behaviour's effects described above (see section 4.3). This value is computed with the predicted agent's need level corresponding to the moment when the behaviour will be realized : a decrease of a need level is considered as a reward, and an increase is considered as a cost.

For example the loss of a resource like a position in a waiting line is a cost for an agent that needs a "Position" type resource, since it causes an increase in agent's need level. This means that the agent will not choose to execute a behaviour which has the only effect to make agent's position lost. By constrast, if this behaviour has the effect to make acquired a position which is better that current agent's position, the agent will select it, because the reward obtained by the new position is greater than the cost entailed by the loss of its current position.

4 Needs and Behaviour Selection

4.1 Computation of Behaviour's Payoff

The execution of a behaviour may change the state of a resource for an agent. A resource can be desired, acquired, threatened, or lost (see section 3.2). If a resource instance that can decrease an agent's need type is acquired or protected for this agent towards a behaviour b, it entails a reward that is a positive value. On the contrary, if such a resource is threatened or lost for this agent, it entails a cost that is a negative value. These values computed before the possible execution of a behaviour b represent the impact of this behaviour on an agent's need level. The predicted payoff at time $t+1$ of a behaviour b for an agent j allows us to proceed behaviour selection (explained in section 4.3). It is computed as :

$$\begin{aligned} P(b,j,t+1) = & \sum_{r \in R_b^+(j) \cup R_b^o(j)} (1+\mu_j^{type(r)}(t)) * C_j^r \\ & - \sum_{r \in R_b^-(j) \cup R_b^\sim(j)} (1+\mu_j^{type(r)}(t)) * C_j^r \end{aligned} \quad (1)$$

4.2 Individual Parameters Influencing Behaviours' Payoff

Some parameters influence rewards and costs perceived by an agent. *Optimism / Pessimism* and *Altruism / Egoism* have been introduced to provide agents with a personality. These parameters are applied before the behaviour selection process and give the payoffs from an agent's point of view.

Optimism and Pessimism. An optimistic agent gives more importance to rewards, and a pessimistic agent gives more importance to costs. This approach is similar to the decision rule of Wald [22], where "decisions are [...] ranked according to the merit of their worst arguments, following a pessimistic attitude. This approach captures the handling of negative affects. Purely positive decisions are sometimes separately handled in a symmetric way, namely on the basis of their best arguments" [3]. Let i be an agent, and $\alpha_i^{rew} \in [0,1]$ a variable representing the importance of rewards. If $\alpha_i^{rew} > 0.5$, i gives more importance to rewards, and the more α_i^{rew} is high, the more rewards are important. If $\alpha_i^{rew} < 0.5$, i gives more importance to costs, and the more α_i^{rew} is low, the more costs are important. The predicted payoff $P_i(b,j,t+1)$ of an agent j from i point of view for behaviour b executable at time $t+1$ taking into account optimism and pessimism is given by equation 2.

$$\forall j \in patients(b), P_i(b,j,t+1) = \begin{cases} P(b,j,t+1) * \alpha_i^{rew}, & \text{if } P(b,j,t+1) > 0 \\ P(b,j,t+1) * (1-\alpha_i^{rew}), & \text{if } P(b,j,t+1) < 0 \end{cases} \quad (2)$$

Egoism and Altruism. Egoistic agents give more importance to their own payoff, and altruistic agents give more importance to other agents' payoff. Let $\alpha_i^{alt} \in [0,1]$ be the altruistic tendency of an agent, and $\alpha_i^{ego} \in [0,1]$ be the egoistic tendency of an agent. For a given behaviour $b \in B_i(t)$ executable by an agent i at time t, the behaviour's payoff foreach patient j of the behaviour, as i considers it, is modified as below :

$$\forall j \in patients(b), P_i(b,j,t+1) = \begin{cases} P(b,j,t+1) * \alpha_i^{alt}, & \text{if } j \neq i \\ P(b,j,t+1) * \alpha_i^{ego}, & \text{else} \end{cases} \quad (3)$$

4.3 Behaviour Selection and Need Value Update

The behaviour selection consists in selecting a behaviour with the maximum positive utility among all activated behaviours of an agent i. Activated behaviours are behaviours that i can realize accordingly to the current state of resources in its architecture (see section 3.3). Given $B_i(t)$ the set of activated behaviours for agent i at time t, $\forall b \in B_i(t)$, $\forall j \in patients(b)$, a payoff $P_i(b,j,t+1)$ has been previously computed, representing the payoff that j will receive from behaviour b at $t+1$ according to i's point of view. Then behaviours' utility for agent i at time t are computed as :

$$\forall b \in B_i(t), U_i(b,t) = \sum_{j \in patients(b)} P_i(b,j,t+1) \quad (4)$$

The selected behaviour $b_i^*(t)$ is :

$$b_i^*(t) = \max_{b \in B_i(t)} \{b : U_i(b,t) > 0\} \quad (5)$$

If no behaviour with a positive utility value exists, then no behaviour is executed. Since our model does not include planification, we assume that it is better for an agent to do nothing than to execute a behaviour which is costly, even if this behaviour could prevent in the future behaviours executed by other agents with worse consequences. If there are more than one behaviour with a maximum positive utility, a behaviour is randomly chosen among them.

Once a behaviour b is executed, agent i's state of resources and need values are updated with behaviour effects. Need values update for acquired resources and lost resources are given respectively by equations 6 and 7.

$$\forall r \in R_b^+(i), \mu_i^{type(r)}(t) = (\mu_i^{type(r)}(t-1) - C_i^r)_{[0,1]} \quad (6)$$

$$\forall r \in R_b^-(i), \mu_i^{type(r)}(t) = (\mu_i^{type(r)}(t-1) + C_i^r)_{[0,1]} \quad (7)$$

with $(x)_{[0,1]}$ meaning that x is bounded between 0 and 1.

5 Directions for Evaluation Procedures

The model has been implemented (see figure 2) and we are now working on the waiting-line scenario to evaluate our approach. Our evaluation procedure is twofold. First, we want to validate our simulation with respect to well-established results from studies in social sciences. Second, we plan on conducting a subjective evaluation, based on the description of affective behaviours by observers.

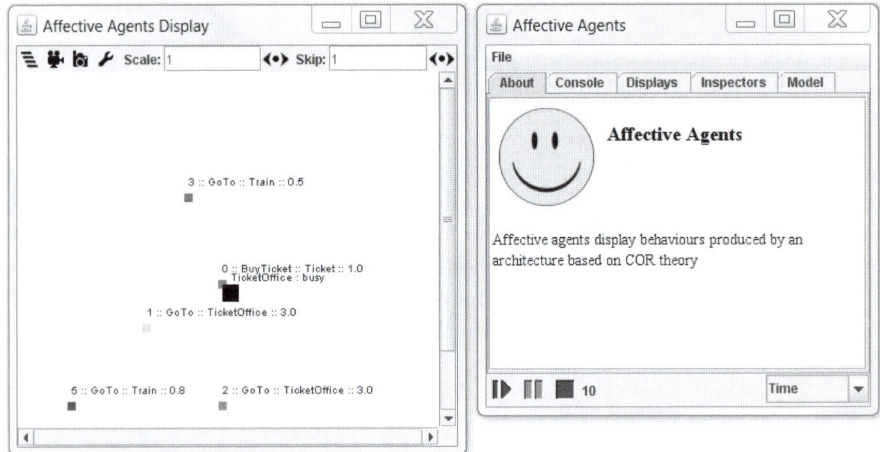

Fig. 2. Example of a 2D simulation of our model with MASON simulator [15] - Agents execute behaviours towards resources with an utility value

The study by [16] shows that in the context of a waiting line, 62% of people react when someone jumps the queue just in front of them, and that people are more likely to react against an intruder if they are in the next 3 positions from the intrusion point. Our simulator's outputs lets us determine which behaviour is selected in each situation. Thus, we are be able to compare numerically our results with social science studies. For example, we aim at obtaining 62% of agents reacting, whereas our code does not contain statistical data.

Our concern is focused on the model's credibility, which can be validated through a subjective evaluation. Our protocol is based on Pfeifer's approach [18]: human users comment on simulations produced by our model and we hope that they describe affective behaviours. To this purpose, we generate N simulations with 20 agents, for which at least 2 are over-constrained (i.e. agents' need for the first position cannot be satisfied at the start of the simulation). Then we prepare two groups of videos, the first containing our simulations, and the second containing videos with behaviours produced by other approaches. These videos should exhibit : 1) agents trying to jump the queue and 2) agents reacting to intrusions. One video from each group will be showed to $6N$ users. First they will be asked to comment freely on them and, in a second time, they will be asked to describe affective behaviours. We will consider the percentage of terms from WordNet-Affect in both situations and we hope that the comparison will show more affective behaviours in the first group. Moreover, we will study the affective terms used to describe behaviours, and we hypothesize that affective behaviours will appear from the observer's point of view for the videos of the first group, but not for the videos of the second group. Last, we will ask people to evaluate the credibility of both simulation of a Likert's scale.

6 Discussion and Future Work

In this paper, we proposed a model aimed at providing virtual agents with affective behaviours. Our hypothesis is that simulating behaviours that can be labelled as "emotional" does not require an architecture grounded on emotion categories. This avoids the definition of a numerical influence of emotions on behaviours, which is a key issue for emotion models handling behaviours. Our architecture relies on the processes of resource acquisition and protection proposed by [13] as the basis for the generation of affective behaviours, with a resource being either a material object (car), a piece of knowledge, an agent, or a psychological element (social image). We think that our architecture is adaptable to many simulation scenarios such as riots, panic escape, social interactions, etc. Our model does not rely on planning like a BDI architecture, since it is a reactive model for the acquisition and protection of resources. We are currently finishing the waiting-line example implementation and we aim at conducting an evaluation in the short term.

However, the model presented here is one module in a complete architecture that should contain other ones. In particular, emotions are essential concepts for communication among agents and reasoning about other's attitudes. There are cultural patterns of facial expressions [4], and the emotion vocabulary is a large part of human langage. This is the reason why our final perspective is to draw a model that combines the model of conservation of resources, aimed at generating behaviours, with models handling emotion categorization, aimed at interpreting the context. This will allow the communication of emotional concepts between our virtual agents. In a longer term, we aim at implementing other examples so as to prove the scalability of our model.

References

1. Bates, J.: The role of emotion in believable agents. Communications of the ACM 37, 122–125 (1994)
2. Burghouts, G.J., Heylen, D., Poel, M., op den Akker, R., Nijholt, A.: An action selection architecture for an emotional agent. Recent Advances in Artificial Intelligence, Proceedings of FLAIRS 16, 293–297 (2003)
3. Dubois, D., Fargier, H.: Qualitative decision making with bipolar information. In: KR, vol. 6, pp. 175–186 (2006)
4. Levenson, R.W.: Autonomic specificity and emotion. In: Davidson, R.J., Scherer, K.R., Goldsmith, H.H. (eds.) Handbook of Affective Sciences, pp. 212–224. Oxford University Press, New York (2003)
5. Ortony, A., Clore, G.L., Collins, A.: The cognitive structure of emotions. Cambridge University Press, New York (1988)
6. Ortony, A., Turner, T.J.: What's basic about basic emotions? Psychological Review 97, 315–331 (1990)
7. Elliott, C.: The affective reasoner: A process model of emotions in a multi-agent system. Northwestern University Institute for the Learning Sciences, Chicago (1992)
8. Russell, J.A.: Core affect and the psychological construction of emotion. Psychol. Rev. 110(1), 145–172 (2003)
9. Ekman, P.: Basic Emotions. In: Dalgleish, T., Power, T. (eds.) The Handbook of Cognition and Emotion, pp. 45–60. John Wiley & Sons, Ltd., Sussex (1999)
10. Russell, J.A.: Culture and the categorization of emotions. Psychological bulletin 110(3), 426–450 (1991)
11. Barrett, L.F.: Solving the emotion paradox: Categorization and the experience of emotion. Personality and Social Psychology Review 10, 20–46 (2006)
12. Gray, K.: The legal order of the queue, University of Cambridge (2007) (unpublished paper)
13. Hobfoll, S.E.: Conservation of resources: A new attempt at conceptualizing stress. American Psychologist 44(3), 513–524 (1989)
14. James, W.: What is emotion? Mind 9(34), 188–205 (1884)
15. Luke, S., Cioffi-Revilla, C., Panait, L., Sullivan, K., Balan, G.: MASON: A multiagent simulation environment. Simulation 81(7), 517 (2005)
16. Milgram, S., Liberty, H.J., Toledo, R., Wackenhut, J.: Response to intrusion into waiting lines. Journal of Personality and Social Psychology 51(4), 683–689 (1986)
17. Miller, D.T.: Disrespect and the experience of injustice. Annual Review of Psychology 52(1), 527–553 (2001)
18. Pfeifer, R.: The "Fungus Eater" Approach to Emotion: A View from Artificial Intelligence. Cognitive Studies (1), 42–57 (1994)
19. Scherer, K.R.: Appraisal theory. In: Dalgleish, T., Power, M. (eds.) Handbook of Cognition and Emotion, pp. 637–663. Wiley, Chichester (1999)
20. Scherer, K.R.: Emotions as episodes of subsystem synchronization driven by nonlinear appraisal processes. In: Emotion, development, and self-organization: Dynamic systems approaches to emotional development, pp. 70–99 (2000)
21. Strapparava, C., Valitutti, A.: WordNet-Affect: an affective extension of WordNet. In: Proceedings of LREC, pp. 1083–1086 (2004)
22. Wald, A.: Statistical decision functions. John Wiley & Sons, Inc., New York (1950)

Emotional Investment in Naturalistic Data Collection

Ian Davies and Peter Robinson

Computer Laboratory, University of Cambridge, UK

Abstract. We present results from two experiments intended to allow naturalistic data collection of the physiological effects of cognitive load. Considering the example of command and control environments, we identify shortcomings of previous studies which use either laboratory-based scenarios, lacking realism, or real-world scenarios, lacking repeatability. We identify the hybrid approach of remote-control which allows experimental subjects to remain in a laboratory setting, performing a real-world task in a completely controlled environment. We show that emotional investment is vital for evoking natural responses and that physiological indications of cognitive load manifest themselves more readily in our hybrid experimental setup. Finally, we present a set of experimental design recommendations for naturalistic data collection.

1 Introduction

As control environments become increasingly complex, understanding the level and effects of cognitive load is becoming ever more important. Drivers are expected to operate their satellite navigation, telephone and in-car entertainment systems without compromising the safety of their driving. Aeroplane cockpits are providing more information to pilots flying in more crowded skies. Air traffic controllers must manage the increasing traffic safely and design the next generation control systems to help their operators avoid cognitive overload. It is essential that we build up an understanding of the effects of cognitive load on human operators, otherwise we rely on guesswork when designing new, usable systems.

This need for understanding has not gone unnoticed. Twenty years ago people were already investigating the effects of stress on physiological responses such as skin conductance and heart rate [2]. These studies were most commonly conducted in laboratory settings with artificial scenarios designed specifically to raise cognitive load in a particular way, such as overloading working memory [3]. Later, as technology for data collection progressed, studies began to focus on real-world scenarios. Healey, Picard and others have conducted in-car studies showing that varying driving conditions can cause different physiological responses [6,10] and that classifiers can be built to identify the conditions based on responses [5]. Lisetti and Nasoz have primarily conducted simulator-based experiments investigating the link between affective states and physiological indicators [8].

S. D´Mello et al. (Eds.): ACII 2011, Part I, LNCS 6974, pp. 467–476, 2011.

These studies were extremely important, initially to show that there is indeed a link between cognitive load and physiological responses, and latterly to verify that these effects can be observed in real-world tasks. Unfortunately the on-road experiments make quantification of the stimuli and effects extremely difficult because of the limited control over experimental conditions, particularly traffic quantity and behaviour. There is also the ethical difficulty of deliberately inducing stress in a driver surrounded by real traffic. Simulator-based studies give researchers the necessary control over the environment, but, as we shall see, may not be suitable for naturalistic data collection due to a lack of emotional investment on the part of the subjects. The issue of naturalistic data collection has come to the fore recently as people start to consider the use of real-world versus acted data in affective computing systems [11].

Here we present two experiments which explore this issue. The first is a simulator-based study of driver stress, where we found that for many subjects physiological responses are not a good indicator of cognitive load. We then hypothesised that participants often did not care about their performance when the scenario was completely artificial and we designed an experiment that provided a real-world control task but maintained our control over the environment.

2 Simulated Car Driving

The objective of the first experiment was to use a driving simulator to replicate results observed by others in real-world scenarios [5,6]. In particular, we hoped to confirm skin conductance and heart rate as good indicators of cognitive load and to investigate correlations with other, less invasive measures such as eye movements.

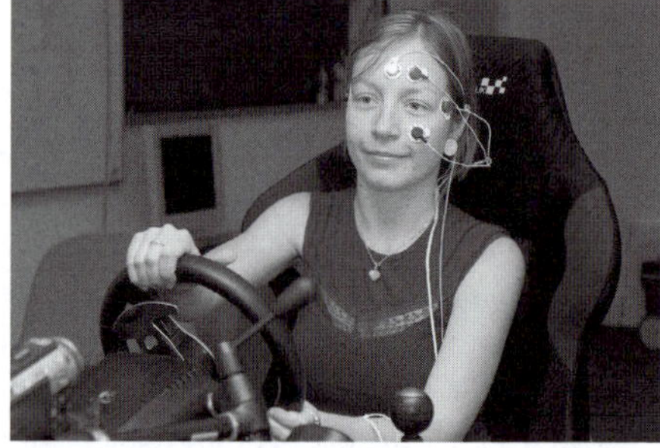

Fig. 1. Participants were asked to drive through several scenarios in our fixed-base driving simulator while wearing EOG, GSR and BVP physiological sensors

2.1 Experimental Setup

Figure 1 shows our fixed-base driving simulator. We use a seat, steering wheel and pedals to give a realistic cab-like environment for our participants, and a projection screen which largely fills the visual field of the driver (around 60° field-of-view). A single PC runs the simulation software which is a slightly modified version of Rockstar Games' "Grand Theft Auto: San Andreas". Modifications allow remote monitoring of controls, speed and road position, as well as control of traffic and weather conditions. The game includes a 6 km x 6 km map with over 500 km of roads, including motorways, city streets and country lanes, which allows long and varied scenarios to be designed. A second PC runs the remote monitoring and control software for the simulator and also controls navigation instructions and secondary tasks. A third and final PC records physiological data gathered from the driver through our NeXus-4 Wireless Physiological Monitoring system. All the computers are synchronised appropriately for logging purposes.

2.2 Subjects

Subjects were recruited through advertisements in the local community. Fifteen subjects participated (nine female, six male), providing twelve sets of complete results. Participants were aged between 20 and 60 years, with about two-thirds below 30 years. All held full European driving licence, and those that required glasses or contact lenses for driving wore them. None had participated in previous studies in our laboratory.

2.3 Procedure

On arrival, participants filled in a pre-study questionnaire for the collection of demographic data. Electrodes were attached for measurement of skin conductance (GSR), blood volume pulse (BVP) and eye movement (EOG) and then they were given time to familiarise themselves with the simulator. They practised for as long as they wanted (typically around 15 minutes) until they were comfortable with the controls and the environment.

The main experiment consisted of six 5-minute scenarios of varying difficulty. Each scenario had a different route, but all routes started on city streets leading to a short section of motorway and finally into country lanes. In all conditions navigation instructions were given verbally by the supervisor. The secondary task consisted of verbal arithmetic questions such as "23 plus 7" in the "simple maths" conditions and "19 minus 76" in the "complex maths" conditions. There were two different weather/traffic conditions (clear weather with no traffic and stormy weather with heavy traffic) and three different secondary task difficulties (navigation only, navigation with simple arithmetic and navigation with complex arithmetic). This gave a total of six scenarios which were randomly ordered for each subject. Between each scenario, participants filled in a questionnaire with questions based on the NASA-TLX self-reporting scheme for workload measurement [4]. They were then given several minutes to relax and drive through open countryside.

2.4 Discussion

The first data analysis step for this experiment was to validate the relative difficulty of the scenarios. Participants' self-report ratings of the scenarios in several categories were ranked, and Friedman tests followed by Wilcoxon Signed Ranks tests showed that navigation plus complex arithmetic was ranked as being significantly more demanding ($p < 0.005$), hurried ($p < 0.05$), frustrating ($p < 0.005$) and stressful ($p < 0.01$). We now compare the results of the "easiest" scenario (clear weather, clear traffic, no arithmetic) to the results of the "hardest" scenario (stormy weather, busy traffic, complex arithmetic).

The results of physiological data analysis were less clear-cut. Some subjects showed strong skin conductance effects correlated with the scenario difficulty, but many bore no relationship. The same was true for heart-rate, blink-rate and heart-rate variability. Figure 2 (a) shows results from a person who showed indications of stress as expected, while Figure 2 (b) is typical of most of our subjects who showed no such response. Figure 2 (c) shows aggregated results from all participants. Note the lack of any significant effect. See Section 3.4 for a detailed description of the physiological data processing procedure. Note that data from several participants was discarded completely following hardware failure. Only complete, valid data sets were analysed.

We consider three possible causes for the disappointing results. Firstly, the possibility that having a supervisor in the room giving navigation instructions and asking arithmetic questions introduced a confounding effect due to social interaction. Secondly, the possibility that the five-minute scenarios were simply too short for the effects of high cognitive workload to manifest themselves. A brief follow-up study where the navigation instructions and secondary task were entirely automated using a speech synthesiser and the scenarios were extended to 20 minutes did not yield clearer results, suggesting that neither of these possibilities was a major source of problems.

The third possible cause we consider is the potential for subjects to lack "emotional investment" in the task when using a simulator. In particular, many subjects would laugh when they crashed, suggesting that they did not really care about their driving performance to the same extent as they would have in on-road studies such as those conducted by Healey and Picard [5,6]. We suspected that this lack of emotional investment meant that although subjects may have been working hard, many did not exhibit the classic indications of stress.

3 Remotely-Controlled Flying

In order to test our hypothesis that participants were not sufficiently invested in their tasks to show signs of stress, we designed a second experiment. We retained the hardware setup of the driving simulator, but this time adapted it for remote control of a real vehicle: a Parrot AR.Drone quadricoptor [1]. This allowed us to maintain complete control over the experimental environment in a way not possible for on-road studies, but also gave our participants a real-world task that was not simulated.

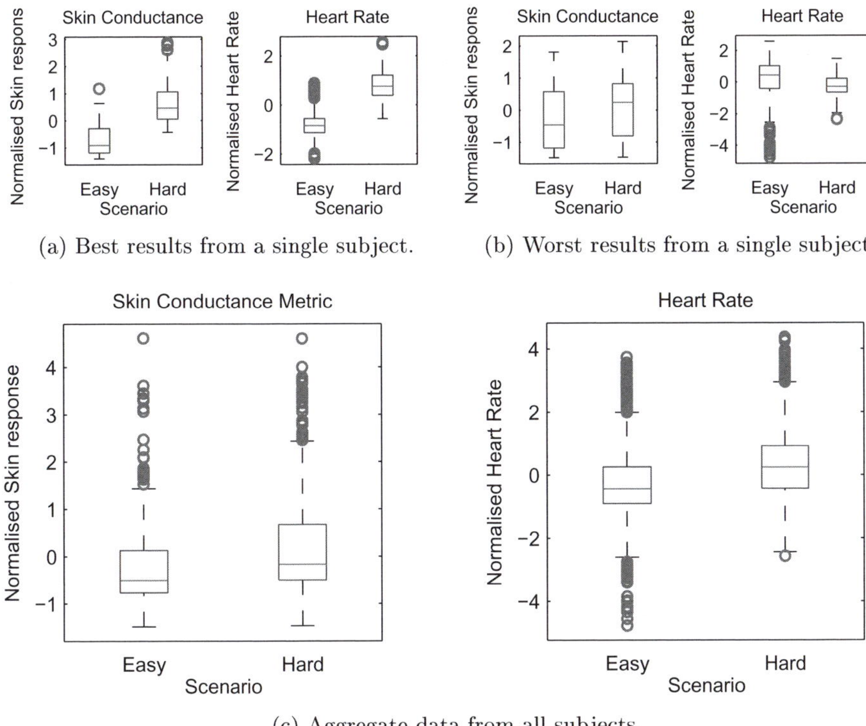

(a) Best results from a single subject.

(b) Worst results from a single subject.

(c) Aggregate data from all subjects.

Fig. 2. Sample results from the simulated driving experiment. Although a small number of subjects showed good results, the aggregate data shows no effect.

3.1 Experimental Setup

The driving simulator described above was repurposed to allow remote control of the quad-rotor drone. This involved the addition of a joystick which allows more realistic control of a flying vehicle than the steering wheel and pedals used previously. The driving simulation software was removed and a live video feed from the forward-facing camera on the drone was projected onto the screen. Figure 3 shows the experimental setup. The drone itself was modified to operate in infrastructure wireless mode, allowing remote control throughout the building using our laboratory wireless network.

3.2 Subjects

Five subjects were recruited locally from within the university. All were 20 – 30 years of age. Some participants had previous experience flying the drone, while others were flying for the first time.

3.3 Procedure

On arrival, participants were instructed in the operation of the drone and given as long as they wanted to practise and get comfortable with the controls. This typically took around 10 minutes. Subjects wore sensors for measurement of skin conductance and blood volume pulse as well as a Dikablis Eye Tracker for measurement of absolute pupil position (which is not possible with EOG).

This experiment consisted of just two conditions, each interleaved and repeated several times. In the first ("easy") condition, participants were asked to fly the drone slowly from one end of a corridor to the other and back several times. In the second ("hard") condition, participants were asked to fly the drone down a corridor that included a 90° bend and then return to their starting point as fast as possible. In this condition they were also required to respond to an n-back secondary task. Single-digit numbers were read to them through a speech synthesiser and every time they heard a number they had to repeat the digit they heard two numbers previously. This type of secondary task has been widely used in previous studies designed to evoke cognitive overload and stress [7]. Whenever the drone crashed, it was reset in the corridor and the experiment continued. We considered the embarrassment of crashing the drone to be sufficient incentive for the subjects to avoid collisions. The experiment lasted approximately 40 minutes for each participant.

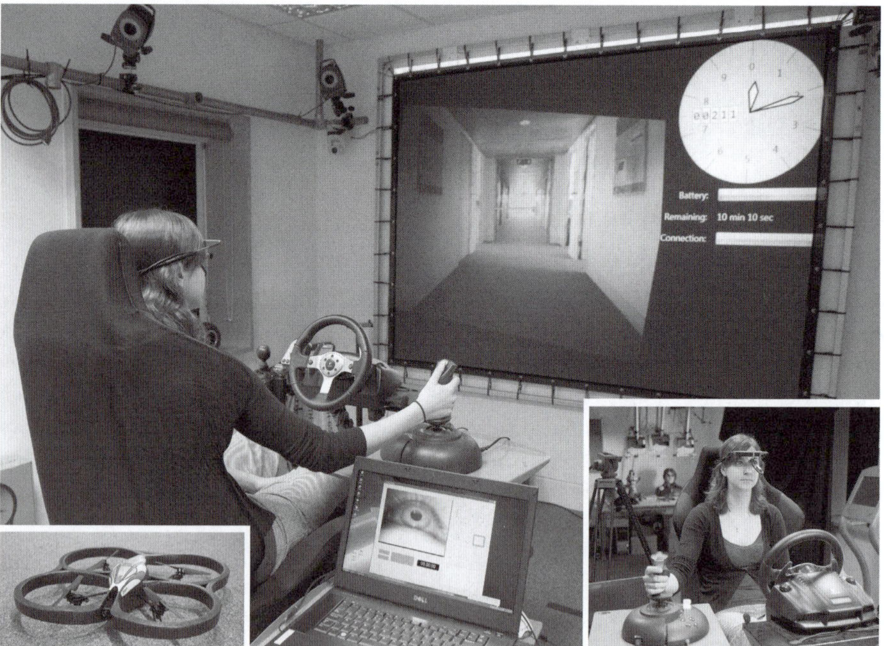

Fig. 3. The driving simulator, adapted for remote control of the Parrot AR.Drone

3.4 Data Analysis

The skin conductance data was bandpassed (0.001 Hz – 0.3 Hz) to remove high-frequency noise and long-term trends. Several features were calculated and then combined into a single "arousal" metric. Peaks were identified along with their preceding trough and then rise-rate and total height calculated. The product of these two features provides a metric which responds strongly to very sharp, tall peaks and largely ignores small, gentle slopes. These features are similar to those used by Healey and Picard in their previous study [5].

The blood volume pulse signal was bandpassed (0.5 Hz – 8 Hz) to remove noise and drift and scaled to mitigate the effects of changing circulation and sensor movement. These processing steps also removed variation between participants. A threshold was then applied to identify peaks corresponding to heart beats. The distribution of peak-heights in the BVP signal was plotted and a threshold chosen which would separate the tall peaks corresponding to heart beats from the others. Continuous beats-per-minute (BPM) were then calculated from the individual beat intervals and smoothed through a 15-beat moving average. The eye-movement data was recorded for future processing, but was not analysed in this experiment.

Both the skin conductance metric and the BPM were normalised for each participant by subtracting the mean and dividing by the standard deviation over the whole experiment. This allows us to compare participants with different physiological baselines on the same scale.

3.5 Discussion

Our intention was that the two scenarios would provide significantly different levels of cognitive load. The participants who could already fly the drone commented that the first condition was quite easy and that the second condition was extremely hard, validating our choice of scenarios for that group. The participants with less experience of the system found both scenarios rather difficult and some were unable to complete the harder of the two. As such, we only consider the results from subjects who completed both tasks. Figure 4 shows the results of the experiment. Readers will note the strong correlation between the heart rate, skin conductance and task difficulty in all individual subjects, and also in the aggregated data.

4 Recommendations

In this section we provide a set of recommendations for the design of experiments intended to measure the effects of varying cognitive load.

4.1 Location

Many previous studies have shown that varying cognitive load can cause measureable effects in drivers [5,10], pilots [12] and others. Most have performed data collection in real-world scenarios where control of the experimental conditions is extremely coarse, such as driving at rush-hour versus driving in light traffic. These studies were essential for stimulating further work on this topic, but make quantification of the effects very difficult. Therefore, it is suggested that further, more controlled experiments are conducted in a laboratory setting. Although commercial moving-base flight simulators give an extremely realistic experience, they are too expensive for most research purposes, requiring an capital investment of around $10m and a recurrent cost of about $200 per hour.

4.2 Scenario

In order to elicit meaningful responses from subjects in a laboratory setting, it is essential that they are emotionally invested in the task undertaken. Entirely simulated scenarios may be suitable for studies of certain behaviours such as visual search [9,10], but if we expect to see genuine indicators of cognitive overload and stress, our subjects must really care about their performance. The approach described in our second experiment overcomes this by using a remote-control scenario where there is a real incentive for the participants not to crash the drone (i.e. it is expensive and could cause damage), but the environment is completely controlled.

4.3 Secondary Task

An important distinction that is rarely considered in the literature is between experiments where there are multiple tasks that are “easy” or “hard” (such as driving at rush-hour versus driving in light traffic) and experiments where a single primary task is performed, accompanied by a secondary task of varying difficulty. We have no reason to believe that the effects of a single task causing a high cognitive load will be equivalent to multiple simpler tasks. Consider the case of a driver in heavy traffic compared with the case of a driver in light traffic trying to operate a satellite navigation system. Both cases are important, but their effects may be very different. Our hybrid experimental environment will allow us to investigate both these types of cognitive load in detail.

4.4 Data Collection and Analysis

When considering metrics for analysis, it is important to bear in mind potential applications. In particular, it is likely that most applications in control systems such as those described will require real-time data about the operator. Therefore, we should choose metrics that are calculable with minimal computation and as short a window of data as possible. All the metrics considered in this paper could be calculated continuously with a lag equal to the window size - generally no more than 10 seconds.

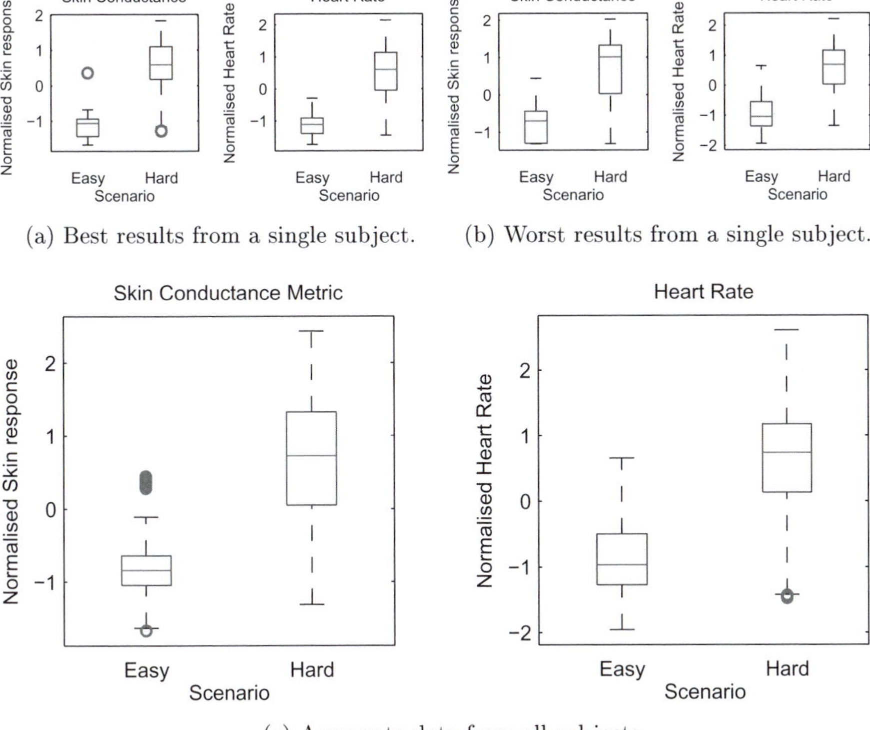

(a) Best results from a single subject. (b) Worst results from a single subject.

(c) Aggregate data from all subjects.

Fig. 4. Results from expert pilots in the remote-controlled flying experiment. Compare to Figure 2, where the distinction between the scenarios in the aggregate data was much less clear.

5 Conclusion

Understanding the effects of cognitive load is an increasingly important area of research, and previous studies have shown that physiological effects are measurable in both laboratory-based and real-world scenarios. However, we argue that laboratory experiments with artificial tasks lack the external validity necessary for generalisation and data collection in real-world situations lacks the internal validity necessary for accurate quantification of the effects.

We have shown through the simulated driving experiment described in Section 2 that simulation of real-world scenarios is not sufficient to evoke consistent responses to cognitive load. Our remotely-controlled flying experiment (Section 3) confirms the hypothesis that this is due to a lack of emotional investment rather than the length of the scenarios or the effect of social interactions. We designed an experiment that provides subjects with a representative real-world task in an experimental environment that is completely controlled. Comparing

Figure 2 (c) with Figure 4 (c) we can see that the results of this experiment are significantly better.

Finally, we presented a set of experimental design recommendations for naturalistic data collection of the effects of operator cognitive load. We argue that, if these recommendations are followed, naturalistic physiological data collection will be possible in controlled experimental environments.

Acknowledgements. This work is supported by the EPSRC and Thales Research and Technology UK Ltd.

References

1. Parrot AR.Drone, `http://ardrone.parrot.com/`
2. Aasman, J., Mulder, G., Mulder, L.J.M.: Operator effort and the measurement of heart-rate variability. Human Factors 29(2), 161–170 (1987)
3. Backs, R.W., Seljos, K.A.: Metabolic and cardiorespiratory measures of mental effort: the effects of level of difficulty in a working memory task. International Journal of Psychophysiology 16(1), 57–68 (1994)
4. Hart, S.O., Staveland, L.E.: Development of NASA-TLX (Task Load Index): Results of empirical and theoretical research (1988)
5. Healey, J.A., Picard, R.W.: Detecting stress during real-world driving tasks using physiological sensors. IEEE Transactions on Intelligent Transportation Systems 6(2), 156–166 (2005)
6. Healey, J.A., Seger, J., Picard, R.W.: Quantifying driver stress: Developing a system for collecting and processing bio-metric signals in natural situations. In: Proceedings of the Rocky Mountain Bio-Engineering Symposium (1999)
7. Jansma, J.M., Ramsey, N.F., Coppola, R., Kahn, R.S.: Specific versus nonspecific brain activity in a parametric N-back task. Neuroimage 12(6), 688–697 (2000)
8. Lisetti, C., Nasoz, F.: Affective intelligent car interfaces with emotion recognition. In: Proceedings of 11th International Conference on Human Computer Interaction (2005)
9. Recarte, M.A., Nunes, L.M.: Mental workload while driving: Effects on visual search, discrimination, and decision making. Journal of Experimental Psychology: Applied 9(2), 119–133 (2003)
10. Reimer, B., Mehler, B., Wang, Y., Coughlin, J.F.: The impact of systematic variation of cognitive demand on drivers visual attention across multiple age groups. In: Human Factors and Ergonomics Society Annual Meeting Proceedings, pp. 2052–2056 (2010)
11. Robinson, P., el Kaliouby, R.: Computation of emotions in man and machines. Philosophical Transactions of the Royal Society B: Biological Sciences 364(1535), 3441 (2009)
12. Veltman, J.A., Gaillard, A.W.K.: Physiological indices of workload in a simulated flight task. Biological Psychology 42(3), 323–342 (1996)

When Do We Smile? Analysis and Modeling of the Nonverbal Context of Listener Smiles in Conversation

Iwan de Kok and Dirk Heylen

Human Media Interaction,
University of Twente
{i.a.dekok,heylen}@utwente.nl

Abstract. In this paper we will look into reactive models for embodied conversational agents for generating smiling behavior. One trigger for smiling behaviour is smiling of the human interlocutor which is used in reactive models based on mimicry. However, other features might be useful as well. In order to develop such models we look at the nonverbal context of smiles in human-human conversation. We make a distinction between three types of smiles - amused, polite and embarrassed - and highlighted differences in context where each type occurs in conversation. Using machine learning techniques we have build predictive models using the nonverbal contextual features analyzed. Results show that reactive models can offer an interesting contribution to the generation of smiling behaviors.

1 Introduction

Within the AI literature, a common distinction is made between deliberative and reactive agents [14]. A deliberative agent is said to possess an explicitly represented, symbolic model of the world. Decisions about what actions to perform are made via symbolic reasoning. A typical model includes representations of beliefs, plans, goals, intentions and emotions. With reactive agents, on the other hand, the actions are selected as a kind of reflex. The agent reacts to external stimuli without much further processing of internal state variables or without planning. The distinction is also used in the literature on conversational agents (see, for instance [13]). Conversational agents often implement a mixture of deliberative and reactive decision making processes in which certain conversational actions are planned and reasoned about, whereas others are simply triggered by external features.

Computational models for the generation of backchannels typically take the form of reactive decision processes, where a few indicators related to the speaker's behaviour (verbal or nonverbal) automatically trigger backchannel responses of the listening agent [10,11]. One can imagine that such an approach works well for some types of contributions to a conversation but is inadequate for others. For instance, utterances with more content might need to take into account

S. D´Mello et al. (Eds.): ACII 2011, Part I, LNCS 6974, pp. 477–486, 2011.

the semantics of sentences uttered before and deal with mutual beliefs, grounding processing, commitments and obligations, etcetera (see again [13]). Also behaviours that may be linked to emotions - such as smiling behaviours - depend on more complex representations and processes (such as appraisal, coping or masking the expression).

In human conversations, smiles may be determined by a multitude of factors. Smiles could be invoked by humourous content, by the emotional state of happiness, but also, as Brunner has shown [4], they may function as backchannels. Whereas some elements of deliberative action selection in an agent simulating human behaviour might need to be involved in the first types of smiles, the latter type might be handled sufficienty well by more reactive models. In [3], a reactive model of smiles is presented that deals with mimicry of smiles. The selection of a smile by an agent is triggered by the detection of smile on the face of the human interlocutor (and some other probabilistic variables). The analysis of Brunner and the attempt to produce smiling behavior in a primarily reactive way, leads us to the question what part reactive models that are based on simple features of the speaker's behaviour can play in deciding on the timing of a smile besides more complex (emotional) models.

To take a first look into this question, we analyze in this paper the nonverbal context of smiles in a human-human corpus. We will analyze the timing of listener smiles in relation to smiles, pauses and gaze behavior of the speaker. Pauses and gaze[1] are also typicaly used in the prediction of backchannels [5,11]. We will perform these analyses on a corpus where three independent listeners are recorded in interaction with the same speaker at the same time. This particular setup allows us to get a wider coverage of the opportunities to smile during a particular interaction.

A distinction will be made between three types of smiles - amused, polite and embarrassed smiles [1] - and differences in context between the three will be analyzed. Furthermore we will build predictive models for these smile types, which we will evaluate on the corpus. First we will present the results of the analyses we did on the human-human corpus in Section 2. This will be followed by the predictive models in Section 3. From these results we will draw our conclusions and discuss future directions in Section 4.

2 Nonverbal Context of Smiles in Human-Human Conversation

In the following sections we will report on our findings of the analyses of human-human conversations. First we will introduce the MultiLis corpus on which the analyses are performed. After that we discuss the three categories, amused, polite and embarrassed smiles, in which these smile are divided for our analyses. Next, the results of our analyses are presented and finally discussed.

[1] Prosody is another factor that is often taken into account in backchannel prediction models. We have experimented with prosodic features but so far did not find any interesting results.

2.1 Corpus

The MultiLis corpus [8] is a Dutch spoken multimodal corpus of 32 mediated face-to-face interactions totalling 131 minutes. Participants (29 male, 3 female, mean age 25) were assigned the role of either speaker or listener during an interaction. The speakers summarized a video they had just seen or reproduced a recipe they had just studied for 10 minutes. Listeners were instructed to memorize as much as possible about what the speaker was telling. In each session four participants were invited to record four interactions. Each participant was once speaker and three times listener.

What is unique about this corpus is the fact that it contains recordings of three individual listeners to the same speaker in parallel, while each of the listeners believed to be the sole listener. The speakers saw one of the listeners, believing that they had an one-on-one conversation. We will refer to this listener, which can be seen by the speaker, as the *displayed listener*. The other two listeners, which can not be seen by the speaker, will be refered to as *concealed listeners*. All listeners were placed in a cubicle and saw the speaker on the screen in front of them. The camera was placed behind an interrogation mirror, positioned directly behind the position on which the interlocutor was projected. This made it possible to create the illusion of eye contact. To ensure that the illusion of a one-on-one conversation was not broken, interaction between participants was limited. Speakers and listeners were instructed not to ask for clarifications or to elicit explicit feedback from each other.

This particular setup allows one to get a wider coverage of the opportunities to smile during a particular interaction. Listeners differ in their behavior. Thus not every opportunity to smile during an interaction might be answered by the recorded listener in a regular corpus. By having two extra listeners the coverage of the smile opportunities in the interaction is wider, since they are likely to also smile at other moments. This will give us a more complete picture of every opportunity in the interaction and allows us to analyze them all.

In the MultiLis Corpus annotations from one annotator of gaze at the listener (speaker only), head (listener only) and mouth movement (including 397 smiles) are available. Furthermore the corpus includes automatically computed speech/silence annotations from the speaker, extracted with the SHoUT software [7].

2.2 Categories of Smiles

As mentioned earlier we will analyze the context of three different types or smiles. We adopt the three types identified by Ambadar et al. [1], which are amused, polite and embarrassed.

The *Amused* smiles appear in contexts where the listener signals a state of amusement to the speaker. Typical contexts in which these smiles arise are funny content in the dialogue of the speaker or funny situations in the interaction.

The *Polite* smiles appear in contexts where the listener signals friendliness or politiness to the speaker. The smile in these contexts are used to regulate communication and affiliate rapport. Typical contexts in which these smiles arise are the start and ending of the interaction. Backchannel smiles and mimicry smiles are also counted as polite smiles.

The *Embarrassed* smiles appear in contexts where the listener signals embarrassment or nervousness to the speaker. The typical context in this particular corpus where this occurs is when the speaker is thinking for a few seconds for the next step in the recipe or story, which they can not immediately recall. To release the tension the interlocutors often smile at each other when their gaze meets.

In the MultiLis Corpus there are 397 smile annotations. Since there are three listeners to the same speaker some of these smiles occur at the same time. When these are counted as the same moment this leaves us with 298 unique smile moments. One annotator categorized each smile into one of the three categories. The distribution of these categories in this corpus is: 140 *amused* smiles, 113 *polite* smiles and 45 *embarrased* smiles.

2.3 The Nonverbal Context of the Smile Categories

In this next section we will analyze the context of the smiles. We will split results for each category to highlight differences between them. Features of the context that we analyze are speaker smiles, speaking/silence of the speaker and the gaze of the speaker.

To look at the relation between *smiles* of the speaker and smiles of the listener we looked at the areas around the start of a listener smile. For every 100ms interval before or after the start of the smile up until 4 seconds we looked whether the speaker was smiling at that time or not. In total the speaker smiles in the corpus 4% of the time, which is our baseline.

In Figure 1 the resulting graph is presented. If we look at the exact time the listener starts smiling (time 0s), we can see mutual smiling for 35% of the *embarrassed* smiles, 25% of the *amused* smiles and 15% for the *polite* smiles. One second before the listener start smiling (time -1s) these percentage are much lower, and for the *embarrassed* smiles the rise is much steeper than for the other categories. Another interesting point is one and a half second after the listener started smiling. There the *amused* category peaks at mutual smile in 34% of the smiles, as high as the *embarrased* category, but also the *polite* category peaks at that time, but at a lot lower percentage (18%).

The same approach was used to investigate the relation between *pause* of the speaker and the listener smiles. We looked at the presence or absence of a pause (no speech from the speaker) at different intervals around a smile. In total the speaker is silent for 32% of the time in this corpus.

In Figure 2 the resulting graph is presented. At the exact time the listener starts smiling (time 0s), we can see that for every smile type the speaker is more often silent than the baseline (32%) suggests (*amused* 40%, *polite* 50%, *embarrassed* 49%). Each smile type has its own pattern if we look before and after that point. For *amused* smiles the speaker is usually talking from 1.5 until 0.4 seconds before the smile. For *polite* smiles starting for 1 seconds before the

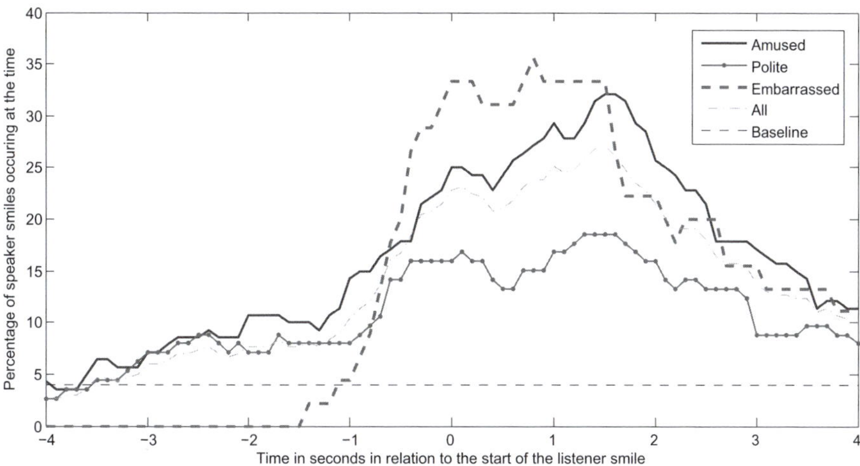

Fig. 1. Graph illustrating the presence or absence of smile of the speaker around the start of a listener smile (time 0s)

smile we see a slight increase in percentage of silence by the speaker until 1 second after. For *embarrassed* smiles the speaker is most often silent in the period before the smile.

The final context feature we analyze is the *gaze* of speaker. We looked at whether the speaker was looking at the listener or not at different intervals around a smile. In total the speaker gazes at the listener for 67% of the time in this corpus.

In Figure 3 the resulting graph is presented. At the time the listener starts smiling (time 0s), we can see that for both *amused* and *polite* smiles (82%) the speaker is looking at them more than the baseline (67%), while at the starts of the *embarrassing* smiles the speaker often looks elsewhere (only 31% the speaker looks at the listener). In both *amused* and *polite* smiles the percentage the speaker looks at the listener starts increasing at around 1.5 seconds before the smile and starts decreasing a few hundred milliseconds after the smile is initiated. For *amused* smiles the speaker looks away more after the smile is initiated until 3 seconds after. For *embarrassed* smiles the speaker is more often looking away. This decrease starts around 5 seconds before the start of the smile (not on the figure) and ends around 2.5 seconds after.

2.4 Discussion

The *amused* smiles are usually preceeded by speech. It is this speech which amuses the listeners and makes them smile. The delay between the speech and the start of the smile is around 400ms, when the pause percentage start to rise again. The speaker starts smiling in a number of cases, but they also answer the smile of the listener with a smile, as can be seen by the continuing rise of the mutual gaze percentage after the start of the listener smile.

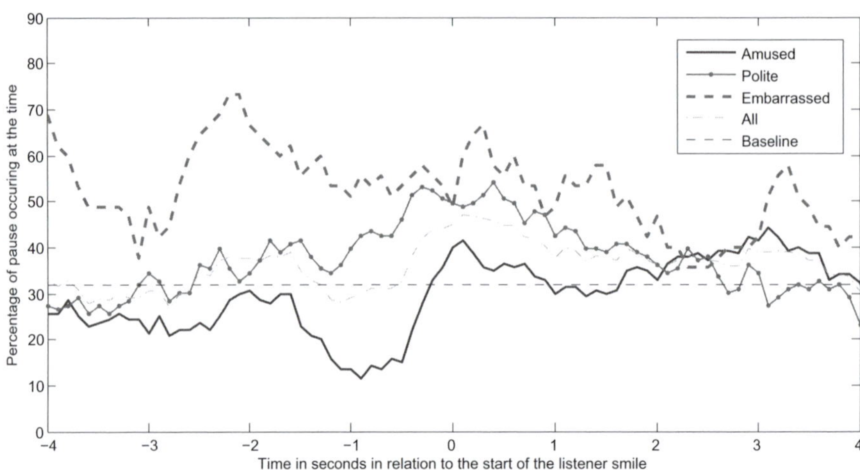

Fig. 2. Graph illustrating the presence or absence of speech of the speaker around the start of a listener smile (time 0s)

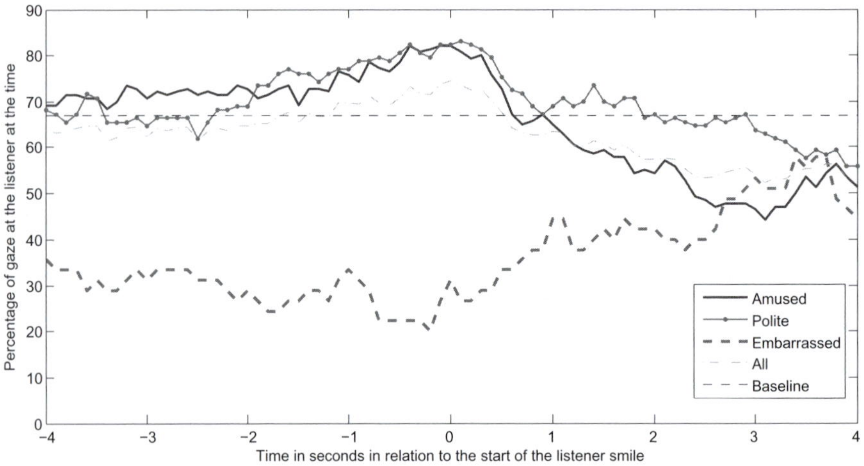

Fig. 3. Graph illustrating whether the speaker was looking at the listener or not around the start of a listener smile (time 0s)

For the *polite* smiles the specific context is less clear. There is a correlation between speaker smiles and polite listener smiles, but less than for the other categories. If we look at the pause analysis, they are situated near the end of an utterance, mostly during the pause, but we do not see a clear pattern as for the amused smile. For gaze we see again a similar pattern as the amused smile, but the drop in gaze percentage is not as sharp.

The *embarrassed* smiles show a high correlation with speaker smiles and are usually situated in areas of long silence and gaze aversion. Note though, that these findings are very corpus specific (even more so than the others) and based on a smaller sample than the other two smile types. In this corpus these smiles mostly occur at times the speaker can not recall an ingredient or part of the story he needs to tell. While thinking the speaker usually averts his gaze and is silent for some time before the listener smiles. This is only one situation in which an embarrased smile may occur. In other corpora the reasons for an embarrassed smile will differ.

3 Predicting the Timing of Smiles in Human-Human Conversation

In the next section we will develop reactive models which predict the timing of smiles in an interaction. The previous analyses have shown that there are differences in the context of the three smile types. Therefore we will compare a general model and individual models for each of the three smile types to each other.

First we will introduce our methodology. After that we will show and discuss the results of the models and reflect on how they used the features analyzed.

3.1 Approach

The approach we use to predict the timing of smiles is introduced by Morency et al. [11]. Based on multimodal features this model is able to learn human behavior from recordings of real life conversations between humans through means of machine learning. The approach uses the sequential probabilistic model Conditional Random Fields [9] to learn the relations between the observations from human-human conversations and the desired behavior, in this case the timing of smiles.

The observations we use to predict the timing of smiles are the following binary features[2]:

- Speaker is smiling
- Speaker is not smiling
- The speaker looks at the listener
- The speaker is not looking at the listener
- The speaker is speaking
- The speaker is silent

The sampling rate of these features is 100Hz. Testing is performed on an hold-out set of 8 randomly selected interactions. The remaining 24 dyadic interactions

[2] Note that even though half of the feature are the inverse of the other half, the model sometimes performs better with the inverse of a binary feature. Performance of both features is not equal.

Table 1. The performance results of the four models and the features selected (in order of selection)

Model	$\mathbf{F_1}$	Prec	Rec	**Features**
All	**0.13**	0.11	0.22	Smile, Pause, Utterance, Not Looking
Amused	**0.17**	0.25	0.15	Pause, Smile, Not Looking
Polite	**0.11**	0.16	0.09	Smile
Embarrassed	**0.01**	0.01	0.04	Looking, Not Looking

were used for learning. All models evaluated in this paper were trained with the same training set and tested on the same test set. The test set does not contain interactions with the same individuals from the training set. Validation of model parameters was performed using a 3-fold strategy on the training set. The objective function of the CRF model contains a regularization term to prevent overfitting. During training and validation, this regularization term was validated with values 10^k, for $k = -3...3$.

The output of a CRF is a smooth probability curve. In this curve peaks represent smile predictions and the height of the peak its associated probability. During validation a threshold is validated which this probability must exceed in order to be a valid prediction. The timing of this prediction is compared to the ground truth labels. These labels are normalized with a 700ms window. We use the F-measure to measure our performance, which is the weighted harmonic mean between precision and recall.

We use the incremental feature selection technique to train our model. We start with training a model using only a single feature. The best performing feature we keep and we train a model with this feature and every other feature. Then again we keep the best performing feature and add on the remaining features. We stop this process once performance remains the same or starts decreasing.

3.2 Results and Discussion

We learn four models in our experiment. One general model, where all smiles are regarded equal, and one for each of the three smile types. The features used in each model and their performance is presented in Table 1.

The first model, where we make no distinction between the three smile types, is based on 298 smiles as ground truth. The performance of this model is 0.13 and it uses the features *smile*, *pause*, *utterance* and *not looking*. The type-specific models for amused, social and embarrassed smiles are based on 140, 113 and 40 smiles respectively. Of these models *Amused* performs better (0.17) than the general model, while the the *Polite* model performs only slightly worse (0.11).

The *Embarrassed* model performs a lot worse (0.01). The difficulty for this model lies in the fact that these smiles are in areas where not much is happening, and what is happening is not captured by the features used. As we have seen in the contextual analysis in Section 2.3 these smiles are usually during long periods of silence, while the speaker is looking away. However the exact timing within these periods varies and no feature used seems to reliably predict this variation. Therefore, a reactive model is not suited for embarrassed smiles.

With these reasonably low performances on replicating smiles in a corpus of human-human interactions, good performance in an interactive embodied conversational agent scenario is not to be expected. Performance needs to be increased before testing in an interactive scenario could be expected to give favorable results. Further exploration of the conversational context into different features, such as prosodic and semantic features, could help to achieve this goal and make the contribution of reactive models more interesting. Reactive models will not replace deliberative models, but both approaches should be combined.

4 Conclusions

In this paper we looked into reactive models for smiling behavior. One trigger for smiling behaviour is smiling of the human interlocutor which is used in reactive models based on mimicry. Besides smiling of the speaker, we also looked at gazing and speaking/not-speaking aspects of the nonverbal context of smiles in human-human conversation. We have made a distinction between three types of smiles and highlighted some differences of these aspects in the context where each type occurs in conversation. With machine learning we have made predictive reactive models using the nonverbal contextual aspects analyzed. Results are promising for amused and polite smiles, but not for embarrassed smiles.

In the development of predictive models of smiling behavior in conversation many challenges still lie ahead. Prosodic features of areas preceeding a smile may hold valuable predictive information for this task. Like backchannels [6], there may be prosodic smile inviting cues. For instance, it has been shown that one can detect a smile in speech [2] by analyzing prosodic features. Since mimicry is a common reason to smile, the use of these features will probably be useful in predicting when to mimic a smile.

Another more challenging task would be to make the agent capable of detecting humor in conversations [12]. This is particulary needed for *amused* smiles. This is not only limited to models to detect funny dialogue based on semantic features and knowledge models, but also the detection of funny situations using visual features as well.

References

1. Ambadar, Z., Cohn, J.F., Reed, L.I.: All Smiles are Not Created Equal: Morphology and Timing of Smiles Perceived as Amused, Polite, and Embarrassed/Nervous. Journal of Nonverbal Behavior 33(1), 17–34 (2009)
2. Aubergé, V., Cathiard, M.: Can we hear the prosody of smile? Speech Communication 40, 87–97 (2003)
3. Bevacqua, E., Hyniewska, S., Pelachaud, C.: Positive influence of smile backchannels in ECAs. In: Interacting with ECAs as Virtual Characters Workshop, the Ninth International Joint Conference on Autonomous Agents and Multi-Agent Systems, AAMAS (2010)

4. Brunner, L.J.: Smiles can be back channels. Journal of Personality and Social Psychology 37(5), 728–734 (1979)
5. Cathcart, N., Carletta, J., Klein, E.: A shallow model of backchannel continuers in spoken dialogue. In: European ACL, pp. 51–58 (2003)
6. Gravano, A., Hirschberg, J.: Backchannel-Inviting Cues in Task-Oriented Dialogue. In: Interspeech 2009, Brighton, pp. 1019–1022 (2009)
7. Huijbregts, M.: Segmentation , Diarization and Speech Transcription: Surprise Data Unraveled. Phd thesis, University of Twente (2008)
8. de Kok, I., Heylen, D.: The MultiLis Corpus - Dealing with Individual Differences of Nonverbal Listening Behavior. In: Esposito, A., Esposito, A., Martone, R., Müller, V.C., Scarpetta, G. (eds.) COST 2010. LNCS, vol. 6456, pp. 362–375. Springer, Heidelberg (2011)
9. Lafferty, J., McCallum, A., Pereira, F.: Conditional random fields: Probabilistic models for segmenting and labeling sequence data. In: Proceedings of International Conference on Machine Learning, pp. 282–289. Citeseer (2001)
10. Maatman, R.M., Gratch, J., Marsella, S.: Natural behavior of a listening agent. In: Panayiotopoulos, T., Gratch, J., Aylett, R.S., Ballin, D., Olivier, P., Rist, T. (eds.) IVA 2005. LNCS (LNAI), vol. 3661, pp. 25–36. Springer, Heidelberg (2005)
11. Morency, L.P., de Kok, I., Gratch, J.: A probabilistic multimodal approach for predicting listener backchannels. Autonomous Agents and Multi-Agent Systems 20(1), 70–84 (2010)
12. Nijholt, A.: Embodied agents: A new impetus to humor research. In: TWLT20 - The Fools Day Workshop on Computation Humor, pp. 101–111. Citeseer, Trento, Italy (2002)
13. Traum, D.R.: A reactive-deliberative model of dialogue agency. In: Jennings, N.R., Wooldridge, M.J., Müller, J.P. (eds.) ECAI-WS 1996 and ATAL 1996. LNCS, vol. 1193, pp. 157–171. Springer, Heidelberg (1997)
14. Wooldridge, M.J.: An introduction to multiagent systems, 2nd edn. Wiley, New York (2002)

Emotional Cognitive Architectures

Usef Faghihi[1], Pierre Poirier[2], and Othalia Larue[3]

[1] Department of computer science, University of Memphis, Memphis, TN,USA
[2] Department of philosophy, UQAM, Montreal, QC, Canada
[3] Department of computer science, UQAM, Montreal, QC, Canada
ufaghihi@memphis.edu,{poirier.pierre,larue.othalia}@uqam.ca

Abstract. We investigate the value of bringing emotional components into cognitive architectures. We start by presenting CELTS, an emotional cognitive architecture, with an aim at showing that the emotional component of the architecture is an essential element of CELTS value as a cognitive architecture. We do so by analyzing the role that the emotional mechanism plays and how respecting the emotion criterion defined by Picard[15] may be a way to address at once several of the architectural features covered by Sun's desiderata[10] or Newell's functional criteria[9].

1 Introduction

Work in affective computing can be divided in two broad classes[6]: 1) devising computer systems that can assess and respond to the emotions of its users (we call these emotionally-sensitive systems. In what follows, we will disregard the fine distinctions that can be made between emotions and affects and effectively take the two words to be synonyms. 2) devising computer systems endowed with emotions. Computer systems can be endowed with emotions either 2a) to provide them with emotional responses (we call them emotional systems) or 2b) to allow their internal processing to be influenced by emotions (we call them emotionally-based systems). Of course, these goals are not mutually exclusive: one might wish to build an emotional system that is emotionally-based and emotionally-sensitive. Alternatively, one might also wish to build an emotional system (e.g., a system that displays happy or sad faces) simply based on production rules such as if the user provides a wrong answers, then display a sad face; else display a happy face.

Emotionally-based systems include emotions in their cognitive architecture. Sun[10] describes a cognitive architecture as the overall, essential structure and process of a domain-generic computational cognitive model, used for a broad, multiple-level, multiple domain analysis of cognition or behavior" (p.4). An emotionally-based system is a cognitive architecture that includes emotions as an essential processing element. That is, to a large extent, a cognitive architecture whose performance is attributable to its emotional mechanism or mechanisms. For instance, Adam [3], Marsella [4], Velsquez [5] and Franklin [23] each proposed their specific emotional model for cognitive architectures or showed the important role emotions can play in cognitive architectures. Working with cognitive

S. D´Mello et al. (Eds.): ACII 2011, Part I, LNCS 6974, pp. 487–496, 2011.

architectures (emotional or not) increases the external validity of the models and simulations developed by cognitive scientists, as the latter are thereby prevented from gerrymandering systems exclusively designed to solve a single problem or model one phenomena. Since models and simulations are devised by setting various parameters offered by the cognitive architecture, one can then hope that different sets of parameters may allow modeling of other phenomena. Be that as it may, the value of using a cognitive architecture to model cognitive phenomena or behaviors depends, of course, on the value of the architecture itself. As Sun[10] remarks, the design of any cognitive architecture is based as much on empirical data (from psychology, biology or neuroscience) as on philosophical arguments and ad hoc working hypotheses. It is thus important for cognitive scientists to assess the value of their architecture. To do so, a number of criteria or desiderata have been recently promoted. The best known is Newell's functional criteria (as expounded by Lebiere and Anderson[9]) and Ron Sun's essential desiderata for cognitive architectures[10].

We start by presenting an emotional cognitive architecture we are working on[1] with an aim at showing that the emotional component of the architecture is an essential element of its value as a cognitive architecture. We do so by analyzing the role that emotional mechanism play in the architecture. In conclusion, we show that emotions may be a way to address at once several of the architectural features covered by Sun's desiderata and Newell's functional criteria. Emotions, we will suggest, may be a way to get many of these important features.

2 Cognitive Criteria Meet Emotions

Since a detailed discussion of proposed criteria and desiderata is beyond the scope of this paper, we will simply list them here (we refer readers to the author's original papers for a justification of the individual criteria). It will, however, be important to detail one criterion in order to see how one goes about applying them. Typically, each criterion is associated with a series of descriptors or diagnostic questions the analyst can pose to assess whether the architecture meets the criterion. For instance, Newell's functional behavioral robustness criterion (criterion 6) can be associated with the two questions: 1) Does the agent behave robustly in the face of error, the unexpected, and the unknown? 2) Can the agent successfully inhabit dynamic environments? One agent may be able to manage error but be unable to manage dynamic environments; another may have the reverse profile. Both will be deemed to meet the behavioral robustness criteria, though not as much, obviously, as one who could manage both error and dynamic environments. It is important to note as well that the criteria are not mutually exclusive. In important cases, this non-exclusivity will be present because of dependence relations between the criteria: one criterion is respected because another one is. For example, a self-aware system (one that thus respects Newell's criterion 8 below) will probably exhibit flexible behavior (thus respecting Newell's criterion 8 below) because its self-awareness may allow it to recognize that some behavior is unsuccessful. For example, a modular system

Table 1. Ron Sun's Desiderata and Newell's criteria

Ron Sun's Desiderata[10]	Newell's functional criteria[8]
Ecological realism	Flexible behavior
Bio-evolutionary realism	Real-time operation
Cognitive realism	Rationality
Eclectism of methodologies and techniques	Knowledgeable in terms of size
Reactivity	Knowledgeable in terms of variety
Sequentiality	Behaviorally robust
Routineness	Linguistic
Trial-and-error adaptation	Self-awareness
Dichotomy of implicit and explicit	Adaptive through learning
Synergistic interaction	Developmental
Bottom-up learning	Evolvable
Modularity	Neurologically realizable

(respecting Sun's criteria 12) will ipso facto be evolutionary realistic if it can be shown that evolution favors modularity [12]. In this paper, we wish to show that cognitive architectures can be set up so that emotions are the way to respect many criteria in the lists, the latter thus being dependent on emotions. We will call such architectures emotional cognitive architectures. An emotional cognitive architecture is one that is set up, by design or evolution, in such a way that at least some of its cognitive capacities are dependent on emotions. We all know that emotions are given an important role by researchers in attention, flexible decision making, learning, social judgment, etc., in humans [13][14]. But we want to go one step further: by showing how cognitive features may be dependent on emotions in some designed architectures, we wish to suggest that many human cognitive capacities may be dependent on emotions, that is, we wish to suggest that the human cognitive architecture may be an emotional cognitive architecture. We illustrate our claim by showing emotions are an integral part of the cognitive processing of the CELTS architecture. At this point, one may wonder what it is for a cognitive architecture to be emotional? In the present context, we'll take this question to mean: What descriptors or diagnostic questions might cognitive scientists use to determine whether a given cognitive architecture is emotional or not. Rosalind Picard[15] has put forward a number of criteria that may serve that purpose: 1) Does the system's behavior arise from emotions? 2) Can emotions allow the system fast/reactive responses to inputs? 3) Does the system have cognitively generated emotions? 4) Is the system aware of its emotions? 5) Are the system's emotions implicated in its cognitive processing, and vice versa? We will use these questions in the same spirit as Newell's or Sun's descriptive questions, that is, as a means to qualitatively assess whether a given architecture meets a proposed criterion. This does not prevent of course using the questions (Picard's criteria) to assess the specific emotional profile of the system, and thus get more precise knowledge of the implementation of emotions in that system. Picard's questions are finer-grained than the general criteria used to assess architectures globally.

3 Emotions and Emotional Learning Mechanisms in CELTS

Conscious Emotional Learning Tutoring System (CELTS)[1] is a hybrid artificial intelligent tutor based on Baars' theory of consciousness[16]. CELTS has many symbolic data structures and has networks (e.g., BN) passing activation in a fashion similar to neural networks. It is partly composed of entities posited at a relatively high level of abstraction, such as behaviors, messages, emotions, etc., and partly of lower level entities such as energy and codelets[1]. In its current implementation, CELTS serves to assist astronauts learn how to operate Canadarm2, the robotic telemanipulator attached to the International Space Station (ISS). CELTS performs through its cognitive cycle, which start with perception and usually end by the execution of an action. CELTS uses its Behavior Network (BN) for action selection, which is based on Maes' Behavior Net[17]. CELTS' BN is a network of partial plans that analyzes the context in order to determine what behavior to set off. Given that CELTS is a tutor, an expert will specify different solutions in the BN to help learners. To improve CELTS tutoring abilities, our team provided CELTS with various types of learning (emotional, episodic and causal learning), all of which depend on emotions[1].

In this section, we present our generic computational model of emotions and explain in details how the peripheral-central[18][19] model and the appraisal theory of emotions[20] are implemented in CELTS. The appraisal theory posits that agent-environment interactions incite appraisal variables in the agent, which leads to the generation of affective states that occur with some intensity and which may set off behavioral and cognitive outcomes. CELTS' emotional states emerge through collaboration between perceptions (sensory input from the virtual world) and inputs coming from interactions between different modules and what is broadcasted through the system by CELTS' consciousness mechanism. For CELTS to make sense of its core affective [2] state, it must be engaged in situated conceptualization that links the core affective state to an object or event. Conceptualization is thus necessary for CELTS to understand its core affective state. To that effect, memories and prior knowledge regarding an object or event are put to use to interpret current sensations. This view on the emergence of the emotions is in accordance with the psychological constructionist model as defended by Lindquist and her colleagues [21].

CELTS can react in two ways when faced with a situation. Information coming from CELTS' Perceptual Mechanism flows along a Short and Long route (ESR and ELR in Fig. 1), which we will describe now.

[1] Based on Hofstadter et al.'s idea, a codelet is a very simple agent, a small piece of code that is specialized for some comparatively simple task. Implementing Baars theory's simple processors, codelets do much of the processing in the architecture. In our case, each information codelet possesses an activation value and an emotional valence specific to each cognitive cycle.

[2] Core affect is a term used to describe the mental representation of bodily changes that are sometimes experienced as feelings of hedonic pleasure and displeasure with some degree of arousal [20].

3.1 CELTS' Long Route (LR)

The LR can be viewed as CELTS' implementation of the appraisal theory. CELTS' cognitive cycle start with perception. When a percept enters working memory (WM) as a single coalition of codelets, emotional codelets inspect the coalition's informational content (the assessment part of appraisal theory), and infuse it with a level of activation proportional to the assessed emotional valence of a perceived situation. This increases or decreases the likelihood that the coalition will draw attention (AM) to itself. CELTS' attention mechanism (Fig. 1), then chooses the information that emotionally influenced by CETLS' Emotional mechanism (Fig. 1, ESR and ELR) and sends it for conscious competition. CELTS' Consciousness mechanism then broadcasts the information through the system for a decision to be made (see ELR rectangle in Fig. 1). In CELTS, the broadcasting of information will cause the appraisal of emotions. CELTS' Attention mechanism in turn influences the emotion mechanism (EM) by providing information regarding the discrepancy between what was expected given an action and what effectively occurred. This information may alter the future valence assigned by EM to the situation, as well as the importance EM gives to the situation. After each cycle of interaction with the environment, CELTS' EM updates its knowledge of the environment (i.e., the emotional valence to be associated with events) for future cycles of interaction with it. This update may also alter current emotional state (e.g., fear to happiness). Thus, the importance given to any situation may increase or decrease when CELTS next encounters it. We can already see that, in our architecture, emotions are implicated in cognitive processing (they influence action selection), and vice-versa (cognitive processing can modify the emotional appraisal, in agreement with Picard's fifth diagnostic question.

3.2 CELTS' Short Route (SR)

The SR (see ESR rectangles in Fig. 1) starts with perception just like the LR. Perception codelets connect in parallel both to CELTS' Behavior Network (BN) and to its emotional codelets. The activation sent directly by perception codelets to emotional codelets is the first stage of the SR (Step 2b, Fig. 1). The emotional codelets in Emotional Mechanism (EM) establishes the positive or negative emotional valance of the event for the system. The valence assigned to the event may result from evolution (an innate valence accorded to evolutionarily important situations) or from learning.

In CELTS, some emotional codelets may correspond to innate (designed) sensitivities (e.g., to excessive speed for Canadarm2, or an imminent collision between the arm and the ISS); others may have learnt the valence of situations from experience. Either way, emotional codelets possess direct connections to behavior nodes in the BN, to which they send positive or negative activations (Step 7,Fig. 1). Some of these emotional codelets react more strongly than others and accordingly send stronger valence activations to the behavior nodes. If the valence activations exceed a behavior node's firing threshold, then the corresponding action will fire automatically. This emotional intervention reflects a direct route between the mechanisms responsible for emotional appraisal, influencing action selection. Because it provides this form of reactive action to situations, typical of some emotional responses, our architecture meets Picard's second diagnostic question. There are other means, of course, to provide for such behaviors, as the growing literature on Type 1 (or heuristic) processes shows[22].

3.3 Expectation Codelets

Whichever route was responsible for an action, short or long, the firing of a behavior node generates one or more expectation codelets, which are a type of attention codelets. These codelets watch for the arrival in WM of a given piece of information, expecting to see within a given time frame some specific result for the action taken by CELTS. The expectation codelets do double duty in CELTS. First, they serve as "environmental reinforcers" to the Action Selection Mechanism in BN. If they see information coming in WM that confirms the behavior's expected result, the expectation codelets directly send reinforcement activation to the behavior nodes that created them (that is, they do not do so through conscious broadcasting). This behavior will accordingly see its base-level activation heightened, making it a more likely choice in similar contexts. In the case of a failure to meet expected results, however, relevant resources need to be recruited, to analyze the cause of the failure, to correct the previous emotional interpretation of the situation (Step 6, Fig. 1), and to allow deliberation to take place concerning supplementary and/or alternative actions. The expectation codelets thus work to have discrepancies brought to the attention of the whole system (in an eventual conscious broadcast of the noted discrepancy) by sending the information to CELTS' WM. Given CELTS previous emotional state, the aforementioned process may cause the appraisal of events (conceptualization and core affect explained by Lindquist). After sending the information to WM, CELTS continues through its cognitive cycles to allow for improved decisions. Thus, the emergence of emotions in CELTS occurs by making sense out of sensory input from different modules and from the virtual world according to prior experiences. The expectation codelets' second duty concerns the Emotional Mechanism itself, in cases where it forced an automatic reaction through the SR, for instance, when it anticipates an imminent collision (in the virtual world). Indeed, when low-level basic information coming from the perception codelets recognize aspects of the situation as highly dangerous, there is no time to think and, through the mechanism described above, the emotional codelets will force an action to fire in the BN. This makes CELTS jump before thinking (ESR's path, red-dotted rectangles and blue arrows, which demonstrate primitive appraisal in Fig. 1); that is, it makes CELTS act before it had time to become "conscious" of the situation and consciously plan a course of action. This corresponds to the first reaction taken by CELTS in our aforementioned example about imminent collisions in the virtual environment.However, the instantaneous, mindless reflex will be evaluated following the more thorough analysis of the situation that comes later, through the LR. When the action thereby proposed comes into WM (step 2), the expectation codelets compare it to the reflex action that was

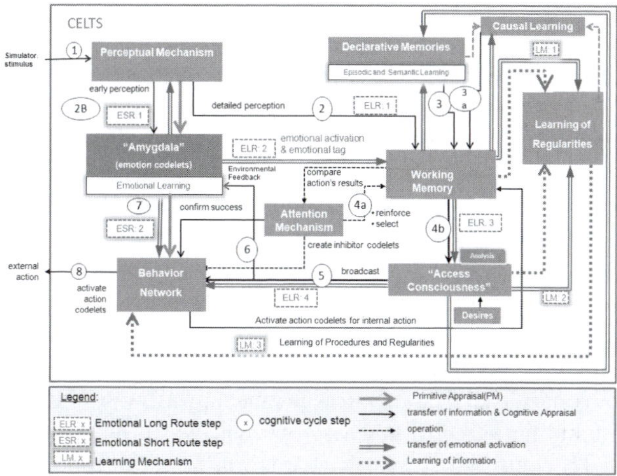

Fig. 1. CELTS' Architecture with Emotion and Learning Mechanisms

prompted. If the initial reaction was right, which will serve, when broadcast, as a reinforcer to the emotional codelet(s) that were instrumental in setting off the reflex. In effect, this will make the Emotional Mechanism reinforce the relevant nodes. However, when the initial reaction diverges from the behavior proposed by the more detailed conscious analysis, the Emotional Mechanism has to alter its initial reaction.

4 Is CELTS an Emotional Cognitive Architecture?

How does CELTS fare with respect to Picard's diagnostic questions? And how do its emotions help CELTS meet Sun's desiderata and Newell's functional criteria? In this last section, we study the relationship between emotions and the capacities of cognitive architecture by answering these two questions. *Does the system's behavior arise from emotions?* Yes. Information is assigned an emotional valence as soon as it enters WM from Perception. Sometimes the valence is strong enough to fire off a behavior immediately (SR). In all cases, emotional valence influences which coalition is at the center of attention, and thus influences which behavior will be set-off.

Can emotions allow the system fast/primary responses to inputs? Yes (see previous answer).

Does the system have cognitively generated emotions? No. Although all higher level conscious processing is influenced by the emotional valence ascribed to events by the emotional codelets, no higher level state of CELTS can properly be called a cognitively generated emotion.

Is the system aware of its emotions? No. There is no mechanism through which CELTS could become aware of its emotions.

Are the system's emotions implicated in its cognitive processing, and vice versa? Yes. As described in question 1 above, all cognitive processing is influenced by emotions. Conversely, higher-level processing may alter the emotional valence ascribed to event by CELTS' emotional codelets (when there is a discrepancy between the event expected by the expectation codelets and the actual event caused by the system's action). This pattern of answers to Picard's diagnostic questions shows, we believe, that CELTS is a basic emotionally-based system but that it lacks the higher-level features associated with emotions in humans: cognitively-generated emotions (i.e., the so-called cognitive emotions - guilt, pride, embarrassment, shame and the like) and awareness of its emotions. While the former are probably beyond CELTS in its current guise, awareness of emotions could be developed by including perception codelets sensitive to the positive and negative valence of CELTS cognitive states. But this matter is beyond the scope of the current paper. Our aim, recall, is to study how emotions in CELTS help the architecture meet Sun's desiderata and Newell functional criteria.

Sun's Desiderata : *Bio-evolutionary realism.* Emotional codelets in CELTS are situated at the same processing level as the WM (observing and tagging WM's content) therefore reproducing the same kind of processing the hypothesized evolutionary old system 1 suggests[22].

Cognitive realism. This is the main advantage gained by adding emotions in our architecture. In the action selection step (step 7, Fig. 1) when the BN starts a deliberation, for instance to build a plan, the plan is emotionally evaluated as it is built (the emotional evaluations from the past experiences). Thus, In CELTS, the emotions play an important role in the action selection[1].

Eclectism of methodologies and techniques. Adding emotions to a cognitive architecture generally favors a variety of methodologies and techniques. In the case of CELTS, a probability approach which consists of a mix of the sequential pattern mining rules and the association rules are used to extract the emotional importance of the events[2].

Reactivity. Reader is referred to the Short Route subsection.

Routineness. Through the emotional valence accorded to actions, emotions in CELTS play a role in procedural learning. In CELTS, those behaviors in the BN that have received emotional tags will be executed faster. They also in some cases (e.g. imminent collisions) bypass consciousness altogether. CELTS' BN may also, in certain cases, delete behaviors that are not emotionally important (see [2])

Dichotomy of implicit and explicit. CELTS implements this distinction generally but not all through its emotional mechanism. The implicit influence of emotions occurs when information arrives at WM. Information in WM that receives higher emotional valence will be chosen faster by CELTS' attentional mechanism. For the explicit emotional influence to the CELTS reader is referred to the CELTS' SR of this chapter.

Trial-and-error adaptation. All actions in CELTS, both reactive and reflective, are influenced by emotional valence and can be adapted by ultimately changing the emotional valence accorded to situations in the environment. Successful actions, as judged by the positive emotional valence accord to the outcome, will see their probability of recurring in similar situations augmented; unsuccessful action, as judged by the negative emotional valence accord to the outcome, will see their probability of recurring in similar situations reduced.

Synergistic interaction. There is synergistic interaction between the ascription of emotional valence by the emotional mechanism and conscious processing. The emotional valence accorded to situations in the environment influences all conscious deliberation and, through the evaluation that conscious deliberation confers on the reactive actions taken be CELTS and on the emotional valence accorded to stituations, conscious processing influences the nature (positive or negative) and degree of emotional valence accorded to situations. There is also synergistic interaction between emotional valence and emotional learning, on the one hand, and higher forms of learning (episodic, procedural, causal) on the other.

Bottom-up learning. Emotional valence provide a value function for all learning in CELTS.

Newell's functional criteria:*Rationality.* Emotions play a role both in CELTS' practical rationality (its ability to achieve its goals) and in CELTS' theoretical rationality (deductive and causal reasoning [1]). Emotions make CELTS more ecologically rational since action selection is made according to the prior emotional valences given to the same stream of actions at prior action executions.

Knowledgeable in terms of size. CELTS selective attention filters large amounts of coming sensory data. Emotions play an important role in CELTS' attentional filtering of information [2]. Attention also provides access to appropriate internal resources that allow the agent to select appropriate actions and using emotional valences to the events CELTS learn from vast amounts of data produced during interactions with learners.

Knowledgeable in terms of variety. See Section 3.

Adaptive through learning. All learning is CELTS depends on emotional evaluation of situations.

5 Conclusion

As can be seen from the two analyses, including emotions in CELTS allows the architecture to meet many, though not all, of Sun's desiderata and Newell's criteria. This reflects, we believe, the centrality of emotions in cognition. On this view, emotions are generatively entrenched[24] in human and animal cognition: it is a basic feature of cognition upon which many other are build or depend on. Although many of the desiderata or criteria can be met without emotions, emotions may be a particularly effective way to get many of the design features they promote.

References

1. Faghihi, U.: The use of emotions in the implementation of various types of learning in a cognitive agent. In: Computer Science. UQAM, Montreal (2011)
2. Faghihi, U., Poirier, P., Fournier-Viger, P., Nkambou, R.: Human-Like Learning in a Conscious Agent. J. Exp. and Theor. Artificial Intelligence, 1–32 (2011)
3. Adam, C.: Emotions: From psychological theories to logical formalization and implementation in a BDI agent. INP, Toulouse, France (2007)
4. Marsella, S., Gratch, J., Petta, P.: Computational Models of Emotion. In: Scherer, K.R., Bnziger, T., Roesch, E. (eds.) A Blueprint for an Affectively Competent Agent. Oxford Univ. Press, Oxford (in press)
5. Velasquez, J.: Modeling Emotions and Other Motivations in Synthetic Agents. AAAI, Menlo Park (1997)
6. Calvo, R.A., D'Mello, S.K.: New Perspectives on Affect and Learning Technologies. Springer, NY (in press)
7. Batson, C.D., Shaw, L.L., Oleson, K.C.: Differentiating Affect, Mood and Emotion. Sage, Newbury Park (1992)
8. Laird, J.E., Newell, A., Rosenbloom, P.S.: Soar 33, 1–64 (1987)
9. Anderson, J.R., Bothell, D., Byrne, M.D., Douglass, S., Lebiere, C., Qin, Y.: An integrated theory of the mind. Psychological Review 111(4), 1036–1060 (2004)
10. Sun, R.: Desiderata for cognitive architectures. Philosoph. Psych. 3, 341–373 (2004)
11. Anderson, J.R., Lebiere, C.: The Atomic Components of Thought. LEA, Mahwah (1998)
12. Calabretta, R., Nolfi, S., Parisi, D., Wagner, G.P.: A case study of the evolution of modularity. In: Proceedings of the Sixth International Conference on Artificial Life, pp. 275–284. MIT Press, Cambridge (1998)
13. Adolphs R, Tranel, D., Damasio, A.: The human amygdala in social judgment. Nature 393(6684) (1998)
14. Phelps, E.A.: Emotion and Cognition. Ann. Rev. of Psy. 57, 27–53 (2006)
15. Picard, W.R.: Affective Computing-Challenges. J. of Human-Computer Studies 59 (2003)
16. Baars, B.J.: In the Theater of Consciousness. Oxford Univ. Press, Oxford (1997)
17. Maes, P.: How to do the right thing. Connection Science 1, 291–323 (1989)
18. LeDoux, J.E.: Emotion circuits in the brain. Annu. Rev. Neurosci. 23 (2000)
19. Cannon, W.: The James-Lange theory of emotion. Am. J. Psychol. 39, 106–124 (1927)
20. Lazarus, R.: Emotion and Adaptation. Oxford University Press, NY (1991)
21. Lindquist, K.A., Wager, T.D., Kober, H., Bliss-Moreau, E., Barrett, L.F.: The brain basis of emotion. In: Behavioral and Brain Sciences. Cambridge University Press, New York (in press)
22. Evans, J.S.B., Frankish, K.: In two minds. Oxford Univ. Press, Cambridge (2009)
23. Franklin, S.: A Cognitive Theory of Everything. In: AGIRI (2006)
24. Wimsatt, W.C.: Developmental Constraints, Generative Entrenchment, and the Innate-Acquired Distinction. In: Integrating Scientific Disciplines, pp. 185–208 (1986)

Kalman Filter-Based Facial Emotional Expression Recognition

Ping Fan[1], Isabel Gonzalez[1], Valentin Enescu[1], Hichem Sahli[1,2], and Dongmei Jiang[3]

VUB-NPU Joint Research Group on AVSP
[1]Vrije Universiteit Brussel, AVSP, Department ETRO; VUB-ETRO, Pleinlaan 2, 1050 Brussels, Belgium
[2] Interuniversity Microelectronics Centre - IMEC, Leuven, Belgium
[3] Shaanxi Provincial Key Laboratory on Speech, Image and Information Processing, Xi'an, China
{pfan,igonzalez,Venescu,hichem.sahli}@etro.vub.ac.be, jiangdm@nwpu.edu.cn
http://www.etro.vub.ac.be/

Abstract. In this work we examine the use of State-Space Models to model the temporal information of dynamic facial expressions. The later being represented by the 3D animation parameters which are recovered using 3D Candide model. The 3D animation parameters of an image sequence can be seen as the observation of a stochastic process which can be modeled by a linear State-Space Model, the Kalman Filter. In the proposed approach each emotion is represented by a Kalman Filter, with parameters being State Transition matrix, Observation matrix, State and Observation noise covariance matrices. Person-independent experimental results have proved the validity and the good generalization ability of the proposed approach for emotional facial expression recognition. Moreover, compared to the state-of-the-art techniques, the proposed system yields significant improvements in recognizing facial expressions.

Keywords: State-space model, Kalman Filter, Hidden States, Emotion Recognition.

1 Introduction

Most of the existing systems for facial emotional expression analysis are based on two-dimensional spatial or spatiotemporal facial features [16]. The former methods [3] use features extracted from a single image to classify the observed expression, while the latter approaches infer the emotion class label of a given frame considering the previous frames [2], or the emotion class label of the full sequence considering the features of all the frames in the sequence [5,21].

Recently, more attention has been put on modeling dynamical facial expressions beyond static image templates. This is mainly due to the fact that the differences between facial expressions are often conveyed more powerfully by dynamic transitions between different stages of an emotion rather than any single state represented by a static (key) frame. Among these works, we can cite

S. D´Mello et al. (Eds.): ACII 2011, Part I, LNCS 6974, pp. 497–506, 2011.

Dornaik et al. [4] who applied Principle Component Analysis(PCA) and Linear Discriminant Analysis(LDA) on high dimensional features to represent an emotion class with low dimensional features; the classification of a given sequence is then done using K-Nearest algorithm. A Bayesian Inference framework has been formulated in [2] to capture the dynamic facial expression transition. Hidden Markov Models (HMMs), have also been used for dynamic facial expression recognition. Both discrete HMMs [24,21], and continuous HMMs [15], have been proposed considering the temporal information both in the training process as well as in the recognition phase. Indeed, since the display of a certain facial expression in video is represented by a temporal sequence of facial motions it is natural to model each expression using an HMM trained for that particular type of expression. HMM uses transition probabilities between the hidden states and learns the conditional probabilities of the observations, in this case the facial motion, given the state of the model. Despite their use, defining the structure and the number of hidden states of such models are still open questions. Thus the assumed number of discrete hidden states, or the vector quantization of continuous features will make the transition on the observation space jump.

Given the temporal nature of facial expressions, and their smoothness and continuous characteristics, in this work we consider using Linear State-Space Models to recognize emotional facial expressions. Kalman Filter is widely used in engineering for combining an inexact forecast of a system's state with an inexact measurement of the state. It provides optimal estimates of the hidden state of any process than can be modeled as a linear dynamic system. The standard Kalman filter is widely used in computer vision in tracking applications, however, most of these approaches have used hard-coded dynamic models inferred from a priori knowledge of the considered task. In this work we propose methods for learning the dynamic model of the observed facial expression. In contrast to HMM, with discrete state space, in Linear Dynamical Systems the state variable vector is real-valued; furthermore, the Kalman filter model is linear with Gaussian noise. Compared to HMM, rather limited state transitions (continuity constraints) are used, but real-valued state vector. Moreover all ARMA models can be written as state space models and non-stationary models (time-varying ARMA) are also state space models, which makes interesting the use of Kalman Filter for facial expression recognition.

The remainder of the paper is structured as follows. Section 2 gives an overview of the used feature extraction approach. In Section 3 we introduce the proposed Linear State-Space model for facial expression recognition and discuss its parameter estimation. In Section 4, the experimental results and the performance of the method are illustrated using the Cohn-Kanade database [12]. Finally in Section 5 we conclude with a discussion of the merits of the proposed approach.

2 Facial Features for Emotion Recognition

In our study, we use the 3D Candide face model [1], formulated as:

$$\mathbf{g}(\boldsymbol{\sigma}, \boldsymbol{\alpha}) = \bar{g} + \mathbf{S}\boldsymbol{\sigma} + \mathbf{A}\boldsymbol{\alpha} \tag{1}$$

where the current face shape $\mathbf{g} = (x_1, y_1, z_1, \ldots, x_N, y_N, z_N)$ and the mean shape $\bar{g} = (\bar{x}_1, \bar{y}_1, \bar{z}_1, \ldots, \bar{x}_N, \bar{y}_N, \bar{z}_N)$ are the (X, Y, Z) coordinates of all vertices in the object coordinate system, respectively; the columns of $\mathbf{S}$ are the Shape Unit Vectors (SUV) and those of $\mathbf{A}$ the Animation Unit Vectors (AUV); the column vectors $\boldsymbol{\sigma}$ and $\boldsymbol{\alpha}$ contain the shape and animation parameters. The values in $\bar{g}$, $\mathbf{S}$ and $\mathbf{A}$ are defined in [1]. Each AUV(SUV) is a column vector combining the displacements of the (X, Y, Z) coordinates of all vertices. The shape parameters describe the overall 3D face shape difference among persons, while the animation parameters describe the local facial expression within one person. In the current work, we have chosen to use all the 11 animation parameters defined in the Candide [1] model, accounting for the following Action Units, AU10 - upper lip raiser, AU26/27 - jaw drop, AU20 - lip stretcher, AU4 - brow lower, AU13/15 - lip corner depressor, AU2 - outer brow raiser, AU42 - eyes closed, AU7 - lid tightener, AU9 - nose wrinkler, AU23/24 - lip pressor, and AU5 - upper lid raiser. These AUs cover most common non-rigid facial motions (eye, eyebrow and mouth movements) conveying expressions.

Given an image sequence, the 11 animation parameters (vector $\boldsymbol{\alpha}(t)$), are recovered, for each frame t , by estimating the optimal alignment between the project 3D Candide model and a 2D shape model (2D feature location) [14], through the optimization of the following equation [9]:

$$\sum_{i=1}^{M} \|\mathbf{u}_i(\mathbf{c}(t)) - \hat{\mathbf{u}}_i(t)\|^2 + \lambda_\alpha \|(\boldsymbol{\alpha}(t) - \boldsymbol{\alpha}(t-1))\|^2 \tag{2}$$

where, λ_α is a regularization parameter set empirically; M the number of considered facial points; $\hat{\mathbf{u}}_i(t)$ is the ith 2D shape point; $\mathbf{u}_i(\mathbf{c}(t))$ is the projection of the ith vertex of the 3D Candide. The projected 3D Candide is given by:

$$\mathbf{u}(\mathbf{c}(t)) = P[\mathbb{R}(\bar{\mathbf{g}} + \mathbf{S}\boldsymbol{\sigma} + \mathbf{A}\boldsymbol{\alpha}) + \mathbf{T}; 1/f] \tag{3}$$

with, P the perspective projection operator; f the camera focal length; $\mathbb{R}$ the $3M \times 3M$ block-diagonal 'rotation' matrix; $\mathbf{T}$ the $3M \times 1$ 'translation' vector [9].

Fig.1 illustrates the variation trends of the animation units of the sequence '010' from the Cohn-Kanade database [12]. Fig.2 2 depicts the shape model of the last frame of the sequence, and Fig.3 demonstrates the fitting of the 3D Candide model using equation 2 and the shape model of Fig.2.

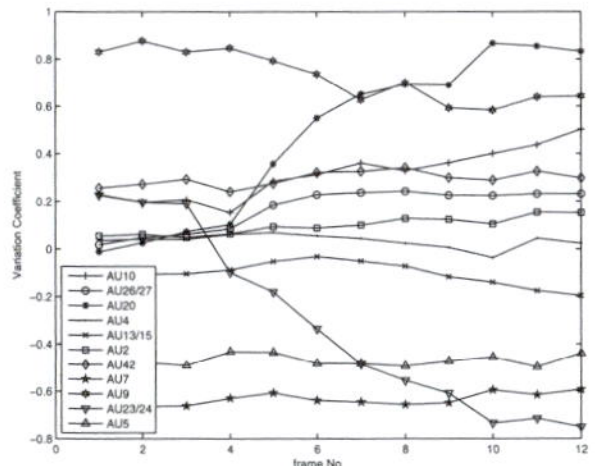

Fig. 1. The 11 facial animation parameters

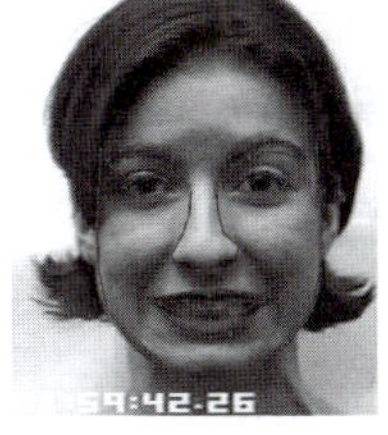

Fig. 2. Shape model

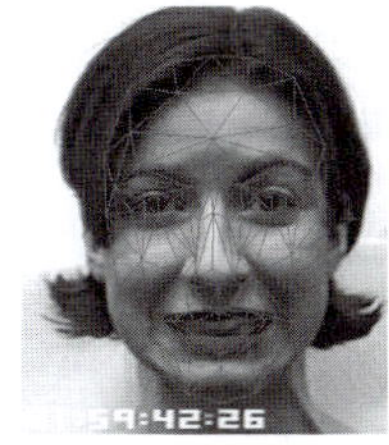

Fig. 3. 3D Candide model

With the idea of inferring the facial expression currently visible from the movement of the face landmarks, the use of a 3D model to estimate the motion parameters as observation, has been designed with the work of Ekman and Friesen [6] in mind. Indeed, the Facial Action Coding System (FACS) [6] describes the muscle activities within a human face. FACS is performed by human observers using stop-motion video, there are clearly defined relationships between FACS and the underlying facial muscles. Action Units (AUs) denote the motion of particular facial parts and state the facial muscles involved. Facial actions are defined by the image changes they produce in video sequences of face images. The 3D Candide model allows inferring information with the deformation parameters $(\boldsymbol{\sigma}, \boldsymbol{\alpha})$ which describe better the constitution of the visible face and the position of the landmarks. Although Candide was developed for the purpose of model-based image coding and facial animation, it exhibit many desirable properties. First, for 3D tracking where the predefined depth and geometrical deformations are used for efficient detection and tracking [9]. Second, for facial expression recognition, where the shape parameters, $\boldsymbol{\sigma}$, are invariant overtime, but specific to each individual, and the animation parameters, $\boldsymbol{\alpha}$, naturally vary over time to describe nonrigid facial animations of different expressions. We, therefore consider $\boldsymbol{\alpha}$ to provide high-level information to the facial expression interpretation process.

3 State-Space Model For Emotion Recognition

3.1 Model Overview

The facial expression recognition could be formulated as follows: we are observing a stochastic process Z_t, defined as the facial animation parameters $\boldsymbol{\alpha}(t)$, based on this process, we wish estimating another stochastic process, Y_t, the facial expression. To model continuous Y_t variables (hidden state), such as the facial expressions, linear State-Space models, i.e. Kalman Filters, are considered in this work.

Formally, let a sequence of T facial images, given by the observations

$$\{Z_1, \ldots, Z_t, \ldots, Z_T\} \triangleq \{\boldsymbol{\alpha}(1), \ldots, \boldsymbol{\alpha}(t), \ldots, \boldsymbol{\alpha}(T)\}$$

Under the state-space model, each D-dimensional observation Z_t is assumed to be a linear projection of a low-dimensional state vector, Y_t, of dimension d. The observed Z_t are corrupted with zero-mean Gaussian noise with covariance matrix R, yielding

$$Z_t = HY_t + v_t \tag{4}$$

where, H is the observation matrix; v_t is zero-mean Gaussian output noise with the covariance R. The temporal evolution of Y_t is modelled by the first-order time-series, or autoregressive (AR) model

$$Y_t = FY_{t-1} + w_t \tag{5}$$

where, Y_t is the hidden state, F is the state transition matrix and w_t a zero-mean Gaussian noise in the emotion dynamics with the covariance Q.

Finally, the initial hidden state Y_1 is assumed as a Gaussian distribution: $Y_1 \sim \mathcal{N}(\mu_1, \Sigma_1)$, where, μ_1 is the mean, and Σ_1 is its covariance.

Kalman Filter defines a probability density over time series of real-valued observation vectors $Z_{1:T} \triangleq \{Z_1, \ldots, Z_t, \ldots, Z_T\}$ by assuming that the observations were generated from a sequence of hidden state vectors $Y_{1:T} \triangleq \{Y_1, \ldots, Y_t, \ldots, Y_T\}$. Given the hidden state vector at one time, the observation vector at that time is statistically independent from all other observation, and the hidden states obey the Markov independence property. Then, considering an emotion class c, its observation $Z_{1:T}$ and considering the presence of the hidden variables $Y_{1:T}$, the joint probability $P(Y_{1:T}, Z_{1:T}|Z_{1:T}, c)$ is factored as [8]:

$$P(Y_{1:T}, Z_{1:T}|Z_{1:T}, c) = P(Y_1)P(Z_1|Y_1)\prod_{t=2}^{T} P(Y_t|Y_{t-1})P(Z_t|Y_t) \tag{6}$$

The probabilities in equation 6 can be derived as follows. From the statistical point of view, Eq.(4) means that $P(Z_t|Y_t)$ is a Gaussian distribution:

$$P(Z_t|Y_t) = \frac{\exp\{-\frac{1}{2}[Z_t - HY_t]'R^{-1}[Z_t - HY_t]\}}{(2\pi)^{\frac{D}{2}}|R|^{\frac{1}{2}}} \tag{7}$$

and, Eq.(5) means that $P(Y_t|Y_{t-1})$ is a Gaussian distribution:

$$P(Y_t|Y_{t-1}) = \frac{\exp\{-\frac{1}{2}[Y_t - FY_{t-1}]'Q^{-1}[Y_t - FY_{t-1}]\}}{(2\pi)^{\frac{d}{2}}|Q|^{\frac{1}{2}}} \tag{8}$$

In summary, the model from which a given facial emotional expression c is drawn will be represented by the parameters $\theta_c = (F, Q, H, R, \mu_1, \Sigma_1)_c$, where H, R model the sequence (emotion) appearance and F, Q its dynamics. A sequence such as $[Z_1, \ldots, Z_t, \ldots, Z_T]$ which is generated from the model is referred to as a realization of the model.

3.2 Emotion Recognition

The facial emotional expression recognition problem is formulated here as follows: given the probe image sequence of features $Z_{1:t}$, the emotion label of frame t is determined by the joint probability $P(Y_{1:t}, Z_{1:t}|Z_{1:t}, c)$. The joint probability $(Y_{1:t}, Z_{1:t}|c)$ is the decision boundaries in statistical pattern recognition which describes the similarity between the testing sequence and the emotion described by the parameters $(F, Q, H, R, \mu_1, \Sigma_1)_c$ of the Kalman Filter of the emotional expression c. Then the emotion of the sequence is recognized as:

$$X_t = \arg\max_c \log P(Y_{1:t}, Z_{1:t}|Z_{1:t}, c) \tag{9}$$

where, X_t is the emotion label of frame t. In this work, we consider recognizing the facial emotional expression displayed by a complete image sequence. Let T the number of frames of a sequence, the facial expression of the sequence is decided by the maximum log joint probability $\log P(Y_{1:T}, Z_{1:T}|Z_{1:T}, c)$. Combining

Eq.(7) and Eq.(8), the recognition is formulated as follows [7]:

$$
\begin{aligned}
X_T &= \arg \max_{c=1,\dots,C} \log P(Y_{1:T}, Z_{1:T}|Z_{1:T}, c) \\
&= \arg \max_{c=1,\dots,C} \log p(Y_1) \prod_{t=2}^{T} p(Y_t|Y_{t-1}) \prod_{t=1}^{T} p(Z_t|Y_t) \\
&= \arg \max_{c=1,\dots,C} \left\{ -\frac{1}{2} \log |\Sigma_1| - \frac{1}{2}(Y_1 - \mu_1)' \Sigma_1^{-1} (Y_1 - \mu_1) \right. \\
&- \frac{T-1}{2} \log |Q| - \sum_{t=2}^{T} \left(\frac{1}{2}(Y_t - FY_{t-1})' Q^{-1} (Y_t - FY_{t-1}) \right) - \frac{T}{2} \log |R| \\
&\left. - \sum_{t=1}^{T} \left(\frac{1}{2}(Z_t - HY_t)' R^{-1} (Z_t - HY_t) \right) - \frac{T(D+d)}{2} \log 2\pi \right\}
\end{aligned} \tag{10}
$$

3.3 Model Parameters Estimation

The state transition, F, and the measurements matrix, H, used by Kalman Filter together encode an internal model of the observed facial expression dynamics of a given expression, c, which should be learned. Three issues should be considered when using Kalman Filter for learning and recognition, (i) the first issue concerns the convergence of the overall learning scheme, in this work we use the Expectation-Maximization (EM) algorithm to learn the Kalman model $\{F, Q, H, R, \mu_1, \Sigma_1\}$ from observed data (image sequences of facial expressions), (ii) the second issue is the initialization of the iterative learning process, in this work we adopt the factor analysis approach of [18], (iii) the third issue is the dimension of the hidden state. Indeed most of the approaches using Kalman Filter define the state using a priori knowledge, in this paper the dimension of the hidden state will be decided upon best recognition results.

Parameters Estimation. We follow the EM algorithm of [17] and [7] to estimated the parameters $\{F, Q, H, R, \mu_1, \Sigma_1\}$ of each emotion c. The E step of EM requires computing the expected log joint probability Eq.(6) over the whole image sequence from frame 1 till frame T. This quantity depends on three expectation: $\hat{Y}_{t|T} \triangleq E[Y_t|Z_{1:T}]$, $P_{t|T} \triangleq E[Y_t Y_t'|Z_{1:T}]$ and $P_{t,t-1|T} \triangleq E[Y_t Y_{t-1}|Z_{1:T}]$ which are estimated using the filtering and the smoothing processes of Kalman Filter. Next, the M-step maximize the expected joint probability $P(Y_{1:T}, Z_{1:T})$ based on the training data the filtering and the smoothing processes of Kalman Filter.

Model Parameters Initialization. It is well known that the initial values of $\{F, Q, H, R, \mu_1, \Sigma_1\}$ affect the final parameters estimated by the EM algorithm. However, there is no generalized way in how to give the best initialization. Here we adopt the factor analysis, trained on the observation data as proposed by Roweis et al. in [18]. As EM for factor analysis has been criticized for being quite slow [19], we applied the MATLAB standard function *factoran* for fitting a factor analysis model [11], which is based on a quasi-Newton optimization algorithm.

Hidden State Dimension. One must note that the dimension of the hidden state is assumed to be known when the state-space model parameters are estimated . In some scenarios, we know exactly the meaning and the components of the hidden state. For example, in tracking applications the hidden states may be the location, velocity or pose of an object. However, in our case we do not have such knowledge, and as discussed by Rene Vidal [22], in the lack of assumptions on the model generating the data there are infinitely many models that produce the same observation. In our implementation the dimension $\hat{d}$ of the state vector is deiced by estimating the parameters $\{F, Q, H, R, \mu_1, \Sigma_1\}$ for various dimensions $d \in [1, D]$ of the hidden state, and then selecting the dimension which provides the best recognition rate.

4 Experiment Results and Evaluation

4.1 Material

The performance of the proposed facial emotional expression has been quantitatively evaluated using the Cohn-Kanade database[12], from which we selected 380 image sequences from the 97 subjects recoded. We then selected as balanced training of 198 sequences consisting of 36 happy sequences, 36 surprise, 32 fear, 29 angry, 35 sad and 30 disgust. The 192 other sequences are used as the testing set, in which 31.8% happy sequences, 25.6% surprise, 14.1% fear, 4.2% angry, 18.2% sad and 6.3% disgust. To achieve person-independent evaluation as well as the assessment of the generalization ability of the proposed approach, the selected subjects for testing are different from the ones used in the training set.

4.2 Dimensionality of the Facial Emotional Expression Hidden States

To select the dimension of the hidden state, the average Information Score (IS) [13], I_a, has been used. The information score of an instance is defined as [13]:

$$I = \begin{cases} -\log P(A) + \log P'(A) & if P'(A) \geq P(A) \\ -\log(1 - P(A)) + \log(1 - P'(A)) & if P(A) < P'(A) \end{cases}$$

with $P(A)$ the prior probability of class A and $P'(A)$ the posterior probability returned by the classifier. The average information score I_a over the test set of N sequences is given by:

$$I_a = \frac{1}{N} \sum_{j=1}^{N} I(j).$$

Fig. 4 depicts the Information Score versus the number of components of the hidden states. As it can be noticed, the best recognition results are obtained using hidden states with 3 components, the second best recognition results are obtained with 5 components.

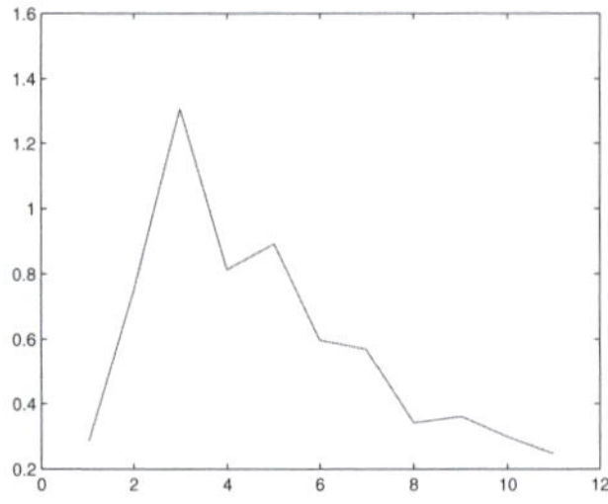

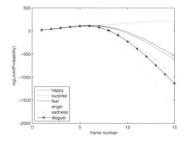

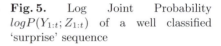

Fig. 4. Information Score versus hidden state dimension

Fig. 5. Log Joint Probability $logP(Y_{1:t}; Z_{1:t})$ of a well classified 'surprise' sequence

For further assessing the proposed approach, we selected $\hat{d} = 3$ as dimension of the hidden state. This choice is justified by the arousal, valence and dominance emotion model proposed by some psychologists [20], and also for the purpose of comparison to state of art methods where Hu et. al [10], decreased the 90 facial landmarks of each image into 3 dimensional feature using Isomap; and Buenaposada et al. [2] transformed the 27-dimensional features into 3 dimension.

4.3 Recognition Performance

Using the estimated facial emotional expression models $\{F, Q, H, R, \mu_1, \Sigma_1\}_c, c \in \{happy, surprise, fear, angry, sad, disgust\}$ using the approach of Section 3, Fig. 5 illustrates the evolution of the log joint probabilities, Eq. (6), given the observation of a testing sequence depicting surprise expression (sequence '052_001' of the Cohn-Kanade database). As it can be seen, the joint probability using the surprise emotion model rises with the frame number, while the joint probability under the other emotion models fall. Hence, using Eq. 10, the sequence is classified as surprise. Considering the full testing set, Table 1 gives the confusion matrix of the obtained recognition results. The overall recognition accuracy is 93.7%.

Table 1. The confusion matrix of Facial Emotional Expression recognition results based on Kalman Filter

	happy	surprise	fear	angry	sad	disgust
happy	95.0%	0%	4.9%	0%	0%	0%
surprise	2.0%	97.9%	0%	0%	0%	0%
fear	3.7%	0%	96.2%	0%	0%	0%
angry	0%	12.5%	0%	75.0%	12.5%	0%
sad	0%	8.5%	2.8%	0%	88.5%	0%
disgust	0%	0%	0%	8.3%	0%	91.6%

Table 2. Comparison to state-of-art methods

Ref	(1)	(2)	(3)	(4)	(5)
happy	95.0%	88.5%	85.2%	98.8%	96.6%
surprise	97.9%	97.9%	97.9%	100%	100%
fear	96.2%	100%	81.4%	73.9%	76.4%
angry	75.0%	62.5%	75.0%	78.4%	100%
sad	88.5%	68.5%	65.7%	82.0%	96.2%
disgust	91.6%	91.6%	100%	87.9%	62.5%
overall	93.7%	88.0%	84.9%	89.1%	90.9%

Finally, we compared our results to the ones reported in [23] and [2]. Both used the Cohn-Kanade database, however with different training and testing sets as the ones we defined. For the purpose of producing effective comparison, we implemented the above two methods using the features as described in section 2, and for the training and testing sets as defined in section 4.1. The comparison is shown in Table 2, where (1) denotes our proposed approach, (2) our implementation of the method in [2], (3) our implementation of the method in [23] using a 3-state HMM, (4) the results reported in [2], and (5) the results reported in [23].

From Table 2, we can conclude that the performance of our emotion recognition with State-Space model gives compraable or slightly better performance than state of art methods. Moreover, the facial features we choose are also good for emotion recognition.

5 Conclusion and Discussion

In this work we proposed Kalman Filter to model and recognize facial emotional expressions. Moreover, we suggested using the EM algorithm for learning the dynamics of facial expressions, by estimating the Kalman Filter parameters, being the State Transition matrix, Observation Matrix, State and Observation noise covariance matrices. To our knowledge, this is the first work which uses Kalman Filter for facial expression recognition. We demonstrated the reliability of the approach by comparing it to state-of-art methods. Future work should consider spontaneous facial emotional expression recognition using switching Kalman Filter for iteratively segmenting the input sequences into regimes (expressions) with approximately linear dynamics and learns the parameters of each of these linear regimes.

Acknowledgments. The research reported in this paper was supported by he CSC-VUB scholarship (grant [2006]6058), the VUB projects HOA8 (Study of Mother-baby Interaction) and HOA26 (Toward Cognitive Adaptive Edu-games), and the EU FP7 project ALIZ-E (grant 248116).

The authors gratefully acknowledge the support of Sam Roweis and Zoubin Ghahramani in providing source codes.

References

1. Ahlberg, J.: Candide-3 - an updated parameterised face (January 2001)
2. Buenaposada, J.M., Muñoz, E., Baumela, L.: Recognising facial expressions in video sequences. Pattern Analysis and Applications 11(1), 101–116 (2007)
3. Cohen, I., Sebe, N., Garg, A., Chen, L.S., Huang, T.S.: Facial expression recognition from video sequences: temporal and static modeling. Computer Vision and Image Understanding: CVIU 91(1-2), 160–187 (2003)
4. Dornaika, F., Davoine, F.: Facial expression recognition in continuous videos using linear discriminant analysis. In: MVA, pp. 277–280 (2005)
5. Dornaika, F., Raducanu, B.: Recognizing facial expressions in videos using a facial action analysis-synthesis scheme. In: AVSS, p. 8. IEEE Computer Society, Los Alamitos (2006)

6. Ekman, P., Friesen, W.: Facial Action Coding System: A Technique for the Measurement of Facial Movement. Consulting Psychologists Press, Palo Alto (1978)
7. Ghahramani, Z., Hinton, G.E.: Parameter estimation for linear dynamical systems. Technical Report (Short Note) CRG-TR-96-2, Department of Computer Science, University of Toronto (February 1996)
8. Ghahramani, Z., Hinton, G.E.: Variational learning for switching state-space models. Neural Computation 12(4), 831–864 (2000)
9. Hou, Y., Fan, P., Ravyse, I., Sahli, H.: 3d face alignment via cascade 2d shape alignment and constrained structure from motion. In: Blanc-Talon, J., Philips, W., Popescu, D.C., Scheunders, P. (eds.) ACIVS 2009. LNCS, vol. 5807, pp. 550–561. Springer, Heidelberg (2009)
10. Hu, C., Chang, Y., Feris, R., Turk, M.: Manifold based analysis of facial expression. In: CVPR Workshop on Face Processing in Video (2004)
11. Jöreskog, K.G.: Some contributions to maximum likelihood factor analysis. Psychometrika 32(4), 443–482 (1967)
12. Kanade, T., Cohn, J.F., Tian, Y.L.: Comprehensive database for facial expression analysis. In: FG, pp. 46–53 (2000)
13. Kononenko, I., Bratko, I.: Information-based evaluation criterion for classifier's performance. Machine Learning 6, 67–80 (1991)
14. Liang, L., Wen, F., Xu, Y., Tang, X., Shum, H.Y.: Accurate face alignment using shape constrained markov network. In: Proceedings of IEEE Conference on Computer Vision and Pattern Recognition, vol. 1, pp. 1313–1319 (2006)
15. Otsuka, T., Ohya, J.: Recognition of facial expressions using hmm with continuous output probabilities. In: 5th IEEE International Workshop on Robot and Human Communication, 1996, pp. 323–328 (November 1996)
16. Pantic, M.: Machine analysis of facial behaviour: Naturalistic and dynamic behaviour. Philosophical Transactions of the Royal Society B: Biological Sciences 364(1535), 3505 (2009)
17. Rosenbaum, T., Zetlin-Jones, A.: The kalman filter and the em algorithm (December 2006)
18. Roweis, S., Ghahramani, Z.: An em algorithm for identification of nonlinear dynamical systems (June 2000)
19. Rubin, D.B., Thayer, D.T.: Em algorithms for ml factor analysis. Psychometrika 47(1), 69–76 (1982)
20. Russel, J.A.: A circumplex model of affect. Journal of Personality and Social Psychology 39(6), 1161–1178 (1980)
21. Uddin, M., Lee, J., Kim, T.: An enhanced independent component-based human facial expression recognition from video. IEEE Transactions on Consumer Electronics 55(4), 2216–2224 (2009)
22. Vidal, R., Chiuso, A., Soatto, S.: Observability and identifiability of jump linear systems (August 2002)
23. Yeasin, M., Bullot, B., Sharma, R.: From facial expression to level of interest: A spatio-temporal approach. In: CVPR (2), pp. 922–927 (2004)
24. Zhu, Y., de Silva, L.C., Ko, C.C.: Using moment invariants and hmm in facial expression recognition. Pattern Recognition Letters 23(1-3), 83–91 (2002)

SARA: Social Affective Relational Agent: A Study on the Role of Empathy in Artificial Social Agents

Sandra Gama, Gabriel Barata, Daniel Gonçalves, Rui Prada, and Ana Paiva

INESC-ID and Instituto Superior Técnico, Technical University of Lisbon, Av. Rovisco Pais, 49, 1050-001 Lisboa, Portugal
{sandra.gama,gabriel.barata}@ist.utl.pt
{daniel.goncalves,rui.prada,ana.paiva}@inesc-id.pt

Abstract. Over the last decade extensive research has been conducted in the area of conversational agents focusing in many different aspects of these agents. In this research, and aiming at building agents that maintain a social connection with users, empathy has been one of those areas, as it plays a leading role in the establishment of social relationships. In this paper we present a relationship model of empathy that takes advantage of Social Penetration Theory's concepts for relationship building. This model has been implemented into an agent that attempts to establish a relationship with the user, expressing empathy both verbally and visually. The visual expression of empathy consists of facial expression and physical proximity representation. The user tests performed showed that while users were able to develop a simple relationship with the agents, they however developed stronger relationships with a version of the agent that is most visually expressive and takes advantage of the proximity element, confirming the significance of our model based on social penetration theory may have and, consequently, the importance of the visual representation of empathic responses.

Keywords: Affective computing, empathic agent, conversational agent, social penetration.

1 Introduction

Empathy plays an important role in the creation of relationships among people and even other species. As such, if we aim at establishing rich relationships with conversational agents we must address that issue. In fact, providing conversational agents with empathic behaviours has proven not only to increase their believability but also enhance their capabilities in building social-emotional relationships with users. It has been shown in [3] that the implementation of empathy in virtual agents enhances cooperation in different contexts, such as counseling and helping, as well as for educational purposes.

But, capturing empathic processes in conversational artificial agents should go beyond the spoken or written dialogues, by taking advantages of other interaction

S. D'Mello et al. (Eds.): ACII 2011, Part I, LNCS 6974, pp. 507–516, 2011.

modalities, such as visual, facial and body expressions. Furthermore, empathy is mediated by many factors, such as similarity, personality or even physical proximity. As such, models of empathy for conversational agents need to take into account some of these factors in order to make the interaction richer and more meaningful.

In that context, we have designed and empathic agent that expresses both emotions and closeness by the use of facial expressions and face proximity, respectively. It also expresses empathy through verbal dialogue. The model takes into account the Social Penetration Theory [1] when building a social relationship between the agent and the user. The main goal of this investigation was to study the role of the visual expression of empathy in the development of a relationship between the user and a conversational agent. So, our research question focuses on how two factors: physical proximity and emotional expressions, impact in the perception of the empathic behaviour of the agent.

With the developed system we have performed a limited set of user tests in order to understand the impact that the visual expression of empathy has in the creation a relationship between the agent and the user. Furthermore, the user tests were designed to find out the degree of importance of these features by comparing the results of different variations of the agent in which either visual expressions of empathy was fully depicted, only facial expression was shown, only closeness was represented or neither visual empathic cues were present. The tests used a standard friendship questionnaire, and the results showed that the presence of the visual elements has a positive impact in some elements found in friendship relations.

This paper is organized as follows. In Section 2 we present some relevant related work that situates our approach in the context of empathic agents. We then present the proposed model and briefly describe the interaction between the user and an agent which implements this model. Finally, we present and discuss the results of user tests that we performed in order to find out the role of the visual representation of empathy in the development of a relationship.

2 Related Work

Conversation plays a leading role in the interaction between users and synthetic characters [6]. As a result, several research studies have been conducted in order to create affective agents that can build relationships with users [2].

In particular, relevant work has been done in the context of the COMPANIONS project [7] [9] [15], in which two virtual companions have been created. The Health and Fitness Companion (HFC) acts as a conversational partner whose overall aim is to build a long-term relationship with the user. Planning the day becomes a compromise between the user and the system. A relationship between the agent and the user is built through dialogue. However, the character acts more as a companion than a personal trainer, since it takes a persistent role in the user's daily life. The second companion agent developed in this project was the Senior Companion (SC), which allows elder people to annotate photographs in order to build up a narrative of their life. Users are allowed to show a friend (the virtual companion) images of their family and friends and the companion prompts users to describe their photos and through conversation the user reminisces about life memories. The information goes through a natural language processing module and is associated with the photographs as annotations. The agent performs face recognition and learns about the user's life, constructing knowledge from it, which contributes to the development of a close relationship.

Another system where the relation between the agent and the user is explored is MAY [6], a conversational companion that implements memory mechanisms in order to create proximity with the user. It is targeted for teenagers and has been created to assist them on self-reflection. The interaction consists of text-based dialogue, and the agent is described as an affective diary, since it reflects the users shared emotional experiences in a timeline form.

Another very interesting agent developed by Bickmore and Picard was LAURA [4], which was integrated on an application (MIT FitTrack) that aimed to motivate users to do physical exercise. The embodied agent supports multiple interactions, contributing to a persistent construction of a relationship. LAURA remembers things about the user's life and refers back to previous interactions. The system's interaction consists entirely of relationship-building dialogue, in which the user selects one of multiple-choice inputs, which are dynamically adapted during each turn of the conversation, while LAURA speaks using synthesized speech. This choice from a set of options can be quite restrictive, because the user is limited to them. In face to face interaction, the emotional display is very important and LAURA has a wide set of non-verbal behaviours associated with the verbal communication, in particular hand gestures, gazing, raising/lowering eyebrows, head nods and walking on and off the screen. These behaviours are automatically generated at compile time. The relational model used in FitTrack considers that initial relations are distant and professional, but gradually become more personal over time. That approach enables a continuous change of behaviour to correspond to user expectations. The user-agent relationship consists of using the relational behaviour, particularly empathy.

More recently, Bickmore et al. [5] have created another agent, Louise, who followed two different approaches to study whether empathic accuracy and user expressivity lead to increasing user-agent social bonds. In the empathic approach, the user is restricted to the way he can express himself, while in the expressive approach users can freely express their feelings conducting to imperfect empathic responses. They concluded that an agent with empathic accuracy is more effective in comforting users, even if their way of expression is restricted.

Bickmore and Picard [4] state that maintaining relationships involves managing expectations, attitudes and intentions. Relationships are supported by emotional interaction and, as such, emotional aspects need to be carefully considered in a companion.

All those systems explore in some way the relation between the user and the agent, exploring somehow the development of more personal relations. Yet none of them adopts any model of social penetration nor explores how such model can be conveyed and perceived by users, which is what we have done.

3 A Model for Empathy Regarding Social Penetration

Our computational model follows a perception-action paradigm and is inspired by the work of Rodrigues et al. [13], which regards empathy as a process, being grounded in the Perception Action Model (PAM) [11] and Vignemont and Singer's research [16]. Our approach consists of the articulation between this model and the Social Penetration Theory [1], which regulates the gradual development of social relationships. According to the Social Penetration Theory, a relationship can go through four stages: (i) Orientation stage; (ii) Exploratory Affective Stage; (iii) Affective Stage; (iv) Stable stage, as depicted in Figure 1. We have adopted this theory to regulate the expression of empathy with the user: it is not until the third stage is achieved that the model allows the agent to perform certain empathic actions, such as comforting and reassuring.

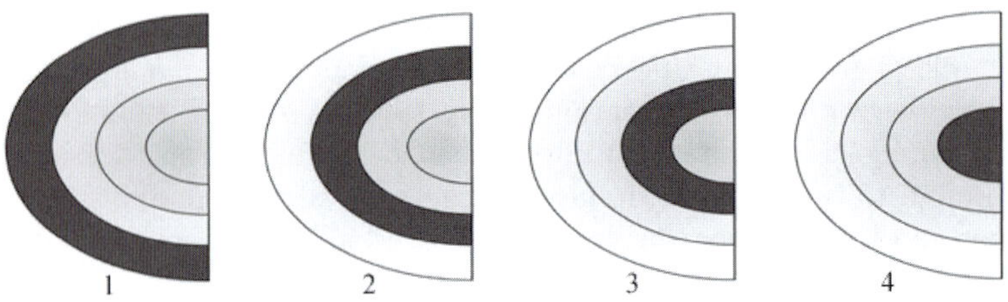

Fig. 1. Social Penetration Theory Stages: (1) Orientation Stage; (2) Exploratory Affective Stage; (3) Affective Stage; (4) Stable Stage

As illustrated in Figure 2, emotion recognition is performed, followed by the generation of an empathic response, depending on the social contextualization of the relationship, congruent with the aforementioned theories. However, while Vignemont and Singer [16] propose several modulation factors, determined by appraisal processes, we perform a social evaluation (based on the Social Penetration Theory) in the two main phases of our model: Empathic Appraisal and Empathic Response.

3.1 Empathic Appraisal

Accordingly with Bickmore et al. [2], even when the user's way of expression is restricted, the agent may be very efficient in comforting users. We have taken advantage of this result by providing the user with four different dialogue options, ranging from uninvolved to warmer responses. Empathic appraisal begins when one option is selected, meaning that the user provided a verbal interaction. This interaction is analyzed through self-projected reasoning, resulting in a potential state of emotion that the agent believes the user to be in. The space

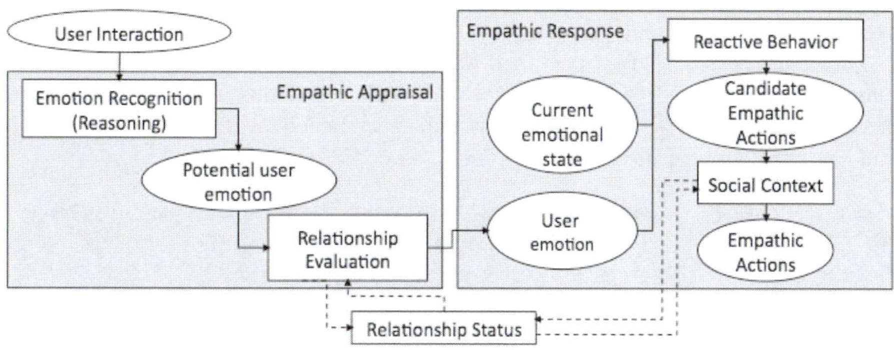

Fig. 2. Model Diagram

of emotions is the same as the agent's: happy, sad, disgusted, angry, surprised, scared, neutral and very happy. The potential user emotion then goes through a social evaluation, which determines whether this emotion is appropriate or not, regarding the relationship's current state of social penetration. As such, the result of Empathic Appraisal is the user's current emotion taking into account both reasoning and social context. For instance, an emotion of strong happiness is more likely to be consistent with more intimate states.

3.2 Empathic Response

The user emotion resulting from Empathic Appraisal is subject to a reactive behaviour which also takes into account the agent's current affective state. Here, potential empathic actions are generated, determing which responses are appropriate given the emotional state of both the agent and the user. However, it is the relationship's intimacy status that determines which actions are most appropriate. As such, a new social evaluation is performed on these candidates, determining the final empathic actions. For instance, when the user's emotion is sadness and the social evaluation allows more intimate actions, not only a close-framed sad face is depicted, but also a verbal comforting emotional reaction is triggered.

Both social evaluation modules perform different tasks - while both are based on the social context, the one on the Empathic Appraisal phase evaluates the user's emotion and the social contextualization on the Empathic Response phase decides which empathic actions are appropriate.

Since relationships are fundamentally social and emotional [2] and people respond to social cues from a computer in the same way that they respond to these cues from other people (even if automatically and unconsciously) [12], one of the most important features of our model is the expression of emotions. In fact, affect leverages the mechanisms of human social cognition, helping to build relationships more naturally [2].

The visual representation of empathy is represented under the form of facial expressions and physical proximity.

Facial Expressions are a powerful way to convey affect [8]. We modelled Ekman and Friessen's [8] six *basic* facial expressions into our agent model: happiness, sadness, surprise, anger, disgust and fear, besides the neutral expression and an expression of increased happiness, as depicted in Fig. 3.

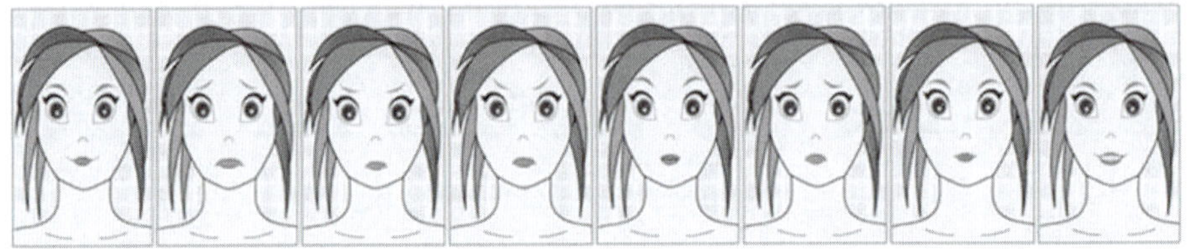

Fig. 3. Facial Expressions (Left to right: happy, sad, disgusted, angry, surprised, scared, neutral and very happy)

Physical Proximity is represented in order to create the feeling of proximity, similarly to Klein et al. [10], who have demonstrated that the use of different proximity frames increases the closeness felt by the user. Furthermore, Bickmore and Picard's research [2] uses 4 conversational frames, with different objectives: a task frame, for task-oriented purposes, a social frame, an empathetic frame and an encouragement frame. We use three different proximity frames (Fig. 4), articulated with the Social Penetration Theory's relationship layers. On less intimate states, the agent is farther, being its body fully shown. As intimacy increases, the face and upper body area are zoomed in. As for more intimate stages, only the face is shown, conveying familiarity.

Fig. 4. Physical Proximity

3.3 User-Agent Interaction

We have implemented an agent that follows our model, capable of interacting through dialogue. At each interaction, the agent recognizes the user's state of emotion through reasoning and social evaluation, The user's emotional state and the current social intimacy status of the relationship are used to generate an empathic response, which is expressed both verbally and visually.

Empathic Actions Example Scenario: Let us consider that the agent and the user have been interacting so that the current social stage is at its innermost, which means that the social evaluation allows the expression of warmer empathic responses and proximity is represented at its maximum. Also, the agent is at a current emotional state of happiness. Regarding the current user-agent intimacy, the agent may ask the user 'Are you alright?'. If the user replies 'I'm not so great today', then the resulting agent's empathic action consists of comforting the user. As such, it shows surprise and replies 'Okay. You know you can trust me if you need to talk about your problems, right?'. This example is illustrated in Fig. 5.

Fig. 5. Empathic Actions Example Scenario

4 Evaluation

In order to test the agent's model, in particular, the Social Penetration Theory's role in the agen'ts capacity to establish a relationship, with focus on the influence of the visual representation of empathy, we performed several user tests.

4.1 Test Scenarios

Given that we have two types of variables to consider (facial expression and proximity), we took into account these two variables and created four versions of the system: **(NP,NE)**: No Proximity, No Expression (control): Both the agent's facial expression and proximity remained constant. The agent was represented both physically distant from the user and showing a neutral facial expression, being thus empathy shown only verbally; **(NP,E)**: No Proximity, Expression: The agent was always represented in the most distant frame but its facial expressions varied. **(P,NE)**: Proximity, No Expression: In this case, proximity frames were used, while facial expressions were not. **(P,E)**: Proximity, Expression: Both proximity frames and facial expressions were used, taking advantage of both forms of visually representing empathy.

4.2 Design and Procedure

Given that the objective was to study the development of social relationships, being friendship a particular type of such relationships, we used an adapted version of the McGill Friendship Questionnaire [14]. The test protocol consisted of a brief presentation of the agent, then allowing users to freely interact with it for at least 10 minutes. Finally, users were asked to fill in a questionnaire, which consisted of a brief set of user profiling questions, followed by the McGill Questionnaire. Since four different control conditions regarding the empathic behaviour have been taken into account, we asked 60 subjects to participate in these tests, 15 per each one of the agent's version, allocated randomly to one of the four conditions. Participants were university students, of different courses and universities, who aged between 18 and 30 years old, of which 52% were female and 48% were male.

4.3 Results

Regarding the visual expression of empathy in the development of a relationship, the general results are depicted in Fig. 6, both for Friendship Functions and Affection. In fact, the combination of facial expressions and physical proximity seems to have a positive impact in building a relationship of friendship, in contrast with the representation of a single visual modality or none. Each part of the questionnaire (Friendship Functions and Affection) was subject to these tests separately.

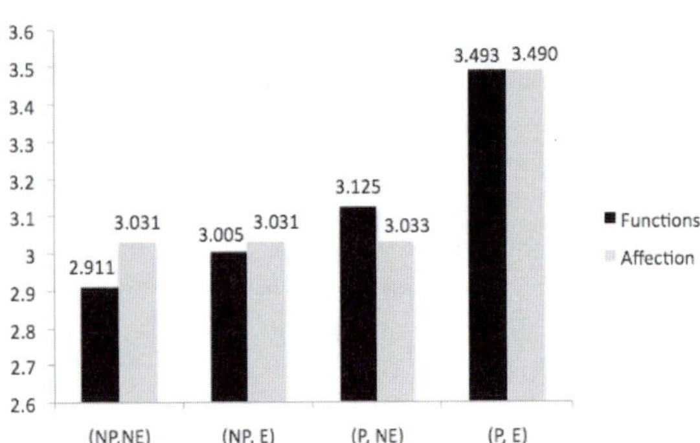

Fig. 6. Average Global Results: Friendship Functions and Affection

A Lilleford Test showed some of the data was non-normal. In fact, for the sets corresponding to the Friendship Functions questionaire, we found no evidence against normality in the second ($L = 0.167, p > 0.1$) and fourth ($L = 0.157, p > 0.1$) sets, yet found evidence against it in the first ($L = 0.204, p < 0.1$) and third sets ($L = 0.229, p < 0.05$). Regarding the Affection questionnaire, we found evidence against normality in the first set ($L = 0.208, p < 0.1$) and signigicant evidence against it in the fourth set ($L = 0.322, p < 0.01$), and no evidence in either the second ($L = 0.118, p > 0.1$) or in the third ($L = 0.143, p > 0.1$).

The fact that some of the data is non-normal suggested the adequateness of a Kruskall-Wallis test to undestand the impact of the visual representation of empathy. We were able to verify that it actually affects significantly Friendship Functions ($H = 10.7, p = 0.0135$), while it also plays an important role in the development of Affection ($H = 6.34, p = 0.0962$).

In order to better understand the impact of the different conditions (combinations of the visual representation of empathy), we performed two sets of Mann-Whitney tests with Bonferroni correction. Each set consisted of the comparrison between each condition (**(NP,E)**, **(P,NE)** and **(P,E)**) and the control group **(NP, NE)**.

Table 1. Mann-Whitney Test Results for Friendship Functions and Affection

Friendship Functions	**(NP,E)** ($Mdn = 2.967$)	**(P,NE)** ($Mdn = 2.900$)	**(P,E)** ($Mdn = 3.367$)
(NP,NE) ($Mdn = 2.700$)	$U = 133.5$ $p = 0.09885$	$U = 147.0$ $p = 0.03965$	$U = 176.5$ $p = 0.00215$
User-Agent Affection	**(NP,E)** ($Mdn = 2.9375$)	**(P,NE)** ($Mdn = 2.9375$)	**(P,E)** ($Mdn = 3.375$)
(NP,NE) ($Mdn = 2.875$)	$U = 115.5$ $p = 0.2301$	$U = 120.5$ $p = 0.18915$	$U = 158.0$ $p = 0.01535$

Concerning Friendship Functions, results have shown that, regarding both Friendship Functions and Affection, **(NP,NE)** does not differ significantly from either **(NP,E)** or **(P,NE)**, while it significantly differs from**(P,E)**.

These results prove the empiric results we had obtained, confirming that the impact of the representation of both facial expression and physical proximity is significant when compared to the presence of only one condition or none of these conditions.

5 Conclusions and Future Work

We have created a model of empathy and implemented it into an agent that expresses empathy through written dialogue and visual cues. One of our main goals was to study and validate the role of the visual expression of empathy in a single interaction with an empathic agent exploring two factors: facial expressions and physical proximity as ways to convey higher states of social affinity.

Evaluation results are encouraging, showing that the visual representation of empathy plays an important role in the creation of a friendship relationship with an artificial agent. It would be interesting, however, to test the model with different agents in order to ascertain whether the agent's appearance has an impact on the results.

Since we have taken into account a single interaction between the user and the agent, it would be interesting to explore the creation and development of a relationship for a series of interactions over time. Being closer to the type of relationships between humans, it would allow us to study the impact of our model in a mid or long-term relationship with a virtual agent.

References

1. Altman, I., Taylor, D.: Social penetration: The development of interpersonal relationships. Holt, New York (1973)
2. Bickmore, T., Picard, R.: Subtle Expressivity by Relational Agents. In: CHI Workshop on Subtle Expressivity for Characters and Robots (2003)
3. Bickmore, T.: Relational Agents: Effecting Change through Human-Computer Relationships Ph.D thesis. MIT, Cambridge, MA (2003)
4. Bickmore, T., Picard, R.: Establishing and Maintaining Long-Term Human-Computer Relationships. In: ACM CHI, pp. 293–327. ACM, New York (2005)
5. Bickmore, T., Schulman, D.: Practical approaches to comforting users with relational agents. In: CHI 2007 Extended Abstracts on Human Factors in Computing Systems, pp. 2291–2296. ACM, New York (2007)
6. Campos, J.: MAY: my Memories Are Yours. An interactive companion that saves the users memories. Master thesis, Instituto Superior Técnico (2010)
7. Cavazza, M., Brewster, C., Charlton, D., Smith, C.: Domain knowledge and multimodal grounding. Technical report, COMPANIONS (2007)
8. Ekman, P., Friesen, W.V.: Manual for the Facial Action Coding System. Consulting Psychologists Press, Palo Alto (1977)
9. Hakulinen, J., Turunen, M., Smith, C., Cavazza, M., Charlton, D.: A model for exible interoperability between dialogue management and do main reasoning for conversational spoken dialogue systems. In: Fourth International Workshop on Human- Compute Conversation, Bellagio, Italy (2008)
10. Klein, J., Moon, Y., Picard, R.: This Computer Responds to User Frustration: Theory, Design, Results, and Implications. Interacting with Computers 14, 119–140 (2002)
11. Preston, S.D., Waal, F.d.: Empathy: Its ultimate and proximate bases. Behavioral and Brain Sciences 25, 1–20 (2001)
12. Reeves, B., Nass, C.: The Media Equation: how people treat computers, televisions and new media like real people and places. Cambridge University Press, Cambridge (1996)
13. Rodrigues, S., Mascarenhas, S., Dias, J., Paiva, A.: I can feel it too! Emergent empathic reactions between synthetic characters. In: 3rd International Conference on Affective Computing and Intelligent Interaction. IEEE, Los Alamitos (2009)
14. Souza, L.K.: Amizade em adultos: adaptação e validação dos questionários McGill e um estudo de diferenças de género. PhD thesis, Universidade Federal do Rio Grande do Sul (2006)
15. Stahl, O., Gamback, B., Hansen, P., Turunen, M., Hakulinen, J.: A mobile tness companion. In: Fourth International Workshop on Human-Computer Conversation, Bellagio, Italy (2008)
16. Vignemont, F.d., Singer, T.: The empathic brain: how, when and why? Trends in Cognitive Sciences 10, 435–444 (2006)

Learning General Preference Models from Physiological Responses in Video Games: How Complex Is It?

Maurizio Garbarino, Simone Tognetti, Matteo Matteucci, and Andrea Bonarini

Politecnico di Milano, IIT Unit, Dipartimento di Elettronica e Informazione,
Piazza Leonardo da Vinci, 32, 20133 Milano, Italy
{garbarino,tognetti,bonarini,matteucci}@elet.polimi.it

Abstract. An affective preference model can be successfully learnt from pairwise comparison of physiological responses. Several approaches to do this obtain different performances. The higher ranked seem to use non linear models and complex feature selection strategies. We present a comparison of three linear and non linear classification methods, combined with a simple and a complex feature selection strategy (sequential forward selection and a genetic algorithm), on two datasets. We apply a strict crossvalidation framework to test the generalization capability of the models when facing physiological data coming from a new user. We show that, when generalization is the goal, complex non-linear models trained using fancy strategies might easily get trapped by overfitting, while linear ones might be preferable. Although this could be expected, the only way to appreciate it has to pass through proper cross-validation, and this is often forgot when rushing in the "best" performance challenge.

Keywords: enjoyment evaluation, physiological signals, feature selection, SFS, neuro evolution, emotion in games, cross validation.

1 Introduction

Learning a general model able to estimate the affective state of a subject from physiological signals is a challenging problem faced by researchers in affective computing. Although a vast amount of literature faces the relation between physiological signals and emotions, a concrete set of guidelines for the design of the experiments and for the analysis of the results is missing. This issue was first raised by van den Broek [1] who presented a review of several recent studies on biosignal-driven classification of emotions. From his analysis it is apparent that a comparison between studies is problematic mainly because of the different settings the research was applied in. In fact, different works reported performances that range from 26% to 97% obtained with different testing frameworks. The same issue was also reported in a recent work by Kolodyazhniy et al. [2] in which the authors claimed the lack of an homogeneous approach for data analysis in affective computing studies.

S. D´Mello et al. (Eds.): ACII 2011, Part I, LNCS 6974, pp. 517–526, 2011.

In this paper, we focus on affective preference models [3,4,5] applied to videogames. As reported by van der Broek [1], when looking for the best method for learning a preference affective model, it is not clear which approach should be used to obtain the maximum performance on new data. It may seem that non linear models and complex feature selection strategies might provide the best model, but the final answer might be different, if the problem is faced properly.

If we aim to investigate on the generalization power of different models obtained through different techniques, it is fundamental to adopt a strict a cross-validation. It must provide a fair and accurate estimation of the generalization capability of the model. This is fundamental in real applications, where a general model able to achieve good performance with data from new users is needed.

In this paper, we describe an example of such framework, used to compare three classification methods (one linear and two non linear) combined with a simple and a complex feature selection strategy (sequential forward selection and a genetic algorithm) on two different datasets.

The final outcome of such comparison highlights that, when generalization is the goal, complex non-linear models trained using complex genetic strategies might easily get trapped by overfitting, while linear ones, having similar performance on test data, might be preferable given their lower computational cost.

2 Case Studies

The analysis presented has been conducted on two real cases datasets. For a thorough description of the experimental protocols, sampling rate and synchronization of physiological signals, window lengths and feature extraction details please refer to the respective original papers for MazeBall [6] and TORCS [7].

In both experiments, physiological signals and self-reported preferences have been collected during a video game session. The two experimental protocols differ in a number of aspects such as the game involved, the hardware for physiological signals acquisition, the questions asked (plain preference vs. single affective state preference) and the answers scheme (2-AFC vs. 4-AFC). They have been selected to test whether we obtain consistent results in our analysis. The difference between protocols is not critical in our analysis since, in this work, we are not concerned with performance comparison between the two datasets but, rather, with the impact of different preference affective models within the same dataset.

2.1 MazeBall Dataset

During the experiment, 36 subjects have been asked to play four pairs of 90 seconds-long games. Each instance of the game (a 3-dimensional prey/predator PacMan-like game) was characterized by a different behavior of the virtual camera: three parameters (height, distance and frame coherence) have been modified to create different variants of the game.

After each pair of game variants, players report their emotional preference using a 4-AFC protocol. Preferences with regards to 7 affective states, anxiety, boredom, challenge, excitement, frustration, fun and relaxation have been collected. Moreover, during the session, Blood Volume Pulse (BVP) and Galvanic Skin Response (GSR) signals have been recorded from bio feedback sensors attached to to the subjects' left hand.

2.2 TORCS Dataset

The cognitive task in the experiment concerns playing a car racing simulation video game. During a session, each participant played 7 races versus one computer driver which was the only opponent. The only difference between races was the skill level of the opponent, set to provide 3 different game experiences: the first variant was against a relatively weak opponent, the second variant was against a challenging opponent, the last variant was against a strong opponent.

During the game session, participants were fitted with several sensors to measure peripheral physiological activity. To allow a consistent comparison with the MazeBall dataset, we kept only two physiological signals (i.e., GSR and BVP). However, for completeness, we also include in the results of a test with the full set of signals. Preference between races has also been collected. At the end of each race, subjects were asked the following question: "Which one did you like most? The last race or the previous one?". The answers are used to identify a preference affective model as reported in Section 4.

2.3 Physiological Features

Several derived features have been extracted from BVP and GSR signals. Heart rate has been derived from BVP (HR_{bvp}); magnitude (SM) and duration (SD) of startle responses have been derived from GSR; upper/lower envelope of BVP (BVP_{up},BVP_l) and their difference ($BVP_d = BPV_{up} - BVP_l$) have been also computed. A vector of statistical features (e.g., mean, standard deviation, first and second differences) $F = [f_1 f_2 \dots f_N] \in \mathcal{R}^N, N = 96$ has been finally obtained by the union of features computed for each mentioned signal during each game as described in detail in [6,4].

3 Cross Validation

The main purpose of this work is to compare different methods for estimating a general affective preference model that will be possibly used to predict preference of a generic user in future experiments. This calls for a rigorous validation method where, in no way, data used for testing have to be considered during the process of model building or feature selection.

In general, if a model is trained on the whole dataset and performance is evaluated on the same dataset, the performance of the obtained preference model result overestimated. In fact, what happens is that the algorithm tends to excessively fit the training data rather than learning a general model. This phenomenon is known as overfitting. One way to overcome this problem is not to

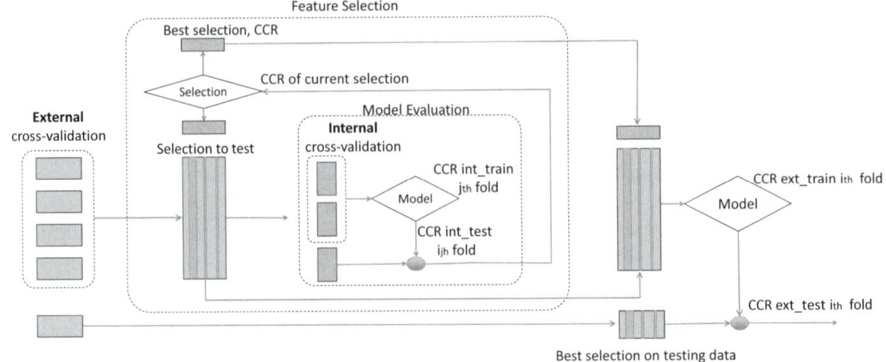

Fig. 1. Nested cross validation. Both feature selection and model training are applied to the training fold. The internal cross validation applied to the feature selection lowers the effect of overfitting and helps to find a subset of features with high generalization power. The resulting external testing CCR is the correct estimation for new data.

use the whole dataset for training the model removing some of the data before training begins. Then, once training is done, the removed data can be used to test the performance of the learned model against totally unseen data.

A very common technique for validation is the K-fold cross validation where the data is first randomly partitioned into K equally (or nearly equally) sized subsets. Subsequently, K iterations of training and validation are performed where, in turn, one fold is held-out for validation while the remaining $k - 1$ folds are used for training. Note that the TORCS dataset has been randomly partitioned on a subject-base criterion (i.e., samples from a given subject are either in the training fold or in the testing fold), this ensures an even more accurate approximation of performance obtainable with unseen users.

To have an accurate estimation of the generalization capability of the final models, it is fundamental to evaluate the performance of the obtained models with completely new data. This is achieved by the external cross validation presented in Figure 1. Feature selection and model learning are applied to training data while the performance of the best model is tested on test data. On the other hand, to obtain a model (and a selection of features) that is not overfitted on training data, a second level of cross validation is applied to the feature selection and model evaluation. Therefore, a nested cross validation scheme has been employed, where the external layer allows accurate estimation of the performance of the model, while the internal cross validation allows to find a general selection of features. Figure 1 shows the nested cross validation technique used in this work. A 5-fold cross validation scheme has been used for the external layer (i.e., model generalization assessment). For each training fold, a feature selection algorithm is applied and, considering only the optimal subset of features, a model of preference is learned on the whole remaining part of the training fold, and tested on the external testing fold.

The internal cross validation loop lowers the effect of overfitting in feature selection and training. The external cross validation guarantees that the reported results are a good estimation of how well the model will do when it is asked to make new predictions for data, or users, it has never seen before.

4 Affective Preference Model

Preference learning [8] is a technique that aims to predict the subject's preference among different elements. A subject expresses a preference $A \succ B$ (we say "A is preferred over B") between two situations A and B when he/she is able to order them with respect to a personal preference criterion which is thus totally subjective. Each situation is described through a set of features $F = [f_1 f_2 \dots f_D] \in \mathcal{R}^D$. The goal of preference learning is to estimate a preference function P that respects the set of N constraints:

$$\forall\, i = 1 \dots N \quad \textbf{if } A_i \succ B_i, \textbf{ then } P(F_i^A) > P(F_i^B) \tag{1}$$

Where F_i^A and F_i^B are the features vectors of elements A and B in the i-th comparison and N is the total number of preferences expressed. Preference learning is a general approach and can be used to model subject's preference from physiological data. Different techniques can be used to estimate P depending on the function used. We have compared linear and a non-linear approaches together with different feature selection methods described in the following sections.

4.1 Linear Model LDA

A linear model is able to exploit the simplest correlation between data. This brings a number of advantages: it is faster to compute; it gives a clear correlation between the model obtained and the features involved; it is less prone to overfit.

The linear technique used is based on Linear Discriminant Analysis [4]. Given a set of N game pairs $A_i \succ B_i$ $i = 1, \dots, N$ where the subject prefers A_i over B_i, the goal is to estimate W in such a way that the user preference is preserved:

$$\forall\, i = 1 \dots N \quad \textbf{if } A_i \succ B_i \textbf{ then } F_i^A W^T > F_i^B W^T \tag{2}$$

where F_i^A and F_i^B are the feature vectors associated to A_i and B_i respectively. We can rewrite the previous inequality as $(F_i^A - F_i^B)W^T = F_i^d W^T > 0$. Where F_i^d is the feature difference between preferred and not preferred games in pair i. We thus reformulate the problem of estimating W as a linear classification problem by considering the dataset $X = \{x_i | i = 1 \dots N\}$, $C = \{c_i | i = 1 \dots N\}$, where $x_i = [F_i^d, -F_i^d]$ and $c_i \in 0, 1$ (i.e., we reduce the problem to 2-classes classification problem assigning class 0 to positive examples F_i^d and class 1 to negative examples $-F_i^d$). Thanks to this reformulation, the problem can be solved with Fisher's projection finding a projection direction W in which classes (i.e., positive and negative examples) are well separated. Then, the obtained W can be used to predict one of the two classes by evaluating the inequality $XW^T > 0$.

4.2 Non-linear Model Neuro Evolution

For complex problems, a linear method might not be the optimal approach. A non-linear model is potentially able to exploit more complex relations within data and, therefore, to achieve better performance. This is generally true if we consider training performance. But does this still hold when a strict cross-validation technique is employed and testing performance are compared? In this paper, we consider a method based on NeuroEvolution [9] that employs a genetic trained neural network as function P. A generational genetic algorithm (GA), whose a fitness function measures the number of correctly predicted pairs (i.e., CCR) is implemented as follows. Each individual is encoded as a set of connection weights from -5 to 5 describing an artificial neural network that adopts the sigmoid (logistic) activation function.

A preliminary study has been performed, where several network topologies and GA parameters have been tested, i.e., Single-Layer Perceptron (SLP), Multi-Layer Perceptron with 1 hidden layer having 2 and 5 hidden neurons (MLP2, MLP5). The outcome of such study suggested that a SLP neural network could provide the best performance. However SLP model is equivalent to logistic regression: to stress the conclusion of this paper, results deriving from extensive tests using SLP and MLP5 topologies are reported.

A population of N_p individuals is evolved for a maximum number of N_g generations. At each iteration, uniform crossover with probability 0.95 and mutation (prob 0.001) is applied. During the preliminary study, the tuning procedure has selected the following optimal parameters : $N_p = 200, N_g = 15$ for the SLP topology, and $N_p = 500, N_g = 30$ for the MLP5 topology. Note that, since MLP5 is a more complex topology (i.e., the search space is larger due to the larger number of weights), the optimal population for learning the model is larger too.

To improve the generalization power and reduce the computational cost of network training, an early stopping technique has been introduced as stop criterion for the algorithm, as described here below. The dataset used by the GA for training the network is divided in 2 subsets: training and validation (90% and 10% of the samples, respectively). For each generation, the best individual of the training subset is evaluated on the validation subset. The algorithm terminates after the maximum number of iterations is reached or when the average performance on the validation subset starts to drop. The best trained network ever returned by the algorithm is the one that reports the maximum performance on the validation subset.

5 Feature Selection

The accuracy of the affective model can be often increased, especially when we aim to general models, by considering only a restricted number of features that, combined together, give the best discriminative power. The models for the estimation of an affective preference previously introduced have been tested against two extremes variants of feature selection algorithms: Sequential Forward Selection (SFS), and two variants of Genetic Feature Selection.

To have a baseline performance for comparison, the maximum performance obtainable by a single feature is evaluated as well. The technique can be thought as a single-step SFS: the feature that maximizes a given score function is selected. This is the simplest and fastest method of feature selection and it selects just a single feature.

5.1 Sequential Forward Selection

Sequential forward feature selection is a greedy search method that aims to find the minimal subset of features that maximizes a given score function. It is a bottom-up algorithm where, at each step, an additional feature is added to the current feature set. The selected feature to be added is selected if its marginal value, with respect to the score function, is maximum among over all candidate features for addition. The search stops when the inclusion of a new feature does not increase the performance any longer.

In our analysis, the simple Correct Classification Rate (CCR) obtained from the model trained with the given feature set has been used as score function. To reduce the chance of overfitting the selection of features, a 3-fold cross validation technique is employed for the evaluation of the score. As showed in Figure 1, the resulting score is the average CCR of 3 testing folds obtained via the internal cross validation.

5.2 Genetic Feature Selection

A Genetic algorithm is a stochastic optimization technique that has been successfully applied in several feature selection tasks [10]. Being a global search method, it could better exploit the relationship between features. For example, in case of multiple features with similar score, the genetic feature selection will consider several combinations of them as opposed to SFS that always takes the one with the highest score. The algorithm considered in this paper is a variant of the one adopted in a previous work [5], where a binary encoding is used for representing the population. Each individual represents a set of features whose success in life is proportional to the CCR of the affective model learned from the selected features. Each chromosome is binary encoded and indicates whether the corresponding feature is included or not (i.e., 0 = *included*, 1 = *not included*). The initial population of $N_f = 96$ chromosomes is created as follows: the i-th chromosome is initialized with all bits but the i-th set to zero. The proposed configuration for the initial population guarantees that all features are considered at least once and minimizes the number of features selected in the optimal subset. The GA runs for 20 iterations and at each iteration, all individuals of the population are evaluated. The value of the fitness is the average CCR of the preference affective model obtained with a 3-fold cross validation (internal cross validation described in Figure 1). The best individual is propagated to the next generation as form of elitism. Then, individuals that will be the parents for crossover operations are selected using stochastic universal sampling [11] as method for fitness proportionate selection. Uniform crossover is then applied

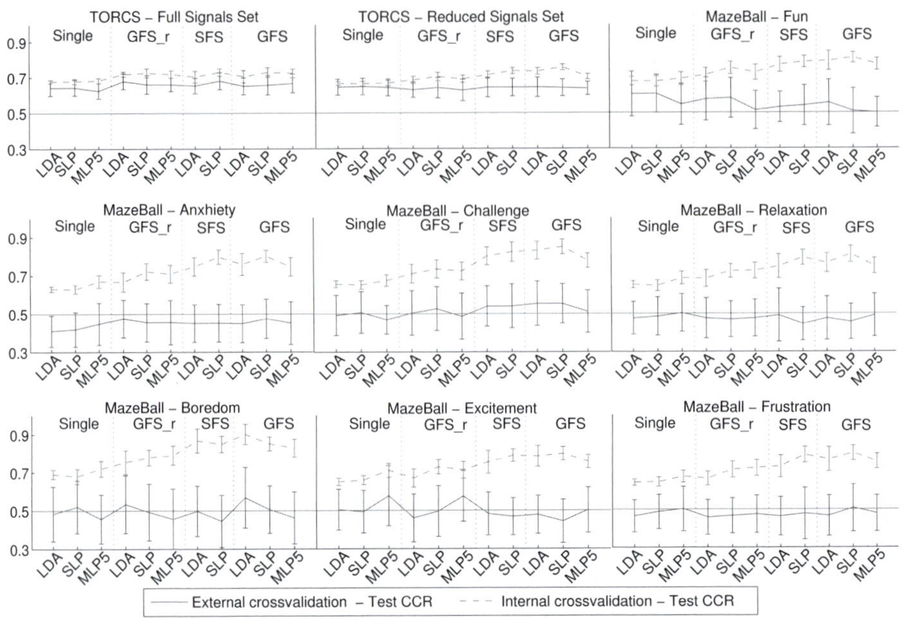

Fig. 2. Internal and external testing CCR comparison. For each dataset, results are reported for different feature selection technique and different preference affective model (i.e., Linear Discriminant Analysis (LDA), Single-Layer Perceptron (SLP), Multi-Layer Perceptron with 5 neurons (SLP5)).

with a probability $P_c = 0.95$ and, finally, mutation of single bits (flipping) occurs at each gene of the offsprings with a probability $P_m = 0.01$.

Classical genetic feature selection often tends to select a large number of features (e.g., 20-30). This is because the number of selected features is not taken into account for the evaluation of the fitness. Often, similar performance can be obtained using a limited number of features and, thus, a simpler and faster to compute model. Moreover, with a limited number of features, the analysis of single contribution for individual features is easier. Two variants of fitness function have been considered: plain CCR and CCR minus a penalization value proportional to the number of features selected. After several tests where we tried to get on average 6 feature selected, we obtained the following formula for the fitness penalization: $fitness = CCR - nSelectedFeatures^{1/8}$ where CCR is the usual Correct Classification Rate of the given selection and $nSelectedFeatures$ is the number of features in the selected subset. The average number of features selected by using a plain CCR fitness function was 11. On the other hand, using SFS, the average number of features selected was 3.5. The chosen fitness function it is a trade-off between the number of features selected by SFS and the number of features selected by GFS employing a plain CCR fitness and it puts pressure on the number of features selected, forcing the algorithm to chose only features with significant additional information.

6 Results and Conclusion

Figure 2 summarizes the results obtained in this work. Each test has been performed 10 times; mean and standard deviation of each result are reported. The first 2 subgraphs show results from the TORCS dataset, while the other 7 subgraphs show results from the MazeBall dataset, one for each affective state investigated. Red values (dashed line) are the internal CCRs of the best subset of features obtained with the feature selection technique (i.e., internal cross validation performances). Blue values are the external testing CCRs obtained from the evaluation of a model learned on the optimal subset of feature of the training fold. The values are grouped by feature selection method: single best feature, SFS, GFS with the penalization on the number of features and GFS. For each feature selection method, 3 methods for preference affective modeling are tested: LDA, SLP and MLP5. Note that the differences among external test CCRs (blue line) are not statistically significant ($p < 0.05$).

- *Feature Selection*: it is apparent from the figure, and statistically significant ($p < 0.05$), that with the increment of complexity for feature selection methods there is an increment in the internal test CCR. This means that a more complex technique of selection can improve performance during the training process. It is not possible to observe a similar pattern in the external test CCR where differences in performance are not related to the complexity of the method of feature selection. Therefore, if we consider the proper performance (obtained trough a strict cross validation framework), complex feature selection strategies are not better than the single best feature. Considering the *single best feature selection* as baseline, SFS was in average 4.4 times slower and GAFS was 20 times slower.
- *Affective Preference Model*: considering the internal test CCR, we observe that with single feature selection performance does not significantly vary among affective preference models. On the other hand, with more complex feature selection methods, i.e., SFS and GFS, we observe that the most complex network topology (i.e., MP5) always yields lower performance. On the other hand, as we stated before, by looking at the external CCR outcome, we observe no statistically significant differences among different affective preference models. Considering LDA as baseline, SLP was 110 times slower and MLP5 was 3500 times slower.

In general, by looking at Figure 2, we note a direct correlation between the internal test CCRs (dashed line) and the complexity of both feature selection methods and preference affective models (except for MLP5 models). However, this does not hold when we consider the external test CCRs (continuous line) since the differences among values are not statistically significant. If we consider the computational cost of different methods, we have a difference of almost 5 orders of magnitude between the simplest LDA+Single feature selection and the most complex MLP5+Genetic feature selection.

In conclusion, we have seen that, in the presented two real cases, no matter how complex a feature selection method or a preference affective method is, the estimated performance of the model on new data does not change significantly. This result is obtainable only when a strong cross validation method is adopted. Otherwise, we may risk to overestimate the performance of a model by considering inappropriate numbers.

Acknowledgments. The research activity described in this paper has been partially supported by IIT. The authors would like to thank Prof. G. Yannakakis of the Center for Computer Games at ITU of Copenhagen for the valuable feedbacks and advices on the topic and for making available the MazeBall dataset.

References

1. Broek, E.L.V.D., Janssen, J.H., Westerink, J.: Guidelines for affective signal processing (asp): From lab to life, pp. 1–6. IEEE, Los Alamitos (2009)
2. Kolodyazhniy, V., Kreibig, S., Gross, J., Roth, W., Wilhelm, F.: An affective computing approach to physiological emotion specificity: Toward subject-independent and stimulus-independent classification of film-induced emotions. Psychophysiology (2011)
3. Yannakakis, G., Hallam, J.: Entertainment modeling through physiology in physical play. International Journal of Human-Computer Studies 66(10), 741–755 (2008)
4. Tognetti, S., Garbarino, M., Bonarini, A., Matteucci, M.: Modeling player enjoyment from physiological responses in a car racing game. In: 2010 IEEE Symposium on Computational Intelligence and Games (CIG), pp. 321–328. IEEE, Los Alamitos (2010)
5. Martínez, H.P., Yannakakis, G.N.: Genetic search feature selection for affective modeling: a case study on reported preferences. In: Proceedings of the 3rd International Workshop on Affective Interaction in Natural Environments, AFFINE 2010, pp. 15–20. ACM, New York (2010)
6. Yannakakis, G., Martínez, H., Jhala, A.: Towards affective camera control in games. User Modeling and User-Adapted Interaction 20(4), 313–340 (2010)
7. Tognetti, S., Garbarino, M., Bonarini, A., Matteucci, M.: Enjoyment recognition from physiological data in a car racing game. In: Proceedings of the 3rd International Workshop on Affective Interaction in Natural Environments, AFFINE 2010, pp. 3–8. ACM, New York (2010)
8. Doyle, J.: Prospects for preferences. Computational Intelligence 20(2), 111–136 (2004)
9. Yannakakis, G.: Preference learning for affective modeling. In: Proceeding of the International Conference on Affective Computing and Intelligent Interaction, ACII 2009, pp. 1–6. IEEE, Los Alamitos (2009)
10. Yang, J., Honavar, V.: Feature subset selection using a genetic algorithm. IEEE Intelligent Systems and Their Applications 13(2), 44–49 (1998)
11. Baker, J.E.: Reducing bias and inefficiency in the selection algorithm, pp. 14–21. Lawrence Erlbaum Associates, Mahwah (1987)

Towards Real-Time Affect Detection Based on Sample Entropy Analysis of Expressive Gesture

Donald Glowinski and Maurizio Mancini

InfoMus Lab, DIST, University of Genova, Italy
{donald.glowinski,maurizio.mancini}@dist.unige.it

Abstract. Aiming at providing a solid foundation to the creation of future affect detection applications in HCI, we propose to analyze human expressive gesture by computing movement Sample Entropy (SampEn). This method provides two main advantages: (i) it is adapted to the non-linearity and non-stationarity of human movement; (ii) it allows a fine-grain analysis of the information encoded in the movement features dynamics. A realtime application is presented, implementing the SampEn method. Preliminary results obtained by computing SampEn on two expressive features, smoothness and symmetry, are provided in a video available on the web.

Keywords: Expressive gesture, Sample Entropy, EyesWeb XMI.

1 Introduction

When do bodily channels convey actual information about a person's emotional state?

Research on nonverbal communication corroborate the view that bodily expressions constitute a relevant source of affective information [22,33,35]. In the last 10 years, an increasing number of affect detection systems have been developed and a great number of features characterizing an affective content have been proposed: movement direction and kinematics, arm extension and so on. As observed by Calvo [2], an assumption in Affective Computing is that emotions occur occasionally during usually affective-free interaction whereas contemporary theories maintain that affect is constantly influencing behavior. The challenge is to "model these perennially present, but somewhat subtle, manifestations of emotion" (p.32, [2]).

In this paper, we address this challenge by considering dynamic entropy of expressive features. Each movement potentially embodies an affect-related information content but this affect-related information content is subtly encoded in the temporal evolution of the movement features. For example, an upward movement may convey several affective meanings: when it follows a still posture, it may convey surprise; when it is a portion of many upward movements expressing anger, it may confirm the subject's angry state.

We develop a real-time affect detection system that is built on the *Sample Entropy* (*SampEn*) method. Tests have been conducted on a reduced amount of visual information related to human upper-body movements [13].

S. D´Mello et al. (Eds.): ACII 2011, Part I, LNCS 6974, pp. 527–537, 2011.

The paper is organized as follows: Section 2 introduces the key concepts of our approach; in Section 3 we detail a realtime application for computing dynamic entropy of movement expressive features; we conclude the paper in Section 4.

2 Background

2.1 Bounding Triangle

Our framework is based on a minimal and efficient representation of human upper body movement. We consider a *bounding triangle* related to the three blobs' centroids of the user's hands and head (see Figure 1). Recent studies [10,13] showed that this minimal representation of human upper body movement provide sufficient information to automatically distinguish between meaningful groups of emotions, related to the four quadrants of the Russel's valence/arousal space [27]. Previous evaluation of emotion recognition performance based on this minimal representation further assessed that human observers could discriminate between high and low arousal emotions [10].

By basing on this minimal user representation we ensure: (i) robust expressivity/emotional analysis; (ii) simplified identification of dynamics factors contributing to the communication of an expressive (e.g., emotional) content; (iii) real-time implementation of our framework.

2.2 Dynamic Expressive Behavior Analysis

Starting from the Kurtenbach and Hulteen's definition of gesture as "a movement of the body that contains information", a gesture is considered *expressive* if the information it carries has an expressive content, i.e., an "implicit message" [6].

Expressive content of a gesture can provide information on the emotional state, mood and personality of the person [34]. Researchers [16][9][34] have investigated human expressive motion and determined qualifiers such as slow/fast, small/large, weak/energetic, unpleasant/pleasant. Behavior expressivity has been correlated to energy in communication, to the relation between temporal/spatial characteristics of gestures, and/or to personality/emotion.

According to Camurri et al.'s framework [4], expressive gesture analysis is accomplished by three subsequent layers of processing: low-level physical measures (e.g., position, speed, acceleration of body parts); overall gesture features (e.g., motion fluency, impulsiveness); high-level information describing semantic properties of gestures (affect, emotion, attitudes).

A growing body of research in affecting computing and in psychology argue that temporal dynamics of human behavior (i.e., timing and duration of behavioral features) can be decisive in distinguishing between observed behavioral expressions [22][18]. [11] extended pilot studies by Castellano et al. [5] and defined a set of dynamics features, derived from the temporal profiles of expressive variations (e.g., the ratio between the gesture movement main peak duration and the total gesture duration, or the number of gesture movement local maxima in a given time span).

The system developed in [13] for characterizing expressive behavior showed that dynamic aspects of motion features are complementary to postural and gesture shape-related information.

2.3 Entropy Measure

The majority of the computational tools used for analyzing behavior dynamics [5] are based on traditional time and frequency domain measures but they fail to account for some properties of human movement: (i) non-linearity (small perturbations can cause large effects) and (ii) non-stationarity (the statistical properties change with time).

The concept of entropy has first been coined in thermodynamics referring to the amount of energy that is inaccessible for work (Shannon [30] applied the concept of information entropy to the development of information theory of communication. First entropy interpretation of human movement variability in terms of information theory constructs were proposed by Fitts to evaluate speed-accuracy task [8]. This classic investigation led to numerous studies examining motor behavior from an information processing perspective ([15] for a review). However, these studies have been often restricted to observing, for example, what happens in single points of a trajectory without considering dynamics, i.e., that consecutive points are part of the same trajectory.

In time series analysis, entropy has been newly defined as a quantity measuring the mean rate of new information production [25]. The Kolmogorov-Sinai (KS) entropy measures the decrease of uncertainty by knowing the current state of the system given its past history. Methods to estimate the K-S entropy were first developed in the field of nonlinear dynamic analysis and chaos [Lake, 16,20] by Grassberger and Procaccia [14], Eckmann and Ruelle [7].

The ApEn statistic and its last, most used modification, *SampEn* (*Sample Entropy*) method, was developed within this conceptual framework, respectively by Pincus [23] and Richman and Moorman [25], to compute the K-S entropy for real-world, noisy time series of finite length. High values of SampEn indicate disorder, smaller values indicate greater regularity. SampEn has been applied to a variety of physiological (heart rate, EMG, see [29] for a review).

Most recent application deal with behavioral data (e.g., investigating postural control mechanisms [24]) and some specifically address affective and social dynamics [12,17].

3 Realtime Implementation

Figure 1 shows the application we developed to perform realtime estimation of entropy in dynamic expressive movement features. The current implementation of our application does not perform any affect analysis: that is, according to the framework described by Camurri et al. [4] our application performs low-level and gesture-level measurements. The application has been implemented in the EyesWeb XMI platform (`http://www.eyesweb.org`), including the EyesWeb Gesture Processing Library for motion features extraction.

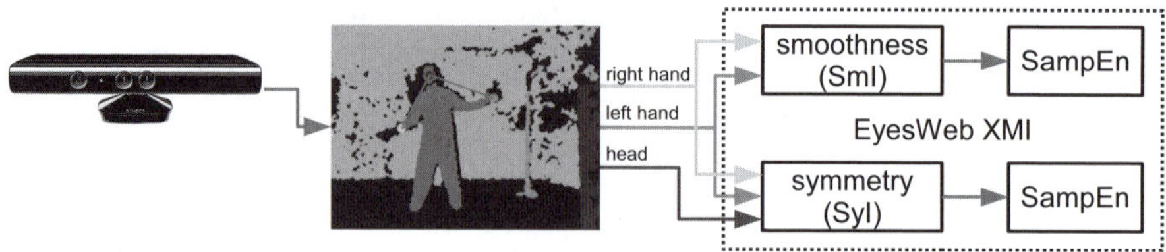

Fig. 1. The user's silhouette is captured through a Kinect acquisition device and body parts are extracted. Head and hands positions are sent to the EyesWeb XMI platform that computes the smoothness and symmetry SampEn.

3.1 Extracting Bounding Triangle Form Human Silhouette

We track the user's body using a Kinect acquisition device (`http://www.xbox.com/en-US/kinect`). Figure 2 shows and example of such tracking: on the left image the user's silhouette is extracted from the background; on the right image the user silhouette is segmented into body parts (e.g., head, shoulders, trunk and so on) by the functions provided by the Kinect open driver OpenNI [20].

Fig. 2. Realtime tracking of user body configuration performed using Kinect

As the user enters the application space for the first time an initialization phase is required: the user must stand for about 3 seconds in the PSI pose (hands up, legs slightly opened).

Then the Kinect tracking is started and 3 user's body parts are considered: (1) head, (2) left hand and (3) right hand. Their 2D coordinates are extracted realtime and provided as input to the computation of dynamic features symmetry and smoothness, see Section 3.2. Finally, the dynamic features values as provided as input to the entropy estimation modules, described in Section 3.3.

3.2 Extracting Dynamic Features: Smoothness and Symmetry Index

As explained in Section 3, we focus movement analysis on a simplification of the human body: the bounding triangle, determined by the user's head as the top vertex and the user's hands as the triangle basis. An example of bounding triangle is shown in Figure 1.

Smoothness Index (SmI). Research in [32] demonstrates a correspondence between (i) smooth trajectories performed by human arms, (ii) minimization of the third-order derivative of the hand position (called *jerk* in physics) and (iii) correlation between hand trajectory curvature and velocity. In our work we use an approach similar to (iii) to determine if a trajectory is smooth or not starting from the trajectory curvature and velocity.

The left and right hand positions (x_l, y_l) and (x_r, y_r) are buffered in two time series consisting of 30 elements. These structures are managed as FIFO buffers, that is, as a new element is pushed in the structure, the oldest element pops out.

The time series are then provided as input to the smoothness computation algorithm: for every sample (x_h, y_h) (where h coiuld be l or r) in the buffer we compute curvature k and velocity v as:

$$k_h(x_h, y_h) = \left| \frac{x_h{}' y_h{}'' - y_h{}' x_h{}''}{(x_h{}'^2 + y_h{}'^2)^{\frac{3}{2}}} \right| \qquad v_h(x_h, y_h) = \sqrt{x_h{}'^2 + y_h{}'^2} \tag{1}$$

where $x_h{}'$, $y_h{}'$, $x_h{}''$ and $y_h{}''$ are the first and second order derivatives of x_h and y_h for hand h. To compute derivatives values we apply a Savitzky-Golay filter [28] that provides as output both the filtered signal and an approximation of the $n-th$ order smoothed derivatives. As mentioned above, we define our algorithm for computing smoothness by taking inspiration from [32], that is, we compute correlation between trajectory curvature and velocity. We consider the Pearson correlation coefficient for two variables, that is, in our algorithm, $log(k_h)$ and $log(v_h)$:

$$\rho_h(k_h, v_h) = \frac{\sigma_{log(k_h), log(v_h)}}{\sigma_{log(k_h)} \sigma_{log(v_h)}} \tag{2}$$

However, k_h and v_h are computed over a relatively "short" time window, so we could approximate the covariance $\sigma_{log(k_h), log(v_h)}$ with 1, as the k_h and v_h variate (or not) approximately at the same time:

$$\rho'_h(k_h, v_h) = \frac{1}{\sigma_{log(k_h)} \sigma_{log(v_h)}} \tag{3}$$

That is, the Smoothness Index SmI_h for hand h is equal to $\rho'_h(k_h, v_h)$. As we compute these value for both the left and right hand, we finally compute the mean value of both hands SmI:

$$SmI = (SmI_l + SmI_r)/2 \tag{4}$$

Symmetry Index (SyI). Symmetry/asymmetry of emotion expression has been first studied in face expressions. Results revealed general hemisphere dominance in the control of emotional expression. A seminal work by [1] using static pictures of emotional expressions with one side of the face replaced by the mirror image of the other (*chimeric face stimuli*) showed that left hemiface is further related to expressivity. Roether et al. recently showed that human gait display lateral asymmetries also in human emotional full-body movement [26]. Motion capture data of twenty four actors recorded during neutral walking and emotionally expressive walking (anger, happiness, sadness) showed that the left body side moved with significantly higher amplitude and energy. Perceptual validation of the results were conducted through the creation of *chimeric walkers* using the joint-angle trajectories of one body half to animate symmetric puppets.

A few studies accounted for the relationship between upper-body movements symmetry and expressivity. Merhabian showed in particular that arm-position asymmetry was a relevant behavioral feature to identify "relax" attitude and relative high social status of a person within a group [19].

Spatial hands symmetry is computed with respect to the vertical axis and with respect to the horizontal axis. Horizontal Symmetry Index ($SyI_{horizontal}$) is computed from the position of the barycenter and the left and right edges of the bounding triangle that relate the head and the two hands (Eq 5).

$$SyI_{horizontal} = \frac{||x_B - x_L| - |x_B - x_R||}{|x_R - x_L|} \tag{5}$$

where x_B is the x coordinate of the barycentre, x_L is the x coordinate of the left edge of the bounding triangle and x_R is the x coordinate of the right edge of the bounding triangle. Similarly, vertical Symmetry Index ($SyI_{vertical}$) is computed by the difference between the y coordinates of hands. A first measure related to spatial symmetry (SyI) results from the ratio of the measures of horizontal and vertical symmetries (Eq 6).

$$SyI = \frac{SyI_{horizontal}}{SyI_{vertical}} \tag{6}$$

Dynamic update of features. Movement features such as symmetry and smoothness are dynamical features, as explained in [3]: their updated values do not only depend on the last frame of the user's movement data (i.e., the last position of the user's head and hands) but it should also consider the recent user movement *history*. We include such dynamic properties by performing an incremental update of movement features, as shown in Figure 3.

To do that, we store the features values at previous times $t - 1$ and $t - 2$: $SyI(t-1), SyI(t-2), SmI(t-1), SmI(t-2)$. At time t, we compute the *detected* movement features values $SyI_{det}(t)$ and $SmI_{det}(t)$, as explained above. Finally we update movement features values by *weighting* the detected values by the difference between the current and previous feature values:

$$SyI(t) = SyI(t-1) + ((SyI_{det}(t) - SyI(t-1)) * |SyI(t-1) - SyI(t-2)|) \tag{7}$$

$$SmI(t) = SmI(t-1) + ((SmI_{det}(t) - SmI(t-1)) * |SmI(t-1) - SmI(t-2)|) \tag{8}$$

In our application, the dynamically updated values of SyI(t) and SmI(t) are used to compute Sample Entropy as described in the following Section.

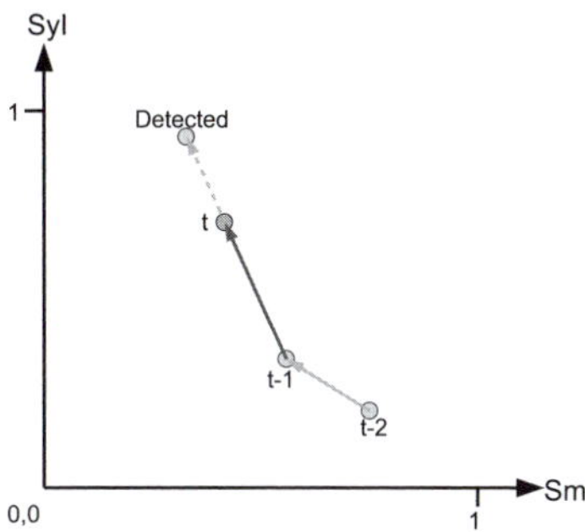

Fig. 3. Dynamic update of movement features

3.3 Computing SampEn

The following algorithm for computing SampEn is introduced in [25].

Given a standardized one-dimensional discrete time series of length N, $X = \{x_1, ..., x_i..., x_N\}$:

1. construct vectors of length m (similarly to the time delay embedding procedure) [31,21],

$$u_i(m) = \{x_i, ..., x_{i+m-1}\}, 1 \leq i \leq N - m \tag{9}$$

2. compute the correlation sum $U_i^m(r)$ to estimate similar subsequences (or *template vectors*) of length m within the time series:

$$U_i^m(r) = \frac{1}{(N - m - 1)} \sum_{i=1, i \neq j}^{N-m} \Theta(r- \parallel u_i(m) - u_j(m) \parallel_\infty) \tag{10}$$

   where $u_i(m)$ and $u_j(m)$ are the template vectors of length m formed from the standardized time series, at time i and j respectively, N is the number of samples in the time series, r is the tolerance (or *radius*), Θ is the Heaviside function, and $\|\|_\infty$ is the maximum norm defined by $\parallel u_i(m) - u_j(m) \parallel_\infty) = max_{0 \leq k \leq m-1} \mid x_{j+k} - x_{i+k} \mid$.
3. calculate the average of U_i^m, i.e., the probability that two vectors will match in the m-dimensional reconstructed state space

$$U^m(r) = \frac{1}{(N - m)} \sum_{i=1}^{N-m} U_i^m(r) \tag{11}$$

4. set $m = m + 1$ and repeat steps 1-4
5. calculate the sample entropy of X_n

$$SampEn(X_n, m, r) = -ln \frac{U^{m+1}(r)}{U^m(r)} \tag{12}$$

Sample Entropy computes the negative average natural logarithm of the conditional probability that subsequences similar for m points in the time series remain similar (as defined by Eq. 3) when one more point $(m + 1)$ is added to those sequences. Small values of SampEn indicate regularity.

In the proposed implementation, we compute SampEn on two time series containing the values of the two dynamic features SmI and SyI, that is, given:

$$SmI_{ts} = \{SmI(t-N), ..., SmI(t)\}, SyI_{ts} = \{SyI(t-N), ..., SyI(t)\} \quad (13)$$

we compute:

$$SampEn(SmI_{ts}, m, r), SampEn(SyI_{ts}, m, r) \quad (14)$$

3.4 Output

An example of the output provided by our application is provided in Figure 4. A demo video is available at:
http://www.mauriziomancini.org/downloads/acii2011.m4v

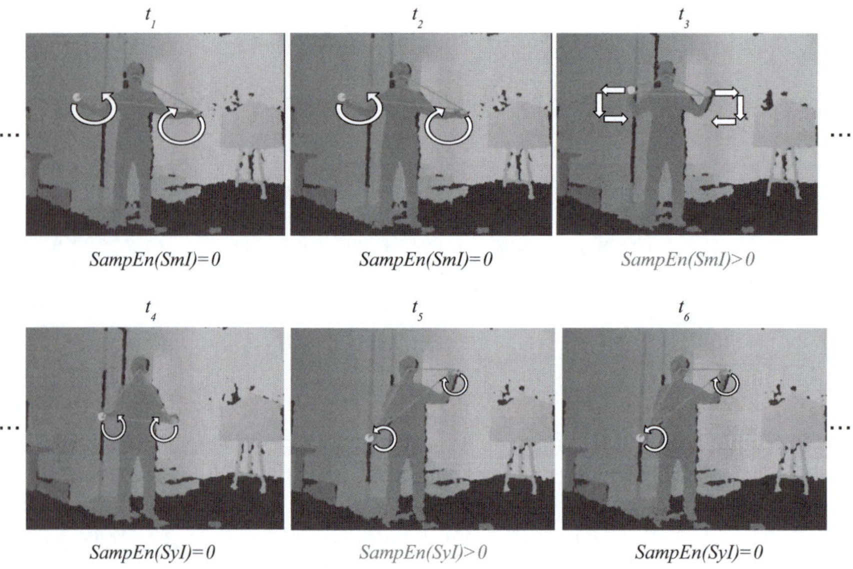

Fig. 4. An example of SampEn computation: user's smoothness is constant (high) between t_1 and t_2, so $SampEn(SmI)$ is zero; then, between t_2 and t_3 smoothness decreases, so $SampEn(SmI)$ increases; user's symmetry decreases between t_4 and t_5, so $SampEn(SyI)$ increases; finally, symmetry is constant (low) between t_5 and t_6, so $SampEn(SyI)$ is zero

4 Conclusion

Our research work aims to contribute to develop affective detection applications. To provide solid foundations for such applications, we suggest that expressive gesture analysis should consider the information content conveyed by movement features such as smoothness and symmetry. We also propose to compute Sample Entropy, a measure adapted to the non-linear dynamics of human movement.

Future work includes: (a) applying the proposed approach to realtime classification of emotion portrayals to refine the evaluation in terms of recognition performance, error analysis and real time aspects; (b) extension to 3D analysis (using the Kinect device) to include other significant information, such as distance and forward or backward movement with respect to camera or person.

Acknowledgements. This work is partly supported by the EU FP7 project MIROR (the project is co-funded by the European Community under the Information and Communication Technologies (ICT) theme of the Seventh Framework Programme, grant agreement 258338).

References

1. Borod, J., Haywood, C., Koff, E.: Neuropsychological aspects of facial asymmetry during emotional expression: A review of the normal adult literature. Neuropsychology Review 7(1), 41–60 (1997)
2. Calvo, R., D'Mello, S.: Affect detection: An interdisciplinary review of models, methods, and their applications. IEEE Transactions on Affective Computing 1(1) (2010)
3. Camurri, A., Ferrentino, P.: Interactive environments for music and multimedia. Multimedia Systems 7(1), 32–47 (1999)
4. Camurri, A., Volpe, G., De Poli, G., Leman, M.: Communicating Expressiveness and Affect in Multimodal Interactive Systems. IEEE Multimedia, 43–53 (2005)
5. Castellano, G., Mortillaro, M., Camurri, A., Volpe, G., Scherer, K.: Automated Analysis of Body Movement in Emotionally Expressive Piano Performances. Music Perception 26(2), 103–119 (2008)
6. Douglas-Cowie, E., Campbell, N., Cowie, R., Roach, P.: Emotional speech: Towards a new generation of databases. Speech Communication 40(1-2), 33–60 (2003)
7. Eckmann, J., Ruelle, D.: Ergodic theory of chaos and strange attractors. Reviews of Modern Physics 57(3), 617–656 (1985)
8. Fitts, P.: The information capacity of the human motor system in controlling the amplitude of movement. Journal of Experimental Psychology 47(6), 381–391 (1954)
9. Gallaher, P.E.: Individual differences in nonverbal behavior: Dimensions of style. Journal of Personality and Social Psychology 63(1), 133–145 (1992)
10. Glowinski, D., Bracco, F., Chiorri, C., Atkinson, A., Coletta, P., Camurri, A.: An investigation of the minimal visual cues required to recognize emotions from human upper-body movements. In: Proceedings of ACM International Conference on Multimodal Interfaces (ICMI), Workshop on Affective Interaction in Natural Environments (AFFINE). ACM, New York (2008)
11. Glowinski, D., Camurri, A., Volpe, G., Dael, N., Scherer, K.: Technique for automatic emotion recognition by body gesture analysis. In: Computer Vision and Pattern Recognition 2008. CVPR Workshops. IEEE Computer Society, Los Alamitos (2008)
12. Glowinski, D., Coletta, P., Volpe, G., Camurri, A., Chiorri, C., Schenone, A.: Multi-scale entropy analysis of dominance in social creative activities. In: Proceedings of the International Conference on Multimedia, pp. 1035–1038. ACM, New York (2010)

13. Glowinski, D., Dael, N., Camurri, A., Volpe, G., Mortillaro, M., Scherer, K.: Towards a minimal representation of affective gestures. IEEE Transactions on Affective Computing (99), 1–13 (2011)
14. Grassberger, P., Procaccia, I.: Measuring the strangeness of strange attractors. Physica D: Nonlinear Phenomena 9(1-2), 189–208 (1983)
15. Hong, S., Newell, K.: Entropy conservation in the control of human action. Nonlinear Dynamics, Psychology, and Life Sciences 12(2), 163 (2008)
16. Johansson, G.: Visual perception of biological motion and a model for its analysis. Perception and Psychophysics 14, 201–211 (1973)
17. Kim, J., Andre, E.: Four-Channel Biosignal Analysis and Feature Extraction for Automatic Emotion Recognition. In: Biomedical Engineering Systems and Technologies, pp. 265–277 (2009)
18. Kleinsmith, A., Bianchi-Berthouze, N., Steed, A.: Automatic recognition of non-acted affective postures. IEEE Transactions on Systems, Man, and Cybernetics, Part B: Cybernetics (99), 1–12 (2011)
19. Mehrabian, A.: Nonverbal Communication. Aldine (2007)
20. OpenNI, `http://www.openni.org`
21. Packard, N., Crutchfield, J., Farmer, J., Shaw, R.: Geometry from a time series. Physical Review Letters 45(9), 712–716 (1980)
22. Pantic, M., Pentland, A., Nijholt, A., Huang, T.: Human Computing and Machine Understanding of Human Behavior: A Survey. In: Huang, T.S., Nijholt, A., Pantic, M., Pentland, A. (eds.) ICMI/IJCAI Workshops 2007. LNCS (LNAI), vol. 4451, pp. 47–71. Springer, Heidelberg (2007)
23. Pincus, S.: Approximate entropy as a measure of system complexity. Proceedings of the National Academy of Sciences of the United States of America 88(6), 2297 (1991)
24. Ramdani, S., Seigle, B., Lagarde, J., Bouchara, F., Bernard, P.: On the use of sample entropy to analyze human postural sway data. Medical Engineering & Physics 31(8), 1023–1031 (2009)
25. Richman, J., Moorman, J.: Physiological time-series analysis using approximate entropy and sample entropy. American Journal of Physiology- Heart and Circulatory Physiology 278(6), H2039 (2000)
26. Roether, C., Omlor, L., Giese, M.: Lateral asymmetry of bodily emotion expression. Current Biology 18(8), 329–330 (2008)
27. Russell, J.A.: A circumplex model of affect. Journal of Personality and Social Psychology 39(6), 1161–1178 (1980)
28. Savitzky, A., Golay, M.J.E.: Smoothing and differentiation of data by simplified least squares procedures. Analytical Chemistry 36(8), 1627–1639 (1964)
29. Seely, A., Macklem, P.: Complex systems and the technology of variability analysis. Crit Care 8(6), R367–R384 (2004)
30. Shannon, C., Weaver, W.: The mathematical theory of information (1949)
31. Takens, F.: Detecting strange attractors in turbulence. In: Dynamical Systems and Turbulence, Warwick 1980 pp. 366–381 (1980)

32. Todorov, E., Jordan, M.I.: Smoothness maximization along a predefined path accurately predicts the speed profiles of complex arm movements. Journal of Neurophysiology 80(2), 696–714 (1998)
33. Vinciarelli, A., Pantic, M., Bourlard, H.: Social signals, their function, and automatic analysis: a survey. In: Proceedings of the 10th International Conference on Multimodal Interfaces, pp. 61–68. ACM, New York (2008)
34. Wallbott, H.G., Scherer, K.R.: Cues and channels in emotion recognition. Journal of Personality and Social Psychology 51(4), 690–699 (1986)
35. Wallbott, H.: Bodily expression of emotion. Eur. J. Soc. Psychol. 28, 879–896 (1998)

Predicting Learner Engagement during Well-Defined and Ill-Defined Computer-Based Intercultural Interactions

Benjamin S. Goldberg, Robert A. Sottilare, Keith W. Brawner, and Heather K. Holden

United States Army Research Laboratory Human Research and Engineering Directorate
Simulation and Training Technology Center, Orlando, FL 32826
{benjamin.s.goldberg,robert.sottilare,keith.w.brawner, heather.k.holden}@us.army.mil

Abstract. This article reviews the first of two experiments investigating the effect tailoring of training content has on a learner's perceived engagement, and to examine the influence the Big Five Personality Test and the Self-Assessment Manikin (SAM) mood dimensions have on these outcome measures. A secondary objective is to then correlate signals from physiological sensors and other variables of interest, and to develop a model of learner engagement. Self-reported measures were derived from the engagement index of the Independent Television Commission-Sense of Presence Inventory (ITC-SOPI). Physiological measures were based on the commercial Emotiv Epoc Electroencephalograph (EEG) brain-computer interface. Analysis shows personality factors to be reliable predictors of general engagement within well-defined and ill-defined tasks, and could be used to tailor instructional strategies where engagement was predicted to be non-optimal. It was also evident that Emotiv provides reliable measures of engagement and excitement in near real-time.

Keywords: learner engagement, well-defined tasks, ill-defined tasks, EEG.

1 Introduction

Simulation-based training environments, although potentially powerful, suffer from the same weaknesses as other computer-based training methods; they lack individualized guidance and feedback. The effectiveness of adaptation in state-of-art computer-based training is limited and is far from producing comparable benefits to those seen in human-to-human instruction. However, incorporating the application of dynamic cognitive-state assessment of a learner can be used to provide additional cues to a training system to facilitate personalized self-directed learning. Emerging evidence suggests that enabling a training system to access affective and cognitive states can enable it to adapt an individual student's learning experience and improve learning outcomes [1]. Personalizing instructional content on the individual level requires real-time cognitive state assessments that aim to interpret the attentional resources a particular student is devoting to a task and to determine a student's readiness to learn [2]. Ultimately, this can lead to enabling training systems to better diagnose student errors and improve learner engagement.

S. D'Mello et al. (Eds.): ACII 2011, Part I, LNCS 6974, pp. 538–547, 2011.

This paper presents the results of an initial study which observed whether and to what degree tailoring of training content (e.g., clarity and flow of task) in a computer-based cultural negotiation trainer had on self-reported levels of engagement. It also evaluated if specific sensors are practical for gathering data for cognitive-state modeling. Engagement is a state of interest. It reflects processes that involve information gathering, visual scanning, and periods of sustained attention [3]. A secondary research objective is to correlate signals from physiological sensors and other variables of interest to arousal leading to development of a model of learner engagement. Longer-term, the results of this study could contribute to establishing the validity of using Commercial Off-The-Shelf (COTS) cognitive-state sensors for manipulations designed to improve engagement and provide inputs sufficient for enabling engagement modeling.

2 The Link of Engagement to Learning

Developing reliable methods to measure and classify learner engagement, as well as better understand its connection to learning has been a research focus within the computer-based tutoring community [4]. A number of empirical studies have shown student engagement to be a critical predictor of learning and personal development [4][6]. Carini et al. [6] found student engagement to be positively correlated with desirable learning outcomes such as critical thinking skills and grades; however, the magnitude of this connection was weak because engagement is only one of a variety of variables that contribute to these particular learning outcomes. Similarly, Rowe et al. [4] found, independent of students' prior domain knowledge and experience, a strong positive relationship between learning outcomes and increased engagement. Thus, engaged interest towards an instructional task can influence cognitive performance, thereby facilitating deeper learning [4][7].

The methods for detecting engagement levels across individuals in real-time rely primarily on physiological sensors. A number of sensors have been empirically tested for detecting engagement levels, including: Electrocardiogram (ECG) [18], Galvanic-Skin Response (GSR) [8], and Electroencephalography (EEG). EEG is the prominent variable of interest for this research because commercial EEG systems have been used to track and model user attention in real time [5]. Fairclough and Venables' [17] experiment revealed EEG measures to reliably correlate with engagement levels and explained 26-42% of the variance for self-reported levels of distress (e.g., tension and confidence associated with negative affect) across prolonged task interaction. By comparison, Stevens, Galloway & Berka [2] found EEG indices of engagement negatively correlate with experience. They consider the metric is responding to the appearance/format of the content rather than the actual content presented.

Results from these studies show a number of variables have an impact on a learner's engagement, and time on task and presentation characteristics of instructional content are directly related. Adaptive tailoring of content can mitigate this effect and extend the time before the onset of disengagement. The primary goal of this effort is to identify predictive influencers of engagement for the adaptation of content and feedback, in real-time, when a classified cognitive state is deemed to have a negative impact on learning.

3 Methodology

Twenty-one adults volunteered to participate in the experiment with seventeen providing usable data. Of the 17 participants, 11 were males (age M = 34, SD = 9.5) and 6 were females (age M = 40, SD = 12). Each participant interacted with the Cultural Meeting Trainer (CMT), a web-browser-based training system prototype in which the learner engages in bilateral conversations with virtual characters representative of Middle Eastern culture. Participants interact with CMT characters through static dialogue choices. No subjects reported experience in inter-cultural conversations or negotiations prior to participating in the study.

A counterbalanced within-subjects experimental design evaluated the effectiveness of an EEG-based cognitive-state sensor during three conversations of (a) varying clarity (one well-defined and two ill-defined) and (b) the presence or absence of interruptions. A well-defined task was one, which followed an unambiguous series of steps, where success was clearly defined. An ill-defined task was one in which the task was vague or ambiguous, where objectives are not clearly stated and there are many possible paths to success.

The second manipulation measured the effect of disruption on engagement, using self-report measures of engagement. In the context of the experiment, participants and characters take turns speaking or acting. Having the character speak unpredictably is a disruption to the pattern of expectancy. This type of disruption occurs in one of the two ill-defined conversations. This manipulation enables the assessment of whether or not there are detectable differences in reported levels of engagement with the inclusion and exclusion of disruptions.

3.1 Procedure

Participants were first given an overview of the research, signed a consent form, were fitted with the EEG recording Emotiv EPOC, and given a demographics questionnaire. Next, initial interaction with the CMT interface was provided through an introductory conversation with a virtual character, followed by three conversation tasks presented to the participants in random order. Before each conversation, participants observed a relaxation video for one to two minutes to place them in a state of calm before conducting the next conversation. This video was intended to mediate the mood state experienced in the previous scenario. At the start of each conversation, participants were given a background briefing on the character they would be conversing with along with guidelines and the purpose of the meeting.

For this study, the participant conversed with three hospital employees following a nearby insurgency attack. The Well-Defined No Interruption (WDNI) task required participants to maintain casual small talk with an in-house physician. The two ill-defined scenarios included an Ill-Defined No Interruption (IDNI) task with the lead physician and an Ill-Defined with Interruption (IDI) task with the hospital administrator. The objective of the conversation with the lead physician was to gather information on the attack without making direct assurances of U.S. pledges to the doctor. The discussion with the administrator was intended to gain U.S. support and identify what the hospital needed to function efficiently. This conversation with the hospital administrator was designed with an interruption in task progression where the character spoke out of turn. Each meeting was approximately five to six minutes in duration.

3.2 Dependent Measures

A demographic questionnaire was administered to each participant. Information included age and education level, prior experience in inter-cultural conversation and negotiation, personality (Big Five Personality Test [9]), and current mood with the Self-Assessment Manikin (SAM) instrument. The Big Five Personality Test provides percentile scores on the Five-Factor Model (FFM) [9] dimensions of openness, conscientiousness, extraversion, agreeableness and neuroticism. Research suggests these dimensions provide insight into how an individual governs their cognitive resources [20].

Subjects' self-reported, engagement levels were collected following each conversational task. A two-part instrument was administered to assess engagement. The first part included 14 engagement-specific (α=.89) questions derived from the Independent Television Commision-Sense of Presence Inventory (ITC-SOPI). The engagement index assesses a subject's attention and involvement during task interaction [12]. This survey was selected because attention signals have been shown to be highly correlated with "presence", which is reasonably correlated with engagement in virtual environments [10, 11]. The second part of the post-conversation survey is the SAM [15], a validated non-verbal graphical approach for evaluating Mehrabian's three dimensions of mood: pleasure, arousal and dominance [16].

Real-time measures of engagement were derived from sensors placed directly on the participant. Data was collected via the Emotiv EPOC Neuroheadset, a commercial-off-the-shelf EEG brain-computer interface. The Emotiv EPOC is composed of 14 electrodes with locations following the American EEG Standard [14]. This device provided rolling continuous measures of associated states, including: Short-Term Excitement (STE), Long-Term Excitement (LTE) and engagement. The Emotiv has previously been used to capture engagement levels within computer-based entertainment games [19]. Collection of sensory data provided concurrent physiological information allowing assessment of dynamically changing cognitive states instead of only evaluating static labels from the administered self-report instruments [13]. Data collected with the initial questionnaire was used to correlate demographic variables with EEG and self-reported data to generate subgroups.

This research evaluated the influence of personality, mood and EEG measures on the prediction of engagement. The following hypotheses were addressed: (1) Assessed measures of personality via Big Five Personality Test and mood via the SAM will correlate with self-reported measures of engagement; (2) Aggregate physiological data (STE, LTE and Engagement from Emotiv) will correlate with self-reported engagement levels (e.g., *feeling of not just watching)*; (3) Self-reported measures of engagement will be significantly higher in the interruption condition (IDI) when compared to scenarios with no interruption (WDNI and IDNI); and (4) Self-reported measures of engagement will be significantly higher in the ill-defined scenarios (IDNI and IDI) when compared to the measures of engagement in the well-defined scenario (WDNI) due to unspecified routines for achieving task objectives. It is believed an interruption in conversation will produce higher engagement scores because the expected interaction routine is broken, resulting in more focused attention to dialogue selections.

4 Results

Analysis was conducted to observe the relationship personality and mood dimensions have on self-reported engagement levels following interaction with a web-based training system. The following tables present Pearson's coefficients for the FFM personality and the SAM mood dimensions in relation to measures derived from the engagement index of the ITC-SOPI (See Table 1, 2, and 3). A Separate analysis conducted for all conditions was based on each of the 14 individual items as well as their mean to produce an overall engagement score. Individual items were examined to gauge causal relationships between variables.

Table 1. Personality (based on FFM) and SAM correlations with reported Engagement scores for individual items within the Well-Defined Conversation Scenario

Engagement Item	Personality Dimension	Correlation
'I paid more attention to displayed environment than I did my own thoughts'	FFM Openness FFM Agreeableness	r(16) = -.564, p = .023 r(16) = -.498, p = .049
'I felt myself being drawn in'	FFM Agreeableness	r(16) = -.524, p = .037
'I felt involved'	FFM Agreeableness	r(16) = -.527, p = .036
'I feel I wasn't just watching something'	FFM Agreeableness	r(16) = -.547, p = .028
'I responded emotionally'	FFM Agreeableness	r(16) = -.546, p = .029
Average Score for All Items	FFM Agreeableness	r(16) = -.767, p = .001
'I felt the characters were aware of me'	SAM Pleasure	r(16) = .516, p = .041
'I feel I wasn't just watching something'	SAM Dominance	r(16) = .596, p = .015

Table 2. Personality (based on FFM) and SAM correlations with reported Engagement scores for individual items within the IDNI Conversation Scenario

Engagement Item	Personality Dimension	Correlation
Average Score for All Items	FFM Agreeableness	r(16) = -.612, p = .012
Average Score for All Items	FFM Neuroticism	r(16) = .535, p = .033
'The experience was intense'	SAM Pleasure	r(16) = .617, p = .011

Table 3. Personality (based on FFM) and SAM correlations with reported Engagement scores for individual items within the IDI Conversation Scenario

Engagement Item	Personality Dimension	Correlation
'I felt involved'	FFM Agreeableness	r(16) = .499, p = .049
'I paid more attention to displayed environment than I did my own thoughts'	FFM Agreeableness SAM Pleasure	r(16) = -.566, p = .022 r(16) = .621, p = .010
'I felt that interacting with the character was difficult'	SAM Dominance	r(16) = -.512, p = .043

Examining the reliability of the assessed personality/mood measures and their influence on self-reported engagement, all variables were accounted for in regression analysis. Variables were trimmed based on coefficients found to not have a significant influence on the prescribed outcome. The results illustrated "*agreeableness and arousal*" to explain a significant portion of variance in *Self-Reported Engagement* scores for the WDNI scenario, adjusted R^2 = .66, F(2, 13) = 15.68, p < .001. The following linear regression model was developed:

$$\textit{Self Reported Engagement} = 4.374 - 0.013 * \textit{agreeableness} - 0.099 * \textit{arousal} \quad (1)$$

Furthermore, results suggest a significant amount of variance in *Self-Reported Engagement* scores (IDNI scenario) is explained by "*agreeableness and neuroticism*", adjusted R^2 = .54, F(2, 13) = 9.89, p = .002, producing the linear regression model shown below:

$$\textit{Self Reported Engagement} = 3.295 - 0.007 * \textit{agreeableness} + 0.010 * \textit{neuroticism} \quad (2)$$

In the interruption scenario (IDI), "*agreeableness*" explained a significant portion of variance in "*feeling of being involved*" scores, adjusted R^2 = .20, F(1, 14) = 4.65, p = .049; and in "*more attention to environment*" scores, adjusted R^2 = .20, F(1, 14) = 6.59, p = .022. Based on these findings, the two models were formed:

$$\textit{Feeling of being involved} = 2.566 + 0.014 * \textit{agreeableness} \quad (3)$$

$$\textit{More attention to environment} = 4.598 - 0.020 * \textit{agreeableness} \quad (4)$$

Subsequently, aggregate physiological data (STE, LTE and Engagement) was analyzed against self-reported engagement scores to identify correlations (See Table 4). This analysis incorporated Resting Engagement (RE) data collected during the two minute phases prior to each individual scenario.

Examining the reliability of self-reported engagement measures in predicting physiological outputs for the WDNI scenario, analysis showed "*surprised by character actions*" to explain a significant portion of variance in RE scores, adjusted R^2 = .21, F(1, 14) = 5.08, p = .041 and "*feeling that character was aware of you*" explained a significant portion of variance in STE scores, adjusted R^2 = .27, F(1, 14) = 6.49, p = .023. The following linear regressions were developed from these results:

$$\textit{STE} = 0.677 - 0.091 * \textit{feeling that character was aware of you} \quad (5)$$

$$\textit{RE} = 0.702 - 0.057 * \textit{surprised by character actions} \quad (6)$$

Table 4. Emotiv STE, LTE, and Engagement correlations with reported Engagement scores for individual items within all Conversation Scenarios (WDNI, IDNI and IDI)

Engagement Item (WDNI, IDNI, IDI)	Emotiv Dimension	Correlation
'I feel I wasn't just watching something' (WDNI)	STE LTE	r(16) = -.523, p = .019 r(16) = -.436, p = .046
'I felt the character was aware of me' (WDNI)	STE LTE	r(16) = -.563, p = .012 r(16) = -.450, p = .040
'I felt that interacting with the character was difficult' (WDNI)	STE	r(16) = .485, p = .029
'I responded emotionally' (WDNI)	LTE	r(16) = -.428, p = .049
'I was surprised by something the character did or said' (WDNI)	Resting Engagement (RE)	r(16) = -.516, p = .020
'I feel I wasn't just watching something' (IDNI)	RE	r(16) = -.455, p = .038
'I lost track of time' (IDNI)	RE	r(16) = -.542, p = .015
'I paid more attention to displayed environment than I did my own thoughts' (IDNI)	RE	r(16) = -.436, p = .046
'I felt myself being drawn in' (IDI)	STE LTE	r(16) = -.447, p = .041 r(16) = -.473, p = .032
'I felt that interacting with the character was difficult' (IDI)	Engagement	r(16) = -.457, p = .037
'I lost track of time' (IDI)	RE	r(16) = -.569, p = .011
'I feel I wasn't just watching something' (IDI)	RE	r(16) = -.440, p = .044

Within the two ill-defined scenarios, two linear regression models that explain significant variance in self-reported scores were found. The item *"lost track of time"* explained a significant portion of variance in RE scores for both the IDNI and IDI scenarios, adjusted $R^2 = .24$, $F(1, 14) = 5.82$, $p = .030$ (IDNI); adjusted $R^2 = .28$, $F(1, 14) = 6.69$, $p = .022$ (IDI). The following linear regression models were developed:

$$RE\ (\text{IDNI}) = 0.722 - 0.063 * \textit{lost track of time} \tag{7}$$

$$RE\ (\text{IDI}) = 0.714 - 0.065 * \textit{lost track of time} \tag{8}$$

The next statistical test evaluated if engagement scores will be significantly higher in the interruption condition (IDI) when compared to scenarios with no interruption (WDNI and IDNI). A non-directional t-Test ($\alpha = .05$) was used to compare the average "interruption" scores with the average "no interruption" score. Only the *"feeling that interaction was difficult"* item, a self-reported measure of engagement, was shown to have a significant difference in the averages within subjects for the WDNI ($M = 2.188$, $SD = 1.05$) and the IDI groups ($M = 2.875$, $SD = 1.02$), $t = -2.63$, p = .019. All other self-reported measures of engagement failed to show any significant differences between the "interruption" and "no interruption" conditions.

In addition, analysis examined if engagement scores were significantly higher in ill-defined scenarios (IDNI and IDI) when compared to the measures of engagement in the well-defined scenario (WDNI). A non-directional student's t-Test ($\alpha = .05$) was used to compare the ill-defined (both with and without interrupts) average scores with the average well-defined score for all ten self-reported measures of engagement.

For *"feeling that interaction was difficult"*, significant differences in the averages of the IDNI group (M = 3.063, SD = 1.12) and the WDNI group (M = 2.188, SD = 1.05), t = 3.12, p = .036 were identified. As well, there were significant differences in the averages of the IDI group (M = 2.875, SD = 1.02) and the WDNI group (M = 2.188, SD = 1.05), t = 2.68, p = .017. For *"surprised by character actions"*, there was no significant difference in averages for the IDI and the WDNI groups, but there was a significant difference between the IDNI (M = 3.375, SD = 1.09) and the WDNI groups (M = 2.75, SD = .93), t = 2.29, p = .036, with a higher mean for the ill-defined task. For *"lost track of time"*, there was no significant difference in the averages of the IDNI group and the WDNI group, but there was a significant difference between the IDI group (M = 2.56, SD = .89) and the WDNI group (M = 3.13, SD = 1.09), t = -2.52, p = .023, with the well-defined scenario showing the larger mean.

5 Discussion

The manipulation of task clarity and sequence of task interaction has shown reliable differences in self-reported scores of engagement. In terms of clarity this conveys that more attentional resources are required for task execution when steps for successful performance are ambiguously defined. As well, it was hypothesized that the interruption scenario would show reliably higher engagement scores when compared to non-interruption conversations. Analysis illustrates that subjects reliably reported the interaction to be more difficult when an interruption in the expected task progression was present. This suggests tailoring training content to incorporate ill-defined rules along with interactions that break expectations can produce visible increases in engagement.

In addition to assessing the effect tailoring of content has on engagement, personality factors, mood factors and physiological factors were evaluated to observe their predictive power in terms of estimating self-reported ITC-SOPI scores. The resulting analysis expressed multiple approaches for reliably predicting learner engagement through static and dynamic assessment techniques. Specifically, the personality dimensions of extraversion, agreeableness, and neuroticism along with the mood dimension of arousal were found to be reliable predictors of engagement when analyzed within individual tasks. For all post-scenario metrics, the dimension of agreeableness (cooperative vs. suspicious) was the only variable to demonstrate predictive power independent of task definition, with the majority displaying negative correlations. This suggests that individuals who are classified with low 'agreeableness' engage in training content on a higher scale due to their preference of questioning events and content they experience.

Furthermore, the specificity of the Emotiv system for predicting engagement scores was evaluated. Specificity defines how precisely a specific cognitive state can be inferred. The protocol attempted to evaluate specificity by comparing self-reported levels of engagement to aggregate states (e.g., STE, LTE) classified by the Emotiv. The results validated relationships between the RE and STE metrics provided by Emotiv with self-reported states of engagement. The RE finding conveys that those subjects exhibiting high engagement in rest states are less apt to be drawn in when training continues due to their attentional resources already being in use.

6 Conclusion and Recommended Future Research

The results of this study show personality factors (agreeableness, neuroticism) are predictors of general engagement and could easily be used to tailor instructional strategies where engagement was not predicted to be optimal. It was also evident that Emotiv provided significant near real-time measures of engagement and excitement where head movement (and thereby signal noise) is restricted. Emotiv would have significant limitations in predicting engagement (or other states) in any interactions where head movement was significant (e.g., natural interfaces like Xbox 360 Kinect).

Following this initial study a more expansive experiment that includes Emotiv and BioPac (ECG and GSR measures) systems will be conducted. ECG and GSR measures have aided EEG in the establishment of an engagement index in order to predict engagement [19]. For future research, we recommend continued efforts to find passive sensors that are portable, durable and indicate the learner's cognitive and affective states to provide a clearer decision point for adaptive instructional strategies.

References

1. Woolf, B., Burleson, W., Arroyo, I., Dragon, T., Cooper, D., Picard, R.: Affect-Aware Tutors: Recognizing and Responding to Student Affect. International Journal of Learning Technology 4, 129–164 (2009)
2. Stevens, R.H., Galloway, T., Berka, C.: Integrating Innovative Neuro-Educational Technologies (I-Net) into K-12 Science Classrooms. In: Schmorrow, D., Reeves, L. (eds.) HCII 2007 and FAC 2007. LNCS (LNAI), vol. 4565, pp. 47–56. Springer, Heidelberg (2007)
3. Berka, C., Levendowski, D.J., Lumicao, M.N., Yau, A., Davis, G., Zivkovic, V.T., Olmstead, R.E., Tremoulet, P.D., Craven, P.L.: EEG Correlates of Task Engagement and Mental Workload in Vigilance, Learning, and Memory Tasks. Aviation Space and Environmental Medicine 78(5), B231–B244 (2007)
4. Rowe, J., Shores, L., Mott, B., Lester, J.: Integrating Learning and Engagement in Narrative-Centered Learning Environments. In: Proceedings of the 10th International Conference on Intelligent Tutoring Systems, Pittsburgh, pp. 166–177 (2010)
5. Peters, C., Asteriadis, S., Rebolledo-mendez, G.: Modelling user attention for human-agent interaction. In: 10th Workshop on Image Analysis for Multimedia Interactive Services, pp. 266–269 (2009)
6. Carini, R.M., Kuh, G.D., Klein, S.P.: Student Engagement and Student Learning: Testing the Linkages. Research in Higher Education 47(1), 1–32 (2006)

7. Wade, S., Buxton, W., Kelly, M.: Using Think-Alouds to Examine Reader-Text Interest. Reading Research Quarterly 34, 194–216 (1999)
8. Dragon, T., Arroyo, I., Woolf, B.P., Burleson, W., el Kaliouby, R., Eydgahi, H.: Viewing Student Affect and Learning through Classroom Observation and Physical Sensors. In: Woolf, B.P., Aïmeur, E., Nkambou, R., Lajoie, S. (eds.) ITS 2008. LNCS, vol. 5091, pp. 29–39. Springer, Heidelberg (2008)
9. McCrae, R.R., John, O.P.: An Introduction to the Five-Factor Model and Its Applications. Special Issue: The Five-Factor Model: Issues and Applications. Journal of Personality 60, 175–215 (1992)
10. Tang, A., Biocca, F., Lim, L.: Comparing Differences in Presence During Social Interaction in Augmented Reality Versus Virtual Reality Environments: An Exploratory Study. In: 7th International Workshop on Presence, Valencia, Spain (2004)
11. Lombard, M., Ditton, T.B., Weinstein, L.: Measuring (Tele)Presence: The Temple Presence Inventory. In: Twelfth International Workshop on Presence, Los Angeles, California, USA (2009)
12. Lessiter, J., Freeman, J., Keogh, E., Davidoff, J.: A Cross-Media Presence Questionnaire: the ITC-Sense of Presence Inventory. Presence 10(3), 282–297 (2001)
13. Inventado, P.S., Legaspi, R., Bui, T.D., Suarez, M.: Predicting Student's Appraisal of Feedback in an ITS Using Previous Affective States and Continuous Affect Labels from EEG Data. In: Wong, S.L., et al. (eds.) Proceedings of the 18th International Conference on Computers in Education, Putrajaya, Malaysia (2010)
14. American Electroencephalographic Society Guidelines for Standard Electrode Position Nomenclature. Journal of Clinical Neurophysiology 8, 200–202 (2001)
15. Bradley, M.M., Lang, P.J.: Measuring emotion: The Self-Assessment Manikin and the Semantic Differential. Journal of Behavior Therapy and Experimental Psychiatry 25(1), 49–59 (1994)
16. Mehrabian, A.: Pleasure-Arousal-Dominance: A General Framework for Describing and Measuring Individual Differences in Temperament. Current Psychology 14, 261–292 (1996)
17. Fairclough, S.H., Venables, L.: Prediction of Subjective States from Psychophysiology: A Multivariate Approach. Biological Psychology 71, 100–110 (2006)
18. Chaouachi, M., Chalfoun, P., Jraidi, I., Frasson, C.: Affect and Mental Engagement: Towards Adaptability for Intelligent Systems. In: Proceedings of the 23rd International FLAIRS Conference. AAAI Press, Daytona Beach (2010)
19. Koutepova, T., Liu, Y., Lan, X., Jeong, J.: Enhancing Video Games in Real Time with Biofeedback Data. In: SIGGRAPH Asia, Seoul (2010)
20. Zhang, L.: Thinking Styles and the Big Five Personality Traits Revisited. Personality and Individual Differences 40, 1177–1187 (2006)

Context-Independent Facial Action Unit Recognition Using Shape and Gabor Phase Information

Isabel Gonzalez[1], Hichem Sahli[1], Valentin Enescu[1], and Werner Verhelst[1,2]

[1] Vrije Universiteit Brussel, AVSP, Department ETRO, VUB-ETRO, Pleinlaan 2, 1050 Brussels, Belgium
{igonzale,hichem.sahli,venescu,wverhels}@etro.vub.ac.be
[2] Institute for Broadband Technology - IBBT

Abstract. In this paper we investigate the combination of shape features and Phase-based Gabor features for context-independent Action Unit Recognition. For our recognition goal, three regions of interest have been devised that efficiently capture the AUs activation/deactivation areas. In each of these regions a feature set consisting of geometrical and histogram of Gabor phase appearance-based features have been estimated. For each Action Unit, we applied Adaboost for feature selection, and used a binary SVM for context-independent classification. Using the Cohn-Kanade database, we achieved an average F_1 score of 93.8% and an average area under the ROC curve of 97.9 %, for the 11 AUs considered.

Keywords: SVM,Adaboost, Facial Action Units.

1 Introduction

Automatic facial expression analysis and recognition has attracted increasing research, the last decade, for applications such as computer vision, affective computing, human centered interfaces, computer graphics and psychology.

The Facial Action Coding System (FACS) [4] proved its efficacy in analyzing facial behavior. FACS employs as basic units, action units (AU) which model facial movements, by associating each AU with the activation of one or more specific facial muscles. As such decomposing facial expressions into a sequence of AUs is considered as an important step in the facial expression recognition process [5].

In the literature two main parameterisations are used for AU recognition, namely geometric, and appearance. The geometric based parameterisation consists of detecting and tracking facial feature points which are then used for classification e.g. by [16] and [19]. Appearance-based features consider motion and texture changes and has been used among others in [1], and [13]. State of the art classification methods are Support Vector Machines (SVM) [1], [14], Neural Networks [18], Hidden Markov Models [12], and Discriminant Analysis [12].

In this work we consider the combination of the geometric and appearance based parametrisation. This has also been used successfully in previous works

S. D´Mello et al. (Eds.): ACII 2011, Part I, LNCS 6974, pp. 548–557, 2011.

[14], [22], with better recognition results. For the shape features we follow the proposed features by [7], [19], and [22]. Among the most successful appearance-based methods for AU recognition Gabor magnitude information have been widely used [18]. However, they still exhibit some shortcomings, as they ensure only partial insensitiveness to illumination changes resulting in the necessity for additional (robust) face descriptors. To tackle the above issues, we propose in this paper the use of histogram of Oriented Gabor phase Congruency. Gabor Phase responses were successfully used for face recognition, e.g. by Zhang et al. [21] who uses as feature vector the local histograms of the phase responses encoded via local binary patterns and showed that over small image regions the Gabor phase patterns exhibit some kind of regularity (in terms of histograms) and contain useful information for the task of face recognition. In this work we propose using the histogram of the 2D phase congruency model of Kovesi [11]. The Kovesi's phase congruency has been also used by Buciu and Nafornita [2] for facial expression analysis, however they consider a 1D representation of the image by lexicographically scanning the image, and apply a "cross - phase Congruency" extracted from a set of aligned images. The effectiveness of orientation histogram has been also shown for AU detection, using SIFT features [17].

For an input image sequence, the above features are estimated for the neutral image and the image showing expression apex, and are fed to a feature selection technique, and classified by Support Vector Machines. The reminder of the paper is as follows. Section 2, gives an overview of the considered features, Section 3 summarizes the approach for feature selection and classification. Experimental results are illustrated in Section 4 and conclusions are give in Section 5.

2 Feature Extraction

The head and facial feature were tracked using the Constrained Shape Tracking approach of [8]. This approach allows an automatic detection of the head and the tracking of a shape model composed of 83 landmarks, located as illustrated in Fig. 1.

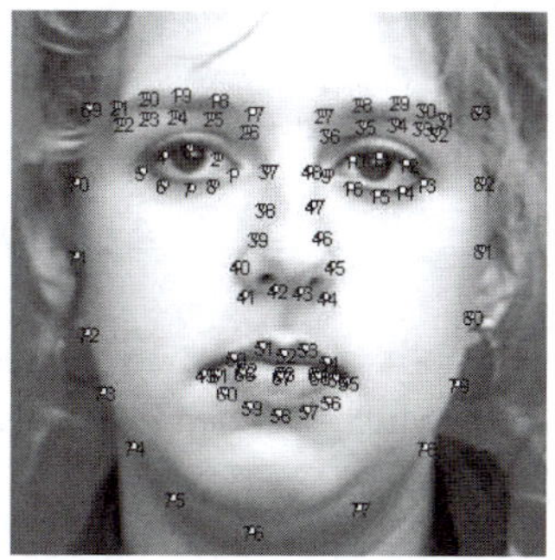

Fig. 1. Facial landmarks

After the facial components have been tracked in each frame, $I(t), t \in \{1..T\}$, a normalization step registers each image with respect to the neutral frame $I(0)$. An affine texture transformation is applied to each image so as to warp the texture into the reference frame. This normalization provides further robustness to the effects of head motion (in-plane rotation, scaling , and translation; and small out-of-plane rotations). Once the texture is warped, the face is subdivided into three areas R_{low}, R_{mid} and R_{up}, and the corresponding landmarks of the shape model are then used to extract the geometry-based, $GF_{low}, GF_{mid}, GF_{up}$, and appearance-based, $AF_{low}, AF_{mid}, AF_{up}$, features for the recognition of the lower, middle and upper AU's, respectively.

2.1 Geometry-Based Features

Let, $P_t = \{p_{i,t}, i \in \{1..83\}\}$ the facial landmarks of frame $I(t)$, with $p^x_{i,t}, p^y_{i,t}$ their horizontal (x) and vertical (y) coordinates, respectively. Let $f_k(p_{i,t}, p_{j,l})$ an operator that would take two landmarks and return a feature estimated using the coordinates of the considered points. We define the following operators:

- the y and the x coordinate deviation of a landmark relative to its position in the first frame [19]:

$$f_1(p_{i,0}, p_{i,t}) = p^y_{i,t} - p^y_{i,0} \ ; \tag{1}$$

$$f_2(p_{i,0}, p_{i,t}) = p^x_{i,t} - p^x_{i,0} \ ; \tag{2}$$

- euclidian distance between each pair of landmarks [19]:

$$f_3(p_{i,t}, p_{j,t}) = ||p_{i,t} - p_{j,t}|| \ ; \tag{3}$$

- displacement of the euclidian distance [19]:

$$f_4(p_i, p_j) = f_3(p_{i,t}, p_{j,t}) - f_3(p_{i,0}, p_{j,0}) \ ; \tag{4}$$

- displacement of the vertical and horizontal distance between each pair of landmarks relative to the first frame:

$$f_5(p_i, p_j) = |p^y_{i,t} - p^y_{j,t}| - |p^y_{i,0} - p^y_{j,0}| \ ; \tag{5}$$

$$f_6(p_i, p_j) = |p^x_{i,t} - p^x_{j,t}| - |p^x_{i,0} - p^x_{j,0}| \ . \tag{6}$$

We also define the following features of the mouth:

- mouth opening, from left corner to center and from right corner to center:

$$fm_1(P_t) = (||p_{A,t} - p_{49,t}|| + ||p_{A,t} - p_{55,t}||) - (||p_{A,0} - p_{49,0}|| + ||p_{A,0} - p_{55,0}||) \ , \tag{7}$$

  with p_A the midpoint between the two mouth corners, computed as in [9] ;
- the size of the red parts of the lips:

$$fm_2(P_t) = ||p_{52,t} - p_{58,t}|| - ||p_{63,t} - p_{67,t}|| \ ; \tag{8}$$

– the difference between the height and the width of the mouth

$$fm_3(P_t) = ||p_{58,t} - p_{52,t}|| - ||p_{55,t} - p_{49,t}|| \ . \tag{9}$$

The last set of geometrical features consider the deviation of certain angles relative to their values in the first frame [22]:

$$fa_1(P_t) = \alpha(p_1, p_5, p_{26})_t - \alpha(p_1, p_5, p_{26})_0 \ ; \tag{10}$$

$$fa_2(P_t) = \alpha(p_9, p_{11}, p_{13})_t - \alpha(p_9, p_{11}, p_{13})_0 \ ; \tag{11}$$

$$fa_3(P_t) = \alpha(p_1, p_3, p_5)_t - \alpha(p_1, p_3, p_5)_0 \ ; \tag{12}$$

$$fa_4(P_t) = \alpha(p_9, p_{13}, p_{15})_t - \alpha(p_9, p_{13}, p_{15})_0 \ ; \tag{13}$$

$$fa_5(P_t) = \alpha(p_1, p_5, p_7)_t - \alpha(p_1, p_5, p_7)_0 \ , \tag{14}$$

where $\alpha(p_i, p_j, p_k)_t$ denotes the angle between the two vectors formed by the three points at frame t.

Considering the sets of landmarks within each of the three face regions, R_{low}, R_{mid}, R_{up}, where the subscript t is omitted:

– $\mathbf{P_{low}} = \{p_1, p_9, p_{49}, p_{52}, p_{55}, p_{58}, p_{71}, p_{76}, p_{81}, p_O\}$, with p_O the center of the nose.
– $\mathbf{P_{up}} = \{p_1, p_3, p_5, p_7, p_9, p_{11}, p_{13}, p_{15}, p_{37}, p_{39}, p_{41}, p_{44}, p_{46}, p_{48}, p_{49}, p_{55}, p_{70}, p_{71}, p_{81}, p_{82}\}$.
– $\mathbf{P_{mid}} = \{p_1, p_3, p_5, p_7, p_9, p_{11}, p_{13}, p_{15}, p_{17}, p_{19}, p_{21}, p_{27}, p_{29}, p_{31}, p_{37}, p_{39}, p_{46}, p_{48}, p_{69}, p_{70}, p_{82}, p_{83}\}$.

the geometrical features are defined as follows:

$$GF^t_{low} = [fm_1(P_t), fm_2(P_t), fm_3(P_t), f_k(p_{i,t}, p_{j,l}), k = 1..6; i, j \in P_{low}],$$
$$\text{resulting in 195 features ;}$$
$$GF^t_{mid} = [f_k(p_{i,t}, p_{j,l}), k = 1..6; i, j \in P_{mid}], \text{ resulting in 442 features ;}$$
$$GF^t_{up} = [fa_1(P_t), fa_2(P_t), fa_3(P_t), fa_4(P_t), fa_5(P_t), f_k(p_{i,t}, p_{j,l}),$$
$$k = 1..6; i, j \in P_{up}], \text{ resulting in 526 features .}$$

2.2 Appearance-Based Features

From the facial feature points, we locate several regions of interest (ROI) as shown in Fig. 2. A number of AU will display wrinkles, bulges or furrows in a particular direction in one or more of the ROI. Since several AUs leave such a display in the same region, we further subdivided , ROI C in 6 subregions, and ROI D in 4 subregions. Table 1 gives an overview of the possible AUs in each ROI.

For each image frame t and each of the ROI'S, $ROI_J; J \in \{A, B, C_1, C_2, C_3, C_4, C_5, C_6, D_{11}, D_{12}, D_{13}, D_{14}, D_{21}, D_{22}, D_{23}, D_{24}, E_1, E_2\}$, we first apply a histogram equalization, and then we compute the Gabor phase congruency (orientation O^t_J) image [11]. From the resulting orientation images, O^t_J, we estimate the normalised orientation histogram, OH^t_J, of 12 orientation bins. Fig. 3(a) and

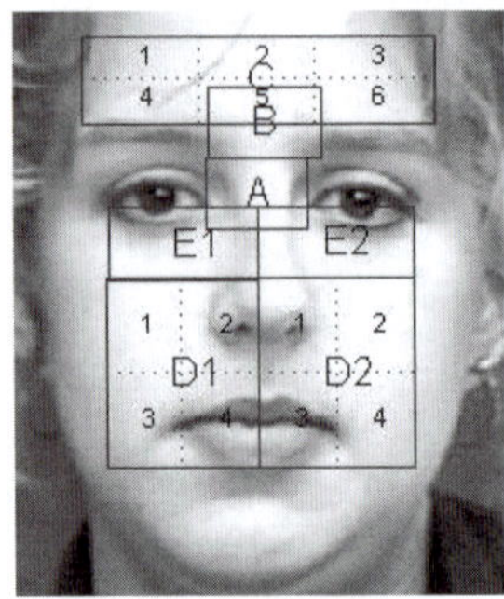

Fig. 2. Regions of Interest for the estimation of appearance features

Table 1. ROI's where one or more action units can be active

ROI_A	ROI_B	ROI_C	ROI_D	ROI_E
AU9 (AU4)	AU4	AU1 AU2 AU4	AU6 AU9 AU12 AU20	AU6 AU7 AU9 AU12

3(b) illustrates the histogram orientation of ROI_A, for the neutral frame $I(0)$ and the apex frame $I(T)$ of a sequence where $AU9$ is strongly active. Finally, the proposed appearance feature for each ROI, AF_J^t, is defined as the difference between the normalized histograms of the the apex frame and the neutral frame:

$$AF_J^t = OH_J^t - OH_J^0 \ . \tag{15}$$

Using the orientation histograms of Fig. 3(a) and 3(b), Fig. 3(c) illustrates the proposed feature within ROI_A, for a sequence where $AU9$ is strongly active, and hence it will display deep horizontal wrinkles in ROI_A. As it can be noticed, orientations 1, 2, and 12 (which are the vertical orientations) are significantly less present in the apex frame T, while orientation 6 (the horizontal orientations), is significantly more present in the apex frame.

Finally, for each of the three face ares, R_{low}, R_{mid}, and R_{up}, we define the appearance features as concatenation of the orientation histograms of the ROI's belonging to the considered are:

- $AF_{low}^t = [AF_{D_1}^t, AF_{D_2}^t, AF_{E_1}^t, AF_{E_2}^t]$;
- $AF_{mid}^t = [AF_A^t, AF_{D_1}^t, AF_{D_2}^t, AF_{E_1}^t, AF_{E_2}^t]$;
- $AF_{low}^t = [AF_A^t, AF_B^t, AF_C^t]$.

2.3 Combination of Geometry-Based and Appearance-Based Features

In this work, considering an image sequence with facial expressions, the geometrical and appearance features are estimated using the first frame, $I(0)$, being the

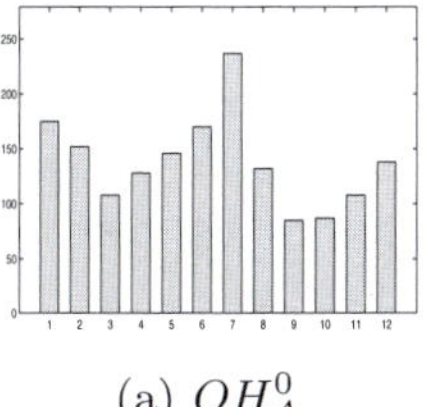

(a) OH_A^0

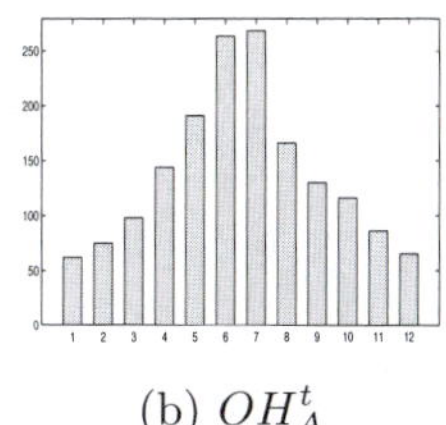

(b) OH_A^t

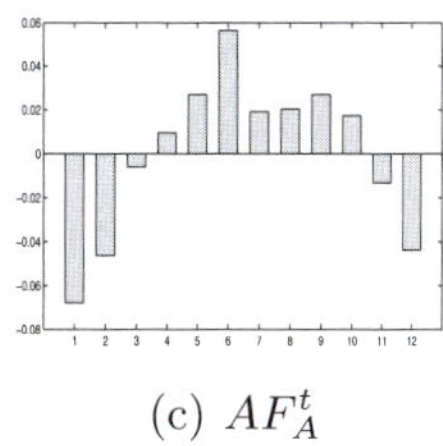

(c) AF_A^t

Fig. 3. Orientation Histograms, 3(a) and 3(b), and appearance-based feature AF_A^t 3(c), of ROI_A

neutral frame, and the last frame, $I(T)$, exhibiting the apex of the expression. The final feature vectors for defined facial areas are obtained by concatenating the geometrical and appearance features as follows:

$$\begin{aligned} F_{low} &= GF_{low}^T \cup AF_{low}^T \ ; \\ F_{mid} &= GF_{mid}^T \cup AF_{mid}^T \ ; \\ F_{up} &= GF_{up}^T \cup AF_{up}^T \ . \end{aligned} \tag{16}$$

F_{low} are used for the classification of lower facial AUs AU12, AU20, AU23, AU25 and AU27; F_{mid} for facial AUs AU6, AU7, and AU9; and F_{up} for AU1, AU2, and AU4.

3 Feature Selection and Classification

For feature selection, the Adaboost algorithm has been used. AdaBoost (Adaptive Boosting) is a strong and fast classification algorithm, introduced by Freud and Schapire [6]. The algorithm makes use of a weak binary classifier that strengthens its decisions in each iteration to end up with a final hypothesis with the lowest error rate. The weak binary classifier (weak learner) is any classifier for which the weighted classification error is expected to be better than chance. More recently, particularly in the Computer Vision community, Boosting has become popular as a feature selection routine, in which a single feature is selected in each Boosting iteration.

In this work, we first use Adaboost as a classifier to find the most suited type (discrete; gentle; logit; and real) and parameters for each AU. Once we find the most suited, i.e. the one with the highest classification rate for a particular AU, we use that type of Adaboost and given parameters as a feature selection method in which the weak classifiers are decision stumps. The result from the feature selection, is a list of selected features with a given quality value. The higher the quality value given by Adaboost, the better the feature.

For AU classification, the Support Vector Machine (SVM) has been used. SVM is a supervised method used for classification and regression, and has a well-founded mathematical theory [20]. Through training, a SVM builds a hyper plane, or set of hyper planes, in a high or infinite dimensional feature space which separates two or more classes. The maximum-margin hyper plane is the hyper plane that maximizes the distance from it to the nearest data point on each side. The larger the margin is, the lower the generalization error of the classifier.

In this paper, the LibSVM [3] has been used to perform 2-class classification for each AU, using the best selected features. Both Linear kernel and Radial Basis Function have been evaluated.

4 Experiments

Our system was trained and tested on the Cohn and Kanade's DFAT-504 dataset [10]. The database consists of 486 sequences of facial displays that are produced by 98 University students from 18 to 30 years old, of which 65% is female. All sequences are annotated by certified FACS coders, start with a neutral face, and end with the apex of the expression.

Overexposed sequences in the database were excluded from the experiment in order to get good appearance based features. This resulted in 418 sequences from 85 subjects. Our system is only trained on the last frame of each sequence, which contains the apex of the expression. Our final goal is to develop a system that detects behavioral patterns in communication between two persons, more specifically between mother and infant. The set of AUs is selected from state of the art work in mother-infant communication, e.g. [15].

We evaluate a SVM for each AU with the first k features selected by AdaBoost, ordered by the given quality value. For example, for AU9, our instances consist of 574 features: 442 geometry-based features and 132 appearance-based. After feature selection, this space is reduced to 73 features (41 geometry-based; and 32 appearance-based). We start evaluating the SVM_{AU9} with $k = 73$, and re-evaluate the SVM in each iteration with $k - 1$ features until $k = 2$. The highest F_1 score for AU9 is achieved when $k = 31$. The best feature set for AU9 consist of 18 geometry-based features; 3 features of area A; 6 of area D; and 4 of area E.

The decision function D is defined as follows:

$$D(\mathbf{x}) = \sum_{i=1}^{l} y_i \alpha_i K(\mathbf{x}_i, \mathbf{x}) + b \; , \tag{17}$$

where $i \in \{1, .., l\}$ are the indices of the support vectors $\mathbf{x}_i$, y_i the labels, and α_i the Lagrange multipliers. The prediction of the instance $\mathbf{x}$ is then made by:

$$\begin{cases} \text{AU present if } D(\mathbf{x}) \geq Ths \; , \\ \text{AU absent if } D(\mathbf{x}) < Ths \; . \end{cases} \tag{18}$$

We also vary the threshold $Ths = -7 : 0.05 : 7$, used for the final classification. Generalization to new subjects was tested using leave-one-subject-out cross validation. In each iteration, all sequences of the test subject are excluded from training, and used for testing. The resulting true positives (tp), negatives (tn), false positives (fp), and negatives (fn) are summed over every subject. The performance was computed using the F_1 score, and the area under the ROC curve. The F_1 score can be interpreted as a weighted average of the precision and recall:

$$F_1 = 2(p.r)/(p+r) \; . \tag{19}$$

with p the precision, and r the recall:

$$p = tp/(tp+fp) \; ,$$
$$r = tp/(tp+fn) \; .$$

The area, A, under the ROC curve is another reliable performance measure which enables us to compare our results with State of the Art work, e.g. [1]. The ROC curve is obtained by plotting the hit rate (tpr), against the false alarm rate (fpr) as the decision threshold varies. An area, A, of 100% represents a perfect test; an area, A of 50% represents a worthless test. A is computed by the trapezoidal integration, which is an approximation of the integral of fpr with respect to tpr. The F_1 score and the area under the ROC curve A are shown in Table 2. For AU7, and AU23 a Linear kernel has been used for the SVM classifier, while for the others Radial Basis Function kernels have been used. AU1, AU7, AU20, and AU23 have a better performance when the threshold $Ths = -0.2$, while the other AUs all perform best when $Ths = 0$. Especially AU20, and AU23 have a higher F_1 score not using the sign of the decision value (or $Thst = 0$), more than 2% and 3% respectively.

Table 2. Results for each AU

AU	1	2	4	6	7	9	12	20	23	25	27
P	117	76	126	90	86	40	96	55	36	251	60
F_1	97.9	98.0	90.9	87.0	81.4	97.5	96.3	93.5	93.0	97.2	99.2
A	98.9	99.5	96.9	96.9	92.6	99.9	99.3	98.4	95.5	98.8	100.0

From Table 2, one can notice that we achieve an average F_1 score of 93.8%, and an average area A of 97.9% for the eleven AUs. Moreover, the ROC curve for AU1, AU2, AU9, AU12, AU25, and AU27, represents an almost perfect test. Finally, we compared our results to the ones of Bartlett et al. [1], where only appearance-based features have been used. The comparison is made by considering the area under the ROC curve as shown in Table 3.

Most of the AUs benefit of using both geometry-based and appearance-based features. AU6, AU7, and AU9 are mainly visible by wrinkles and bulges, incorporating geometry-based features does not add (much) advantage. While a combination of geometry-based and appearance is clearly an advantage for AU20. If we compare the lower facial AUs to the work of Gonzalez etal. [7], who uses only geometry-based features, we see that the higher performance of AU23 is more to

Table 3. Proposed approach v.s. Bartlett et al. [1]

AU	1	2	4	6	7	9	12	20	23	25	27	Avg
A	98.9	99.5	96.9	96.9	92.6	99.9	99.3	98.4	95.5	98.8	100.0	**97.9**
A[1]	95	92	91	96	95	100	98	84	70	93	100	**92.18**

the geometry-based features than to appearance-based features, while AU27 has a similar performance using either geometry-, appearance-, or a combination of both.

5 Conclusion

We have presented a technique for context-independent Action Unit Recognition. We divided the face in three main regions, and constructed a feature set according those facial regions. Each feature set contains geometry- and appearance-based features. For each Action Unit, we applied Adaboost for feature selection, and used a binary SVM for context-independent classification. We achieve an average F_1 score of 93.8% and an average area under the ROC curve of 97.9%. Comparing our result to State of the Art work that use only geometry-based, or only appearance-based learns us that most action units benefit from using a combination of both. Some of the action units, e.g. AU23, performs better only geometry-based features, while e.g classification of AU27 has similar performance using either set of features.

Acknowledgments. The research reported in this paper was supported by the EU FP7 project ALIZ-E grant 248116, and the VUB HOA projects Mother-Child Interaction and Toward Cognitive Adaptive Edu-games.

References

1. Bartlett, M., Littlewort, G., Frank, M., Lainscsek, C., Fasel, I., Movellan, J.: Fully automatic facial action recognition in spontaneous behavior. In: Proceedings Of the 7th International Conference on Face and Gesture Recognition, pp. 223–230 (2006)
2. Buciu, I., Nafornita, I.: Feature extraction through cross - phase congruency for facial expression analysis. International Journal of Pattern Recognition and Artificial Intelligence, Special Issue on Facial Image Processing and Analysis 23(3), 617–635 (2009)
3. Chang, C.C., Lin, C.J.: LIBSVM : a library for support vector machines (2001), software `http://www.csie.ntu.edu.tw/~cjlin/libsvm`
4. Ekman, P., Friesen, W., Hager, J.: The Facial Action Coding System on CD ROM. Network Information Research Center, Salt Lake City (2002)
5. Fasel, B., Luettin, J.: Automatic facial expression analysis: A survey. Pattern Recognition 36(1), 259–275 (2003)

6. Freund, Y., Schapire, R.E.: A decision-theoretic generalization of on-line learning and an application to boosting. Journal of Computer and System Sciences 55(1), 119–139 (1997)
7. Gonzalez, I., Sahli, H., Verhelst, W.: Automatic recognition of lower facial action units. In: Proceedings of the 7th International Conference on Methods and Techniques in Behavioral Research, pp. 8:1–8:4. ACM, New York (2010)
8. Hou, Y., Sahli, H., Ravyse, I., Zhang, Y., Zhao, R.: Robust shape-based head tracking. In: Blanc-Talon, J., Philips, W., Popescu, D., Scheunders, P. (eds.) ACIVS 2007. LNCS, vol. 4678, pp. 340–351. Springer, Heidelberg (2007)
9. el Kaliouby, R.: Mind-reading machines: Automated inference of complex mental states (2005)
10. Kanade, T., Cohn, J., Tian, Y.: Comprehensive database for facial expression analysis. In: 4th IEEE International Conference on Automatic Face and Gesture Recognition, Grenoble, France, pp. 46–53 (2000)
11. Kovesi, P.: Image features from phase congruency. Videre: A Journal of Computer Vision Research 1(3) (1999)
12. Lien, J.J.J., Kanade, T., Cohn, J., Li, C.: Detection, tracking, and classification of action units in facial expression. Journal of Robotics and Autonomous Systems (1999)
13. Littlewort, G., Bartlett, M., Fasel, I., Susskind, J., Movellan, J.: Dynamics of facial expression extracted automatically from video. Image and Vision Computing 24, 615–625 (2006)
14. Mahoor, M., Cadavid, S., Messinger, D., Cohn, J.: A framework for automated measurement of the intensity of non-posed facial action units. In: Computer Vision and Pattern Recognition Workshop, pp. 74–80 (2009)
15. Messinger, D.S., Mahoor, M.H., Chow, S.M., Cohn, J.F.: Automated measurement of facial expression in infant-mother interaction: A pilot study. Infancy 14(3), 285–305 (2009)
16. Reilly, J., Ghent, J., McDonald, J.: Modelling,Classification and Synthesis of Facial Expressions. In: Affective Computing: Emotion Modelling, Synthesis and Recognition, pp. 107–132. InTech Education and Publishing (2008)
17. Simon, T., Nguyen, M.H., De La Torre, F., Cohn, J.: Action unit detection with segment-based svms. In: IEEE Conference on Computer Vision and Pattern Recognition (CVPR), pp. 2737–2744 (2010)
18. Li Tian, Y., Kanade, T., Cohn, J.: Evaluation of gabor-wavelet-based facial action unit recognition in image sequences of increasing complexity. In: 5th IEEE International Conference on Automatic Face and Gesture Recognition, pp. 229–234 (2002)
19. Valstar, M., Pantic, M.: Combined Support Vector Machines and Hidden Markov Models for Modeling Facial Action Temporal Dynamics. In: Lew, M., Sebe, N., Huang, T.S., Bakker, E.M. (eds.) HCI 2007. LNCS, vol. 4796, pp. 118–127. Springer, Heidelberg (2007)
20. Vapnik, V.: The Nature of Statistical Learning Theory, 2nd edn. Springer, New York (1999)
21. Zhang, S., Shang, X., Chen, W.G.: Histogram of gabor phase pattern (hgpp): A novel object representation approach for face recognition. IEEE Transactions on Image Processing 16(1), 57–68 (2007)
22. Zhang, Y., Ji, Q.: Active and dynamic information fusion for facial expression understanding from image sequences. IEEE Transactions on Pattern Analysis and Machine Intelligence 27(5), 699–714 (2005)

Conveying Emotion with Moving Images: Relationship between Movement and Emotion

Rumi Hiraga[1] and Keitaro Takahashi[2]

[1] Tsukuba University of Technology
4-3-15, Amakubo, Tsukuba 305-8520, Japan
[2] Musik-Akademie der Stadt Basel
Hochschule für Musik
Leonhardsstrasse 6 Postfach 4003 Basel, Switzerland

Abstract. We investigated the relationship between movement and conveying emotion with moving images. We developed a software system for generating moving images in which movement is specified with moving effects consisting of a few elements. We prepared eight movements from the Vertex Noise moving effect, which consists of the three elements of speed, density, and strength, by giving each element different values and combined them with still images and sound data to generate moving images that would convey emotions. Subjects looked at moving images without sound and determined whether they felt certain emotions. The results showed the the higher density value affects the conveyance of any emotions with moving images, and strength distinguishes the conveyance of anger from fear and sadness. Anger is the most recognizable emotion, and fear and sadness are difficult to distinguish from movements.

Keywords: Moving Image, Emotion, Moving Effect, Effect Element, Movement.

1 Introduction

We have been working on developing a performance assistance system with which hearing-impaired people can enjoy playing music. Since our focus is on communication with music through emotion, we investigated the possibility of smoother musical communication between a player and listeners or among players during a musical performance for expressing a certain emotion with visual information conveying the same emotion as that from the musical performance [7][8][9]. To determine what visual information is useful for communicating emotion through music, we studied the relationship between the physical attributes of still images of abstract shapes and the emotions they convey [10]. The relationship between the movement of moving images and conveying emotions is another interest for using the appropriate visual information.

With our performance assistance system prototype, called Motion Picture with Music (MPM), a still image moves with the sound input and assigned moving effects, to generate a moving image. The combination of movement and

S. D´Mello et al. (Eds.): ACII 2011, Part I, LNCS 6974, pp. 558–567, 2011.

a still image, when both convey a certain common emotion, can be effective supplemental visual information for a musical performance. Insight into the relationship between movement and conveying emotion helps us in using visual information in MPM, as well as it gives us clues in creating effective animations and motion pictures. We describe the causality of conveying emotion in terms of moving effects and their elements.

2 Related Work

We focused on the movement of moving images and conveying emotions using a single type of media contents. On the other hand, there have been studies investigating the conveyance of emotions using multimodal interfaces.

A musical performance, a single medium content, conveys emotional messages. Emotion in musical research is a significant area of interest both for performers and listeners. Juslin introduced methods for analyzing the conveyance of emotion in music [12]. Senju, a professional violinist, and Ogushi investigated the possibility of emotional communication through music by studying Senju's own musical performances [19]. Emotions conveyed from facial expressions has attracted attention in computer science (e.g., [6][11][13]). The causal relationship between conveying emotions and still images was also investigated (e.g., [10][15][17]), and Eyben et al. studied on linguistic features and the conveyance of emotion [5].

Expressing emotion using multimodal interfaces involves understanding the relationship between two or more media sources. Schubert and Fabian analyzed piano performances by using a Chernoff face [18], Parke et al. analyzed how music supports movies [16], Castellano et al. analyzed gestures for giving audio-visual feedback [3], and we investigated the conveyance of emotion from musical performances with and without visual information with hearing-impaired people and those with hearing abilities [9].

3 MPM

Motion Picture with Music (MPM) is a software system that generates moving images with a still image, sound data, and moving effects. It uses a still image as a seed, sound information as a trigger for the still image to move, and moving effects that specify how the still image will move. For creating moving images, users select a still image and moving effects available in MPM, assign values to the elements of the selected moving effects, and provide sound either from recorded data or dynamic input through microphone. Motion of moving images vary according to the moving effects' element values even when using the same moving effect, still image, and sound information.

Figure 1 is a screen shot of MPM. The moving effect with selected element values and generated moving images can be saved as a text file and a video file, respectively. Sound information is analyzed to obtain amplitude, brightness, and attack.

MPM, running on Mac OS X, is an application of Cycling 74 MaxMSP [2] with Digital Image Processing with Sound (DIPS) [14], which provides a set of Max objects that handle OpenGL functions, OpenGL Shading Language (GLSL) [20], and Apple Core Image, apart from real-time visual-image-processing events. MPM has other sets of objects for effects and generating video files.

3.1 Moving Effects of MPM

The moving effects of MPM are implemented either with GLSL or Apple Core Image. Altogether 19 types of moving effects are prepared in MPM. One of the moving effects of MPM is Vertex Noise, which is made with a noise function of GLSL. Other moving effects include several types of distortions and blurs rendered with Apple Core Image functions. Each moving effect is defined by two to three elements.

3.2 Moving Effect Elements (Vertex Noise)

Users specify the degree of each element of a moving effect to generate a movement. When using the moving effect of Vertex Noise, users can specify the values of the three elements of speed, density, and strength as shown in the top right

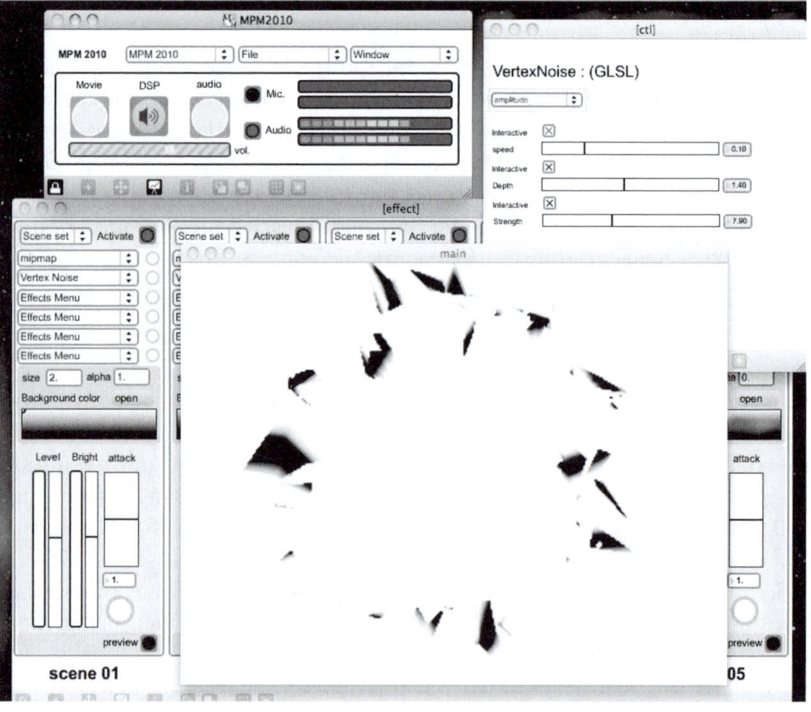

Fig. 1. Screen shot of MPM

window in Figure 1. DIPS receives the values from MPM then calls the *noise3* function of GLSL.

Each of these elements (speed, density, and strength) corresponds to and affects how fast, how smooth, and how much a shape varies, respectively. A higher speed value moves the still image more quickly, a higher density value adds more notches to contours of objects, and a higher strength value changes the position and size of objects.

4 Experiment

The purpose of the experiment is to investigate which element affects the conveyance of emotion with moving images. Subjects looked at moving images, determined and scored the intensity of the emotions they felt from them.

4.1 Still Image

With the purpose of the experiment, a still image that moves in MPM should arouse as little emotion as possible to limit its effect in conveying emotion. We prepared eight Attneave-style nonrepresentational polygons [1], with 6, 8, 10, and 12 edges by using the ShapeFamily function on Matlab [4]. We modified the shapes using the spline function to obtain similar shapes with curved lines. With the eight Attneave-style shapes, eight corresponding spline-curved shapes, a line, and a circle, we conducted the experiment by asking 16 subjects (10 male and 6 female, both aged between twenties and fifties) if they felt joy, fear, anger, or sadness, which are used in music cognition research, from these shapes. They scored the intensity of each emotion they felt from each shape on a scale from 0 to 100. More than one emotion could be rated. For example, if a subject felt joy strongly and sadness slightly with a shape, then he or she rated 80 for joy and 20 for sadness, respectively.

We then selected those shapes that had the lowest scores for the four emotions. Figure 2 shows the still images we selected from the experiment and used in our moving image experiment. Shape Nos. 2 and 7 are Attneave-style shapes and shapes Nos. 1 and 3 are the corresponding curved shapes.

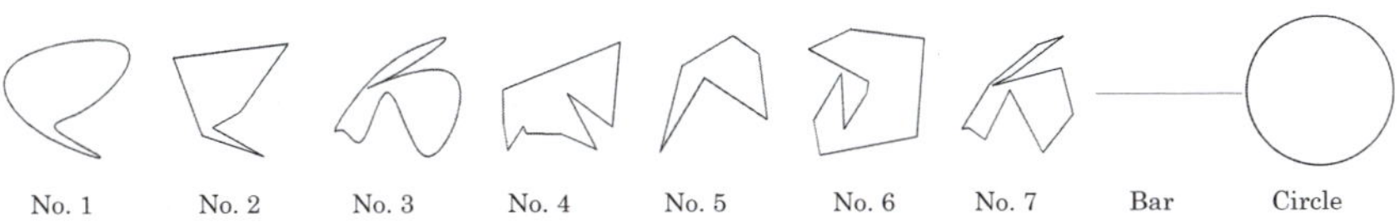

Fig. 2. Nine still images, Nos.1 to 7, bar, and circle, used in experiment

4.2 Moving Effect

We used the Vertex Noise effect as the moving effect, which consists of the three elements of speed, density, and strength. We prepared eight movements by using two values (low and high) for each of the three elements. Low is 10% to the maximum value for speed and strength, and is 0 for density. A still image does not move in MPM when either the elements of speed or strength is specified with the value of 0. High is 90 % of the maximum value for all the elements. We denote the eight movements as Eabc, where a is the value for speed, b is that for density, and c is that for strength. A, b, c is either 1, 0, or 9 where 1 and 0 are low values and 9 is the high value. Therefore we prepared movements E101, E109, E191, E199, E901, E909, E991, and E999. For example, E909 means that speed and strength is specified with high values, while density is specified with low value.

4.3 Sound Data

We created beat data of tempo of 90 beats per minute (BPM) with sequence software (XGworks ST by Yamaha) using the sound source of basic drum. Though the sound data is not presented to subjects at the experiment, it is used as trigger to give movement to a still image in MPM.

4.4 Moving Image

We used nine still images, built eight moving images with eight movements for each still image with the sound data, generated a total of 72 moving images, and recorded them in MPM.

Figure 3 shows snapshots of every sixth frame from three of the moving images. From top to bottom, the frames were extracted from a moving image made with E109 and the circle, from one made with E199 and the circle, and from one made with E991 and still image No. 4.

4.5 Procedure

We asked 20 subjects (12 male and 8 female, both aged between twenties and fifties) to specify the emotions they felt by looking at moving images without sound. Subjects scored the intensity of each emotion they felt from each moving image between 0 and 100. Any number of emotions could be rated.

A moving image had a maximum of 400 points because a subject could give up to 100 points to each emotion. Thus each moving image had had a maximum of 8,000 points (400 points by 20 subjects) and each movement 72,000 points (8,000 points by nine still images). We analyzed these data using Matlab and its Statistics Toolbox.

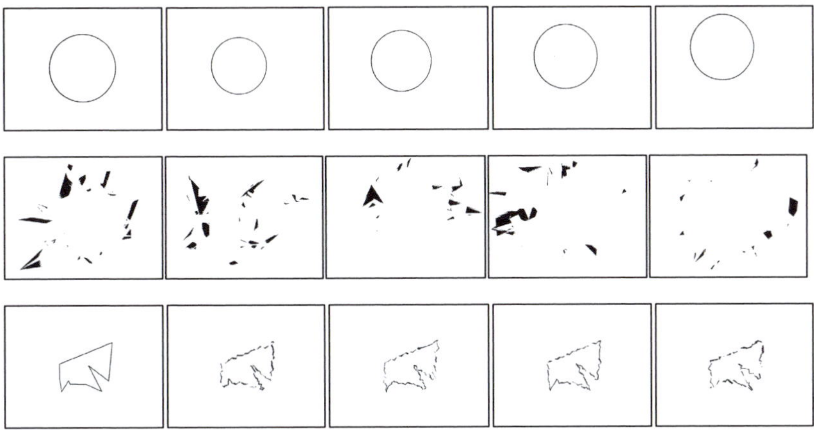

Fig. 3. Snapshots of every sixth frame in moving images. From top, moving image made with E109 and circle, E199 and circle, and E991 and still image No. 4.

5 Results

5.1 Difference in Emotion Conveyed among Still Images

One-way analysis of variance (ANOVA) showed that there were no significant differences among the still images in emotions conveyed (p-value=0.528, df=8).

5.2 Movement in Conveying Emotion

Table 1 lists the movements and their scores. We analyzed the effectiveness of the eight movements using one-way ANOVA. There were significant differences in intensity scores among the eight movements (p-value=0 to four decimal places, df=7). A multiple comparison test showed that both E101 and E109 significantly differed from all the other movements. E901 was different from E199 and E991 and also from E101 and E109.

Table 2 lists the most conveyed emotions for each movement based on the intensity scores from the subjects. All moving images generated with E199 and E999 were mostly determined as conveying anger. Moving images generated with E191 and E991 were almost evenly determined as conveying fear or sadness.

Table 1. Movements and their scores. Each movement had a maximum 72,000 points. Average 15,825, sigma 2,272, and skewness -1.43.

Movement	E991	E199	E999	E191	E909	E901	E109	E101
Points	17,858	17,457	17,248	16,755	16,720	15,676	13,611	11,272

Table 2. The number of most conveyed emotion with moving images based on intensity scores from subjects. For example, all moving images generated with E199 and E999 were mostly determined as conveying anger.

Emotion	E101	E109	E191	E199	E901	E909	E991	E999
Joy	3	9	0	0	0	2	0	0
Fear	0	0	4	0	6	1	5	0
Anger	0	0	1	9	3	6	0	9
Sadness	6	0	4	0	0	0	4	0

5.3 Emotion

We performed two-way ANOVA to see the difference of conveyed emotions on each movement. All the p-values for the four emotions, the eight movements, and the interaction were 0 to four decimal places. Table 3 lists which movement was most effective in conveying a certain emotion and their scores (maximum 72,000 points). The table is consistent with Table 2.

Table 3. Movements with the highest and second highest scores for each emotion and their points

	Most recognized movement		Second recognized movement	
	Movement	Points	Movement	Points
Joy	E109	7,697	E909	5,125
Fear	E991	8,342	E901	7,345
Anger	E999	12,296	E199	11,768
Sadness	E991	7,861	E191	7,091

6 Discussion

A moving image is generated with a still image, a movement, and sound data. We can take the basis of conveying emotions with moving images as the movements because (1) there were no differences in the conveying of emotions among the still images, and (2) there were no sounds for the subjects to listen to while looking at the moving images.

6.1 Role of Elements

The three elements –speed, density, and strength– had different roles for moving images to convey emotions to the subjects.

Density. The element of density affects the conveyance of emotions.@ Table 1 shows that the best four movements are E*9* where * is either 1 or 9. This means density affects the conveyance of emotions with moving images. Since a higher density value notches the contour of an object, the contour as the result of motion has the most effect in conveying a certain emotion.

Strength. The element of strength controls the kind of conveyed emotion. By comparing the emotions conveyed with moving images generated with E199 and E191 as well as with that of those with E991 and E999 (Table 2), we can see that moving images with E191 and E991 convey fear or sadness while E199 and E999 convey anger: 1 for fear and sadness, 9 for anger. Thus, the role of strength is to discriminate emotions, especially anger from fear and sadness. Since a higher strength value makes a still image move position and change in size more, the motion of fear and sadness is small, while that of anger is large.

Speed. To determine the role of speed in conveying emotion, we compared the movements by paring the different speed values. The pairs were (E101, E901), (E109, E909), (E191, E991), and (E199, E999). From Table 2, we can come to the following conclusion:

- For the pairs with large density values, (E191, E991) and (E199, E999), the conveyed emotions were quite similar between the two movements. Thus, the element of density on conveying emotion exceeds that of speed.
- Though the conveyed emotions in the other two pairs are reciprocal, it is not easy to describe the specific role of speed in conveying emotion from moving images.

6.2 Emotion

The movements generated with the moving effect of vertex noise can convey a certain emotion to some extent, as shown in Table 3. Though we should be careful with the scores, the table shows that E*09 is effective for conveying joy, E9*1 for fear, E*99 for anger, and E*91 for sadness. The asterisk means either 0, 1, or 9.

Joy. Moving images generated with E*09 show floating movement, with a small density value (less notches) and large strength value (large position movement). The top row in Fig. 3 shows the moving image mostly conveyed joy.

Anger. Since anger obtained the largest score, it is easier to convey with moving images. The middle row in Fig. 3 shows the moving image mostly conveyed anger.

Fear and Sadness. From Table 2, we can see that fear and sadness were not easy to discriminate from movement. In Table 3, we can see the strength value is 1 for fear and sadness. The bottom row in Fig. 3 shows the moving image mostly conveyed fear (still image No.4 with E991 obtained a score of 977 for fear and 723 for sadness).

6.3 Future Works

So far, we have examined a type of movement of a shape and its inducing emotions. In order to explain the generalized reason of why do humans respond with certain emotions to the animated shapes, we want to investigate other possibilities in generating moving images.

- Using different moving effects. In this experiment, we used only one type of moving effect–vertex noise. Since there are many moving effects in MPM, we should try using other moving effects or combining several types of moving effects.
- Using different sound data. We used beat data with a tempo 90 BPM. Using a faster or slower tempo may affect the conveyance of emotion.
- Using different still images. Since we used simple closed drawings to reduce the causality of conveying emotion with still images, we should use still images with several other attributes, such as texture or color.

We need to know whether we can create a moving image that either clearly conveys fear or sadness. This may be difficult, so we need still images that clearly convey one of these two emotions. Thus, we also need to accomplish the following.

- Determine whether it is possible to create a still image that clearly conveys fear or sadness.
- Determine whether the combination of a moving effect and a still image that are both appropriate for a certain emotion can amplify the conveyance of that emotion.

Acknowledgments. This research is supported by Special Research Funds from the Tsukuba University of Technology.

References

1. Attneave, F., Arnoult, M.D.: The Quantitative study of shape and pattern perception. Psychological Bulletin 53(6), 452–471 (1956)
2. Blum, F.: Digital Interactive Installations: Programming interactive installations using the software package Max/MSP/Jitter. VDM Verlag (2007)
3. Castellano, G., Bresin, R., Camurri, A., Volpe, G.: User-centered control of audio and visual expressive feedback by full-body movements. In: Paiva, A.C.R., Prada, R., Picard, R.W. (eds.) ACII 2007. LNCS, vol. 4738, pp. 501–510. Springer, Heidelberg (2007)
4. Collin, C.A., McMullen, P.A.: Using Matlab to generate families of similar Attneave shapes. Behavior Research Methods 34(1), 55–68 (2002)
5. Eyben, F., Wöllmer, M., Graves, A.: On-line emotion recognition in a 3-D activation-valence-time continuum using acoustic and linguistic cues. Journal on Multimodal User Interfaces 3-1-2, 7–19 (2010)
6. Fellenz, W.A., Taylor, J.G., Tsapatsoulis, N., Kollias, S.: Comparing template-based, feature-based and supervised classification of facial expressions from static images. In: Proc. of Circuits, Systems, Communications and Computers, pp. 5331–5336 (1999)
7. Hiraga, R., Kato, N., Matsuda, N.: Effect of visual representation in recognizing emotion expressed in a musical performance. In: Proc. of IEEE ICSMC, pp. 131–136. IEEE, Los Alamitos (2008)
8. Hiraga, R., Takahashi, K., Kato, N.: Toward music communication with supplemental visual information. In: Proc. of ICoMusic 2009, pp. 34–37 (2009)

9. Hiraga, R., Kato, N.: First steps toward determining the role of visual information in music communication. Ubiquitous Computing and Communication Journal, Special Issue of Media Solutions that Improve Accessibility to Disabled Users, 32–41 (2010)
10. Hiraga, R., Matsuda, N.: Emotion-intending drawings–relationship between image properties and emotion elicited. In: Proc. of IEEE ICSMC, pp. 2163–2168. IEEE, Los Alamitos (2010)
11. Hupont, I., Cerezo, E., Baldassarri, S.: Sensing facial emotions in a continuous 2D affective space. In: Proc. of IEEE ICSMC, pp. 2045–2051. IEEE, Los Alamitos (2010)
12. Juslin, P.N.: Communicating emotion in music performance: a review and a theoretical framework. In: Juslin, P.N., Sloboda, J.A. (eds.) Music and Emotion, Theory and Research, pp. 309–340. Oxford University Press, Oxford (2004)
13. Kumano, S., Otsuka, K., Yamato, J., Maeda, E., Sato, Y.: Pose-invariant facial expression recognition using variable-intensity templates. Int'l Journal of Computer Vision 83(2), 178–194 (2009)
14. Miyama, C., Rai, T., Matsuda, S., Ando, D.: Introduction of DIPS programming technique. In: Proc. of ICMC, pp. 459–462. ICMA (2003)
15. Oyama, T., Miyano, H., Yamada, H.: Multidimensional scaling of computer-generated abstract forms. In: Proc. of the Int'l Meeting of the Psychometric Society, p. 551 (2001)
16. Parke, R., Chew, E., Kyriakakis, C.: Quantitative and visual analysis of the impact of music on perceived emotion of film. ACM Computers in Entertainment 5(3) (2007)
17. Pavlova, M., Sokolov, A., Sokolov, A.: Perceived dynamics of static images enables emotional attribution. Perception 34, 1107–1116 (2005)
18. Schubert, E., Fabian, D.: An experimental investigation of emotional character portrayed by piano versus harpsichord performances of a J.S. Bach excerpt. In: Mackinlay, E. (ed.) Aesthetics and Experience in Music Performance, pp. 77–94. Cambridge Scholars Press (2005)
19. Senju, M., Ogushi, K.: How are the player's ideas conveyed to the audience? Music Perception 4(4), 311–323 (1987)
20. Rost, R.J., Licea-Kane, B.: OpenGL Shading Language, 3rd edn. Addison Wesley, Reading (2009)

Hybrid Fusion Approach for Detecting Affects from Multichannel Physiology

Md. Sazzad Hussain[1,2], Rafael A. Calvo[2], and Payam Aghaei Pour[2]

[1] National ICT Australia (NICTA), Australian Technology Park, Eveleigh 1430, Australia
[2] School of Electrical and Information Engineering, University of Sydney, Australia
{Sazzad.Hussain,Rafael.Calvo,Payam.Aghaeipour}@sydney.edu.au

Abstract. Bringing emotional intelligence to computer interfaces is one of the primary goals of affective computing. This goal requires detecting emotions often through multichannel physiology and/or behavioral modalities. While most affective computing studies report high affect detection rate from physiological data, there is no consensus on which methodology in terms of feature selection or classification works best for this type of data. This study presents a framework for fusing physiological features from multiple channels using machine learning techniques to improve the accuracy of affect detection. A hybrid fusion based on weighted majority vote technique for integrating decisions from individual channels and feature level fusion is proposed. The results show that decision fusion can achieve higher classification accuracy for affect detection compared to the individual channels and feature level fusion. However, the highest performance is achieved using the hybrid fusion model.

Keywords: Affective computing, physiology, multimodality, feature extraction, machine learning, information fusion.

1 Introduction

Multimodal approaches to affect recognition are becoming increasingly popular. This is because using just one modality or channel is not enough to consistently detect human affective states. Humans, for example, interact with each other interpreting affective states using multiple modalities like facial expressions, speech and metalinguistic information, behavior and posture, breathing and physiology (through for example, flushed cheeks and changes in breathing patterns). Many researchers believe that computers that aim to have similar detection accuracy should also use multimodal approaches [1, 2]. Affective computing researchers are using facial expressions, vocalization, gestured behavior, physiological changes, or the combination of all as indicator of affect. Computer reasoning and pattern recognition applied to a combination of all these modalities could lead to the most accurate affect detection. Features are extracted and analyzed using machine learning techniques to discriminate the various affective reactions that take place after a certain amount of cognitive processing.

Until recently, much of the research in affective computing has involved the analysis of single modality for affect detection (for detailed review see [3]).

S. D´Mello et al. (Eds.): ACII 2011, Part I, LNCS 6974, pp. 568–577, 2011.

However, single channel could be less reliable and accurate, so multichannel/ multimodal approaches for affect recognition are desired. Recent affect detection studies tend to use features from audio-visual, speech-text, dialog-posture, face-body-speech, and speech-physiology, face-physiology, and multi-channel physiology (for detailed review see [3]). We have been using physiological signals (amongst others) to study affect during naturalistic learning interactions with intelligent tutoring systems (ITS) [4, 5]. Detecting affects and finding their correlations with specific physiological signal is very challenging, therefore fusing variety of physiological channels is desirable for better detection accuracy. In this paper, heart and facial muscle activity, skin response, and respiration are used for affect recognition. Unlike previous studies in affect recognition using physiology, this study considers each channel as a modality and integrates them using multimodal fusion techniques. Therefore, each channel is considered independently, allowing them to contribute to the fusion model equally.

Information fusion techniques combine multichannel or multimodal information to improve accuracy. Most multimodal studies in affective computing have focused on feature fusion, merging features from all modalities. Decision fusion is often considered more suitable for multimodal affect detection, especially for channels that are less coherent (e.g. physiological signals) [1]. However, studies have tended to show poorer accuracy for decision fusion compared to feature fusion. This paper presents a framework for fusing multichannel physiology to improve the accuracy of affect recognition over the individual channels. The performances of feature level and decision level fusion along with individual channel performances are evaluated using physiological data. The feature level fusion is adopted from [6] which proposes the use of equal number of features from each channel for feature level fusion. Furthermore, we propose a hybrid fusion model using information from individual channels and feature level fusion.

Section 2 gives a brief background on multimodal information fusion and multimodality in affective computing. Section 3 and 4 explains the data collection procedure and the computation framework. The results for this study are presented in section 5 followed by conclusion in section 6.

2 Background

2.1 Multimodal Information Fusion

Data from multiple modalities, channels, or sensors can be combined synchronously to provide more reliable and accurate information in less time, and at a lesser cost [7]. Multimodal data fusion can be accomplished at three levels: data, feature, and decision [1]. Data fusion is the lowest level of fusion which involves integration of raw sensory information. Fusion at this level can only occur in the case when the sensors' information is of the same type. During feature level fusion, each stream of sensory data is first analyzed for features, and the features themselves are combined. Decision level fusion is based on the fusion of the individual mode decisions. This level of fusion uses a set of similar or different type of classifiers having similar or different features. Decision level fusion is considered to be the most robust and resistant to individual sensor and computationally less expensive than feature fusion

[1, 2]. Features are the most important part of information for classifiers. Not all features are necessarily useful for classifiers, such as noisy, redundant, distorted and confusing features can degrade the performance. Therefore, selecting the most useful set of features from channels is very important for both feature level and decision level fusion. For instance, features which are weakly related to class information should be avoided. Once the suitable subset of features for the individual channels are extracted from the original set, the features from multiple channels can be concatenated for feature level fusion [8].

2.2 Information Fusion in Affective Computing

Previous works on multimodal affect recognition tried to make use of both feature level and decision level fusion, but have mostly achieved better performance for feature fusion. Busso et al. [10] integrated facial expression and speech at both feature and decision level using support vector machine (SVM) to recognize four emotions – sadness, happiness, anger and neutral. They reported classification results of 89.1% for the bimodal model using feature fusion. The result for their decision level fusion was slightly lower than the feature level. Jonghwa Kim [11] evaluated feature level, decision level, and hybrid fusion performance integrating multichannel physiological signals and speech signal for detecting valance and arousal using linear discriminant analysis (LDA) classifier. Their fusion scheme reported results for feature, decision, and hybrid fusion, where the performance for the feature fusion was highest. Castellano et al. [12] presented a multimodal emotion recognition approach which integrated information from facial expression, gesture, and speech and used a Bayesian classifier. Data were fused at the feature and decision level. Both fusion techniques performed greater than the individual channels but feature level fusion (78.3%) had higher accuracy compared to decision level (74.6%). More recently, D'Mello and Graesser [6] proposed a multimodal semi-automated affect detector that combines dialog, posture, and facial expression in the feature level and used LDA to discriminate between affective states (boredom, engagement/flow, confusion, frustration, delight, and neutral). The Cohen's kappa score was calculated for the individual channels and multichannel model. Their affect detector was based on feature fusion where their analysis indicated that the accuracy of the multichannel model was statistically higher than the individual channels for the fixed but not spontaneous judgments. They also investigated decision fusion but the classification accuracy rates were similar to feature fusion.

3 Data Collection: Participants, Sensors, Procedure

Participants were 20 healthy volunteers (8 males and 12 females) age ranged from 18 to 30 years. They signed an informed consent prior to the experiment and were rewarded with $20 book vouchers for their participation. Due to sensor failure and loss of data from two subjects, results are presented for 18 subjects.

Each trial lasted approximately 1 hour and involved a 40 min recording of multiple physiological signals while participants viewed emotionally stimulated photos from the International Affective Picture System (IAPS) collection [13]. Sensor setup and the explanation of experiment protocol took around 20 minutes.

For physiological recording, participants were equipped with electrocardiogram (ECG), electromyogram (EMG), respiration, and galvanic skin response (GSR) sensors. BIOPAC MP150[1] system with AcqKnowledge software was used to acquire the physiological signals at a sampling rate of 1000 Hz for all channels. Two electrodes were placed on the wrists for collecting ECG. Two channels recorded EMG activity from two facial muscles regions (zygomatic and corrugator) respectively. GSR was recorded from the index and middle finger of the left hand and a respiration band was strapped around the chest.

As for the experiment, three blocks of 30 images (total 90 images from IAPS) were selected; each image was presented for 10 seconds, followed by 6 seconds pauses showing blank screen between the images. The images were categorized based on IAPS normative ratings so that the valence and arousal scores for the stimulus spanned a 3×3 valence/arousal space. After each image was shown, participants clicked radio buttons on the appropriate location of a 3×3 valence/arousal grid as part of self report [14]. In this paper, results are presented using the normative ratings instead of self reports. Therefore, the computational model was trained and tested using a balanced class distribution, which could be suitable for evaluating accuracies of classification without applying any up or down sampling techniques. The normative ratings are useful because they are standardized scientifically for assessing basic and applied problems in psychology [13]. Moreover, many people do not know how to recognize, express and label/scale their own feelings, therefore self reports sometimes can be unreliable [15]. However, self reports provide important information and should not be ignored; therefore the collected self ratings will be used as an extension of this work in future studies.

4 Computational Model

4.1 Feature Extraction, Selection and Classification

Statistical features were extracted from the different physiological channels using the Augsburg Biosignal toolbox (AuBT)[2] in Matlab. Normative ratings for the presented IAPS image were synchronized with the physiological signals and features were extracted using a 10 seconds window (same length as image presentation). The feature vectors were also labeled with the normative ratings (1-3 degrees of valence/arousal). Some features were common for all signals (e.g. mean, median, and standard deviation, range, ratio, minimum, and maximum) whereas other features were related to the characteristics of the signals (e.g. heart rate variability, respiration pulse, frequency). A total of 214 features were extracted from the five physiological channel signals (84 from ECG, 42 from EMG, 21 from GSR, and 67 for respiration).

PRTools[3], a data mining package for Matlab, was used for the feature selection and classification. To reduce the dimensionality of the large number of features, a Forward Feature Selection (FFS) technique was used for ranking the best features with respect to the class, in this case affective states. Five machine learning

---

[1] BIOPAC: http://www.biopac.com/data-acquisition-analysis-system-mp150-system-windows.

[2] AuBT: http://mm-werkstatt.informatik.uni-augsburg.de/project_details.php?id=%2033

[3] PRTools: http://www.prtools.org/

algorithms; LDA, quadratic discriminant analysis (QDA), linear kernel SVM, nonlinear poly kernel SVM, and k-nearest neighbor (KNN, k=3) were selected for classification. Finally, a vote classifier for combining the classifiers was applied [16]. The training and testing for the IAPS dataset were performed with a 10-fold cross validation. The kappa statistic was used as the overall classification performance metric and the F1 (F-measure) value was calculated as an indication of how well each affective state was classified. For the classification scores of precision (P) and recall (R), the F-measure (F1) is calculated by; $F1=2((P*R)/(P+R))$.

4.2 Hybrid Information Fusion

The hybrid fusion proposed here consists of mainly three steps: (a) obtain classification decision from the individual channels, (b) obtain classification decision from feature fusion, and (c) perform decision fusion over all decisions.

(a) Individual channel classification: FFS algorithm considers equal number of features from each channel using equation (1).

$$f_{equal1} = \min(f_{ch1}, f_{ch2}, \ldots, f_{chN}) \tag{1}$$

Where, f_{ch1}, f_{ch2}, f_{chN}, are the number of features for the channels (1, 2, …, N) respectively (for this study, $f_{equal1}=20$). Classify individual channels (selected features) using the classification techniques explained in section 4.1.

(b) Feature level fusion: The contribution of equivalent number of features for the fusion model is suitable so that each modality is equally represented. Equation (1) and (2) are used for selecting features for the fusion model [6].

$$f_{equal2} = f_{equal1} / N \tag{2}$$

Where, f_{equal2} is the number of features that each channel contributes, and N is the number of channels. For this study, $f_{equal2}=5$ *and* $N=4$. FFS algorithm was used for selecting the f_{equal2} features from each channel. All selected features were then merged to achieve the feature fusion. Even though only small subset of features are considered from each channel, they are the best subset of features out of all.

(c) Decision level fusion: A weighted majority voting technique [8] was applied for achieving decision fusion and hybrid fusion. The classification decision (D_i) from the individual channels and the feature fusion model are obtained. The weight coefficients (ω_i) are calculated using their kappa scores of the individual channels. The combiner adopts the weighted majority vote for every sample using the rule in equation (3).

$$\sum_{i=1}^{m} \omega_i . d_{ik} = \max_{j=1}^{c} \sum_{i=1}^{m} \omega_i . d_{ij} \text{ ; } with \ d_{ik} = \begin{cases} 1 \text{ if } \mathrm{D_i} \text{ has the label class k} \\ 0 \qquad \text{otherwise} \end{cases} \tag{3}$$

Where, c and m represents the number of classes and the number of channels respectively. Classification decision from the individual physiological channels and their feature fusion are fused using this technique to obtain hybrid fusion.

The following section gives the results obtained for the IAPS dataset using this computational framework.

5 Results and Discussions

This section presents the classification results for detecting 1-3 degrees of arousal (low, medium, high) and valence (positive, neutral, negative) from physiological features averaged across subjects for the following:

1. Individual physiological channels (ECG, GSR, EMG, & Resp) having equal features (=20).
2. Feature Level Fusion 1 (FF1): Merge all physiological features and then select 20 features.
3. Feature Level Fusion 2 (FF2): Select equal number of features (=5) from each channel and then merge all features (=20) to achieve the feature level fusion.
4. Decision Level Fusion (DF): Select equal number of features (=20) from each channel and perform classification separately. Then fuse classification decision using weighted majority vote technique.
5. Hybrid Fusion (HF): Select equal number of features (=20) from each channel and perform classification separately. Fuse classification decision from individual channels and FF2 using weighted majority vote technique.

The kappa score is used for reporting the overall accuracy of detecting the degrees of arousal and valence. Figure 1 and figure 2 presents the mean, maximum and minimum kappa scores for detecting 1-3 degrees of arousal and valence respectively from physiological channels and the fusion models. The standard deviation of the kappa scores for the individual channels (ECG, GSR, EMG, Resp) and the fusion models (FF1, FF2, DF, HF) were 0.13, 0.09, 0.10, 0.09, 0.09, 0.10, 0.09, and 0.09 respectively for arousal and 0.09, 0.12, 0.13, 0.09, 0.15, 0.11, 0.09, and 0.12 respectively for valence.

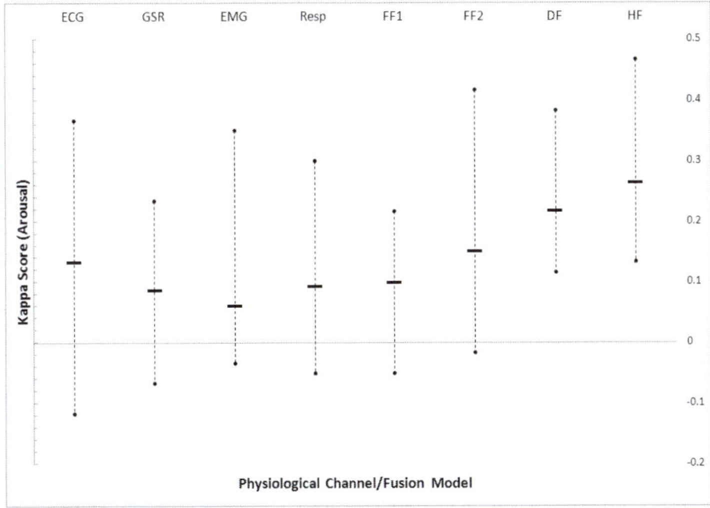

Fig. 1. Mean, maximum and minimum kappa scores for detecting 1-3 degrees of arousal from physiological signals and fusion models across subjects. [The means are represented with '–'].

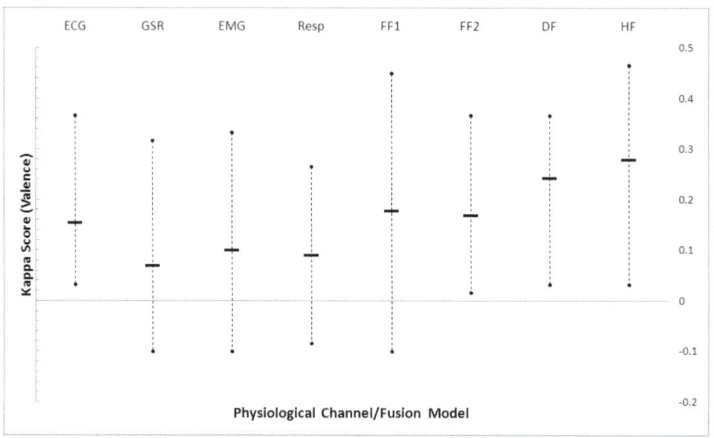

Fig. 2. Mean, maximum and minimum kappa scores for detecting 1-3 degrees of valance from physiological signals and fusion models across subjects. [The means are represented with '–'].

According to the figures, it can be observed that the overall performance of the fusion models for detecting both arousal and valence is higher than the individual channels. Despite the lower detection accuracy of the physiological channels, fusing features or channel decisions can improve the overall accuracy. However, the decision fusion and hybrid fusion approaches show better detection accuracy over the feature level fusion models. This is apparent because the feature level fusion approaches either consider large subset of features for certain channels and very small subsets for other channels (FF1) or considers equal number of a small subset of features from all channels (FF2), whereas the decision fusion models (DF & HF) are allowing equal and large subset of features from all channels.

The one-way ANOVA of the individual channels and the fusion models show $F(7,136)=9.2$, $p<0.05$ and $F(7,136)=7.51$, $p<0.05$ respectively for arousal and valence. The post-hoc test with *bonferroni* revealed that the HF model exhibits significant differences from all the physiological channels and DF model exhibits significant differences from all channels except ECG. The other two fusion models (FF1 & FF2) failed to show any significant differences from any of the individual channels. The statistical test also confirms the significant improvement of the decision fusion and hybrid fusion approaches for detecting arousal and valence over the physiological channels.

While the overall performance measurement is reflected using the kappa score, the F1value represents how well the individual affective levels of arousal/valence were classified. The F1 values for only the fusion models (FF1, FF2, DF, HF) are presented here. Table 1 and Table 2 give the mean F1 values across the 18 subjects for detecting 1-3 degrees of arousal and valence respectively.

Table 1. F1 values for detecting 1-3 degrees of arousal from fusion models across subjects

	FF1	FF2	DF	HF
High Arousal	0.45	0.47	0.53	0.56
Medium Arousal	0.35	0.37	0.40	0.43
Low Arousal	0.34	0.46	0.47	0.50

Table 2. F1 values for detecting 1-3 degrees of valance from fusion models across subjects

	FF1	FF2	DF	HF
Pos Valence	0.49	0.53	0.53	0.57
Neutral Valence	0.31	0.30	0.39	0.37
Neg Valence	0.49	0.45	0.53	0.55

From Table 1, it is observed that the HF model was best at detecting all three degrees of arousal compared to other fusion models. It is also noticeable that DF is the next best model followed by FF2 and FF1 for detecting arousal. As for detecting the three degrees of valence (Table 2), HF model is best at detecting *positive valence* and *negative valence* but the DF model is better at detecting *neutral valance*. The DF model is also good at detecting *positive valence* and *negative valence* compared to the FF1 and FF2 models.

From the results it is obvious that the performance of the DF model is reasonably good but having a hybrid fusion model (individual channel decision with FF2 decision) can greatly improve the performance of detecting the degrees of valance and arousal. The FF1 model is the common trend for fusing physiological data [4, 5], but it is now evident that decision fusion can improve accuracy of affect detecting over the FF1 model. Moreover, the FF2 model considers equal number of features from every channel for the fusion which is suitable for evaluating feature fusion performance over individual channels [6]. Thus, the performance of the HF model, which makes use of the individual channel decisions and the FF2 model decision is very good even compared to the DF model. The overall average improvement of accuracy for detecting degrees of arousal and valence of the hybrid fusion model over the individual physiological channels is given in Table 3.

Table 3. Overall performance improvement (% accuracy) of HF over the individual physiological channels

Physio Ch	Arousal	Valence
ECG	8.70 %	8.33 %
GSR	12.03 %	14.01 %
EMG	14.07 %	11.98 %
RESP	11.48 %	12.65 %

6 Conclusion and Future Works

Fusion of multimodal data is a big challenge, where the reliability of affect recognition depends on the choice of channels and the fusion techniques. Despite the challenges of affect recognition from physiological signals, this study presents a model for fusing multichannel physiological signals with the support of a systematic experimental setup, feature selection techniques, and machine learning approaches. We have used the normative IAPS ratings instead of self-reports, yet the results are good considering artifacts and individual differences in the expression of emotion, especially with physiological signals. The same IAPS dataset can be analyzed using the self reports applying up or down sampling techniques. Even though the results are presented for multichannel physiological signal, the proposed framework is also suitable for information and features from other modalities. The feature selection technique and the vote classifier for this framework can adapt to other machine learning algorithms besides the ones presented in this paper. Other techniques [8] for fusion (especially decision fusion) can be explored to improve the overall performance. Furthermore, the sensor fusion techniques and relevant modalities should follow theories of human sensory system to achieve the realistic nature of affect recognition. Neuroscientists [17] have proposed that the nervous system seems to combine sensory information with a technique similar to a maximum-likelihood integrator. This study has also collected physiological data for the same subjects while they interacted with an ITS. The proposed framework can be tested on this dataset which may improve accuracy of detecting learning affective states in naturalistic ITS interactions compared to results in [5] for the same dataset.

Acknowledgments. M. S. Hussain was supported by Endeavour Award and National ICT Australia (NICTA). NICTA is funded by the Australian Government as represented by the Department of Broadband, Communications and the Digital Economy and the Australian Research Council through the ICT Centre of Excellence program.

References

1. Sharma, R., Pavlovic, V.I., Huang, T.S.: Toward multimodal human-computer interface. Proceedings of the IEEE 86, 853–869 (1998)
2. Pantic, M., Rothkrantz, L.J.M.: Toward an affect-sensitive multimodal human-computer interaction. Proceedings of the IEEE 91, 1370–1390 (2003)
3. Calvo, R.A., D'Mello, S.: Affect Detection: An Interdisciplinary Review of Models, Methods, and their Applications. IEEE Transactions on Affective Computing 1, 18–37 (2010)
4. Aghaei Pour, P., Hussain, M.S., AlZoubi, O., D'Mello, S., Calvo, R.: The Impact of System Feedback on Learners' Affective and Physiological States. In: Aleven, V., Kay, J., Mostow, J. (eds.) ITS 2010. LNCS, vol. 6094, pp. 264–273. Springer, Heidelberg (2010)
5. Hussain, M.S., AlZoubi, O., Calvo, R.A., D'Mello, S.: Affect Detection from Multichannel Physiology during Learning Sessions with AutoTutor. In: Biswas, G., Bull, S., Kay, J., Mitrovic, A. (eds.) AIED 2011. LNCS (LNAI), vol. 6738, pp. 131–138. Springer, Heidelberg (2011)

6. D'Mello, S., Graesser, A.: Multimodal semi-automated affect detection from conversational cues, gross body language, and facial features. User Modeling and User-adapted Interaction 20, 147–187 (2010)
7. Hall, D.L., McMullen, S.A.H.: Mathematical techniques in multi-sensor data fusion. Artech House Publishers, Boston (2004)
8. Utthara, M., Suranjana, S., Sukhendu, D., Pinaki, C.: A Survey of Decision Fusion and Feature Fusion Strategies for Pattern Classification. IETE Technical Review 27, 293–307 (2010)
9. Paleari, M., Lisetti, C.L.: Toward multimodal fusion of affective cues. In: Proceedings of the 1st ACM International Workshop on Human-Centered Multimedia, pp. 99–108. ACM, New York (2006)
10. Busso, C., Deng, Z., Yildirim, S., Bulut, M., Lee, C.M., Kazemzadeh, A., Lee, S., Neumann, U., Narayanan, S.: Analysis of emotion recognition using facial expressions, speech and multimodal information. In: Proceedings of the 6th International Conference on Multimodal Interfaces, pp. 205–211. ACM, New York (2004)
11. Kim, J.: Bimodal emotion recognition using speech and physiological changes. In: Robust Speech Recognition and Understanding. I-Tech Education and Publishing, Vienna (2007)
12. Castellano, G., Kessous, L., Caridakis, G.: Emotion recognition through multiple modalities: face, body gesture, speech. In: Peter, C., Beale, R. (eds.) Affect and Emotion in Human-Computer Interaction. LNCS, vol. 4868, pp. 92–103. Springer, Heidelberg (2008)
13. Lang, P.J., Bradley, M.M., Cuthbert, B.N.: International affective picture system (IAPS): Technical manual and affective ratings. The Center for Research in Psychophysiology, University of Florida, Gainesville, FL (1997)
14. Russell, J.A.: A circumplex model of affect. Journal of Personality and Social Psychology 39, 1161–1178 (1980)
15. Picard, R.W.: Affective computing: challenges. International Journal of Human-Computer Studies 59, 55–64 (2003)
16. Kuncheva, L.I.: Combining pattern classifiers: methods and algorithms. Wiley-Interscience, Hoboken (2004)
17. Holmes, N.P., Spence, C.: Multisensory integration: space, time and superadditivity. Current Biology 15, 762–764 (2005)

Investigating the Suitability of Social Robots for the Wellbeing of the Elderly

Suzanne Hutson[1], Soo Ling Lim[2], Peter J. Bentley[2], Nadia Bianchi-Berthouze[1], and Ann Bowling[3]

[1] UCLIC, University College London
[2] Department of Computer Science, University College London
[3] Department of Primary Care and Population Sciences, University College London
Gower Street, London WC1E 6BT, United Kingdom
suzi.hutson@yahoo.co.uk,
{s.lim,p.bentley}@cs.ucl.ac.uk,
{n.berthouze,a.bowling}@ucl.ac.uk

Abstract. This study aims to understand if, and how, social robots can promote wellbeing in the elderly. The existing literature suggests that social robots have the potential to improve wellbeing in the elderly, but existing robots focus more on healthcare and healthy behaviour among the elderly. This work describes a new investigation based on focus groups and home studies, in which we produced a set of requirements for social robots that reduce loneliness and improve psychological wellbeing among the elderly. The requirements were validated with the participants of our study. We anticipate that the results of this work will lead to the design of a new social robot more suited to improving wellbeing of the elderly.

Keywords: Wellbeing, elderly, social robots.

1 Introduction

With old age, major life challenges are increasingly likely to occur. Elderly people are at greater risk of social isolation compared to the general population, because of the increased likelihood of health problems, and major life-events (e.g., death of relatives and friends) [1]. As a result, the psychological wellbeing of millions of older people is detrimentally affected in the UK[1].

Psychological wellbeing is not simply an absence of ill-being [2-4]. It is about lives going well: the combination of feeling good and functioning effectively. Feeling good involves having positive emotions of happiness and contentment, interest, engagement, confidence and affection [2]. Functioning effectively involves the development of one's potential, having some control over one's life, having a sense of purpose, and experiencing positive relationships [2]. The science of wellbeing is concerned with what makes people flourish, i.e., they "have enthusiasm for life and are actively and productively engaged with others and in social institutions" [2, 5]. A study in 2002 reported that only 17% of the US adult population was flourishing [6].

[1] Age UK (http://www.ageuk.org.uk/).

S. D´Mello et al. (Eds.): ACII 2011, Part I, LNCS 6974, pp. 578–587, 2011.

Better psychological wellbeing leads to better physical health [2]. Yet much of the existing healthcare robots and literature about social robots for the elderly focuses on devices that can provide assistance or support to people with physical or mental health problems. This work focuses on the promotion of positive psychological wellbeing, for people who are physically and mentally healthy. Our study aims to understand if, and how, social robots can help improve this form of wellbeing in the elderly. We examine whether there are social robots currently available which might reduce loneliness and improve psychological wellbeing among the elderly, and whether they can be designed to be acceptable and desirable to people. Our research questions are:

- What devices are currently available and are they able to reduce loneliness and improve psychological wellbeing?
- If current devices are inadequate, can requirements be elicited for a social robot that can reduce loneliness and improve psychological wellbeing?

The remainder of the paper describes our approach to answer the research questions. We first assess the literature and existing social robot devices. Then, we conduct focus groups with the elderly, in which we present participants with existing social robots and elicit their feedback on each robot. We report on home studies in which the elderly participants live with the social robots and document their experiences with the robots. Based on the results of the focus groups and home studies, we identify the needs of the elderly and map their needs to requirements. We then conduct a final focus group to validate the requirements.

2 Literature Review

In this study we regard a social robot as "an autonomous or semi-autonomous robot that interacts and communicates with humans by following the behavioral norms expected by the people with whom the robot is intended to interact" [7]. Among the different kinds of social robots, service-type robots are designed to provide functional help; companion-type robots are designed to enhance psychological wellbeing [8].

Social robots are widely studied in the fields of Socially Assistive Robotics (SAR), Socially Interactive Robotics (SIR) and Assistive Robotics (AR) [9]. In these fields, a number of areas are important foci for research: embodiment (bodily presence), personality, empathy, engagement, adaptation (the robot's ability to learn about the user and adapt its capabilities according to the user's personality, needs and preferences), and transfer (the ability of a robot to bring about long-term behavioural change in the user) [10, 11]. In previous studies, participants have found that physical robots are more "watchful" and enjoyable than virtual ones [12].

Existing social robots focus on providing companionship, entertainment (albeit often aimed for adults), communication, and healthcare (Table 1). Social robots specifically developed for the elderly focus on companionship or healthcare, which is only one aspect of psychological wellbeing. Other aspects, such as sense of purpose and interest, are not specifically investigated.

Table 1. Main Features of Existing Social Robots (See below for table key and robot URL)

Robot name	Main Focus	Type	Material	Target	Emotions?	Responds to:	Connectivity	Behaviour
Aibo [8]	E	Aml (dog)	P	A	☺	T, So, Si, Sp	W, B	Sp, So, Mo
CareBot	H	Rbt	P	All	☻	Si, Sp	W	L, Sp, Mo
CompanionAble [13]	C	Rbt	P	E	☺	T, Sp, Si	I	L, Mo, Sp
FurReal Cat	E	Aml (cat)	F	C	☺	T	/	So, Mo
Hasbro I-Cat	E	Dvt (cat)	P	A	☺	T, So	/	L, Mo, So
Heart Robot	C	Hmd	C	All	☺	T	/	L, Mo
Homie [14]	C	Aml (dog)	F	E	☺	Sp, T	B, S	L, Sp, So
Hopis [13]	H	Aml (dog)	C	All	☻	/	W	Sp
Huggable [15]	C	Aml (bear)	F	C	☺	T, So, Si	I	Sp
iCat [8]	C	Aml (cat)	P	All	☺	T, Sp	U	L, Sp, Mo
KASPAR [16]	H	Hmd	R	D, C	☺	T, So, Si Mo, Sp	U	Mo
Keepon	H	Dvt (snowman)	R	C	☺	So, Si	/	Mo
Mood Lamp	E	Dvt (mushroom)	P	C	☺	To, So	B	L, So
Nabaztag	T	Dvt (rabbit)	P	A	☺	Sp	I, R	L, Sp, Mo, So
NeCoRo [17]	C	Aml (cat)	F	All	☺	T, So, Si	/	So, L
Nursebot [13]	H	Rbt	P	E	☺	To, Sp, Si	I	L, Mo, Sp
Paro [18, 19]	C	Aml (seal)	F	All	☺	T, So, Si, Sp	/	So, Mo
PC Mascot	T	Dvt (parrot)	P	A	☻	/	U	L, Sp, Mo
Pleo	C	Aml (dinosaur)	R	All	☺	T, So, Si		So, Mo
Probo [20]	C	Aml (elephant)	C	C	☺	T, So, Si, Sp	/	L, Mo, Sp
Robosapien	E	Hmd	P	C	☻	T	Ir	Sp
Teddy Phone	T	Dvt (bear)	F	A	☻	So	T	So, Mo
USB Robot Owl	E	Dvt (owl)	P	A	☻	/	U	Mo
Wakamaru-bot [13]	C	Hmd	P	E, D	☺	Si, Sp	I	Sp
Yorisoi Ifbot	C	Hmd	P	E	☺	Sp	I	L, Sp, Mo

KEY	
Main Focus	H: healthcare, C: companion, E: entertainment, T: communication
Type	Aml: animal, Hmd: humanoid, Rbt: robot, Dvt: device-type
Material	C: cloth, P: plastic, F: fur, R: rubber
Target	All: all ages, E: elderly, D: disabled, A: adults, C: children
Expresses emotion?	☺: yes, ☻: no
Responds to / Behaviour	Sp: speech, T: touch, L: light, Si: sight, So: sound, Mo: movement
Connectivity	W: WiFi, I: Internet, R: RFID, B: Bluetooth, Ir: Infrared, U: USB, T: phone line, S: SMS

URL: CareBot (www.geckosystems.com), CompanionAble (www.companionable.net), Hasbro FurReal Cat, Hasbro Mood Lamp, and Hasbro I-Cat (www.hasbro.com), Heart Robot (www.heartrobot.org.uk), Huggable (robotic.media.mit.edu/index.html), KASPAR (kaspar.feis.herts.ac.uk), Keepon (beatbots.net), Nabaztag (www.nabaztag.com), PC Mascot (www.parrotchronicles.com/reviews/pcmascot/pcmascot.htm), Pleo (www.pleoworld.com), Robosapien (www.wowwee.com), Teddy Phone (no longer available), USB robot owl (www.thinkgeek.com), Yorisoi Ifbot (www.techdigest.tv/2009/01/ces_2009_yoriso.html)

A recent review of social robots for the wellbeing of the elderly found that most studies: (1) use Paro and Aibo (other robots should be investigated), (2) are conducted in Japan (but robot perception is culturally dependent), (3) are conducted with elderly people in nursing homes (but not with those still living in their own house, despite a growing number of these) [8].

To summarise, although some social robots have been designed to provide companionship for the elderly, few have been designed specifically to improve psychological wellbeing among the elderly. Those that have been investigated in this respect (such as Paro and Aibo) do not necessarily meet all the needs of the elderly, e.g., they do not provide mental challenges, improve social interaction, or they are too heavy or large [8]. The lack of suitable devices designed specifically to improve psychological wellbeing among the elderly suggests the need to understand the requirements for a wellbeing robot for the elderly.

3 Focus Groups and Home Studies

This study aims to understand if, and how, social robots can help improve wellbeing in the elderly. A user-centered approach, which consisted of 3 focus groups and 9 home studies, was used to identify the design requirements for the social robot. Ten existing social robots from Table 1 were selected and where feasible acquired for the study. The selection of robots represented a range of different robot types: "animal-type" (Pleo, Huggable and FurReal Cat), "device-type" (Keepon, Mood Lamp, I-Cat, Nabaztag, and Teddy Phone), and "humanoid" (Robosapien and Heart). These robots have different materials (fur or smooth), functionalities (walking, speaking, or Internet enabled), and interaction methods (touch, light, or sound).

Six elderly participants were recruited by the Social Care Workforce Research Unit[2] to participate in the study and represented people from a range of different backgrounds (Table 2). The participants were not too elderly or confined to home so that they could travel to the focus groups.

[2] A multi-disciplinary national centre at King's College London for research into issues relating to the social care workforce (https://www.kcl.ac.uk/schools/sspp/interdisciplinary/scwru/).

Table 2. Participants and Home Study

ID	Sex	Age Range	Former Occupation	Home Study Device(s) and Duration
P1	F	76-85	-	FurReal Cat (5 days), Mood Lamp (7 days)
P2	M	76-85	Mechanical engineer	Pleo (17 days), Mood Lamp (7 days)
P3	M	66-75	Patent examiner	N/A (Only took part in focus groups)
P4	F	76-85	Therapist	Pleo (7 days), Nabaztag (7 days)
P5	F	Unknown	-	I-Cat (7 days), Teddy Phone (7 days)
P6	F	66-75	Theatre producer	FurReal Cat (7 days)

In Focus Group 1, the participants were briefed about the purpose of the study to understand if, and how, social robots can help improve wellbeing in the elderly. In three consecutive sessions a selection of existing robots was presented and discussed. Where possible the robots were physically presented. For Keepon, Huggable, and Heart robot, publically available video demonstrations were shown instead. For each device, the main capabilities were shown, and participants were given the opportunity to interact with and handle the devices. We asked the participants to discuss their opinions about each robot in terms of what they thought of the robot, what they liked and disliked about it, how the robot could help them, how it could be improved and whether they wanted the robot in their homes. They also discussed what their ideal robot would do and what it would look like. At the end of the focus group, participants were asked if they were prepared to participate in home studies with robots, and if so, which robots they preferred.

Home studies were conducted after Focus Group 1, in which the participants lived with the social robots and documented their daily experiences. Robots were assigned to the participants based on their preferences (e.g., P2 was assigned Pleo as it was in his top 3 preferences, P6 was assigned FurReal Cat as she disliked cats and was curious about her reaction to a robot cat) and the technology in their homes (e.g., P4 was assigned Nabaztag because she was the only participant with Wi-fi). Five participants took part in the home study (Table 2). The duration and number of home studies were constrained by the availability of the participants, and the practicality of having them provide daily notes. The McCarthy and Wright framework [21] was used to record the experience of the participants.

For each home study, the participant completed a pre-study questionnaire about their impressions on the robot. For example, if the robot was Pleo, they were asked to rate from 1 – 'completely untrue' to 5 'completely true' the following questions: (1) Pleo looks/feels/sounds attractive to me, (2) I find Pleo interesting/stimulating, (3) I find Pleo entertaining/fun, (4) I feel attached to Pleo, (5) I think Pleo could enhance my sense of wellbeing, and (6) I would like to own Pleo. We also conducted a semi-structured interview with the participant about their anticipated experience with the device, and the impact of the device on their behaviour and relationship with others.

For each day the participant lived with the device, they were asked to enter the following details in the diary forms we provided: how many times they noticed or engaged with the device, any positive and negative experience they had with the device, what surprised them about the device, if they found any technical or practical problems with the device, and other thoughts and observations they have about the device. At the end of each home study, we asked the participant to complete a post-study questionnaire with the same questions as the pre-study questionnaire described above. We also conducted a post-study interview with the participant to elicit their responses to the device and their experiences engaging with the device. For participants who conducted home studies with two devices, the new device was given to them on collection of the old device and the process was repeated.

In Focus Group 2, for each robot used in the home studies in turn, the participants shared their experiences in their home studies, in terms of the ability of the robot to provide companionship, its functionality, and its ability to provide entertainment. The participants also discussed the advantages and disadvantages of current social robots, and what is needed for future social robots. Following the second focus group, results were collated and analysed from the literature review, focus groups, and home studies. A set of overall requirements was generated from this data.

In Focus Group 3 (which occurred several weeks later), each requirement was presented in turn to the participants. An open discussion was conducted with the participants to gather their feedback and assessment of the requirements. Specifically, the discussion points focused on the user profile for such a device, context of its use, user needs and desired user experience, functional and maintenance requirements.

4 Results

The results from our study indicate that the participants were mostly unsatisfied with the social robots. Most of the robots did not meet the participants' expectations: out of the nine home studies, six had a lower post-study score compared to their pre-study score. In the final questionnaire, only P1 (on FurReal Cat), P4 (on Nabaztag), and P5 (on I-Cat) provided a score of more than 20 out of a maximum of 30.

The participants expected animal-type robots (Pleo and FurReal Cat) to behave like real animals. They compared these robots with house pets, both favourably and unfavourably. P4 found herself talking to Pleo, anthropomorphising, and caring for it. She reported feeling responsible for its welfare, and "extricated it when it became entangled with a chair leg." Her affection towards Pleo was evident in the post-study interview, referring to Pleo as "a clever little dinosaur." P2's experience with Pleo was less positive. He initially referred to Pleo as "he" but after the study reverted to "it." He felt that Pleo was "not sufficiently lifelike" and became bored of it after a few days. This is consistent with a study by Shibata [22], which found that unfamiliar animal-type robots are more acceptable to humans than human-type or familiar animal-type, as people are less able to compare them unfavourably with the actual animal. However, our study found that unfamiliar animal-type robot Pleo was still compared unfavourably with animals. For example, P2 compared Pleo to a puppy, which, unlike Pleo, would give a "personal response" to its owner.

Several participants said that they saw the potential of such devices in encouraging conversation in those who are lonely or housebound. The device's effect on the participants' self image is crucial to their acceptance of the device. P5 and P6 disliked the toy-like appearance of Teddy Phone and FurReal Cat respectively. P5 comments' in the first three days of having the Teddy Phone were positive: she found its moving face "very novel" and described it as "entertaining" and "friendly to look at." However, she felt that it was "a bit childish" when a guest asked her why she had a

Teddy Bear. P1, P5 and P6 mentioned the possession of social robots has to maintain their self-image as independent. This is consistent with Broadbent et al.'s [13] findings that older adults may not use assistive robots if they feel that this portrays them as "disabled, dependent, weak or feeble."

Several participants mentioned the importance of being able to control the devices. P5 wanted I-Cat to have a volume control but was otherwise very positive about the simple device; P6 wanted to be able to stop FurReal Cat from "yowling" using a vocal command. P6 did not like cats and was allergic to them, a response mirrored in the artificial cat. Her ratings in the post-study questionnaire for FurReal Cat were very low. She found the loud meowing of the cat very irritating and distracting, and stopped touching it because she felt it evoked an allergic reaction similar to that of real cats. By the end of the study she no longer wanted to interact with it. This observation is consistent with a study by Shibata et al., which found that those who do not like animals or pets in general tend not to engage with robotic animals [23].

Similar to Broadbent et al.'s study of healthcare robots [13], we found that one design is unlikely to suit everyone. A customisable experience is essential, for example of gender, voice, shape, for improved perceived user autonomy. For instance P4 did not like one of the voices used by Nabaztag, but in other ways was very happy with this device. Likewise her objections to the touch of Pleo might have been overcome by using a different surface material.

Based on the focus groups and interviews with the participants, the target user for the social robot should be over 75 (i.e., the older elderly) and in need of intellectual stimulation, companionship, and empathy. The user may have limited independence, and is possibly housebound with limited mobility. The user may have moderate visual or auditory impairment and/or motor impairment. The user may have limited social contact and be somewhat isolated. The user may have little or no cognitive/speech impairment. The device should be used in the home environment or in a care home. The device should usually be used by one person, but a friend, relative, or care person may set up the device and communicate with the user using the device. The functional, user experience and maintenance requirements are summarised as follows.

Functional Requirements. All participants wanted the robot to respond to voice and touch. They agreed that devices must respond to voice in order to be a satisfactory companion but were divided as to what such a response entailed. One participant suggested that the robot could respond by talking back, but another was strongly against this. A participant suggested that voice response could be as simple as the FurReal Cat meowing if one spoke to it. The robot should respond to the user and the environment (audio or visual recognition). It should recognise and respond to user's emotions/mood (possibly from their tone of voice), and influence or alter its "mood" in some way by its response. For example, P3 wanted something he could shout at, and that would know he was shouting at it.

The robot should provide one or more useful functions promoting wellbeing, such as facilitate communication with relatives, friends and carers, contact with the outside world, and promote creativity by intellectual stimulation. Participants wanted to be able to tell stories to the device (which could be transmitted to grandchildren or collated as memoires). This is consistent with the literature that the elderly enjoy activities that enable them to add value to society and connect them to others [24].

Participants welcomed the idea of combining animal-type and device-type properties in the way that 'Huggable' does, i.e. an animal-like robot which is comforting to hold, but also enables communication and other activities. Participants mentioned that communication robots could help the elderly stay in touch with younger relatives and with the world in general. There was consensus on the benefits of intellectual stimulation to wellbeing, and the participants agreed that some form of intellectual challenge such as learning to play music (which participants had unsuccessfully attempted with the Mood Lamp) or solve puzzles could be of benefit. An ideal robot could also provide accurate and reliable reminders, for instance to take pills, take exercise, or for appointments.

User Experience Requirements. The robot should be pleasing to touch or stroke, but the touch and feel should be customisable. Physical aspects of animal-like devices (e.g., purring and the sensation of fur when stroked) were found by some participants to be soothing and relaxing but were undesirable to others. Some participants found the rubber skin of Pleo, the mechanics under the skin of Pleo, and the synthetic feeling of the fur in FurReal Cat to be undesirable. The sounds made by the device or voices should be pleasing and not irritating, and should be customisable. Over-loud meowing of FurReal Cat was irritating for some. Although P4 enjoyed the quirky random comments from Nabaztag, she disliked a synthesised female voice used by Nabaztag for reminders.

The appearance of the device should not resemble a children's toy. Older people prefer robots with a serious aspect [13]. A participant mentioned being self-conscious when guests saw them with child-like robots such as Teddy Phone. All the participants described Heart as "creepy" and half of them said that the Furreal Cat was scary. These two robots may have suffered from the *uncanny valley* effect: when the robot looks too much like a living creature, it is no longer judged by the standards of a robot trying to act like a creature, but judged by the standards of normal behaviour for the living creature [25].

The robot should exhibit personality traits, such as curiosity and humour. P4 found the "witty unexpected comments" from Nabaztag entertaining (e.g., "I need a hug"). The personality of the robot is important for its acceptance. Most participants disliked Robosapien due to its rude "caveman speech" and "grotesque" built-in behaviours.

The robot should provide auditory and visual stimuli, i.e., changing colours or sounds, which provide a pleasing background but do not require attention. For example, participants liked the lights on Mood Lamp, I-Cat and Nabaztag. Devices that have a "presence" have the potential to provide companionship. Similar to Heerink et al. [26], we also found that improved social abilities in robots promotes improved sense of presence, which has a positive effect on perceived enjoyment by users. For example, P4 let Pleo roam around the space whilst occupied cooking the dinner. Despite being very busy and active, she willingly gave it time from her other commitments. Similar to P4, the other participants also reported talking to Pleo, FurReal Cat, and Nabaztag.

The robot should not require action to give a reaction. Unpredictability, i.e., not knowing what the robot is going to do next, was desired. The participants found it interesting to observe what Pleo would do next, and what Nabaztag would say next.

Maintenance Requirements. The device should be continuously powered, or require low-maintenance battery operation. In the home studies, participants found the short battery life of Pleo to limit their engagement. Participants commented that a device does not have to be able to move around to give pleasure or have a presence. The device should be robust (not easily damaged by dropping, not easily dirtied). Participants found the white fur for FurReal Cat impractical, as it may get dirty easily.

Device operation should be accessible for those with moderate visual, auditory or dexterity impairments. There should be no small switches or text to read, and voices from the robot should be clear and audible (Nabaztag required an expert to spend two hours installing and configuring it). Size and weight should be manageable for those with reduced mobility. Participants commented that devices such as Pleo might be too heavy for those with reduced mobility or strength. (Pleo's weight, which is 1.6 kg, should be the maximum). This is consistent with the existing literature: Paro was found to be too heavy to pick up and this limited interactions with elderly people [27]. Finally, the device should be independent and not require a lot of care and attention.

5 Conclusion

This study aimed to understand if, and how, social robots can help improve wellbeing in the elderly. We found that social robots have the potential to improve wellbeing in the elderly, but existing robots focus more on healthcare and healthy behaviour among the elderly. Based on our focus groups and home studies, we produced a set of requirements for social robots that reduce loneliness and improve psychological wellbeing among the elderly. The requirements were validated with the participants of our study. Future work involves mapping the requirements to design specification, making an initial prototype design and validating the design with the participants. Their feedback will be used to improve the design and a real prototype will be developed for testing.

Acknowledgments. This project was funded by UCL CRUCIBLE.

References

1. Machielse, A.: Social isolation and the elderly: causes and consequences. In: Shanghai Int. Symp. on Caring for the Elderly, Workshop on Community & Care for the elderly (2006)
2. Huppert, F.A.: Mental capital and well-being: making the most of ourselves in the 21st Century. Government Office for Science (2008)
3. Ereaut, G., Whiting, R.: What do we mean by "wellbeing"? And why might it matter. Department for Children, Schools and Families, London (2008)
4. Huppert, F.A., Whittington, J.E.: Evidence for the independence of positive and negative well-being: Implications for quality of life assessment. British J. of Health Psychology 8, 107–122 (2003)
5. Keyes, C.L.M. (ed.): Promoting a life worth living: human development from the vantage points of mental illness and mental health. Sage, CA (2002)
6. Keyes, C.L.M.: The mental health continuum: From languishing to flourishing in life. J. of Health and Social Behavior 43, 207–222 (2002)

7. Bartneck, C., Forlizzi, J.: A design-centred framework for social human-robot interaction. In: Int. Workshop on Robot and Human Interactive Communication, pp. 591–594 (2004)
8. Broekens, J., Heerink, M., Rosendal, H.: Assistive social robots in elderly care: a review. Gerontechnology 8, 94–103 (2009)
9. Feil-Seifer, D., Mataric, M.J.: Defining socially assistive robotics. In: 9th Int. Conf. on Rehabilitation Robotics, ICORR 2005, pp. 465–468 (2005)
10. Tapus, A., Mataric, M.J., Scassellati, B.: The grand challenges in socially assistive robotics. IEEE Robotics and Automation Magazine 14, 35–42 (2007)
11. Lee, K.M., Jung, Y., Kim, J., Kim, S.R.: Are physically embodied social agents better than disembodied social agents?: The effects of physical embodiment, tactile interaction, and people's loneliness in human-robot interaction. Int. J. of Human-Computer Studies 64, 962–973 (2006)
12. Mataric, M.J., Eriksson, J., Feil-Seifer, D.J., Winstein, C.J.: Socially assistive robotics for post-stroke rehabilitation. J. of NeuroEngineering and Rehabilitation 4, 5 (2007)
13. Broadbent, E., Stafford, R., MacDonald, B.: Acceptance of Healthcare Robots for the Older Population: Review and Future Directions. Int. J. of Social Robotics 1, 319–330 (2009)
14. Kriglstein, S., Wallner, G.: HOMIE: an artificial companion for elderly people. In: CHI 2005 Extended Abstracts on Human Factors in Computing Systems, pp. 2094–2098 (2005)
15. Stiehl, W.D., Lee, J.K., Breazeal, C., Nalin, M., Morandi, A., Sanna, A.: The huggable: a platform for research in robotic companions for pediatric care. In: Proc. of the 8th Int. Conf. on Interaction Design and Children, pp. 317–320 (2009)
16. Dautenhahn, K., Nehaniv, C.L., Walters, M.L., Robins, B., Kose-Bagci, H., Mirza, N.A., Blow, M.: KASPAR - a minimally expressive humanoid robot for human-robot interaction research. Applied Bionics and Biomechanics 6, 369–397 (2009)
17. Libin, A.V., Libin, E.V.: Person-robot interactions from the robopsychologists' point of view: the robotic psychology and robotherapy approach. Proc. of the IEEE 92, 1789–1803 (2004)
18. Wada, K., Shibata, T., Kawaguchi, Y.: Long-term robot therapy in a health service facility for the aged-A case study for 5 years. In: IEEE Int. Conf. on Rehabilitation Robotics, ICORR 2009, pp. 930–933 (2009)
19. Taggart, W., Turkle, S., Kidd, C.D.: An interactive robot in a nursing home: Preliminary remarks. In: Towards Social Mechanisms of Android Science, pp. 56–61. Cognitive Science Society, Stresa (2005)
20. Goris, K., Saldien, J., Lefeber, D.: Probo: a testbed for human robot interaction. In: ACM/IEEE Int. Conf. on Human Robot Interaction, pp. 253–254 (2009)
21. McCarthy, J., Wright, P.: Technology as experience. Interactions 11, 42–43 (2004)
22. Shibata, T.: An overview of human interactive robots for psychological enrichment. Proc. of the IEEE 92, 1749–1758 (2004)
23. Shibata, T., Wada, K., Ikeda, Y., Sabanovic, S.: Cross-cultural studies on subjective evaluation of a seal robot. Advanced Robotics 23, 443–458 (2009)
24. De Schutter, B., Vanden Abeele, V.: Meaningful play in elderly life. In: Annual Meeting of the Int. Communication Association (2008)
25. MacDorman, K.F., Ishiguro, H.: The uncanny advantage of using androids in cognitive and social science research. Interaction Studies 7, 297–337 (2006)
26. Heerink, M., Ben, K., Evers, V., Wielinga, B.: The influence of social presence on acceptance of a companion robot by older people. J. of Physical Agents 2, 33–40 (2008)
27. Kidd, C.D., Taggart, W., Turkle, S.: A sociable robot to encourage social interaction among the elderly. In: Proc. of the 2006 IEEE Int. Conf. on Robotics and Automation, pp. 3972–3976 (2006)

The Effects of Emotionally Worded Synthesized Speech on the Ratings of Emotions and Voice Quality

Mirja Ilves[1], Veikko Surakka[1], and Toni Vanhala[1,2]

[1] Tampere Unit for Computer-Human Interaction, School of Information Sciences, FI-33014 University of Tampere, Finland
[2] VTT Technical Research Centre of Finland, P.O. Box 1300, FI-33101 Tampere, Finland
{mirja.ilves,veikko.surakka}@cs.uta.fi, toni.vanhala@vtt.fi

Abstract. The present research investigated how the verbal content of synthetic messages affects participants' emotional responses and the ratings of voice quality. 28 participants listened to emotionally worded sentences produced by a monotonous and a prosodic tone of voice while the activity of corrugator supercilii facial muscle was measured. Ratings of emotions and voice quality were also collected. The results showed that the ratings of emotions were significantly affected by the emotional contents of the sentences. The prosodic tone of voice evoked more emotion-relevant ratings of arousal than the monotonous voice. Corrugator responses did not seem to reflect emotional reactions. Interestingly, the quality of the same voice was rated higher when the content of the sentences was positive as compared to the neutral and negative sentences. Thus, the emotional content of the spoken messages can be used to regulate users' emotions and to evoke positive feelings about the voices.

Keywords: Emotions, speech synthesis, facial expression, voice quality.

1 Introduction

In human interaction, speech is the most important means to communicate ideas, intentions, and emotions, for example. For this reason, it is evident that for the development of human-computer interaction (HCI) and communication speech offers big potential. The use of synthetic speech in HCI is perhaps the most straightforward approach for creating human-like expressive verbal behavior for computers.

The importance and potential of synthesized spoken messages is highlighted in studies, which have shown that people respond to speech similarly whether it comes from a human or a computer [1]. Our approach is to support the use of speech in HCI by studying how emotional messages produced by speech synthesis affect emotional experiences and physiological responses of humans. More specifically, the focus of our research is to study the role of the verbal content in activating human emotional system.

There is evidence that the emotional content of synthetic speech has both significant effects on human emotional processing in general and potential benefits for HCI in particular. It has been found that emotionally charged messages produced by a monotonous voice can evoke emotion related subjective and physiological

S. D´Mello et al. (Eds.): ACII 2011, Part I, LNCS 6974, pp. 588–598, 2011.

responses in listeners [2,3]. Further, cognitive processing can be facilitated by giving emotionally worded feedback during a computerized problem-solving task [4].

On the other hand, we have suggested that the naturalness of voice affects the experienced emotions. Synthesized speech can be created with different techniques that sound more or less humanlike. We have found that when emotional messages were delivered by two synthesizers, only the more humanlike synthesizer evoked emotion related facial electromyographic (EMG) responses as well as more emotion-related variation in the ratings of arousal and in pupil responses [2,3]. In addition to synthesis technique, the naturalness of prosody is a central component for natural sounding voice. The naturalness of voice can easily be increased by adding prosodic variation to speech that would otherwise be monotonous. This enables us to study whether emotional effects could be enhanced by increasing the prosodic variation of the speech. In the present research, emotionally worded sentences were produced by unit selection technique with a monotonous and a prosodic speaking style.

Naturalness, clearness and pleasantness are central factors when people rate the quality of speech synthesis [5]. Adding prosodic variation to the synthesized speech probably enhances the quality of voice, but it is interesting to study if the ratings of voice quality are affected also by the content of the message. Fogg and Nass [6] found that interaction with a computer that flatters was rated more positively than the interaction with a computer that gave generic feedback. Thus, the second interest of the present study is related to the question: Is the verbal content of the spoken message so powerful that it affects the ratings of voice quality, even though the voice remains similar? If a synthesizer speaks in a positive way about a listener, does the listener rate the voice more positively than when the synthesizer produces negative statements about the listener? Does this happen even when there is no real interaction between the human and the computer?

Dimensional theory of emotions defines emotions through a set of dimensions [7]. The most important and widely used dimensions are valence, which refers to the pleasantness of the experienced emotion and arousal, which relates to the experienced level of activation.

Emotions cause changes both in subjective experiences and physiological activity. For example, there is evidence that the activation of facial muscles is related to emotional valence. It has been shown that there is a linear effect of valence on activity over corrugator supercilii [8]. In other words, the activity of corrugator supercilii increases during negative emotions and relaxes during positively valenced emotions. Based on this, we chose to investigate emotion related physiological responses by measuring the activity of corrugator supercilii in the present study. However, it is important to remember when viewing the results that corrugator activity may be influenced also, for example, by cognitive factors like concentration [9].

In summary, the aim of the present research was to study how synthetic verbal stimulation with emotional content might affect the perceiver. First aim was to study, if there is a difference between the emotional effects of same messages delivered either without or with prosodic variation. Second aim was to study whether the ratings of voice quality are affected by the emotional content of the spoken message. First, participants listened to a set of emotionally worded sentences produced by a monotonous and a prosodic tone of voice, while their corrugator EMG activity was measured. Following this, ratings of emotional experiences and speech quality were collected.

2 Methods

2.1 Participants

31 volunteers from an introductory course of Computer Science participated in the study. Data from three subjects was discarded, because post-experiment interview revealed that they were aware of the facial muscle activity being measured. Thus, data from 28 subjects were used for the analysis (21 females, mean age 22.93 years, range 18-41 years). The participants were native speakers of Finnish, and had normal hearing by their own report. The participants were compensated with a movie ticket for their participation.

2.2 Equipment and Physiological Measurement

Stimuli were created with Finnish-speaking speech synthesizer Bitlips' Unit Selection [10]. The stimulus presentation and rating were controlled by E-Prime© [11] stimulation software running on a PC computer with a Windows XP operating system. The stimuli were presented via earphones.

Facial EMG was registered from the left side of the face above the corrugator supercilii muscle site using Ag–AgCl sintered electrodes. The ground electrode was over the mastoid bone and an active reference on the forehead close to the center of the hairline. Guidelines of Fridlund and Cacioppo [12] were followed. EMG was measured using a NeXus-10 physiological monitoring device (Mind Media B.V.) that was connected to a laptop computer using a wireless Bluetooth communications link. The sampling rate was 2048 Hz. Analog high-pass filter of .5 Hz was used and EMG was further digitally pass-band filtered (4-th order Butterworth) from 20 to 500 Hz.

2.3 Stimuli

Vocal stimuli consisted of 12 different sentences[1] with emotional content. Emotional categories were happiness, anger, and neutral. Happiness and anger were selected because they are located on the opposed ends of valence scale. Emotional words expressing happiness and anger were selected and translated to Finnish from the list of causative emotions by Johnson-Laird & Oatley [13]. In addition, neutral sentences were created so that the sentences in different categories matched for word length.

The sentences were produced by a male voice of synthesizer with both a monotonous and a prosodic tone of voice. The monotonous tone of voice means that fundamental frequency (F0) variation was set as flat as possible. The prosodic tone of voice means that variation in F0 was not manipulated, that is, variation in F0 was not flattened nor any emotional cues were added. Besides the variation of F0, the voice parameters of the sentences were similar to each other as shown in Table 1.

---

[1] Sentences (roughly translated from Finnish): Happiness: I am content with you, You please me, You make me delighted, You make me exhilarated; Anger: I am irked by you, You irritate me, You make me annoyed, You make me infuriated; Neutral: You seem to be normal, You are average, You seem to be decent, You seem to be ordinary.

Table 1. ANOVA results for the duration (in seconds), loudness (dB), fundamental frequency (F0), and variability of fundamental frequency (F0 sd) of the stimulus sentences produced by the monotonous and prosodic tone of voice

	Duration (s)	dB	F0 (Hz)	F0 (Hz) sd
Monotonous	1,33	72,63	89,37	3,31
Prosodic	1,33	73,21	89,39	7,94
ANOVA	$F(1, 18) = 0.00$, ns	$F(1, 18) = 1.26$, ns	$F(1, 18) = 0.00$, ns	$F(1, 18) = 152.52$, $p < .001$

2.4 Experimental Procedure

First, the sound attenuated and electromagnetically shielded laboratory was introduced and the participant was seated in a chair. She/he was explained that the aim was to study how people react to synthesized speech. The participant was told a cover story that the purpose of the electrodes was to measure the humidity of her/his skin, and then the electrodes were attached.

To familiarize the participants to listening to synthetic speech, three speech samples spoken by three different speech synthesizers were presented before the actual experiment. Then, the participant was instructed to relax, listen carefully with an open mind the sentences, and to fixate to a small cross in the center of the screen whenever the cross was within sight. Finally, the lights of the laboratory were dimmed and the experimental phase began.

The stimulus sentences were presented randomly with fifteen seconds pause between the stimulus presentations. Fixation-cross appeared five seconds before the stimulus onset and disappeared five seconds after the stimulus offset. The presentation of the stimulus sentences lasted approximately 8 minutes.

After the experimental phase, the electrodes were detached and the participant gave the ratings of the stimuli. First, the participant rated her/his emotional experiences evoked by the stimuli on nine-point bipolar scales. The valence-scale ranged from negative to positive and the arousal-scale from calm to aroused. Secondly, the participant rated on five-point scales how pleasant, natural, and clear the voice was. These questions were selected from a modified mean opinion score (MOS) scale [5]

Before the rating sessions, the scales were explained to the participant. The scales were presented in the computer screen and a keyboard was used to give the ratings. After the ratings, the participant was interviewed whether she/he was aware that her/his facial muscle activity had been measured. Finally, the participant was debriefed about the purpose of the study, and she/he gave a written consent.

2.5 Data Preprocessing and Analysis

EMG responses were extracted by averaging rectified sample values. A 500 ms pre-stimulus baseline correction was performed. Mean EMG responses of three seconds from the stimulus offset were analyzed.

Subjective data was analyzed using repeated measures ANOVAs. Greenhouse-Geisser adjusted degrees of freedom were used when necessary. For the multiple post-hoc comparisons, Bonferroni corrected p-values were used.

3 Results

3.1 Ratings of Emotional Experiences

Figure 1 shows the mean ratings and standard error of the means (SEM) for valence and arousal. 2 x 3 two-way (voice x emotion category) ANOVAs were performed separately for the ratings of valence and arousal. For the ratings of valence, there was a statistically significant main effect of emotion category, $F(1, 36)= 42$, $p< .001$. The main effect of voice and the interaction of voice and category were not statistically significant. Post-hoc pairwise comparisons showed that the ratings were significantly lower for the negative sentences than for the neutral, $t(27)= -3.98$, $p< .001$ and positive sentences, $t(27)= -6.98$, $p< .001$. The ratings for the positive sentences were significantly higher than for the neutral sentences, $t(27)= 6.59$, $p< .001$.

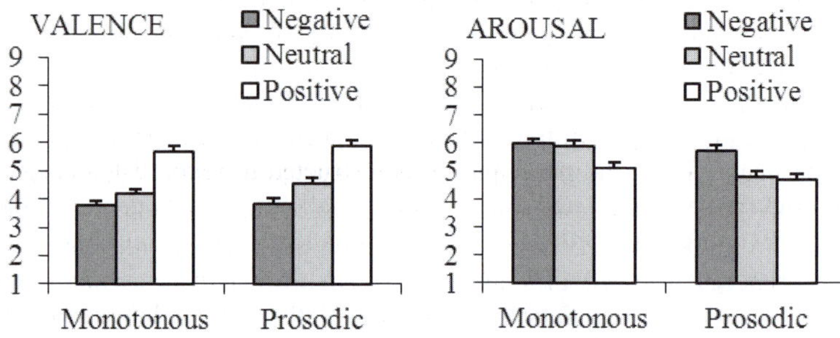

Fig. 1. Mean ratings (and SEM) of valence and arousal

For the ratings of arousal, ANOVA revealed a statistically significant main effect of voice, $F(1, 27)= 12.79$, $p< .01$ and emotion category, $F(2, 54)= 10.47$, $p< .001$. Because the interaction effect was also significant, $F(2, 54)= 6.76$, $p< .01$, one-way ANOVAs with emotion category as a factor were conducted separately for both voices. The results are reported in Table 2.

Table 2. Results of the effect of the voice on the ratings of arousal

Tone of voice	ANOVA	Pairwise comparisons
Monotonous	$F(2, 54) = 7.89$, $p< .001$	Negative > Positive $t(27) = 3.54$, $p< .01$ Neutral > Positive $t(27) = 2.98$, $p< .05$
Prosodic	$F(2, 54) = 11.35$, $p< .001$	Negative > Positive $t(27) = 4.30$, $p< .001$ Negative > Neutral $t(27) = 4.03$, $p< .01$

In addition, pairwise comparisons between the voices were conducted separately for the different emotion categories. The neutral sentences produced by the monotonous voice were rated as more arousing than the neutral sentences spoken by the prosodic tone of voice, $t(27)= 4.61$, $p< .001$. The arousal ratings of the positive sentences produced by the monotonous voice were higher than the arousal ratings of the positive sentences produced by the prosodic tone of voice, t(27)= 2.70, p< .05. The difference between the arousal ratings of the negative sentences was not statistically significant.

3.2 Ratings of Voice Quality

The average ratings of the voice are shown in Figure 2. Three 2 x 3 two-way (voice x emotion category) ANOVAs were performed separately for each ratings. For the ratings of pleasantness, there was a statistically significant main effect of voice, F(1, 27)= 57.84, p< .001 and emotion category, F(2, 54)= 25.89, p< .001, and a significant interaction of voice and category, F(2, 54)= 11.40, p< .001. For the ratings of naturalness, there was a statistically significant main effect of voice, F(1, 27)= 76.29, p< .001 and emotion category, F(2, 54)= 25.54, p< .001, and a significant interaction of voice and category, F(2, 54)= 7.89, p< .001. Also, for the ratings of clearness, there was a statistically significant main effect of voice, F(1, 27)= 62.38, p< .001 and emotion category, F(2, 54)= 39.57, p< .001, and a significant interaction of voice and category, F(2, 54)= 6.82, p< .01.

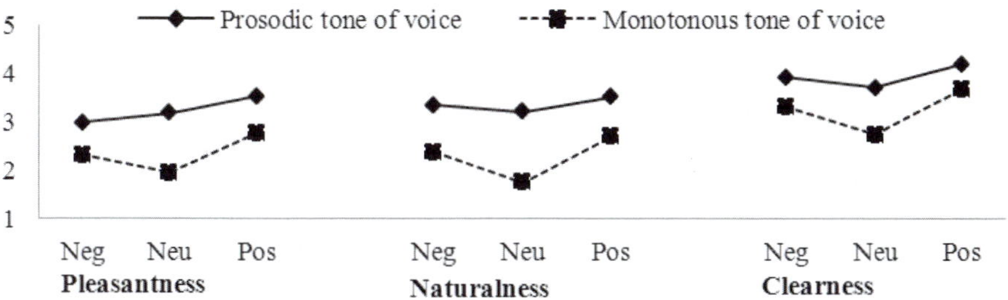

Fig. 2. Mean ratings of pleasantness, naturalness, and clearness of the voice separately for both voices and each emotion category

Table 3. Results of the effect of the emotion category on the ratings of the pleasantness, naturalness, and clearness of the monotonous voice

Rating scale	ANOVA	Pairwise comparisons
Pleasantness	F(2, 54) = 29.06, p < 0.001	Positive>Neutral t(27) = 7.22, p < .001 Positive>Negative t(27) = 4.50, p < .001 Negative>Neutral t(27) = 3.36, p < .01
Naturalness	F(2, 44) = 40.78, p < 0.001	Positive>Neutral t(27) = 12.05, p < .001 Positive>Negative t(27) = 2.78, p < .05 Negative>Neutral t(27) = 5.14, p < .001
Clearness	F(2, 54) = 48.33, p < 0.001	Positive>Neutral t(27) = 9.96, p < .001 Positive>Negative t(27) = 3.95, p < .01 Negative>Neutral t(27) = 5.60, p < .001

Pairwise comparisons between the voices showed that the prosodic tone of voice was rated as more pleasant, $t(28)= 7.61$, $p< .001$, natural, $t(28)= 8.73$, $p< .001$, and clear, $t(28)= 7.90$, $p< .001$ than the monotonous voice.

Because of the significant interaction, one-way ANOVAs with emotion category as a factor were performed separately for the both voices. The emotional content of the sentences affected the ratings of voice quality as can be seen from Tables 3 and 4.

Table 4. Results of the effect of the emotion category on the ratings of the pleasantness, naturalness, and clearness of the prosodic tone of voice

Rating scale	ANOVA	Pairwise comparisons
Pleasantness	$F(2, 54) = 13.10$, $p < .001$	Positive>Neutral $t(27) = 3.28$, $p < .01$
		Positive>Negative $t(27) = 4.62$, $p < .001$
Naturalness	$F(2, 54) = 2.38$, $p > .05$	
Clearness	$F(2, 54) = 9.24$, $p < .001$	Positive>Neutral $t(27) = 4.13$, $p < .001$
		Positive>Negative $t(27) = 3.05$, $p < .05$

3.3 Electromyographic Responses

Mean corrugator responses to stimulus categories are presented in Figure 3. Interestingly, the mean corrugator response to all stimulus categories was relaxing. First, the effect of the voice on corrugator muscle activity was tested. Pairwise comparison between the voices did not reveal a statistically significant difference between the voices, $t(27) = 1.67$, ns. Because the degree of the relaxation seemed to be divergent to different stimulus categories, the activity change of the corrugator muscle was compared to the baseline level. Statistically significant relaxations from the pre-stimulus baseline were found by one-sample t-test for the neutral sentences, $t(27) = -2.15$, $p < .05$. Relaxation from the pre-stimulus baseline for the positive sentences approached statistical significance, $t(27) = -1.894$, $p < .07$. Mean corrugator response to negative sentences did not differ significantly from the baseline level, $t(27) = -0.93$, $p >$ ns.

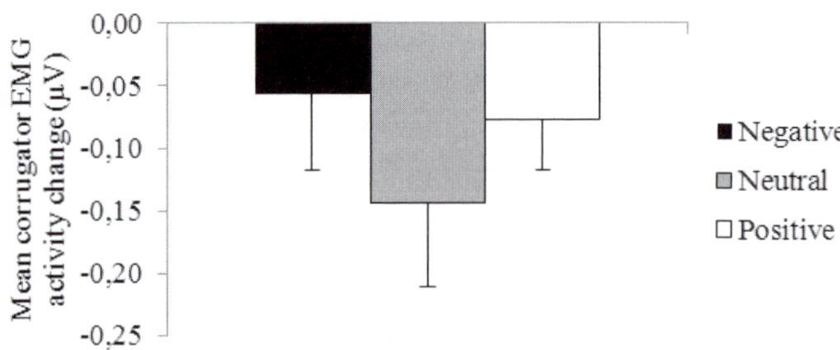

Fig. 3. Mean corrugator supercilii EMG responses (and SEM) to negative, neutral, and positive sentences during three-second period after stimulus offset

4 Discussion

The ratings of valence were significantly affected by the emotional contents of the sentences. The ratings were significantly different for all stimulus categories. The tone of voice had no significant effect on the ratings of valence. In line with the valence ratings, corrugator supercilii activity was not affected by the tone of voice. Instead, frowning activity significantly decreased from the pre-stimulus baseline level during the three seconds following a neutral stimulus. After negative and positive sentences, frowning activity was not significantly different from the baseline.

The ratings of arousal were affected by the voice. The neutral and positive sentences produced by the monotonous voice evoked higher ratings of arousal than the positive and neutral sentences produced by the prosodic tone of voice.

The tone of voice had an effect also on the ratings of the quality of the voice. The prosodic tone of voice was rated as more pleasant, natural, and clear than the monotonous voice. In addition, the verbal content of the sentences had interestingly an effect on the ratings of voice quality. The prosodic tone of voice was rated as more pleasant and clear when the content of the sentence was positive compared with the neutral and negative sentences. The monotonous tone of voice was rated similarly as more pleasant and clear, and also more natural, when the content of the sentence was positive in comparison to the neutral and negative sentences. The ratings of monotonous voice were also more positive when the content of the sentence was negative in comparison to the sentences with neutral content.

The current findings support the previous findings that emotional responses can be evoked by the lexical emotional content of the spoken messages [2,3]. At the present study, the ratings of valence were significantly different for all emotion categories but the ratings were not affected by the tone of voice. We have previously found [14] that even short emotional words produced by a very machinelike voice can evoke congruent emotion-related ratings in the participants, but the experienced valence and approachability can be enhanced when the words are spoken by a more humanlike voice. On the other hand, at the previous study, the differences between two concatenative synthesizers (i.e. more humanlike voices) were not significant. Thus, it seems that, when the voice is experienced humanlike enough, experienced valence is not enhanced even if the naturalness of the voice is increased by using the technique that sounds even more humanlike or increasing the prosodic variation of the voice. There are similar findings also for human speech. In the study of Bertels et al. [15], people rated the valence of positive words similarly when the words were uttered by a neutral tone of human voice compared with the emotionally congruent tone of human voice.

However, the arousal of the sentences was rated significantly differently depending on the tone of voice. The arousal of the neutral and positive sentences was rated significantly higher when the sentences were produced by the monotonous voice compared with the prosodic tone of voice. When we look at the averages of the ratings, it can be seen that the ratings of the positive and neutral sentences produced by the prosodic tone of voice were actually more emotion-relevant than the positive and neutral sentences produced by the monotonous voice. That is because the arousal of the neutral sentences produced by the prosodic tone of voice was judged closer to neutral experience (the center of the scale) than the arousal of the neutral sentences produced by the monotonous tone of voice. Further, the arousal ratings of the positive sentences produced by the monotonous voice were very close to neutral experience whereas the arousal ratings of the positive sentences produced by the prosodic tone of voice were more different from the neutral experience and were judged a little bit calming.

It has been shown that perceiving emotionally negative stimulus increases corrugator supercilii EMG activity and emotionally positive stimulus decreases the activity [8]. At the present study, the average corrugator response during three seconds period after stimulus offset was below pre-stimulus baseline level for all emotion categories. Relaxing corrugator response to speech synthesis has also been found in previous studies [2,4]. Significant decrease from the pre-stimulus baseline was found for the neutral sentences, whereas the activity of the muscle site did not differ significantly from the pre-stimulus baseline after the negative and positive sentences. Thus, the current EMG responses do not seem to reflect emotional reactions. Even though the correlation between the facial muscle activity and emotion has been frequently found, there exist also studies where this correlation has not been found [see 16]. It has also been reported that the activity of corrugator is associated with cognitive processing, like mental effort [17] and concentration [9]. It might be that corrugator activity at the present research did not reflect emotions but cognitive processing instead. Because the corrugator activity decreased significantly after the neutral sentences but not after the negative and positive sentences, it may be that the participants concentrated less on the processing of the neutral sentences than the processing of the emotionally loaded sentences. This is supported by memory studies, where it has been found that emotionally valenced words are remembered better than nonvalenced words, and this has suggested resulting, for example, from the facilitated attention to emotional words [18].

One of the most interesting findings of the current study was that the content of the spoken message affected how people rated the voice quality. In spite of the fact, that the same voice produced negative, neutral, and positive sentences and the participants were instructed to specifically rate the voice, the sentences with positive content evoked more positive ratings of the voice quality than the negative or neutral sentences. This was true for both prosodic styles. In addition, when the voice was monotonous, even the negative emotional content of the sentence had pronounced effects on the ratings of voice quality as compared to the neutral content. It has been previously found that the interaction with computer is rated more positively when the computer sincerely or insincerely praises the participant than when the computer gives only some generic feedback [6]. Our study showed that the positive content has so strong effect on people that just listening to the positive comments, without any interaction, affects the ratings of voice.

In summary, our results confirmed previous findings that emotional responses can be evoked by the lexical content of the synthetic speech. Speech itself seems to be so powerful means of communication that even the monotonous tone of voice can be used quite effectively to communicate the emotional messages. In addition to previous findings that the emotional effects of emotionally worded messages can be enhanced through the synthesized nature of the speech, emotional effects can further be enhanced by increasing the naturalness of the prosodic variation. However, because the voice itself was quite natural, increasing the naturalness through the prosodic variation did not seem to have great effects on the emotional responses. Instead, the pleasantness, naturalness, and clearness of the voice were rated clearly higher when the prosodic variation was more natural compared with the monotonous speaking style. Further, the impression of the voice quality was affected by the content of the spoken message. Thus, the emotional content of the spoken messages in general can be used to regulate users' emotions and positive language in particular can be used to enhance positive feelings about the voices.

Acknowledgments. The authors would like to thank all the participants of the study. This research was supported by the Graduate School in User-Centered Information Technology (UCIT).

References

1. Nass, C., Brave, S.: Wired for speech: How voice activates and advances the human-computer relationship. The MIT Press, Cambridge (2005)
2. Ilves, M., Surakka, V.: Subjective and physiological responses to emotional content of synthesized speech. In: Magnenat-Thalmann, N., Joslin, C., Kim, H. (eds.) Proc. of CASA, pp. 19–26 (2004)
3. Ilves, M., Surakka, V.: Emotions, Anthropomorphism of Speech Synthesis, and Psychophysiology. In: Izdebski, K. (ed.) Emotions in the Human Voice. Culture and Perception, vol. III, pp. 137–152. Plural Publishing Inc., San Diego (2009)
4. Partala, T., Surakka, V.: The effects of affective interventions in human-computer interaction. Interacting with Computers 16(2), 295–309 (2004)
5. Viswanathan, M., Viswanathan, M.: Measuring speech quality for text-to-speech systems: development and assessment of a modified mean opinion score (MOS) scale. Computer Speech and Language 19(1), 55–83 (2005)
6. Fogg, B.J., Nass, C.: Silicon sycophants: the effects of computers that flatter. International Journal of Human-Computer Studies 46(5), 551–561 (1997)
7. Bradley, M.M., Lang, P.J.: Measuring emotions: the self-assessment manikin and the semantic differential. Journal of Behavioral Therapy and Experimental Psychiatry 25(1), 49–59 (1994)
8. Larsen, J.T., Norris, C.J., Cacioppo, J.T.: Effects of positive and negative affect on electromyographic activity over zygomaticus major and corrugator supercilii. Psychophysiology 40(5), 776–785 (2003)
9. Cacioppo, J.T., Petty, R.E., Morris, K.J.: Semantic, evaluative, and self-referent processing: memory, cognitive effort, and somatovisceral activity. Psychophysiology 22(4), 371–384 (1985)
10. Bitlips, `http://www.bitlips.fi/index.en.html` (retrieved March 30, 2011)
11. Schneider, W., Eschman, A., Zuccolotto, A.: E-Prime User's Guide. Psychology software Tools Inc., Pittsburgh (2002)
12. Fridlund, A.J., Cacioppo, J.T.: Guidelines for human electromyographic research. Psychophysiology 23(5), 567–589 (1986)
13. Johnson-Laird, P.N., Oatley, K.: The language of emotions: an analysis of a semantic field. Cognition and Emotion 3(2), 81–123 (1989)
14. Ilves, M., Surakka, V.: Subjective emotional responses to synthesized speech with lexical emotional content: The effect of the naturalness of the synthetic voice. Submitted for publication in Behaviour & Information Technology (under review)

15. Bertels, J., Kolinsky, R., Morais, J.: Norms of emotional valence, arousal, threat value and shock value for 80 spoken french words: comparison between neutral and emotional tones of voice. Psychologica Belgica 49(1), 19–40 (2009)
16. Tassinary, L.G., Cacioppo, J.T.: The skeletomotor system: Surface electromyography. In: Cacioppo, J.T., Tassinary, L.G., Berntson, G.G. (eds.) Handbook of Psychophysiology, 2nd edn., pp. 163–199. Cambridge University Press, New York (2000)
17. Van Boxtel, A., Jessurun, M.: Amplitude and bilateral coherency of facial and jaw-elevator EMG activity as an index of effort during a two-choice serial reaction task. Psychophysiology 30(6), 589–604 (1993)
18. Doerksen, S., Shimamura, A.P.: Source memory enhancement for emotional words. Emotion 1(1), 5–11 (2001)

Evaluating a Cognitive-Based Affective Student Model

Patricia A. Jaques[1], Rosa Vicari[2], Sylvie Pesty[3], and Jean-Claude Martin[4]

[1] PIPCA/UNISINOS, Brazil
[2] PGIE/UFRGS, Brazil
[3] LIG, France
[4] LIMSI, France

Abstract. Predicting students' emotion raises several questions about the data on which these predictions should be grounded. This article describes an empirical evaluation of a cognitive-based affective user model accomplished with 7th grade students. The affective model is based on the OCC psychological theory of emotions in order to infer the students' emotions from their actions and choices in the interface of the learning system. The model relies on a BDI model to implement the process of inference of students' emotions in a web-based learning environment. Two experiments were conducted based on a direct and an indirect approach. The results of the evaluation are discussed and some ideas of improvement for the experiments protocol are presented.

Keywords: Affective Computing, Inference of Emotions, BDI.

1 Introduction

In order for a computing system to recognize users' emotions, two main steps are necessary. First, the system should be able to capture some users' data from which it could infer their emotions. Researchers are currently developing system aiming at recognition of emotion from the different modalities: (*i*) voice; (*ii*) facial expressions [1, 2]; (*iii*) physiological signs (blood volume pulse, muscle tension, skin conductivity, breathing) [3], and (*iv*) behavioural data, i. e. user's actions in the system interface (for example, chosen options and typing speed) [1, 4-6]. Second of all, the system should have a user model that enables to predict her/his emotional states from previously recognised emotions and also from the captured data.

Users' **behavioral data** may be a path to predict, recognize and interpret their affective states. In this case, the system is conceptually grounded on a psychological model of emotions that follows a cognitive approach in order to infer the users' emotions from their actions and choices in the computing system. This approach was denominated **Cognitive-Based Affective User Modeling (CB-AUM)** [4]. One of the most employed cognitive-based psychological models for inference of emotions in computing environments is Ortony, Clore and Collins Cognitive Structure of Emotions [7], generally called OCC model. The OCC model aims at explaining the appraisal, the cognitive process that elicits an emotion, of twenty-two categories of emotions.

Several works are using the OCC model for users' inference of emotions [5, 8]. Conatti and colleagues [5, 9] proposed a probabilistic approach, using Bayesian

S. D'Mello et al. (Eds.): ACII 2011, Part I, LNCS 6974, pp. 599–608, 2011.

networks, for the inference of 6 emotions (joy, distress, pride, shame, admiration and reproach) according to OCC model. Eyharbide et al. [8] use an ontology in order to predict students' emotions when interacting with a quiz about Java programming. These two approaches are domain dependent. So, the proposed models cannot be integrated to other learning environments. In a Bayesian network, as in Conati, it is just possible to know the goals that elicited the emotions, but not the event, since it does not interfere directly in the goals. An explicit knowledge of the reasons that elicit an emotion is important for systems like intelligent tutoring systems, where the tutor should take into account that type of information in order to decide the best action to apply in order to motivate or increase the student self-confidence.

This paper describes the evaluation of a cognitive-based affective student model, which is conceptually founded on the OCC model in order to infer students' emotions from their behavioural data in the context of a web-based learning environment. The used approach is independent of domain and platform. The model follows a mental states approach, more specifically it profits from the reasoning capacity of the Belief-Desire-Intention (BDI) architecture in order to infer students' appraisal, which allows the agent knowing the reasons that elicited an emotion.

This affective information about the student is used by an animated pedagogical agent called Pat [6, 10]: a domain and platform independent agent, which is responsible for motivating students, encouraging them to make more efforts as well as increasing their motivation. Two main modules compose the architecture of this agent: the Body (responsible for presenting verbal and physical behaviours of the character) and the Mind (responsible for emotions inference and affective scaffolding). Although Mind Module accomplishes both goals (scaffolding and emotions inference), this paper focuses on the evaluation of the affective model and on the inference of emotions.

The remainder of this paper is organised as follows: the next section explains the psychological and pedagogical theories that found the proposed model. Section 3 explains the BDI process of reasoning responsible for emotions inference. Section 4 presents the experiment protocol, and Section 5 the results of the evaluation. Finally, Section 6 suggests some improvements in the experiments protocol and mentions ideas for future work.

2 Modelling User's Emotions

The model described in this work is able to recognise the emotions *joy, distress, satisfaction, disappointment, gratitude, anger*, and *shame*, based on the cognitive psychological model of emotion OCC [7]. These emotions were chosen, because, among the emotions types presents in OCC, they are the most relevant for learning environments.

Due to space limitation, let us see the appraisal for the emotion joy and distress in OCC and how our model tries to infer this appraisal in order to recognise these emotions (for the other emotions, it works similarly). According to OCC, *joy* and *distress* are elicited when a person focuses on the desirability of an event in relation to individual's goals. Joy occurs when a person is pleased about a desirable event that takes place and distress when he is displeased about an undesirable one. For instance, for a certain student who has the intention of pleasing the teacher and his parents, obtaining a good grade is a desirable event. For recognising joy, it is necessary to verify when a learning event is desirable for the student (according to his goals) and when s/he is pleased because this desirable event took place.

Some events have been defined that can happen in the learning environment and which can elicit an emotion. They are 11 events, as for example, the student did not accomplish the task, the student provided an incorrect response for an exercise, the student asked for help, the student disabled the agent (due to space limitation, only some examples of 11 events are cited here).

Furthermore, it was necessary to determine the student's goals in order to verify the desirability of events. As the affective model was applied in a web-based domain-independent learning environment, the goals should be sufficiently generic. According to Ames [11], students can have *mastery* or *performance oriented* objectives, which are the reasons that they engage in learning and choose to take on in academic tasks. Students who have a *learning/mastery goal* are oriented in developing new skills and abilities and try to understand their work, improve their level of competence, and learn new things. When students have *performance goals* they believe that performance is important and they want to demonstrate that they have abilities. They feel successful when they please the teacher or do better than other students, rather then when they understand something new. In order to identify the student's objectives, the *Motivated Strategies for Learning Questionnaire (MSLQ)[12]* is applied the first time the student accesses the learning system.

Finally, once the student's objectives are known and that her actions and the software events are collected, it is possible to determine the desirability of the events and when the student is pleased/displeased with them. The events have been classified according to their desirability based on what psychology and pedagogy researchers know about students who have mastery or performance goals [11, 13].

The information about students' goals and event pleasantness is inserted in the BDI model as the agent beliefs. Based on this information, the agent reasons in order to infer students' appraisal and, therefore, their emotions. This reasoning process is described in the next section.

3 Emotions' Inference

The Pat's Mind, responsible for inferring emotions, is a BDI agent that was implemented in X-BDI. X-BDI is a tool for the implementation of an agent's cognitive module based on the Belief-Desire-Intention (BDI) approach [14]. This approach enables to design a system as a rational agent having certain mental attitudes of belief, desire and intention, respectively representing the informative, motivational and deliberative states of the agent [15]. The Mind module of Pat (responsible for inferring student's emotions and also for the affective scaffolding) was implemented in X-BDI. The other components of the agent's architecture (such as Body module, sensors, effectors and interface) were programmed in Java and communicate with X-BDI through *sockets*.

The following scenario was chosen as an illustration of how the X-BDI cognitive kernel (Pat's mind) infers the students' emotions: a female student has performance goals and she is disappointed because she provided an incorrect response to an exercise (the event).

The sensors notify the BDI cognitive kernel that the student has performance goals and her effort was high, and that the student provided an incorrect response to the exercise. The student's **effort** in the resolution of an exercise is classified in function of his persistence in the resolution of problems with or without asking for help assistance. It is calculated by the number of attempts to solve an exercise, or by the number of steps made. A great number of steps means a higher degree of effort made by the student.

Pat should know the student's emotions in order to decide which affective tactic to apply. It infers the student's emotions from the following beliefs (represented by the predicates *bel*):

```
bel (Pat,event_pleasantness (not_correct_answer, displeased))  if
bel (Pat, student_goal(performance)),
bel (Pat, event(not_correct_answer)).

bel (Pat, is_prospect_event(not_correct_answer)) if
bel (Pat,event(not_correct_answer)).

bel (Pat, student_emotion(disappointment)) if
  bel(Pat, event_pleasantness(Event,displeased)),
bel (Pat,-is_mediador_action), bel (Pat,is_prospect_event (Event)).

bel (Pat, student_emotion(distress))  if
bel (Pat, event_pleasantness(Event,displeased)),
bel (Pat, -is_mediador_action).
```

The student is displeased with the event, because the event consequences are undesirable, or it is desirable but it did not occur. When the student is displeased, she experiences a distress emotion and also disappointment if it is the prospect of an event that was confirmed (*is_prospect_event* predicate). It is the case of the event *not_correct_task_answer,* as long as the student accomplishes a task she hopes to obtain a good grade. Distress is used in this article as an emotion type, as described in the OCC model. An emotion type is a distinct kind of emotion that can be realized in a variety of recognizably related forms and, which are differentiated by their intensity. For example, fear is an emotion type that can be manifested in varying degrees of intensity, such as "concern" (less afraid), "frightened", and "petrified" (more afraid).

The variables that affect the emotion's intensity in the OCC model are effort, realization, unexpectedness and undesirability for disappointment, and undesirability for distress. Their values are estimated and sent to Pat by the sensor of the body module. It is responsible for identifying the value of these variables with questionnaires and student's observable behavior. For example, performance oriented students desire more strongly to obtain a high grade and in this way the sensor considers that this event has a high desirability.

```
bel (Pat, emotion_intensity(disappointment, high)) if
bel (Pat, effort(high)), bel (Pat,student_emotion(disappointment)).
```

4 Experiment Protocol

Only few works describe the evaluation of affective students models [3, 5, 16]. When the interest is in affective models based on appraisal, the only one that these authors are aware of is Conati's work [5]. Following [9], there are just two approaches to evaluate affective models. The *direct approach* specifically measures the accuracy of the affective model, i. e., it obtains a reliable measure of student's emotions in order to compare this data with the one inferred by the model. The *indirect approach* evaluates the performance of an application that uses an affective model in order to adapt itself to the user. One of the limitations of the indirect approach is that the model evaluation can be damaged by the introduction of other variables in the user's interaction with the system [9]. However, it can be used in order to complement the results of the direct approach. This way, we use both approaches in this paper.

A possible way to obtain information about students' emotions is from their self-report [5]. One possibility is asking the student to describe their emotions after the interaction with the system. One limitation of this approach is that students can no longer remember their emotions after the interaction with the software; mainly if this interaction was long, as it usually happens in learning environments. Another option is to record the students interacting with the application and to show this video to them after the session. This approach requires recording the interaction of each student with the system, which can be impracticable due to the amount of equipment required. Besides, students have difficulties to self annotate their facial expressions.

For this experiment the approach developed by [9] and applied by [5] has been adopted: users were asked to report their emotions in a pop-up dialog box. This approach was chosen because it was created to be applied in cognitive-based affective model, and it was improved after some tests. [5, 9] suggest presenting in the screen a *permanent dialog box* in which the students can report their emotions. The emotions reported by the student are compared with those inferred by the affective model in order to define its success rate. As users can distract themselves with the options in the learning environment and forget to notify their emotions [9], it is also suggested pop-upping the same dialog box in two situations: (*i*) if the user has not related his emotions for a long period, (*ii*) if the system detects a change in student's emotions.

In [9], it was observed that no great level of frustration was reported by students. This suggests that a dialog box does not generate too much user frustration and, in this way, might not interfere in the affective model evaluation as one might expect.

5 Evaluation Results

Twenty-four pupils, whose ages vary between 12 and 19 years old, were initially recruited to participate in the experiment. They were 7th grade students who were enrolled at a local public school in Canoas, Brazil. Pat was integrated to a web-based learning environment called JADE for the evaluation experiment of the affective model. JADE [17] is as web-based learning environment that can be customized to any domain subject of interest, as long as it presents the pedagogical content in sessions composed by pages of theoretical content and exercises. Although JADE is a simplistic learning environment and not an intelligent one (like intelligent tutoring systems), it was chosen because one of the goals of this work was to verify how hard it is to infer students' emotions in a domain independent environment, and how useful and motivating would be an affective animated pedagogical agent in a not so intelligent learning system. JADE was adapted to the pedagogical content of Earth time zones. This domain was selected because in Brazilian schools this content is taught in just one class (with 1-3 hours of duration), the foreseen duration for our experiment. Another reason is that this content was not taught for the student that participated in the evaluation.

We opted for letting the agent active during the evaluation experiment of the affective model, since most tactics by Pat can interfere in student's emotions. For example, some inferred emotions, such as shame, are emotions that the student feels towards the agent, because, according to OCC model, someone may feel shame if it disapproves his own action. For example, asking for help may mean for a performance-oriented student that he is not able to accomplish the task alone. In this case, the agent asks the student if he feels uncomfortable in asking help. If the response is positive, it means that he disapproves his attitude of showing to Pat that he is not able to accomplish the activities alone, and feels shame.

Initially, students were informed about the experiment goals, the voluntary character of their participation, as well as about the complete confidentiality of collected data. It was explained that they would interact with an animated pedagogical agent in a web-based learning environment that would try to adapt itself to their needs and help them to learn better the content of the class. The students were encouraged to inform their emotions sincerely in the dialog boxes, whenever there were changes. Afterwards, students had a brief explanation on JADE.

Students were also told that they would have access to two dialog boxes in which they should report their emotions. The first one is a permanent dialog box and they should use it each time that they feel a new emotion. The second one is a pop-up dialog box that would appear after an interval (each 10 minutes) and after each event that can elicit an emotion (each 2.9 minutes in average). The content of the two dialog boxes are identical. The reason for using the two dialog boxes is that we do not want to block the interaction to force the student to report his emotions, because it could irritate him. Figure 1 (translated from Portuguese) illustrates the dialog boxes used by students to report their emotions. The emotions disappointment and distress are grouped, as well as the emotions joy and satisfaction. This was done because all events in the learning environment generate the emotions disappointment/distress and joy/satisfaction simultaneously. This is due to the fact that these four emotions are elicited by the evaluation of the consequences of the events: the consequences of an event are evaluated as desirable (joy/satisfaction) or undesirable (disappointment/distress) by students according to their goals. What differentiates these emotions is the expectation if the event will occur or not; when there is an expectation satisfaction and disappointment may arise; otherwise the students might feel joy/distress. For instance, when a student accomplishes an exam, he waits for the assessment. This generates an expectation by the student (for instance, obtain a good grade). When there is an expectation, emotions disappointment (if a good expectation was disconfirmed) and satisfaction (or confirmed) may occur when the event is confirmed. So, when the student receives the result of an assessment, he may feel joy/distress if he just focuses on the consequence of the event and/or satisfaction/disappointment if he had some expectation for the consequence. Another possibility, which we re considering in this work, is that the student experiences a "mixture of emotions resulting from considering the situation from these different perspectives" [7].

From twenty-four students that participated in the experiment, eight did not report any emotion at all. This happened because the pop-up dialog box was not modal, which allows the student to close the window without selecting an answer option. As in this dialog box the students have the option to report that they feel no emotion, the data from these eight students were not considered in the analysis. We discarded these data because the lack of information from these students does not mean that they feel no emotion, but that they do not want to report it. This could have happened either because the students did not feel comfortable to report their emotions or they felt disturbed by the presence of the pop-up dialog boxes. Only 8% of the students in the post-questionnaire reported that they felt uncomfortable in telling their emotions. Among the students that informed their emotions at least once, 18% abstain of the occurrence of the pop-up dialog boxes. As the dialog box allows the students to report that they felt no emotion, these cases were not considered in the evaluation.

The emotions reported by the students (which were stored in a log file) were matched with those inferred by the affective model. For this analysis one-minute time frame was considered since we observed that students took up to one minute to report their emotions in the dialog box whenever it appears.

Table 1 shows the success rate for the affective model inference. For each emotion inferred, the percentage of emotions reported by the student that agrees with it has been verified. The model obtained a good success rate for the emotions joy/satisfaction: 77%. In 13% of the situations, the students informed that they felt joy/satisfaction and the model did not infer any emotion. In the other 10% of situations, the model inferred a different emotion. This is a fairly good rate if we consider that humans have a success rate with emotional recognition of the basic emotions by face of 87% and by voice 65% [18].

On the other hand, the emotions disappointment, gratitude and anger were not so well predicted. A possible explanation for this is that the students liked the presence of the agent so much that they informed to be grateful for it almost all the time. This can happen by the fact that students misinterpret the emotion gratitude with admiration or because the fact that they liked to interact with the agent. The students probably did not report distress and disappointment for the same reason. As Table 1 illustrates, in 72% of the time in which students notified being grateful to the agent, it was not inferred by the model. Regarding anger, there were only two situations that were expected to elicit this emotion in students, which were students asks for or deny agent's help. Therefore, there is not enough information to interpret the inference accuracy for this emotion.

The *indirect evaluation* provided results about the effect of affective tactics in students learning. Another experiment was conducted with two groups of 13 students. The first group (control group) interacted just with the web-based learning system (JADE), while the second one (experimental group) made use of Pat. The average duration of the test was 13 minutes in the web-based condition and 8 minutes in the Pat condition, although students had 1 hour to interact with the environment. Table 2 summarizes the results of the pre-tests and post-tests. Although, the mean in the pre-test was almost the same for both groups, the students that interacted with Pat obtained a relatively greater mean in the post-test. The t-test shows that there is significant evidence that students in group 2 obtained better gains in the post-test rather than students in group 1 [$F(21.842) = -2.5039$, $p=0.01013$]. Besides this, the application of the t-test to verify students' gains in the post-test in relation to the pre-test allows to verify that there was an important difference between pupils in the means for the group 2 [$F(21.773) = 4.6757$, $p<0.01$]. As emotions are a important information in order for the agent to decide an affective scaffold, these findings give some evidence that the inferred emotions were very close to those that were experienced by students. We believe that this allowed Pat to apply the appropriate affective tactics and this way to improve students' results in the post-test. In another paper [10], we discuss in more details the comparison among three versions of the environment in order to evaluate the effectiveness of the pedagogical affective tactics: (i) a first group interacted with JADE, without the presence of the animated pedagogical agent; (ii) the second group had access to JADE with a non-affective version of Pat. For this group, the agent had just the role of providing hints and help, without applying affective tactics. In this group the agent does not know the user's emotions; (iii) the third group interacted with a full version of Pat (able to infer emotions and apply affective tactics).

Table 1. Inference accuracy of the affective model

	success rate	Incorrect Inference	n. of reports
joy/satisf.	77%	23%	39
distress/disap	0%	100%	17
gratitude	22%	78%	35
anger	0%	100%	2
total			93

Fig. 1. Dialog box for students' emotions report

After the interaction with JADE, the students were invited to answer a questionnaire in order to verify to which extent the dialog box for reporting emotions interfered with their emotions. The questions (adapted from [5]) and the students' answers on a Likert scale from 1 (strongly disagree) to 5 (strongly agree) are presented in Table 3. Table 3 suggests that students were indifferent to the number of times that the dialog box popped-up and that it did not interfere in their studies. These results are consistent with the fact that few students reported feeling disappointment or anger. Furthermore, results show that students do not mind to report their emotions to the system. This is important because the feeling of being obligated to report their emotions make the student become distressed [9]. If students feel uncomfortable in reporting their feelings, they can omit this information or lie about the emotions they are feeling.

6 Discussion and Conclusions

This paper presented two evaluations conducted for assessing the proposed affective student model. Regarding the indirect approach evaluation, the better results observed in the post-test compared to the pre-test of the students who used the affective version of the agent give an indication that the model provides useful affective information about the student. As the agent uses the predictions of students' emotions to guide its affective scaffold, the better gains of the group that interacted with the affective version of Pat in relation to the other groups indicate that the information provided by the affective model is close to the students real emotions. This allows the agent to choose the adequate affective tactic and, indirectly, improve their learning.

Table 2. Pre and Post-tests results in experiments

	Pre-test		*Post-test*	
	Mean	*Std. Dev.*	*Mean*	*Std. Dev.*
JADE	4.04	1.54	5.87	1.79
Pat	4.52	1.81	7.40	1.30

Table 3. Average scores for the post-questionnaire

1. The pop-up dialog box appeared very frequently	3.30
2. The pop-up dialog box interfered in my studies	2.35
3. The permanent dialog box interfered in my studies	2.00
4. The questions in the dialog boxes were clear	3.96
5. I felt uncomfortable to report my emotions	2.08

The outcomes of the direct evaluation were not so promising. We suggest three directions for improvement. First, it is very important to have the popup dialog box. It was observed that only 11% of students reported emotions by their own initiative in the permanent dialog box. Second, it is important that this popup window be modal. Experimenters that participated in the evaluation verified that students have the reflex of closing the popup window without reading it. This can be observed in the results. From 24 students that participated in the experiment, only eight reported no emotion. Third, students have a simple conception about emotion. They see emotions only as those feelings that have a very strong behavioural/mental reaction. This was verified in another post-questionnaire where students should relate the moments during which they felt greater emotional intensity. Some students said that it was very difficult to report their emotions, since they did not feel any emotion during the interaction with the environment. Nevertheless, these same students reported some emotional situations in the post-questionnaire. They became distressed, for instance, with the presence of the agent because they thought the agent could criticize them. The OCC states that each emotion in the model represents a group of emotions (emotion type) that are triggered by the same appraisal, but have different intensities. Some students misinterpreted emotions as being affects with great intensity, which hardly occurs in a learning environment. It was also observed that students misinterpret liking the agent with being grateful to it. These misconceptions can be corrected by asking students about their appraisal, for example, how they feel about their performance or concerning an agent action, instead of asking directly about their emotions.

Finally, the BDI model is a convenient tool for the implementation of cognitive-based affective user models. It allows the agent to predict the student's affective state by reasoning about the cognitive evaluation made by him that elicited a specific emotion (his appraisal) based on his personal information (events that are happening and the student's goals). This allows the affective model to infer the reasons that elicited the emotion, since it estimates the student appraisals. This knowledge will be important for the agent to decide which affective tactic to apply to improve student's learning. An important limitation of the BDI implementation of the affective model is that it is difficult to infer the emotions intensity. This is due to the fact that the appraisal psychological models do not provide any statistical information in which to base the inference of the intensity. A way of having the information about intensity is to combine an emotional inference mechanism based on physiological information.

This second model will be responsible for predicting when the student had the emotion, while the BDI model will inform the agent of the reasons that elicited the emotion.

References

1. Calvo, R., D'Mello, S.: Affect Detection: An Interdisciplinary Review of Models, Methods, and Their Applications. IEEE Transactions on Affective Computing 1, 18–37 (2010)
2. Wehrle, T., Kaiser, S.: Emotion and Facial Expression. In: Paiva, A. (ed.) IWAI 1999. LNCS, vol. 1814, pp. 49–63. Springer, Heidelberg (2000)
3. Picard, R.W., Vyzas, E., Healey, J.: Toward Machine Emotional Intelligence. IEEE Transactions Pattern Analysis and Machine Intelligence 23, 1175–1191 (2001)
4. Martinho, C., Machado, I., Paiva, A.: A Cognitive Approach to Affective User Modeling. In: Paiva, A. (ed.) IWAI 1999. LNCS, vol. 1814, pp. 64–75. Springer, Heidelberg (2000)
5. Conati, C., Maclare, H.: Evaluating A Probabilistic Model of Student Affect. In: Lester, J.C., Vicari, R.M., Paraguaçu, F. (eds.) ITS 2004. LNCS, vol. 3220, pp. 55–66. Springer, Heidelberg (2004)
6. Jaques, P.A., Viccari, R.M.: A BDI approach to infer student s emotions in an intelligent learning environment. Computers & Education 49, 360–384 (2007)
7. Ortony, A., Clore, G., Collins, A.: The Cognitive Structure of Emotions. Cambridge University Press, Cambridge (1988)
8. Eyharabide, V., et al.: An Ontology for Predicting Students' Emotions During a Quiz. In: IEEE Symposium Series on Computational Intelligence- Paris (2011)
9. Conati, C.: How to evaluate models of user affect? In: André, E., Dybkjær, L., Minker, W., Heisterkamp, P. (eds.) ADS 2004. LNCS (LNAI), vol. 3068, pp. 288–300. Springer, Heidelberg (2004)
10. Jaques, P.A., Lehmann, M., Pesty, S.: Evaluating the Affective Tactics of an Emotional Pedagogical Agent. In: ACM Symposium on Applied Computing, vol. 1. ACM, Hawaii (2009)
11. Ames, C.: Motivation: What teachers should know. Teachers College Record. 91, 409–421 (1990)
12. Pintrich, P.: A Manual for the Use of the Motivated Strategies for Learning Questionnaire. The Reg. of the University of Michigan (1991)
13. Meece, J., McColskey, W.: Improving Student Motivation (2001)
14. Móra, M.C., Lopes, J.G., Viccari, R.M., Coelho, H.: BDI Models and Systems: Reducing the Gap. In: International Workshop on Agent Theories, Architectures, and Languages (1998)
15. Rao, A.S., Georgeff, M.: BDI Agents: from Theory to Practice. Australian Artificial Intelligence Institute, Melbourne, Australia (1995)
16. Burleson, W., Picard, R.W.: Gender-Specific Approaches to Developing Emotionally Intelligent Learning Companions. IEEE Intelligent Systems 22, 62–69 (2007)
17. Silveira, R.A., Vicari, R.M.: Developing distributed intelligent learning Environment with JADE. In: Cerri, S.A., Gouardéres, G., Paraguaçu, F. (eds.) ITS 2002. LNCS, vol. 2363, pp. 105–118. Springer, Heidelberg (2002)
18. Sebe, N., Cohen, I., Gevers, T., Huang, T.S.: Multimodal Approaches for Emotion Recognition: A Survey. In: Internet Imaging VI. EUA, San Jose (2005)

Audio Visual Emotion Recognition Based on Triple-Stream Dynamic Bayesian Network Models

Dongmei Jiang[1,2], Yulu Cui[1,2], Xiaojing Zhang[1,2], Ping Fan[3], Isabel Ganzalez[3], and Hichem Sahli[3,4]

VUB-NPU Joint Research Group on AVSP
[1] Northwestern Polytechnic University, Xi'an, China
[2] Shaanxi Provincial Key Laboratory on Speech, Image and Information Processing
[3] Vrije Universiteit Brussel (VUB) - AVSP, Department ETRO
[4] Interuniversity Microelectronics Centre – IMEC, VUB-ETRO Pleinlaan 2, 1050 Brussels, Belgium
jiangdm@nwpu.edu.cn, cuiyulu1024@163.com, {pfan,igonzale,hichem.sahli}@etro.vub.ac.be

Abstract. We present a triple stream DBN model (T_AsyDBN) for audio visual emotion recognition, in which the two audio feature streams are synchronous, while they are asynchronous with the visual feature stream within controllable constraints. MFCC features and the principle component analysis (PCA) coefficients of local prosodic features are used for the audio streams. For the visual stream, 2D facial features as well 3D facial animation unit features are defined and concatenated, and the feature dimensions are reduced by PCA. Emotion recognition experiments on the eNERFACE'05 database show that by adjusting the asynchrony constraint, the proposed T_AsyDBN model obtains 18.73% higher correction rate than the traditional multi-stream state synchronous HMM (MSHMM), and 10.21% higher than the two stream asynchronous DBN model (Asy_DBN).

Keywords: triple stream DBN model, asynchronous, MSHMM, Asy_DBN.

1 Introduction

Emotion recognition has attracted increasing attention of researchers from various fields, such as psychology, cognition and pattern recognition. There are two main representation methods on emotions, namely discrete and continuous representations. The well known discrete categorical description is six primary emotions [1]: happiness, surprise, anger, sadness, fear and disgust. Therefore emotion recognition problem normally becomes a pattern classification problem on these emotions.

Most research in emotion recognition considers separately the audio information [2, 3] and visual information [4, 5]. In recent years, increasing efforts have been made in multimodal emotion recognition using different approach of fusing audio and video information. For example, [6, 7] adopt the early fusion strategy. Emotion recognition performance of such approach could be reduced due to the increasing feature space. To overcome such problem, the decision fusion strategy has been proposed in [8, 9].

S. D´Mello et al. (Eds.): ACII 2011, Part I, LNCS 6974, pp. 609–618, 2011.

The disadvantage of such strategy is the loss of the mutual correlation between the audio and visual modalities. [10] explores an Adaboost multi-stream hidden Markov model (AMHMM) framework in which the visual features and audio features are integrated, and an Adaboost learning scheme is used to build a HMM fusion. [11] presents a Multi-stream Fused HMM to build an optimal connection among multiple streams from audio and visual channels according to the maximum entropy and the maximum mutual information criterion. In [10] and [11], prosody features from pitch and RMS energy are extracted as audio features, and the local preserving projection (LPP) of facial texture images are adopted as visual features. To reasonably integrate the information from speech and facial expressions, [12] proposes a tripled hidden Markov model (triple-HMM) based emotion recognition system modeling the correlation of three component HMMs that are based individually on upper face, lower face, prosodic dynamic behaviors, and allows unlimited state asynchrony between these streams. Moreover, in [10 -12] it has been showed that the audio visual multi-modal emotion recognition performs much better than the mono-modal emotion recognition, i.e. audio emotion recognition from prosodic features, or facial expression recognition from 2D or 3D facial features.

Nevertheless, due to the rigid structure of HMM, the above mentioned HMM based fusion models cannot describe reasonably the correlation and asynchrony between the audio and visual emotion features. To model the asynchrony in a more flexible way, it has been proposed in [13] a two stream dynamic Bayesian network model (Asy_DBN) using as audio inputs the perceptual linear prediction (PLP) coefficients, and as visual inputs facial shape features. This model allows the audio-state and visual-state to be asynchronous but within certain constraints. Experimental results showed that by setting the appropriate maximum asynchrony constraint between the audio and the visual streams, the Asy_DBN model performs better than the audio or visual single stream HMM, and state synchronous multi-stream HMM (MSHMM).

In the Asy_DBN model, the most commonly adopted features in audio emotion recognition, i.e. the prosodic features, are missing. Moreover, the visual features only consider the geometric features of the upper face. Based on the Asy_DBN model, in this paper, with the aim of obtaining increased emotion recognition accuracy, we propose the following extensions: i) Features extraction. For the audio stream, apart from the Mel filterbank cepstrum coefficient (MFCC) features, we propose also using the PCA coefficients of the local prosodic features. For the visual features, to efficiently capture the Action Units [14] activation/inactivation, we propose using the PCA coefficients of both 2D facial features and 3D geometric deformation features using the Facial Animation Units of the Candide model. ii) As the recognition model, we propose a triple stream DBN model (T_AsyDBN) in which the two audio streams, i.e. the local prosodic features and the MFCC features, are synchronous at the state level, while they are asynchronous with the visual stream within controllable constraints. Emotion recognition experiments are carried out on the eNERFACE'05 audio visual speech database. Results show that by setting the appropriate asynchrony constraint between the audio and the visual feature streams, T_AsyDBN gets 10.21% higher correction rate than the audio visual Asy_DBN model, and even 18.73% higher than the traditional MSHMM.

The remainder of the paper is organized as follows. In section 2, we summarize the used audio and visual features. Section 3 defines the structure and conditional probability distributions of the nodes in the T_AsyDBN models. The experimental results are discussed in section 4, and section 5 discusses conclusions and future work.

2 Audio Visual Feature Extraction

2.1 Audio Features

The following audio features are considered:

MFCC. MFCC features are extracted using the HMM toolkit HTK [15] with window size of 30ms and frame rate of 10ms. 14 MFCC features, together with their first-order and second-order differential coefficients, resulting in an audio feature vector of 42 dimension.

Local Prosodic Features. After extracting pitch and energy features from the speech signal using window size of 30ms and window shift of 10ms, we calculate their maximum, minimum, median, mean, as well the maximum, minimum and median of their slopes in a local period of 130ms, with the time shift of the local period as 10ms. Finally, 28-dimensional feature vectors of 100 frames/s are obtained using the above features and their first order differentials. To reduce the data redundancy, we further perform PCA on these features. In our experiments, 16-dimension local prosodic feature vectors are obtained, with the contribution of the principle components around 90%.

2.2 Visual Features

2D Facial Features. In this work, we adopt the constrained Bayesian tangent shape model (CSM) algorithm [16] to detect and track a shape model defined by 83 facial landmarks. Fig.1(a) shows an example of the tracking results, while the locations and sequence numbers of the 83 facial landmarks are shown in Fig. 1(b).

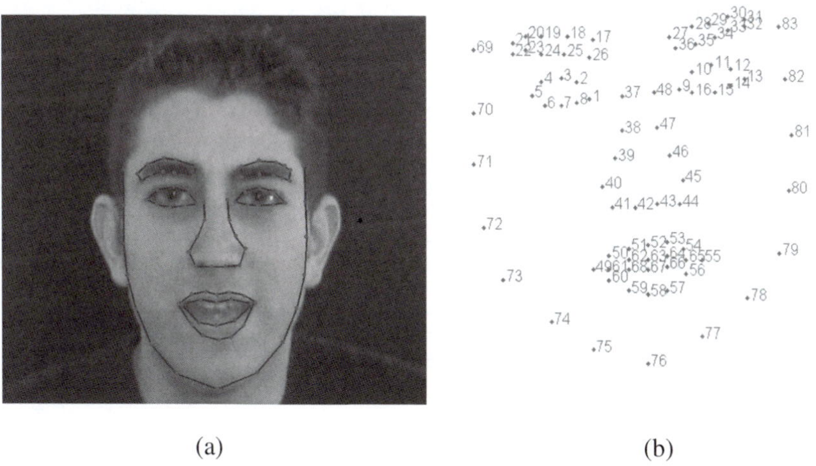

Fig. 1. Face detection/tracking results and position description of the 83 facial points

Table 1. 8 facial geometric features

ID	definition	description
1	dis(26, 36)	distance between the left and right eyebrows (lower)
2	dis(27,17)	distance between the left and right eyebrows (upper)
3	disV (84, 26)	vertical distance between nose apex and inner right eyebrow
4	disV (84, 36)	vertical distance between nose apex and inner left eyebrow
5	disV (84, 21)	vertical distance between nose apex and outer right eyebrow
6	disV (84, 31)	vertical distance between nose apex and outer left eyebrow
7,8	dis(3,7), dis(11,15)	right eye opening and left eye opening

Table 2. The 18 proposed 2D facial features

ID	Name	Description
1	disV(52,15)	vertical distance between the upper lip center and the left eye
2	disV(52,7)	vertical distance between the upper lip center and the right eye
3	dis(52,O)	distance between the upper lip center and the nose apex
4	dis(52,58)	mouth height
5	dis(44,41)	width of the nose wings
6	dis(A,49)	distance between the right mouth corner and the mouth center
7	dis(A,55)	distance between the left mouth corner and the mouth center
8	dis(55,9)	distance between the left mouth corner and the inner corner of left eye
9	dis(49,1)	distance between the right mouth corner and the inner corner of right eye
10	dis(55,49)	mouth width
11	disV(15,29)	vertical distance between the left lower eyelid center and the left upper eyebrow center
12	disV(7,19)	vertical distance between the right lower eyelid center and the right upper eyebrow center
13	dis(9,27)	distance between the left inner eye corner and the left inner corner of eye-brow
14	dis(1,17)	distance between the right inner eye corner and the right inner corner of eyebrow
15	dis(J,J')	distance between the inner corners of eyebrows
16	dis(15,11)	left eye opening
17	dis(7,3)	right eye opening
18	dis(B,B')	distance of upper and lower inner lips

Table 3. Intermediate points in the definitions of Table 2

Point	Description	x-coordinate	y-coordinate
A	Midpoint of the left and right mouth corners	$x_A = \frac{k(y_1 + y_9) + (x_1 + x_9) - 2k(y_{49} - kx_{49})}{2(1+k^2)}$ $y_A = k(x_A - x_{49}) + y_{49} \quad k = \frac{y_{49} - y_{55}}{x_{49} - x_{55}}$	
O	nose apex	$x_O = \frac{x_{42} + x_{43}}{2}$	$y_O = \frac{y_{42} + y_{43}}{2}$
J	inner center point of the left eyebrow	$x_J = \frac{x_{27} + x_{36}}{2}$	$y_J = \frac{y_{27} + y_{36}}{2}$
J'	inner center point of the right eyebrow	$x_{J'} = \frac{x_{17} + x_{26}}{2}$	$y_{J'} = \frac{y_{17} + y_{26}}{2}$
B	mean inner upper lip center	$x_B = \frac{x_{62} + x_{63} + x_{64}}{2}$	$y_B = \frac{y_{62} + y_{63} + y_{64}}{2}$
B'	mean inner lower lip center	$x_{B'} = \frac{x_{66} + x_{67} + x_{68}}{2}$	$x_{B'} = \frac{y_{66} + y_{67} + y_{68}}{2}$

In [13], an 8-dimensional feature vector, describing the movements of eyes and eyebrows in the upper face, has been used. For the sake of completeness, these features are summarized in Table 1, where point 84 has been defined as the midpoint between landmarks 41 and 43, representing the nose apex. dis(i, j) and disV(i, j) are the Euclidian distance and vertical distance between the landmarks i and j, respectively.

In this paper, following the Facial Action Coding System (FACS) [15] which describes facial expressions by Action Units (AUs) designed to detect subtle changes in facial features, we define the 2D facial features as listed in Table 2, while the intermediate point variables are defined in Table 3. This set of features allows taking into account the full shape of the face and the movements of the landmarks.

Facial Animation Units (FAU) Features. To obtain more accurate facial expression information, in this study, we use the Candide 3D face model, and we have chosen the following seven Animation Units (AU): AUV6-eyes closed, AUV3-brow lower, AUV5-outer brow raiser, AUV0-upper lip raiser, AUV11-jaw drop, AUV2-lip stretcher, and AUV14-lip corner depressor. In this work, we track the head and facial actions using the face tracking of [17].

For each image frame, we define as visual features vector the concatenation of the 18 2D facial features of Table 2, and the 7 Animation Units features, together with their first order derivatives, resulting in 50-dimension feature vectors with frame rate of 25 frames/s. To match the frame rate of the audio features, the visual features are linearly interpolated to the frame rate of 100 frames/s. Finally, the dimensions of the resulting visual features are reduced by PCA. In our experiments, 19-dimension visual features are obtained with the contribution of the principle components around 90%.

3 Triple Stream Asynchronous DBN (T_AsyDBN) Model

In [13], a two stream state asynchronous DBN model (Asy_DBN) has been proposed. In this paper, to combine the MFCC features, local prosodic features and visual emotion features more reasonably, we extend the Asy_DBN model to a triple stream audio visual asynchronous DBN (T_AsyDBN) model, as shown in Fig. 2. The model contains three parts: a Prologue part to initialize, a Chunk part that is repeated every frame with the evolution of the audio visual features, and a closure of sentence with an Epilogue frame.

The key nodes of the model are:

a) AS/VS: index of the current audio /visual state.
b) AT/VT: indicate when the current audio/visual state transits to the next state. when $AT = 1$ / $VT = 1$, the audio-state/visual-state is allowed to transit, and when $AT = 0 / VT = 0$, the transition is not allowed.
c) o^{a1} , o^{a2} , o^{v} : observation vector of MFCC feature, local prosodic feature, and visual feature.
d) CheckAsy(CA): checks the degree of asynchrony between the audio and visual states.

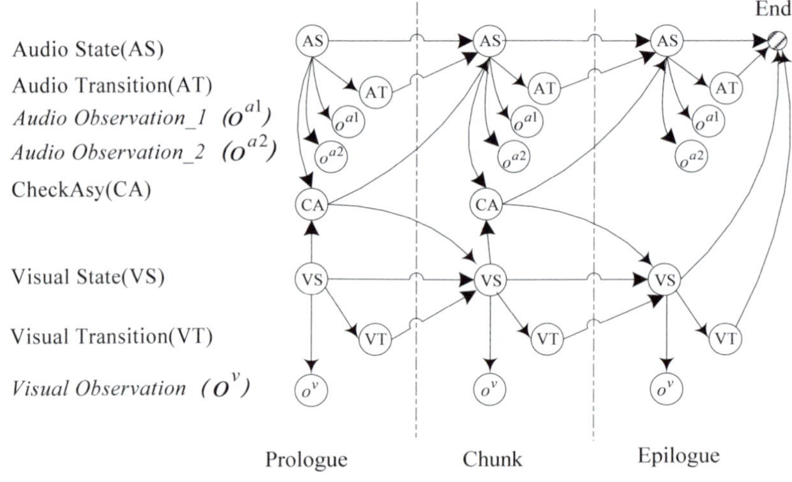

Fig. 2. Structure of the triple stream DBN model

The two audio features streams o^{a1} and o^{a2} , i.e. MFCC and local prosodic features, are both associated to the same audio-state, thus they are forced to be synchronous at the state level. However, the visual features are associated only to the visual-state. The audio-state and visual-state can transit individually in their corresponding streams, but their asynchrony is constrained through the node CheckAsy (CA), which is measured as the distance between the indices of the audio- and visual-states.

The conditional probability distributions (CPD) of the key nodes are defined as follows.

$$p(\mathrm{CA}_t = i \mid \mathrm{AS}_t = j, VS_t = k) = \begin{cases} 1 & i = j - k \\ 0 & otherwise \end{cases} \tag{1}$$

Let the number of audio-state and visual-state be AN and VN respectively (both set as 8 in our experiments), and the allowed maximum asynchrony between the audio-state and visual-state is m, the CPD of AS and VS are defined as

$$p(AS_t = i \mid AS_{t-1} = j, AT_{t-1} = k, CA_{t-1} = l) = \begin{cases} 1 & i = j \quad and \quad k = 0 \\ 1 & i = j \quad and \quad j = AN \\ 1 & i = j+1 \ and \quad k = 1 \quad and \quad j < AN \quad and \quad l \in [-m, m-1] \\ 1 & i = j \quad and \quad k = 1 \quad and \quad j < AN \quad and \quad l \notin [-m, m-1] \\ 0 & otherwise \end{cases} \tag{2}$$

$$p(VS_t = i \mid VS_{t-1} = j, VT_{t-1} = k, CA_{t-1} = l) = \begin{cases} 1 & i = j \quad and \quad k = 0 \\ 1 & i = j \quad and \quad j = VN \\ 1 & i = j+1 \ and \quad k = 1 \quad and \quad j < VN \quad and \quad l \in [-m+1, m] \\ 1 & i = j \quad and \quad k = 1 \quad and \quad j < VN \quad and \quad l \notin [-m+1, m] \\ 0 & otherwise \end{cases} \tag{3}$$

According to Equation (2), the audio-state AS might not change if it is not allowed to transit ($k = 0$), or it has reached the final state of the audio stream ($j = AN$), or even it is not at the final state and allowed to transit but the asynchrony between the audio and visual states exceeds the constraint ($k=1 \ and \ j<AN \ and \ l \notin [-m, m-1]$). The same rule will be applied to the visual-state according to the CPD of Equation (3).

At each time slice, the probability of the audio visual states emitting the observation feature vectors is defined as a production of Gaussian mixture models (GMMs).

$$\begin{aligned} & p(o_t^{a1}, o_t^{a2}, o_t^{v} / AS_t = i, VS_t = k) \\ & = p(o_t^{a1}, o_t^{a2}, o_t^{v} / S_t = j) = \prod_{d \in \{ a1, a2, v \}} \left[\sum_{n=1}^{N} c_{jn}^{d} N(O_t^{d}, \mu_{jn}^{d}, \Psi_{jn}^{d}) \right]^{\lambda_d} \end{aligned} \tag{4}$$

where $S_t = j$ is the combined audio visual state. For each feature stream d ($d \in (a1, a2, v)$), c_{jn}^{d}, μ_{jn}^{d} and Ψ_{jn}^{d} are the GMM parameters (weight, mean and covariance matrix) of the Gaussian mixture n of the state j, respectively. N is the number of Gaussian mixtures. λ_d is the weight adjusting the influence of the stream d, with the constraint $\lambda_{a1} + \lambda_{a2} + \lambda_v = 3$. In the training process of the T_AsyDBN models, λ_{a1}, λ_{a2} and λ_v are set to 1, respectively.

In the training process, for each of the six emotions anger, disgust, happiness, fear, sad and surprise, a T_AsyDBN model is trained using the extracted, on the training samples, MFCC, local prosodic features and facial features. For each combined audio visual state, the GMM parameters c_{jn}^{d}, μ_{jn}^{d} and Ψ_{jn}^{d} for the feature streams $d \in (a1, a2, v)$ are estimated using the Expectation Maximization (EM) algorithm. In our experiments, the number of Gaussian mixtures N is fixed to 4. In the recognition process, the emotion model which obtains the highest likelihood probability is chosen as the recognition result.

Both the training and recognition processes of the T_AsyDBN models are implemented using the Graphical Models Toolkit (GMTK) [18].

4 Experiments and Results

In this work, we carried out audio visual emotion recognition on the eNERFACE'05 database [19]. Due to the limited data set, the jack-knife strategy is adopted: for each of the six emotions anger, disgust, happiness, fear, sad and surprise, 30 sentences have been set as the training data, and another 81 sentences of all emotions as testing data. For an emotion, the correction rate is the ratio of the number of correctly recognized sentences to the number of testing sentences of that emotion. Then in each turn, for each emotion, 10 sentences are exchanged between the training and testing data. The final correction rate is the average of the correction rates of these turns.

Table 4. Correction rates of audio and visual single stream emotion recognition (%)

Model	anger	disgust	fear	happiness	sad	surprise	Avg
AHMM(MFCC)	54.55	41.67	35.42	66.67	78.95	35.90	52.19
AHMM(Prosody_16)	30.30	19.44	33.33	33.33	61.40	21.80	33.27
VHMM(GF_16)	30.30	50.00	35.42	26.67	29.82	32.23	34.07
VHMM(GF+FAU_19)	18.18	63.89	45.83	66.67	33.33	52.75	46.78

To verify the effectiveness of the proposed local prosodic features (Prosody_16) and the 19-dimension facial features (GF+FAU_19), we firstly apply audio and visual single stream emotion recognition experiments based on HMM. Results are shown in Table 4. One can notice that audio emotion recognition (AHMM) using local prosodic features, is not as good as that using MFCC features. But the visual emotion recognition (VHMM), using the 19-dimension visual features, gets 12.71% higher correction rate than that using the 8 geometric features (GF_16) in Table 1.

Table 5. Correction rates of multi-modal audio visual emotion recognition (%)

Model	anger	disgust	fear	happiness	sad	surprise	Avg
MSHMM	66.67	22.22	33.33	63.33	60.25	41.09	47.81
Asy_DBN(1)	60.61	36.11	45.83	66.67	71.93	53.84	55.83
Asy_DBN(2)	**60.61**	**36.11**	**47.92**	**70.00**	**77.19**	**46.15**	**56.33**
Asy_DBN(3)	63.64	38.89	43.75	70.00	77.19	43.59	56.18
T_AsyDBN(1)	69.70	61.11	33.33	73.33	77.19	46.15	60.14
T_AsyDBN(2)	78.79	55.56	47.92	66.67	70.17	41.02	60.02
T_AsyDBN(3)	**81.82**	**58.33**	**58.33**	**83.33**	**78.95**	**38.46**	**66.54**

Table 5 gives the emotion recognition results using MSHMM and the asynchronous DBN models, with (m) meaning that the asynchrony constraint is set as m. In MSHMM and Asy_DBN, the 42-dimension MFCC features, and the 19-dimension facial features are adopted as audio features and visual features, respectively. In T_AsyDBN, the 16-dimension local prosodic features are added as another audio feature stream.

One can notice that since the asynchrony between the audio and visual features is not modeled appropriately, MSHMM gets even lower average correction rate than the AHMM using MFCC features. On the other side, by adjusting the asynchrony constraint m properly, the asynchronous DBN models Asy_DBN and T_AsyDBN both can get their highest average correction rates. The proposed T_AsyDBN(3) model obtains the highest average correction rate of 66.54%, which is 10.21% higher than the Asy_DBN(2) model, and even 18.73% higher than the traditional MSHMM.

5 Conclusions and Future Work

In this paper, we proposed a triple stream DBN model (T_AsyDBN) for audio visual emotion recognition, in which the two audio feature streams—MFCC features and local prosodic features – are forced to be synchronous at the state level, while they are asynchronous with the visual emotion features – the PCA coefficients of facial geometric features and facial animation unit vectors – within controllable constraints. Experimental results show that the T_AsynDBN model obtains higher performance than the two stream asynchronous DBN model Asy_DBN, and even 18.73% improvement compared to traditional MSHMM. In our future work, we will be investigating how to normalize the audio and visual features to reduce the influence of different speakers in the database.

Acknowledgements. This work is supported within the framework of the LIAMA-CAVSA project, the EU FP7 project ALIZ-E (grant 248116), Shaanxi Provincial Key International Cooperation Project(2011KW-04), and the NPU Foundation for Fundamental Research (NPU-FFR-JC200943).

References

1. Ekman, P., Friesen, W.V.: Constants across Cultures in the Face and Emotion. Journal of Personality and Social Psychology 17(2), 124–129 (1971)
2. Lee, C.M., Narayanan, S.S.: Toward Detecting Emotions In Spoken Dialogs. IEEE Tran. on Speech and Audio Processing 13(2), 293–303 (2005)
3. Neiberg, D., Elenius, K., Laskowski, K.: Emotion Recognition In Spontaneous Speech Using GMMs. In: Proceedings ICSLP 2006, Pittsburgh, pp. 809–812 (2006)
4. Wang, J., Yin, L., Wei, X., Sun, Y.: 3D Facial Expression Recognition Based on Primitive Surface Feature Distribution. In: Proc. IEEE Int. Conf. on Computer Vision and Pattern Recognition, pp. 1399–1406 (2006)
5. Zeng, Z., Fu, Y., Roisman, G.I., Wen, Z., Hu, Y., Huang, T.S.: Spontaneous Emotional Facial Expression Detection. Journal of Multimedia 1(5), 1–8 (2006)

6. Busso, C., Deng, Z., Yildirim, S., Bulut, M., Lee, C.M., et al.: Analysis of Emotion Recognition using Facial Expressions, Speech and Multimodal Information. In: ACM Int. Conf. on Multimodal Interfaces, pp. 205–211 (2004)
7. Schuller, B., Müller, R., Hörnler, B., et al.: Audiovisual Recognition of Spontaneous Interest Within Conversations. In: ACM Int. Conf. on Multimodal Interfaces, pp. 30–37 (2007)
8. Pal, P., Iyer, A.N., Yantorno, R.E.: Emotion Detection from Infant Facial Expressions and Cries. In: Proc. ICASSP, vol. 2, pp. 721–724 (2006)
9. Petridis, S., Pantic, M.: Audiovisual Discrimination between Laughter and Speech. In: Proc. ICASSP, pp. 5117–5120 (2008)
10. Zeng, Z., Hu, Y., Roisman, G.I., Wen, Z., Fu, Y., et al.: Audio-Visual Emotion Recognition in Adult Attachment Interview. In: Int. Conf. on Multimodal Interfaces, pp. 139–145 (2006)
11. Zeng, Z., Tu, J., Pianfetti, et al.: Audio-visual Affective Expression Recognition through Multi-stream Fused HMM. IEEE Transactions on Multimedia 10(4), 570–577 (2008)
12. Song, M., You, M., Li, N., Chen, C.: A Robust Multimodal Approach for Emotion Recognition. Neurocomputing 71(10-12), 1913–1920 (2008)
13. Chen, D., Jiang, D., Ravyse, I., Sahli, H.: Audio-Visual Emotion Recognition Based on a DBN Model with Constrained Asynchrony. In: Proc. ICIG, pp. 912–916 (2009)
14. Ekman, P., Friesen, W.V.: Facial Action Coding System. Consulting Psychologist Press, Palo Alto (1978)
15. Young, S., Kershaw, O.D., Ollason, J., Valtchev, D.V., Woodland, P.: The HTK Book. Entropic Ltd., Cambridge (1999)
16. Hou, Y., Sahli, H., Ravyse, I., Zhang, Y., Zhao, R.: Robust Shape-based Head Tracking. In: Blanc-Talon, J., Philips, W., Popescu, D., Scheunders, P. (eds.) ACIVS 2007. LNCS, vol. 4678, pp. 340–351. Springer, Heidelberg (2007)
17. Hou, Y., Fan, P., Ravyse, I., Sahli, H.: 3D Face Alignment via Cascade 2D Shape Alignment and Constrained Structure from Motion. In: Blanc-Talon, J., Philips, W., Popescu, D., Scheunders, P. (eds.) ACIVS 2009. LNCS, vol. 5807, pp. 550–561. Springer, Heidelberg (2009)
18. Bilmes, J., Zweig, G.: The Graphical Models Toolkit: An Open Source Software System for Speech and Time Series Processing. In: Proc. ICASSP, pp. 3916–3919 (2002)
19. Martin, O., Kotsia, I., Macq, B., et al.: The eNTERFACE'05 Audio-visual Emotion Database. In: Proceedings of the 22nd Int. Conf. on Data Engineering Workshops (2006)

Author Index